Economic Statecraft

Economic Statecraft

David A. Baldwin

PRINCETON UNIVERSITY PRESS

Copyright © 1985 by Princeton University Press
Published by Princeton University Press,
41 William Street, Princeton, New Jersey 08540
In the United Kingdom: Princeton University Press,
Chichester, West Sussex

LIBRARY OF CONGRESS CATALOGING-IN-PUBLICATION DATA

Baldwin, David A. (David Allen), 1936–
    Economic statecraft.

    Bibliography: p.
    Includes index.
    1. International economic relations.
2. International relations.   I. Title.
HF1411.B2327   1985   337   85-42672
ISBN 0-691-07687-1
ISBN 0-691-10175-2 (pbk.)

This book has been composed in Linotron Times Roman

Princeton University Press books are printed on acid-free
paper, and meet the guidelines for permanence and durability
of the Committee on Production Guidelines for Book
Longevity of the Council on Library Resources

Printed in the United States of America by Princeton Academic Press

10   9   8   7   6   5

In Memory of
Harold Sprout
and
Jacob Viner

CONTENTS

TABLES AND FIGURE

PREFACE

Pinpointing the origins of this book is difficult. I have been trying to integrate the disciplines of economics and political science in studying foreign policy and international relations for more than twenty-five years. I first publicly advocated the concept of economic statecraft when I organized and chaired a panel on that topic for the International Studies Association in 1969. During 1969–70 I worked full-time on this project but encountered formidable theoretical and methodological problems in making power analysis compatible with the concept of economic statecraft. Foreign aid obviously had to be included; yet standard political science treatments of power tended to focus on negative sanctions and ignore or deny the possibility that power could be based on positive sanctions. Foreign trade also fell within the rubric of economic statecraft; yet standard treatments tended to deny that mutually beneficial exchange relationships could or should be viewed in terms of power. The costs of economic statecraft were obviously an important consideration; yet the role of costs in power analysis was frequently ignored. Thus, for a decade I concentrated on the development and elaboration of the concepts of positive sanctions, power costs, and exchange. Much of this work was a matter of transplanting the ideas and insights of the social power literature into the field of international relations, which, despite its long-standing emphasis on power, had become relatively isolated from the post-1950 revolution in power analysis.

Friends and colleagues familiar with my work in international political economy during the 1960s would often ask why I seemed to have abandoned that field just when it was on the verge of becoming a popular intellectual fad in the 1970s. The answer was always the same—I had not lost interest in either international political economy or the study of economic statecraft. Every article on power that I wrote during the 1970s was intended to lay the foundations for this book. If political economy is about wealth and power, it behooves those who would call themselves political economists to take power analysis more seriously than has heretofore been the case.

In many ways this is a rather old-fashioned piece of work. The research is not a team effort; interviews, surveys, and statistical analysis play little or no role; and many of the references are to works written many years ago. Three reasons for emphasis on the older literature should be mentioned: (1) The quality of such works is often very high. The scholarship of Jacob Viner, Quincy Wright, Harold Sprout, Albert O. Hirschman, or Eli Heckscher, for example, endures and has not yet been superseded by superior treatments. (2) The generation of newly minted or recently converted international political economists that grew up in the 1970s was largely oblivious to the older tradition of international political economy and seemed to believe that the field was either nonexistent prior to 1970 or populated entirely by Marxists.[1] Academic specialists "pay their dues" by acquainting themselves with the scholarly literature in their field. In the case of international political economy, the dues are higher than the generation of the 1970s has been led to believe. (3) The growth of cumulative knowledge requires that some effort be made to relate current scholarship to past scholarship. Among contemporary social scientists, oddly enough, it is often the most vociferous advocates of cumulative knowledge who ignore anything more than ten years old.

Another sense in which this study is old-fashioned is in its blindness to disciplinary boundaries. I have drawn on economics, political science, philosophy, psychology, history, law, and sociology as well as on traditional works in international relations. Although specialists in each field will no doubt find fault with my analysis, I hope that the synthesis will be valuable enough to offset such objections. Both international political economy and international relations have traditionally been synthetic disciplines.

Three questions have been raised often enough at various stages of this project to justify the expectation that they will occur to others: First, why is so much attention devoted to "stage-setting" in the early chapters? When comments were solicited on early drafts of the manuscript, the most frequent reactions concerned the need to clarify the concept of economic statecraft and to justify aggregation of so many foreign policy tools into a single category. Thus, the first few chapters are in response to such concerns. Second, why go out of the way to identify differences between this approach and those of other scholars? I believe that the spirit of scientific inquiry—indeed, the spirit of scholarly inquiry in general—creates an obligation to set one's ideas in the context of work by others. This obligation means not only giving credit where it is due, but also giving criticism where it is due. Scholars seem to be much better at fulfilling the first than the second of these obligations. Thus, works with which one disagrees are often ignored or referred to only vaguely as "opposing schools

---

[1] When I first discussed this project with Susan Strange in 1969, she asked me to name other American scholars primarily interested in international political economy. Other than myself, I could only come up with Klaus Knorr; and I had to admit that his work during the 1960s seemed to be more military than economic. Although there must have been others, my answer even today would be the same *with respect to 1969*. This situation, of course, was to change rapidly during the 1970s.

of thought'' or ''common beliefs,'' leaving the reader wondering precisely what one has in mind. This escape from scholarly duties is eschewed in the pages that follow. Whenever I present a line of argument that conflicts with the views of other scholars, I try to inform the reader precisely how and why my views differ from those of others. I realize that this approach may give the impression of a polemical or adversarial style, but this is neither my intention nor desire. I attribute this impression to the relative dearth of professional scholarly criticism in international relations and in social science in general. To take another's work seriously enough to submit it to critical review is not a sign of disrespect but rather the highest compliment one scholar can pay another. This approach should not be trivialized as the mere scoring of debating points; it is the heart of the scientific process. Morton Kaplan trenchantly summarizes this approach as follows:

> Although individual great minds may be responsible for spectacular advances in science, the progress of science requires community. . . . If those working in a field fail to address similar problems, or fail to do so in a manner that permits genuine comparison, then it is possible neither to build on previous efforts nor to discover the inadequacies of current efforts. *Rejection of, as well as development from, the past is an integral part of the scientific process. Formulation and criticism are opposite sides of the same scientific coin.*[2]

Third, why is so much material in footnotes? Although I am well aware of the contention that footnotes ''interfere'' with the reader and should therefore be minimized, I do not believe that this contention has had a healthy effect on scholarship. In scholarship truth takes precedence over readability. If a footnote is needed to support a point or to expand on a related point, I have not hesitated to ''interfere'' with the reader's thought processes.[3] This book is addressed to scholars, not to speed-readers. The effort to suppress footnotes has even reinforced the desire of publishers to save money by placing footnotes at the end of a book. This practice is not only a nuisance, but also antithetical to the spirit of science insofar as it hinders verification of the sources on which an argument is based. On the assumption that scholars are supposed to facilitate rather than impede verification of their sources, the footnotes in this book appear on the same page as the text to which they refer.

I am indebted to a number of people who have commented on various stages of this project and have thereby forced me to rethink, clarify, abandon, or bolster certain positions. They include Charles W. Baldwin,

---

[2] *Toward Professionalism in International Theory* (New York: Free Press, 1979), p. 1. Italics added.

[3] For a brilliant and witty defense of scholarly footnotes, see Jacob Viner, *The Long View and the Short* (Glencoe, Ill.: Free Press, 1958), pp. 376-377.

David Deese, Margaret Doxey, Henry Ehrmann, Frank W. Fetter, Alexander George, Robert Gilpin, Albert O. Hirschman, Peter Katzenstein, Robert O. Keohane, Gene Lyons, James Mayall, John Odell, Richard Stuart Olson, Robert Paarlberg, Robert Packenham, Laurence Radway, Susan Strange, Bernard Segal, and Oran Young. Sole responsibility for the final product, however, rests, as always, with the author. I should also record my appreciation for the stimulating atmosphere of the Department of International Relations at the London School of Economics and Political Science, where much of the early research was carried out. Jan Barry and Gail Patten provided able typing assistance, while Emily Baldwin and Rebecca Baldwin helped with proofreading, translating, duplication, and humoring the author.

I am grateful to Dartmouth College for faculty fellowships and research support and to the German Marshall Fund of the United States for a fellowship that enabled me to complete the manuscript. It somehow seems appropriate that a fund to memorialize an act of economic statecraft—the Marshall Plan—should be the vehicle for financing the final stages of this study.

This book is dedicated to two former teachers who greatly influenced the way I think about international political economy—and about other things for that matter. The two shared many characteristics, including a view of scholarship as a craft to be practiced meticulously, a belief that familiarity with the history of one's discipline is important, a healthy disrespect for disciplinary boundaries, and, above all, the view that a scholar's most important obligation is to speak the truth as he or she believes it to be.

Economic Statecraft

CHAPTER 1

INTRODUCTION

The best service peace research could offer to
the world today probably consists, not so much in
understanding conflicts better, as in providing
politicians with an enormous repertoire of actions
short of violence that can be applied in
conflict situations.[1]

* * *

One of the main purposes for which social
scientists use the concept of A's power over B is for
the description of the policy possibilities open to A.[2]

In Quincy Wright's landmark work, *The Study of International Rela-*
tions, he observes that "the fields of economics and politics overlap"—
on the one hand, a shortage of resources may generate political rivalry,
while on the other hand, one group may influence another by "offering
economic rewards or withholding economic advantages. Politics may therefore be an instrument of economics and economics may be an instrument
of politics."[3] This is a study of economics as an instrument of politics.
Although economic techniques of statecraft have been used throughout
history, in recent years they have received renewed attention because of
the Arab oil embargo in 1973, the American grain embargo protesting the
Soviet invasion of Afghanistan, the freezing of Iranian assets during the
hostage crisis in 1980, and other well publicized cases. Most of these
events have been accompanied by journalistic background stories pointing
out that such measures rarely work and citing the widespread scholarly
consensus on this point. Thus, although few scholars would deny Wright's
contention that "economics may be an instrument of politics," most would
add the caveat that it is not a very useful instrument.

A puzzlement arises: Why do statesmen continue to practice economic
statecraft when "everybody knows" that it does not work? Is this but
another example of failure to take accumulated academic wisdom into

---

[1] Johan Galtung, "On the Meaning of Nonviolence," *Journal of Peace Research*, no. 3
(1965), p. 251.

[2] John C. Harsanyi, "Measurement of Social Power, Opportunity Costs, and the Theory
of Two-Person Bargaining Games," *Behavioral Science* VII (January 1962):69.

[3] Quincy Wright, *The Study of International Relations* (New York: Appleton-Century
Crofts, 1955), p. 239.

account leading to bad policy decisions? Are policy makers adopting measures they know are futile in order to appease the public's demand for action? Although either of these explanations is plausible, a third explanation also deserves consideration: Is it possible that the conventional wisdom is wrong? That economic tools of foreign policy work better than is generally supposed? That statesmen are making more or less rational attempts to adapt foreign policy means to foreign policy ends? What "everybody knows" easily becomes what "everybody takes for granted"; and what "everybody takes for granted" easily becomes what nobody submits to critical review.

PURPOSES OF THE STUDY

This study has three main purposes: The first is to submit the conventional wisdom regarding economic statecraft to critical review. The basic concepts, underlying assumptions, logic, and supporting evidence are all examined. My thesis is that the utility of economic techniques of statecraft has been systematically underestimated by most analysts since 1945. The second purpose is to stimulate increased awareness of and thinking about the many forms of economic statecraft. My thesis is that the study of economic instruments of foreign policy has been neglected relative to the study of other policy tools. And the third purpose is to develop an analytical framework with which to reassess the utility of economic techniques of statecraft. My thesis is that the social power literature developed since 1950 provides a useful framework within which to study economic statecraft.

STRUCTURE OF THE STUDY

The approach proposed here assumes that economic instruments of foreign policy should be analyzed and evaluated in the same way as other means for making influence attempts. Even a sympathetic reader, however, is unlikely to regard such a statement as self-explanatory. Precisely how should these "other means" be studied? What are the various forms of statecraft, and how does one distinguish economic from noneconomic statecraft? How has economic statecraft been viewed in the past, and why has it not been analyzed and evaluated in the same way as other foreign policy tools? Chapters 2 through 7 deal with such questions. Chapter 8 reviews several of the classic cases of alleged failure of economic statecraft. Indeed, most of the cases discussed in chapters 8, 9, and 10 were chosen precisely because they are widely regarded as examples of failure. This case selection strategy thus focuses on the crucial cases supporting the conventional wisdom. Since utility is not the only basis for evaluating economic statecraft, chapter 11 surveys the legal and moral norms relevant to such measures.

LIMITS OF THE STUDY

It is important to be clear as to what this book is *not* about. First, it has little to say about the wisdom with which foreign policy makers choose their goals. A judgment that economic statecraft was "successful" in a particular case refers to the statesman's adaptation of means to ends and implies little or nothing about whether the ends were good or bad, wise or foolish. Second, specific policy proposals for particular countries are beyond the scope of this study. The emphasis here is on *how* rather than *what* to think about such matters. And third, domestic politics in the country using economic statecraft has been largely ignored. This omission is not intended to imply that domestic politics is unimportant in understanding economic statecraft. Its inclusion, however, would add to the length and complexity of the argument without affecting the basic thrust of that argument in any fundamental way. Domestic political costs and benefits can be incorporated into the cost/benefit calculus of decision makers without altering the basic structure of the argument presented here. An additional reason for omitting domestic politics is that even those who most vigorously deny the utility of economic instruments for foreign policy purposes often admit the domestic political utility of such measures. Thus, the important thing to be demonstrated is that economic techniques can be useful even when domestic politics is ignored. A fourth limitation on this study arises from the case selection strategy. A focus on those cases most often cited as examples of failure, i.e., the hardest cases, is useful for critical assessment of the conventional wisdom; but it is not appropriate for generalizing about typical cases. Such generalizations should be based on study of the whole universe of *comparable* cases or on a random sample of such cases. For reasons that will be discussed later (especially in chapter 8), identifying a set of *comparable* cases suitable for statistical analysis is likely to be more difficult than is generally recognized.

IMPLICATIONS

What difference does it make whether the full range of economic techniques available to statesmen is recognized or whether the utility of such measures has been underestimated? There is no guarantee, of course, that better understanding of policy alternatives will lead to better policy. However, in a world where some policy options can have devastating global consequences, extraordinary efforts to elucidate less dangerous alternatives seem worthwhile. If we are to have war, let it not be because of a lack of imagination in identifying policy alternatives or because of miscalculation regarding the probable utility of such options.

Is social science needed to estimate the utility of economic statecraft? Not everyone thinks so. The American Committee on East–West Accord, composed of distinguished academics, business people, journalists, and former public officials, suggests that "common sense" should determine American policy with respect to trade with the Soviet Union.[4] This committee tends to favor détente, accommodation, and coexistence in East–West relations and advocates expanded trade with the Soviet Union as a step in that direction. Although sympathetic with this approach, I am wary of relying on "common sense." Consider, for example, the following "common-sense" truths put forward by the committee:

> *Economic boycotts never work.*—Economic warfare is an ineffective weapon. In modern times it has never worked. . . .[5]
> * * *
> Grain embargoes are a grievous mistake. . . . They are self-defeating and counterproductive abroad. They are not even any good for "sending the Soviets a message."[6]
> * * *
> About American economic sanctions against the Soviet Union, two things are of significance above all others: One, they haven't worked. Two, they can't work.[7]
> * * *
> Events of the past decade have proven that embargoes or other economic "sticks" do not increase leverage and control over another nation. Both common sense and historical data suggest just the opposite.[8]

"Common-sense" knowledge usually has the admirable quality of avoiding extreme statements, but these examples are hardly moderate. To say that economic sanctions against the Soviet Union "never work" or "can't work" is to take an extreme position on a policy issue of immense importance. Even if such propositions seem "commonsensical," one must ask whether this is enough. When stakes are high and issues are complex, rigorous analysis is in order. Neither good intentions nor common sense suffice. In medicine, as Karl Deutsch points out, a "well-meaning ignoramus is not a doctor but a quack." In international politics, well-meaning,

---

[4] Margaret Chapman and Carl Marcy, eds., *Common Sense in U.S.–Soviet Trade* (Washington, D.C.: American Committee on East–West Accord, 1983).

[5] Harold B. Scott, "U.S.–Soviet Trade 1970-1982: Twelve Years a Hostage to Politics and Unrelated Foreign Policy," in ibid., p. 24.

[6] Walter B. Saunders, "Soviet Agriculture and World Grain Trade," in ibid., p. 124.

[7] Fred Warner Neal, "Economic Sanctions: How to Damage Ourselves Without Hurting the Soviet Union," in ibid., pp. 140-141.

[8] Carol Brookins, "Misconceptions in U.S.–Soviet Trade," in ibid., p. 163.

but ill-informed, policy recommendations can be even more disastrous than in medicine. "We must study international relations, therefore, as deeply, as carefully, and as responsibly as our limited time and resources permit."[9] The Committee on East–West Accord may indeed be right in advocating increased trade with the Soviet Union, but it is wrong in suggesting that "common sense" is sufficient justification for such a policy recommendation.

[9] Karl W. Deutsch, *The Analysis of International Relations*, 2d ed. (Englewood Cliffs, N.J.: Prentice-Hall, 1978), p. 5.

CHAPTER 2

TECHNIQUES OF STATECRAFT

*Students of politics are expected to have something
pertinent to offer about the probable effects of
adopting one form of government or another, or one
policy or another relating to power.*[1]

International economic policies may be studied from the perspective of
law, economics, international organization, or the the international system.
To treat such measures as techniques of statecraft, however, is to adopt a
perspective different from any of these. Before economic statecraft can be
understood, the general nature and implications of the statecraft perspective
must be clarified. This chapter will therefore focus on the nature of statecraft, the scholarly neglect of this topic, ways to classify techniques of
statecraft, and the relationship between the statecraft perspective and the
perspectives of foreign policy, international politics, and policy science.
In addition, some objections to the statecraft orientation will be considered.

THE NATURE OF STATECRAFT

Statecraft has traditionally been defined as the art of conducting state
affairs. Such a definition, of course, could include both the foreign and
domestic dimensions of public policy; but in contemporary usage the term
has been virtually abandoned by students of domestic affairs.[2] Among
students of foreign policy and international politics the term is sometimes
used to encompass the whole foreign-policy-making process, but more
often it refers to the selection of means for the pursuit of foreign policy
goals. Thus, for Harold and Margaret Sprout "statecraft embraces all the
activities by which statesmen strive to protect cherished values and to attain
desired objectives vis-à-vis other nations and/or international organizations."[3] Similarly, K. J. Holsti defines "statecraft as the organized actions
governments take to change the external environment in general or the
policies and actions of other states in particular to achieve the objectives

---

[1] Harold D. Lasswell, *Politics: Who Gets What, When, How* (New York: Meridian Books,
1958), p. 187.

[2] For a significant exception, see Charles W. Anderson, *Statecraft: An Introduction to
Political Choice and Judgment* (New York: John Wiley, 1977).

[3] *Toward a Politics of the Planet Earth* (New York: Van Nostrand, 1971), p. 135.

that have been set by policy makers.''[4] Insofar as such definitions depict statecraft as governmental influence attempts directed at other actors in the international system, they correspond to the conception of statecraft employed here. The only qualifications are that, in contrast to the Sprouts, nonstate actors in addition to international organizations are included as possible targets of influence attempts; and, in contrast to Holsti, changes in beliefs, attitudes, opinions, expectations, emotions, and/or propensities to act are included in addition to changes in behavior.[5]

THE NEGLECTED STUDY OF STATECRAFT

To study statecraft, as conceived here, is to consider the instruments used by policy makers in their attempts to exercise power, i.e., to get others to do what they would not otherwise do. Two traditional foci of political science research—policy and power—are thus linked by this undertaking. Paradoxically, neither policy analysts nor power analysts have given much attention to the instruments or techniques of influence.[6] Analysts of both foreign and domestic policy have focused their attention on policy-making processes and have tended to ignore the content or output of those processes. "How are policies made?" is the question that has preoccupied policy analysts, not "By what means are they carried out?" Writing in 1968, Austin Ranney noted that "at least since 1945 most American political scientists have focused their professional attention mainly on the *processes* by which public policies are made and have shown little concern for their contents."[7] Ranney purported to see "signs of increasing discontent among political scientists . . . with the discipline's post-1945 focus on process" and to hear "a growing number of voices . . . urging more attention to policy contents."[8] Ranney's optimism regarding the desire for more emphasis on policy content was partially justified by the appearance in 1975 of *Policies and Policymaking* as one of the eight volumes in the *Handbook of Political Science*.[9] Unfortunately, the instruments of policy receive very little attention in the essays in that volume.

Foreign policy analysts have displayed a similar tendency to emphasize

[4] "The Study of Diplomacy," in *World Politics*, ed. James N. Rosenau, Kenneth W. Thompson, and Gavin Boyd (New York: Free Press, 1976), p. 293.

[5] On this point see Jack H. Nagel, *The Descriptive Analysis of Power* (New Haven: Yale University Press, 1975), p. 12.

[6] The terms "power" and "influence" will be used interchangeably throughout this book.

[7] Austin Ranney, ed., *Political Science and Public Policy* (Chicago: Markham, 1968), p. 3.

[8] Ibid., p. 13.

[9] Fred I. Greenstein and Nelson W. Polsby, eds., *Handbook of Political Science*, vol. 6, *Policies and Policymaking* (Reading, Mass.: Addison-Wesley, 1975).

policy-making processes and to ignore policy content. An article on "Foreign Policy" in the *International Encyclopedia of the Social Sciences*, published in 1968, focuses mostly on how policy is made while virtually ignoring policy instruments.[10] A similar article in the *Handbook of Political Science* identifies "the concentration on policy process and the neglect of policy output" as "one of the major deficiencies in the study of foreign policy."[11]

The neglect of scholarly attention to techniques of statecraft is usually noted with some regret—if it is noted at all. An important exception is James N. Rosenau's *International Politics and Foreign Policy: A Reader in Research and Theory.*[12] Rosenau defends the exclusion of selections on the "tools or techniques of statecraft" from his collection of readings on the grounds that such matters have been thoroughly treated and "pose no major theoretical or methodological problems" (p. 174).

> Unlike the goals of state action, its forms have proved easy to clarify and analyze. The nature, implications, and consequences of diplomatic action, for example, are the subject of a vast literature not marked by controversy or confusion. The purposes, types, and limits of diplomacy are readily classified, and one is hard put to think of any major methodological problems which might inhibit the investigation of diplomatic practices and processes. Much the same can be said of the other tools and techniques of "statecraft." Propaganda, subversion, economic action, military action (or the threat of it), and other techniques have all been thoroughly explored, and none has presented insoluble substantive or procedural problems. (p. 169)

Although economic techniques of statecraft are the main concern of this book, it should be noted in passing that even Rosenau's remarks about diplomacy are questionable. The works of Robert Jervis[13] and Thomas Schelling[14] have demonstrated numerous theoretical and methodological problems and have generated many new insights about this technique of statecraft. The lack of fungibility of power resources, the possibilities and

[10] Bernard C. Cohen, "Foreign Policy," *International Encyclopedia of the Social Sciences*, vol. 5 (New York: Free Press, 1968), pp. 530-535.

[11] Bernard C. Cohen and Scott A. Harris, "Foreign Policy," in *Handbook*, vol. 6, *Policies*, pp. 382-383.

[12] Rev. ed. (New York: Free Press, 1969), pp. 167-174.

[13] *The Logic of Images in International Relations* (Princeton: Princeton University Press, 1970) and *Perception and Misperception in International Politics* (Princeton: Princeton University Press, 1976).

[14] *The Strategy of Conflict* (Cambridge: Harvard University Press, 1960) and *Arms and Influence* (New Haven: Yale University Press, 1966). See also Alexander L. George, David K. Hall, and William R. Simons, *The Limits of Coercive Diplomacy* (Boston: Little, Brown, 1971).

incentives for secrecy and deception, and the subtleties of strategic bargaining are only a few of the important theoretical and methodological problems associated with the study of diplomatic statecraft.[15] Rosenau's reader provided several generations of graduate students with a useful overview of the field of international politics and foreign policy, but it seriously misled them by implying that there were no worthy intellectual challenges in the study of "the nature, implications, and consequences" of statecraft.[16]

Policy analysts might try to justify ignoring influence techniques by arguing that such matters should be addressed by students of power relations. Unfortunately, power analysts have been just as oblivious to policy instruments as the policy analysts. In Robert Dahl's classic article, "The Concept of Power," he notes that the "main problem . . . is not to determine the existence of power but to make comparisons."[17] For Dahl, however, and for most political scientists, this implies a comparison of actors rather than a comparison of techniques. "Who governs?" rather than "By what means?" has been the dominant concern of most power analysts. What kinds of influence attempts are most likely to succeed? Is the carrot more effective than the stick? Is napalm more useful than economic aid? Are economic embargoes more likely to work than military invasions? Political scientists have had little to say in answer to such questions.

In an inventory of "scientific findings" in the field of comparative foreign policy, Patrick J. McGowan and Howard B. Shapiro found that "the effect of the foreign policy tool used has been a neglected area of research."[18] They expressed both surprise and concern about this finding,

[15] Any attempt to discuss the consequences or outcomes of an influence attempt must deal with counterfactual conditions, one of the most difficult methodological problems in social science. Also, the inclusion of positive sanctions—actual or promised rewards—in a treatment of influence attempts leads to a consideration of the relationship between exchange relations and power relations, one of the most fundamental conceptual problems in all of social science. See David A. Baldwin, "Power and Social Exchange," *American Political Science Review* LXXII (December 1978):1229-1242.

[16] Ironically, although Rosenau belittles the importance of studying techniques of statecraft, he has written one of the most valuable treatises on the subject, a work that deserves far more attention than it has received. James N. Rosenau, *Calculated Control as a Unifying Concept in the Study of International Politics and Foreign Policy*, Research Monograph No. 15, Princeton University Center of International Studies (February 10, 1963). While others preach without practicing, Rosenau apparently prefers to practice without preaching.

[17] *Behavioral Science* II (July 1957):206.

[18] *The Comparative Study of Foreign Policy: A Survey of Scientific Findings* (Beverly Hills, Calif.: Sage, 1973), p. 193. A similar comment nearly a decade later suggests that the situation has not changed much. See Patrick Callahan, Linda P. Brady, and Margaret G. Hermann, eds., *Describing Foreign Policy Behavior* (Beverly Hills, Calif.: Sage, 1982), p. 257.

and their rhetorical question is worth pondering—"Since the purpose of foreign policy is to bring about some consequence . . . why study foreign policy if you are going to ignore the outcomes which decision-makers hope to bring about with that policy?" (p. 211).

This book does not purport to fill the need for more study of the nature, implications, and consequences of techniques of statecraft. It is intended to take some steps in this direction, however, by clarifying some basic concepts, by constructing an analytical framework, and by treating in some depth the least studied and most misunderstood techniques of statecraft—the economic ones.

Classification of Techniques

In making influence attempts foreign policy makers may choose from among a wide variety of alternative ways to promote their goals. Foreign policy "tools," "means," "instruments," "levers," and "techniques" all refer to the policy options available to decision makers in pursuing a given set of objectives; and these terms will here be used interchangeably.[19] To reduce the multitude of techniques of statecraft to manageable proportions, a classification scheme that facilitates reference to broad categories of statecraft is useful. The selection of a particular taxonomy, however, is not a purely arbitrary undertaking, but rather should proceed according to specified criteria.

The criteria employed here are as follows:

1. Conformity with scientific canons requiring parallel categories to be mutually exclusive and exhaustive of all cases.
2. Avoidance of unnecessary departures from common usage. Ideally, categories would be consistent with common usage by laymen, academics, and policy makers.
3. Utility in identifying and clarifying policy options for modern statesmen. The important thing is to capture the richness and variety of available techniques without overwhelming the policy maker with a huge number of categories.

Some scholars reduce all techniques of statecraft to two categories—war and diplomacy. Both Raymond Aron and Hans Morgenthau illustrate this tendency to use "diplomacy" to refer to all the means of conducting

[19] It should be noted that "resources," "power bases," and "capabilities," which are sometimes used interchangeably with the terms noted in the text, are not so used in this book for reasons that will be discussed in the section on statecraft and international politics.

relations with other states short of war.[20] While such an approach may be reasonably consistent with the first two criteria, it is seriously deficient in terms of the third criterion. It is simply not very helpful to present a policy maker with only two sets of options. Even the busiest statesman is likely to regard such categorization as overly simple and not especially useful. The trick is to give the policy maker a set of alternatives that is simple enough to be readily understood yet complex enough to call attention to alternatives that might otherwise be ignored.

Charles F. Hermann[21] has developed a taxonomy of foreign policy instruments based on eight categories: diplomatic, domestic political, military, intelligence, economic, scientific/technological, promotive, and natural resources. Although this thought-provoking list is more useful than the simple dichotomy suggested by Aron and Morgenthau, some of the categories are not mutually exclusive (e.g., "economic" and "natural resources"); and, more importantly, this taxonomy may involve too many categories to be useful to a policy maker. Bewildering complexity is as undesirable as oversimplification.

If common usage is a desirable characteristic, an old taxonomy may be more useful than a more recent one, since there has been more time for such categories to become accepted. Harold Lasswell's classic work, *Politics: Who Gets What, When, How*, sets forth a classification scheme that seems well suited to the study of policy instruments.[22] In a "postscript" to this book written in 1958, Lasswell suggests that his "fourfold division of policy instruments is particularly convenient when the external relations of a group are considered: information, diplomacy, economics, force (words, deals, goods, weapons)."[23] Lasswell's formulation provides the basis for the following taxonomy of techniques of statecraft employed in this book:

1. *Propaganda* refers to influence attempts relying primarily on the deliberate manipulation of verbal symbols.
2. *Diplomacy* refers to influence attempts relying primarily on negotiation.
3. *Economic statecraft* refers to influence attempts relying primarily

---

[20] Raymond Aron, *Peace and War: A Theory of International Relations* (Garden City, N.Y.: Doubleday, 1966), pp. 5, 24; and Hans J. Morgenthau, *Politics Among Nations*, 3d ed. (New York: Alfred A. Knopf, 1964), pp. 539 ff. For a similar conception of diplomacy see Adam Watson, *Diplomacy* (New York: McGraw-Hill, 1983); and Hedley Bull, *The Anarchical Society* (New York: Columbia University Press, 1977), p. 162.

[21] "Instruments of Foreign Policy," in *Describing Foreign Policy Behavior*, ed. Callahan, Brady, and Hermann, pp. 159-161.

[22] (New York: McGraw-Hill, 1936).

[23] Pp. 204-205. Cf. Harold D. Lasswell, *World Politics Faces Economics* (New York: McGraw-Hill, 1945), p. 9.

on resources which have a reasonable semblance of a market price in terms of money. (This category will be developed in chapter 3.)

4. *Military statecraft* refers to influence attempts relying primarily on violence, weapons, or force.

Actual influence attempts by states, of course, will often involve varying degrees of more than one of these elements; but in most cases it is possible to make a reasonable judgment as to the primary basis of the influence attempt. Words, for example, are often involved in diplomatic, economic, and military statecraft; but that does not mean that all such influence attempts must be classified as propaganda. As in all classification schemes, borderline cases exist that require the analyst to make judgments. With a reasonable amount of imagination and judgment the requirements that categories be mutually exclusive and that they exhaust all cases can be satisfied, at least adequately if not perfectly.

These categories have the advantage of corresponding closely to common usage by both laymen and academics.[24] The scheme also corresponds roughly with the organizational arrangements of most governments. Almost all governments have specialized institutional machinery for the conduct of diplomacy and military statecraft, and almost all have separate institutions for dealing with economic matters. Thus, the scheme also corresponds with categories familiar to policy makers.

The number of categories is small enough to be readily comprehended yet large enough to remind policy makers of the broad spectrum of available alternatives. If further complexity is desired, each category can be subdivided in terms of such distinctions as conditional versus unconditional usage, multilateral versus bilateral channels, positive versus negative sanctions, and covert versus overt operations.

The main concern of this book is with economic techniques of statecraft; so why bother with a taxonomy of other techniques? The answer lies partly

[24] Although some scholars add one or two additional categories, the four categories suggested by Lasswell are usually included. See, for example, William T. R. Fox and Annette Baker Fox, "International Politics," *International Encyclopedia of the Social Sciences*, vol. 8 (New York: Free Press, 1968), pp. 50-60; K. J. Holsti, *International Politics: A Framework for Analysis*, 4th ed. (Englewood Cliffs, N.J.: Prentice-Hall, 1983), pp. 161-310; Harry Howe Ransome, ed., *An American Foreign Policy Reader* (New York: Thomas Y. Crowell, 1965); U.S. Senate, Committee on Foreign Relations, *United States Foreign Policy*, "Economic, Social, and Political Change in Underdeveloped Countries and Its Implications for United States Policy," a study prepared by the Center for International Studies, Massachusetts Institute of Technology, Committee Print, 86th Cong., 2d sess., 1960, pp. 4-6; Howard H. Lentner, *Foreign Policy Analysis: A Comparative and Conceptual Approach* (Columbus, Ohio: Charles E. Merrill, 1974), pp. 216-220; and Myres S. McDougal and Florentino P. Feliciano, *Law and Minimum World Public Order* (New Haven: Yale University Press, 1961), pp. 27-33.

in the nature of policy making and partly in the peculiar nature of *foreign* policy making. Policy making involves making decisions, and decision making involves choosing among alternative courses of action. The advantages and disadvantages of various policy options acquire significance primarily by comparison with other policy options. Thus, in any decision-making situation, decision makers are always going to want *comparative* information about the costs and benefits of their perceived alternatives. There is an important difference, however, between business firms and nation-states in evaluating policy options. If a business firm discovers that all of its options have unattractive cost/benefit ratios, it can always decide to go out of business and employ its assets in a more lucrative way. Although technically speaking, nation-states have the option of ceasing to exist, this alternative is likely to be so unthinkable to foreign policy decision makers that for practical purposes it is irrelevant. No matter how tough the going, no matter how unpleasant the situation, no matter how many alternatives have unattractive consequences, the statesmen usually cannot elect to "go out of business."

Instead they must choose from among the alternative courses of action as they perceive them—no matter how unpleasant. From the standpoint of the decision maker, information about the costs and benefits of only one technique (or category of techniques) of statecraft is utterly useless without some implicit or explicit assumptions about the pros and cons of alternative (categories of) techniques. Indeed, the concepts of cost and benefit necessarily imply the existence of at least one policy alternative. In a world in which everyone can have his cake and eat it too, there are no policy decisions to be made. The same is true of a world in which everyone can have his cake but no one can eat it. Costs and benefits make sense *only* within the context of a choice situation. In evaluating the utility of techniques of statecraft, it is wise to keep in mind the answer given by the octogenarian in response to an inquiry as to whether he was enjoying old age—"I enjoy it very much—considering the alternative!" Before leaping to conclusions about the utility (or disutility) of economic statecraft in a given situation, one should consider the alternatives.[25]

STATECRAFT AND FOREIGN POLICY: ENDS, MEANS, AND TARGETS

One of the main themes of this book is that economic techniques of statecraft should be described and evaluated using the same intellectual

---

[25] On the importance of considering alternative courses of action, see Herbert A. Simon, *Administrative Behavior*, 3d ed. (New York: Free Press, 1976), pp. 61-67, 178-180, et passim.

apparatus that is used to analyze other techniques of statecraft. The primary intellectual perspective is foreign policy; it is not international organization, international law, or international economics. Thus, some general comments on the nature of foreign policy are in order.

Foreign policy is generally viewed as purposive behavior, i.e., activity oriented toward some end, goal, objective, or aim. As such, foreign policy is an "instrumental activity," i.e., activity carried out because of the results it is expected to produce rather than for its own sake.[26] When a scholar suggests that economic sanctions can be understood better as "expressive" rather than "instrumental" behavior, he is adopting an analytical perspective quite different from that of most foreign policy analysis.[27] Although abandoning the "mainstream" is legitimate and sometimes enlightening, those who do so have a responsibility to explain and justify their actions. Departing from the normal paradigm in a casual or off-hand way is a questionable scholarly practice.

Means-ends analysis is complicated by the fact that very few ends are ultimate or final values; most are intermediate or instrumental in some sense. Thus, the same activity may be viewed as a means in one context and a goal in another. There is no reason to despair, however; as long as care is taken to specify the ends and means in the particular situation being analyzed, this approach can be very useful.[28]

Noting this difficulty, inherent in all means-ends analysis, scholars sometimes describe the distinction between instruments and objectives as "no more than a convenient analytical device."[29] For those interested in the effectiveness, efficiency, utility, or rationality of a given policy or technique of statecraft, however, the distinction is more than a "convenient analytical device"; it is a necessity. As Graham Allison has observed, for analyzing the utility of alternative ways to solve a problem, "there is no clear alternative to this basic framework."[30]

It is useful to distinguish between the targets (or domain) of an influence

[26] Cf. ibid., pp. 62, 182; Sprout and Sprout, *Politics of the Planet Earth*, p. 109; Graham T. Allison, *Essence of Decision* (Boston: Little, Brown, 1971), pp. 1-38, 252-257; and James N. Rosenau, "Comparative Foreign Policy: Fad, Fantasy, or Field?" *International Studies Quarterly* XII (September 1968):323-324. On the distinction between "instrumental" and "intrinsic" goals, see also Harold D. Lasswell and Abraham Kaplan, *Power and Society* (New Haven: Yale University Press, 1950), pp. 16-17, 240.

[27] For examples see chapter 6.

[28] For discussions of means-ends analysis, see Simon, *Administrative Behavior*, pp. 61-73; and Vernon Van Dyke, *Political Science: A Philosophical Analysis* (Stanford: Stanford University Press, 1960), pp. 10-13, 154-157.

[29] Peter J. Katzenstein, "Domestic Structures and Strategies of Foreign Economic Policy," *International Organization* XXXI (Autumn 1977):882.

[30] *Essence of Decision*, p. 268.

attempt and the objectives (or scope) of the attempt.[31] The distinction refers to who is to be influenced (the target) and in what ways (the scope). Targets and objectives vary in number, specificity, and importance. In any given influence attempt, states may—and usually do—pursue more than one goal with respect to more than one target. The policy maker's image of his goals may be specific, as in a positive vote on Resolution No. 412 in the General Assembly on the day after tomorrow, or general, as in enhanced respect in the indefinite future. Likewise, the policy maker's image of the targets may be specific, as in the Brazilian government, or general, as in the Third World. Not all goals or targets are equally important, but none is intrinsically unimportant. Thus, it may be useful to sort out the primary, secondary, and perhaps even tertiary goals and targets of a given influence attempt; but it is a mistake to assume that the content of such categories never varies. James Barber's[32] distinctions among the primary, secondary, and tertiary objectives of economic sanctions are valuable contributions insofar as they call attention to the multiplicity and variable significance of such objectives; but they are unfortunate insofar as certain kinds of goals and targets are permanently assigned to specific categories. The particular state with which trade is embargoed may or may not be the primary target of the influence attempt.[33] When one chooses to "make an example" out of someone, the usual implication is that other targets matter more than the immediate one. The teacher who chooses to "make an example" out of a misbehaving student is often more interested in the deterrent effects on the other children than in the effects on the particular recipient of the punishment.[34] Changing the behavior of the embargoed state may indeed be—and often is—more important than influencing the perceptions and attitudes of onlookers; but sometimes the reverse is true. Determination of the relative importance of targets and goals should be treated as an empirical matter rather than based on *a priori* assumptions embedded in a conceptual framework that assigns primary importance to

[31] The terms "scope" and "domain" come from Lasswell and Kaplan, *Power and Society*, pp. 73-76.

[32] "Economic Sanctions as a Policy Instrument," *International Affairs* LV (July 1979):367-384.

[33] In a widely cited article Johan Galtung defines economic sanctions in terms of "senders" and "receivers." In context it is clear that the "receivers" are the immediate and direct targets of the sanctions. There is no consideration of the possibility that there might be targets of such influence attempts other than, or in addition to, the sanctioned states. Johan Galtung, "On the Effects of International Economic Sanctions: With Examples from the Case of Rhodesia," *World Politics* XIX (April 1967):378-416, esp. 379.

[34] "Throughout history, and especially for the great powers since 1945, states have often cared about specific issues less for their intrinsic value than for the conclusions they felt others would draw from the way they dealt with them. This is often not understood." (Jervis, *Logic of Images*, p. 7.)

objectives having to do with the behavior of the immediate target and secondary or tertiary importance to objectives having to do with the perceptions of third parties or with the structure and operations of the international system. The number, specificity, and relative importance of targets and goals are all researchable topics and should be so treated by the foreign policy analyst.

Recognition that a given influence attempt may involve multiple goals and targets of varying generality and significance is an important first step for assessing the utility of various techniques of statecraft, especially economic ones. Case studies of economic sanctions, for example, based on consideration of a single goal with respect to a single target should be scrutinized with particular care. No case study, of course, can ever capture all of the complexities of a situation; but oversimplified case studies may be quite misleading. The fact that many of the case studies of economic statecraft have been produced by economists, international lawyers, and specialists in international organization justifies wariness on the part of the foreign policy analyst. Factual details essential to judging the utility of a technique of statecraft from the standpoint of a foreign policy maker may be of little or no importance to a scholar interested in maximizing global economic welfare, strengthening the international legal order, or improving the viability of the United Nations.

STATECRAFT AND INTERNATIONAL POLITICS

To treat techniques of statecraft as the means by which statesmen make influence attempts on other actors is to say that such activities are political acts. For most political scientists political processes are defined in terms of power or influence, that is, situations in which some people change the actions or predispositions of other people in some way.[35]

Although power analysis has been a concern of political thinkers for centuries, Robert Dahl maintains that "the systematic empirical study of power relations is remarkably new."[36] He attributes the "vast improvement in the clarity" of power concepts to the fact that "the last several decades probably have witnessed more systematic efforts to tie down these concepts than have previous millenia of political thought."[37] Exact turning points in intellectual history are difficult to pinpoint, but many would regard the publication of Lasswell and Kaplan's *Power and Society* in 1950 as the

[35] See Robert A. Dahl, *Modern Political Analysis*, 3d ed. (Englewood Cliffs, N.J.: Prentice-Hall, 1976), pp. 1-41; Lasswell and Kaplan, *Power and Society*, esp. pp. xii-xiii, 53, 75; and Quincy Wright, *The Study of International Relations* (New York: Appleton-Century-Crofts, 1955), esp. pp. 130-131.

[36] "Power," *International Encyclopedia of the Social Sciences*, vol. 12, p. 414.

[37] *Modern Political Analysis*, p. 26.

watershed between the older, intuitive, and ambiguous treatments of power and the clarity and precision of more recent studies.[38] Since then, Herbert Simon, James March, Robert Dahl, Jack Nagel, Frederick Frey, Felix Oppenheim, and others have developed power analysis to the point that the social power literature stands today as one of the most impressive achievements of modern social science.[39]

One need not accept all—or any—of the particulars of this literature in analyzing power in the international arena, but one should not ignore it. Unfortunately, students of international politics and foreign policy have paid little attention to the revolution in power analysis spawned by Lasswell and Kaplan.[40] One of my main purposes in this book is to introduce some of the basic concepts and analytical tools of modern social power analysis into the study of techniques of statecraft and to demonstrate that even the most primitive use of such analytical tools can greatly improve understanding of the efficacy of economic techniques of statecraft.

A preliminary review of the principles of power analysis to be applied later may be helpful at this point. Although some power analysts might object to particular aspects of this list, most should find it both familiar and compatible with the social power literature in general.[41]

[38] In an early and influential article, Herbert A. Simon described his discussion as "a series of footnotes on the analysis of influence and power by Lasswell and Kaplan." "Notes on the Observation and Measurement of Political Power," *Journal of Politics* XV (November 1953).301. On this point, see also Jack H. Nagel, "Some Questions about the Concept of Power," *Behavioral Science* XIII (March 1968):129.

[39] Simon, *Models of Man* (New York: Wiley, 1957); James G. March, "An Introduction to the Theory and Measurement of Influence," *American Political Science Review* XLIX (June 1955):431-451; Dahl, "Concept of Power" and "Power"; Nagel, *Descriptive Analysis of Power*; Frederick W. Frey, "On Issues and Nonissues in the Study of Power," *American Political Science Review* LXV (December 1971):1081-1101; and Felix E. Oppenheim, *Political Concepts: A Reconstruction* (Chicago: University of Chicago Press, 1981), pp. 1-52. Excellent reviews of the literature on power, reflecting both consensus and healthy intellectual dispute, are the following: Dorwin Cartwright, "Influence, Leadership, Control," in *Handbook of Organizations*, ed. James March (Chicago: Rand McNally, 1965), pp. 1-47; Dahl, "Power"; James T. Tedeschi and Thomas V. Bonoma, "Power and Influence: An Introduction," in *The Social Influence Processes*, ed. James T. Tedeschi (Chicago: Aldine-Atherton, 1972), pp. 1-49; and Nagel, *Descriptive Analysis of Power*.

[40] On this point see Rosenau, *Calculated Control*, pp. 2-3; David A. Baldwin, "Inter-Nation Influence Revisited," *Journal of Conflict Resolution* XV (December 1971):471-486; and "Power Analysis and World Politics: New Trends versus Old Tendencies," *World Politics* XXXI (January 1979):161-194.

[41] For further discussion of these principles, see Baldwin, "Money and Power"; "Inter-Nation Influence Revisited"; "The Power of Positive Sanctions," *World Politics* XXIV (October 1971):19-38; "The Costs of Power," *Journal of Conflict Resolution* XV (October 1971):145-155; "Power and Social Exchange"; "Power Analysis"; and "Interdependence and Power: A Conceptual Analysis," *International Organization* XXXIV (Autumn 1980):495-504.

1. *Power is a relational concept.* It refers to a relationship between two or more people, not to a property of any one of them. In order to make a meaningful statement about an (actual or potential) influence relationship, one must (explicitly or implicitly) specify who is influencing (or has the capacity to influence) whom (domain) with respect to what (scope).

2. *Power can be defined broadly to include all relationships in which someone gets someone else to do something that he or she would not otherwise do.*[42] Although such a broad definition is ill suited for some kinds of research, it is especially useful if one is interested in identifying and assessing the probable efficacy of the options available to a policy maker. Since that is one of the main purposes of this book, the terms power and influence will be used interchangeably in this broad sense.

3. *Both positive sanctions (actual or promised rewards) and negative sanctions (actual or threatened punishments) are means to exercise power.* The important point here is to include positive sanctions, an often overlooked means of influencing others.[43] Both political scientists in general and students of international politics in particular have tended to ignore the role of positive sanctions.

4. *Power may rest on various bases, and no one form of power is basic to all the others.* Lasswell and Kaplan are emphatic on this point:

> Political science is concerned with power in general, with all the forms in which it occurs. Failure to recognize that power may rest on various bases, each with a varying scope, has confused and distorted the conception of power itself, and retarded inquiry into the conditions and consequences of its exercise in various ways. . . .
>
> In particular, it is of crucial importance to recognize that power may rest on various bases, differing not only from culture to culture, but also within a culture from one power structure to another. . . .
>
> In short, the concepts of influence and power are extremely general, and have reference to a wide range of interpersonal relations. The analysis can be carried to whatever level of refinement is required by the particular problem at hand. But political phenomena are only obscured by the pseudo simplification attained with any unitary conception of power as being always and everywhere the same (violence

---

[42] Dahl used similar phraseology in the first edition of *Modern Political Analysis* (1963), p. 40, to refer to the "common-sense notion" of influence. Critics have pointed out that a focus on observable behavior may exclude changes in beliefs, attitudes, opinions, expectations, emotions, and/or predispositions to act. This is a valid criticism, but it is easily taken care of by simply subsuming such matters under the general term behavior. Unless otherwise specified, all references in this book to one actor's influence on another actor's behavior or actions should be interpreted as including these matters. See Nagel, *Descriptive Analysis of Power*, p. 12.

[43] See Baldwin, "Positive Sanctions."

or economic power or . . .). What is common to all power and influence relations is only effect on policy. What is affected and on what basis are variables whose specific content in a given situation can be determined only by inquiry into the actual practices of the actors in that situation.[44]

The position of Lasswell and Kaplan may be contrasted with frequently voiced views that "in the last resort, influence depends upon the will to use force";[45] "that the *ultima ratio* of power in international relations is war";[46] that "in the final analysis, force is the ultimate form of power";[47] or that "a study of power, in the last analysis, is a study of the capacity to wage war."[48] Such views imply that military force is a more fundamental base of power, at least in international politics, than other bases of power. While admitting that there are many situations in which military force is more important than other power resources, the argument in this book follows Lasswell and Kaplan in not prejudging the relative importance of force and in treating this question as one to be answered in the context of particular cases.[49]

5. *Power is multidimensional.* Power varies in degree with respect to several dimensions, including scope, weight, domain, and cost. Thus, analyzing the outcomes of influence attempts in terms of simple dichotomies or single dimensions can be misleading *even in the unusual situation in which statesmen are pursuing a single objective with respect to a single target.*

6. *Power is not necessarily a zero-sum game.* It is frequently asserted that an increase in the power of one actor necessitates a decrease in the power of another actor.[50] One state's gain in power is another state's loss. Once the multidimensional nature of power is recognized, however, it is

[44] *Power and Society*, pp. 85, 92.

[45] J. B. Condliffe, "Economic Power as an Instrument of National Policy," *American Economic Review* XXXIV (March 1944):308.

[46] Edward Hallett Carr, *The Twenty Years' Crisis: 1919-1939*, 2d ed. (London: Macmillan, 1946), p. 109.

[47] Robert Gilpin, *U.S. Power and the Multinational Corporation* (New York: Basic Books, 1975), p. 24.

[48] Ray S. Cline, *World Power Assessment: A Calculus of Strategic Drift* (Boulder, Colo.: Westview, 1975), p. 8.

[49] On the tendency of students of international politics to exaggerate the importance of military bases of power, see Sprout and Sprout, *Politics of the Planet Earth*, pp. 167-168; and Baldwin, "Power Analysis," pp. 180-183.

[50] For examples, see Albert O. Hirschman, *National Power and the Structure of Foreign Trade* (Berkeley: University of California Press, 1945), p. 6; R. G. Hawtrey, *Economic Aspects of Sovereignty* (London: Longmans, Green, 1930), p. 27; Gilpin, *U.S. Power and the Multinational Corporation*, pp. 22-25, 34; Gilpin, *War and Change in World Politics* (Cambridge: Cambridge University Press, 1981), p. 94; and Charles P. Kindleberger, *Power and Money: The Economics of International Politics and the Politics of International Economics* (New York: Basic Books, 1970), p. 20.

easy to show that such a view is fallacious.[51] It is quite possible—and common—for two actors to increase their power over one another with respect to similar or different aspects of behavior simultaneously. Mutual influence is a ubiquitous phenomenon. It is especially important for the student of economic statecraft to avoid this fallacy since politics and economics are often alleged to be zero-sum and positive-sum games respectively. Such characterizations, it will be argued, impede fruitful thinking about economic statecraft.

7. *Power analysis always requires consideration of counterfactual conditions.* If power relations involve some people getting other people to do something they would not otherwise do, the question of *what would otherwise have been done* cannot be ignored. The necessity of dealing with this question makes power analysis inherently messy, difficult, and frustrating. Nothing very significant can be said about the utility of economic techniques of statecraft without addressing the question of what would have happened if they had not been used or if some other technique had been used. Such discussions may amount to little more than "educated guesses," but this is preferable to ignoring the problem.

The relational nature of the concept of power noted in the first principle has implications for the analysis of techniques of statecraft that are seldom acknowledged. These implications may be illuminated in terms of the difference between "relational concepts" and "property concepts."[52] The population, geographic area, and wealth of a country are all properties; they can be defined and measured without reference to other countries. Similarly, policies, decisions, influence attempts, intentions, and instruments of statecraft are properties of a state in that one does not need to know anything about other states in order to describe them. They are in a sense possessed by and under the control of the state to which they belong. In contrast to such properties are terms like influence, capabilities, power bases, and power resources. These terms are relational in the sense that they say something about an actual or potential relationship between two or more actors.[53] It is impossible to describe actor A's capabilities without saying or implying something about the value system of actor B. A gun, for example, may be a property belonging to A; and, as such, it can be used by A in an *attempt* to influence B. The determination of whether A will actually succeed in influencing B, however, is not entirely within A's control; it depends on B's value system. Some people are afraid of guns; others are not. In some situations guns are power resources; in others they are not. Table 1 categorizes terms commonly used by students

[51] See Baldwin, "Money and Power," pp. 605-606; "Power Analysis," pp. 186-187; and "Power and Social Exchange."
[52] For a discussion, see Oppenheim, *Political Concepts*, pp. 4-8.
[53] See Baldwin, "Power Analysis," pp. 163-175.

Table 1

Relational and Property Concepts Employed in International Relations

Property Concepts	Relational Concepts
Foreign policy	International politics
Lever	Leverage
Weapon	War
Policy	Power
Intentions	Capabilities
Undertakings	Outcomes
Influence attempts	Influence
Decisions	Results
Policy instruments	Power bases (or power resources)
Technique of statecraft	Influence technique

of international politics and foreign policy in terms of the distinction between property and relational concepts.

The study of techniques of statecraft is complicated and confused by the tendency to treat the capabilities (power resources, power assets, or power bases) of states as if they were property rather than relational concepts. Thus, statesmen are often described as "employing" or "using" their "capabilities" or "power bases" as if these were possessions of a single state.[54] And techniques of statecraft are often classified according to the kind of "power base" being "employed"—e.g., economic, military, propaganda, or diplomatic. Thus, economic techniques are said to exercise economic power, military techniques are said to exercise military power, and so on.

If influence attempts always succeeded and if the success of economic techniques of statecraft was always due to economic bases of power, this approach might be acceptable. Influence attempts, however, often fail; yet this is logically impossible if they really rest on "power bases" or "base values" as conceived by Lasswell and Kaplan. The "influence base" as defined by Lasswell and Kaplan (pp. 83-84) refers to the causal condition that gives influence its effectiveness. Thus, by definition, ineffective influence attempts cannot employ "influence bases." Since Lasswell and

---

[54] For examples, see Hermann, "Instruments of Foreign Policy," p. 154; Klaus Knorr, *The Power of Nations: The Political Economy of International Relations* (New York: Basic Books, 1975), p. 6; and Richard L. Merritt, ed., *Foreign Policy Analysis* (Lexington, Mass.: Lexington Books, 1975), p. 1. In the 1958 "postscript" to *Politics: Who Gets What, When, How* (p. 204), Lasswell also fails to distinguish between power bases and policy bases. The taxonomy of policy instruments described earlier is therefore developed from—but not identical with—Lasswell's.

Kaplan invented the concept in order to explain why some influence attempts succeed, this was a sensible way for them to proceed. Problems have arisen from efforts to use this same terminology to describe and analyze influence *attempts*. In short, whereas Lasswell and Kaplan were trying to explain *outcomes*, subsequent scholars have tried to use their concept of "influence bases" to explain and describe *undertakings*.

What is clearly needed is a conception of the instruments of policy that is independent of the causal conditions that determine success, i.e., the bases of power. The instruments of policy, or techniques of statecraft, should thus be treated as properties of a single state and should be discussed without implying anything whatsoever about the probable effectiveness of an influence attempt employing a particular instrument. In short, the concept of policy instruments belongs to the realm of policy analysis, not capability analysis. For the same reason that a clear distinction must be maintained between undertakings and outcomes, a clear distinction must also be made between the bases of influence *attempts* and the bases of influence.[55]

An additional reason to distinguish between the bases of influence and the instruments used in making influence attempts is that failure to do so obscures the dynamics of the influence process. Economic techniques of statecraft are often used to exercise economic power, i.e., power in which the causal condition of success is an economic base value. But economic techniques of statecraft may also be used to exercise noneconomic forms of power. Thus, economic sanctions may be effective not because of their economic impact, which may be nil, but rather because of the signal they send about the intentions of the state imposing the sanctions.

An embargo, for example, might be interpreted by the target state as a veiled threat to use military force if compliance is not forthcoming. In such a situation, the causal condition of success (the influence base) is military rather than economic. It would be misleading, however, to argue that since the actual success of the influence attempt was based on the perceived (or misperceived?) threat to use force, no economic policy instrument was used in the first place. The description of policy options and the description of the causal condition(s) of success are best kept separate if one wants to understand how techniques of statecraft work. In sum, policy instruments used to make influence attempts should be described in ways that imply nothing whatever about either the probability of success or the causal condition of success. Trying is one thing; succeeding is another.

---

[55] On the importance of distinguishing clearly between foreign policy analysis and capability analysis, between undertakings and outcomes, see Harold Sprout and Margaret Sprout, *The Ecological Perspective on Human Affairs: With Special Reference to International Politics* (Princeton: Princeton University Press, 1965). Cf. Rosenau, *Calculated Control*, pp. 36-37.

STATECRAFT AND POLICY SCIENCE

The study of statecraft is based predominantly on case studies rather than on experimental or statistical research approaches. This does not mean, however, that such cases cannot be approached in the spirit of science.[56] To approach specific cases in the spirit of science is to treat them as specific examples of a more general category of events rather than as unique historical phenomena. Thus, the United States trade embargo against Cuba can be viewed as a specific event in a larger category of events called negative economic sanctions, which, in turn, is a part of the category of techniques of statecraft based on negative sanctions, which is one type of statecraft in general. To depict the Cuban embargo this way is to lay the groundwork for such questions as the following: If the embargo seems to be a failure, one might ask what the success rate is for influence attempts in general in the international arena before drawing conclusions about the effectiveness of such measures. If the embargo generates popular support for the Cuban regime, one might ask whether this is a typical side effect of inter-nation influence attempts based on negative sanctions before inferring that such side effects are peculiar to economic sanctions. And if the embargo seems costly, one might inquire as to the costliness of other techniques of statecraft before making a judgment about the utility of economic sanctions. Merely to pose such questions is to expose the intellectual weaknesses in much of what has been written about economic statecraft, for most of these writings do not even acknowledge the existence of such questions, let alone answer them. Case studies of particular instances can enhance our understanding of the techniques of statecraft, but only if we have some general framework in terms of which to judge the significance of a given case. The facts never speak for themselves.

It is sometimes suggested that an emphasis on generalization is relevant only for those interested in developing theories and not for those interested in advising policy makers. The concept of policy science, however, denies the validity of a rigid distinction between theoretical knowledge and knowledge relevant to policy making.[57] Without trying to provide specific rec-

[56] For two especially useful essays on science and case studies, see Alexander L. George, "Case Studies and Theory Development: The Method of Structured, Focused Comparison," in *Diplomacy: New Approaches in History, Theory, and Policy*, ed. Paul Gordon Lauren (New York: Free Press, 1979), pp. 43-68; and Harry Eckstein, "Case Study and Theory in Political Science," in *Handbook of Political Science*, vol. 7, *Strategies of Inquiry*, pp. 79-137.

[57] Lasswell and Kaplan conceived of the whole discipline of political science as "one of the policy sciences" (p. xii). A more recent discussion of the need for "policy-relevant theory" in international relations appears as an appendix in Alexander L. George and Richard Smoke, *Deterrence in American Foreign Policy: Theory and Practice* (New York: Columbia University Press, 1974), pp. 616-642. See also Harold Sprout and Margaret Sprout, *Foundations of International Politics* (Princeton: D. Van Nostrand, 1962), pp. 28-29.

ommendations for dealing with specific problems, scholars can provide theories and analytical tools that help policy makers clarify their goals, identify policy options, and assess the likely utility of various alternatives.

The study of the efficacy of various techniques of statecraft is based on what William H. Riker has called a "recipe-like" concept of causality, which focuses attention on the manipulative techniques by which a given effect can be made to occur. Riker contrasts this with "the necessary and sufficient condition kind of causality," which focuses on a "full explanation" of the effect rather than on manipulative techniques.[58] Although Riker may be correct in asserting the superiority of the latter concept of causality for some types of science, the former concept is more useful in the policy sciences and will therefore be employed here.

Efforts to study politics scientifically are often marked by impatience with conceptual problems and a resultant preoccupation with operationalization and measurement. Conceptual problems are brushed aside as "mere semantics" in an effort to get on with the important job of testing hypotheses. The result is often a misleading impression of precision about something that was never very clear in the first place.

The primary goal of this book is to develop basic concepts and to construct an analytical framework that will encourage thinking about statecraft in general, and economic statecraft in particular, in ways that are both scientifically respectable and relevant to the needs of policy makers. Neither grand theories of economic statecraft nor definitive studies of particular historical cases will be attempted. The value of Graham Allison's study of the Cuban missile crisis, *Essence of Decision*, lay not so much in his development of a theory nor in his identification of historical details overlooked by others—though he did both—but rather in demonstrating that analytical frameworks have tremendous ramifications for both theory building and policy making. It is in this spirit that particular attention will be devoted to conceptual frameworks in this book.

WHY STUDY STATECRAFT?

Helping the prince to clarify his goals, identify his policy options, and assess the utility of various courses of action may be scientifically respectable, but is it worthwhile? Does the modern prince deserve a handbook? Does adoption of this analytical perspective imply that one is preoccupied with cynical Machiavellian manipulation of foreign policy for ignoble purposes, that one might even approve of such practices, that one's

[58] "Some Ambiguities in the Notion of Power," *American Political Science Review* LVIII (June 1964):346-348.

commitment to world order, peace, or justice is questionable, or that one subscribes to a "hard-nosed realist" view of international politics?

Objections to the princely perspective of statecraft might be based on either globalist or Marxist grounds. The globalist might complain that the study of statecraft views the world from the statesman's perspective, that it focuses on his conception of the "national interest" and his effectiveness in pursuing it. This perspective, a globalist might argue, is narrowly concerned with national goals and is either irrelevant to, or incompatible with, concern for global values of welfare, security, or justice. To the extent that national interests coincide with global interests, however, the statecraft perspective can be useful in promoting such values by helping policy makers to understand the nature of the overlap. In an interdependent world, states have mutual interests as well as conflicting ones; indeed, interdependence has traditionally been defined in terms of the mutual interests of states.[59] Contrary to popular belief, growing interdependence necessitates not the abandonment of the national-interest perspective but rather the development of a national-interest perspective that takes account of the overlap among national interests.[60]

From a Marxist standpoint, increasing the potential for statesmen to pursue their goals efficiently is not likely to seem very worthwhile. After all, if policy makers are merely the servants of a ruling class dedicated to exploiting other classes, increasing the efficiency of their activities would appear to have a rather low moral standing. Even Marxists, however, must live in an interdependent world. When survival is one of the stakes in the conduct of statecraft, it is in everyone's interest to ensure that statesmen do not endanger that value by misunderstanding the range of their options or the consequences thereof. Even one who believes that the world is plagued with evil statesmen should prefer well-informed to ill-informed statesmen.

Some might object to the emphasis on power in the study of statecraft. To approach the study of statecraft this way, however, does not imply anything about the importance of power as a *goal* of statecraft; nor does it imply approval of the goals sought by statesmen. The justification for the approach is rooted in the view that influence is a pervasive phenomenon that cannot be eliminated from any sphere of social life. Human beings, as Plato and Aristotle noted long ago, are political animals. As long as states continue to exist, statesmen will make influence attempts. In an

---

[59] On the evolution of the concept of interdependence, see Baldwin, "Interdependence and Power."

[60] For an opposing line of argument, see Miriam Camps, *The Management of Interdependence: A Preliminary View* (New York: Council on Foreign Relations, 1974), pp. 7, 63-64, et passim.

interdependent and dangerous world, greater understanding of the capabilities and limitations of various techniques of statecraft is imperative.

The idea of a handbook for the prince has antidemocratic overtones that should not be applied to the study of statecraft as conceived here. In a democracy the people must pass periodic judgment on the prince's performance. And in doing so, they need to evaluate not only the goals pursued on their behalf but also the efficiency with which such activities are undertaken. Thus, a study that clarifies goals, identifies policy options, and assesses their utility for various purposes can be useful not only to those who make policy but to those who must decide whether to retain such policy makers in office or replace them with others. Improved understanding of statecraft is one of the most valuable contributions that scholars can make to the functioning of democratic political processes.

CHAPTER 3

WHAT IS ECONOMIC STATECRAFT?

Concepts for the study of influence must be changed or invented when influence is sought by novel means or under changed conditions. In epochs of rapid development, there is need to reassess the relevance of intellectual effort.[1]

"The vocabulary of statecraft," according to Margaret and Harold Sprout, "has never been very precise." They are not optimistic about the prospects for bringing order out of what they consider to be a state of "semantic chaos":

> Operations of statecraft are expressed, and will continue to be expressed, mainly in the conventional vocabulary, however imprecise and otherwise inadequate it may be. The most that one can do . . . is to alert readers to some of the ambiguities, tidy up the existing terminology a little, introduce a few new terms to designate salient concepts more precisely, and suggest some simple categories and typologies to bring the processes and styles of statecraft into somewhat sharper focus for purposes of description and comparison.[2]

No portion of the vocabulary of statecraft is more in need of conceptual tidying up than that relating to economic techniques. In a study of U.S. foreign economic policy one author asserts that most of those who have written on this subject "are narrators of events rather than conceptualizers" and that "there are few important terms which are used so often and so loosely."[3]

Some writers are hostile to conceptual analysis. Sidney Weintraub, for example, refers to such questions as matters of "semantic taste." Expressing his wish not "to be diverted by a semantic distinction," he asserts that the cases in his book "speak for themselves about the extent of persuasion, pressure, and coercion being used."[4] In a similar spirit, Angela Stent explicitly declines to define "economic or political levers," the two

---

[1] Lasswell, *Politics*, pp. 7-8.

[2] Sprout and Sprout, *Politics of the Planet Earth*, p. 136.

[3] Robert A. Pastor, *Congress and the Politics of U.S. Foreign Economic Policy, 1929–1976* (Berkeley: University of California Press, 1980), pp. 7, 26n.

[4] Sidney Weintraub, ed., *Economic Coercion and U.S. Foreign Policy: Implications of Case Studies from the Johnson Administration* (Boulder, Colo.: Westview, 1982), pp. x, 4.

central concepts in her study of economic statecraft in West German–
Soviet relations. Noting that such definitions "would be too abstract for
the purposes of this analysis," she announces her intention to "distinguish
between economic and political levers in a concrete context."[5] To imply
that such distinctions can be made in "concrete contexts" without reference
to abstract criteria is tantamount to "letting the facts speak for themselves."
The facts, however, never "speak for themselves," but rather must be
interpreted in terms of a conceptual framework imposed by the analyst.
Conceptual analysis is neither impossible nor merely a matter of taste; it
is a necessary first step toward clear thinking about economic statecraft.

In selecting a concept of economic statecraft for this study, two criteria
are especially important. First, does the concept help with the identification
and evaluation of policy options? And second, does it avoid unnecessary
departures from common usage?[6] "Ordinary language," however, does
not necessarily mean the way most people would define the term, but rather
the "set of rules they implicitly follow when applying it to a given
situation."[7]

In the previous chapter economic techniques of statecraft were defined
as governmental influence attempts relying primarily on resources that have
a reasonable semblance of a market price in terms of money. Although
the rationale for defining techniques of statecraft in terms of influence
attempts was covered in the previous chapter, the justification for defining
"economic" in terms of money prices was postponed until now.

Not everyone would agree that this is worthwhile. Klaus Knorr, for
example, focuses his attention on explicating the concepts of power and

---

[5] Angela Stent, *From Embargo to Ostpolitik: The Political Economy of West German–
Soviet Relations, 1955–1980* (Cambridge: Cambridge University Press, 1981), p. 16. Stent
cites Albert O. Hirschman, *A Bias for Hope: Essays on Development in Latin America* (New
Haven: Yale University Press, 1971), p. 12, in support of her position. In the passage she
cites, however, Hirschman is arguing that the economic and political dimensions of a given
situation are often difficult to disentangle; he is not denying either the possibility or desirability
of distinguishing between the *concepts* of political and economic dimensions. Reasoning
analogous to Stent's would lead to the conclusion that because neither pure monopoly nor
pure competition is ever found in the real world, the distinction between the two concepts
at an abstract level is worthless.

[6] On conceptual analysis in general and the criterion of conventional usage in particular,
see Rev. T. R. Malthus, *Definitions in Political Economy, preceded by An Inquiry into the
Rules Which Ought to Guide Political Economists in the Definition and Use of Their Terms;
with Remarks on the Deviations from these Rules in their Writings* (London: John Murray,
1827); Fritz Machlup, *Essays on Economic Semantics* (Englewood Cliffs, N.J.: Prentice-
Hall, 1963); Alfred Marshall, *Principles of Economics*, 9th (variorum) ed., vol. 1 (New
York: Macmillan, 1961), p. 51; and Felix E. Oppenheim, "The Language of Political Inquiry:
Problems of Clarification," in *Handbook of Political Science*, ed. Greenstein and Polsby,
vol. 1: *Political Science: Scope and Theory*, pp. 307-309.

[7] Oppenheim, "Language of Political Inquiry," p. 307.

influence, while virtually ignoring economic concepts. He defends this by asserting that "the conceptualization of economic phenomena . . . [can be taken] for granted, because it is highly standardized and easily accessible in good textbooks."[8] Thus, when Knorr defines "economic power" in terms of "economic policy,"[9] it is presumably all right since one has only to consult a "good textbook" in order to ascertain criteria for distinguishing economic from noneconomic policy. The best known textbook available, however, is not very helpful in this respect. Paul A. Samuelson's *Economics* lists six different definitions of economics and notes that the list could be extended "many times over."[10] Some of these are clearly unacceptable for differentiating economic from noneconomic statecraft. For example, to define economic activities as those which involve exchange transactions among people regardless of whether money is used is to include many areas of social life not normally considered to be "economic." The social exchange theorists have demonstrated that the exchange of status, favors, respect, love, friendship, and so on are ubiquitous in social life;[11] yet few economists or noneconomists would label such exchanges as "economic." Similarly, to define economics as the "study of how to improve society"[12] is too broad to be helpful in defining economic statecraft. An equally broad definition favored by some economists depicts economics as "a science responsible for the study of human behavior as the relationship between ends and means which have alternative uses."[13] So defined, it encompasses the whole field of means-ends analysis and is utterly worthless for distinguishing economic techniques of statecraft from other techniques. In defining economic statecraft or economic power, as in other areas of intellectual inquiry, it is risky to take agreement on basic concepts for granted.[14]

---

[8] *The Power of Nations*, p. x.

[9] Ibid., pp. 79-80.

[10] 10th ed. (New York: McGraw-Hill, 1976), p. 3. The term "economic policy" does not appear in the index of this text. See also Charles J. Hitch's warning "that no one has ever defined the content of economics to the general satisfaction of economists, and that there exists in consequence some disagreement about what is and what is not an 'economic' problem or aspect of a problem." ("National Security Policy as a Field for Economics Research," *World Politics* XII [April 1960]:435.)

[11] See Peter M. Blau, *Exchange and Power in Social Life* (New York: John Wiley, 1964); George C. Homans, *Social Behavior: Its Elementary Forms*, rev. ed. (New York: Harcourt, Brace, Jovanovich, 1974); and David A. Baldwin, "Power and Social Exchange."

[12] Samuelson, *Economics*, p. 3.

[13] J. M. Letiche, "The History of Economic Thought in the *International Encyclopedia of the Social Sciences*," *Journal of Economic Literature* VII (June 1969):424.

[14] In my opinion Knorr gets things backward. In the last three decades it is power analysis that has attended to conceptual matters, while economics has tended to neglect conceptual analysis. With the notable exception of Fritz Machlup, economists today show little interest in the explication of abstract basic concepts. One is more likely to find useful conceptual

Definition of the ''economic'' aspect of social life in terms of the production and consumption of wealth that is measurable in terms of money corresponds with long-standing usage by the classic textbooks[15] of economics and is descriptive of the interests of most contemporary economists. In addition, such usage captures the basic intuitive notion of economic activities used by laymen and policy makers.

There are, as always, borderline cases that are hard to classify. For example, should the sale or gift of military hardware be considered as economic or military statecraft? In general, the relevant distinction is between firing (or threatening to fire) weapons and selling (or promising to sell) them. Insofar as a market price for such items exists, these transactions could reasonably be labeled economic statecraft. A plausible case could also be made for classifying them as military since some items, e.g. nuclear bombs, may have no ''going market price.'' Also, since providing weapons is so closely related to military statecraft, some might want to treat it as such. Depending on the particular research interest at hand, one might decide to classify them either way. The existence of such borderline cases, however, does not do serious harm to the value of this concept of economic statecraft for most purposes.

The concept of economic statecraft elucidated thus far has the following three basic components:

1. Type of policy instrument used in the influence attempt, i.e., economic.
2. Domain of the influence attempt, i.e., other international actor(s).
3. Scope of the influence attempt, i.e., some dimension(s) of the target(s') behavior (including beliefs, attitudes, opinions, expectations, emotions, and/or propensities to act).

It was noted in the previous chapter that such a conception necessarily makes economic statecraft a political act. It should be reemphasized that the scope of an influence attempt based on an economic technique may be *any dimension* of the target's behavior. The political quality of the act depends on the magnitude of the influence that the statesman is attempting to wield—not on the intrinsic qualities of any particular scope value. Thus

---

distinctions between political and economic phenomena in political science texts, such as Robert A. Dahl's *Modern Political Analysis*, 3d ed. (Englewood Cliffs, N.J.: Prentice-Hall, 1976) or Quincy Wright's *The Study of International Relations*, than in economics textbooks.

[15] See, for example, John Stuart Mill, *Principles of Political Economy*, new ed. (London: Longmans, Green, 1923), pp. 1-3, 9; and Marshall, *Principles of Economics*, vol. 1, pp. 1, 14, 22, 27, 49, 57. See also Kindleberger, *Power and Money*, pp. 3, 14; and H. Van B. Cleveland, ''Economics as Theory and Ideology,'' *World Politics* VI (April 1954):295-296. For a brilliant comparison of political and economic life that focuses on money as the distinctive feature of the latter, see G.E.G. Catlin, *The Science and Method of Politics* (New York: Alfred A. Knopf, 1927).

an influence attempt intended to effect another state's tariff levels, economic growth rate, attitude toward private foreign investment, or economic welfare is a political act. To repeat, the political quality of the act is a function of the total (actual or potential) influence relationship; it is not a function of scope.[16]

ALTERNATIVE CONCEPTS

As with policy options, the value of a particular conceptualization is best measured by comparing it with available alternatives. Whereas economic statecraft is defined in terms of means, alternative concepts are usually defined in terms of actual or intended effects of a policy or in terms of the process by which the policy was made.

Foreign Economic Policy

The term "foreign economic policy" is sometimes used in much the same way as "economic statecraft" is used here. Other uses, however, should be noted. Benjamin Cohen and Robert Pastor define it in terms of governmental actions intended to affect the international economic environment.[17] An important drawback to this conception is that it makes it definitionally impossible to consider foreign economic policy as an option when a statesman wants to affect the *noneconomic* aspects of the international environment, say the international climate of opinion with respect to the legitimacy of the government of Rhodesia. Rational adaptation of means to ends in foreign policy making is not facilitated by defining some policy options in terms of particular ends. Still another objection to this definition is that it says nothing about the *means* to be used, thus leaving open the possibility that the use of noneconomic techniques, such as threats of violence, could be considered foreign economic policy. Such a possibility strays needlessly from common usage.

I. M. Destler offers a definition of "foreign economic policy" in terms of the actual impact of governmental actions on foreign and economic

---

[16] Although this point is continually misunderstood, it corresponds to the position of a wide variety of scholars. For examples, see the following: "The ends of politics may be anything" (Wright, *Study of International Relations*, p. 132); "The goals that might be pursued by nations in their foreign policy can run the whole gamut of objectives that any nation has ever pursued or might possibly pursue" (Morgenthau, *Politics Among Nations*, 3d ed., p. 9); "A's decisions may affect, say, ... [B's] shaping and enjoyment of economic values" (Lasswell and Kaplan, *Power and Society*, p. 76).

[17] Benjamin J. Cohen, ed., *American Foreign Economic Policy: Essays and Comments* (New York: Harper and Row, 1968), p. 10; and Pastor, *Congress*, p. 12.

concerns.[18] This definition implies nothing whatever about either the means used or the effect intended; instead it focuses on the actual effects—intended or not. Thus, a nuclear war could be labeled as "foreign economic policy" if it had important side effects on foreign economic matters. Any conception of foreign economic policy that cannot differentiate between nuclear attack and trade restrictions is hopelessly at odds with common usage. Any conception of "policy" that ignores both means and ends is unlikely to be of much use in assessing the rationality of a given policy.

International Economic Policy

Stephen D. Cohen argues that the term "international economic policy" is preferable to the more commonly used phrase, "foreign economic policy." He contends that "international economic policy must be viewed as being a separate phenomenon, not a tool for use by either foreign policy or domestic economic policy officials." The reasons underlying Cohen's position can be summarized as follows: (1) "International economic policy" is the "preferable term because . . . policy making in this area must take account of too many questions of domestic . . . policy to be considered 'foreign.'" (2) "The term 'foreign economic policy' usually connotes a subdivision of foreign policy as a whole and is therefore an oversimplification." And (3) acceptance of international economic policy as a distinct policy area is the "best and quickest way" to improve understanding of the "forces of economics in international economic policy" and of "the global political impact of U.S. international economic policy."[19] The following points, however, should be noted in response to Cohen's position: (1) Foreign policy has traditionally been defined in terms of attempts to influence foreigners, not in terms of the factors that should be taken into account in formulating the policy. The fact that making international economic policy requires consideration of foreign and domestic political and economic factors in no way distinguishes it from traditional conceptions of foreign economic policy. (2) It is not self-evident that treating foreign economic policy as a subdivision of foreign policy as a whole constitutes "oversimplification." Cohen provides little evidence or argument to support this contention. Indeed, from an *a priori* standpoint, it would seem simpler to consider international economic policy by itself than to treat it as part of a larger whole. Treating more variables may lead to overcomplexity, but it rarely leads to oversimplification. And (3) the question of whether Cohen's approach is the "best and quickest way" to enhance

[18] *Making Foreign Economic Policy* (Washington, D.C.: Brookings Institution, 1980), p. 7.

[19] *The Making of United States International Economic Policy: Principles, Problems, and Proposals for Reform* (New York: Praeger, 1977), p. xvii-xxiii.

understanding is best answered after consideration of alternative approaches, a matter to which Cohen devotes scant attention. Indeed, Cohen's admissions that "economic relations with other countries have become a principal means of pursuing medium-to-longer-term U.S. foreign-policy goals" and that "instruments of economic warfare are being resorted to more frequently as a surrogate for military confrontation" raise serious doubts about the wisdom of treating foreign policy and international economic policy as separate and distinct topics.

Economic Diplomacy

The term "economic diplomacy" is sometimes used in much the same sense that "economic statecraft" is used here.[20] The primary disadvantage of such a definition is that it broadens the concept of "diplomacy" so much that it makes it difficult to think in terms of diplomatic alternatives to economic techniques.

Economic Leverage

Klaus Knorr uses the term "economic leverage" to discuss how economic factors can be used "*as means* to achieving state policy."[21] Such usage might appear similar to the concept of "economic statecraft."[22] There is a difference, however, between "levers" and "leverage" a difference that is crucial to understanding the dynamics of influence attempts. "Lever" is a property concept, while "leverage" is a relational concept. Some levers permit the exercise of leverage; others do not. For reasons explained in chapter 2, policy instruments should be treated as property rather than relational concepts.

Economic Sanctions

At least three common meanings of the term "economic sanctions" may be identified. The first is a rather narrow concept referring to the use of economic measures to enforce international law. The second refers to

[20] Pastor, *Congress*, p. 9; and John Pinder, "Economic Diplomacy," in *World Politics: An Introduction*, ed. James N. Rosenau, Kenneth W. Thompson, and Gavin Boyd (New York: Free Press, 1976), pp. 312-336.

[21] "International Economic Leverage and Its Uses," in *Economic Issues and National Security*, ed. Klaus Knorr and Frank N. Trager (Lawrence: Regents Press of Kansas, 1977), p. 99.

[22] One fundamental difference between Knorr's concept of "leverage" and the concept of "influence" used here stems from his insistence that pure exchange relationships do not involve either leverage or power (p. 101). This point will be discussed later.

the types of values that are intended to be reduced or augmented in the target state.[23] And the third usage corresponds to the concept of economic techniques of statecraft as used here.

The first is narrowly legalistic and therefore unsuitable for general foreign policy analysis. The second emphasizes intended effects rather than the means for achieving those effects. The difficulty is that any or all of the policy instruments discussed in the previous chapter can be used to affect the economic values in a target state. Diplomatic pressure on other states can be used to discourage trade with the target; propaganda can be used to undermine confidence in the target state's currency; and military attack can be used to destroy factories. Thus, conceiving of economic sanctions in terms of the intended effects on the receiving state is no help at all in distinguishing economic from noneconomic tools of statecraft.

The term "economic sanctions" is used in so many different ways that there is much to be said for avoiding it altogether. Unfortunately, the term is so deeply embedded in the literature of economic statecraft that ignoring it is impossible. Later chapters will therefore use this term, but only in its third sense.

Economic Warfare

Some conceptions of "economic warfare" emphasize means, while others emphasize effects. Thus, some writers portray the bombing of industrial targets during World War II as economic warfare.[24] This conception, which Knorr contends is "the standard one,"[25] would be classified as a form of military statecraft according to the taxonomy developed in the previous chapter. While military analysts may indeed consider an attack on industrial targets as economic warfare, the basic intuitive notion of most people is that firing weapons and dropping bombs are military undertakings.

Yuan-li Wu conceives of economic warfare in terms of "international economic measures" that enhance the "strength" of a country relative to an actual or potential "enemy."[26] The context of Wu's discussion makes it clear that he conceives of "strength" as war-making potential. War-making potential, of course, may take various forms, depending on the type of war to be fought. Wu seems to have World War II in mind, and the subtitle of his chapter on World War II reveals a tone that infuses the whole book—"The Test of Economic Power." Since the utility of any

[23] See, for example, Galtung, "International Economic Sanctions."

[24] Margaret P. Doxey, *Economic Sanctions and International Enforcement*, 2d ed. (New York: Oxford University Press, 1980), p. 13.

[25] *Power of Nations*, p. 139.

[26] *Economic Warfare* (New York: Prentice-Hall, 1952), pp. 1-2, 6, 366.

technique of statecraft varies from one policy-contingency framework to another,[27] no overall assessment of the utility of a technique can be based on a single set of assumptions about who is trying to influence whom, when, where, and how. Although the "international economic measures" discussed by Wu are similar to the "economic techniques of statecraft" discussed here, Wu's concentration on the utility of such techniques for promoting a particular kind of war-making ability severely restricts the applicability of his analysis to other kinds of situations.[28]

Robert Loring Allen defines "economic warfare" as "state interference in international economic relations for the purpose of improving the relative economic, military, or political position of a country."[29] By using the term "economic" in the definition, Allen, like Wu, leaves it undefined. By confining economic warfare to instances in which a state is trying to improve its relative position in the international "hierarchy of power,"[30] Allen, like Wu, makes it impossible to apply this concept to the full range of influence attempts based on economic statecraft. Sometimes policy makers use economic statecraft to improve (what they believe to be) their relative position in the "power hierarchy," and at other times they use such techniques to pursue other goals. Improving one's position in (what one perceives to be) the "power hierarchy" is not synonymous with the exercise of power in international relations. For analyzing the full range of influence attempts that might employ economic techniques, Allen's concept of "economic warfare," like Wu's, is too restrictive.

The concept of "economic warfare" most closely related to the concept of "economic statecraft" is Thomas Schelling's. He defines it in terms of the "*economic* means by which damage is imposed on other countries or

---

[27] For a discussion of the concept of policy-contingency frameworks in the context of capability analysis, see Sprout and Sprout, *Politics of the Planet Earth*, pp. 176-178; and Baldwin, "Power Analysis."

[28] "It is only with the greatest caution that the results and methods of war economy can be used as a basis for criticizing the substantive rationality of forms of economic organization. In war time the whole economy is oriented to what is in principle a single clear goal. . . . Hence, however illuminating the experience of war-time and post-war adjustments is for the analysis of the possible range of variation of economic forms, it is unwise to draw conclusions from the type of accounting in kind found under war conditions for their suitability in a permanent peacetime economy." Max Weber, *The Theory of Social and Economic Organization*, trans. A. M. Henderson and Talcott Parsons, ed. Talcott Parsons (New York: Free Press, 1947), p. 209.

[29] "Economic Warfare," *International Encyclopedia of the Social Sciences*, vol. 4, p. 467.

[30] Ibid., p. 468. Some would question the utility of the concept of a single international power hierarchy. On this point, see Baldwin, "Power Analysis," pp. 192-194; and Kjell Goldmann, "The International Power Structure: Traditional Theory and New Reality," in *Power, Capabilities, Interdependence*, ed. Kjell Goldmann and Gunnar Sjostedt (London: Sage, 1979), pp. 7-36.

the threat of damage used to bring pressure on them."[31] He specifically rules out the use of military means to inflict economic damage, and he makes it clear that economic warfare can be used to pursue a wide variety of foreign policy goals, not merely economic ones. Although superior to most other concepts of "economic warfare," Schelling's concept includes only techniques intended to impose negative sanctions and is therefore too narrow to serve in place of "economic statecraft."

Economic Coercion

The concept of "economic coercion" is rarely defined by those who use it.[32] Knorr's work stands as an admirable exception to this rule.[33] The concept of "coercion" developed by Knorr, however, diverges substantially from conventional usage. The basic intuitive notion of coercion refers to a high degree of constraint on the alternative courses of action available to (i.e., perceived by) the target of an influence attempt.[34] To be more precise, coercion usually refers to a situation in which one actor (A) is able to manipulate the cost/benefit ratios of the alternatives perceived by another actor (B) so that the latter would be foolish to choose any alternative other than X, where X represents either a single alternative or a category of alternatives. There are essentially five ways for A to do this: (1) by threats of punishment; (2) by promised rewards; (3) by actual punishment; (4) by actual rewards; and (5) by conveying correct or incorrect information to B with respect to the cost/benefit ratios of his alternatives. Thus, the most common examples of coercion include the following: "Your money or your life!"; "Sink or swim!"; "Surrender or die!"; "An offer you can't refuse!"; and "Water for a person dying of thirst." The most often overlooked ways for A to coerce B are actual rewards and punishments.[35]

---

[31] *International Economics* (Boston: Allyn and Bacon, 1958), p. 487. Despite its age, this text is invaluable to the student of economic statecraft. Schelling's emphasis on the foreign policy aspects of international economics is exemplary—and, regrettably, unique among economics texts.

[32] See, for example, Weintraub, *Economic Coercion*, pp. ix-28; Anna P. Schreiber, "Economic Coercion as an Instrument of Foreign Policy: U.S. Economic Measures Against Cuba and the Dominican Republic," *World Politics* XXV (April 1973):387-413; and Richard Stuart Olson, "Economic Coercion in World Politics: With a Focus on North-South Relations," *World Politics* XXXI (July 1979):471-494.

[33] *Power of Nations*, pp. 4-5, 14-15, et passim.

[34] See Dahl, *Modern Political Analysis*, pp.48-49; and Lasswell and Kaplan, *Power and Society*, pp. 97-99.

[35] On this point, see John C. Harsanyi, "Measurement of Social Power, Opportunity Costs, and the Theory of Two-Person Bargaining Games," *Behavioral Science* VII (January 1962):71; Robert A. Dahl and Charles E. Lindblom, *Politics, Economics, and Welfare: Planning and Politico-Economic Systems Resolved into Basic Social Processes* (New York:

Adding to or subtracting from B's capabilities to do X, however, can be effective means of coercion. Common parlance implicitly recognizes this with references to actors as "being so weak as to have no choice but to do X" or "being so strong that they cannot resist the temptation to do X." Knorr's conception of coercion refers only to situations in which B's choice is affected by A's threats and explicitly rules out the use of punishment to coerce. Thus, Knorr denies that destroying "part of a potential opponent's military capacity" is coercive.[36] For most people, however, bombing the enemy to the point at which it perceived itself as having to choose between surrender and total annihilation would be an example *par excellence* of coercion. The logic of this situation is directly analogous to that involved in throwing someone into a lake—one does not even have to say "sink or swim"; the person in the lake will immediately perceive these as his most important alternatives—and he is likely to feel coerced! Such a substantial departure from ordinary language might be justified if there were important advantages accruing to the definition that could not be attained by adhering more closely to conventional usage. Until such advantages have been demonstrated, however, the student of economic statecraft should be wary of Knorr's conception of "economic coercion."

In the study of techniques of statecraft the most important disadvantage of the concept of "economic coercion" is that it is a relational concept, not a property concept. Thus, attempts to treat it as an instrument of foreign policy are likely to blur the distinction between undertakings and outcomes. To describe an influence attempt as "coercive" says as much about B's perceptions and value system as it does about A's policy choice. A may choose to stop sending aid to B or to stop trading with B; but the coerciveness of such actions depends as much on B as on A. As a relational concept coercion is more useful in describing outcomes than in describing undertakings.

Choosing a concept of economic statecraft is not merely a matter of "semantic taste," at least not if that is meant to imply that "there is no disputing matters of taste." Some concepts are better suited for the analysis of governmental influence attempts than others. In comparison with available alternatives, the concept of "economic statecraft" has several advantages. The most important of these can be summarized as follows:

1.   "Economic statecraft" emphasizes means rather than ends. This usage is probably closer to ordinary language than definitions in terms of ends. Bombing a library is not called cultural warfare; bombing homes is not called residential warfare; bombing nuclear reactors (with conventional

---

Harper and Row, 1953), pp. 98-106; and Baldwin, "Inter-Nation Influence Revisited," pp. 476, 481-482.

[36] *Power of Nations*, p. 5.

bombs) is not called nuclear warfare; and bombing factories should not be labeled economic warfare.

2.   ''Economic statecraft'' does not restrict the range of goals that may be sought by economic means. It makes it conceptually possible to describe the empirically undeniable fact that policy makers sometimes use economic means to pursue a wide variety of noneconomic ends.

3.   ''Economic statecraft'' treats policy instruments as property concepts, thus facilitating the maintenance of a clear distinction between undertakings and outcomes.

4.   Unlike most alternative concepts, the definition of ''economic statecraft'' includes a definition of ''economic.'' It thus provides criteria for distinguishing economic techniques of statecraft from noneconomic techniques.

FORMS OF ECONOMIC STATECRAFT

The concept of economic statecraft employed here is intentionally broad, as it must be if it is to subsume all of the economic means by which foreign policy makers might try to influence other international actors. Some of the myriad specific forms of economic techniques of statecraft are listed in table 2 and table 3. These tables are intended to illustrate the wide variety of economic techniques and do not purport to be exhaustive. Table 2 contains examples of policy instruments usually associated with attempts to threaten or punish while table 3 provides examples of tools of statecraft normally associated with attempts to promise or provide rewards.

It should be noted that blacklisting and preclusive buying are especially instructive examples of the need to distinguish between the target of an influence attempt and the immediate recipient of a particular sanction. When describing the Arab blacklisting of Japanese firms that did business with Israel or the American purchase of wolfram from Spain in order to preclude its sale to Nazi Germany, it is more helpful to designate Israel and Germany as the targets than it is to focus on the intermediate targets of Japan and Spain.

Depending on the particular situation, any of the policy instruments listed in tables 2 and 3 could be used for either positive or negative sanctions. The tables reflect only the typical use of such techniques. Such techniques have been or might be employed by statesmen to pursue a wide variety of foreign policy goals, including the following: weakening or strengthening the leadership of another state, changing the political system of another state, changing the domestic or foreign policies of another state, changing the capabilities of another state, promoting a particular ideology, deterring war, acquiring or maintaining allies, weakening or strengthening alliances of other states, stopping or reducing the level of violence of an

Table 2

Examples of Economic Statecraft: Negative Sanctions

Trade	Capital
Embargo	Freezing assets
Boycott	Controls on import or export
Tariff increase	Aid suspension
Tariff discrimination (unfavorable)	Expropriation
Withdrawal of "most-favored-nation	Taxation (unfavorable)
treatment"	Withholding dues to international
Blacklist	organization
Quotas (import or export)	Threats of the above
License denial (import or export)	
Dumping	
Preclusive buying	
Threats of the above	

NOTE:

Embargo—prohibition on exports, sometimes used to refer to a ban on all trade.

Boycott—prohibition on imports.

Tariff increase—increase in taxes on imports from target state(s).

Tariff discrimination—imports from target countries may be treated less favorably than those from other countries.

Withdrawal of mfn—ceasing to treat imports from a country as favorably as similar imports from any other country are treated.

Blacklist—ban on doing business with firms that trade with the target country.

Quotas—quantitative restrictions on particular imports or exports.

License denial—refusing permission to import or export particular goods.

Dumping—deliberate sale of exports at prices below cost of production, e.g., to disrupt economy of target country by depressing world price of a key export or to gain foothold in a world market.

Preclusive buying—purchase of a commodity in order to deny it to the target country.

Freezing assets—impounding assets, denying access to bank accounts or other financial assets owned by the target country.

Controls on import or export of capital—restrictions on who can transfer how much capital for what purposes into or out of a country.

Aid suspension—the reduction, termination, or slow-down of aid transfers.

Expropriation—seizing ownership of property belonging to target state.

Taxation—assets of target state may be taxed in a discriminatory manner.

Withholding dues to international organization—nonpayment, late payment, or reduced payment of financial obligations agreed to in the past.

Threats of the above—making use of any of the above techniques conditional on certain kinds of behavior by the target.

ongoing war, affecting the tariff policy of another state, changing the rate of economic growth in another state, changing the economic system in another state, acquiring access to the goods or services of another state, denying another state access to the goods or services of a third state, changing the level of economic welfare in another state, speeding up or slowing down the rate of economic recovery from war in another state, and so on. In each case a political act is taking place insofar as a state is

Table 3

Examples of Economic Statecraft: Positive Sanctions

Trade	*Capital*
Tariff discrimination (favorable)	Providing aid
Granting "most-favored-nation" treatment	Investment guarantees
Tariff reduction	Encouragement of private capital exports
Direct purchase	or imports
Subsidies to exports or imports	Taxation (favorable)
Granting licenses (import or export)	Promises of the above
Promises of the above	

NOTE:

Tariff discrimination—import duties favoring imports from target state(s).

Granting mfn treatment—promising to treat imports from target state as favorably as imports of similar products from any other source.

Tariff reduction—lowering of tariffs in general or on particular products.

Direct purchase—payment for service or goods, e.g. purchase of Louisiana Territory by United States government.

Subsidies to exports or imports—exports to or imports from the target state may be subsidized, e.g., arms sales to Third World countries or above market prices paid for Cuban sugar by United States prior to 1960.

Granting licenses—permission to import or export particular goods.

Providing aid—extension or continuation of aid via bilateral or multilateral channels in the form of grants or loans.

Investment guarantees—governmental insurance against some of the risks of private foreign investors.

Encouragement of private capital exports or imports—variety of incentives to import or export capital.

Taxation—especially favorable taxation of foreign capital investment.

Promises of the above—making use of any of the above techniques conditional on certain kinds of behavior by the target.

attempting to affect the actual or potential behavior of another international actor.

SOME NOT-SO-OBVIOUS FORMS OF ECONOMIC STATECRAFT

Several of the forms of economic statecraft, such as trade embargoes and foreign aid, are obviously in conformity with conventional usage. Others, however, are less obvious and diverge from common usage. Closer scrutiny of some less obvious forms is therefore in order.

Purchase

Economic exchange may be viewed from three perspectives—the seller's, the buyer's, or the independent observer's. The independent observer is likely to describe the relationship as one in which each participant in the exchange voluntarily surrenders something of value for something he values even more. Each benefits, and neither is likely to feel coerced. This relationship is at odds with popular conceptions (or misconceptions) of power relations as zero-sum games, as involving a victim and a victor, as relations between unequal actors, as exploitative, coercive, and unpleasant from the standpoint of the actor being influenced. Some power relations, of course, do take this form and should be differentiated from normal economic exchange relationships. It does not follow, however, that all power relations take this form; nor does it follow that the basic intuitive notion of power elucidated by power theorists is necessarily incompatible with the common notion of economic exchange. Indeed, it can be shown that all exchange relationships can be described in terms of conventional power concepts without twisting the common-sense notions that underlie such concepts.[37] Direct monetary payment is one of the most common ways for some people to get other people to do things they would not otherwise do.

Knorr contends that ''purely economic exchange'' involves neither politics nor power.[38] Thus, he states:

> Strictly commercial exchanges . . . do not, in our opinion, involve economic power, unless they are affected by monopolist market power. For example, no use of power takes place when two trading states negotiate an exchange of exports without any insertion of threats or blandishments designed to affect the behavior of the other side. Although the actors are governments, the transaction is equivalent to a commercial contract between private firms. When the United States purchased the Louisiana territory from France in 1803 for $12 million, Florida from Spain in 1819 for $5 million, and the Virgin Islands from Denmark in 1917 for $25 million, it used wealth, but there was no application of economic power.[39]

The advantages of denying that the Louisiana Purchase involved politics or power are not immediately obvious. If President Thomas Jefferson

[37] For discussion and further references on these points, see Baldwin, ''Power and Social Exchange''; ''Money and Power''; and Oppenheim, *Political Concepts*, pp. 40-43.

[38] *Power of Nations*, p. 80.

[39] Ibid., p. 81. Knorr discusses two other situations that resemble economic exchange— ''reward power'' and ''nonpower influence.'' He also excludes economic exchange from either of these categories. (See ibid., pp. 7, 310-311.) Even Knorr's own definition of ''economic power,'' which includes the ability of a state to benefit itself by using economic or financial policy to benefit another state (pp. 79-80), does not exclude economic exchange. It is only by introducing two additional requirements, not alluded to in his definition of ''economic power,'' that he can deny that economic exchange involves politics or power. These supplementary requirements are that the actors be ''unequal'' (p. 7) and that the weaker actor be ''harmed'' by the transaction (p. 311).

wanted to acquire this territory from France, he obviously had a number of policy options, including military force, from which to choose. Direct purchase was one of several means by which he could attempt to get France to do something it would not otherwise do, i.e., transfer title to this land to the United States. This way of describing the Louisiana Purchase is compatible with standard notions of power employed by social power theorists. In addition, it helps to clarify the policy alternatives available to President Jefferson. These two advantages suggest that regarding direct purchase as a form of economic statecraft is a potentially fruitful way to think about foreign policy.

If one adopts the perspective of either the buyer or the seller, it is easy to view such transactions as influence attempts. The buyer is trying to induce the seller to sell, while the seller is trying to induce the buyer to buy. The consummation of the exchange occurs if, and only if, both influence attempts succeed. Two hundred years ago Benjamin Franklin maintained that purchase was preferable to war as a means of acquiring territory. Forty years ago Nicholas John Spykman published a widely read book entitled *America's Strategy in World Politics* containing a chapter on "Power Politics and War," which includes "purchase" as one of the "great variety of techniques designed to win friends and influence people."[40] This viewpoint, however, has been neglected in subsequent scholarship in the area of international politics and foreign policy. Indeed, recent scholarship explicitly denies that purchase should be regarded as an influence technique. For the student of economic statecraft, this is a step in the wrong direction.

Free Trade

Is a policy of free trade a technique of economic statecraft, or is it the very antithesis of economic statecraft?[41] Some writers depict free trade as "a weapon" of economic warfare[42] or as a tool for promoting imperialist foreign policy goals.[43] Others, however, assert that "the free trade doctrine

[40] Gerald Stourzh, *Benjamin Franklin and American Foreign Policy*, 2d ed. (Chicago: University of Chicago Press, 1969), p. 240; and Nicholas John Spykman, *America's Strategy in World Politics* (New York: Harcourt, Brace, 1942), p. 12.

[41] A "policy of free trade," strictly speaking, implies the complete absence of trade barriers and nondiscrimination among foreign suppliers. Loosely speaking, the term refers to policies moving toward freer trade by lowering trade barriers and reducing discrimination. Although the latter usage is employed here, the comments on free trade as a technique of statecraft apply equally well to a policy of pure free trade.

[42] P.J.D. Wiles, *Communist International Economics* (Oxford: Basil Blackwell, 1968), p. 473.

[43] Bernard Semmel, *The Rise of Free Trade Imperialism: Classical Political Economy, the Empire of Free Trade, and Imperialism, 1750-1850* (Cambridge: Cambridge University Press,

. . . denies the validity of the use of economic instruments for political ends'' and compare a policy of free trade to disarmament.[44] Thus Knorr observes:

> It must be understood that after World War II the world's leading trading countries . . . agreed to disarm themselves regarding the power uses of trade . . . between themselves, especially in support of non-economic objectives. They did so by establishing the GATT in 1947. Thereby, they created an international economic order characterized by the joint goal of freer trade on the basis of the most-favored-nation principle that precluded discrimination. And power uses of trade are essentially discriminatory.[45]

Disarmament, however, whether military or economic, does not necessarily constitute the forswearing of statecraft. Military techniques of statecraft were defined in chapter 2 as influence attempts relying primarily on violence, weapons, or force. The essence of such techniques is the adoption of a policy stance vis-à-vis violence, weapons, or force with the intention of thereby influencing other actors. Therefore, a specific commitment not to shoot first, not to use certain kinds of weapons, or to disarm completely *is* a military technique of statecraft if this commitment is undertaken for the purpose of influencing other actors. Military and economic disarmament do not necessarily signal the renunciation of statecraft. As Thomas C. Schelling has pointed out, sophisticated understanding of the relationship between arms and influence entails recognition that some influence attempts, e.g., nuclear deterrence, are more likely to succeed if one forgoes certain kinds of arms, e.g., first-strike weapons.[46] As Gene Sharp has shown, a commitment to nonviolence can be an instrument of policy in the same sense as a commitment to violence.[47] One way to ''use'' violence is to commit oneself not to use it. The apparent contradiction here is due solely to the looseness of the term ''use.''

A policy of free trade, i.e., lower and less discriminatory trade barriers, was employed by the United States after World War II in order to pursue a number of foreign policy objectives, including strengthening military

---

1970); and John Gallagher and Ronald Robinson, ''The Imperialism of Free Trade,'' *The Economic History Review* VI (1953):1-15.

[44] Pinder, ''Economic Diplomacy,'' pp. 313-314. See also a similar comment by J. Henry Richardson: ''As long as the Government maintained a *laissez-faire* policy it was not able to reinforce its political foreign policy by economic means. . . .'' *British Economic Foreign Policy* (London: George Allen and Unwin, 1936), p. 11.

[45] *Power of Nations*, pp. 159-160.

[46] *Strategy of Conflict*, pp. 207-254.

[47] *The Politics of Nonviolent Action*, 3 vols. (Boston: Porter Sargent, 1973). See also Johan Galtung, ''On the Meaning of Nonviolence,'' *Journal of Peace Research*, no. 3 (1965), pp. 228-257.

alliances, promoting economic recovery from the war in Western Europe and Japan, ensuring access to strategic raw materials, stimulating economic development in poor countries, creating markets for American exports, and creating an international atmosphere conducive to peace and security.[48] Rather than disarming itself, the United States used its policy of free trade to shape the postwar international political and economic order.

Although one can imagine a world economy based entirely on state trading with neither trade barriers nor discrimination, the concept of free trade often connotes an emphasis on private firms. Free trade in this sense is frequently depicted as "nonpolitical" or "depoliticized" trade. Thus, Kindleberger contends that "the glory of free trade is that it decentralizes decisions about trade to non-political levels."[49] Private international trade, however, is carried on within a framework of laws and policies created and maintained by governments of sovereign states. Attempts by statesmen to influence the pattern of international trade through manipulating this legal and political framework can be regarded as acts of economic statecraft. Policies of free trade may not be obvious economic techniques of statecraft, but they can be and have been important ones.

Tariffs

Are tariffs a form of economic statecraft? The answer is not obvious. Students of economic statecraft frequently go out of their way to deny that tariffs, at least certain kinds of tariffs, should be viewed as instruments for influencing the behavior of foreigners. Consider the following examples:

Immediately following a definition of economic warfare that includes "all those foreign economic policies that may have as their long-run objective the enlargement of a country's sphere of economic influence," Yuan-li Wu inserts a discussion of the "difference between economic warfare and a protective trade policy." Noting that among the most frequently advanced arguments in favor of trade barriers are protection of domestic wage levels, increased domestic employment, and enhanced self-sufficiency, he states that "obviously, only the last argument could be related to economic warfare."[50]

---

[48] For discussion and further references regarding the goals of postwar American trade policy, see Clair Wilcox, *A Charter for World Trade* (New York: Macmillan, 1949); Commission on Foreign Economic Policy, *Staff Papers* (Washington, D.C.: U.S. Government Printing Office, 1954); and David A. Baldwin, *Economic Development and American Foreign Policy: 1943–62* (Chicago: University of Chicago Press, 1966).

[49] *Power and Money*, p. 132.

[50] *Economic Warfare*, pp. 6, 8-9. In fairness to Wu, it should be noted that he does include a discussion of tariffs as tools of economic warfare (pp. 66-67). It is only certain kinds of

Immediately after defining economic power in terms of the deliberate use of economic policy to modify the behavior or capabilities of other states, Klaus Knorr states his desire to

> exclude uses of foreign economic policy that, although instrumentally suited to the exercise of power, are adopted only to satisfy a domestic interest. Thus, protective import tariffs may be introduced to benefit the interests of politically influential domestic producers, to shape national production capacity in the interest of economic military potential, or to curtail domestic unemployment. Any effects on other states are purely incidental; there is no intent to wield power internationally.[51]

Immediately after defining economic warfare as "state interference in international economic relations for the purpose of improving the relative economic, military, or political position of a country," Robert Allen exempts tariffs aimed primarily at "support of domestic industry to achieve purely domestic economic or political goals."[52]

Immediately after describing a group of state actions having in common "the manipulation of economic relations for political objectives," Henry Bienen and Robert Gilpin exclude from this group tariffs intended to "protect domestic economic interests, to retaliate against foreign trade barriers, or to force economic concessions from other countries." The primary purpose of such actions, according to Bienen and Gilpin, is "economic rather than political."[53]

The common theme of such authors is that tariffs imposed primarily for domestic purposes should not be viewed as techniques of statecraft, i.e., as attempts to influence foreigners.[54] The effects on foreigners of such

---

protective tariffs that Wu seems to exclude. Wu's conclusion that only self-sufficiency can be related to economic warfare is unjustified even in terms of his own definition. It is easy to imagine a scenario in which wage and employment levels might affect a country's economic influence. The morale of the labor force is likely to be of some interest in assessing its economic power base.

[51] *Power of Nations*, p. 80.

[52] "Economic Warfare," pp. 467-468.

[53] "An Evaluation of the Use of Economic Sanctions to Promote Foreign Policy Objectives, with Special Reference to the Problem of Terrorism and the Promotion of Human Rights," report prepared for the Boeing Corporation, April 2, 1979, p. I,2. The pages of this report are not numbered consecutively; therefore, page numbers here and in subsequent references will be designated with Arabic numerals while chapters will be identified by Roman numerals. Although this report is unpublished, it has achieved prominence through the *New York Times* (January 13, 1980); *Forbes* (February 18, 1980); and Gilpin's testimony to Congress (U.S. Senate, Subcommittee on International Trade of the Committee on Finance, *Hearings, U.S. International Trade Strategy*, 96th Cong., 2d sess., 1980, pp. 160-161).

[54] The contention of Bienen and Gilpin that even tariffs used to "retaliate against foreign trade barriers" or to "force economic concessions from other countries" do not constitute

measures should be viewed as incidental, unintended, and perhaps even unwanted. The difficulty with this position stems mainly from two sources. The first is the hierarchy of ends inherent in the nature of means-ends analysis, and the second is the rhetorical smokescreen that usually enshrouds the imposition of a tariff for allegedly domestic purposes.

In chapter 2 it was noted that means-ends analysis is complicated by the instrumental nature of most human goals. What is treated as a goal by one may be viewed as an instrument for achieving some higher goal by another. Thus, a tariff on autos might be viewed in terms of the following hierarchy of ends:

1. Getting Japan to export fewer cars to the United States, which is in turn a means to
2. Supporting the price of domestically made autos, which is in turn a means to
3. Ensuring the survival of the domestic automobile industry, which is in turn a means to
4. Promoting the U.S. ''national interest,'' which is in turn a means to
5. Serving God's will by saving the world from the scourge of atheistic communism, which is in turn a means to
6. Ensuring peace for one's soul in the hereafter.

There is, of course, no single level in this hierarchy that is ''right'' while others are ''wrong.'' Whereas a focus on levels 1, 4, or 5 gives a foreign-policy tinge to the analysis, a focus on levels 2 or 3 emphasizes the domestic dimension, while a focus on level 6 smacks of otherworldliness. Although there is no mathematically precise formula for choosing an appropriate level of analysis, the decision need not be arbitrary. ''Rules of thumb,'' or, as the lawyers might say, ''rules of reason,'' may be used to eliminate at least some of the alternative levels of focus. The inclusion of level 1 suggests that it is neither ''wrong'' nor implausible to treat a protective tariff as an influence attempt on foreigners. The question remains, however, as to whether this is the most useful focal point. The rule of thumb employed, of course, depends on the topic one seeks to illuminate. Here the concern is with understanding what policy makers do and why they do it. No matter what rule of thumb is employed, the same rule should be used for analyzing all policy instruments.

Although it is true that statesmen almost never—well, hardly ever—impose tariffs solely for the purpose of influencing the behavior of for-

---

''the manipulation of economic relations for political objectives'' will not be discussed here. Such actions obviously constitute influence attempts on foreign actors and would be so considered by most writers.

eigners, the same could also be said of almost any other foreign policy undertaking. Getting other states to export fewer autos, refrain from nuclear attack, support certain United Nations resolutions, join military alliances, or any other foreign policy goal is seldom the ultimate goal, i.e., an end pursued for its own sake. In fact, almost all foreign policy goals are, in turn, means to promote the welfare and/or security of the domestic populace or some segment thereof. American foreign policy makers do not—generally speaking—threaten the Soviet Union with nuclear attack solely, or even primarily, because of some sadistic desire to instill fear in foreigners. They do it because they believe—rightly or wrongly—that such threats make the domestic populace safer. In short, they do it for "domestic reasons." Thus, the logic of denying that protective tariffs are attempts to influence foreigners would require similar treatment of most other foreign policy undertakings. Almost everything would become a "domestic matter," and precious little would be left of "foreign policy."

A reasonable way to proceed is to ask what the usual effects of a technique are, whether there is reason to suspect that policy makers are aware, at least in a general way, of these effects, and whether such effects are intended. To determine whether the effects are intended, one might ask whether policy makers could be expected to make the same policy choice once the likely effects were explained to them. When a state goes to war, casualties are a normal consequence; and it is reasonable to assume that the policy makers who chose to go to war were aware of the likelihood of these consequences. The statesman who plunges his country into war while treating casualties as incidental and unintended side effects is likely to be viewed as a liar, a fool, or both.

Is it reasonable to assume that policy makers who impose tariffs know what they are doing? Tariffs "will normally produce customs revenue, protect domestic output, reduce consumption of the protected product, and reduce imports."[55] With the exception of the first, none of these effects can occur without affecting the behavior of foreigners.[56] To say that a tariff reduces American auto imports from Japan is the same as saying that it reduces Japanese auto exports to America. It is nonsense to advocate the one and oppose the other. An American tariff on autos is likely to be defended with language that obscures the nature of the undertaking. Thus, "we want to help American workers," not "we want to hurt Japanese workers"; "we want to improve America's terms-of-trade," not "we want to harm Japan's terms-of-trade"; "we want to reduce American imports,"

[55] W. M. Corden, "Tariffs and Protectionism," *International Encyclopedia of the Social Sciences*, vol. 8, p. 114. For a discussion of tariffs that treats them as techniques of statecraft, see Wilcox, *Charter for World Trade*, pp. 3-4.

[56] An exception is made for the special case when price elasticities are such that the entire customs revenue is paid by domestic importers.

not "we want to reduce Japanese exports"; "we want to increase employment levels in America," not "we want to depress employment levels in Japan." When the intended effects of a tariff—say, protection of the auto industry—can be achieved *only* through influence on foreigners, it seems reasonable to regard such undertakings as influence attempts on foreigners. When four people are dividing a pie, one may insist that he would like half for himself while proclaiming that this is for purely "personal reasons," denying any intention or desire to reduce the amount of pie available to the others. He may say he views such effects as incidental, unintended, and unwanted side effects of his purely "domestic" decision. His protestations are unlikely to be accepted at face value by either his companions or by observers. It is best to characterize as "incidental side effects" only those things that really are incidental. To characterize the necessary causal condition of success of a protective tariff—i.e., its effect on foreigners—as an "incidental side effect," however, is difficult to justify.

It is possible, of course, that policy makers do not understand the inherent tendency of tariffs to affect foreigners. There are two reasons for rejecting this contention. First, tariffs are rarely, if ever, imposed on products not produced elsewhere in the world. This would seem to suggest that the impact of a tariff on foreigners is more than just an unintended incidental side effect. The very term "protective tariff" suggests protection against foreigners. Second, unofficial descriptions of protective tariffs by journalists and the "man-in-the-street" are quite likely to depict such undertakings as influence attempts on foreigners. Even the most lowly paid American auto worker is likely to view a tariff on autos in terms of "getting back at the Japanese." Indeed, apart from official rhetoric, academics are about the only people who do not view protective tariffs this way!

Like other techniques of statecraft, the purposes of tariffs are many and varied. Like other techniques of statecraft, these purposes often include a significant concern for domestic implications. It is quite reasonable to emphasize these domestic matters and to depict tariffs as means for achieving domestic ends. It is not reasonable, however, to deny that tariffs almost always involve attempts to influence foreigners. Clear understanding of world affairs is more likely if tariffs are treated as techniques of statecraft than if they are conceived solely as domestic undertakings not involving any "intent to wield power internationally."

CHAPTER 4

THINKING ABOUT ECONOMIC STATECRAFT

Economics as a separate science is unrealistic,
and misleading if taken as a guide in practice. It is
one element—a very important element, it is true—
in a wider study, the science of power.[1]

One of the purposes of this book is to think about economic statecraft, but an additional and related purpose is to think about thinking about economic statecraft. This chapter will consider the treatment of economic statecraft in the international relations literature, discuss a variety of obstacles to clear thinking about economic statecraft, and address the question of why it is useful to think about economic statecraft.

THE LITERATURE ON ECONOMIC STATECRAFT

The two most salient characteristics of the literature on economic statecraft are scarcity and the nearly universal tendency to denigrate the utility of such tools of foreign policy. The paucity of studies of economic statecraft should be considered in the context of the dominant research foci in the two most closely related academic disciplines—economics and political science. Although Bertrand Russell may describe economics as part of "the science of power," few economists would agree. "If we look at the main run of economic theory over the past hundred years," observes K. W. Rothschild, "we find that it is characterized by a strange lack of power considerations. . . . The whole power problem has been badly neglected in economic literature and has never been systematically treated."[2] Noting that there is not much difference between classical and Keynesian economics with respect to this point, P.J.D. Wiles observes that "Keynes and his followers have produced virtually nothing on economic warfare," which Wiles attributes to "the narrowing and unscientific tradition of 'purity'

---

[1] Bertrand Russell, *Power: A New Social Analysis* (New York: W.W. Norton, 1938), p. 135.

[2] K. W. Rothschild, ed., *Power in Economics: Selected Readings* (Middlesex: Penguin, 1971), p. 7, 16. While agreeing with Rothschild's characterization of economics, one might point to exceptions like Albert O. Hirschman, John Kenneth Galbraith, John C. Harsanyi, Klaus Knorr, Thomas C. Schelling, Peter Wiles, Charles Kindleberger, Kenneth Boulding, and Yuan-li Wu.

among economists; who suppose that they should only ask questions to which economics alone has the answer.''[3] In addition to questions of power, economists have also neglected questions of foreign policy. Thus, Benjamin J. Cohen points out that although "foreign economic policy is part of a country's total foreign policy and to some extent serves the same goals," it is "not often discussed from this point of view.''[4] Cohen's point is supported by the *International Encyclopedia of the Social Sciences,* which includes five articles on "International Trade Controls," none of which treats the topic within a foreign policy framework and none of which discusses the use of such means to pursue general foreign policy goals.[5]

The neglect of economic statecraft in political science is partly explained by the tendency to focus on policy-making processes and to ignore policy techniques and outputs, noted in chapter 2. As with the discipline of political science in general, the subfield of international politics has devoted little attention to techniques of statecraft. Economic techniques have been doubly neglected since until recently the economic aspects of international politics attracted the attention of only a handful of scholars. For example, a review of the first twelve volumes of the *Journal of Conflict Resolution* reported "the nearly complete absence of articles relating international conflict to international trade and international finance.''[6] And Susan Strange, writing in 1970, noted the serious scholarly neglect of foreign economic policy in general and of economic warfare in particular.[7] Although the decade since then has seen the rejuvenation of the field of international political economy, relatively little attention has been focused on economic statecraft.

Chapter 2 noted James N. Rosenau's contention that the forms of statecraft were "easy to clarify and analyze," that economic techniques were "the subject of a vast literature," and that "thorough discussions" could

---

[3] *Communist International Economics,* pp. 6, 455. One textbook writer bold (or foolish?) enough to include a chapter on trade warfare relied heavily on a single unpublished doctoral dissertation described as "the only substantial work in the field." A later edition of the book published in 1969 omits this chapter altogether. See Murray C. Kemp, *The Pure Theory of International Trade* (Englewood Cliffs, N.J.: Prentice-Hall, 1964), pp. 208-217; and Henry York Wan, Jr., "A Contribution to the Theory of Trade Warfare," Ph.D. dissertation, Massachusetts Institute of Technology, 1961.

[4] Cohen, ed., *American Foreign Economic Policy,* p. 1.

[5] See "International Trade Controls," *International Encyclopedia of the Social Sciences,* vol. 8, pp. 113-139. Although articles in the encyclopedia usually direct readers to related topics elsewhere in the encyclopedia, not one of the articles on international trade controls cross-references the article on "Economic Warfare." It would appear that economists see little connection between international trade controls and economic warfare.

[6] Elizabeth Converse, "The War of All Against All," *Journal of Conflict Resolution* XII (December 1968):486.

[7] "International Economics and International Relations: A Case of Mutual Neglect," *International Affairs* XLVI (April 1970):308-309.

be found in "standard texts."[8] With respect to economic statecraft, at least, these assertions gave a misleading impression of the state of the literature. Of sixteen textbooks in print at the time of Rosenau's comment, only five devoted separate chapters to economic statecraft; three contained significant parts of chapters on the subject; and eight gave little or no attention to the topic.[9] The techniques of statecraft most likely to be discussed were military and diplomatic, while economic techniques were the least likely to be considered. Those texts that did include discussions of economic techniques of statecraft were generally lacking in analytical or theoretical depth. A convenient indicator of such depth is whether the text cites Albert O. Hirschman's classic study of the relationship between foreign trade and national power, a test passed by only one.[10] Contrary to Rosenau, the treatment of economic statecraft in standard textbooks has been neither plentiful nor thorough.

The literature on economic statecraft tends to be narrowly focused and

---

[8] *International Politics and Foreign Policy: A Reader in Research and Theory*, rev. ed. (New York: Free Press, 1969), pp. 169, 174.

[9] Raymond Aron, *Peace and War*; Cecil V. Crabb, Jr., *Nations in a Multipolar World* (New York: Harper and Row, 1968); Ivo D. Duchacek, *Nations and Men*, 2d ed. (New York: Holt, Rinehart, and Winston, 1971); David V. Edwards, *International Political Analysis* (New York: Holt, Rinehart, and Winston, 1969); Fred Greene, *Dynamics of International Relations* (New York: Holt, Rinehart, and Winston, 1964); Frederick H. Hartmann, *The Relations of Nations*, 3d ed. (New York: Macmillan, 1967); K. J. Holsti, *International Politics: A Framework for Analysis*, 2d ed. (Englewood Cliffs, N.J.: Prentice-Hall, 1967); W. W. Kulski, *International Politics in a Revolutionary Age*, 2d ed. (New York: J. B. Lippincott, 1968); Hans J. Morgenthau, *Politics Among Nations*, 4th ed. (New York: Knopf, 1967); Norman D. Palmer and Howard C. Perkins, *International Relations*, 3d ed. (New York: Houghton Mifflin, 1969); Norman J. Padelford and George A. Lincoln, *The Dynamics of International Politics*, 2d ed. (New York: Macmillan, 1967); A.F.K. Organski, *World Politics*, 2d ed. (New York: Knopf, 1968); Herbert J. Spiro, *World Politics: The Global System* (Homewood, Ill.: Dorsey Press, 1966); John W. Spanier, *World Politics in an Age of Revloution* (New York: Praeger, 1967); John G. Stoessinger, *The Might of Nations*, 4th ed. (New York: Random House, 1973); and Vernon Van Dyke, *International Politics*, 2d ed. (New York: Appleton-Century-Crofts, 1966). Those with separate chapters include Van Dyke, Stoessinger, Padelford and Lincoln, Palmer and Perkins, and Holsti. Those with significant parts of chapters on the subject are Kulski, Hartmann, and Aron.

[10] Morgenthau lists Hirschman's book, *National Power and the Structure of Foreign Trade*, in the bibliography. References to that book also provide useful indicators of interest in economic statecraft in scholarly journals. Between 1948 and 1970 *World Politics* contained only three citations of this work, one by the present writer. Between 1950 and 1970 *International Organization* did not contain a single citation. And from 1960 to 1970 the *International Studies Quarterly* included but one reference to it—in an article by the present writer. For those who would like to apply a measure of theoretical depth to textbooks currently in print, references to works of fundamental theoretical importance such as the following might be considered: Hirschman; Thomas C. Schelling, *International Economics*; and Yuan-li Wu, *Economic Warfare*. Even Holsti's relatively sophisticated treatment of economic statecraft includes a reference only to Hirschman—and that was not added until 1983. See K. J. Holsti, *International Politics: A Framework for Analysis*, 4th ed., p. 239.

topical rather than general and theoretical. Typical foci include the Alliance for Progress, foreign aid to India, the Arab oil "weapon," sanctions against Rhodesia, food as an instrument of U.S. policy, and the wisdom of transferring technology to the Soviet Union. In 1970 Strange observed that "what is noticeably missing from the picture are more general studies of international economic relations—whether of problems or issue areas— treated analytically, with the political analysis predominating over the economic analysis."[11] With the notable exception of Knorr's *The Power of Nations: The Political Economy of International Relations*, the situation has changed little since 1970.[12] Various techniques, such as foreign aid, have been studied in isolation, but they are rarely treated as part of a larger category of similar techniques. There are general studies of propaganda, general studies of diplomacy, and a veritable mountain of general studies of military force; but comparable treatments of economic statecraft are rare.[13]

[11] Strange, "International Economics," p. 308.

[12] Additional treatments of economic techniques at a high level of generality are Wu's *Economic Warfare*; the introductory chapters in Sidney Weintraub, ed., *Economic Coercion*, pp. ix-70; and a few chapters in Schelling's *International Economics*, pp. 424-462, 487-532. Knorr, Wu, Weintraub, and Schelling are all economists; thus, it may be an exaggeration to say that political analysis predominates over economic analysis in their work. Nevertheless, they make a serious effort to incorporate political dimensions into their theories.

[13] General studies of propaganda include Martin L. John, ed., *Propaganda in International Affairs* (Philadelphia: Annals of the American Academy of Political and Social Science, 1971); Terence H. Qualter, *Propaganda and Psychological Warfare* (New York: Random House, 1962); and Harold D. Lasswell, Daniel Lerner, and Hans Spier, eds., *Propaganda and Communication in World History*, 3 vols. (Honolulu: University Press of Hawaii, 1979, 1980).

General studies of diplomacy are, for example, Fred C. Iklé, *How Nations Negotiate* (New York: Harper and Row, 1964); Harold Nicolson, *Diplomacy*, 3d ed. (New York: Oxford University Press, 1963); and Adam Watson, *Diplomacy*.

For general studies of military force see, for example, Bernard Brodie, *War and Politics* (New York: Macmillan, 1973); Thomas C. Schelling, *Arms and Influence* (New Haven: Yale University Press, 1966); Oran Young, *The Politics of Force* (Princeton: Princeton University Press, 1968); Robert E. Osgood and Robert W. Tucker, *Force, Order, and Justice* (Baltimore: Johns Hopkins Press, 1967); Fred S. Northedge, *The Use of Force in International Relations* (New York: Free Press, 1974); Klaus Knorr, *On the Uses of Military Power in the Nuclear Age* (Princeton: Princeton University Press, 1966); Carl von Clausewitz, *On War*, ed. and trans. Michael Howard and Peter Paret (Princeton: Princeton University Press, 1976); and Robert Gilpin, *War and Change in World Politics* (Cambridge: Cambridge University Press, 1981).

A major study of economic sanctions financed by the Twentieth Century Fund in the 1930s ended by recommending a series of case studies in hopes that "out of such a broad study we might fairly draw conclusions of some validity regarding the types of economic pressure which can best be employed, and upon the results which may fairly be expected from each." Evans Clark, ed., *Boycotts and Peace* (New York: Harper, 1932), p. 260. If such studies were ever conducted, they are not well known to students of international relations. More than thirty years later, Johan Galtung stated that he knew "of no systematic study of economic

Within the category of economic statecraft broadly defined, are three clusters of overlapping foci, economic sanctions, economic warfare, and foreign aid. The economic sanctions literature tends to focus on multilateral influence attempts, reflecting the interest of the authors in international law and organization. This literature is characterized by an emphasis on the use of negative sanctions to stop or deter a war. Much of the economic warfare literature was generated by World Wars I and II, and to some extent by the cold war. The focus tends to be on using economic techniques to help win a war by inflicting negative sanctions on the enemy. The foreign aid literature, much of it written by economists or former government officials, has emphasized the use of aid as a positive sanction to promote economic development in the third world. In none of these three subareas of economic statecraft have students of foreign policy and international politics played a predominant role. Perhaps as a consequence of this lack, there is no overarching conceptual framework that ties these three clusters together; nor is there much evidence of a desire to integrate studies of economic sanctions, economic warfare, or foreign aid with the mainstream literature of foreign policy/international politics in particular or of social science in general.[14]

The second salient characteristic of the literature on economic statecraft is the tendency to denigrate the utility of such techniques. Witness the following examples:

> Blessing: "In general, then, it can be argued that the suspension of aid does not appear to have been a very effective means of inducing change in recipient behavior. This conclusion is in general agreement with the conclusions of numerous other studies which show that neither the granting of aid nor the use of economic sanctions have been effective mechanisms of inducing behavior change in recipient countries."[15]

> Bienen and Gilpin: "The analysis of these cases lends support to the nearly unanimous conclusion of scholars that sanctions seldom

---

sanctions in the world community of nations" ("On the Meaning of Nonviolence," p. 247). See also Wiles' comment that although "there is a fair amount of descriptive literature in this field, . . . the bite of theory has been very feeble" (*Communist International Economics*, p. 455).

[14] The omission of the "*dependencia*" literature as a subtype of economic statecraft literature is deliberate. Although this literature does integrate power considerations with economic factors, the emphasis is on systemic determination of national and subnational behavior. This deterministic and systemic orientation is difficult to reconcile with the statecraft perspective, which emphasizes the choices of statesmen rather than the systemic determinants of their behavior.

[15] James A. Blessing, "The Suspension of Foreign Aid: A Macro-Analysis," *Polity* XIII (Spring 1981):533.

achieve their purposes and more likely have severe counter-productive consequences."[16]

Wallensteen: "The general picture is that economic sanctions have been unsuccessful as a means of influence in the international system."[17]

Kindleberger: "Most sanctions are not effective."[18]

Taubenfeld and Taubenfeld: "In modern times at least, economic sanctions against a non-belligerent do not ever appear to have achieved the stated aims of the sanctionists."[19]

Knorr: "On the whole, the power to give foreign aid only has ordinarily uncertain effectiveness and decidedly low utility when used for purposes of coercing other states or of establishing a position of unequal influence over them. This finding parallels our similar conclusion regarding the use of trade policy for these purposes."[20]

Strack: "There seems to be a consensus among scholars that sanctions are not only an ineffective means to secure policy objectives, but may well be dysfunctional or counterproductive, producing results opposite to those desired by the initiators of sanctions."[21]

Weintraub: "Most theorists insist that the economic coercion is rarely successful."[22]

Adler-Karlsson: "The burden of proof is clearly on those who claim that an embargo policy is an efficient instrument of foreign policy. Experience seems to indicate the contrary."[23]

[16] Bienen and Gilpin, "Evaluation," pp. III,2-3. See also Bienen and Gilpin, "Economic Sanctions as a Response to Terrorism," *Journal of Strategic Studies* III (May 1980):89.

[17] Peter Wallensteen, "Characteristics of Economic Sanctions," *Journal of Peace Research*, no. 3 (1968), p. 262.

[18] Kindleberger, *Power and Money*, p. 97.

[19] Rita Falk Taubenfeld and Howard J. Taubenfeld, "The 'Economic Weapon': The League and the United Nations," *Proceedings of the American Society of International Law* LVIII (1964):203-204. The Taubenfelds pose the question of whether "even the most perfectly applied, full economic measures [can] be expected to interfere seriously with a state's ability to achieve its goals, aggressive or otherwise" (p. 188). The context of their discussion clearly implies that the answer is no.

[20] Knorr, *Power of Nations*, pp. 205-206.

[21] Harry R. Strack, *Sanctions: The Case of Rhodesia* (Syracuse, N.Y.: Syracuse University Press, 1978), pp. xi-xii.

[22] Weintraub, *Economic Coercion*, p. 23. It should be noted that Weintraub merely notes this position; he does not subscribe to it.

[23] Gunnar Adler-Karlsson, *Western Economic Warfare, 1947–1967: A Case Study in Foreign Economic Policy* (Stockholm: Almqvist and Wiksell, 1968), p. 10.

Holsti: "If aid as an instrument of diplomatic influence has only a mixed record, it matches that of other economic techniques. . . . Past experience suggests that little is to be gained from using these instruments. . . ."[24]

Doxey: "In none of the cases analyzed in this study have economic sanctions succeeded in producing the desired political result."[25]

Wilkinson: "Turning next to the economic means of policy, we shall find that their direct utility as tools of action is strictly limited. . . ."[26]

Olson: "It is worth noting at the outset that there is a consensus in this literature that economic sanctions are largely ineffective."[27]

Galtung: "In this article the conclusion about the probable effectiveness of economic sanctions is, generally, negative."[28]

Losman: "The three boycotts studied have thus far failed to accomplish their political ends, and it seems unlikely that economic measures alone will fare better in the future."[29]

It would be difficult to find any proposition in the international relations literature more widely accepted than those belittling the utility of economic techniques of statecraft.[30] Some writers explain this striking consensus in terms of allegedly inherent weaknesses in economic tools of statecraft,[31] while a few question the basis of the consensus by suggesting bias in the

[24] Holsti, *International Politics*, p. 239. For a similarly pessimistic treatment in a textbook, see Robert L. Wendzel, *International Politics: Policymakers and Policymaking* (New York: John Wiley, 1981), pp. 239-263.

[25] Doxey, *Economic Sanctions and International Enforcement* (1971), p. 139.

[26] David O. Wilkinson, *Comparative Foreign Relations: Framework and Methods* (Belmont, Calif.: Dickenson, 1969), p. 47.

[27] Richard Stuart Olson, "Economic Coercion in World Politics: With a Focus on North-South Relations," *World Politics* XXXI (July 1979):473. Like Weintraub, Olson notes the consensus without joining it.

[28] Galtung, "International Economic Sanctions," p. 409. Unlike most writers, Galtung specifically warns his readers that "nothing of what has been said should be taken to imply that there are no conditions under which economic sanctions will work" (p. 410).

[29] Donald L. Losman, *International Economic Sanctions: The Cases of Cuba, Israel and Rhodesia* (Albuquerque: University of New Mexico Press, 1979), p. 140.

[30] The difference between "effectiveness" and "utility" is important and will be discussed later. Few of the writers cited in footnotes 15-29 distinguish clearly between the two concepts, and most use the terms interchangeably. Rarely do writers ascribe both low effectiveness and high utility to economic techniques. For an exception to this general rule, see Herbert S. Levine, Francis W. Rushing, and Charles H. Movit, "The Potential for U.S. Economic Leverage on the USSR," *Comparative Strategy* I (1979):371-404.

[31] See, for example, Taubenfeld and Taubenfeld, " 'Economic Weapon,' " pp. 187-188, 194.

selection of cases to be studied.[32] A third approach, however, contends that the consensus is best explained in terms of the analytical frameworks within which such conclusions are reached. *The main thesis of this book is that the utility of economic techniques of statecraft has been systematically underestimated primarily because of inadequacies in the analytical frameworks used to make such estimates.* Although Weintraub and Olson are correct in pointing to biases in case selection, their challenge to "the conventional wisdom" does not go far enough. For if an appropriate analytical scheme is used, even the cases usually cited in support of the conventional wisdom bolster it less than is generally supposed. Thus, rather than developing new case studies, the analysis in the following chapters will reexamine some of the same cases that make up the "overwhelming historical evidence" that is alleged to support the conventional wisdom.[33]

OBSTACLES TO THINKING ABOUT ECONOMIC STATECRAFT

Logically prior to—and perhaps more important than—the question of *what* to think about economic statecraft is the question of *how* to think about it. One way to clarify the problem is to identify some of the intellectual stumbling blocks that inhibit clear thinking about economic statecraft.

Economic Liberalism

The governmental monopoly on control of diplomatic and military techniques of statecraft has been generally accepted since the beginnings of the nation-state system. Not so with economic techniques. The proper relationship between government and the economy has been the focus of vigorous debate, off and on, for more than three centuries.[34] As was noted in chapter 3, a policy of free trade logically can—and should—be viewed

---

[32] See, for example, Olson, "Economic Coercion in World Politics," p. 473; and Weintraub, *Economic Coercion*, pp. 23-24.

[33] Cf. Knorr, *Power of Nations*, pp. 181, 183; and Bienen and Gilpin, "Evaluation," p. IX,3. On the scientific utility of focusing on "crucial cases," see Harry Eckstein, "Case Study and Theory in Political Science," in *Handbook of Political Science*, vol. 7, *Strategies of Inquiry*, pp. 113-123.

[34] On the implications of economic liberalism for international relations, see Carr, *The Twenty Years' Crisis*, pp. 43-46, 113-132; Anthony Harrison, *The Framework of Economic Activity: The International Economy and the Rise of the State* (London: Macmillan, 1967); Wiles, *Communist International Economics*, pp. 1-8, 495; Baldwin, *Economic Development*, pp. 8-10, 25-27, 51-57, 101-105, 146-152; Gilpin, *U.S. Power*, pp. 25-43; Cleveland, "Economics as Theory and Ideology," pp. 289-305; and David S. McLellan and Charles E. Woodhouse, "The Business Elite and Foreign Policy," *Western Political Quarterly* XIII (March 1960):172-190.

as a technique of economic statecraft. This is not to say, however, that the economic doctrine of *laissez-faire* liberalism is conducive to viewing free trade this way, at least not in the twentieth century. On the contrary, beliefs that the economy and the polity can and should be insulated from one another, that governmental management of economic relations should be minimal, hinder thinking about economic statecraft. Any doctrine firmly committed to one—and only one—technique of statecraft is not likely to encourage speculation about alternative techniques.

In Great Britain, the homeland of the doctrine of economic liberalism, "the separation of foreign economic policy from traditional diplomatic and security concerns of foreign policy . . . [was] deeply embedded" and "large areas of foreign economic policy were therefore taken as given: not closely linked with foreign policy because they were not seen as proper or as available instruments of foreign policy."[35] And in the United States, which clung tenaciously to the doctrine for several years after most other states had abandoned it, similar conceptual blinders have retarded inquiry into the subject of economic statecraft. Shortly after service on the National Security Council staff, Samuel P. Huntington discussed several "formidable obstacles" to "harnessing economic power to foreign policy goals." Among them was the fact that "in dramatic contrast to military power [there is] a pervasive ideology that sanctifies the independence, rather than the subordination, of economic power to government."[36] Viewed against this background, the lack of academic attention to economic statecraft in these two countries is not hard to understand.

Abnormality

The doctrine of economic liberalism fosters a tendency to depict economic statecraft as "abnormal" activity. Robert Loring Allen, for example, suggests that the concept of economic warfare "can best be understood against a background of what economists consider 'normal' international economic relations," by which he means the ideal world of economic liberalism.[37] Yuan-li Wu comments that "to those of us who still regard peace and international good will as a normal state of affairs, . . . economic warfare is the negation of normal international economic relations."[38] Weintraub argues that "trade as an instrument of economic coercion must

[35] William Wallace, *The Foreign Policy Process in Britain* (London: Royal Institute of International Affairs, 1975), pp. 156-157. See also J. Henry Richardson, *British Economic Foreign Policy* (London: George Allen and Unwin, 1936), p. 11.

[36] "Trade, Technology, and Leverage: Economic Diplomacy," *Foreign Policy*, no. 32 (Fall 1978), p. 71.

[37] "Economic Warfare," p. 467.

[38] *Economic Warfare*, pp. 3-4.

involve non-routine uses of trade for the purpose of applying economic pressure on a target nation,''[39] although he provides little guidance with respect to how "routine" uses of trade may be identified. Yet another example of the tendency to link a concept of normality with economic analysis is Kindleberger's contention that "economics proceeds in a context framed by law and order, established by politics. Economic life continues in wartime and in periods of revolution and anarchy, but under conditions that must be regarded as pathological.''[40]

Although Carr's assertion that "economics presupposes a given political order''[41] is undoubtedly correct, it does not follow that this political order must be characterized by law and order. Kindleberger's argument is especially tricky when applied to the international arena, since international relations are frequently characterized by war, revolution, and anarchy, and seldom by law and order. If extended, the logic of such a position could lead to the conclusion that all international economic relations are pathological because the international order is anarchical.

Far from being the best background against which to analyze economic statecraft, the concept of "normal international economic relations" is about the worst imaginable background for understanding the role of such policy instruments in the twentieth century. As was suggested in the discussion of free trade in the previous chapter, "routine" trade can be and has been used as a technique of statecraft throughout history. Indeed, it is precisely the routine, day-to-day uses of trade as a technique of statecraft that are least well understood and therefore most in need of illumination. Fruitful thinking about economic statecraft is impeded by the widespread belief that "it is possible somehow to escape" the "intimate connection between international trade and 'power politics' and to restore trade to its 'normal and beneficial economic functions.' ''[42] As Hirschman demonstrated, such a belief is delusory. In a world in which international economic relations always have a power dimension, it is not very helpful to posit a concept of normality that denies this dimension. In a world characterized by revolutionary change—exploding populations, more than a hundred new states since 1945, unprecedented spread of multinational corporations, rising expectations in the Third World, rapidly changing military technology, new methods of communication and transportation, record high volumes of trade and standards of living, and so on—the concept of "normality" is highly misleading. Economic statecraft is not a bizarre, abnormal, nonroutine, extraordinary, unusual occurrence, but rather a normal, routine, everyday, ordinary, commonplace activity. Power relations

[39] Weintraub, *Economic Coercion*, p. 15.
[40] *Power and Money*, p. 15.
[41] *The Twenty Years' Crisis*, p. 117.
[42] Hirschman, *National Power*, p. 78.

infuse every aspect of social life; there is no reason to make an exception for international economic relations.

High Politics/Low Politics

The distinction between "high politics" and "low politics" has also, hindered thinking about economic statecraft. It is often implied that "high politics," concerned with diplomatic and military affairs, is more important than "low politics," dealing with such mundane and unimportant matters as trade and investment. Some writers even suggest that "low politics" should not be considered foreign policy at all. T. B. Millar, for example, argues that foreign trade policy "is" foreign policy only "when it has some evident bearing on the security of the country or its capacity to get along in the world."[43] To the extent that the distinction between "high" and "low" politics implies that foreign economic policy is either unimportant or outside the scope of foreign policy in general, it discourages inquiry about economic statecraft.

The distinction between "high" and "low" politics is usually made by those concerned with the former. The reverse phenomenon, with equally pernicious effects on the study of economic statecraft, sometimes occurs among economists. In this version economic activity is depicted as serious business, while politics is treated as frivolous or irresponsible meddling. Thus, Kindleberger uses such phrases as "puerile political nonsense" and "children's parties with prizes for everyone" to refer to the political dimension of international economic relations.[44] And the Taubenfelds refer to "playing political games with world trade or with unilateral economic aid."[45] Regardless of the intentions of the authors, such rhetoric is no more conducive to objective thinking about the utility of economic statecraft than the "high politics–low politics" distinction. The student of economic statecraft should regard both economics and politics as serious and important.

Economic Means and Ends

Although seldom explicitly stated, it is often implied that economic means must have economic ends. An illustration of this tendency is economist Joseph A. Pechman's contribution to the *Handbook of Political Science*, which, without explicitly defining "economic policy," gives the

---

[43] "On Writing About Foreign Policy," in *International Politics and Foreign Policy: A Reader in Research and Theory*, ed. James N. Rosenau, rev. ed. (New York: Free Press, 1969), p. 57.

[44] *Power and Money*, pp. 12, 132.

[45] Taubenfeld and Taubenfeld, " 'Economic Weapon,' " p. 194.

impression that economic policies have economic goals.[46] Noneconomic goals in general and noneconomic foreign policy goals in particular receive little attention despite the fact that Pechman's remarks are addressed to an audience of political scientists.[47] This implicit assumption that economic means have economic goals often makes it difficult for Pechman and his fellow economists to comprehend disagreements with their policy recommendations. Thus, Pechman maintains that "most of the difficulties economists encounter in persuading others result from their [the economists'] emphasis on efficiency" (p. 43). Not so. The difficulties are more likely to arise from different assumptions about the goal(s) to be pursued. Few are really opposed to efficiency and in favor of waste. The efficient conduct of foreign policy, however, may require sacrifices in the efficiency with which goods are produced and/or distributed. The important question is, efficiency in doing what?

Even when economists turn their attention to economic sanctions or economic warfare, the fixation with economic ends is likely to persist. Thus, Morris Bornstein contends that "the aim of economic sanctions is to deprive the country . . . subject to them of goods and services"; Richard C. Porter views economic sanctions as imposed "for the purpose of reducing the economic welfare of the target country"; and Murray Kemp treats "trade warfare" as an attempt by one country "to reduce the income of its victim to a certain maximum level *provided the trade war does not depress its own income below some critical level.*"[48] If taken literally, such descriptions of the goals of economic statecraft can be very misleading. Inflicting economic harm on the target country may well be the instrumental, or intermediate, goal of the influence attempt, but it is almost never an end in itself. There is almost always some higher echelon of the hierarchy of ends *in terms of which the policy makers are defining the situation.*

Since very few foreign policy goals are final, objections to treating the goals of economic sanctions in terms of economic effects may seem to be

---

[46] "Making Economic Policy: The Role of The Economist," in *Handbook of Political Science*, vol. 6, *Policies and Policymaking*, pp. 23-78.

[47] Pechman does note that some economists have recently become interested in "such major social issues as eradicating poverty, broadening educational opportunities, eliminating discrimination, improving the quality of life, moderating the tax burden on the poor, and increasing the fiscal resources of hard-pressed state and local governments"; but foreign policy goals are strikingly absent from this list (p. 59). See also the five articles on "International Trade Controls" in the *International Encyclopedia of the Social Sciences*, none of which discusses the use of such techniques to pursue noneconomic foreign policy goals.

[48] Morris Bornstein, "Economic Sanctions and Rewards in Support of Arms Control Agreements," *American Economic Review* LVIII (May 1968):417; Richard C. Porter, "Economic Sanctions: The Theory and the Evidence from Rhodesia," *Journal of Peace Science* III (Fall 1978):93; and Kemp, *Pure Theory of International Trade*, p. 209.

quibbling. After all, most goals are intermediate. There are, however, two important counter arguments. First, it is desirable to state the objectives of a policy in terms of higher levels of the hierarchy of ends insofar as this can be done without losing a reasonable degree of specificity.[49] Thus, although stating the goals of economic sanctions in terms of vague ends such as "promoting the national interest," "maximizing power," or "doing good" would not be very helpful in understanding policy, focusing on higher-level, but still rather specific, foreign policy goals is essential. To describe United Nations sanctions against Rhodesia without reference to majority rule in Rhodesia or the 1973 Arab oil embargo without reference to Israel is to misrepresent seriously the rationale of these two influence attempts.

A second objection is that focusing on the immediate economic effects of sanctions may impede assessment of the utility of such undertakings in terms that are relevant to the concerns of policy makers. Thus, such a focus easily leads to the conclusion that the Arab oil "embargo against the United States and the Netherlands was not effective as an embargo because available oil was shifted around the world."[50] If, however, the goal was to cause those countries to reconsider the intensity of their support for Israeli policies, the failure of the embargo is less obvious. Similarly, the conclusion that "sanctions against Rhodesia clearly did not succeed"[51] cannot be supported merely by demonstrating the lack of economic effects on Rhodesia. If support for Israeli policies was weakened and if Rhodesia did move toward majority rule, the possibility that the embargoes may have worked through noneconomic influence bases must at least be considered before attributing failure to them. Embargoes may trigger a sense of shame, impose a sense of isolation from the world community, signal a willingness to use more radical measures, or simply provoke reexamination of policy stances in the target country. Any or all of these effects can occur without *any economic effects whatsoever on the target.* Economic sanctions may have diplomatic, psychological, political, military, or other effects even when their economic effect is nil. Ignoring this fact severely impairs one's ability to evaluate the costs and effectiveness of economic sanctions as instruments of foreign policy.

Some writers go beyond merely focusing on intermediate economic goals and argue that economic techniques of statecraft can succeed *only* through economic effects on the target. Losman, for example, distinguishes between the political and economic effectiveness of economic sanctions and asserts that the former is a prerequisite to the latter.[52] That is, Losman

[49] On this point see Simon, *Administrative Behavior*, p. 176.
[50] Weintraub, *Economic Coercion*, p. xiv.
[51] Porter, "Economic Sanctions," p. 107.
[52] Losman, *International Economic Sanctions*, pp. 1, 125, 128, 139.

views infliction of economic damage on the target country as a necessary but not sufficient condition for political success. Although such a proposition may be treated as an empirical hypothesis to be tested, it seems unwise to rule out in advance the possibility that economic techniques may succeed because of their connection with noneconomic causal conditions.

The tendency to attribute economic ends to economic means probably stems from the image projected by economic liberalism that the economy is a relatively autonomous sphere. This attitude is summed up by Kindleberger's denial that Clausewitz's famous dictum about the relationship between politics and war could be used to characterize economics.[53] The point of Clausewitz's frequently misunderstood dictum, however, was precisely to deny that war was an end in itself, i.e., that it was an autonomous sphere separate from the broad context of national policy:

> This unity [of politics and war] lies in *the concept that war is only a branch of political activity; that it is in no sense autonomous.*
>
> It is, of course, well known that the only source of war is politics— the intercourse of governments and peoples; but it is apt to be assumed that war suspends that intercourse and replaces it by a wholly different condition, ruled by no law but its own.
>
> We maintain, on the contrary, that war is simply a continuation of political intercourse, with the addition of other means. We deliberately use the phrase "with the addition of other means" because we also want to make it clear that war in itself does not suspend political intercourse or change it into something entirely different. In essentials that intercourse continues, irrespective of the means it employs. . . . Is war not just another expression of . . . thoughts, another form of speech or writing? Its grammar, indeed, may be its own, but not its logic.
>
> If that is so, then war cannot be divorced from political life; and whenever this occurs in our thinking about war, the many links that connect the two elements are destroyed and we are left with something pointless and devoid of sense.[54]

---

[53] Kindleberger, *Power and Money*, p. 15. For a similar view see Frank D. Graham, "Economics and Peace," in *The Second Chance: America and the Peace*, ed. John B. Whitton (Princeton: Princeton University Press, 1944), p. 115.

[54] Clausewitz, *On War*, p. 605. The most frequently quoted version of Clausewitz's dictum is found in a short paragraph in his first chapter—"It is clear . . . that war is not a mere act of policy but a true political instrument, a continuation of political activity by other means" (p. 87). The passage quoted in the text appears later in the book and provides the context within which the dictum should be interpreted. On the popular misunderstanding of the dictum see Brodie, *War and Politics*, pp. 1-11. Although Wu does not cite Clausewitz, his logic is strikingly similar—"For economic warfare, like every other form of warfare, does not aim at winning a war for its own sake. Wars are fought for certain purposes, and it is important to insure that the methods used in winning them do not prevent the realization of these purposes" (*Economic Warfare*, p. 3).

Properly understood, Clausewitz's words are as applicable to the economic sphere as to the military. Thus, both military and economic activities must be considered and evaluated in terms of an overarching set of values and priorities. Neither war nor economic activity—production, consumption, saving, investment, or whatever—should be treated as a separate enclave of social life with its own ends. Neither war nor economics can be divorced from politics; each must be judged as an instrument serving the higher goals of the polity. The fallacious view that economic means must imply economic ends is precisely analogous to the equally fallacious view that war has its own purposes. In this sense Clausewitz's dictum can and should be used to characterize economics. The concept of economic statecraft is consistent with this perspective. Although economic policy instruments may be used to pursue economic ends, their use is not confined to such aims. Clausewitz argues that what is peculiar about war "is simply the peculiar nature of its means."[55] Likewise, the distinguishing characteristic of economic statecraft lies not in its goals but rather in the "peculiar nature of its means."

WHY THINK ABOUT ECONOMIC STATECRAFT?

Should tariffs, foreign aid, embargoes, preclusive buying, investment guaranties, direct purchase, and so on be treated in terms of a broad concept of economic statecraft? Why bother to group them all together? Even if one grants the need for increased attention to economic techniques, it would be possible to favor continued separate treatment for each technique. What is to be gained, after all, by conceptual aggregation at such a high level of abstraction? It is one thing to show that such aggregation is possible, but it is another to show that it is desirable.

There are at least three reasons for thinking in terms of a broad concept of economic statecraft: (1) because others do; (2) because economic techniques are peculiar; and (3) because other techniques of statecraft are treated at this level of generality. If the concept of economic statecraft involved lumping together activities that are not usually considered to be members of a single category, some justification for the departure from common usage would be called for. In the case of economic statecraft, however, no such obligation exists. Both in social science and in ordinary language the economic dimension of social life—defined roughly the way it is here—is often treated as an analytical category. Conventional usage includes frequent references to "the economy," "the economic system," "economic activities," and "economic organizations." There is nothing unusually broad about the term "economic" as used here. Categorization at this level of generality occurs in daily newspapers, social science textbooks,

---

[55] *On War*, p. 87

library catalogues, everyday conversation, and in governmental organizations at every level. Furthermore, the distinction corresponds with the conventional division of academic disciplines. There are few departments of foreign aid, international trade, foreign investment, or taxation; instead, such academic interests are usually lumped together in a department of economics. The burden of proof lies with those who would deny that a conceptual category employed so often in other spheres of life should be applied to thinking about foreign policy techniques.

A second reason for thinking in terms of economic statecraft is that these techniques share certain characteristics that differentiate them from noneconomic techniques of statecraft. Both money and markets are unusual institutions. Thus, Gilpin argues that "what is unique about the modern world is that the economic aspects of social life have become more differentiated from other aspects because of the rise of a market economy."[56] And Alfred Marshall observes that "the problems, which are grouped as economic, because they relate specially to a man's conduct under the influence of motives that are measurable by a money price, are found to make a fairly homogeneous group."[57] If money and markets are peculiar, those techniques of statecraft closely associated with them are likely to share some peculiarities. One of the purposes of this book is to identify some of these.

The most compelling argument, however, for treating economic techniques at a high level of generality is that other techniques are so treated. Thus, Charles F. Hermann identifies the following examples of "a single broad type of instruments": propaganda, military, diplomacy, and foreign assistance.[58] The striking thing about this list is that the first three are on a much higher level of generality than the fourth. Unlike propaganda, military instruments, and diplomacy, foreign aid is *not* a broad category but rather a relatively narrow one. It is simply not comparable to the level of generality of the other three types of foreign policy tools.

From the policy maker's standpoint—and from the standpoint of rational policy analysis—the *only* characteristics of policy instruments that matter are those helpful in choosing among them. Information about the utility of a single technique or category of techniques *has no significance whatever* for decision making until it is set in the context of explicit or implicit assumptions about the comparative utility of alternative techniques. To the

[56] *War and Change*, p. 68.

[57] *Principles of Economics*, vol. 1, p. 27. On monetary exchange as a distinguishing characteristic of economic activities, see also Peter M. Blau, *Exchange and Power in Social Life*, pp. 8, 93-95, 253-282; Catlin, *The Science and Method of Politics*, pp. 206-279; Baldwin, "Power and Social Exchange," and "Money and Power."

[58] "Instruments of Foreign Policy," p. 155.

statesman only the *relative* utility of policy instruments matters.[59] Comparative studies of techniques or rational consideration of policy options by statesmen require thinking about various techniques or categories of techniques on similar levels of generality. If there are books on *War and Politics* (Brodie), there should be books on economic statecraft and politics; if there are books on *Arms and Influence* (Schelling), there is a need for books on economic techniques and influence; if there are books on *The Politics of Force* (Young), there must be some on the politics of economic statecraft; if there are books on *The Use of Force in International Relations* (Northedge), then comparable books on the use of economic statecraft are required; if there are books *On the Uses of Military Power in the Nuclear Age* (Knorr), there ought to be some on the uses of economic power in the nuclear age; if there are books on *Force, Order, and Justice* (Osgood and Tucker), there is a need for some on economic statecraft, order, and justice; and if there are books on *War and Change in World Politics* (Gilpin), there should be studies of economic statecraft and change in world politics. Any generalization about the utility of military force as a technique of statecraft made without reference to the utility of alternative techniques is likely to be both intellectually misleading and socially irresponsible. Given the plethora of studies of military statecraft at a high level of generality, most of which make no serious attempt to consider alternative techniques, scholars are derelict in fulfillment of their social responsibilities if they fail to provide studies of alternative techniques of statecraft at comparable levels of generality. It is possible, of course, to argue that studies of military statecraft should be conducted on a lower level of generality, emphasizing the differences among nuclear war, convention war, guerilla war, and so on. This might be a compelling line of argument were it not for the existence of numerous treatments of military force at a high level of generality. Since the books on military statecraft cannot be unwritten, the only socially responsible alternative is to generate studies of alternative policy techniques at comparable levels of generality. Only then can a fair and objective evaluation be made of the relative merits of military force.

The preceding three arguments concern the level of abstraction on which economic statecraft should be approached. A fourth argument focuses not on the conceptual level of analysis but rather on the need for more thinking about economic techniques of statecraft at all levels. Some assert that economic techniques of statecraft have increased, and are increasing, in importance. Thus, in 1962 the Sprouts argued that "economic techniques of statecraft have gained in importance and seem likely to increase still

---

[59] Strictly speaking, the concept of relative utility is redundant—as King Midas learned.

more in the future."[60] And in 1966 Knorr concluded that "the use of economic support and denial" and, indeed, "all non-military bases of international influence . . . have gained in value."[61] Support for such arguments is provided by the increased importance of international economic relations and by the decline in the utility of military force. Gilpin sees a long-term trend toward increased importance of economic factors in international relations coinciding with "the expansion of a highly interdependent world market economy" and suggests that this has "enhanced the role of economic power as an instrument of statecraft."[62]

The proposition that the utility of military statecraft has declined rests on purported changes in the goals and costs of such techniques. As territorial conquest recedes, and economic, ideological, and political goals gain in importance, it is argued, force loses its utility. The most important reason for the alleged decline in the utility of military instruments, however, is the vast increase in their costs. The monetary cost of weapons production is probably the least important of such costs. The two most important costs stem from the radical decline in the legitimacy of military force and the risks associated with the incredible destructive effects of nuclear weapons.[63]

Reduced to essentials, then, the argument for the increased utility of economic statecraft as a result of the reduced utility of military statecraft is as follows: The costs of military statecraft have substantially increased. Assuming that statesmen will continue to want to influence other states or nonstate actors, they are likely to find nonmilitary measures, such as economic techniques of statecraft, increasingly attractive. If this is true, enhanced understanding of the capabilities and limitations of such policy instruments would seem desirable.

Balanced and judicious discussion of the comparative utility of military and economic techniques of statecraft is scarce. Contentions that military force is totally worthless or that economic techniques have completely displaced military techniques are so extreme that they are easily refuted. In addition, such views draw attention away from the more moderate positions that deserve serious debate. Both sides need to develop an analytical framework that will allow rigorous systematic evaluation of the

---

[60] *Foundations of International Politics*, p. 437.

[61] *Uses of Military Power*, p. 171.

[62] *War and Change*, pp. 68-69, 218.

[63] For discussion of these matters see Knorr, *Uses of Military Power*; and Quincy Wright, *A Study of War*, 2d ed. (Chicago: University of Chicago Press, 1965). The former is the most sophisticated study of the utility of military statecraft available, and the latter is a monumental work, the most thorough and comprehensive treatment of war in any language. When the second edition was published, Wright added a "Commentary on War Since 1942," which suggests several reasons for the declining utility of military statecraft. This work deserves far more attention than it gets from contemporary writers on military affairs. In the study of statecraft, newer does not necessarily mean better.

comparative utility of alternative policy instruments. In the nuclear age, it is especially important, nay imperative, to understand the capabilities and limitations of alternatives to military force. It may well be that none exists, but the stakes are too high to permit basing the conclusion on any but the most careful research. Studies that purport to assess the utility of military techniques while ignoring their costs or while giving only the scantiest attention to nonmilitary alternatives do not begin to satisfy this need.[64]

[64] For an example of an attempt to assess the utility of military statecraft without reference to cost considerations, see Barry M. Blechman and Stephen S. Kaplan, *Force Without War: U.S. Armed Forces as a Political Instrument* (Washington, D.C.: Brookings Institution, 1978).

CHAPTER 5

ECONOMIC STATECRAFT IN INTERNATIONAL THOUGHT

*We hold that for the mastery of a speculative and
controversial science a certain multiplication of
authorities is desirable. The false tendency of
teachers to inculcate, and pupils to learn by rote,
the very phrases and metaphors of a favourite
author can only be corrected by dividing the
allegiance of those who, like the Romans of old,
"rush to slavery." Hence the history of theory is
particularly instructive in political economy as in
philosophy.*

(F. Y. Edgeworth)

Both the theory and practice of economic statecraft are centuries old.
The relationship between foreign policy goals and economic resources has
been discussed by Plato, Aristotle, Machiavelli, Locke, Bacon, Montesquieu, Hume, Smith, Kant, Hamilton, List, John Stuart Mill, Woodrow
Wilson, John Maynard Keynes, and many others. No comprehensive or
detailed history of thought about economic statecraft will be attempted
here. Rather, this chapter will provide an overview of thinking on this
subject for the last twenty-five centuries.

ANCIENT AND MEDIEVAL THOUGHT

"In the ancient Greek and Roman classics is to be found the doctrine
that differences in natural conditions in different countries made trade
between these countries mutually profitable."[1] To the ancient Greeks,
however, the profitability of foreign trade did not necessarily make it
desirable. The Greek ideal of city-states as self-sufficient, independent
entities gave rise to the view that foreign trade was more a necessary evil
to be endured than an advantageous opportunity to be encouraged. Sir
Alfred Zimmern summarizes this view as follows:

> It was a tradition and a boast of Greek cities to be sovereign States
> wholly independent of foreign claims. Their fierce love of independ-

[1] Jacob Viner, *Studies in the Theory of International Trade* (New York: Harper, 1937), p.
100.

ence had been nourished by centuries of isolation, and was . . . one of the strongest forces in the national life. But we shall be merely following the bad example of so many nineteenth-century traders and pioneers if we interpret this sentiment in a strictly political sense. It was in origin and essence, in Greece as elsewhere, every whit as much economic as political: for politics and economics, State government and State housekeeping, are to simple people (as they should be to us) merely two aspects of the same thing. So it provided what was for centuries the bedrock of Greek economic policy. If a State was to be independent it must not only govern itself in its own way, but also feed and clothe itself in its own way. It must not only manage its own affairs but supply its own needs. Home Rule and Self-sufficiency . . . are, in the traditional Greek view, almost convertible terms. How strong was the tradition may be seen by the way it lingered on, years after Greek traders had begun pouring in goods from East and West, in the political economy of the philosophers.[2]

The Greek emphasis on self-sufficiency grew less out of concern for military security or desire to protect domestic producers than from fear of the corrupting effects of foreign influences on the polity.[3]

These ideas are reflected in the writings of the Greek philosophers Plato and Aristotle, who both regarded self-sufficiency as a desirable attribute in a state and who were concerned primarily with the internal rather than the external life of the state.[4] In the *Republic* Plato rather grudgingly admits that foreign trade will be necessary since "it will be next to impossible to plant our city in a territory where it will need no imports."[5] In the *Laws* Plato's hostility toward foreign trade leads him to locate the ideal state inland away from good harbors that would tempt traders. "Trade and commerce were regarded as harmful in that they fostered greed and sharp practices, thus tending to render a city faithless to itself and the rest of the world."[6]

Aristotle's outlook on foreign affairs is similar to Plato's. He criticizes Plato for neglecting foreign affairs[7] but does not do much better himself

---

[2] *The Greek Commonwealth*, 5th ed. (London: Oxford University Press, 1931), pp. 286-287.

[3] Ibid., pp. 323-324.

[4] George H. Sabine, *A History of Political Theory*, rev. ed. (New York: Henry Holt, 1950), pp. 123-129; and Frank M. Russell, *Theories of International Relations* (New York: D. Appleton-Century, 1936), pp. 51-74.

[5] *The Republic of Plato*, trans. F. M. Cornford (New York: Oxford University Press, 1945), p. 57.

[6] Russell, *Theories*, p. 67.

[7] *The Politics of Aristotle*, trans. Earnest Barker (London: Oxford University Press, 1958), pp. 57-58.

in this regard. He notes that "it is a hotly debated question whether connexion with the sea is to the advantage, or the detriment, of a well-ordered state"; but states his own position as favoring a coastal location so as to facilitate both military security and the importation of "a good supply of material necessities."[8] Thus, although Aristotle shared Plato's preoccupation with the internal life of the (nearly) self-sufficient state, he was somewhat more tolerant of "a temperate and regulated intercourse with other states."[9]

The idea that foreign economic policy should be formulated with an eye to preserving the autonomy of the domestic life of the state is not merely a vestige of the ancients; it is an important element in the twentieth-century debate over strategies for coping with international interdependence.

The lack of enthusiasm for trade found in the works of Plato and Aristotle is also reflected in medieval thought. Medieval otherworldliness tended to depict commerce as a temptation to become overly interested in the material life to the detriment of the spiritual life. Worth noting, however, is Pierre Dubois, an adviser to the king of France, who proposed a federation of Christian states that contained some of the elements found in later peace plans. Especially notable is the idea of an economic boycott directed against any member making war on another, thus preceding the "sanctions of the covenant of the League of Nations by over six centuries."[10]

THE MERCANTILIST ERA: 1500–1750

"Mercantilism" is a label applied by nineteenth-century German scholars to the doctrines and practices of European states with respect to international economic relations in the period roughly from 1500 to 1750. The vigorous attack on mercantilism by Adam Smith in *The Wealth of Nations* and by his nineteenth-century followers was so successful that many economists came to look upon mercantilist ideas "not only with disapproval but also with contempt."[11] Even today the pejorative connotations of "mercantilism" linger on, and one is usually safe in assuming that those who label the policies of a contemporary state as "neomercantilism" disapprove of such practices.

In addition to a number of little known pamphleteers, the ranks of the

[8] Ibid., p. 294.

[9] Russell, *Theories*, p. 69.

[10] Sylvester John Hemleben, *Plans for World Peace Through Six Centuries* (Chicago: University of Chicago Press, 1943), p. 3. See also Russell, *Theories*, pp. 106-110; and F. Melian Stawell, *The Growth of International Thought* (London: Thornton Butterworth, 1929), pp. 63-68.

[11] Joseph A. Schumpeter, *History of Economic Analysis* (New York: Oxford University Press, 1954), p. 336.

mercantilists include Montaigne, Montchrétien, Bacon, and Locke.[12] Since mercantilism is often associated with the idea of a strong state, the inclusion of Locke, the apostle of limited government, may come as a surprise. Even more surprising, however, is the absence of Machiavelli, founder of the "power politics" school of realism, from the ranks of the mercantilists.

With so many writers contributing over so many years, it is small wonder that the content of mercantilist doctrine is a matter of dispute. Jacob Viner has identified five propositions summarizing the essentials of mercantilist doctrine:

> (1) Policy should be framed and executed in strictly nationalistic terms, that is, national advantage alone is to be given weight; (2) in appraising any relevant element of national policy or of foreign trade, great weight is always to be put on its effect, direct or indirect, on the national stock of the precious metals; (3) in the absence of domestic gold or silver mines, a primary national goal should be the attainment of as large an excess of exports over imports as is practicable, as the sole means whereby the national stock of the precious metals can be augmented; (4) a balance of trade "in favor" of one's country is to be sought through direct promotion by the authorities of exports and restriction of imports or by other measures which will operate indirectly in these directions; (5) economic foreign policy and political foreign policy are to be pursued with constant attention to both plenty and "power" (including security under this latter term) as coordinate and generally mutually supporting national objectives, each capable of being used as a means to the attainment of the other.[13]

These propositions, according to Viner, "constituted the solid core of mercantilist doctrine, from which there was little dissent before the 1750s by writers on economic matters."[14] Although the mercantilists have sometimes been accused of sharing King Midas's preoccupation with collecting precious metals as an end in itself, others have argued that mercantilists viewed precious metals as means to other ends. The mercantilists, for example, were well aware that precious metals could be used to "finance

[12] For discussions of mercantilist views, see Eli F. Heckscher, *Mercantilism*, trans. Mendel Shapiro, rev. ed., 2 vols. (New York: Macmillan, 1955); Jacob Viner, "Power Versus Plenty as Objectives of Foreign Policy in the Seventeenth and Eighteenth Centuries," *World Politics* I (October 1948):1-29; Viner, "Economic Thought: Mercantilist Thought," in *International Encyclopedia of the Social Sciences*, vol. 4, pp. 435-443; and Edmund Silberner, *La Guerre dans la Pensée Économique du XVIᵉ au XVIIIᵉ Siècle* (Paris: Librairie du Recueil Sirey, 1939), pp. 7-122.

[13] Viner, "Mercantilist Thought," p. 436.

[14] Ibid.

and equip armies and navies, hire foreign mercenaries, bribe potential enemies, and subsidize allies."[15]

The relationship between war and mercantilism is also a matter of dispute. Eli Heckscher and Edmund Silberner portray mercantilism as a doctrine that subordinates economic concerns to war preparation and perhaps thereby increases the probability of war.[16] Jacob Viner, while not denying the mercantilist concern with military preparedness, argues that wealth was also a concern and denies the existence of any clearcut priority for either goal.[17] Joseph Schumpeter develops yet another line of argument to the effect that the warlike nature of nation states during the mercantilist era stemmed from their social structures.[18] The implication of this line of argument is that states adopted mercantilist policies because they were warlike; they did not become warlike because of mercantilist policies. In sum, although there is little doubt that the mercantilists were concerned about military preparedness, questions regarding the importance of this goal relative to others and regarding the effects of such policies on the probability of war have not been resolved.

The prevalence of mercantilist ideas during the period 1500–1750 justifies calling it the "mercantilist era"; but this label does not mean that other writers were silent with respect to economic statecraft. Diplomatists, international lawyers, and proponents of world peace plans also discussed economic statecraft.

The most famous treatise on statecraft written in this period was Machiavelli's *The Prince*. In view of the mercantilists' emphasis on power and national interest, one might expect Machiavelli to have embraced their views. Not so. Machiavelli seems to have had little interest in economic statecraft of any kind. Shortly before writing *The Prince*, he wrote as follows to a friend:

> Fortune has decreed that, as I do not know how to reason either about the art of silk or about the art of wool, either about profits or about losses, it befits me to reason about the state.[19]

[15] Ibid., p. 438.

[16] See also Frank D. Graham, "Economics and Peace," p. 116; and Edward Mead Earle, "Adam Smith, Alexander Hamilton, Friedrich List: The Economic Foundations of Military Power," in *Makers of Modern Strategy: Military Thought from Machiavelli to Hitler*, ed. Edward Mead Earle (Princeton: Princeton University Press, 1943), pp. 118-119.

[17] "Power Versus Plenty." The question of establishing priorities with respect to wealth and power was not of much interest to the mercantilists since they viewed these two goals as compatible—perhaps even inseparable. Cf. Albert O. Hirschman, *National Power and the Structure of Foreign Trade*, pp. 4-5. Robin Renwick (*Economic Sanctions* [Cambridge: Harvard University Center for International Affairs, 1981], p. 4) appears to be quite alone in contending that the objectives of the mercantilists were economic rather than political.

[18] Schumpeter, *History of Economic Analysis*, p. 146.

[19] Quoted by Hirschman, *National Power*, p. xv.

Albert Hirschman interprets this comment as revealing "the complete failure of Machiavelli to perceive any connection between economics and politics."[20] Machiavelli may have been the first political scientist, but he certainly was not the first political economist.

The content of *The Prince* lends support to Hirschman's view of Machiavelli. Military statecraft fascinates and preoccupies Machiavelli. In considering how the strength of states should be measured, the discussion is cast in military terms.[21] In considering the duties of a prince, he advises him to "have no other aim or thought . . . but war and its organization and discipline, for that is the only art that is necessary to one who commands."[22] Clearly, military techniques of statecraft dominate Machiavelli's thought.

In the *Discourses*, Machiavelli attacks the widely held mercantilist view that "money is the sinews of war." Asserting that there cannot "be a more erroneous opinion," he argues that good soldiers are more important than gold in war, since "gold alone will not procure good soldiers, but good soldiers will always procure gold."[23] Thus, not only was Machiavelli not a mercantilist, he went out of his way to dispute one of the most widely accepted tenets of mercantilism in his time.

A less well known treatise on statecraft published in 1716 by François de Callières is primarily concerned with diplomacy but mentions possible uses of money.[24] Indeed, a section is devoted to the art of offering bribes to foreign officials (pp. 24-26). And in a discussion of the difficulties inherent in bargaining between parties of unequal power, the author suggests the possibility that "a large outlay of money" by the more powerful state may be a useful way to "harmonise the interests of the parties concerned" (p. 110).

The early international law thinkers, Francis of Vittoria and Hugo Grotius, also touched on economic statecraft in some of their works. Vittoria, writing in 1532, "maintained that nothing would justify cutting off commerce with another state in time of peace,"[25] thus asserting a right of commercial intercourse that would, if adhered to, seriously limit the prac-

---

[20] Ibid. See also Albert O. Hirschman, *The Passions and the Interests* (Princeton: Princeton University Press, 1977), p. 41.

[21] Niccolò Machiavelli, *The Prince and the Discourses* (New York: Modern Library, 1950), pp. 39-41. (*The Prince* was written in 1513 but not published until 1532.)

[22] Ibid., p. 53. On the immense importance Machiavelli attached to the art of war, see H. Butterfield, *The Statecraft of Machiavelli* (London: G. Bell, 1940), pp. 93-94.

[23] Machiavelli, *The Prince and the Discourses*, pp. 308-312.

[24] *On the Manner of Negotiating with Princes*, trans. A. F. Whyte (Notre Dame, Ind.: University of Notre Dame Press, 1963).

[25] Janice Catherine Simpson, "The Position in International Law of Economic Measures of Coercion Carried on Within a State's Territory" (Ph.D. dissertation, University of Chicago, 1935), p. 13. See also, Russell, *Theories*, pp. 139-140.

tice of economic statecraft. Vittoria may have derived this principle at least in part from the belief that "God had endowed different regions with limited but varied products in order to give mankind an incentive to trade, so that through a world economy they would learn to love each other," a common belief in the sixteenth century.[26] Writing at the beginning of the seventeenth century, Hugo Grotius followed Vittoria in arguing that international commerce had divine approval and that to interfere with trade was to interfere with the natural order of things. He did not, however, assert a country's right to sell abroad, but only to buy what was needed. This idea that free trade, peace, and international harmony are related was to play an important role in the eighteenth and nineteenth centuries.[27]

Two proposals for world peace, one from the seventeenth and the other from the eighteenth century, are also important landmarks in the intellectual history of economic statecraft. In 1623 Émeric Crucé published *Le Nouveau Cynée*, a work ostensibly intended as advice to rulers with respect to the achievement of universal peace.[28] This was the first recorded plan for a universal international organization with peace as its primary objective. The idea—if not the actual terminology—of international economic interdependence as the key to world peace is deeply embedded in Crucé's argument. He disparages the tendency to extol military virtues and glorifies the social utility of the merchant class. Noting Crucé's advocacy of free or nearly free trade as a way to promote peace, Silberner summarizes his contribution as follows: "A century and a half before Smith, more than two centuries before Cobden, he worked out a line of thought that engaged the most important liberals of the 18th and 19th centuries. To the ancient and feudal ideal of the warrior, he opposed the modern bourgeois ideal of the peaceful worker."[29] The idea of a link between free trade and peace, of course, carried over into the twentieth century and is reflected, for example, in the thought of Sir Norman Angell, Woodrow Wilson, Ramsay Muir, and Cordell Hull.

In 1713 the Abbé de Saint-Pierre published *A Project for Making Peace Perpetual in Europe*, which followed Crucé in challenging the mercantilist notion that trade was a zero-sum game. He also espoused the idea that "international exchange creates favorable conditions for universal

---

[26] Viner, *Studies in International Trade*, p. 100. See also Jacob Viner, *The Role of Providence in the Social Order* (Philadelphia: American Philosophical Society, 1972), pp. 27-54; and Hirschman, *Passions and Interests*, p. 60.

[27] See Simpson, "Economic Measures of Coercion," p. 14; Russell, *Theories*, pp. 151-152, 294; and Hirschman, *Passions and Interests*, pp. 79-81.

[28] *The New Cyneas*, trans. Thomas Willing Balch (Philadelphia: Allen, Lane and Scott, 1909); Russell, *Theories*, pp. 163-169; Hemleben, *Plans for World Peace*, pp. 21-31; and Silberner, *La Guerre*, pp. 128-138.

[29] Silberner, *La Guerre*, p. 137.

peace."[30] Thus, although mercantilism was the dominant doctrine of the period 1500-1750, alternative ways of thinking about economic statecraft were not unknown; and some of these were to achieve prominence as the mercantilist consensus broke down in the latter part of the eighteenth century.

ECONOMIC LIBERALISM

Although few would quarrel with the depiction of mercantilism as a theory of economic statecraft, similar characterization of the free trade doctrines of economic liberalism is likely to raise some scholarly eyebrows. Clearly, mercantilism was concerned with the pursuit of foreign policy goals (i.e., wealth and power) by economic means, but can liberalism, supposedly the very antithesis of mercantilism, be so described?[31] The mercantilist emphasis on active state intervention in economic life in contrast with the liberal emphasis on limiting such interference by the state easily leads to portrayal of liberalism as postulating economics and politics as separate, distinct, and autonomous spheres of social life. Adam Smith is credited with having severed the mercantilist link between politics and economics, between the study of such "mean things" as "national rivalries and national power" and "the study of national wealth."[32] From there it is easy to assert that "the free trade doctrine . . . denies the validity of the use of economic instruments for political ends."[33]

Mercantilism, however, is not synonymous with economic statecraft; it is merely one doctrine emphasizing particular policy instruments and particular goals. Mercantilism is only one of many forms of economic statecraft. Economic statecraft implies nothing about the degree or kind of state intervention in the economy. Its fundamental characteristic is simply that economic policy be deliberately formulated so as to promote the foreign policy goals of the state—whatever those may be.

The best known link between the free trade doctrines of liberalism and foreign policy objectives is the proposition that trade promotes peace.[34]

[30] Ibid., pp. 160-170. Quote is from p. 163. See also Russell, *Theories*, pp. 188-196; and Hemleben, *Plans for World Peace*, pp. 56-82.

[31] Cf. Silberner: "In all its doctrinal elements liberalism is opposed to mercantilism" (*La Guerre*, p. 125. See also p. 265).

[32] William Cunningham, *The Growth of English Industry and Commerce in Modern Times*, 3d ed., vol. 1 (Cambridge: Cambridge University Press, 1903), p. 594n.

[33] John Pinder, "Economic Diplomacy," in *World Politics: An Introduction*, ed. James N. Rosenau, Kenneth W. Thompson, and Gavin Boyd (New York: Free Press, 1976), p. 314.

[34] See Russell, *Theories*, pp. 179-203; 282-313; Hirschman, *National Power*, pp. 6-10; Silberner, *La Guerre*, pp. 125-269; and Edmund Silberner, *The Problem of War in Nineteenth Century Economic Thought*, trans. Alexander H. Krappe (Princeton: Princeton University Press, 1946).

The strong form of this proposition maintained that peace would be the inevitable result of universal free trade, but more moderate versions asserted merely that free trade lowered the probability of war. Of course, if liberals had viewed war as desirable, such an observation would not necessarily qualify as a theory of economic statecraft; but since they tended to regard war avoidance as a desirable foreign policy goal, the proposition clearly concerned the kind of economic statecraft they thought could and should be practiced—peace was the goal and free trade was the means.

The case for free trade as a way to prevent war rests on three types of arguments. First, mercantilist beliefs and practices were viewed as a prime cause of war. Thus, the mere absence of such doctrines and policies would enhance the probability of peace. Second, by strengthening the influence of the bourgeoisie, presumed to be less bellicose than the aristocracy, countries would be less likely to pursue warlike policies.[35] And third, since war is likely to interrupt trade, the increased level of international economic interdependence produced by free trade creates vested interests in peace.

The last proposition, regarding the pacifying effects of international economic interdependence, can be traced to Crucé and has served as a powerful argument for the link between trade and peace ever since. The following quotations are but some of the more famous observations on this topic:

> The natural effect of commerce is to bring about peace. Two nations which trade together, render themselves reciprocally dependent: if the one has an interest in buying the other has an interest in selling; and all unions are based on mutual needs.[36]

> Just as nature wisely separates the nations which the will of each state would like to unite under its sway either by cunning or by force, . . . so also nature unites nations which the concept of a cosmopolitan or world law would not have protected from violence and war, and it does this by mutual self-interest. It is the *spirit of commerce* which cannot coexist with war, and which sooner or later takes hold of every nation. For, since the money power is perhaps the most reliable among all the powers subordinate to the state's power, states find themselves impelled (though hardly by moral compulsion) to promote the noble peace and to try to avert war by mediation whenever it threatens to break out anywhere in the world.[37]

---

[35] Unlike many nineteenth-century free traders, Adam Smith himself was not a pacifist. Indeed, he regarded the decline of the "martial spirit" as "a bad effect of commerce." (Hirschman, *Passions and Interests*, pp. 105-106.)

[36] Charles-Louis de Montesquieu, *De l'Espirit des Lois* (1748), book XX, chap. II, quoted by Hirschman, *National Power*, p. 10n.

[37] Immanuel Kant, "Essay on Eternal Peace" (1795), reprinted in appendix to Carl Joachim Friedrich, *Inevitable Peace* (Cambridge: Harvard University Press, 1948), pp. 264-265.

* * *

It is commerce which is rapidly rendering war obsolete, by strengthening and multiplying the personal interests which are in natural opposition to it. And it may be said without exaggeration that the great extent and rapid increase of international trade, in being the principal guarantee of the peace of the world, is the great permanent security for the uninterrupted progress of the ideas, the institutions, and the character of the human race.[38]

Similar passages are to be found in twentieth century works by Sir Norman Angell (1914), Francis Delaisi (1925), and Ramsay Muir (1933).[39]

To depict mercantilism and economic liberalism as subgroups of a larger class of theories of economic statecraft is to imply some similarities between the two doctrines. Indeed, the common tendency to emphasize the differences between mercantilism and liberalism makes it difficult to conceive of them as members of this larger group of theories. Robert Gilpin, for example, differentiates mercantilism from liberalism with respect to "the nature of economic relations, the goal of economic activity, the assumed nature of the actors in international economic relations, and the relationship of economics and politics."[40] Gilpin contends that the differences between the two doctrines with respect to these matters are "fundamental," "decisive," and "critical."[41] Although Gilpin is primarily concerned with elucidating contemporary theoretical viewpoints with respect to foreign investment strategies, the criteria he sets forth provide a convenient organizing framework for discussing the historical evolution of these doctrines with respect to economic statecraft in general.[42] The question here, then, is the extent to which Gilpin's discussion of mercantilism and liberalism is helpful in understanding the historical evolution of thinking about economic statecraft.

The Nature of Economic Relations

Liberal and mercantilist conceptions of the nature of economic relations, according to Gilpin, differ in the former's view of trade as a "positive-

---

[38] John Stuart Mill, *Principles of Political Economy* (1848), p. 582.

[39] Angell, *The Foundations of International Polity* (London: William Heinemann, 1914); Delaisi, *Political Myths and Economic Realities* (London: Noel Douglas, 1925); and Muir, *The Interdependent World and Its Problems* (Boston: Houghton Mifflin, 1933). See also Baldwin, "Interdependence and Power."

[40] Robert Gilpin, "The Political Economy of the Multinational Corporation: Three Contrasting Perspectives," *American Political Science Review* LX (March 1976):185; and *U.S. Power*, pp. 25-43.

[41] "Political Economy," pp. 185-186; and *U.S. Power*, pp. 26, 28. Gilpin also includes Marxism in his discussion.

[42] An additional reason for using Gilpin's discussion as a reference point is that his characterization of these doctrines has been very influential among international relations scholars.

sum game'' and the latter's view of trade as ''essentially a zero-sum game.''[43] Although this seems to be an accurate characterization of an important—perhaps the most important—difference between the two doctrines, it is still possible to classify both as forms of economic statecraft.[44] This difference affects the way liberals and mercantilists define a problem but not its basic nature as a problem in economic statecraft. Neither view rules out the possibility of trying to promote foreign policy goals using economic means.

As long as the ''harmony of interests'' attributed to liberalism is confined to the economic sphere, there is little reason to question it. The liberals believed trade was—or could be—mutually advantageous; the mercantilists did not. This does not mean, however, that liberals believed that all interests in all spheres of life were always perfectly harmonious. Adam Smith saw clearly that what was mutually beneficial from an economic standpoint might not be so from a political standpoint when he observed that the ''wealth of a neighbouring country'' might be ''dangerous in war and politics'' even though ''certainly advantageous in trade.''[45]

The Goal of Economic Activity

Gilpin describes the liberal goal as ''maximization of global welfare'' and the mercantilist goal as ''maximization of national interest.'' Whereas the former is concerned with the ''efficient use of the world's scarce resources,'' the latter is concerned with ''the distribution of employment, industry, and military power among nation-states.''[46] Elsewhere, Gilpin describes mercantilism ''as the striving after security through economic means.''[47] Gilpin summarizes his position by comparing it with a frequently quoted passage by Viner:

> What then is the correct interpretation of mercantilist doctrine and practice with respect to the roles of power and plenty as ends of national policy? I believe that practically all mercantilists, whatever the period, country, or status of the particular individual, would have subscribed to all of the following propositions: (1) wealth is an ab-

[43] *U.S. Power*, pp. 26-27.

[44] Viner, Heckscher, and Hirschman seem to agree with Gilpin. See Viner, ''Power vs. Plenty,'' p. 10; Heckscher, *Mercantilism*, vol. 2, pp. 316-324; and Hirschman, *National Power*, pp. 4-10.

[45] Adam Smith, *An Inquiry into the Nature and Causes of the Wealth of Nations* (1776), ed. Edwin Canaan (New York: Modern Library, 1937), p. 461.

[46] *U.S. Power*, p. 27. Silberner's view is similar to Gilpin's. See *La Guerre*, p. 265.

[47] ''Economic Interdependence and National Security in Historical Perspective,'' in *Economic Issues and National Security*, ed. Klaus Knorr and Frank H. Trager (Lawrence: Regents Press of Kansas, 1977), p. 28.

solutely essential means to power, whether for security or for aggression; (2) power is essential or valuable as a means to the acquisition or retention of wealth; (3) wealth and power are each proper ultimate ends of national policy; (4) there is long-run harmony between these ends, although in particular circumstances it may be necessary for a time to make economic sacrifices in the interest of military security and therefore also of long-run prosperity.[48]

Neither the passage cited nor the article from which it was taken provides support for the contention that the goals of mercantilists were fundamentally different from the goals of the liberals. Viner was attacking Heckscher's interpretation of mercantilism for exaggerating the importance of power and neglecting the role of wealth as goals of mercantilist policy—thus his third proposition attributes to them the view that *both* wealth and power were "proper ultimate ends of national policy." The implication of Viner's argument was that Heckscher had exaggerated the differences between liberal and mercantilist goals. He points out that in the eighteenth century power and plenty were viewed as proper policy goals by patriotic citizens *regardless of whether they were mercantilists or not.* "Adam Smith," observes Viner, "though not a mercantilist, was speaking for mercantilists as well as for himself when he said that 'the great object of the political economy of every country, is to increase the riches and power of that country.' "[49] And with respect to the idea that mercantilists were interested in military power while liberals were interested in global economic welfare, the following comment by Viner is instructive: "It is not without significance that it was an anti-mercantilist economist, Adam Smith, and not the mercantilists, who laid down the maxim that 'defence is more important than opulence.' "[50] Indeed, Viner's general position was that "the moderate mercantilist could often sound like a moderate exponent of laissez faire."[51]

In comparison with Gilpin's view of fundamental differences between mercantilist and liberal goals, the differences between Viner and Heckscher are minimal. Even Heckscher did not regard the differences between liberal and mercantilist goals as critical, as the following passages indicate:

It is true that one important difference between mercantilism and *laissez-faire* referred to ends: mercantilism was especially concerned

[48] Viner, "Power vs. Plenty," p. 10, cited by Gilpin, *U.S. Power*, p. 37.

[49] "Power vs. Plenty," p. 13. Cf. Smith, *Wealth of Nations*, p. 352.

[50] "Power vs. Plenty," p. 17. Actually, Viner uncharacteristically misquotes Smith, whose comment is even stronger than Viner implies: "As defence, however, is of *much* more importance than opulence. . . ." (Smith, *Wealth of Nations*, p. 431. Italics added.)

[51] Jacob Viner, "The Intellectual History of Laissez Faire," *The Journal of Law and Economics* III (October 1960):46.

with wealth as a basis for state power, while *laissez-faire* regarded it mainly as valuable to the individual and thus desirable on that account. But in actual fact this difference meant much less than might have been expected, for wealth as such was the centre of interest and dominated economic thought and dealings to an equal degree in both, far more in fact than the question of its ultimate application. To this extent mercantilism and *laissez-faire* were in agreement on the question of ends.[52]

[The] fact that they represented essentially different, if not directly opposed, opinions in matters of economic policy was due to the wide gap between their views as to the proper means. Mercantilists and *laissez-faire* politicians or economists agreed in directing their attention primarily to such questions as "How does a state become powerful?" "What should one do to bring it to prosperity and well-being?" "What is it that creates the 'increase and decline' of countries, the 'wealth of nations'?" But to tackle these problems, they offered quite different if not entirely opposite solutions.[53]

[One] is perfectly justified in considering mercantilism as a nationalist system.

It must, however, be pointed out that this approach does not lead to any fundamental explanation of the essence of mercantilism. . . . From certain points of view, free trade provides the strictest contrast with mercantilism. But paradoxical as it may seem, free trade on its first premises was likewise entirely preoccupied with the interests of the native country. Only in its consequences was it cosmopolitan. . . . From the point of view of economic policy, . . . the most important aspect to note is that it was out of a concern for the interests of their own country that free trade theorists demanded free exchange with other countries. . . . The interests of the native country were the deciding factor in determining policy both under free trade and under mercantilism. The differences between the two lay in another direction.[54]

It is true that several mercantilists considered it an exclusive feature of their times that interest in power should be applied to the economic sphere. . . . But still it may be asserted that, on this point, mercantilism was not fundamentally different from the policy which was later to supersede it. This is particularly clear in the remarks of Adam Smith. He showed himself in profound agreement with measures

[52] Heckscher, *Mercantilism*, vol. 1, p. 25.
[53] Ibid., p. 26.
[54] Ibid., vol. 2, pp. 13-14.

precisely in the sphere of the policy of power, which, in view of his general attitude, would not on other grounds have met with his approval.[55]

Time and again Heckscher compares the goals of the mercantilists with those of the liberals, and each time he concludes that the differences are superficial and misleading rather than fundamental and revealing. To depict the goals of the liberals as economic and global in contrast with the political and nationalistic goals of the mercantilists is to distort both doctrines. Both were concerned with national power and national wealth. The fundamental differences between them had to do with means not ends. Viner and Heckscher differed in their interpretation of mercantilism, but both would have profoundly disagreed with Gilpin's description of the goals of mercantilism and liberalism.

The Nature of the Actors

According to Gilpin the mercantilists view nation-states as "the real actors in international economic relations . . . national interest determines foreign policy." He contrasts this view with the liberal emphasis "on the individual consumer, firm, or entrepreneur."[56] This characterization flows naturally from Gilpin's contention that mercantilist goals were defined in terms of national interests while liberal goals were defined in terms of global welfare.

If Adam Smith's book had been entitled "An Inquiry into the Nature and Causes of the Wealth of Consumers, Firms, and Entrepreneurs," of course, Gilpin's point would be strengthened. The actual title, however, is difficult to reconcile with Gilpin's description of liberalism. The quotations from Viner and Heckscher in the foregoing discussion of goals are relevant here but need not be repeated. Mercantilists and liberals agreed that states were important actors in international economic relations, that policies should be defined in terms of the national interest, and that wealth and power were both important components of the national interest. Mercantilists and liberals differed as the degree to which national interests, rightly defined, were likely to conflict and as to the specific state policies best suited to pursuit of the national interest. The idea that "the nation-state has no meaning as an economic entity"[57] may characterize the views of some contemporary "economists, . . . businessmen, and American

[55] Ibid., pp. 15-16.
[56] U.S. Power, p. 28.
[57] Ibid., p. 25.

officials'';[58] but it was not the view of Adam Smith and other classical economic liberals.

The Relationship Between Politics and Economics

Gilpin attributes to liberalism the view that politics and economics are ''relatively separable and autonomous spheres of activities'' and that ''economic rationality *ought* to determine political relations.'' ''The essence of the mercantilistic perspective,'' according to Gilpin, ''is the subservience of the economy to the state and its interests.'' Although these characterizations represent stereotypical images of the two schools of thought, caution is in order. In the first place, the proposition that liberals believed that ''the pursuit of wealth should determine the nature of the political order'' requires more documentation than Gilpin provides.[59] It is, after all, rather difficult to reconcile the idea that ''the pursuit of wealth should determine the nature of the political order'' with Adam Smith's assertion that ''the first duty of the sovereign . . . [is] that of protecting the society from the violence and invasion of other independent societies.''[60] Smith believed that the ''*material* welfare of 'the whole society' is advanced when everyone is allowed to follow his own private interest'';[61] but he did *not* believe that material welfare was so important that the political order should be subordinated to it. He did not say, after all, that opulence is more important than defense! And although he may have had a low opinion of politicians, the view of businessmen expressed below does not suggest that he wanted to subordinate the political order to their views:

> The capricious ambition of kings and ministers has not, during the present and the preceding century, been more fatal to the repose of Europe, than the impertinent jealousy of merchants and manufacturers. The violence and injustice of the rulers of mankind is an ancient evil, for which, I am afraid, the nature of human affairs can scarce admit of a remedy. But the mean rapacity, the monopolizing spirit of merchants and manufacturers, who neither are, nor ought to be, the rulers of mankind, though it cannot perhaps be corrected, may very easily be prevented from disturbing the tranquility of any body but themselves.[62]

The question of whether ''subservience of the economy to the state and its interests'' differentiates mercantilism from liberalism should also be

---

[58] Ibid., p. 28. Cf. the discussion of the role of nation-states in international trade theory in Viner, *Studies in International Trade*, pp. 594-601.

[59] *U.S. Power*, pp. 25, 29.

[60] Smith, *Wealth of Nations*, p. 653.

[61] Hirschman, *Passions and Interests*, p. 111. Italics added. See also pp. 104-113.

[62] Smith, *Wealth of Nations*, p. 460.

approached with caution. The mere fact that mercantilists believed that extensive state intervention in the economy was in the national interest while liberals did not does not mean that liberals were indifferent to state interests. Their primary difference with the mercantilists concerned *how*, not *whether*, to adapt the economic policy of the state so as to serve state interests. *Most liberals believed that laissez faire was in the best interests of the state.* As Viner points out in the following passage, the differences between liberals and mercantilists on the question of state intervention should not be exaggerated:

> Even between extreme mercantilists and extreme advocates of laissez faire the difference in avowed general principle might consist only in that the mercantilist would stress the duty of intervention unless, by exception, good reason existed for leaving things alone, while the laissez faire doctrinaire would insist that the government should leave things alone unless by exception special reasons existed why it should intervene.[63]

Actually, it is difficult to determine the precise position of liberalism with respect to the subservience of the economy to the interests of the state, of economics to politics. The liberal assumption of harmony between political and economic interests meant that they rarely faced the issue of which should give way in the event of conflict. For many nineteenth-century liberals, free trade was the best policy for achieving *both* economic welfare *and* national security. Gilpin's description of mercantilism as "the striving after security by economic means"[64] in no way distinguishes it from the views of liberals who believed that free trade was the best means to ensure national security.[65] Both mercantilists and liberals believed that the policies they advocated were conducive to the economic welfare and military security of the state.

On those few occasions when liberals perceived an actual or potential conflict between economic and political goals, they usually resolved the conflict by subordinating economics to politics. Thus, both Adam Smith, writing in 1776, and John Stuart Mill, writing in 1848, approved of the Navigation Acts, which restricted trade on national security grounds.[66] Edward Mead Earle states Smith's position clearly as follows:

> [The] critical question in determining his [i.e., Smith's] relationship to the mercantilist school is not whether its fiscal and trade theories were sound or unsound but whether, when necessary, the economic

---

[63] Viner, "Intellectual History of Laissez Faire," p. 56.

[64] Gilpin, "Economic Interdependence," p. 28.

[65] See Russell, *Theories*, p. 295; Silberner, *La Guerre*, p. 282; and Hirschman, *National Power*, p. 6.

[66] Silberner, *The Problem of War*, p. 63; Earle, "Adam Smith," pp. 121-122.

power of the nation should be cultivated and used as an instrument of statecraft. The answer of Adam Smith to this question would clearly be "Yes"—that economic power should be so used.[67]

Adam Smith's willingness to subordinate the economy to what he perceived as overriding political interests in no way distinguishes his views from those of many of the nineteenth-century advocates of free trade. However, since many of them were pacifists and he was not, his conception of what constituted overriding political interests was not necessarily theirs. The pacifist Richard Cobden, who has been described as "the towering figure among the free traders and internationalists of the first half of the nineteenth century,"[68] was also willing to subordinate economics to politics when conflict arose. "If free trade conflicted with peace, as in the case of loans for armaments to foreign governments, he opposed free trade. 'No free trade in cutting throats.' "[69] Indeed, for Cobden and other members of the so-called Manchester School, the international political order was of overriding importance. "All his economic ideas were subordinated to a theory of foreign relations which sprang from something close to pacifism. He worked for free trade because he wanted peace, not for peace because he wanted free trade."[70] For the liberals, writes Silberner, "political economy is the science *par excellence* of peace."[71] In sum, the free trade advocates of the nineteenth century believed that a peaceful international political order was in the interest of the state, and they believed that economic relations should be subservient to this interest. On these grounds they advocated free trade except when it came into conflict with their vision of the desirable political order. Adam Smith and most nineteenth-century free traders were as willing as the mercantilists to make economics subservient to politics; their differences concerned the specific policies that would truly benefit the political order.

Writing in 1948, Viner warned against uncritical acceptance of prevailing stereotypes:

> The foreign policy implications of the nineteenth century economics, I believe, need investigation as much as do the aims of mercantilism. Until such investigation is systematically made, comparisons with mercantilism are liable to be misleading with respect to the true position of both bodies of doctrine.[72]

[67] Earle, "Adam Smith," pp. 123-124.
[68] Russell, *Theories*, p. 296.
[69] F. H. Hinsley, *Power and the Pursuit of Peace* (London: Cambridge University Press, 1963), p. 97. See also Silberner, *The Problem of War*, p. 62.
[70] Hinsley, *Power*, p. 96. Cf. Schumpeter, *History of Economic Analysis*, p. 398.
[71] *The Problem of War*, p. 282.
[72] "Power vs. Plenty," p. 6n.

The preceding discussion is no substitute for the kind of rigorous analysis Viner was calling for, but it does suggest that his warning is as relevant today as it was then. The differences between mercantilism and liberalism were, as Gilpin maintains, fundamental, critical, and decisive. These differences, however, did not concern the goals of economic activity, the nature of the actors in international economic relations, or the subservience of the economy to the political order. Mercantilism and liberalism differed primarily with respect to the conceptions of social causation underlying their views and with respect to the means most appropriate to furthering the national interest. Their differences concerned *how*, not *whether*, to practice economic statecraft.

PROTECTIONISM

Liberalism was not the only theory of economic statecraft in the nineteenth century. In 1800 the German philosopher Johann Gottlieb Fichte published *The Closed Commercial State*, which argued for complete autarky in international economic relations.[73] Rejecting both mercantilism and the liberal doctrine of free trade, Fichte maintained that commercial rivalry caused war; therefore, complete economic independence was the path to peace.

The best known and most sophisticated statements of protectionism, however, were Alexander Hamilton's "Report on the Subject of Manufactures," presented to Congress in 1791, and Friedrich List's *The National System of Political Economy*, published in 1841. Since Hamilton's views will be considered later, along with those of other Americans, the discussion here will focus on List.[74]

Although List is often portrayed as a mercantilist,[75] his views are actually a blend of mercantilist and liberal ideas mixed with some peculiarly Germanic perspectives. List shares the mercantilist emphasis on the conflictual aspects of international economic and political relations and their preoccupation with preparation for war. Paradoxically, he also shares the liberal vision of a peaceful and harmonious world based on free trade. For List, protectionism is a temporary stage in the transition to ultimate free trade and peace. Thus, although he shares the mercantilist view of the conflictual nature of international relations, he denies that this is the inherent or

[73] For discussion of Fichte's views, see Russell, *Theories*, pp. 213-217; Silberner, *The Problem of War*, pp. 164-166; and Michael A. Heilperin, *Studies in Economic Nationalism* (Geneva: Librairie E. Droz, 1960), pp. 82-96.

[74] For discussion of List's views, see Silberner, *The Problem of War*, pp. 131-171; Earle, "Adam Smith," pp. 139-154; and Marcello de Cecco, *Money and Empire* (Oxford: Basil Blackwell, 1974), pp. 9-13.

[75] E.g., Gilpin, *U.S. Power*, pp. 25, 31; and Earle, "Adam Smith," p. 153.

necessary state of affairs. It is simply a particular stage in international history.

List criticizes the classical economists for overemphasizing economic welfare and underemphasizing politics and accuses them of neglecting the nation-state in their concern for global welfare. Although List's criticisms of the classical economists are often unfair and misleading, he is certainly correct in contending that Adam Smith's admission that defense is more important than opulence opens the door, at least in principle, to a whole host of protectionist policies under some conditions. Identification of those conditions, in fact, helps in understanding List's similarities and differences with the liberals. List's interest in protection for industry grows out of his estimate of the likelihood of war and his consequent concern with the military implications of differing levels of industrial development among nations. Since liberals were also concerned with national security, how can one explain the divergent views of List with respect to foreign economic policy? Whereas List estimates the probability of war as high, the liberals tend to estimate it as low; and whereas List emphasizes the security problems of countries like Germany, the classical economists' views reflect the security problems of Britain. The tendency of the classical economists to assume, at least implicitly, that the economic and military interests of Great Britain were much like those of other countries may have been naive, but it is at least as indicative of national parochialism as it is of cosmopolitanism. The differences between List and the liberals, like those between the mercantilists and the liberals, flow from the question of how, not whether, to practice economic statecraft. Earle summarizes this view succinctly:

> The thinking of Adam Smith, Alexander Hamilton, and Friedrich List was conditioned by the fact that they were, respectively, British, American, and German. But in certain fundamentals of statecraft their views were surprisingly alike. They all understood that military power is built upon economic foundations and each of them advocated a national system of economics which would best meet the needs of his own country.[76]

THE AMERICANS

The role of economic statecraft in American political thought has been interpreted variously, depending on whether early American foreign policy is viewed as "isolationist," as "idealist and internationalist," or as "realist and nationalist." The isolationist interpretation emphasizes the desire for withdrawal and noninvolvement in international politics and often implies

---

[76] Earle, "Adam Smith," p. 154.

repudiation of economic statecraft in early American theory and practice. Thus, two scholars writing during World War II, when isolationist interpretations of American diplomatic history were common, attribute to the Founding Fathers the belief that trade and politics could and should be kept separate:

> To both Washington and Jefferson it seemed quite possible to divorce trade from politics, to have close trading relationships and, therefore, interdependence with other nations, and yet to stay free of any political associations.[77]

> [The] belief is widespread that it is possible somehow to escape this intimate connection between international trade and "power politics" and to restore trade to its "normal and beneficial economic functions." How deep-rooted this conviction is, especially in Anglo-Saxon tradition, may be seen by the famous sentence of Washington's Farewell Address: "The great rule of conduct for us, in regard to foreign nations, is, in extending our commercial relations, to have with them as little political connection as possible."[78]

Others have argued, however, that "the isolationist interpretation is one-sided and incomplete," pointing out that many of the ideas embodied in American foreign policy derived from the European *philosophes*.[79] The *philosophes* were not isolationists, but rather wanted to replace the traditional "power politics" diplomacy of the time with free trade, which they viewed as a way to promote a peaceful international order. Thus, the repudiation of "power politics" concerned the secret diplomacy and military alliances that typified eighteenth-century foreign policy undertakings; it did not involve abandoning attempts to change the behavior of other states. On the contrary, the *philosophes* "saw in commerce a great instrument for bringing about a new age of peace" in which "the need for a political diplomacy with alliances and balance of power would disappear from the scene." American foreign policy, according to this line of argument, was "idealistic and internationalist no less than isolationist."[80]

A third interpretation suggests that the emphasis on commercial policy in early American foreign policy can also be viewed as "realist and nationalist," implying a desire to promote the national interest through economic means that was at least as important as idealist and internationalist goals. Noting that "economics may be, and very often is, a tool of pol-

---

[77] Graham, "Economics and Peace," p. 119.

[78] Hirschman, *National Power*, p. 78.

[79] Felix Gilbert, *To the Farewell Address: Ideas in Early American Foreign Policy* (Princeton: Princeton University Press, 1961), p. 72.

[80] Ibid., pp. 68-69, 72.

itics,'' one author suggests that American policy did not necessarily imply repudiation of ''balance-of-power'' politics but could be plausibly interpreted as realistic practicing of such policies based on an assessment of America's capabilities at the time.[81]

The ''idealist-internationalist'' view and the ''realist-nationalist'' view depict the *goals* of American policy in somewhat different terms, but both agree that economic instruments were being used to pursue such goals. Washington's ''Farewell Address'' is not the clearcut repudiation of economic statecraft that it seems to be. Both the ''idealist-internationalist'' and the ''realist-nationalist'' interpretations suggest that it can just as plausibly be read as an exhortation to practice a particular kind of economic statecraft.[82]

The importance of economic statecraft in thinking about early American foreign policy is illustrated in the ideas of Benjamin Franklin, Thomas Paine, Alexander Hamilton, and Thomas Jefferson. Franklin, one of America's earliest and greatest diplomats, was a mercantilist in his early years but later abandoned this view in favor of free trade.[83] This conversion, however, did not mean that Franklin lost interest in promoting national goals through economic means; he merely changed his mind as to the economic policies most appropriate to this end. He saw economic instruments as potentially useful in pursuing what he regarded as America's two most important foreign policy objectives—security and national expansion. Well aware that threats to American security were likely to originate in Europe, he suggested that America should consider offering its commerce in exchange for the friendship of European states, a proposal that struck ''the note which was to dominate the diplomacy of the new country in its first stage.''[84] Franklin's desire for continental expansion was potentially in conflict with his love of peace. However, Franklin had a rather low opinion of the utility of war as an instrument of statecraft, believing that wars for territory or commercial advantage were likely to be ''futile and a waste of manpower and money.''[85] Therefore, he advocated purchase as an alternative to military conquest in acquiring territory. He specifically proposed the purchase of Canada, ''and he envisaged the same procedure for the Spanish possessions in the South.''[86] Clearly, economic statecraft

[81] Gerald Stourzh, *Benjamin Franklin and American Foreign Policy*, 2d ed. (Chicago: University of Chicago Press, 1969), pp. 129-132.

[82] On interpretation of Washington's ''Farewell Address,'' see Burton Ira Kaufman, ed., *Washington's Farewell Address: The View from the 20th Century* (Chicago: Quadrangle Books, 1969).

[83] The discussion of Franklin's ideas here is based on the excellent book by Stourzh, *Benjamin Franklin and American Foreign Policy*.

[84] Ibid., p. 116.

[85] Ibid., p. 240.

[86] Ibid., p. 251.

played an important role in Franklin's thinking about American foreign policy.

Although Thomas Paine is sometimes depicted as "a founding father of the American tradition of isolationism,"[87] there is ample reason to regard him as an advocate of economic statecraft. His famous pamphlet, *Common Sense*, foreshadowed Washington's "Farewell Address" in its warning against political alliances with Europe and its emphasis on trade.

> Our plan is commerce, and that, well attended to, will secure us the peace and friendship of all Europe; because it is the interest of all Europe to have America a free port. Her trade will always be a protection. . . . As Europe is our market for trade, we ought to form no partial connection with any part of it. It is the true interest of America to steer clear of European contentions. . . .[88]

Rather than a call for America to opt out of international politics, this passage may be interpreted as a suggestion for using economic statecraft to play off European states against each other in international politics. The basic idea is that by providing European states with equal access to American ports, each will have an interest in preventing others from threatening American independence.

Paine's belief in the utility of economic statecraft is also reflected in his proposal for an international organization of neutral states based on economic sanctions. Noting that attempts to protect neutral rights through armed force are often "inconvenient, expensive, and ineffectual," Paine favors the "much easier and more powerful means" of economic and financial sanctions against offending belligerent powers. Were the neutral nations to do this, Paine argued, England "dare not molest them, and France would not."[89]

Not all of the Founding Fathers subscribed to the view that free trade enhances national security. Alexander Hamilton explicitly rejected the contention that "the spirit of commerce has a tendency to soften the manners of men and to extinguish those inflammable humors which have so often kindled wars" and suggested that commercial rivalry had caused

[87] Arnold Wolfers and Laurence W. Martin, eds., *The Anglo-American Tradition in Foreign Affairs* (New Haven: Yale University Press, 1956), p. 130.

[88] Quoted in Stourzh, *Benjamin Franklin*, p. 117. See also Gilbert, *To the Farewell Address*, pp. 42-43.

[89] Paine, "The Eighteenth Fructidor," in Wolfers and Martin, eds., *Anglo-American Tradition*, pp. 136-138. Given Paine's favorable view of the utility of economic statecraft, it is not surprising to find him advising Thomas Jefferson to try to acquire Louisiana by purchase (Joseph Dorfman, *The Economic Mind in American Civilization*, vol. 1 [New York: Viking Press, 1946], pp. 457).

as many wars as disputes over "territory or dominion."[90] For Hamilton, military force was the primary guarantor of national security, but this did not cause him to ignore economic statecraft. On the contrary, he was a strong advocate of such measures, for whom "commerce was a weapon in the struggle of power politics."[91]

Although it is frequently asserted that "the tariff was a domestic issue only" in the early years of the Republic,[92] this view is difficult to reconcile with Hamilton's famous "Report on Manufactures" delivered to Congress in 1791. That document, which has been described as "the strongest presentation of the case for protection which has been made by any American statesman,"[93] set the tariff question squarely in a foreign policy context. Thus, the preamble focuses attention on the means of promoting such manufactures "as will tend to render the United States independent on foreign nations for military and other essential supplies."[94] And later in the report, Hamilton observes:

> Not only the wealth, but the independence and security of a country appear to be materially connected with the prosperity of manufactures. Every nation, with a view to those great objects, ought to endeavor to possess within itself all the essentials of national supply. . . . The extreme embarrassments of the United States during the late war, from an incapacity of supplying themselves, are still matter of keen recollection. A future war might be expected again to exemplify the mischiefs and dangers of a situation to which that incapacity is still in too great a degree applicable, unless changed by timely and vigorous exertions.[95]

For Hamilton the question of industrial protection was inextricably linked with the foreign policy questions of national independence and national security. This point of view is reflected in Edward Mead Earle's evaluation of Hamilton:

> As one who combines economics with politics and statecraft, . . . Hamilton ranks with the great statesmen of modern times. He is, in fact, an American Colbert or Pitt or Bismarck. The power and effect

---

[90] *The Federalist*, no. 6. On Hamilton's foreign policy views, see also Earle, "Adam Smith," pp. 128-138; Wolfers and Martin, eds., *Anglo-American Tradition*, pp. 139-154; and Gilbert, *To the Farewell Address*, pp. 111-136.

[91] Gilbert, *To the Farewell Address*, p. 131.

[92] Charles P. Kindleberger, "U.S. Foreign Economic Policy, 1776-1976," *Foreign Affairs* LV (January 1977):396.

[93] F. W. Taussig, *State Papers and Speeches on the Tariff* (Cambridge: Harvard University Press, 1893), p. iv.

[94] Ibid., p. 1.

[95] Ibid., pp. 55-56. Cf. Carr, *The Twenty Years' Crisis*, pp. 121-122.

of his ideas was indelibly impressed upon succeeding generations of Americans, so that in the realm of government and industry his influence is more marked than that of any of his contemporaries except Jefferson.[96]

The two arch-rivals, Hamilton and Jefferson, were usually on opposite sides of the political fence. Thus, in 1789 Jefferson advocated tariff discrimination against Britain in an attempt to achieve more favorable treatment for American traders, a move opposed by Hamilton.[97] This dispute, however, concerned the particular case at hand and did not indicate fundamental disagreement with respect to the general principle that economic statecraft could be a valuable foreign policy tool. Jefferson, in his own way, was just as enthusiastic about economic statecraft as Hamilton.[98] He believed that economic sanctions could be used to bring peaceful pressure on other states and used an embargo to protect American seamen and avoid war with Britain when he was president. His most successful use of economic statecraft, the Louisiana Purchase in 1803, was supported by Hamilton. Although he had been opposed to the protectionist views expressed in Hamilton's "Report on Manufactures," Jefferson later adopted a position very much like that of his departed political enemy. In 1815 he wrote to the French economist Jean Batiste Say that during wartime "the interception of exchanges . . . becomes a powerful weapon in the hands of the enemy" and extolled protectionism as a means by which the country may be secured "against a relapse into foreign dependency."[99] Whatever differences Hamilton and Jefferson may have had, they did not include the question of whether economic instruments could or should be used to pursue foreign policy goals. On this point the views of Franklin, Paine, Hamilton, and Jefferson all converge.

A century later the views of Woodrow Wilson likewise reflected the belief that economic means were appropriate for pursuing foreign policy goals.[100] Wilson's attitude toward economic statecraft is easy to misconstrue because his foreign policy "was characterized by a vigorous denunciation of Dollar Diplomacy."[101] Wilson's repudiation of Dollar Diplomacy, however, was concerned more with the ends than the means of this policy. The following passage summarizes his objections to the goals of Dollar Diplomacy:

[96] Earle, "Adam Smith," p. 138.
[97] Jerald A. Combs, "Embargoes," in *Encyclopedia of American Foreign Policy*, ed. Alexander de Conde, vol. 1 (New York: Charles Scribner's, 1978), pp. 310-314.
[98] See Wolfers and Martin, *Anglo-American Tradition*, pp. 163-164.
[99] Earle, "Adam Smith," p. 137.
[100] The discussion here is based on William Diamond, *The Economic Thought of Woodrow Wilson* (Baltimore: Johns Hopkins University Press, 1943), pp. 131-192.
[101] Ibid., pp. 141-142.

If American enterprise in foreign countries, particularly in those foreign countries which are not strong enough to resist us, takes the shape of imposing upon and exploiting the mass of the people of that country it ought to be checked and not encouraged. I am willing to get anything for an American that money and enterprise can obtain except the suppression of the rights of other men. I will not help any man buy a power which he ought not to exercise over his fellow-beings.[102]

Wilson viewed Dollar Diplomacy as a misuse of economic instruments of foreign policy, but he did not want to eliminate such instruments from the repertoire of American foreign policy makers. On the contrary, he saw economic statecraft as a useful means for promoting what he believed to be the appropriate foreign policy goals of the country. Strongly influenced by the nineteenth-century view that free trade promotes peace, Wilson did not see exploitation or infringement of human rights as necessary—or even normal—consequences of economic statecraft. Wilson believed that America had a "peculiar mission to spread the ideals and institutions of democracy among the less advanced peoples of the world,"[103] and he saw trade as a mechanism for accomplishing this mission. Thus, the promotion of American trade was not only a way to enhance America's economic welfare but also a means of pursuing the political and ideological goals of peace and democracy throughout the world.

As president, Wilson envisioned a postwar world free of economic warfare except for the economic sanctions duly authorized by the League of Nations. Thus, the third of his fourteen points concerned "the removal, so far as possible, of all economic barriers and the establishment of an equality of trade conditions."[104] He was, however, quite willing to contemplate economic pressure as a means of winning the war and in order to force other countries to accept his plans for organizing the postwar world.[105] No less than Franklin, Paine, Hamilton, and Jefferson, Wilson favored the pursuit of foreign policy goals by economic means.

Neither the theory nor the practice of economic statecraft is peculiar to the twentieth century. During the last twenty-five centuries, isolationists, internationalists, nationalists, warmongers, pacifists, and ideological crusaders have advocated economic statecraft in pursuit of their goals. Insulating the domestic society from the pernicious effects of foreign influences, enhancing national security through military preparedness, enhancing national security through reducing the need for military pre-

---

[102] Quoted in ibid., p. 142.
[103] Ibid., p. 136.
[104] Ibid., p. 165.
[105] Ibid., pp. 138, 166.

paredness, promoting national economic welfare, punishing aggressors, and spreading democracy throughout the world have all been proposed as appropriate goals of economic statecraft. "The ideas of economists and political philosophers, both when they are right and when they are wrong," observed John Maynard Keynes, "are more powerful than is commonly understood. Indeed the world is ruled by little else."[106] Retaining the spirit of Keynes but changing the wording, one might add that today's practical statesmen, advocating some form of economic statecraft and believing themselves to be quite exempt from any intellectual influences, are usually the slaves of some defunct political economist.[107]

[106] *The General Theory of Employment, Interest, and Money* (New York: Harcourt, Brace, 1936), p. 383.
[107] Cf. ibid.

CHAPTER 6

BARGAINING WITH ECONOMIC STATECRAFT

The political interactions of various persons and groups are constituted by patterns of influence and power, *manifested in and affected by* symbols, *and stabilized in characteristic political* practices.[1]

International bargaining processes subsume more than mere diplomatic negotiations. Bargaining situations, according to Thomas C. Schelling, are those "in which the ability of one participant to gain his ends is dependent to an important degree on the choices or decisions that the other participant will make."[2] He notes:

> Analytically, . . . the essence of bargaining is the communication of intent, the perception of intent, the manipulation of expectations about what one will accept or refuse, the issuance of threats, offers, and assurances, the display of resolve and evidence of capabilities, the communication of constraints on what one can do, the search for compromise and jointly desirable exchanges, the creation of sanctions to enforce understandings and agreements, genuine efforts to persuade and inform, and the creation of hostility, friendliness, mutual respect, or rules of etiquette.[3]

Trade embargoes, most-favored-nation treatment, aid programs, aid suspensions, tariffs, and investment guaranties can all be used to bargain in this sense. This chapter focuses on economic statecraft as a form of bargaining behavior.

IMAGES AND SYMBOLS

Much of what Schelling describes as the "essence of bargaining" is involved in the symbolic uses of economic statecraft. Employing economic techniques this way is often derided as a sign of national immaturity, an excessive concern with image rather than matters of substance, a self-indulgent expression of righteous indignation, a futile gesture, a national

[1] Lasswell and Kaplan, *Power and Society*, p. 53.
[2] Schelling, *The Strategy of Conflict*, p. 5.
[3] *Arms and Influence*, p. 136n.

temper tantrum, or a venting of feelings of frustration based on recognition that nothing can be done.

The distinction between expressive and instrumental behavior is frequently introduced in order to explain the use of economic statecraft—especially negative economic sanctions—for symbolic purposes. Whereas instrumental behavior is depicted as intended to influence other actors, expressive behavior has no objective other than the release of internal tensions.[4] Thus, although instrumental behavior is a means to an end, expressive behavior is an end in itself. When applied to economic statecraft the usual implication is that such measures were undertaken in order to pacify domestic public opinion rather than because policy makers viewed them as instruments of statecraft.

The instruments of economic statecraft—like those of military statecraft—may indeed be used in expressive behavior in Johan Galtung's sense, but this does not mean that the symbolic use of such techniques is never instrumental. The tendency to classify economic sanctions as expressive behavior is closely linked with the tendency to underestimate the utility of such techniques of statecraft. Thus, when analysts are unable to detect the instrumental effects of economic techniques of statecraft, they are likely to conclude that such measures are serving purely expressive purposes. However, if the failure to detect instrumental effects is caused by faulty analytical frameworks—as this book contends—the incidence of expressive acts is likely to be exaggerated. Statesmen usually behave as if others were watching, i.e., they usually consider the effects their behavior may have on such onlookers.[5] Before designating (what appear to be) foreign policy actions as expressive behavior, analysts should make a vigorous effort to identify plausible hypotheses that would explain such actions in instrumental terms.

Galtung rightly notes the existence of situations in which "military action is impossible for one reason or another," in which "doing nothing is seen as tantamount to complicity," and in which something must be done "that at least serves as a clear signal to everyone that what the receiving nation [of the economic sanctions] has done is disapproved of."[6] But it does not follow that the use of economic sanctions in such situations is expressive rather than instrumental. Such sanctions may be intended to serve as a

---

[4] The most frequently cited source in discussions of economic statecraft is Johan Galtung, "On the Effects of International Economic Sanctions." For an understanding of Galtung's view of the distinction, it is useful to consult his "Pacifism from a Sociological Point of View," *Journal of Conflict Resolution* III (1959):69-72; and Talcott Parsons and Robert F. Bales, *Family, Socialization and Interaction Processes* (Glencoe, Ill.: Free Press, 1955), pp. 45-47. Cf. Simon, *Administrative Behavior*, pp. 48-50, 61-78.

[5] Even small children rarely throw temper tantrums when they are alone.

[6] Galtung, "Economic Sanctions," pp. 411-412.

warning to the offending state or to other states that similar actions in the future will be punished. When a state—especially a powerful state—goes out of its way to clarify its values and intentions for others, such actions are neither frivolous nor pointless.

Peter Wallensteen uses Galtung's distinction between expressive and instrumental behavior to analyze ten cases involving negative trade sanctions.[7] Wallensteen's attempt to operationalize the concepts of instrumental and expressive behavior illustrates the tendency to ignore symbolic instrumental uses of economic statecraft. If the state imposing sanctions was vague about the conditions under which sanctions would be lifted, he classifies the action as expressive. Others have argued, however, that influence attempts based on vague demands may be more useful than those based on specific demands.[8] For example, it is usually easier for the target to comply with a vague demand. If the imposing state combined sanctions with a threat to undertake further negative actions, such as breaking diplomatic relations, Wallensteen classifies the behavior as expressive. Others, however, might view economic sanctions as a useful way to strengthen the credibility of such threats in much the same way that Schelling suggests that rocking the boat a little adds credibility to the threat to rock it still harder if compromise is not forthcoming.[9] And if the imposition of sanctions is accompanied by condemnation of the target state, Wallensteen classifies the action as expressive once again. Since negative sanctions are almost always used to demonstrate disapproval, it is small wonder that such methods lead to the "finding" that eight of the ten cases were expressive rather than instrumental. Since Wallensteen's criteria for classifying instrumental and expressive behavior continually ignore plausible instrumental interpretations of the actions of the sanction-imposing state, his conclusions that most uses of economic sanctions are expressive and that such measures are not very successful means of influence are not surprising. With such an analytical framework, it would be difficult to imagine different conclusions.

The occasional "expressive" use of economic statecraft should not be permitted to divert attention from the many uses of such techniques that are *both* symbolic and instrumental. The symbolic aspects of politics are not merely decorative. In *Power and Society* Harold D. Lasswell and Abraham Kaplan devote considerable attention to "the role of symbols in the political process," noting that "nonlinguistic symbols" are especially

---

[7] "Characteristics of Economic Sanctions," pp. 252-253.

[8] Schelling, *Arms and Influence*, pp. 84-85; Robert Jervis, *The Logic of Images in International Relations* (Princeton: Princeton University Press, 1970), pp. 123-130; and David A. Baldwin, "Thinking About Threats," *Journal of Conflict Resolution* XV (March 1971):75-76.

[9] *Strategy of Conflict*, pp. 195-199.

likely to play a role in politics. Political symbols, according to them, "function directly in the power process, serving to set up, alter, or maintain power practices."[10]

In the foreign policy arena symbols are also important. James N. Rosenau argues that foreign policy "involves a degree of manipulation of symbols that is unmatched in any other political situation."[11] If Rosenau is right the tendency to disparage the symbolic aspects of economic statecraft is difficult to understand. For governments to be concerned about preserving a desired image or "saving face" is not necessarily a sign of excessive pride. Their reputations as political actors may be at stake. Did the removal of Soviet missiles from Cuba while leaving behind 15,000 troops constitute a "defeat" for the Soviets or a "defeat" for the United States?[12] Did the Tet offensive constitute a "defeat" or a "victory" for the North Vietnamese? The answers to such questions depend to a large extent on how such events are perceived. Is it worthwhile to fight in order to "save face"? Insofar as a country's reputation for action is at stake, Schelling contends, "this kind of face is one of the few things worth fighting over."[13]

Symbolic acts are undertaken not only for expressive purposes but for instrumental ones as well. Concern about an actor's image does not indicate indifference to power. "A desired image," according to Robert Jervis, "can often be of greater use than a significant increment of military or economic power. An undesired image can involve costs for which almost no amount of the usual kinds of power can compensate and can be a handicap almost impossible to overcome."[14] Although Jervis is not particularly concerned with economic statecraft, much of his analysis is relevant to understanding the symbolic uses of such techniques:

> Throughout history, and especially for the great powers since 1945, states have often cared about specific issues less for their intrinsic value than for the conclusions they felt others would draw from the way they dealt with them. This is often not understood. A state may be conciliatory and make sacrifices on a small issue or may not take advantage of the temporary weakness of another state. Observers who pride themselves on their hard-headed realism may claim that such actions are a foolish attempt to gain ephemeral good will at the price of concrete and valuable interests. In other circumstances a state may be willing to pay a high price or take risks to win a minor symbolic

---

[10] Pp. xviii, 10-11, 103-141. See also Harold D. Lasswell, *World Politics and Personal Insecurity* (New York: McGraw-Hill, 1935).

[11] "Comparative Foreign Policy: Fad, Fantasy, or Field?" *International Studies Quarterly* XII (September 1968):328.

[12] Schelling, *Arms and Influence*, pp. 93-94.

[13] Ibid., p. 124.

[14] *Logic of Images*, p.6.

victory. Critics may charge that such a policy is a wasteful and unrealistic pursuit of prestige. Or a state may refuse to retreat on a trivial
matter. In such instances the actors themselves may speak of "national
honor" and commentators often observe an unfortunate concern with
"saving face."

But good will, prestige, and saving face are often not ephemeral
goals pursued by politicians courting domestic support or foolish
statesmen unappreciative of the vital role of power. Rather these are
aspects of a state's image that can greatly contribute to its pursuit of
other goals. . . .

This of course is not to deny that efforts to gain good will, prestige,
or to save face may fail, be unnecessary, or involve inordinate risks.
But they cannot be dismissed merely as efforts that sacrifice valuable
resources to win domestic votes or the short-term approval of foreign
opinion. For if they succeed they can bring rewards all out of proportion to their costs by influencing the psychological environments
and policies of other decision-makers.[15]

Jervis' argument should be kept in mind when evaluating treatments of
economic sanctions that depict them merely as ways to register disapproval
without noting the possible instrumental value of such registrations, that
portray them as little more than efforts to appease domestic opinion, or
that label arguments emphasizing the symbolic functions of economic
sanctions as "the last-ditch defense" of the advocates of such measures.[16]

Discussions of the utility of military instruments of statecraft often point
out that the utility of such techniques depends not only—perhaps not even
primarily—on their actual use in warfare but also on the standing threat
to use them implied by awareness of their existence. Thus, the implicit
threat of war is said to underlie international politics or to pervade the
psychological atmosphere within which statecraft is conducted.[17] Without
denying the pervasiveness of statesmen's concern for military security, it
should be recognized that the desire to preserve and improve national
economic welfare also permeates the international psychological atmosphere. The assertion that the possibility of war is always in the back of a
statesman's mind does not justify the conclusion that military power is the
essence of statecraft. There may be other things at the back of a statesman's
mind, such as awareness of the ability of sovereign states to extend or
withdraw economic cooperation.[18] Once the Pandora's box of vague, amor-

---

[15] Ibid., pp. 7-8.

[16] Cf. Bienen and Gilpin, "Evaluation," p. IX,3.

[17] Schelling, *Arms and Influence*, pp. 33-34; and Osgood and Tucker, *Force, Order, and Justice*, pp. 27-28.

[18] On this point see Hirschman, *National Power*, pp. 15-17, 77-78.

phous, implicit threats is opened, it cannot be confined to the military sphere but must be extended to include nonmilitary threats and promises as well.

INDICATORS OF CAPABILITY

Images matter. Statesmen care about how policy makers in other countries perceive their capabilities and intentions. Economic instruments can be—and have been—used to affect such images. In the seventeenth and eighteenth centuries, for example, the accumulation of precious metals, especially gold, was perceived as an important indicator of national power. In the twentieth century, with more systematic and widespread collection of economic statistics, Gross National Product has become an important symbol of national power. The symbolic importance of manipulating GNP growth rates and per capita GNP growth rates has not gone unnoticed by foreign policy makers. Since World War II American policy makers have pointed to the need to stimulate domestic economic growth in order to demonstrate to other countries the superiority of the American economic system and thereby to increase the probability that this model will be emulated.[19] In emerging countries, "where nationalism is strongest," Edward Banfield has argued that economic development "is valued less for itself (it may even be thought intrinsically undesirable) than as a means of symbolizing, or of asserting, the power and glory of the nation."[20] And in the Soviet Union the interest in promoting emulation by demonstrating superior economic performance is presumably of some concern.

Currency exchange rates have also been endowed with symbolic importance that goes beyond their use to facilitate international economic exchange. Charles P. Kindleberger has pointed out that "a country's exchange rate is more than a number. It is an emblem of its importance in the world, a sort of international status symbol."[21] And in discussing the "abuse of convertibility" as a technique of economic warfare, P.J.D. Wiles refers to the period 1873–1914 as one in which "by a curious mixture of

[19] See Sprout and Sprout, *Foundations of International Politics*, pp. 426-449 passim; U.S. Senate, Committee on Foreign Relations, *United States Foreign Policy*, "Worldwide and Domestic Economic Problems and their Impact on the Foreign Policy of the United States," a study prepared by the Corporation for Economic and Industrial Research, Committee Print, 86th Cong., 1st sess., 1959, pp. 2, 5, 35, 39, 49; and numerous comparisons of U.S. and Soviet economic performance published by the Joint Economic Committee of the U.S. Congress since the mid-1950s. See also W. W. Rostow, *The Stages of Economic Growth: A Non-Communist Manifesto* (Cambridge: Cambridge University Press, 1960).

[20] Edward C. Banfield, *American Foreign Aid Doctrines* (Washington, D.C.: American Enterprise Institute, 1963), p. 20.

[21] *Power and Money*, p. 204. On the psychological implications of currency depreciation see also Wu, *Economic Warfare*, pp. 124-125.

Social Darwinism with sound money, a nation was judged not only by the strength of its currency but also by the rate at which its government could borrow abroad. This was held to be an index not merely of its diplomatic strength but of its citizens' prosperity.''[22] Contemporary concern about the debt-servicing capacity of many countries suggests the longevity of the pre-World War I attitudes described by Wiles.

INDICATORS OF INTENTION

The use of economic statecraft to indicate capabilities is important but not so subtle or complex as the use of such techniques to communicate the intentions of a state. Economic instruments may be used to signal narrowly specific intentions or to project general foreign policy orientations. Both are ways to affect the predictions of others about a state's behavior. Thus, providing another country with economic aid is regarded as an indication of a positive or supportive orientation toward the recipient even though it may not imply approval of specific policies or actions. Refusal to engage in economic intercourse with another country, however, projects an image of disapproval and hostility.[23] The projection of a vague overall policy orientation may, of course, be ambiguous as to specific intentions; but this may be precisely what is intended.

Sometimes it is useful to clarify a commitment; at other times it is desirable to blur it. Economic statecraft is potentially useful for either purpose. Thus, "you have our support" is regarded as less ambiguous and more specific if it is accompanied by foreign aid. Similarly, "we disapprove" is clearer if combined with aid suspension.[24]

The use of economic statecraft to clarify commitments is widely recognized as a common occurrence, but the use of such techniques to create ambiguity is less often acknowledged. Thus, there are times when a policy maker wants to make a commitment, but not too much of a commitment. Such commitments might be described as "soft," "deniable," "ambig-

---

[22] *Communist International Economics*, p. 461.

[23] Some writers refer to such broad foreign policy orientations in terms of "affect." See Margaret G. Hermann, Charles F. Hermann, and Gerald L. Hutchins, "Affect," in *Describing Foreign Policy Behavior*, ed. Callahan, Brady, and Hermann, pp. 207-222. On the use of international commercial relationships to influence national images, see also Richard L. Merritt, "Transmission of Values Across National Boundaries," in *Communication in International Politics*, ed. Richard L. Merritt (Urbana: University of Illinois Press, 1972), pp. 3-32; and Robert E. Klitgaard, "Sending Signals," *Foreign Policy*, no. 32 (Fall 1978), pp. 103-106.

[24] For a study of "specificity" in foreign policy, see Dean Swanson, "Specificity," in *Describing Foreign Policy Behavior*, ed. Callahan, Brady, and Hermann, pp. 223-241.

uous," or "qualified."[25] There is a difference between "you have our support up to a point" and "you have our unqualified support for anything you might attempt." Techniques of statecraft vary in the degree to which they allow states to make ambiguous and limited commitments. Thus, one might rank various ways for the United States to express support for the government of El Salvador in terms of the degree of ambiguity implied:

1. Verbal support (most ambiguous and limited)
2. Economic aid
3. Military aid
4. U.S. military advisors
5. U.S. combat troops
6. Military alliance
7. All of the above (least ambiguous and limited)

Although this ranking is disputable, it illustrates the essential point that how one expresses a commitment matters. Most people would agree, however, that economic aid represents a less ambiguous commitment than a verbal pat on the back and that committing combat troops to foreign soil is less ambiguous than providing economic aid.

The United States has used economic statecraft to project a number of dimensions of its foreign policy orientation. The following list is illustrative:

1. *Opposition to communism.*
    The embargo against Cuba, the Truman Doctrine, and the embargo on trade with communist countries provide obvious examples.
2. *Commitment to a nondiscriminatory international trading system.*
    The British Loan (1946), the promotion of tariff reductions via the General Agreement on Tariffs and Trade (GATT), and resistance to Third World demands for tariff preferences (1948–1965) are examples.
3. *Commitment to human rights.*
    Support for United Nations sanctions against Rhodesia, making aid conditional on progress in human rights, and conditioning most-favored-nation treatment for the Soviet Union on the treatment of Jewish emigrants provide examples.
4. *Commitment to popularly based governments.*
    The Alliance for Progress is perhaps the best example.
5. *Interest in and sympathy with the plight of the Third World.*
    Development aid is the best example.

[25] See the discussion of "Signals and Ambiguity" in Jervis, *Logic of Images*, pp. 113-138.

6. *Willingness to use force.*

    The sanctions against Japan in 1940, the sanctions against Iran during the hostage crisis, the Carter grain embargo, the "destroyers for bases" deal, and Lend Lease aid all had overtones indicating that these were first steps intended to demonstrate American resolve.

7. *Support for international law and organization.*

    Participation in the United Nations sanctions against Rhodesia and the payment of dues to international organizations furnish examples. (Of course, the United States has also witheld dues to indicate lack of support for international organizations.)

8. *Commitment to friends and allies.*

    The Marshall Plan and the encouragement of trade discrimination against the United States via European integration are salient cases.

9. *Commitment to private enterprise system.*

    Promotion of private foreign investment by guaranties against risks and attempts to ensure that foreign aid programs did not compete with private investment are examples.

10. *Demonstration of commitment to moderation and restraint.*

    The sanctions against Iran during the hostage crisis and those against Cuba could be interpreted this way.

Is the use of economic instruments of statecraft a sign of weak and pusillanimous statesmanship or an indication of firm commitment? No general rule can answer this question since the situational context is likely to be crucial in determining the symbolic importance of any given instance. Threatening to suspend aid to a country that is bombing your capital city is unlikely to communicate strong resolve, but the same response to mispronouncing the name of your country in a United Nations speech is likely to seem like impetuous overreaction.

Judging the degree of commitment demonstrated by the use of economic statecraft is further complicated by the multiple goals—or mixed motives—that are usually involved. Economic sanctions lie somewhere in between war and appeasement in terms of a continuum of "toughness." Thus, they often get denounced by both sides. Those favoring a "soft line" are likely to criticize them as too coercive and confrontational, while "hard-liners" are likely to see them as demonstrating a lack of commitment. This is understandable since economic sanctions are often intended to combine elements of appeasement and hostility, to demonstrate simultaneously both commitment and restraint. For this reason they are easily misunderstood. They are stronger than diplomatic protests but weaker than military attack. They are likely to appeal to reasonable but firm policy makers but not to cowards or jingoists. They are neither heroic nor saintly measures. They are often designed to deter and reassure simultaneously. Techniques that enable policy makers to demonstrate firmness while reassuring others of their sense of proportion and restraint can be highly useful, especially to nuclear powers.

In order to understand the symbolic uses of economic sanctions—or other economic techniques of statecraft—the existence of mixed motives must be recognized. Thus Fredrik Hoffmann rightly concludes that economic sanctions are unlikely to appeal to policy makers who are "extremely motivated for destroying" their opponents and that such measures are likely to appeal to those who feel "a need for doing 'something' but not 'too much.' "[26] It is misleading, however, for Hoffmann to portray the latter situation as one in which motivation is "low."[27] Intensity of commitment to destruction should not be the sole criterion for measuring motivation. It would be more appropriate to label the motivation of those who use sanctions as "complex" rather than "low." Indeed, the two situations described by Hoffmann should make economic sanctions highly appealing to rational statesmen. Single-minded determination to destroy one's opponents is hardly a characteristic of responsible statesmanship; the *only* sensible position for a rational decision maker is one of "doing something" but not "too much"! A rational statesman is likely to be highly committed *both* to "doing something," i.e., achieving benefits, *and* to not doing "too much," i.e., incurring excessive costs. To describe such policy makers as lacking in motivation is both unfair and misleading.

One study lists among "principal failures" of the League of Nations sanctions against Italy "the limited nature of the measures, involving a total refusal to consider any measures that, by promising to succeed, might have offended Italy seriously enough to provoke retaliation in the form of war."[28] Here again the motives of those imposing the sanctions seem to have been a mixture of desires to apply pressure on Italy on the one hand, while avoiding the evocation of a militant response on the other. Given such mixed motives the League sanctions were remarkably successful in doing what they were supposed to do.

Henry Bienen and Robert Gilpin correctly note that the use of economic sanctions "has a detrimental impact on foreign perceptions of the United States."[29] They aptly compare damage to America's image as a reliable trading partner as a result of using economic sanctions with damage to America's image as a reliable military ally that would result from aban-

[26] "The Functions of Economic Sanctions: A Comparative Analysis," *Journal of Peace Research*, no. 2 (1967), p. 154.

[27] Ibid., p. 155.

[28] Taubenfeld and Taubenfeld, "The 'Economic Weapon,' " p. 186.

[29] "Evaluation," p. VII,4.

doning Taiwan.[30] But such observations do not constitute an overall assessment of the impact of a policy of economic sanctions on America's image. America's reputation as a reliable trading partner is only one element in the U.S. image, albeit an important one. Participation in United Nations sanctions against Rhodesia strengthened America's image as an opponent of racism, a friend of the Third World, and a supporter of international organization even though it may have shaken confidence in her as a reliable trading partner. Likewise, the abandonment of Taiwan as a military ally might improve America's image by demonstrating a lack of rigidity, a willingness to admit mistakes, and a prudent recognition of the need to come to terms with China even though it might weaken perceptions of America's commitments to allies. Whether such cases add up to a net loss or a net gain for the American image may be reasonably disputed, but the need to add up the impacts on various dimensions of the American image is beyond dispute. Promoting the American image abroad is a mixed motive game in which failure on one dimension may be offset by success on another. Any attempt to assess the overall net impact of using economic sanctions on the U.S. image abroad must take account of the multidimensional nature of that image.

The mixture of motives underlying most uses of economic sanctions is captured by Wiles' portrayal of Soviet and American use of such sanctions as reactions "with dignified restraint to a moral leper." Both the moral disapproval on the one hand and the moderation on the other should be noted. Economic sanctions, Wiles contends, "are the style most suited to an ideological age, in which nationalism may no longer appear naked, and military war has become a little dangerous."[31]

ECONOMIC STATECRAFT AND THE ART OF COMMITMENT

The projection of credible images is difficult for sovereign states. In the absence of an overarching authority capable of enforcing agreements, it is often difficult for statesmen to convince others that they mean what they say. The work of Thomas Schelling suggests that making credible commitments is an art, one that can be practiced skillfully or clumsily.[32] Although Schelling concentrates most of his attention on military affairs, many of his insights are applicable to economic statecraft. Three dimensions of the art of commitment will be considered: (1) the process of binding oneself; (2) the interdependence of commitments, and (3) the circumventing of an adversary's commitments.

[30] Ibid., p. VII,7.
[31] Wiles, *Communist International Economics*, p. 496.
[32] *Arms and Influence* and *Strategy of Conflict*.

Are American policy makers really committed to opposing the spread of communism? Are they really in favor of majority rule in Africa? Do they really care how other states treat their own citizens? Do they really care about poverty in the Third World? Are they really upset by Soviet actions in Afghanistan? In augmenting the credibility of such commitments, costs play a paradoxical role that is seldom recognized or appreciated. Although costs, defined as value forgone, are usually regarded as necessary evils to be minimized insofar as possible, there are circumstances in which costliness is a *desirable* attribute in a policy alternative. This is especially true when one is trying to send a credible signal. The assertion by Bienen and Gilpin that "there is very little evidence to suggest that economic sanctions are any more effective than other means of registering disapproval of a repugnant government"[33] ignores this point. Actually the evidence suggesting that economic sanctions are likely to be more effective than other means of registering disapproval is so abundant that it is deeply embedded in such everyday sayings as "Talk is cheap," "Do you want to bet on that?" "Put your money where your mouth is!" and "If he gave me such an expensive gift, he must really love me." Each of these phrases implies that incurring costs adds to the credibility of mere words. Costs are widely regarded as a standard indicator of the intensity of one's resolve. In statecraft, observes Schelling, "words are cheap, not inherently credible when they emanate from an adversary. . . . Actions also prove something; significant actions usually incur some cost or risk, and [thus] carry some evidence of their own credibility."[34]

In comparison with other techniques, economic statecraft is likely to be especially useful in registering approval or disapproval. Economic techniques usually cost more than propaganda or diplomacy and thus tend to have more inherent credibility. Military techniques, of course, usually entail higher costs and therefore even more credibility; but their costs may be too high. Economic techniques are likely to represent an appealing

---

[33] "Evaluation," p. IX,3.

[34] *Arms and Influence*, p. 150. Schelling quotes President Lyndon Johnson with respect to the Vietnam War: "I wish it were possible to convince others with words of what we now find it necessary to say with guns and planes." And President John F. Kennedy with respect to Khrushchev: "That son of a bitch won't pay any attention to words; he has to see you move" (p. 150). On the value of costs in augmenting the credibility of signals, see also Jervis, *Logic of Images*. According to Thucydides, Pericles understood this principle quite well. With respect to the the image Athens should project to its enemies, he says: "And if I could persuade you to do it, I would urge you to go out and lay waste your property with your own hands and show the Peloponnesians that it is not for the sake of this that you are likely to give in to them" (*History of the Peloponnesian War*, trans. Rex Warner [New York: Penguin, 1972], p. 122). There is no more striking reference to the use of self-inflicted costs to strengthen perceptions of a state's resolve anywhere in the literature of international relations.

combination of costs that are high enough to be effective yet low enough to be bearable. Contrary to much that has been written, the costs of economic statecraft are not an unmitigated drawback but rather are often a blessing in disguise.[35]

Publicity, it is often argued, is likely to hinder the effectiveness of negative economic sanctions.[36] And so it may insofar as it challenges the target state in a way that makes compliance awkward. Compliance with specific demands relating to the immediate issue at hand, however, may not be the most important foreign policy consideration. The question of whether the government of El Salvador or Cuba calls itself ''Marxist'' may matter less because of immediate specific implications for United States interests than for the symbolic challenge to American hemispheric dominance. In such a situation the imposition of economic sanctions may be primarily aimed at reinforcing the image of American resolve to resist communism and only secondarily at compliance with specific demands. In such situations publicity may augment the credibility of the signal being sent. Bienen and Gilpin are right to point out that trade boycotts are highly publicized actions that thereby engage ''the prestige of both the sanctioning and sanctioned state''; but they are wrong in depicting this as evidence of the ''highly pernicious nature'' of such techniques of statecraft.[37] It is precisely because they engage ''the prestige and credibility of the participants'' that such instruments are potentially useful for projecting images. If they could not be coupled with the prestige of the user, they would be worthless for symbolic purposes. The fact that highly publicized trade boycotts engage the prestige of the states involved should be noted as a characteristic of such techniques of statecraft that is advantageous in some situations and disadvantageous in others. To imply that it is necessarily pernicious is to mistake a drawback peculiar to a particular policy-contingency framework with a weakness inherent in the instrument itself.

This is not to deny that publicity can, and often does, undermine the effectiveness of economic sanctions by making compliance difficult for the target state, although the same could be said of any technique of statecraft. One series of case studies of the Johnson administration found that publicity ''may be either fatal to or necessary for success, depending on the objectives actually being sought.''[38] This suggests that the conven-

[35] The advantage of costliness for sending credible signals is seldom recognized by writers on economic statecraft. The only examples I have found are Klitgaard, ''Sending Signals,'' p. 106; Galtung, ''Economic Sanctions,'' p. 412; and Patrick Callahan, ''Commitment,'' in *Describing Foreign Policy Behavior*, ed. Callahan, Brady, and Hermann, pp. 177-206.

[36] See Weintraub, ed., *Economic Coercion*, pp. 19-20, 50-54.

[37] ''Evaluation,'' p. II,7.

[38] Weintraub, ed., *Economic Coercion*, p. 51.

tional view that publicity is detrimental to the effectiveness of economic measures may need more qualification than it has thus far received.

Any actor, state or individual, has interdependent commitments.[39] The credibility of a commitment in one area often cannot be eroded without affecting the credibility of commitments in other areas. Commitments, credibility, and symbols are basically psychological phenomena. Logically, it is quite possible to love your spouse and forget your anniversary; but psychologically, it may be difficult to convince your spouse that the two are not related. Logically, economists can demonstrate that trading with the enemy, even during wartime, may be economically justifiable;[40] but psychologically, it would be quite difficult.

International economic intercourse has symbolic significance regardless of the desires of the policy makers involved. Although "linkage" of political and economic affairs is in one sense a policy to be pursued at will, it is also a fact of international life that must be taken into account by policy makers. When Ronald Reagan assumed the presidency, he was on record as opposing his predecessor's use of a grain embargo against the Soviet Union to protest the Soviet invasion of Afghanistan. Repeal of the embargo, however, would have called into question his commitment to a "hard-line" approach to dealing with the Soviets. Thus, he could not obliterate the symbolic significance of repealing the embargo simply by declaring how he wished the action to be interpreted. Recognizing this fact, he delayed repeal of the embargo. Decisions as to whether to grant most-favored-nation trading status to the Soviet Union, to buy Cuban sugar, or to support a loan to Brazil by the International Monetary Fund have symbolic significance for foreign statesmen whether one wants them to or not. The American imposition of economic sanctions on Cuba sent one kind of signal, but continuance of "business as usual" would also have sent a signal. President Carter's grain embargo may not have had all of the desired effects, but one must recognize that doing nothing would also have had effects on the U.S. image. Commitments are interdependent; U.S. behavior in the diplomatic and military sphere cannot be psychologically insulated from its behavior in the economic sphere. Even the most ardent foes of "linkage politics" must recognize this kind of linkage. Universal implicit recognition of the interdependence of commitments in the economic and political spheres is demonstrated by the nearly complete absence of any serious argument, then or now, that the United States should have continued normal economic relations with Germany during World War II.

[39] See Schelling, *Arms and Influence*, pp. 55-59.
[40] See Schelling, *International Economics*, pp. 496-497; and Wiles, *Communist International Economics*, pp. 460, 465-468, 495-496.

Economic techniques of statecraft can be used not only to make commitments but to circumvent the commitments of others. Commitments are never absolute; there is always some room for interpretation. Thus, a butcher may be committed not to give salami away free; but if one asks to taste a single slice each day, one may eventually consume the whole salami over a long period. The essence of such "salami tactics"[41] is the slow, cumulative effect of a series of influence attempts no one of which crosses the threshhold that makes the commitment operative. There are times when techniques that produce slow, cumulative, undramatic effects are preferable to those that produce sudden, dramatic effects. In such situations economic sanctions may be useful as ways to apply unobtrusive pressure to comply without seeming to challenge the target's commitment to noncompliance. Schelling illustrates the point as follows:

> Landlords rarely evict tenants by strong-arm methods. They have learned that steady cumulative pressures work just as well, though more slowly, and avoid provoking a violent response. It is far better to turn off the water and electricity, and let the tenant suffer the cumulative pressure of unflushed toilets and candles at night and get out voluntarily, than to start manhandling his family and his household goods. Blockade works slowly; it puts the decision up to the other side. To invade Berlin or Cuba is a sudden identifiable action, of an intensity that demands response; but to cut off supplies does little the first day and not much more the second; nobody dies or gets hurt from the initial effects of a blockade. A blockade is comparatively passive; the eventual damage results as much from the obstinacy of the blockaded territory as from the persistence of the blockading power. And there is no well-defined moment before which the blockading power may quail, for fear of causing the ultimate collapse.[42]

Although Schelling refers to a blockade, which is properly a military rather than an economic instrument, his reasoning can easily be applied to economic sanctions. Compared to other techniques of statecraft, economic measures are likely to exert more pressure than either diplomacy or propaganda and are less likely to evoke a violent response than military instruments. In mixed motive games in which applying pressure and avoiding the evocation of a violent response are both important goals, economic tools are likely to be especially attractive. In such situations economic sanctions are not just "second-best" techniques, but rather techniques that promise to be effective in ways that military force could not be. They are not merely inferior substitutes for force but rather superior, "first-best" policy alternatives. It should be noted that economic sanctions, with the

---

[41] See Schelliing, *Arms and Influence*, pp. 66-69.
[42] Ibid., pp. 68-69.

possible exception of Japan in 1941, have never triggered a violent response against those imposing them. The so-called mad dog response that many feared would occur in response to the League of Nations sanctions against Italy appears to be an imaginary drawback of economic sanctions. Italy did not attack League members; Cuba did not attack the United States; Rhodesia did not attack United Nations members; and the Soviet Union has never attacked those imposing economic sanctions against it. There can be little doubt, however, that had the sanctioning states used military force instead of economic measures, a military response would have occurred in each of these cases. The surest way to evoke a violent response from a country is to attack it. Economic statecraft often works slowly, but this is not necessarily the "inherent weakness" it is often made out to be. Quicker is not always better.[43]

One historic instance of the use of economic statecraft to circumvent an adversary's commitment, a strikingly successful instance, seems to have been overlooked by students of economic statecraft. Schelling relates it as follows:

> President Truman appreciated the value of this tactic in June 1945. French forces under de Gaulle's leadership had occupied a province in Northern Italy, contrary to Allied plans and American policy. They announced that any effort of their allies to dislodge them would be treated as a hostile act. The French intended to annex the area as a "minor frontier adjustment." It would have been extraordinarily disruptive of Allied unity, of course, to expel the French by force of arms; arguments got nowhere, so President Truman notified de Gaulle that no more supplies would be issued to the French army until it had withdrawn from the Aosta Valley. The French were absolutely dependent on American supplies and the message brought results. This was "nonhostile" pressure, not quite capable of provoking a militant response, therefore safe to use (and effective). A given amount of coercive pressure exercised over an extended period of time, allowed to accumulate its own momentum, is a common and effective technique of bypassing somebody's commitment.[44]

RISK AND ECONOMIC STATECRAFT

In the literature on war prevention two major themes or schools of thought emerge. One emphasizes tension reduction, conciliation, appeasement, and positive sanctions, while the other emphasizes increasing tension

---

[43] Cf. Gary Clyde Hufbauer and Jeffrey J. Schott, *Economic Sanctions in Support of Foreign Policy Goals* (Washington, D.C.: Institute for International Economics, 1983), pp. 79-80.

[44] Schelling, *Arms and Influence*, p. 69.

through deterrence, military preparedness, toughness, and negative sanctions. This debate raises questions that go far beyond the scope of this study, and no attempt will be made here to resolve the issues involved. Each school of thought has formidable proponents whose arguments cannot be dismissed lightly. Discussions of economic statecraft, however, often fail to acknowledge that both approaches are potentially relevant to the use of economic techniques. Thus, the fact that economic sanctions may increase the risk of war is usually treated as a disadvantage of such instruments.

Negative economic sanctions, like other kinds of negative sanctions, are risky in that they may increase the risk of war. Robin Renwick notes that one of the lessons learned from the League of Nations experience with economic sanctions was that it is "impossible to make sanctions effective without running the risk of war."[45] Bienen and Gilpin observe that economic sanctions "carry with them the possibility of war if they are to be effective."[46] And Muriel J. Grieve points out that economic sanctions could, "if effectively applied, challenge a . . . [target] state in as direct and positive a manner as a threat of war. When war is actually threatened, a sanctions policy, rather than reducing tension . . . would serve to enhance it."[47] To the extent that such comments call attention to one of the implications of using economic sanctions, they serve as valuable warnings against careless use of such measures; but insofar as they imply that increasing the risk of war is never desirable, they may be quite misleading. Sometimes risky techniques of statecraft are preferable to safe ones.

Risking war is a kind of cost; and like other costs, it may be used to add credibility to a signal. Thus, if economic sanctions are intended to warn the target state that the sanction-imposing state feels strongly and is willing to risk war if more acceptable behavior is not forthcoming, the riskiness of the sanctions may make the implied threat more credible—"In order to demonstrate to you the strength of my resolve, I am risking war to send you this message. I am really serious about this; so think twice before proceeding."

There is an analogy here between the role of risk in economic statecraft and Schelling's portrayal of limited war. He contends that "one of the functions of limited war . . . is to pose the deliberate risk of all-out war, in order to intimidate the enemy and to make pursuit of his limited objectives intolerably risky to him. . . . The supreme objective may not be to *assure* that it stays limited, but rather to keep the risk of all-out war

[45] *Economic Sanctions*, p. 23.

[46] "Evaluation," p. IIIa,9.

[47] "Economic Sanctions: Theory and Practice," *International Relations* III (October 1968):433.

within moderate limits *above zero.*"[48] If this is the case, Schelling points out, estimates of the utility of limited war or of a state's capacity to fight such a war often go awry because they fail to take into account these larger strategic implications of what is often treated as an isolated tactical operation. An inferior local military force matched against a superior force in a limited war may not be able to "win" but may be able to increase the risk of a larger war. "One does not have to be able to win a local military engagement to make the threat of it effective. Being able to lose a local war in a dangerous and provocative manner may make the risk . . . outweigh the apparent gains to the other side."[49]

This line of reasoning has two important implications for thinking about economic statecraft. If the imposition of economic sanctions really generates a risk of war, as is often alleged, such measures can perform functions similar to those of limited war. When Bienen and Gilpin point out that "the imposition of sanctions has a dynamic all its own and can trigger an action-reaction process which leads to dire consequences which neither sanctioned nor sanctioning state desired," they portray this as a cost or disadvantage of such measures.[50] Such a situation, however, corresponds almost perfectly with that described by Schelling in discussing "threats that leave something to chance":

> Brinkmanship is thus the deliberate creation of a recognizable risk of war, a risk that one does not completely control. It is the tactic of deliberately letting the situation get somewhat out of hand, just because its being out of hand may be intolerable to the other party and force his accommodation.[51]

It may well be that economic sanctions have a dynamic of their own that cannot be completely controlled, but it may also be precisely this quality that makes the actual or threatened use of them effective. Such a quality would allow the escalation process to begin at a lower level and thus allow more time for each party to reconsider. Thus, they could be considered a "generator of risk" that is safer to use than limited war. The real drawback here is not that economic sanctions are risky but that they may not be risky enough to produce the desired moderating effects.

The second implication of Schelling's line of reasoning concerns methods of estimating the utility of economic statecraft. In the same way that it is misleading to judge the utility of limited war or threats thereof in

---

[48] *Strategy of Conflict*, p. 193. The relevant chapters are those on "The Threat that Leaves Something to Chance" in *Strategy of Conflict* and "The Manipulation of Risk" in *Arms and Influence*.

[49] *Arms and Influence*, pp. 104-105.

[50] "Evaluation," p. II,7.

[51] *Strategy of Conflict*, p. 200.

isolation from the larger strategic implications of such undertakings, it may also be inappropriate to judge economic instruments without reference to underlying strategic purposes. To judge the utility of the anticommunist trade restrictions for the United States without reference to the overall framework of American policy toward communism, to estimate the utility of the U.S. embargo against Cuba without reference to the larger implications for U.S.–Soviet and U.S.–Latin American relations, to measure the utility of U.S. sanctions against Iran solely in terms of effects on the Iranian economy, would all result in misleading conclusions. Even those who believe that economic sanctions nearly always "fail" might usefully ponder Schelling's conclusion that fighting or threatening to fight a limited war can be a potent technique of statecraft *"even when there is little expectation that one could win it."*[52]

The analysis of risk is risky business. Optimizing the riskiness of a given technique of statecraft requires thorough and subtle scrutiny of the situation. Before depicting the riskiness of economic sanctions as an inherent weakness of such policy instruments, serious attention should be given to the difficult subject of the role of risk in international politics. And there is no better place to begin than with Schelling's *The Strategy of Conflict* and *Arms and Influence*.

[52] *Arms and Influence*, p. 109. Italics added.

CHAPTER 7

NATIONAL POWER AND ECONOMIC STATECRAFT

*Let us examine carefully, however, how financial
diplomacy can be made to contribute to the
national strength, since some of the current ideas
and stereotypes on this question are fallacious or
highly questionable.*[1]

Techniques of statecraft are ways for foreign policy makers to make influence attempts on other states or nonstate actors in the international arena. The preceding chapters have laid the groundwork for asking the question "How useful are economic techniques of statecraft for such purposes?" The overall impression one derives from the literature is that economic statecraft is so obviously useless as to raise questions about the good judgment of any policy maker who gives serious consideration to using such techniques. How well does economic statecraft work? How can we tell whether it is working? What do we mean by "work"? This chapter will examine the difficulties of answering such questions.

BIASED CONCEPTS

Concepts matter. No amount of detailed historical research on the effectiveness of economic statecraft will help if the conceptual basis of the research is hopelessly biased. To some extent the tendency to denigrate the effectiveness of economic instruments is caused by concepts that make it *definitionally* difficult for them to succeed. Influence, to reiterate, involves A getting B to do something he would not otherwise do. Now one of the most important foreign policy goals for most countries is how to get other countries to contribute to enhancement of their economic welfare. Consider the alternatives available to statesmen in pursuing this goal: (1) Propaganda could be used to exhort other countries to donate goods in the name of charity, justice, or whatever. As Third World statesmen will testify, however, this technique of statecraft is not strikingly successful. (2) Diplomacy could be used to offer a diplomatic quid pro quo in return for economic support. When Haiti exchanges its vote in the United Nations

[1] Jacob Viner, *International Economics* (Glencoe, Ill.: Free Press, 1951), p. 343.

or the Organization of American States for American economic aid, it could be viewed as using this technique. Since some quid pro quo is involved, this approach is likely to work better than mere "jaw-boning." (3) Military force could be used to threaten or subjugate other countries in order to extract part of their wealth. Indeed, imperialism is often described as just such an influence attempt. The question of whether this kind of imperialism was worthwhile has been vigorously debated, but there is general agreement that it no longer pays.[2] (4) Economic statecraft, in the form of allowing and possibly even promoting private international trade, however, is by far the most effective—and cost-effective—way for one country to acquire the goods or services of another.[3] No other technique of statecraft even begins to approach international trade for effectiveness in promoting this important foreign policy goal. International economic exchange is one of the most spectacularly successful examples of international influence in history; yet it is rarely so described. Why? Because routine, mundane, day-to-day economic exchange is often *defined* as either not involving power or as not being "real" foreign policy.[4] Such conceptions of power or foreign policy have important effects on conclusions about the efficacy of economic techniques of statecraft.

In general it is easier to make successful influence attempts when dealing with "low politics" issues than when dealing with "high politics" issues. This is probably true for any technique of statecraft, economic or not. Thus, it is often said that much of diplomacy involves small issues, mundane, unglamorous issues that nevertheless have a cumulative effect that should not be underestimated. Negotiating peace treaties, the United Nations Charter, or major disarmament treaties are atypical diplomatic undertakings—and less likely to succeed. Similarly, it is said that military force has important effects on the day-to-day conduct of statecraft in subtle, continuing, and pervasive ways that are not often recognized. Well and good, such comments serve as reminders that the cumulative effect of a large number of undramatic influence attempts can be impressive over a long enough period of time. Similar comments, however, are rarely made with respect to economic techniques of statecraft. On the contrary, one is more likely to find that routine use of such instruments is conceived of as "nonpolitical." Thus, Henry Bienen and Robert Gilpin observe that "an economic threat is most often successful" if it is used "to gain economic

---

[2] See Kenneth E. Boulding and Tapan Mukerjee, eds., *Economic Imperialism* (Ann Arbor: University of Michigan Press, 1972), esp. pp. ix-xviii, 240-261. See also the comment by Quincy Wright with respect to the "dubious value" of war as a means of solving economic problems. (*A Study of War*, pp. 281-283.)

[3] Note that it is not the decisions of the private traders themselves that constitute economic statecraft, but rather the statesman's decision to permit or encourage such trade.

[4] See previous discussion in chapter 3.

concessions.''[5] Since they have previously excluded such measures from the broad category of state actions that "have in common the manipulation of economic relations for political objectives,''[6] however, this observation in no way hinders their pessimistic conclusions regarding the efficacy of economic sanctions in promoting foreign policy objectives. Similarly, Robin Renwick excludes the "numerous instances in which countries have sought to exert economic pressure to achieve commercial objectives, restraints on exports, changes in tariffs, etc." from consideration in his study of economic sanctions, noting that "in current international usage sanctions are conceived essentially as the imposition of economic penalties to bring about a change in the political behavior of the country against which they are directed.''[7] One can only wonder what those responsible for negotiating changes in the European Community's Common Agricultural Policy or Japan's automobile export restraints would think about the contention that such actions do not entail changes in "political behavior''!

A still more important conceptual bias in the study of economic statecraft is the denial that economic exchange processes involve power or influence. Klaus Knorr, for example, distinguishes between economic exchange on the one hand and transactions involving politics and power on the other hand.[8] Thus, although he admits that the "extraction of economic gain" may be a foreign policy goal, he ignores the one technique of statecraft most likely to be effective in pursuing that goal, i.e., mutually satisfactory economic exchange:

> We are not concerned here with mutually satisfactory exchanges that come about without the insertion of power, as when governments agree on reciprocal tariff concessions or when state-trading governments import or export goods in free markets. We are concerned with the use of economic power to achieve unequal exchanges of valued things.[9]

And in discussing foreign aid as a technique of statecraft Knorr disregards "so-called aid that is given and received strictly as a quid pro quo, as a payment for something specific, whether it is an air base or a vote on an issue in the United Nations,''[10] thus ruling out of consideration the form of aid most likely to succeed. Having conceptually eliminated the forms

---

[5] "Evaluation," p. II,14.

[6] Ibid., pp. I,1-2.

[7] *Economic Sanctions*, p. 2. For a similar view that excludes "from foreign policy goals the normal realm of objectives sought in banking, commercial, and tax negotiations between sovereign states," see Hufbauer and Schott, *Economic Sanctions*, p. 2.

[8] *Power of Nations*, pp. 80-81, 135, 171, 310-314.

[9] Ibid., p. 135.

[10] Ibid., p. 171.

of economic statecraft with the highest probability of success, it is not surprising that Knorr has a low opinion of the efficacy of aid and trade as techniques of statecraft.[11]

It is easy to overestimate the importance of the spectacular, the unusual, the dramatic, the extraordinary while underestimating the cumulative impact of everyday things that we take for granted. The "low politics" of economic exchange may not be very noticeable on any given day; but over the long haul, it is one of the most important influence mechanisms in the world. The standing implicit threat not to cooperate unless others do is often hard to detect, but it underlies most forms of international economic exchange. The twin principles of "If you do, I will; and if you don't, I won't" are as important in international trade negotiations or foreign aid transactions as they are in disarmament talks.

COMPARING COSTS AND BENEFITS

Assessing the utility of a technique of statecraft is essentially a matter of estimating and comparing the costs and benefits associated with alternative ways to pursue a given set of foreign policy goals. Although this

[11] Knorr realizes that his rigid separation of power and exchange leaves some important dimensions of international influence unaccounted for. Instead of tracing the difficulty back to his concepts of power and exchange, however, he creates a new conceptual category with the awkward label of "nonpower influence." Problems arise when he tries to differentiate this new category from power, on the one hand, and exchange, on the other. In distinguishing "nonpower influence" from power, he asserts that power is necessarily harmful to the weaker actor. This puts Knorr in the position of denying that power can be a symmetrical relationship between actors of equal strength (thus making it hard to understand mutual deterrence) and in the position of seeming to rule out power based on positive sanctions. The latter is especially awkward for Knorr since he has explicitly stated his desire to include "reward power" in his concept of power. Positive sanctions, by definition, are beneficial rather than harmful to the target. Even less satisfactory is Knorr's attempt to differentiate between exchange and nonpower influence. Although admitting that some exchanges may look like nonpower influence, he argues that the latter is distinguished from the former by the lack of any "stipulated payment" in return for value received (p. 311). Later, however, he depicts a situation in which nonpower influence can be fully reciprocal, with each actor providing the other with something of value (p. 314). Apparently, the *only* difference between this situation and an exchange transaction is the degree of specificity of the quid pro quo.

Knorr's assertion that there has been "astonishingly little systematic study" (p. 310) of nonpower influence is rather misleading. Once exchange is recognized as a particular kind of power relationship, most of the conceptual difficulties encountered by Knorr disappear; and the amount of relevant academic literature grows to gigantic proportions, i.e., all the literature on social and economic exchange becomes relevant. There is nothing that Knorr's concept of nonpower influence can account for that cannot be adequately dealt with by conventional concepts of power and exchange. For further discussion of these issues, see Baldwin, "Power and Social Exchange"; "The Power of Positive Sanctions," *World Politics* XXIV (October 1971):19-38; "Power Analysis and World Politics"; Oppenheim, *Political Concepts*, pp. 40-43; and Dahl, *Modern Political Analysis*, 3d ed., p. 50.

may sound simple, analytical pitfalls abound. They include (1) ignoring costs; (2) misleading cost comparisons; (3) failure to compare alternative techniques; and (4) misleading cost estimates.

Ignoring Costs

Choices are costly.[12] Choosing to use economic statecraft—or any other kind of statecraft for that matter—costs something. The TANSTAAFL principle[13] should figure prominently in any assessment of the utility of economic techniques of statecraft. Unfortunately, this is not always the case. Sometimes the neglect of costs is casual and implicit. Although it is possible to estimate power, i.e., the effectiveness of an influence attempt, without reference to the costs of making the attempt, such an estimate by itself would be of little or no help to a foreign policy decision maker.[14] Without a cost estimate, policy makers cannot make judgments as to how worthwhile the influence attempt is likely to be. In the twentieth century— and certainly in the latter part of that century—social scientists are expected to distinguish between "effectiveness" and "efficiency," between "effectiveness" and "utility." Whereas "efficiency" and "utility" imply something about the relationship between inputs and outputs, between costs and benefits, "effectiveness" relates only to outputs or benefits.[15] Casual neglect of costs occurs when techniques of statecraft are discussed using "effectiveness" and "utility" (or "efficiency") interchangeably with no explicit mention of costs and no warning that the terms are being used in an unusual way.[16]

[12] This is not merely an empirical generalization; it is a logical necessity. The concepts of choice and cost are integrally related. One implies the other. On this point see Frank H. Knight, "Fallacies," pp. 592-593; David A. Baldwin, "The Costs of Power," *Journal of Conflict Resolution* XV (October 1971):145-155; and Armen A. Alchian, "Cost," *International Encyclopedia of the Social Sciences*, vol. 3, p. 404.

[13] "There ain't no such thing as a free lunch." Cf. Edwin G. Dolan, *TANSTAAFL* (New York: Holt, Rinehart, and Winston, 1971), p. 14.

[14] John C. Harsanyi has suggested that both the costs to A (the maker of the influence attempt) and to B (the target) should be incorporated into the concept of power. Although his arguments are cogent, they will not be used here. Although the costs to B of noncompliance are implied in the concept of power employed here—as, I believe, they must be in any sensible concept of power—the costs to A will be treated separately. This is solely for the purpose of making the argument easier to follow, however, and does not imply any basic disagreement with Harsanyi's point. See Harsanyi, "Measurement of Social Power, Opportunity Costs, and the Theory of Two-Person Bargaining Games," *Behavioral Science* VII (January 1962):67-80.

[15] On this point see Simon, *Administrative Behavior*, pp. 180-182.

[16] For examples see Kindleberger, *Power and Money*, pp. 56, 65; Blechman and Kaplan, *Force Without War*, esp. pp. 17-20, 58-85, 517-518, 532-534; and Robert W. Tucker, *The Inequality of Nations* (New York: Basic Books, 1977), p. 93.

Some writers go beyond casual neglect to deny explicitly that the costs of an influence attempt are a relevant consideration. E. H. Carr, for example, contends that the lesson of the League of Nations sanctions against Italy was that "in sanctions, as in war, the only motto is 'all or nothing.' "[17] Another writer observes that when economic sanctions are used for "purely political" purposes, they are "no longer connected with the question of whether we hurt ourselves or not."[18] And John D. Montgomery questions whether it is possible to "set a price" on such foreign policy objectives as keeping "South Vietnam out of communist hands for a decade," insuring "Taiwan's freedom after the fall of mainland China," promoting "a prosperous, reasonably united Europe," or "a reconstructed Japan."[19] Perhaps such observations were not meant to be taken at face value; or perhaps the writers simply overlooked the logical implications of their statements. In any case, no rational justification for ignoring costs is possible, whether in war, trade restrictions, or foreign aid. Costs always matter to the rational decision maker, and cost estimates must be made no matter how difficult that may be. "All or nothing" is a decision rule for fanatics, not for rational and prudent statesmen.

Misleading Comparisons

Even those who recognize that costs matter may fail to make it clear precisely how costs affect the utility of a given technique of statecraft. Thus, it is sometimes argued that the significance of costs is to be found in the relative magnitude of the costs incurred by the state making the influence attempt (the sender) and those incurred by the target. "Trade sanctions," observes Sidney Weintraub, "may be more costly to the sending nation than to the target."[20] "Economic sanctions," asserts Milton Friedman, "are likely to do us as much harm as they do their intended target."[21] "The probable success of economic sanctions," argue Bienen and Gilpin, "may very well turn on whether the ultimate costs involved are higher for the sanctioned or the sanctioning state."[22] "It is not irrational

---

[17] Carr, *The Twenty Years' Crisis*, p. 119.

[18] Otto Wolff von Amerongen, "Commentary: Economic Sanctions as a Foreign Policy Tool?" *International Security* V (Fall 1980):167.

[19] *Foreign Aid in International Politics* (Englewood Cliffs, N.J.: Prentice-Hall, 1967), pp. 72-73. Montgomery's later comment that the "alternatives to continuing some form of aid are almost unthinkable" (p. 85) indicates that he does recognize, at least implicitly, that opportunity costs matter.

[20] Weintraub, ed., *Economic Coercion*, p. 11.

[21] *Newsweek*, January 21, 1980, p. 76.

[22] "Evaluation," p. II,8. See also comments by Gilpin in *New York Times*, January 13, 1980, and U.S. Senate, Committee on Finance, Subcommittee on International Trade, *Hearings, U.S. International Trade Strategy*, 96th Cong., 2d sess., 1980, p. 156. Hufbauer and

to do the enemy absolute good, provided we do ourselves more good; nor again to do ourselves harm, provided we do him more harm,'' contends P.J.D. Wiles.[23] In the hypothetical world of pure zero-sum games, comparing A's costs with B's makes sense, since *by definition* A's costs are B's benefits; but in the mixed motive games that characterize international behavior in the real world, this comparison can be quite misleading.[24] The question of whether trade sanctions are more costly to the target than to the sender may be beside the point. The significance of the costs of trade sanctions *to the foreign policy maker imposing or considering such measures* is a function of the costs and benefits associated with the other policy alternatives which the policy maker perceives as available in a given situation. The rational statesman will compare the costs and benefits of a policy alternative with the costs and benefits of other alternatives. The question of whether it is rational to impose sanctions that hurt the sender more than the target cannot be answered a priori (except in zero-sum games), but rather must be approached in terms of the sender's value system and his perceived alternatives. In some situations policy makers may have no choice because all of their policy alternatives involve bigger costs for themselves than for the target. Rational but stern fathers cannot be counted on to cease and desist after asserting, ''This is going to hurt me more than it hurts you.'' Quite the contrary. For the rational statesman the relevant cost comparison is not between his country and the target but rather between *his* costs and *his* benefits with respect to *his* alternatives.

Another pitfall involves direct comparisons between the costs of one policy instrument and the costs of another rather than comparing the cost-benefit combination. Even K. J. Holsti, whose treatment of economic statecraft is more sophisticated than that in any comparable textbook, concludes as follows: ''Past experience suggests that little is to be gained

---

Schott seem to share this view insofar as they portray the precept that a country using sanctions ''should seek to maximize the ratio of costs inflicted to costs incurred'' as an unattainable ideal rather than as a ridiculous precept (*Economic Sanctions*, pp. 63-64).

[23] *Communist International Economics*, pp. 465-466. Wiles refers to the ''principle of relative gain'' (p. 465). Cf. Wu, *Economic Warfare*, p. 11.

[24] Thomas C. Schelling's principle of ''net advantage'' is basically the same as Wiles' ''principle of relative gain.'' Contrary to Wiles, however, the implication of Schelling's discussion is that the principle has little normative or predictive value when the parties do not have completely conflicting relative priorities. See Schelling, *International Economics*, pp. 496-497. Schelling makes this point more clearly in his later work, when he says: '' 'Winning' in a conflict does not have a strictly competitive meaning; it is not winning relative to one's adversary. It means gaining relative to one's own value system'' (*Strategy of Conflict*, pp. 4-5). Strictly speaking, the concept of ''costs'' is not needed in zero-sum games; since one party's gains are the other's losses, the payoffs represent values that have already taken costs into account. Schelling addresses all of these points cogently in ''The Strategy of Inflicting Costs,'' in *Issues in Defense Economics*, ed. Roland N. McKean (New York: National Bureau of Economic Research, 1967), pp. 105-127.

from using these [economic] instruments. . . . Compared to other techniques, particularly subversion and warfare . . . they might seem particularly inexpensive. That is not to say, they are more effective."[25] Such a conclusion is misleading as to the comparative utility of economic techniques of statecraft. The question of what is to be "gained" by choosing to rely on economic techniques rather than, say, military ones, cannot be answered in the way Holsti implies. Herbert Simon has pointed out why this is so:

> An administrative choice is incorrectly posed, then, when it is posed as a choice between possibility A, with low costs and small results, and possibility B, with high costs and large results. For A should be substituted a third possibility C, which would include A *plus* the alternative activities made possible by the cost difference between A and B.[26]

Thus, in order to determine the utility (i.e., gain) of using economic rather than military statecraft in attempting to influence Vietnam in the period 1963–1973, American policy makers would have to consider not only the immediate costs and effectiveness of such measures but also the other policy goals that could have been promoted with the resources saved by not using expensive military measures.[27] Although economic instruments might have been less effective in accomplishing U.S. goals (if, indeed, that is possible), they would certainly have cost less. By comparison with the Vietnam War—the most counterproductive influence attempt in American diplomatic history—the United States would probably have "gained" substantially if it had used economic rather than military techniques. To the extent that military statecraft is more expensive than economic statecraft—which is usually the case—the resources saved by using economic rather than military techniques in a given situation should be considered in calculating the costs and benefits. The fact that economic techniques are usually less costly *and* less effective does not mean that they are *less useful* than military techniques. If one were to consider the comparative utility of economic and military techniques with respect to opposing Mussolini's invasion of Ethiopia, promoting majority rule in Rhodesia, pro-

[25] *International Politics*, 4th ed., p. 239.

[26] *Administrative Behavior*, p. 179. On the tendency to ignore "the essential cost-benefit nature of all decisions" in evaluating the utility of economic statecraft, see Levine, Rushing, and Movit, "Potential for U.S. Economic Leverage," p. 374.

[27] The costs of the Vietnam War have been estimated at $900 billion not counting costs unmeasurable in terms of money, such as 56,000 lives, detrimental effects on the U.S. image abroad, and damage to domestic institutions. See Robert Warren Stevens, *Vain Hopes, Grim Realities: The Economic Consequences of the Vietnam War* (New York: Franklin Watts, 1976).

testing the Soviet invasion of Afghanistan, or resisting communism in Cuba, it is not obvious that economic techniques would be judged less useful than military techniques if the comparison were conducted as Simon suggests. There is, after all, something unfair about basing the conclusion that military force is more useful or more effective than economic aid on a comparison of five billion dollars worth of aid with one hundred billion dollars worth of military force.

Failure to Compare

The most common and most serious shortcoming in most assessments of the utility of techniques of statecraft is failure to cast the analysis in comparative terms. No matter how much evidence and argument are amassed to demonstrate the uselessness of economic statecraft, little has been said that is relevant to policy making until one states or implies the existence of more useful policy instruments. Shooting oneself in the foot is normally viewed as a counterproductive undertaking, and rightly so; but for the rational and unpatriotic soldier who values living more highly than helping his country win a war and who sees the alternative as certain death, it may be the most rational thing he could do. The utility of a technique of statecraft is a function of the situation and not a quality intrinsic to the particular technique.[28]

Robin Renwick introduces his study of economic sanctions as follows:

> In deciding whether to impose economic sanctions, governments frequently find themselves responding to an international crisis on the basis of three broad options: (a) to do nothing; (b) to consider taking some form of military action; (c) to seek to impose economic penalties. A decision to impose sanctions may be taken less on its intrinsic merits than because of its attractions in relation to the alternatives.[29]

Despite the rather disconcerting reference to the fruitless concept of "intrinsic merits" and the overly simple range of policy options, which ignores propaganda and diplomacy, this passage plunges very near the heart of the matter—the relative attractiveness of economic sanctions in comparison with alternative techniques. Unfortunately, Renwick ignores the logical implications of this opening paragraph, which dictate structuring an assessment of the utility of economic sanctions in terms of comparative costs and benefits. Instead, having noted the importance of comparing alternative

---

[28] The question of utility as an intrinsic quality versus utility as "value in use" has been a major theme in the evolution of the discipline of economics. Many of these issues are relevant to determining the utility of techniques of statecraft. See Nicholas Georgescu-Roegen, "Utility," *International Encyclopedia of the Social Sciences*, vol. 16, pp. 236-265.

[29] *Economic Sanctions*, p. 1.

ways to solve a given problem, he virtually ignores this perspective throughout most of the book, returning to it only in the last chapter when he again observes that "sanctions frequently—one might almost say, generally—are decided in large measure as a consequence of the lack of feasible alternatives."[30] Although Renwick seems to believe that economic sanctions are more useful than is generally believed, his failure to focus on "the lack of feasible alternatives" vitiates the force of his argument.

In considering the "efficiency of embargo policies" Gunnar Adler-Karlsson concludes:

> It seems to be a valid conclusion that those who today propose embargo actions . . . should at least be required to show that a considerable degree of probability exists that the proposed actions are likely to lead to the desired results. . . . The burden of proof is clearly on those who claim that an embargo policy is an efficient instrument of foreign policy.[31]

Even those who agree with Adler-Karlsson as to the location of the "burden of proof" must admit that the test he proposes is unnecessary and inappropriate. It is not necessary to "show that a considerable degree of probability does exist that the proposed actions are likely to lead to the desired ends"; it is only necessary to show that the probability of reaching the desired ends—no matter how low that may be—is higher for the proposed embargo than for alternative policy options.[32] In a world characterized by uncertainty and national sovereignty, Adler-Karlsson's proposed test might rule out *every* alternative including doing nothing. Such a test is not likely to be very helpful in either making policy or passing judgment on its efficiency.

Rita Falk Taubenfeld and Howard J. Taubenfeld construct a "firm *prima facie* case against economic measures" by examining the costs and benefits associated with such actions.[33] Rather than setting the discussion in the context of the comparative utility of alternative policy options, however, the Taubenfelds describe their analysis as "speculation on the inherent potentialities" of such policy instruments.[34] Later in the article, having

---

[30] Ibid., p. 85.

[31] *Western Economic Warfare*, p. 10.

[32] "Doing nothing," of course, is one of the policy options that should be considered. I am assuming that Adler-Karlsson means by "desired ends" the maximization of value based on consideration of both costs and effectiveness. In view of the fact that this section on "efficiency of embargo policies in general" contains no reference whatever to costs, this may be an overly generous interpretation. For a later article in which Adler-Karlsson also fails to distinguish clearly between "efficiency" and "effectiveness," see "The U.S. Embargo: Inefficient and Counterproductive," *Aussenwirtschaft* XXXV (June 1980):170-187.

[33] "The 'Economic Weapon,' " pp. 188-195.

[34] Ibid., pp. 187-188, 194.

already constructed their "firm *prima facie* case," they note: "For a more complete evaluation of the economic weapon, we would of course need to consider . . . the costs of economic sanctions to the [international] organization and its members, relative to the costs of alternative action open to them."[35] This qualification, however, is too little and too late. Comparison of alternative policy options is not merely a step to be taken by those who seek a "more complete evaluation" that goes beyond the "firm *prima facie* case," but rather a step that must be taken in order to construct even a "minimally acceptable" *prima facie* case against the use of economic measures, let alone a "firm" or "more complete" case.

Bienen and Gilpin construct a series of case studies of the utility of economic sanctions purporting to show that such measures tend to be low in effectiveness and high in costs. They pay little or no attention, however, to the comparative costs and effectiveness of alternative courses of action. Although they promise to "suggest a number of alternatives to a sanctions policy," their "policy recommendations" identify no such alternatives. Instead they confine themselves to suggestions as to when, where, and how to implement economic sanctions.[36] Bienen and Gilpin conclude that "in the light of so much evidence against the utility of sanctions, the burden of proof that sanctions against a country will serve any useful purpose lies squarely on those individuals who advocate them."[37] Until more useful policy instruments have been identified, however, this conclusion seems premature.

The most sophisticated attempt to assess the utility of economic techniques of statecraft is Knorr's *The Power of Nations*. Although Knorr considers both military and economic statecraft, his judgments as to the utility of various techniques of statecraft are usually based on examination of the costs and benefits of one technique at a time rather than on comparison of alternative ways to cope with a given problem. Thus, his conclusion that both aid and trade policies have low utility as techniques of statecraft implies little or nothing about the *relative* utility of such measures in comparison with propaganda, military statecraft, or diplomacy.[38]

---

[35] Ibid., p. 196. Although they mention in this passage the need to compare policy options, the rest of the article contains few such comparisons.

[36] "Evaluation," pp. I,4-XI,2 et passim.

[37] Ibid., p. IX,3. Oddly, Bienen and Gilpin note that for the target state the costs of compliance should be compared with the costs of alternative courses of action (p. I,6); but they fail to apply similar logic to the costs of the sanctioning state. In testimony before Congress Gilpin asserted that "the history of sanctions shows that they don't work, that they are counterproductive and that other measures are to be preferred in international politics." (U.S. Senate, Committee on Finance, *U.S. International Trade Strategy: Hearings*, p. 161.) Gilpin did not elaborate, however, as to what these "other measures" are or why they "are to be preferred."

[38] See pp. 165, 188, 205-206. But for an exception to this tendency, see p. 140.

The logic of Knorr's position becomes clear near the end of *The Power of Nations* when he acknowledges his assumption that "the costs of using power have risen, and its effectiveness has decreased. The world has become less coercible" (p. 318). Thus, Knorr's argument could be summarized as follows: "Changes in underlying world conditions, such as the diffusion of power, increased nationalistic sensitivities, and so on, have created a situation in which the value, i.e., utility, of making influence attempts, regardless of the technique used, is lower than it used to be. Making influence attempts may be a little more useful than doing nothing, but not much; it may even be worse than doing nothing."[39] In effect, Knorr is telling statesmen that they are in a difficult and frustrating line of work, in which successes are few and defeats are many.

Although this insight provides valuable counsel to foreign policy makers not to expect too much when making influence attempts and not to neglect giving serious consideration to doing nothing, it is not much help to the statesman who has already decided that something must be done. When someone is seeking advice as to which exit to use in fleeing a burning house, it is not very helpful to tell him that all the exits are very small and hard to get to. Likewise, unless statesmen are willing to stop making influence attempts altogether, they are going to require advice as to the *relative* utility of alternative techniques of statecraft in given situations.[40] The world may indeed be "less coercible" than it used to be, but it is also true that some instruments of coercion work better than others.

The possibility of a general decline in the utility (and perhaps the effectiveness also) of all techniques of statecraft gives rise to some tricky analytical problems. The following excerpts from Robert Tucker's *The Inequality of Nations* illustrate the nature of these problems:

---

[39] This is not a quote from Knorr; it is my attempt to paraphrase the thrust of his argument. Technically, the concept of opportunity costs (or opportunity benefits for that matter) implies the existence of at least one policy alternative as a matter of logical necessity. Thus, strictly speaking, the statement that Knorr's utility estimates are made without reference to "alternative ways to cope with a given problem" is incorrect. In most cases the alternative he implies seems to be doing nothing. Thus, the utility of aid giving is judged with reference to the utility of not giving aid; and the utility of an embargo is judged with reference to the alternative of no embargo. It is to Knorr's credit that he recognizes that doing nothing may also entail costs (e.g., p. 194), but one might wish he had emphasized this point more.

[40] In addition to his *The Power of Nations*, Knorr's treatment of the utility of military statecraft is to be recommended as the clearest, most rigorous, and most conceptually sophisticated assessment available. (*On the Uses of Military Power in the Nuclear Age* and "On the International Uses of Military Force in the Contemporary World," *Orbis* XXI (Spring 1977):5-27.) The earlier work, published in 1966, gives more consideration to alternative techniques of statecraft (pp. 14-16) than either *The Power of Nations* or the article published in 1977.

Nor is it reasonable to expect that a growing disutility of military power will have no effect on the economic power wielded by the strong. . . . Power may not be indivisible, but the burden of proof is on those who would argue that, though the utility of military power has markedly declined, there need be no devaluation in the efficacy of economic power. Curiously, it is precisely the opposite conclusion that is drawn—or simply assumed—by most observers today. For the prevailing view finds the decline in the utility of military power largely compensated by the rise in the utility of economic power. In this view "power" remains, as it were, a constant. Hence the decline in one form of power (military) must be expected to result in the rise of another form (economic). Is this doctrine of the "substitutability" of power valid, or even approximately so? One must seriously doubt that it is. . . . Although it may be true that military power has . . . declined, it does not follow that economic power has accordingly risen. Instead, it may be that power itself is increasingly at a discount and what military power can no longer do economic power also can no longer do. (pp. 81-82)

Tucker's tendency to equate "utility" with "effectiveness" sometimes and to use it as if it took account of costs at other times necessitates discussing this passage from two perspectives. First, let us assume that Tucker is using "utility" the way most other twentieth-century social scientists do—to refer to net advantages. From this perspective there is nothing "curious" at all about the assumption that a decrease in the utility of one kind of statecraft implies increased utility of other kinds of statecraft. Such a view does not require the assumption that power is a constant. It is merely an application of the "law of diminishing marginal utility," which states that, other things being equal, the less of something one has, the higher the value of a single unit; and the more of something one has, the lower the value of a single unit. Thus, statesmen who find themselves with fewer feasible techniques of statecraft, other things being equal, are likely to value the remaining ones more highly.[41] Although one might rightly object to the assumption that other things remain equal, "the burden of proof" should not lie with those who are merely applying one of the most widely accepted laws in social science. On the contrary, the burden of proof must rest on those who purport to have found exceptions to this law. The existence of this law, of course, is the underlying rationale for

---

[41] Knorr makes this important point in *On the Uses of Military Power in the Nuclear Age* (pp. 14-16), but he does not draw out its implications. Unfortunately, the point seems to disappear completely in his later treatments of the utility of military power. Cf. *Power of Nations* and "International Uses of Military Force."

evaluating the utility of techniques of statecraft in a comparative context. The utility of any one "unit" of statecraft is affected by how many other "units" are available.

Suppose that in the quoted passage Tucker really means to ignore costs and focus exclusively on effectiveness. Although it may be true that the effectiveness of "power itself," i.e., statecraft itself, has declined, it does not follow that the relative attractiveness of economic and military "power" has remained unchanged. If the effectiveness of "military power" is declining at a faster rate than "economic power," then the *relative effectiveness* of "economic power" is increasing even while its overall effectiveness is falling. As with Knorr, Tucker's contention that "power itself" has become less effective says nothing whatever about the relative effectiveness (or utility for that matter) of alternative types of statecraft. One cannot refute assertions of increased *relative* attractiveness of economic statecraft simply by arguing that the efficacy or the utility of all policy instruments is low or falling.[42]

Estimating Costs

To insist that cost estimates are necessary is not to say that they are easy. The terms "costs" and "benefits" can easily give a misleading impression of more precision than actually exists. The tools of economic statecraft involve things measurable in terms of money, but that does not mean that the costs of using such techniques are measurable solely in economic terms. The costs of using economic statecraft, like the costs of any other kind of influence attempt, may be political, military, or psychological as well as economic.[43] To pretend that the costs or benefits of influence attempts can be calculated with great precision by even the most rational of decision makers would be false and misleading.[44]

Regardless of the label—"advantages and disadvantages," "pros and cons," "goods and bads"—the basic idea is to identify the desirable and undesirable consequences of making a decision, i.e., choosing one alternative rather than another. It follows that only values forgone *as a result of the decision* are properly called costs. Thus, Knorr may be right in

[42] A rise in the costs of statecraft in general, causing a fall in the utility of all techniques of statecraft, has the paradoxical result of lowering the cost of choosing one technique of statecraft rather than another. If military force is worth less, then one gives up less in choosing to use some other technique instead of military force.

[43] For an example of a study that treats both the costs incurred by the country using sanctions and the costs inflicted on the target state as if they were measurable in monetary terms, see Hufbauer and Schott, *Economic Sanctions*, esp. pp. 97-100.

[44] For some cogent objections to overly precise cost-benefit analysis with respect to foreign aid, see Jacob Kaplan, *The Challenge of Foreign Aid: Policies, Problems, and Possibilities* (New York: Praeger, 1967), pp. 88-89.

counting among the costs of the U.S. embargo against Cuba "a considerable loss of respect and goodwill in western Europe and the underdeveloped world, including much Latin American public opinion."[45] But one might well ask how much of this "loss of respect and goodwill" would have occurred anyway. To allow the Soviet Union to establish what Secretary of State Dean Rusk called a "communist outpost in the Western hemisphere"[46] or to ignore the anti-American posture of Castro without responding in any way might well have meant an even greater loss of respect.[47] Whereas diplomacy and propaganda might have been perceived as weak responses, a military invasion would certainly have been viewed as overreaction. In short, on an *a priori* basis, it is not obvious that a "considerable loss of respect and goodwill" is properly attributable as a cost of the embargo. Unless it can be shown that an alternative to the embargo would have resulted in less loss of "respect and goodwill," this loss should not be attributed in any way to the embargo. One has to prove that the value forgone was related to the choice made in order to establish cost.

One of the biggest advantages of using economic instead of military statecraft derives from avoiding the costs associated with military statecraft. An accurate assessment of the utility of economic statecraft, therefore, depends to some extent on an accurate estimate of the costs of military statecraft. If the costs of military statecraft are underestimated, the utility of economic statecraft is also likely to be undervalued. Robert Gilpin's *War and Change in World Politics* provides an example of how the costs of military statecraft can be underestimated:

> Despite contemporary criticisms of the "warfare state," there appears today to be less of a tendency than in the past for the costs of war to rise at a faster rate than national income. . . . At the same time that the destructiveness of war has been greatly magnified, the relative cost of military power has actually declined; in other words, the cost of protection claims a smaller share of national income. (p. 163)[48]

Two types of errors are illustrated here. First, the "costs of war" should not be measured exclusively in monetary terms. The cost of the Vietnam

---

[45] *Power of Nations*, p. 149. See also Bienen and Gilpin, "Evaluation," p. IIId,1.

[46] Quoted in Knorr, *Power of Nations*, p. 149.

[47] Anna P. Schreiber notes that the State Department "feared that the United States had come to look weak, and that other Latin American revolutionaries might take heart in the face of apparent American inability to deal strongly with Castro." ("Economic Coercion," p. 392.)

[48] A similar point is made by Alan S. Milward, *War, Economy and Society, 1939-1945* (Berkeley: University of California Press, 1977), pp. 1-4.

War, for example, has been estimated at $900 billion;[49] but that does not include moral costs, lives lost, damage to the U.S. image, the weakening of domestic institutions, and so on. Second, the most spectacular increase in the cost of military statecraft since World War II does not involve the economic cost of supporting the military establishment, but rather the risks ("expected value") associated with the destructiveness of modern weapons. To ignore such risks or "expected values" in calculating the costs of military statecraft is to underestimate seriously the costs of such techniques and, thereby to undermine one of the most potent arguments in favor of economic statecraft.[50]

MEASURING EFFECTIVENESS

According to conventional wisdom economic statecraft often "fails." Numerous case studies of economic statecraft characterize effectiveness in terms of a single word—usually "success" or "failure," more often the latter.[51] Less attention has been focused on the questions of what "failure" means, how we are to know it when we see it, and what pitfalls are to be avoided in assessing it. Since techniques of statecraft are defined here as instruments for making influence attempts, it seems reasonable to assess their efficacy using standard power measurement concepts.

The Lump-of-Failure Fallacy

Robert Dahl refers to "The Lump-of-Power Fallacy" as the belief that power is "a single, solid, unbreakable lump."[52] The use of simple dichotomies, such as success or failure, to describe the outcome of an influence attempt tends to give an impression of lumpiness even when a few borderline cases are classified as "ambiguous" or "mixed." In the absence of a specific definition, what meanings might plausibly be attributed to the statement that economic statecraft "failed" in a given instance?

[49] Stevens, *Vain Hopes*, pp. 186-187.

[50] In a footnote Gilpin notes that "it may very well be that the increased destructiveness of modern weapons is responsible for the decreased cost of protection" (p. 163). Precisely the opposite is closer to the truth. It is the increased destructiveness of modern weapons that is responsible for the *increased* cost of protection by military means. On risks as costs of statecraft, see Schelling, *Strategy of Conflict*, pp. 177-178; Knorr, *Uses of Military Power*, pp. 12, 37-38, 80-137; and Baldwin, "Costs of Power," pp. 147-148. Ironically, Gilpin *includes* the risks of war in calculating the costs of economic sanctions. See Bienen and Gilpin, "Evaluation," p. I,8.

[51] For examples, see Knorr, *Power of Nations*, pp. 150-152, 180-181, 336, 338-339; Blessing, "Suspension of Foreign Aid"; and Peter Wallensteen, "Characteristics of Economic Sanctions."

[52] *Modern Political Analysis*, 3d ed., p. 26.

1. *The costs outweighed the benefits.*

Comment: Since costs are defined in terms of alternatives forgone, this implies that there was at least one alternative with more desirable consequences. Although this would be an acceptable way to view failure, it requires identification of the superior alternative—something that is rarely done.

2. *Another alternative would have been more effective.*

Comment: Although this meaning ignores costs, it at least focuses attention on alternative policies.

3. *The "minimum acceptable" degree of success was not attained.*

Comment: The primary difficulty with this meaning is determining the cut-off point. Some foreign policy goals, such as securing passage of a United Nations resolution, may seem like "either-or" situations; but most influence attempts by statesmen do not involve clear-cut indicators of minimum acceptable success.

4. *Some goals were not completely attained.*

Comment: This is the most common and the most misleading meaning. In statecraft, indeed, in most influence attempts of whatever kind, goals are usually approximated rather than reached. "Attainment of objectives," according to Simon, "is *always* a matter of degree."[53] When confronted with an observation that none of several cases of economic sanctions "has been wholly successful,"[54] the appropriate response is, "Has any influence attempt ever been wholly successful?" Although World War II is regarded by most Americans as a rather successful influence attempt from the standpoint of U.S. policy, it was hardly "wholly successful." Surely World War II would have been even more successful if it had been shorter, less costly in terms of lives and money, and so on.

In judging the success of influence attempts the concept of the "wholly successful" influence attempt is a snare and a delusion. More appropriate reference points would be the following principles: (1) influence is a matter of degree; and (2) "TANSTAAPIA" ("There ain't no such thing as a perfect influence attempt").

Multiple Dimensions of Power

Power varies not only in degree but on several dimensions, including scope, domain, and cost. Thus, a simple dichotomy of "success/failure" obscures not only variations in degree but also the various dimensions for measuring success. Establishing the intended scope and domain of an influence attempt is a basic first step in assessing effectiveness. This step

---

[53] Simon, *Administrative Behavior*, p. 177.
[54] Doxey, *Economic Sanctions*, 1st ed., p. 2.

is more difficult than is often recognized.[55] To view the use of economic statecraft strictly in terms of securing compliance with explicit and publicly stated demands is to load the dice in favor of failure. Third parties, secondary goals, implicit and unstated goals are all likely to be significant components of such undertakings.[56] Case studies from the Johnson administration show that implicit goals were sometimes more important than explicit ones and that "when all objectives are determined and attention given to them rather than solely to the objectives stated formally for the record, success is much more common than the critics of economic coercion have led us to believe."[57]

Another dimension of power is cost. Although both the costs of the would-be power wielder and the costs of the intended target are sometimes incorporated into the concept of power, only the latter are being considered a dimension of effectiveness here. To the extent that actor A can increase the costs to actor B of not doing X (or decrease the costs of doing X, which amounts to the same thing), A may be said to have power over B with respect to X.[58] Thus, to the extent that economic sanctions increase a target country's costs of noncompliance, power is being exerted *even though no change occurs in the policies of the target country*. Although this point is widely recognized by power analysts, it is not well understood by students of economic statecraft. Studies of economic sanctions, for instance, usually admit that costs are imposed on target countries by such measures but deny that influence is occurring unless an actual policy change occurs.[59] Thus, a typical conclusion is that sanctions succeeded in increas-

[55] Indeed, the step is not always taken. Renwick's discussion of the U.S. embargo against Cuba contains no reference to American goals other than describing the embargo as being "in response to developments in Cuba in the 1960's" (*Economic Sanctions*, pp. 64-66). Similarly, Donald L. Losman defines boycotts as "essentially political acts, representing instruments of foreign policy by which one state tries to bring about a change in the domestic or foreign policies of another"; but his analysis gives scant attention to determining what changes in which states the boycotts he studies are intended to bring about. (*International Economic Sanctions*, p. 1.)

[56] For a study that acknowledges the importance of multiple goals and targets but ignores them in its analysis, see Hufbauer and Schott, *Economic Sanctions*, esp. pp. 10-11, 29, 31, 42, 55.

[57] Weintraub, ed., *Economic Coercion*, pp. 57-58.

[58] See Harsanyi, "Measurement of Social Power," pp. 67-80; David A. Baldwin, "Inter-Nation Influence Revisited"; and "Costs of Power," pp. 151-153. Schelling asks whether "my adversary should buy a bullet knowing that I can nullify his investment with a bulletproof vest." He concludes that the adversary has "wasted his money if the vest is cheap, made a splendid investment if the vest is expensive, *and if asked what he accomplished by buying his bullet should have the good sense to say that he imposed a cost on me, not that he hoped to kill me and was frustrated*" ("The Strategy of Inflicting Costs," p. 111. Italics added).

[59] See Losman, *International Economic Sanctions*, pp. 44, 79, 124-125, 139; Renwick, *Economic Sanctions*, pp. 76-92; Harry R. Strack, *Sanctions*, pp. 238, 252-253; Bienen and Gilpin, "Evaluation," p. IIIe,2; and Adler-Karlsson, *Western Economic Warfare*, pp. 10, 213.

ing the costs of intransigence to the target but failed to produce a political effect. From the standpoint of conventional power analysis, however, *increased costs are political effects*. Not all influence is manifest in terms of changes in policy; changes in the costs of noncompliance also constitute influence. The tendency to overlook this point contributes to underestimating the effectiveness of economic statecraft.

This problem may also be viewed in terms of the target country's costs of compliance. The higher the costs of compliance, the more difficult the undertaking, and the higher the costs of noncompliance will have to be if the costs of compliance are to be offset by the influence attempt. This is just another way of saying that difficult things are harder to accomplish. This truism, however, is a reminder that levels of difficulty should be taken into account when assessing the effectiveness of an influence attempt. Just as competitive divers get extra points for difficult dives, so techniques of statecraft should be judged according to the difficulty of the task. Many of the best known applications of economic statecraft involve extraordinary levels of difficulty. Examples include the following:

1. Getting Italy to abandon its invasion of Ethiopia after it had already begun.
2. Getting Castro to step down.
3. Getting Israel to abolish itself.
4. Getting Rhodesian whites to accept majority rule.
5. Getting the Soviet Union to change its political system.
6. Promoting economic development and democracy in countries that have never known either.
7. Getting the United States to change its policy of support for Israel in response to a public demand based on an oil embargo.

In each case the cost of compliance was perceived as enormous by the target countries. To judge economic techniques of statecraft to be weak and ineffective because they could not produce such results is to ignore the difficulty of the undertaking and thereby to underrate the effectiveness of the policy instrument being used. The diver who executes a difficult dive poorly is not necessarily less competent than one who performs an easy dive well.

Observability of Success

Not all techniques of statecraft have effects that are easy to observe. Whereas the effects of military statecraft tend to be exaggerated, the effects of economic statecraft tend to be underestimated. In the case of military techniques, this bias is caused partly by the frequent failure to distinguish between destruction and influence. It is all too easy to be seduced by seemingly hard indicators of success, such as body counts, ships sunk, or villages controlled, while ignoring the overall purposes of the war. Phrases like "Pyrrhic victory," "destroying the village in order to save it," and "winning the war while losing the peace" suggest that the Tet offensive was not an isolated event but rather part of a long history of battles that seem to have been won but were really lost. The ability of military force to wreak spectacular death and destruction can lead observers to treat such effects as measures of success. This can be quite misleading; shooting a horse may indicate little or nothing about one's ability to lead him to water.

Economic statecraft has the opposite problem with respect to the salience of its effects. The effects of economic statecraft are rarely sudden or dramatic but rather tend to be slow, circuitous, and unexciting. "Economic variables," as Gilpin observes, "tend to be accretive. Although sudden and dramatic economic changes can and do take place, in general the influence of economic changes tends to be cumulative, building up over decades or even centuries."[60] This low profile makes it easy to overlook the effects of economic statecraft.

Another characteristic of economic statecraft that tends to obscure its effects is its intimate connection with organized markets. When exchange occurs outside a market, as in the case of disarmament negotiations, the process is clumsy and the quid pro quo is usually obvious; but when exchange takes place within a market, the dynamics of influence are often obscured. As Kenneth E. Boulding notes, "The organizing power of the market is so quiet and persistent that it is largely imperceptible."[61] To the extent that statesmen work through the market in making influence attempts, the effects of their efforts may be difficult to identify.

EXPLAINING EFFECTIVENESS

A power "base" refers to the causal condition that makes a successful influence attempt possible. The three most important things to remember about power bases are: (1) They may or may not correspond with the policy instrument used in making the influence attempt; that is, the success of economic techniques does not necessarily rest on economic bases of influence.[62] (2) They depend as much on the target's perceptions and values

---

[60] *War and Change*, p. 69. See also Kindleberger, *Power and Money*, p. 13; and David A. Baldwin, "Economic Power," in *Perspectives on Social Power*, ed. James T. Tedeschi (Chicago: Aldine, 1974), pp. 402-410.

[61] "The Economics of Human Conflict," in *The Nature of Human Conflict*, ed. Elton B. McNeil (Englewood Cliffs, N.J.: Prentice-Hall, 1965), p. 180. See also Kenneth E. Boulding, *A Primer on Social Dynamics: History as Dialectics and Development* (New York: Free Press, 1970), p. 26; and Baldwin, "Power and Social Exchange," p. 1232.

[62] It is also possible, of course, for noneconomic tools of statecraft to work through economic base values. Bombing factories is an obvious example, but more subtle uses are also possible. In the 1950s President Eisenhower was convinced that the Soviet military

as on the policy instrument used; e.g., threats work better against cowards than against masochists. (3) The bases of power are many, and no one of them is basic to all the others; e.g., military force is not the ultimate measuring rod in terms of which to measure all other power bases.[63] Harold D. Lasswell and Abraham Kaplan identify eight "base values" that can serve as bases of power, and any of these could serve as the causal condition of success for an influence attempt using economic techniques of statecraft.[64] Thus, a large number of explanations for success are conceivable. Consider the possibilities that follow:

1. *Power*—Economic statecraft may remind the target that the power wielder is a powerful state with other forms of power at its disposal. Compliance may be forthcoming not because of the immediate economic effects of the influence attempt but in order to forestall further influence attempts using noneconomic techniques. Perhaps the U.S. economic sanctions against Iran with respect to the hostage crisis served as a reminder to Iran and others of American power and determination.

2. *Respect*—Economic statecraft may be used to show respect, as in the conferring of most-favored-nation status, or to show disrespect, as when most-favored-nation status is denied or withdrawn.

3. *Rectitude*—Economic statecraft may be a means of expressing moral disapproval, as when sanctions are imposed on a human rights offender. It is conceivable, not to say likely, that the target state may care more about its moral standing in the international community than about the effects of such sanctions on its economic welfare.

4. *Affection*—Foreign aid, perhaps in response to a natural disaster, may generate feelings of affection for the donor that make the aid recipient want to reciprocate the favor.

5. *Well-being*—Economic sanctions may be used to communicate a threat of military attack, thus endangering the physical well-being of the target.

6. *Wealth*—The use of economic statecraft to threaten or damage the wealth of the target is, of course, the example most often

---

threat was intended to force upon the United States "an unbearable security burden leading to economic disaster. . . . Communist guns, in this sense, . . . [were aimed] at an economic target no less than a military target." (Quoted in Samuel P. Huntington, *The Common Defense* [New York: Columbia University Press, 1961], p. 66.)

[63] See chapters 2 and 4.

[64] *Power and Society*, pp. 86-92. It should be noted that Lasswell and Kaplan do not contend that the eight base values they discuss exhaust the list of possible base values.

cited. The use of positive sanctions to enhance the wealth of the target is less often noted, but it is also a possibility.

7.   *Skill*—Economic aid may be used to develop another country in order to demonstrate one's skill in such matters. Concern about demonstrating the efficacy of free enterprise in promoting economic development is not unknown among American foreign policy makers.

8.   *Enlightenment*—Foreign aid may be used to enlighten others through financing schools, scholarships, books, or technical advisers.

To discuss economic statecraft in terms of these eight base values is not intended to imply that the hypothetical examples cited are actual or likely cases. Rather, it is intended to illustrate the wide range of potential explanations for the success of an influence attempt using economic instruments. Most attempts to assess the effectiveness of economic statecraft consider only the economic power base.[65]

Johan Galtung's study of the effects of international economic sanctions against Rhodesia has been especially important in reinforcing the tendency to view such sanctions in terms of a single causal mechanism.[66] It not only is widely cited but is often treated as a basic reference point for discussions of economic sanctions.[67] A close look at Galtung's article, therefore, may be helpful in understanding much that has been written since 1967. Galtung defines the purpose of his study as being "in the direction of general theory. . . . a pilot study for a more thorough investigation both of the general theory of economic sanctions and other sanctions in the international system. . . . not as anything more pretentious" (pp. 378-379). He then proceeds to outline and criticize something he calls "the general theory of economic sanctions,"[68] which is based on a simple chain of causal reasoning: Economic value deprivation leads to economic distintegration, which leads to political disintegration, which in turn leads to compliance. Galtung points out two weaknesses in this theory. First, it ignores the

[65] See, for example, Hufbauer and Schott, *Economic Sanctions*, esp. p. 58. Losman is quite explicit about the causal conditions that permit economic sanctions to succeed: "For sanctions to be successful, . . . the economic damage inflicted *must* be sufficient to unleash domestic political pressures that will either topple an intransigent regime or bring about the adoption of new policies more in accord with the norms of boycotting nations" (p. 128, italics added). Precisely why this is the *only* way sanctions may work is not addressed by Losman. For a line of reasoning similar to Losman's, see Porter, "Economic Sanctions"; and Adler-Karlsson, "U.S. Embargo," p. 173.

[66] "On the Effects of International Economic Sanctions."

[67] For examples, see Bienen and Gilpin, "Evaluation," pp. I,1-5; Strack, *Sanctions*, pp. 11-15; and Olson, "Economic Coercion in World Politics," pp. 472-478.

[68] Later in the article he uses the phrase "theory of economic warfare," but there is no indication that this is different from "the theory of economic sanctions." Cf. pp. 388-393.

"rally round the flag" effect of increased political integration as a response to economic sanctions; and second, it ignores the many counter measures available to the target state that tend to nullify the degree of economic disintegration.

If Galtung's "general theory of economic sanctions" were interpreted as merely one causal mechanism through which economic sanctions might work—a not-so-general theory as it were—it would be a more useful contribution to understanding economic statecraft. Unfortunately, his reference to "*the* general theory of economic sanctions" (italics added) tends to give the impression either that there is some generally agreed upon body of literature setting forth this theory—so widely agreed upon, in fact, that none of it need be cited—or that there is no literature at all on the subject, thus giving Galtung a free hand in creating such a theory. Neither impression is accurate. Although some theoretical works on economic sanctions existed at the time Galtung was writing,[69] most of the literature was a hodge-podge of intuitive hunches, idealistic hopes, and specific policy prescriptions generated during the interwar period.[70] To call this "the general theory of economic sanctions" is stretching things more than a little.

To describe Galtung's ideas as a theory of *economic* sanctions is also somewhat misleading. Actually, a more accurate description is that he uses economic sanctions to illustrate some propositions about the role of negative sanctions in general. His theory of economic sanctions is of little or no help in distinguishing the effects of economic sanctions from those of noneconomic sanctions.[71] He specifically notes the similarities between his "theory of the effects of economic warfare" and the "theory of the effects of military warfare" (p. 388) and concludes "that very much of what we have said in this article about economic sanctions would apply *a fortiori*

---

[69] The three most important systematic theoretical works were Hirschman, *National Power and the Structure of Foreign Trade*; Wu, *Economic Warfare*; and Schelling, *International Economics*, pp. 487-532. None is cited by Galtung. The failure to cite Hirschman's work is an especially glaring omission since a large chunk of Galtung's article is devoted to developing the concept of economic vulnerability, ground that Hirschman had covered more cogently in 1945. Galtung (p. 386n) does cite Michael Michaely, *Concentration in International Trade* (Amsterdam: North-Holland, 1962), which uses some of Hirschman's ideas about how to measure trade concentration. Michaely's book, however, virtually ignores the main thrust of Hirschman's argument, which had to do with the political implications of international trade.

[70] For a bibliography of this literature, see Doxey, *Economic Sanctions*, 1st ed., pp. 149-153.

[71] To some extent the problem is conceptual. Galtung defines economic sanctions in terms of the type of value deprivation experienced by the target (pp. 381-383). In effect, this amounts to defining economic sanctions in terms of economic bases of power, thus making it impossible even to conceive of the possibility that economic sanctions might work through noneconomic causal mechanisms. See discussion in chapter 2.

to . . . other types of sanctions'' (p. 414). If this is true, of course, Galtung's general theory is not a theory of economic sanctions *per se* but rather a theory of (negative) sanctions *in general*. In a sense the point that really interests Galtung is demonstrating the limitations of negative sanctions and exhorting readers to direct their attention to positive sanctions. Subsequent commentators often overlook the general applicability of Galtung's argument and give the impression that his comments, especially on weaknesses, have some peculiar applicability to *economic* sanctions. The tendency of internal cohesion to increase when external negative sanctions are applied in highly publicized crisis situations, however—the "rally round the flag" effect—is a characteristic of *all* negative sanctions, including those based on propaganda, military force, and diplomacy. Although Galtung's article is brilliant and insightful, it can easily mislead one as to the causal conditions of success and the peculiar traits of economic sanctions.

A DOUBLE STANDARD?

This chapter has attempted to show how the concepts, the methods of comparing policy alternatives (or not comparing them), and the criteria used to define and measure success have tended to lead to overly pessimistic conclusions about the utility and/or effectiveness of economic techniques of statecraft. In concluding this chapter a number of propositions commonly found in writings about economic statecraft will be reviewed. The underlying question in each case is not so much the truth or falsity of these propositions but whether they imply an analytical double standard that hinders a fair and objective judgment of the utility and efficacy of economic statecraft.[72]

1. *The effects of economic sanctions are difficult to predict.*[73]

Comment: Of course this is true, but it in no way distinguishes economic sanctions from other techniques of statecraft.[74] Diplomacy may result in appeasement; propaganda may be misinterpreted; and military force may not have the intended effects. Capability analysis is tricky business.

---

[72] This list of propositions is illustrative rather than exhaustive. Although most are drawn from the final chapter of Renwick's study of economic sanctions, each is relatively easy to find elsewhere in the literature on economic statecraft. The precise wording of each proposition is not necessarily Renwick's, but the gist is the same. The choice of Renwick's study as a source for these propositions is especially appropriate since he is more sympathetic to economic techniques than most writers. Drawing these propositions from a friendly treatment of economic techniques illustrates that even the friends of economic statecraft tend to underestimate it.

[73] Renwick, *Economic Sanctions*, p. 77; Bienen and Gilpin, "Evaluation," p. IIIb,8. Cf. Knorr, *Power of Nations*, p. 140.

[74] See Gilpin, *War and Change*, p. 202; Knorr, *Power of Nations*, p. 22; and Osgood and Tucker, *Force, Order, and Justice*, pp. 255-256.

2. *The implementation of economic sanctions is beset by many difficulties.*[75]

Comment: It is not obvious that economic statecraft involves more administrative difficulties than other kinds of statecraft. Most modern states maintain professionally trained cadres to implement diplomacy and military statecraft, but few have similar staffs to administer economic statecraft. The fact that nation states find it necessary to maintain such professional cadres suggests the existence of implementation problems to be overcome. Furthermore, the difficulties of implementing economic sanctions may say more about the organization of contemporary states for the conduct of foreign affairs than about the inherent drawbacks of economic sanctions. It is usually easier to do something if one is organized to do it.

3. *The effectiveness of economic sanctions depends on the extent of national support for the policy.*[76]

Comment: True enough, but the same could be said of any other technique of statecraft. The Korean War, the Vietnam War, the Peloponnesian War, or World War II could be cited. When a diplomat says, "My countrymen would never stand for that," he is likely to be more effective if it is really true.

4. *Third parties may take steps to offset or nullify the effects of economic sanctions.*[77]

Comment: This shortcoming is not peculiar to economic measures. It is also a common response to influence attempts based on diplomacy or military force. Indeed, balance-of-power theory suggests that third party moves of this type are to be expected.

5. *Economic sanctions are likely to increase the degree of state intervention in the economy of the sanctioning state and/or the target state.*[78]

Comment: This trait would seem to differentiate between diplomacy and propaganda on the one hand and economic and military statecraft on the other. Whether it distinguishes between economic and military statecraft, however, is another matter. Nothing is so effective as war in injecting the state into economic life.[79]

6. *Economic sanctions work slowly.*[80]

[75] Renwick, *Economic Sanctions*, p. 78; Taubenfeld and Taubenfeld, "The 'Economic Weapon,' " pp. 197-202.

[76] Renwick, *Economic Sanctions*, p. 79.

[77] Ibid., pp. 79-80; Bienen and Gilpin, "Evaluation," p. IX,2; and Adler-Karlsson, "U.S. Embargo," p. 171.

[78] Renwick, *Economic Sanctions*, p. 80; and Condliffe, "Economic Power," p. 311. Condliffe takes the rather extreme position that "only when control of the domestic economy is absolute . . . [can] economic power . . . be used effectively in this way as an instrument of national policy" (p. 311).

[79] See Harrison, *Framework of Economic Activity*, pp. 37-39, 73-77; and Milward, *War, Economy and Society*, pp. 99-131.

[80] Renwick, *Economic Sanctions*, p. 81.

Comment: It seems difficult to contest this point, but caution is in order. Patience, it is often said, is desirable in a diplomat, thus suggesting that instant success is not necessarily to be expected from diplomacy. The same could probably be said of propaganda. Although military techniques can produce spectacular effects rapidly, the cases of Vietnam, the Arab-Israeli conflict, World War II, World War I, and the Peloponnesian War suggest that military statecraft may be overrated with respect to its ability to produce desired results speedily. Also, as the previous chapter pointed out, speed is not always a desirable trait in a technique of statecraft.

7.   *There is always a cost attached to economic sanctions.*[81]

Comment: The TANSTAAFL principle applies to all techniques of statecraft, not just the economic ones. When confronted with an assertion that economic statecraft entails "costs" or "high costs," the appropriate response is "Compared to what?" Neither diplomacy nor propaganda is costless, although they are usually cheaper than economic statecraft. In comparison with military statecraft, however, economic statecraft is almost always less expensive. It should also be reiterated that costliness can increase the effectiveness of a technique of statecraft in some situations.[82]

8.   *The costs of economic sanctions tend to be unevenly distributed.*[83]

Comment: Equitable cost sharing within or among states is difficult at best, no matter what policy instruments are used. Two points should be noted. First, the lack of a generally agreed upon measuring rod for costs makes it hard to divide them up fairly. Economic costs, however, *unlike noneconomic costs*, are measurable in terms of a standardized measure of value—money. Thus, other things being equal, costs of an influence attempt tend to be easier to measure and divide up the higher the proportion of economic costs to total costs. Although economic techniques are not the only type of statecraft involving economic costs, such costs probably tend to be relatively more important for economic statecraft than for noneconomic statecraft. To the extent that this is true, it should, in principle, be easier to share the costs of economic statecraft than to share the costs of any other type of technique if—and a big "if" it is—equitable cost sharing is desired by all. A second point to be noted is that the costs of war tend to be even more unevenly distributed than those of economic statecraft. In most societies such costs fall disproportionately on males between the ages of eighteen and thirty. Within the United States the costs of the Vietnam War were borne disproportionately by the young, the poor,

---

[81] Ibid.; Taubenfeld and Taubenfeld, "The 'Economic Weapon,' " p. 198; Bienen and Gilpin, "Evaluation," pp. II,8; VII,1; IX,1.

[82] See chapter 6.

[83] Renwick, *Economic Sanctions*, p. 82; Bienen and Gilpin, "Evaluation," p. II,9; Taubenfeld and Taubenfeld, "The 'Economic Weapon,' " pp. 198-200; and von Amerongen, "Commentary," pp. 159-167.

the nonwhite, the male, and the less well educated parts of the population.[84] By comparison, the effects of President Carter's grain embargo were probably distributed much more fairly. In 1915 a report on economic sanctions prepared by the U.S. Chamber of Commerce commented, "to the contention that . . . [economic sanctions] would bear with undue hardship upon individuals of special trades and industries, it may be replied that so does war."[85] This telling response, which has been neglected in the ensuing decades, deserves reiteration today. Before bemoaning the difficulties of sharing the costs of economic statecraft equitably, it is wise to consider the alternatives.

9. *Economic sanctions may have undesirable side effects on neighboring countries.*[86]

Comment: Any technique of statecraft may have such side effects in some situations. Military statecraft is especially prone to have such effects—ask the inhabitants of Cambodia, Laos, or Thailand about the side effects of the Vietnam War! Ask anyone in the world about the potential side effects of the Cuban missile crisis! There is no conceivable use of economic statecraft that endangers the human race the way military statecraft can.

10. *Economic sanctions may be difficult to terminate.*[87]

Comment: This point is usually made with reference to sanctions imposed by international organizations. It calls attention to aspects of the decision-making process in such organizations, but it says little about economic sanctions *per se*. World War I, World War II, the Vietnam War, the Korean War, the Arab-Israeli conflict, and disarmament negotiations do not provide much assurance that difficulty of termination is peculiar to influence attempts using economic sanctions. As a general rule, wars are almost always harder to terminate than economic measures.

11. *Economic sanctions may have perverse (counterproductive) effects on the target country.*[88]

Comment: Supportive evidence is not hard to find, but it is not clear that economic techniques are more likely to have such effects than other kinds of statecraft.[89] Diplomatic efforts to appease may generate contempt;

[84] See Lawrence M. Baskir and William A. Strauss, *Chance and Circumstance: The Draft, the War, and the Vietnam Generation* (New York: Alfred A. Knopf, 1978).

[85] Quoted in Evans Clark, ed., *Boycotts and Peace* (New York: Harper, 1932), p. 245.

[86] Renwick, *Economic Sanctions*, pp. 82-83.

[87] Ibid., pp. 83-84.

[88] Ibid., p. 85; Doxey, *Economic Sanctions*, 1st ed., pp. 121, 126-127; Strack, *Sanctions*, p. 13; Bienen and Gilpin, "Evaluation," pp. IX,1; and Adler-Karlsson, "U.S. Embargo," pp. 172, 185-187.

[89] Some of the "evidence" cited, however, is not especially convincing. Renwick, for example, notes that in the case of Italy "the loss of exports [caused by League of Nations sanctions] was accompanied by a cutback in imports which actually resulted in an *improvement*

propaganda may engender skepticism and mistrust; and military force may have perverse effects, such as the famous statement of the need to destroy a Vietnamese city in order to save it. Investment in military statecraft may well have been a counterproductive investment for Japan in the twentieth century.[90]

12. *Economic sanctions may stiffen the will to resist in the target country.*[91]

Comment: Influence attempts involving highly publicized negative sanctions in a confrontational situation are likely to evoke this response *no matter what form they take.*[92] No matter how true this is of economic sanctions, it is probably even more true of military sanctions. Nothing unifies a country faster or more effectively than military attack. Dependency theorists might even point out that quietly implemented economic sanctions often divide the target country rather than unite it and may weaken rather than strengthen its will to resist the influence attempt.[93]

13. *Economic sanctions do not automatically bring about the desired political effects.*[94]

Comment: To state this proposition is to imply that some serious people believe that the desired political effects will automatically follow from economic sanctions. I have never been able to identify such a person. The important thing here is to make it clear that the TANSTAAPIA principle applies to all forms of statecraft.

14. *Economic sanctions are often accompanied by overly optimistic public expectations of success.*[95]

Comment: In democracies it is often necessary for policy makers to "oversell" in order to generate domestic support for a foreign policy undertaking. Whether this tends to be more true of economic techniques than of other kinds of statecraft is not obvious. Arguments in favor of quiet, behind-the-scenes diplomacy often seem to grow out of fears that diplomatic techniques are also vulnerable to excessive optimism. In the

---

in the trade balance" (p. 85). Any sovereign state, of course, can achieve such an "improvement" by simply stopping all imports and exports, thereby achieving instant and perfect balance—zero in and zero out!

[90] Kenneth E. Boulding and Alan H. Gleason, "War as an Investment: The Strange Case of Japan," in *Economic Imperialism*, ed. Kenneth E. Boulding and Tapan Mukerjee (Ann Arbor: University of Michigan Press, 1972), pp. 240-261.

[91] Renwick, *Economic Sanctions*, p. 88; Galtung, "International Economic Sanctions," pp. 388-391; Losman, *International Economic Sanctions*, p. 131; Bienen and Gilpin, "Evaluation," pp. II,13-14, IX,1; and Adler-Karlsson, "U.S. Embargo," pp. 172, 176.

[92] See Baldwin, "The Power of Positive Sanctions," pp. 32-33.

[93] See Olson, "Economic Coercion in World Politics," pp. 479-485.

[94] Renwick, *Economic Sanctions*, p. 89; Losman, *International Economic Sanctions*, p. 139.

[95] Renwick, *Economic Sanctions*, pp. 77, 91-92.

early stages of the Vietnam War the American public was often led to believe that there was "light at the end of the tunnel" or that the "troops would be home by Christmas," indicating that unrealistic expectations are not the exclusive province of economic statecraft.

15. *Economic sanctions increase international tensions and thereby increase the probability of war.*[96]

Comment: Compared to propaganda and diplomacy this proposition seems to hold, at least in most situations. Compared to military statecraft its validity is dubious at best. The surest way to get into a war with most countries is to attack them. The question of whether appeasement or deterrence is the better way to prevent war lies outside the scope of this book. It is important to recognize, however, that this question is separate from that of whether economic sanctions cause war. Policy makers can stand up to a potential aggressor with diplomacy, propaganda, economic statecraft, or military force. In any case, the strategy of confrontation is likely to be more important than the particular policy instrument used. There are many ways to increase international tension.

16. *Economic sanctions are more effective when used in conjunction with other techniques of statecraft.*[97]

Comment: This is true, of course; but it is not the peculiar deficiency of economic statecraft it is often implied to be. To evaluate economic warfare during World Wars I and II in terms of whether such measures alone could have ensured victory is pointless and misleading. Pointless because the answer is obvious and misleading to the extent that a peculiar limitation of economic statecraft is implied. The same could be said—but rarely is—about the infantry, the artillery, or aerial bombardment. The relevant question is not whether economic measures were "decisive"— whatever that may mean—but whether they had a significant effect on the length, outcome, or intensity of the war. Actually, any technique of statecraft works poorly in isolation from the others. War without diplomacy is likely to become pointless butchery, and diplomacy that is not backed up by implicit or explicit threats or promises of using other techniques of statecraft is not very effective. More generally, Lasswell and Kaplan note that this proposition is applicable to all forms of power:

> The forms of power are interdependent: a certain amount of several forms of power is a necessary condition for a great amount of any form. . . . Each form of power always involves a number of others,

[96] Ibid., p. 23; Bienen and Gilpin, "Evaluation," p. IIIa,9; and Grieve, "Economic Sanctions," p. 433.

[97] Condliffe, "Economic Power," pp. 305-314; James Barber, "Economic Sanctions," p. 367; Renwick, *Economic Sanctions*, pp. 72-73; and Carr, *The Twenty Years' Crisis*, pp. 118, 132.

to degrees and in ways which must be separately determined, in principle, in each case. . . . In short, none of the forms of power can stand alone: each requires, for its acquisition as well as maintenance, the simultaneous exercise of other forms of power as well.[98]

The sixteen propositions stated above and others like them pervade the literature on economic statecraft. Individual authors, no doubt, could point to particular qualifications that are ignored in the foregoing formulations. The point, however, is not to consider the precise wording of each individual author but rather to convey the overall pattern of such comments. Most of these propositions are true in some sense of that word; yet in context they can easily give the impression that some peculiar characteristic of economic statecraft is being discussed, something that differentiates it from noneconomic forms of statecraft. Most of these propositions are as applicable to noneconomic as to economic statecraft, *mutatis mutandis*; and this is precisely the problem. It is, of course, important for policy makers to understand the general characteristics of techniques of statecraft; but it is more important for them to know the distinctive traits of different kinds of statecraft. For, unlike academics and journalists, policy makers must choose among alternative techniques. If academics and journalists are to say something about economic statecraft that is potentially useful to policy makers, they must clearly label comments applicable to statecraft in general as opposed to those that differentiate one kind of statecraft from another. If propositions similar to those enumerated above were as common in discussions of other techniques of statecraft, especially military ones, as they are in discussions of economic statecraft, the problem would be less acute. Unfortunately, this is not the case; therein lies the analytical "double standard." In assessing the utility of economic statecraft, writers are prone to accentuate the negative and downplay the positive aspects of such measures.

[98] *Power and Society*, pp. 92-94. They cite R. H. Tawney and Bertrand Russell in support of their position that economic power is not the fundamental form of power from which other forms, such as war and propaganda, derive. This reaction to the economic determinism of the 1930s is likely to seem odd to the contemporary reader immersed in the military determinism of the postwar world.

CHAPTER 8

"CLASSIC CASES" RECONSIDERED

Our government is being charged by Soviet
statesmen with practicing "dollar diplomacy,"
meaning presumably the use of our financial
resources as an instrument of our high foreign
policy. In this sense, all of the great Powers of
modern times have at one time or another practiced
financial diplomacy.[1]

* * *

I think I can claim to have written one of the
shortest serious letters to The Times *(published*
December 10, 1966). It read: "Have sanctions
against any country ever worked?" I received a
number of long replies direct, all *of which asserted*
that the answer was "No."
(G. C. Bird, letter to the editor, *The Times*
(London), November 17, 1980)

A few cases have received so much attention in discussions of economic statecraft that they might well be dubbed "classic cases." They include the League of Nations sanctions against Italy (1935–1936), the United States embargo against Japan (1940–1941), the restrictions on trade with communist countries imposed by the United States and Western Europe (1948–the present), United States sanctions against Cuba (1960 to the present), and the United Nations sanctions against Rhodesia (1966–1979). These cases are mentioned with great frequency and are usually cited as examples of the failure of such measures.[2] Indeed, these cases form the bedrock on which the conventional wisdom about economic statecraft rests. The purpose of this chapter is to review these "classic cases" from the analytical perspective developed in previous chapters.[3] The word "review" is used advisedly, since there is no intent to provide full-blown, detailed case studies, but rather to evaluate existing case studies in terms of this analytical perspective. The intent is not to prove that economic statecraft

---

[1] Viner, *International Economics*, p. 341.

[2] All of these cases are mentioned by Wallensteen, "Characteristics of Economic Sanctions"; Knorr, *The Power of Nations*; and Bienen and Gilpin, "Evaluation." All except the U.S.–Japan case are treated by Doxey, *Economic Sanctions*.

[3] The anticommunist trade embargo will be reviewed in the following chapter.

"succeeded" in these instances, but rather that the cases do not provide the "clear-cut," "obvious," "self-evident," "indisputable," "overwhelming" historical support for the alleged ineffectiveness or uselessness of economic techniques that is often implied. Before considering particular cases, however, some general characteristics of the case study approach should be noted.

CASE STUDIES: GENERAL CONSIDERATIONS

History does not present itself tied up in neat bundles of facts clearly labeled "case no. 1," "case no. 2," etc. The boundaries that delimit a particular case are not "discovered" by the researcher; they are created by him. This has some implications that deserve emphasis. The number of historical "cases" of economic statecraft is limited only by the imagination of the analyst. One analyst may treat World War II as a single instance of economic warfare, while another may treat each day of the war or each bilateral interstate relationship as a separate case. The Marshall Plan could be treated as a single instance of economic aid, or, if treated country by country and year by year, it could be viewed as subsuming more than sixty cases. The U.S. embargo against Cuba could be broken into individual years or even decades, and the embargo imposed by the Western allies on communist states over three decades could be broken down in terms of time periods (days, years, decades?), states involved (United States–Soviet Union, France–Hungary, etc.), or commodities (food, medicine, military hardware, technology, toys, etc.) to which the embargo applies. None of these is an inherently silly way to delimit a case; each could be useful for certain purposes. There is no one "right way" to do it. It does suggest, however, that the number of possible "cases" is infinite and that any claim to have studied *all* the cases of economic statecraft in a given period of time should be viewed with suspicion.[4]

The artificial nature of cases also suggests wariness about attempts to compare the number of "successful" cases with the number of cases of "failure." What is one to do when a leading text tells students that "one study of 18 cases in which total economic sanctions were employed . . . indicates that only two worked effectively"?[5] Should it be pointed out that these cases include Soviet sanctions against Yugoslavia (1948–1955), which Knorr treats as two separate cases; the League of Nations sanctions against Italy, which lasted nine months; and the Western allies' embargo

[4] For example, see Wallensteen, "Characteristics of Economic Sanctions," p. 249. See also Robert Gilpin's testimony: "A colleague and I did a long study of this subject about 18 months ago and looked at all past cases of economic sanctions. . . ." (U.S. Senate, Committee on Finance, *U.S. International Trade Strategy: Hearings*, p. 160.)

[5] K. J. Holsti, *International Politics*, 3d ed., p. 252. Holsti is referring to Wallensteen's article.

on the Soviet Union and China, which had been in existence for two decades at the time the study was published? What are we to make of Knorr's twenty-two cases of trade sanctions, of which four "succeeded" and thirteen "clearly failed"? Knorr infers from this that "the dramatic use of economic power in the form of trade restrictions [is] apt to fail in the large majority of instances."[6] Such an inference, however, implies that the cases are comparable; yet the list treats the Arab oil embargo of 1973 as two separate cases, one directed against the United States and another against the countries of western Europe and Japan.[7] Similarly, Knorr identifies twenty-five "notorious cases" of actual or threatened aid cutoffs occurring since World War II, of which two "succeeded," nineteen "failed," and four had mixed results. This leads Knorr to observe that "the historical record does not establish the coercive use of foreign economic or military aid as a generally effective measure" (pp. 180-181). Even ignoring the possibility that twenty-five notorious post–World War II cases may not coincide with "the historical record," this is a questionable inference. One case, for example, includes the U.S. threat to cut aid to its European allies if they did not support the anticommunist embargo. This threat was directed at sixteen countries over a period of several years and, as Knorr admits, was successful as long as the target countries were dependent on U.S. aid. Thus, it could be treated as sixteen (successful!) influence attempts per year, an approach that would change Knorr's "historical record" significantly. Since Knorr treats U.S. aid cutoffs to Peru from 1965 to 1969 as four separate cases of failure, it might have been appropriate to treat the U.S. threat against its allies in a similar manner.[8] The point here is not to suggest that Knorr is wrong, but rather to point out that attempts to establish a scoreboard of "successes" and "failures" may be misleading if cases are not defined in a comparable way. One man's case may be another man's sixteen cases.

Some ways of delimiting cases have implications that make economic statecraft seem less useful than it is. Two of these concern the relation between low salience and effectiveness and the actor's perspective. It is often asserted that well-publicized influence attempts based on clear-cut demands are less likely to succeed since compliance is more difficult for the target state.[9] This has prompted some writers to suggest that case studies of economic statecraft based on well-publicized confrontations—e.g., all

[6] Knorr, *Power of Nations*, p. 152.

[7] Ibid., p. 336. For another example of a study that attempts to make statistical generalizations about "cases," some of which lasted less than a year and some of which lasted more than thirty years, see Hufbauer and Schott, *Economic Sanctions*.

[8] *Power of Nations*, pp. 338-339. It is especially difficult to compare threats to cut off aid with actual aid suspensions.

[9] See Weintraub, ed., *Economic Coercion*, pp. 19, 23, 50; Olson, "Economic Coercion in World Politics," pp. 473, 477, 479, 483-485; and Knorr, *Power of Nations*, p. 156.

of the "classic cases," all of Knorr's twenty-two cases of trade sanctions, and all of Knorr's twenty-five "notorious" aid suspensions—may lead to overly pessimistic estimates of the efficacy of economic techniques.[10] To the extent that economic statecraft is more likely to work through low-profile, continuous processes than other techniques of statecraft there may be a tendency to underestimate its efficacy. Whether this bias is more applicable to economic than to noneconomic policy tools, however, is a question that should not be prejudged. Until further research has been conducted on this topic, it is well to treat this as an open question.

The perspective of the actor making the influence attempt is usually taken for granted in constructing a case study of economic statecraft; yet this dimension is not "dictated" by the situation, but rather "chosen" by the analyst. Thus, typical interpretations are the following:

> *USSR-Yugoslavia.*   The Soviet Union used economic sanctions in attempts to squelch Tito's independence between 1948 and 1958, but each time these attempts failed because Western countries were willing to step in and help Yugoslavia.
>
> *U.S.-Cuba.*   The United States used economic sanctions in an attempt to topple Castro and/or to change his foreign policy, but this attempt failed because the Soviet Union stepped in and helped Cuba.
>
> *UN-Rhodesia.*   The United Nations used economic sanctions in an attempt to topple the white regime and/or to get it to accept majority rule, but this attempt failed because South Africa stepped in and helped Rhodesia.

Each of these cases involves not one but two influence attempts. On the one hand, economic statecraft is used by the first party in an attempt to influence the second party; and on the other hand, a third party is also using economic techniques in an attempt to nullify the influence attempt of the first party. In terms of the zero-sum assumptions implied by most such analyses, if the first party's influence attempt is classified as a failure, the third party's influence attempt should be judged as a success—but it never is. When the efficacy of economic statecraft is added up, these cases are usually recorded as three failures rather than as three failures and three successes. It is as if the efficacy of military force were to be assessed solely by looking at wars from the losers' point of view. If this were done, of course, the conventional wisdom about the effectiveness of military statecraft might be somewhat different. Since history tends to be written by war winners, however, one suspects that there may be an understandable tendency to exaggerate the utility of military force as a technique of state-

---

[10] Weintraub, ed., *Economic Coercion*, p. 23; Olson, "Economic Coercion in World Politics," p. 485; and Baldwin, "Economic Power," p. 408.

craft. Whether a telescope makes things larger or smaller depends on which end of it one looks through, and whether a case of economic statecraft succeeds or fails may depend on which actor's perspective one adopts.

Before examining particular cases, it would be well to summarize the analytical perspective developed in previous chapters. This will be done by presenting a checklist of questions one should ask when evaluating a case study of economic statecraft.

1. *Has the policy-contingency framework been carefully established at the beginning?*[11]   The single most important step in capability analysis is establishing who is trying to get whom to do what. Since goals are taken as given, one should be able to assess the efficacy or utility of economic techniques to Hitler without endorsing his goals. Likewise, one's assessment of the utility of economic statecraft to the United States in dealing with the Soviet Union or Cuba should not be colored by approval or disapproval of U.S. policy goals.[12] (Beware of discussions that disguise underlying disagreement with policy goals as attacks on the means used.) One indicator of care in constructing a policy-contingency framework is the positing of multiple targets and objectives. Statesmen may sometimes undertake an influence attempt with only one goal and one target in mind, but this is surely the exception rather than the rule.

2. *Is the level of difficulty taken into account?*

3. *Is the utility of economic statecraft discussed in terms of alternative policy options?* (Beware of "it hurts us more than it hurts them.")

4. *Is success treated as a matter of degree?* (Beware of dichotomies and "obvious," "total," "clear-cut," "complete," or "absolute" failures.)

5. *Are the generalizations commensurate with the evidence?* (Beware of leaps from examination of a few atypical cases to "history teaches us that," "the historical record suggests that," or "the overwhelming historical evidence is that" economic statecraft does not work.)

6. *Does the author allow for multiple bases of power?* (Beware of the contention that sanctions must bite in order to work.)

7. *Are certain foreign policy goals treated as inherently inferior or*

[11] On policy-contingency frameworks and capability analysis, see Sprout and Sprout, *The Ecological Perspective on Human Affairs*; and Baldwin, "Power Analysis."

[12] This is not a matter of asserting that complete objectivity is possible. Of course, it is not; but one can at least *try* to be as objective as possible.

perhaps even as "unreal"? (Beware of the tendency to denigrate symbolic goals.)
8. *Are the costs of noncompliance treated as a measure of power?* (Beware of "although the sanctions imposed great costs on the target, the influence attempt was a total failure.")
9. *Is the relevance of counterfactual conditions acknowledged?* It is not easy to estimate what Castro's foreign policy would have been in the absence of U.S. sanctions, but no meaningful statement about the efficacy of U.S. policy can be made without such an estimate.

With this checklist in mind let us turn to particular cases.

THE MEGARIAN DECREE

In 432 B.C., Athens imposed a trade boycott on Megara, a Spartan ally, excluding her from access to ports in the Athenian empire and the market of Athens. The subsequent refusal to lift the boycott in response to pressure from Sparta was popularly believed to have caused the Peloponnesian War. Although this case is not one of the "classic cases" underlying the conventional wisdom, it is worth discussing for three reasons. First, it is a valuable reminder that economic sanctions are not a twentieth-century phenomenon. Second, the case is considered by Thucydides, who has had a profound and lasting influence on thinking about international politics.[13] And third, the case is sometimes used to buttress the contention that economic sanctions are costly and ineffective techniques of statecraft.[14]

According to Bienen and Gilpin:

It was the imposition of the Athenian trade boycott of Megara and Athens' refusal to lift it in response to the Spartan ultimatum that precipitated the Great Peloponnesian War which led to the weakening of Greek civilization and its eventual conquest by Macedonian imperialism.

The point of this dramatic event is that the imposition, the compliance with, or even the lifting of a trade boycott of whatever magnitude involves unanticipated and potentially very high costs. A trade boycott is an act of economic warfare and, as is the case in any act of war, should not be undertaken lightly.[15]

[13] Thucydides, *The History of the Peloponnesian War*, trans. Crawley (New York: Modern Library, 1951), pp. 78-83.

[14] Bienen and Gilpin, "Evaluation," pp. I,7-8. See also Gilpin, *War and Change*, p. 218; and U.S. Senate, Committee on Banking, Housing, and Urban Affairs, *Hearings: U.S. Embargo of Food and Technology to the Soviet Union*, 96th Cong., 2d sess., 1980, p. 169.

[15] Bienen and Gilpin, "Evaluation," p. I,8. Hufbauer and Schott portray the decree as

Although Bienen and Gilpin may be right in linking the Megarian Decree with the fall of Greek civilization, the argument of Thucydides runs counter to such an interpretation. The majority of ancient popular opinion regarded the Megarian Decree as the main cause of the war, but then, as now, public opinion as to the causes of war was likely to commit the *post hoc ergo propter hoc* fallacy. Thucydides was well aware of this widespread popular belief and was attempting to refute it.

> It is precisely the prevalence of this interpretation, we may suspect, that explains Thucydides treatment of the Megarian Decree. . . . [The] Thucydidean account of the causes of war is a "latent polemic" against the popular interpretation. Thucydides was persuaded that the war was inevitable from the time Athens became an imperial power. He was convinced that forces were at work beyond the control of individuals. . . . Although he believed this was generally true, it was especially important to emphasize it in the case of Athens, for there the vulgar view had taken hold that one man, Pericles, had brought on the war by rigid adherence to a single policy, the affirmation of the Megarian Decree. To his mind that interpretation was altogether wrong. The decree was really a measure in the preliminary maneuverings of a war that was already determined, if not in progress. . . . The slight importance he allotted to the decree was a most artistic way of making the point of its insignificance. His intelligent readers would not miss the point.[16]

Thucydides reacted to popular opinion about the way a contemporary college professor would react to an undergraduate paper blaming World War I on the assassination of an Archduke. Indeed the speech he attributes to Pericles explaining why the boycott should not be lifted sounds as if it had been written by Thomas Schelling. The excerpt from Thucydides quoted by Bienen and Gilpin is as follows:

> I hope that you will none of you think that we shall be going to war for a trifle if we refuse to revoke the Megara Decree, . . . the revocation of which is to save us from war. . . . Why, this trifle contains the whole seal and trial of your resolution. If you give way, you will instantly have to meet some greater demand, as having been frightened into obedience in the first instance; while a firm refusal

---

having "contributed to the Peloponnesian War" (*Economic Sanctions*, p. 23). The question of whether the boycott did in fact constitute an "act of war" will not be taken up here. For a cogent argument that the boycott did not constitute a breach of the peace, see Donald Kagan, *The Outbreak of the Peloponnesian War* (Ithaca, N.Y.: Cornell University Press, 1969), pp. 266-267.

[16] Kagan, *Peloponnesian War*, p. 271.

will make them clearly understand that they must treat you more as equals.[17]

Pericles' point is that it is unwise to establish a precedent for willingness to negotiate under duress. He argues that the particular issue at hand is essentially irrelevant, since the important task is to send a message to Sparta. If it were not this issue, it would be some other issue, he is saying. The issue here is willingness to negotiate under duress, not economic sanctions.[18]

Thucydides, of course, may have misjudged the wisdom of Pericles, whom he greatly admired. The Megarian Decree may be viewed as an instance of economic statecraft without becoming entangled in Thucydides' theories about the causes of war. Although Gilpin notes that the decree "sought to bring economic ruin to the Megarians,"[19] this does not provide an adequate policy-contingency framework. One must ask how this goal related to overall Athenian foreign policy and why economic instruments of statecraft were used. Donald Kagan suggests that the problem arose because Megara joined Corinth in fighting against Corcyra, an ally of Athens, at Sybota.[20] At the time Corinth was trying to involve other members of the Peloponnesian League in her quarrel with Athens, but the Spartans were opposed to this. Thus, Megara's action was not only a hostile act toward Athens but also one that had been carried out against the advice of Sparta. Thus, if Pericles wanted to avoid war, there was no easy or obvious way to do it. If he allowed the Megarian attack to go unpunished, Sparta might find it increasingly difficult to keep other League members from joining Corinth the next time; but if he were to yield to domestic hawkish pressure for a military attack on Megara, Sparta would have little choice other than to come to the aid of her ally. By choosing the middle ground between military attack and doing nothing, he might be able to avoid a technical breach of the peace and thus give Sparta an excuse to stay out of it. After all, if Megara had followed Sparta's advice, she would not have incurred Athenian wrath.

Pericles' choice of economic sanctions, therefore, could be viewed as

[17] Thucydides, *History* (Modern Library ed.), pp. 79-80.

[18] For a similar interpretation of this passage, see Osgood and Tucker, *Force, Order, and Justice*, p. 201. Indeed, Gilpin seems to agree with this interpretation, but he fails to recognize that it conflicts with his assertion that the Megara Decree precipitated the war. Cf. Gilpin, *War and Change*, pp. 93, 191, 199-200, 218, 236.

[19] Gilpin, *War and Change*, p. 218n. The description by Hufbauer and Schott (*Economic Sanctions*, pp. 4, 23) of the decree as in response to Megarian expansion and the kidnapping of three women is equally unsatisfactory.

[20] Kagan, *Peloponnesian War*, pp. 265-266. The discussion here is based on ibid., pp. 251-272.

a prudent and sophisticated influence attempt with multiple goals and targets along the following lines:

Message to Megara.   Those who join Corinth in opposing us will be punished. If you do it again, punishment could be worse next time.

Message to Friends of Corinth.   Beware, what happened to Megara could happen to you.

Message to Corinth.   Beware, after what happened to Megara, members of the League will be less eager to help you in your quarrel with us.

Message to Sparta.   Naturally, we could not allow an attack on our ally to go unpunished, but note the moderation of our response, which is intended to reassure you of our desire to avoid war with you. Note also, however, that the sanctions have weakened your ally, Megara, thus strengthening our strategic position and making war with us even less advisable than it was before.

Message to Athenian allies.   You can count on us to retaliate against your enemies, as we did against the Megarians.

The scenario presented by Sir Alfred Zimmern is slightly different from the one depicted above but is similar in its emphasis on Sparta as an additional target—perhaps even the primary target—and in portraying the Megarian Decree as an attempt to prevent war by signaling a threat. Zimmern even suggests that the immediate economic impact on Megara was substantial:

Pericles was not anxious for war, but he rightly felt that the city had gone too far to draw back. . . . There was only one possible way by which war might yet be averted—by a display of Athenian power which might serve as an object-lesson to the Peloponnesians as to the nature of the war on which they were being asked to engage. Pericles determined to give a demonstration of what sea-power really meant. The victims selected for the purpose were the Megarians, against whom Athens had had a grudge ever since they had ungratefully deserted her alliance and butchered their Athenian garrison at a moment of grave difficulty thirteen years before. A decree of boycott was issued closing all the harbours of the Empire and all the markets of Attica to Megarian ships and Megarian goods. Thus at a single blow Megara was practically isolated from the world, and thrown back for her subsistence upon the old self-sufficient agricultural basis. How severely she felt the pinch we know, not only by the part she played in the final deliberations at Sparta, but by Aristophanes' picture of the poor Megarian who disguises his daughters as pigs and smuggles them across the border into the Athenian market for sale. What Athens could do for Megara she could do also, so soon as war was declared, for the other maritime cities of the Peloponnesian League, and Pericles was anxious that, in their councils of war, this fact should be duly weighed.

The Spartans were frightened, as well they might be.[21]

Although Pericles' action failed to deter war, the probability of war was fairly great to begin with; and perhaps nothing he could have done would have avoided it. Given the tense and complex situation, the imposition of economic sanctions may well have been the policy option with the highest probability of success—even though it was very low. Taking into consideration the difficulty of the task, the policy alternatives available, and the complexity of the situation, it seems as plausible to say that the Peloponnesian War occurred *despite* Pericles' prudent—perhaps even ingenious—attempt to head it off via the Megarian Decree as it does to say that the decree "precipitated" the war.

The League of Nations

When Italy invaded Ethiopia in October 1935, the League of Nations, in accordance with Article 16 of its Covenant, imposed economic sanctions consisting of a boycott of Italian products and a limited embargo. When the sanctions were lifted nine months later, they were generally viewed as having failed and have been so regarded ever since. Indeed, since 1936 the very mention of economic sanctions calls up memories of the League's great debacle.[22] These memories have colored thinking about economic sanctions for more than forty years.

"It was impossible to avoid the impression," writes Martin Wight, "that failure to impose effective sanctions against Italy in 1935–36 was a turning point in international history that has conditioned everything since, a seminal failure, the generator of a whole series of other failures."[23] The

[21] Sir Alfred Zimmern, *The Greek Commonwealth*, 5th ed. (London: Oxford University Press, 1931), pp. 426-427.

[22] In 1980, after President Carter had used economic sanctions in response to the Iranian seizing of hostages and the Soviet invasion of Afghanistan, a spate of articles appeared in the popular press explaining why sanctions do not work, and nearly all cited the League sanctions as evidence. See Donald L. Losman, "Those Sanctions Just Won't Work," *Philadelphia Inquirer*, May 1, 1980; Ann Crittenden, "Warfare: Trade as a Weapon," *New York Times*, January 13, 1980; "Economic Sanctions: An Obsolete Weapon?" *Forbes*, February 18, 1980; and Roger Fisher, "Sanctions Won't Work," *Newsweek*, January 14, 1980.

[23] Martin Wight, *Power Politics*, ed. Hedley Bull and Carsten Holbraad (New York: Holmes and Meier, 1978), p. 208.

association of economic sanctions with this important historical turning point, however, has not encouraged objective evaluation of the utility of this technique of statecraft. In the 1930s economic sanctions was a codeword for fundamental differences of opinion about international relations. To be favorably disposed toward economic sanctions was to be pro-League and antiwar. Although the original drafters of the League Covenant had envisioned military and economic sanctions as mutually reinforcing measures, the Pact of Paris (Kellogg-Briand Pact, 1928), in which states renounced war as an instrument of national policy, strengthened the view that economic sanctions were to be used instead of military force. In a sense this was true, since the Covenant implied that the *initial response* to aggression should be economic *rather than* military; but this was more a matter of timing than of principle.[24]

In the 1930s there was little or no interest in assessing the utility of economic sanctions as a general foreign policy instrument; the only question that mattered was how to deter or respond to aggression. The underlying issue was what role, if any, military force should play in national policy. The failure to stop Mussolini's invasion of Ethiopia and the coming of World War II seemed to vindicate those who had warned that the democracies were lacking in military preparedness. Since the primary arguments against an arms build-up had emphasized reliance on the League and economic sanctions, it was understandable that those who believed it foolhardy and naive to abandon force as an instrument of national policy should focus their attention on discrediting the proposed alternative to military force—economic sanctions.

The "realist" school of international relations emerged after World War II largely as a reaction to the overly optimistic expectations associated with the League of Nations. It was the "utopian" ideas associated with the League that provided grist for the "realists'" mill; therefore, it was only natural that economic sanctions, as the policy instrument most closely identified with the League in the public mind, should also be denounced. Whereas military force symbolized hard-headed "realism," economic sanctions symbolized fuzzy-minded "idealism" and unwillingness to face up to the hard facts of international life.

The alleged failure of the League's sanctions against Italy has been blamed for contributing to both the breakdown of the League and the onset of World War II; yet neither charge is fair. Although the sanctions against Italy called attention to the weaknesses of the League, they were not responsible for them. In the first place, the League envisioned in the

---

[24] See Carr, *The Twenty Years' Crisis*, p. 118; and Royal Institute of International Affairs, *International Sanctions* (London: Oxford University Press, 1938). The Pact of Paris is the recurrent touchstone in Clark, ed., *Boycotts and Peace*.

Covenant never came into existence, primarily because of America's refusal to join; thus, the League was substantially, perhaps even fatally, weakened from the beginning.[25] In the second place, the withdrawal of Japan and Germany in the early 1930s and the failure even to consider seriously economic sanctions against Japan for her occupation of Manchuria in 1931 were further indications of the League's impotence.[26] And in the third place, if the influence attempt did damage the League, the harm was more likely to have been caused by the half-hearted and insincere commitment demonstrated by Britain and France than by the sanctions themselves. For the strength of the League, like any international organization, depended on the support of its members.

The contention that economic sanctions were a contributing cause of World War II can be supported by three arguments—(1) that Franco-British relations were exacerbated; (2) that Hitler was encouraged by the timid and vacillating policies of Britain and France; and (3) that sanctions drove Italy into the arms of Hitler.[27] In response, it should be noted that—(1) the fundamental problem was not sanctions but rather how to coordinate British and French responses to Italy's invasion of Ethiopia. Sanctions were the symptom, not the disease; (2) economic sanctions did not *cause* British and French reluctance to use or threaten to use force; they simply demonstrated what Hitler already (rightly) suspected to be true; and (3) if sanctions had not been imposed, Italy might not have been pushed into Germany's camp; but Hitler would have been even more encouraged. If, on the other hand, force had been used, the probability of Mussolini's turning to Hitler was even higher. All things considered, it is at least as plausible to suggest that the League's *failure* to impose sanctions earlier— especially with respect to Japan—was responsible for the weakening of the League and the onset of World War II as it is to suggest that the *imposing* of sanctions had such effects. The League's problem was not that it used sanctions but rather that it did not use them earlier and more often.

The structure of the League's influence attempt on Italy contained several complex and partially incompatible elements. Although international lawyers tend to assess the efficacy of this undertaking in terms of the Covenant, such a legalistic view can be seriously misleading as to the actual goals of the statesmen involved. Since Britain and France were the dominant

[25] Inis L. Claude, Jr., *Power and International Relations* (New York: Random House, 1962), pp. 154-155.

[26] F. P. Walters, *A History of the League of Nations* (London: Oxford University Press, 1952), pp. 465-499.

[27] See Bienen and Gilpin, "Evaluation," pp. IIIa,9-10; and George W. Baer, "Sanctions and Security: The League of Nations and the Italian-Ethiopian War, 1935-1936," *International Organization* XXVII (Spring 1973):178. For a somewhat different discussion of the goals of League sanctions, see Barber, "Economic Sanctions as a Policy Instrument."

actors, it is the goals of their statesmen that must be understood. The goals and targets of the League sanctions may be summarized as follows:

Germany. The primary target was not Italy at all; it was Hitler. "The main argument for League action in 1935," George Baer points out, "was to test the association's capacity to stand against Hitler's revisionism"[28]—although it would probably be more accurate to describe the main object as demonstrating that the association had the *will* to resist Hitler.

Italy. Although stopping the aggression is usually perceived as the primary goal with respect to Italy, it appears that *avoiding war* with Italy was even more important, at least as far as Britain and France were concerned. Were it not so, they would presumably have been willing to use military force to stop Italy; and this they were unwilling to do. Secondary goals with respect to Italy included persuading Mussolini to stop fighting and negotiate; imposing costs on Italy for noncompliance with the demand to stop fighting; convincing Mussolini not to join Hitler (this was probably the most important of the secondary goals); and preserving the stability of the Italian body politic. There was a desire to avoid undermining the Fascist regime, which, it was feared, might cause social chaos or bring a communist government to power.[29] (Ironically, failure to undermine the domestic position of Mussolini is sometimes cited as evidence of the failure of the sanctions!)[30]

Expressing condemnation of Italy's aggression was probably a goal of tertiary importance.

Ethiopia. Expressing sympathy with Ethiopia's plight and encouraging her to hang on until sanctions could take effect may also have been a goal. If it were a goal, it was probably of tertiary importance.[31]

How successful were the League sanctions in approximating these objectives?

Impressing Hitler

The sanctions were counterproductive with respect to this goal. According to Albert Speer, "Hitler concluded that both England and France were loath to take any risks and anxious to avoid any danger. Actions of

---

[28] Baer, "Sanctions and Security," p. 166.

[29] Ibid. See also Wright, *A Study of War*, pp. 943-944.

[30] See, for example, Bienen and Gilpin, "Evaluation," p. IIIa,9.

[31] Note that domestic public opinion is not treated as one of the targets. Although this was an important consideration, especially in Britain, it seems more appropriate to think of this as a determinant than as a target of British foreign policy. Foreign policy, by definition, is aimed at foreigners.

his which later seemed reckless followed directly from such observations. The Western governments had . . . proved themselves weak and indecisive."[32] Hitler, of course, was not interested in a demonstration of willingness to impose economic sanctions; he was interested in whether the democracies were willing to fight. Since the British and the French went out of their way to leave no doubt as to their desire to avoid war with Italy, it is not surprising that Hitler's preexisting views of them were confirmed. It is possible to use economic sanctions to demonstrate resolve and even to convey an explicit or implicit threat to use force. Indeed, this seems to have been the underlying premise of Article 16 of the Covenant. However, sanctions are more effective in demonstrating resolve when the resolve actually exists. In this case, not only was the resolve to fight if necessary lacking, but British and French statesmen went to great lengths to insure that everyone understood this. As E. H. Carr put it, "what paralysed sanctions in 1935–36 was the common knowledge that the League Powers were not prepared to use the military weapon."[33]

Avoiding War

The degree of success in attaining this objective, of course, undermined the ability to impress Hitler. Bienen and Gilpin argue that "there was a failure on the part of the sanctioning states to appreciate the enormity of the decision they had taken. The imposition of economic sanctions is an act just short of the declaration of war."[34] Considering the amount of handwringing by British and French statesmen, it would seem more accurate to say that they not only appreciated the enormity of their decision, they worried about little else.[35]

Stopping the War

Since the Italian victory came earlier than was expected, there was little or no success with respect to this goal.

Imposing Costs

Sanctions were at least somewhat successful in imposing economic and financial costs on Italy as punishment for noncompliance.[36] The limited nature of the sanctions, the month's delay in implementing them, and prior

[32] *Inside the Third Reich*, trans. R. and C. Winston (New York: Macmillan, 1970), p. 72, quoted by Baer, "Sanctions and Security," p. 178.

[33] Carr, *The Twenty Years' Crisis*, p. 119n.

[34] Bienen and Gilpin, "Evaluation," p. IIIa,9.

[35] See Baer, "Sanctions and Security," for several examples.

[36] See M. J. Bonn, "How Sanctions Failed," *Foreign Affairs* XV (January 1937):350–361; Renwick, *Economic Sanctions*, pp. 9-24, 76, 95-98; and Hufbauer and Schott, *Economic Sanctions*, p. 94.

stockpiling by Italy combined to limit these costs. The standard textbook explanation for the failure of the League sanctions is that oil was not included on the list of embargoed items.[37] This interpretation gains credence in the light of Mussolini's reported remark to Hitler that "if the League had extended sanctions to include oil, he would have had to withdraw from Ethiopia 'within a week.' "[38]

Preventing a Hitler-Mussolini Alliance

Although sanctions had little or no success with respect to this goal, it is not clear that they drove Italy into German arms. The obvious compatibility of Fascism and Nazism as ideologies and political systems may have been a more important consideration.

Avoiding Revolution in Italy

This goal was not only achieved, it was "overachieved" in the sense that the sanctions generated Italian nationalism and support for Mussolini. As one study put it, "International opprobrium, rather than weakening the aggressor's government, was turned into a tool for uniting the Italian people behind the Fascists in defiance of the League."[39] Although this "rally round the flag" effect is commonly noted as an unintended and unwanted side effect of the sanctions, three points should be noted in interpreting the significance of this reaction. First, part of the Italian resentment had more to do with *who* was imposing the sanctions, i.e., Britain and France, than with the nature of the sanctions themselves. Since these two countries already dominated Africa, it seemed more than a little hypocritical to the Italians for the British and the French to deny them a piece of the pie.[40] Second, much of the reaction was to "international opprobrium" itself rather than to the instrument through which this was being expressed. Noneconomic sanctions, especially military attack, would have elicited a similar response. And third, although Britain and France did not want to strengthen Mussolini's domestic support, they did not want to weaken it very much either.

[37] See, for example, Thomas A. Bailey, *A Diplomatic History of the American People*, 10th ed. (Englewood Cliffs, N.J.: Prentice-Hall, 1980), p. 700. Despite the prominence of the view that oil was the critical omission from the League's embargo lists, one sometimes encounters references to "the League of Nations oil embargo against Italy"! See Kindleberger, *Power and Money*, p. 97; and C. Fred Bergsten, Robert O. Keohane, and Joseph S. Nye, "International Economics and International Politics: A Framework for Analysis," *International Organization* XXIX (Winter 1975):9.

[38] Doxey, *Economic Sanctions*, 1st ed., p. 57.

[39] Taubenfeld and Taubenfeld, "The 'Economic Weapon,' " 185.

[40] Renwick, *Economic Sanctions*, p. 23.

Condemning Aggression

As a symbolic condemnation of blatant aggression on behalf of the international community, the influence attempt was highly successful. It began to sensitize the Western democracies to the need to oppose aggression and may have made it easier to arouse public support in subsequent years.

Support for Ethiopia

Although Ethiopia would have preferred stronger measures, there must have been some satisfaction from the League's support.

The difficulty of approximating all of these goals to any great extent was very high. This level of difficulty was due to five factors: (1) This was the first time the League had undertaken economic sanctions; so no precedents or standard operating procedures were available as guides to action. (2) The level of Mussolini's commitment to the war was so high that it was hard for him to back down. Stopping a war—like stopping a stampede—is easier to do before it has begun. (3) The sanctions were limited in scope and implemented a month after the decision had been made to impose them. No attempt to deter Mussolini with a threat of economic sanction prior to the war was made. (4) The influence attempt was based on faulty intelligence estimates. "Every general staff thought the Italian army would take at least two years to conquer Ethiopia."[41] Although the difficulty of predicting the effects of economic sanctions is often noted as a drawback of such measures, it should be noted that the critical intelligence failure with respect to the League's sanctions did not concern economic measures but rather the effects of Italy's *military* efforts. (5) The most important source of the difficulty of the League's undertaking, however, grew out of the complex and contradictory combination of objectives being pursued. It was impossible to succeed on all dimensions. To impress Hitler it was necessary to risk war; yet avoiding the risk of war was one of the primary goals. Condemning and punishing Italy on the one hand made it extremely difficult to court her as an ally against Germany on the other hand. And the desire to generate domestic pressure on Mussolini to withdraw was offset by the fear of destabilizing the Fascist regime. Considering the difficulty of the undertaking, the sanctions against Italy were more effective than should have been expected. As Samuel Johnson said about dogs who walk on their hind legs, "The wonder is not that they do it badly but that they do it at all!" Overall, the League was able to condemn aggression in a way that imposed costs on the aggressor without evoking a violent response and without undermining the political stability of the target state; but it was unsuccessful, even counterproductive in its attempt to impress Hitler and stop the war.

[41] Baer, "Sanctions and Security," p. 174.

Given the goals of British and French statesmen in this situation, would noneconomic techniques of statecraft have worked better? Although propaganda might have been more effective in avoiding war and in retaining the friendship of Italy, it would have been less effective than sanctions with respect to all of the other objectives. Doing nothing had about the same advantages and disadvantages as propaganda. Diplomatic action could have included expulsion from the League or offers to mediate the dispute, but, like doing nothing and propaganda, these were likely to be more effective than economic measures only with regard to appeasing Italy.[42] Military techniques, it is usually implied, would have worked better than economic ones in this situation. This is probably true with respect to every goal except avoiding war and retaining Italy as a possible ally against Germany. In retrospect, it seems that the League's influence attempt would have worked better if the sanctions had been accompanied by at least the implicit threat to use military force at some later time. That this was not done indicates how much value the British and French placed on avoiding war and retaining close relations with Italy. The costs of military techniques, at least in the eyes of the British and French statesmen, were just too high. Given their priorities, it would be difficult to identify an alternative to economic sanctions that would have approximated more of their goals at an acceptable cost.

Can or should "lessons" be drawn from the League experience? Lessons that do not take account of the complex set of goals and targets, of the availability of alternative policy options, and of the extraordinary level of difficulty of the undertaking are likely to be misleading. On balance, it is probably prudent not to draw lessons from such an unusual case.[43] Still, lessons have been suggested; so the matter cannot be ignored. Let us therefore review some of the conclusions that others have drawn from this case.

[42] Bienen and Gilpin argue that "whether more judicious diplomacy could have found a peaceful solution to the Ethiopian-Italian problem remains unclear" ("Evaluation," p. IIIa,8). They do not spell out what form "judicious diplomacy" might have taken; nor do they cite anyone who has seriously argued that "judicious diplomacy" would have stopped Italy. Even if it had found a "peaceful solution," such a technique would have been less effective than economic sanctions with respect to the goals of impressing Hitler, condemning aggression, and imposing costs on Italy.

[43] The Taubenfelds note the dangers of generalizing on the basis of one or two case studies, but they nevertheless proceed to generalize not only about limited negative economic sanctions imposed under difficult circumstances but also about the ability of "even the most perfectly applied, full economic measures . . . to interfere seriously with a state's ability to achieve its goals, aggressive or otherwise?" ("The 'Economic Weapon,' " pp. 187-188). From limited negative sanctions imperfectly applied to full economic measures perfectly applied, from stopping a war to interfering seriously with any kind of foreign policy goal, from one or two cases to "history suggests that . . ." (p. 191) is a long leap.

Lesson No. 1: *Economic sanctions are useless and counterproductive techniques of statecraft.*[44]

> If ever the imposition of collective sanctions would succeed this seemed to be the case, and members of the League gave them a fair chance of success. That they did not illustrates the problem of making sanctions work under the best of circumstances.[45]

Comment: For reasons mentioned above, the situation hardly constituted ideal conditions for giving economic sanctions a fair test. League members and popular opinion at the time were mistaken in their belief that the sanctions had a "fair chance of success."

> It can be argued that the Italian case was no fair test of the concept of all-out economic sanctions. . . . Fear of war with Italy, fear of the loss of Italian political support against resurging Germany, . . . and even sympathy with Italy's position imposed the real limits to the action taken.[46]

Comment: Having succinctly summarized the case against generalizing from the League experience, the Taubenfelds proceed to generate a number of sweeping generalizations not only about economic sanctions but about the "inherent weaknesses" of "even the most comprehensive, well-administered economic measures."

> Judged from the point of view of the immediate political aims of several important League Members, economic measures against Italy did not fail.[47]

Comment: Having based their whole argument on the assumption that the League's sanctions failed, the Taubenfelds pause midway through to observe that "when international collective measures fail, we must suspect a major cause to be a failure of the members to agree to succeed."[48] Rather than first determining what goals League members were pursuing, they begin by noting that "failure" and proceed to explain this "failure" in terms of the League members' pursuit of the wrong goals. It would seem more appropriate, however, to get the cart of judging the degree of success behind the horse of determining the goals of the influence attempt.

> The course of events in 1935 and 1936 . . . compels the conclusion that the sanctions policy, at least in so far as Britain and France were

---

[44] This is the most common lesson according to popular opinion and represents the gist of the argument by Taubenfeld and Taubenfeld and Bienen and Gilpin.

[45] Bienen and Gilpin, "Evaluation," p. IIIa,1.

[46] Taubenfeld and Taubenfeld, "The 'Economic Weapon,' " p. 185.

[47] Ibid., p. 201.

[48] Ibid.

concerned, was not designed to coerce Italy to any significant degree, but would be more accurately described as a face-saving exercise in half-hearted punishment, in which no more than the forms of the Covenant were observed.[49]

Comment: Although somewhat oversimplifying the complex set of British and French objectives, Doxey's conclusion wisely cautions against generalizing about the inherent capabilities of economic sanctions on the basis of this case.

This failure was due mainly to obstructionist tactics employed by British and French leaders who, for various reasons, were not disposed to use strong economic, not to mention military, measures.[50]

There had been a misinterpretation of circumstances, a failure of leadership in the higher circles of government in Britain and in France.[51]

Comment: Both quotes suggest that the case tells us more about British and French foreign policy than about the inherent capabilities or limitations of economic sanctions.

It would seem that Sanctions did not work simply and only because the League did not work. I can find no fault with the notion itself; not even with its unimaginative selection of weapons from the armory of economic war. . . . If ever an economic war was ill organized, it was that of the League of Nations against Italy: oil was never embargoed, nor was the Suez Canal closed. So craven and foolish was the application that the idea itself seems hardly to have lost respectability.[52]

Comment: This suggests that the experience tells us more about the vagaries of international organization than about economic sanctions *per se*. Wiles is wrong however, about the implications of the League experience for the "idea itself," for the idea of economic sanctions has been stigmatized ever since by its association with the League debacle.

It cannot be said that sanctions failed. For pressure which has not been exercised cannot have failed.[53]

Comment: This suggests that the League experience was hardly a fair test of economic sanctions.

[49] Doxey, *Economic Sanctions*, 1st ed., p. 93.
[50] John B. Whitton, "Institutions of World Order," in *The Second Chance*, ed. Whitton, p. 109.
[51] Baer, "Sanctions and Security," p. 178.
[52] Wiles, *Communist International Economics*, p. 496.
[53] Bonn, "How Sanctions Failed," p. 359.

Chamberlain and Laval did not want the sanctions to succeed. Chamberlain's England was anxious not to deepen its conflict with Mussolini's Italy and to divert it from Franco's Spain. Laval's France was interested in keeping Mussolini's attention diverted from Tunisia. Under England's and France's leadership only imperfect types of economic sanctions were applied. The oil sanctions were never put into real effect. . . . The Suez Canal was never closed, either for Italian ships and Italian commerce, or even for the Italian African invasion army and its supplies. The climax was reached when Chamberlain's sister-in-law met in Rome with Mussolini and reached a secret agreement. The sanctions were sabotaged by Paris and London, time and strength were given to Italy to crush Abyssinia's resistance. When Italy proclaimed that country's annexation, the sanctions were declared ended.

The defeat of the sanctions was not the result of an inherent inadequacy of "economic sanctions" as such. It was the result of a premeditated policy of the leading great European Western Powers not to use really effective economic sanctions which would defeat Italy's expansion in Abyssinia. The types of economic sanctions which were applied were merely lip service rendered to the League of Nations by Chamberlain and Laval.[54]

Comment: When the Taubenfelds had finished delivering their paper demonstrating the "inherent weaknesses" of economic sanctions to the American Society of International Law, Ivan Soubbotitch, who had been a member of the "Committee of 18" entrusted with implementing the sanctions by the League of Nations, arose during the discussion period and made this comment. It speaks for itself.

Lesson No. 2: *In order to be effective economic sanctions must be comprehensive and universally applied.*[55]

The League's experience provides as much evidence against as it does for this proposition. The surprising thing about the League sanctions was that such limited measures by so few states had so great an impact. Italy's imports and exports were cut by 40 percent, and Mussolini was apparently genuinely worried by the threatened oil embargo despite estimates that Italy probably would have had enough oil to sustain the war effort.[56]

[54] Ivan Soubbotitch, comment during discussion of paper delivered by Taubenfeld and Taubenfeld. (Addendum to Taubenfeld and Taubenfeld, "The 'Economic Weapon,' " pp. 215-216).

[55] Taubenfeld and Taubenfeld, "The 'Economic Weapon,' " p. 197; Knorr, *Power of Nations*, p. 162; and Bienen and Gilpin, "Evaluation," p. IIIa,10.

[56] Renwick, *Economic Sanctions*, p. 20; and Royal Institute of International Affairs, *International Sanctions*, pp. 60-75.

Lesson No. 3: *In order to be effective, economic sanctions must be backed by the threat to use force if necessary.*[57]

Once again, considering the amount of effort exerted to dissociate the League sanctions from even the hint of a threat to use force, the striking thing is how much rather than how little effect they had. In any event, this lesson would be applicable only to a narrow range of goals, such as deterring or stopping a war, and would not necessarily be relevant to all foreign policy goals.

Renwick laments that "by the time of the second great sanctions experiment [i.e., United Nations sanctions against Rhodesia] the lessons of the first had been forgotten almost in their entirety."[58] But what were these lessons? If lessons must be drawn from the League experience, something along the following lines is about all that seems appropriate: If statesmen try to pursue a large number of difficult and partially incompatible goals vis-à-vis several targets, using very limited economic sanctions, implemented late, with little or no prior planning or precedents to guide them, based on faulty intelligence estimates, the degree of success is unlikely to be very high.

UNITED STATES AND JAPAN

In 1937 Japan invaded China and became bogged down in war there until the end of World War II. The sympathies of the American government and public opinion were definitely with the Chinese victims of the aggression. Isolationist sentiments and legislation were strong in the United States, however, and American attempts to influence the Japanese were confined to diplomatic protests, propaganda (e.g., President Roosevelt's "Quarantine Speech," October 1937), and a "moral embargo" on the sale of aircraft to Japan. The United States also made loans available to the Chinese, but the effects were somewhat offset by the fact that America continued to export vital war materials—especially oil and scrap iron—to Japan from 1937 to July 1941. Economic sanctions were imposed piecemeal by the United States from July 1940 to July 1941. The first round consisted of licensing of certain exports and a ban on the sale of aviation fuel for Japan. These sanctions were imposed after Japan indicated an interest in acquiring the Pacific colonies of France and the Netherlands, both of which had fallen to Germany in June. The second round, consisting of an embargo on sales of iron and steel scrap to Japan, was imposed in response to the signing of the Tripartite Alliance. And a third round freezing

---

[57] Carr, *The Twenty Years' Crisis*, p. 119; Knorr, *Power of Nations*, p. 162; and Renwick, *Economic Sanctions*, p. 23.

[58] *Economic Sanctions*, p. 18.

Japanese assets and imposing a de facto embargo on all trade including oil was imposed in July 1941 in response to Japanese occupation of southern Indochina. Four months later Japan attacked Pearl Harbor.

The U.S. economic sanctions against Japan, especially the measures taken in 1941, are often cited as an example of the clear failure of an influence attempt intended to deter aggression. Indeed, many go further and suggest that the sanctions not only failed but were actually counterproductive in that they evoked the very response they were intended to deter. Knorr classifies the case as one that "clearly failed" and suggests the possibility that the oil embargo intended to induce Japan "to abandon military aggression in Asia had the perverse effect of contributing to the Japanese invasion of southwest Asia (Sumatran oil!), and perhaps even to the subsequent decision to attack Pearl Harbor."[59] Bruce Russett shares Knorr's view of the sanctions as a failure of deterrence, but goes beyond Knorr's tentative speculation as to the "possibility" that sanctions were counterproductive and asserts "the Japanese attack would not have come but for the American, British, and Dutch embargo."[60] And Chihiro Hosoya adopts a position similar to Russett's in stating that "the economic sanctions, rather than serving as a 'deterrent to a southern advance,' produced precisely the opposite effect."[61] The most extreme indictment of the sanctions, however, comes from Bienen and Gilpin:

> From the perspective of the United States, the application of an oil boycott against Japan in August 1941 is the most momentous example of the dangers and ultimate ineffectiveness of economic sanctions. The oil boycott not only failed to achieve its purpose of deterring Japan but it triggered the Japanese attack on Pearl Harbor and the Second World War in the Pacific. . . . The ostensible purpose of sanctions, . . . and most historians agree, was to deter Japanese aggression in Asia. From this perspective, economic sanctions were not only a failure but they were actually counter productive in that they stimulated further Japanese aggression in southeast Asia and against the United States itself.[62]

[59] Knorr, *Power of Nations*, pp. 152-155. Knorr presumably means to refer to "southeast" Asia.

[60] Bruce M. Russett, *No Clear and Present Danger: A Skeptical View of United States Entry into World War II* (New York: Harper and Row, 1972), p. 45. See also Bruce M. Russett, "Pearl Harbor: Deterrence Theory and Decision Theory," *Journal of Peace Research*, no. 2 (1967), pp. 89-105.

[61] Chihiro Hosoya, "Miscalculations in Deterrent Policy: Japanese-U.S. Relations, 1938-1941," *Journal of Peace Research*, no. 2 (1968), p. 108.

[62] "Evaluation," p. IIIb,1. Having identified economic sanctions as a "precipitator" of the Peloponnesian War and a "contributory cause" of the Second World War in Europe, Bienen and Gilpin now depict them as having "triggered" the Second World War in the Pacific!

The depiction of U.S. sanctions against Japan as solely intended to deter aggression illustrates the dangers of viewing influence attempts in terms of a single objective. In addition to deterring Japanese aggression, the sanctions were intended (1) to deny vital resources to a potential enemy in case deterrence failed; (2) to impose costs on Japan for failure to comply with American demands that it withdraw from China and southern Indochina; and (3) to provide indirect support for Chinese resistance to Japan and European resistance to German aggression.[63] It is not even clear that deterrence was the most important of these goals, since those who believed that war with Japan was "inevitable" probably placed higher priority on denying the "inevitable" enemy the resources for waging war.[64] There is no evidence that any American decision makers were absolutely sure that oil sanctions would deter Japan, and there were certainly those who were skeptical but who favored an embargo for other reasons. Thus, in the fall of 1940 Secretary of the Interior Harold Ickes wrote to the president as follows:

> We didn't keep Japan out of Indo-China by continuing to ship scrap iron, nor will we keep Japan out of the Dutch East Indies by selling it our oil. When Japan thinks that it can safely move against the Dutch East Indies, and is ready to do so, it will go in, regardless. It will make it all the more difficult for it to go in if it is short on oil and gasoline.[65]

And the position of U.S. Army intelligence (G-2) in July 1941 was as follows:

> Effective economic sanctions against Japan . . . would not, in the opinion of this Division, force Japan to take any steps in the way of aggressive action which she does not plan to take anyway, when a favorable opportunity arises. . . . On the contrary, by adopting such a policy we will be able to conserve for Britain and for ourselves supplies which . . . are being worse than wasted when we place them in Japanese hands.[66]

[63] For a concise summary of the perceptions of U.S. and Japanese policy makers, see Glenn H. Snyder and Paul Diesing, *Conflict Among Nations: Bargaining, Decision Making, and System Structure in International Crises* (Princeton: Princeton University Press, 1977), pp. 124-129, 553-555. See also Gordon W. Prange, *At Dawn We Slept: The Untold Story of Pearl Harbor* (New York: McGraw-Hill, 1981), pp. 165-171; and Herbert Feis, *The Road to Pearl Harbor* (Princeton: Princeton University Press, 1950).

[64] The term "inevitable" has no place in the vocabulary of the social scientist, but others use it so frequently in this context that it seems appropriate in describing their views. It should be interpreted, I presume, as meaning "highly probable."

[65] Quoted in William L. Langer and S. Everett Gleason, *The Undeclared War, 1940-1941* (New York: Harper, 1953), p. 35.

[66] Prange, *At Dawn We Slept*, p. 165.

Although both statements favor an oil embargo, neither is based on the goal of deterrence. Rather than trying to affect Japan's *intentions*, both Ickes and G-2 were advocating an attempt to influence Japan's *capabilities*.

Figure 1

U.S. and Japanese Strategies

		JAPAN	
		Contraction	Expansion
U.S.	Trade	2, 3	4, 1
	Embargo	1, 4	3, 2

If the oil embargo is viewed in terms of the legitimate and reasonable concerns of U.S. policy makers with *both* defense and deterrence, it emerges not as the reckless, naive, and counterproductive undertaking that Bienen and Gilpin describe, but rather as a prudent rational "minimax" strategy. Consider the 2 x 2 matrix in figure 1. Japan's strategies are to "contract" by giving up its plans for the New Order for East Asia and withdrawing from southern Indochina and China or to continue to expand in pursuit of Asian dominance.[67] The U.S. strategies are to continue trade or impose an embargo. Each country's rank ordering of preferred outcomes was as follows:

United States

1. An embargo plus contraction by Japan would change *both* Japanese intentions and capabilities in ways preferred by the United States
2. Continued trade combined with Japanese contraction would be preferable to any alternative involving Japanese expansion.

[67] Russett contends that the attack on Pearl Harbor was not evidence of "unlimited expansionist policy" by the Japanese, but rather a consequence of the "much less ambitious goal" of consolidating its position in China (*No Clear and Present Danger*, pp. 56-57). Since the United States was adamantly opposed to both, this point is irrelevant to the analysis here. Those who object to calling Japan's second strategy "expansion" may call it "consolidation"; the outcome is still the same.

3. An embargo in the event of Japanese expansion would at least mean a weaker Japan.
4. Continued trade with an expanding Japan is the least preferred outcome from the U.S. point of view.

Japan

1. Asian dominance plus trade with the United States.
2. Asian dominance despite a U.S. embargo.
3. Contraction plus trade with United States.
4. Contraction plus a U.S. embargo.

In this situation an embargo guarantees the United States either its first or third choice, while expansion guarantees Japan either its first or second choice. Clearly, the rational strategy for the U.S. is to impose an embargo.[68]

The estimate of the probability of war with Japan is crucial to determination of the wisdom of the U.S. embargo. If it is estimated as low, then the argument that an embargo was an unnecessarily provocative act carries more weight; but if it is estimated as high, the embargo seems more attractive, since providing a likely enemy with the "sinews of war" makes little sense. Also, if war were "inevitable," i.e., highly probable, the imposition of sanctions cannot be blamed—at least not very much—for "causing" a war that was going to happen anyway. With respect to the probability of war between Japan and the United States, it is interesting to note that numerous scholars using different analytical approaches have concluded that war was highly likely. Traditional historian Gordon Prange concludes that "no one can say with certainty that had the United States not frozen Japanese assets and embargoed oil, Japan would have accepted the status quo. The evidence of history suggests that it would not." Snyder and Diesing employ formal models of bargaining depicting the situation as one in which war is "inevitable." And Quincy Wright calculates that war between the United States and Japan was highly probable from 1937 onward. Indeed, his estimates of the probability of war between twenty pairs of great powers as of July 1939 ranked war between the United States and Japan eighth—by the time the United States imposed the oil embargo, four of these pairs were already at war, thus moving the United States and

---

[68] Snyder and Diesing depict the basic structure of the situation in a similar but not identical way and conclude that war was inevitable. (*Conflict Among Nations*, pp. 124-129.) Although 2 x 2 matrices of this type usually oversimplify foreign policy decision making and imply misleading zero-sum aspects of the situation, in this case the matrix is useful for two reasons. First, the perceptions—but not the reality, as Snyder and Diesing point out—of each side did approximate a zero-sum outlook. And second, in comparison with treatments of deterrence as the sole objective of the United States, the use of a 2 x 2 matrix makes the situation more complex and realistic by bringing in the objective of defense in case deterrence fails.

Japan even higher on the list.[69] For American foreign policy makers to base their decision to impose economic sanctions on the assumption that war with Japan was likely was hardly reckless; on the contrary, it was reasonable, responsible, and prudent statesmanship.[70]

How cost-effective were the economic sanctions imposed on Japan? Although Japan was not deterred, this says little about the effectiveness of sanctions. It is not clear that Japan could have been deterred from her goal of Asian dominance. With respect to the proposition that deterrence failed *because* sanctions were imposed, it seems that at least as strong a case can be made that deterrence in 1941 failed because sanctions had *not* been imposed against Japan in 1931 or 1937. There is general agreement that the first step in Japan's effort to establish an Asian empire was in 1931. Although there was some thought of responding to Japan's aggression in Manchuria with economic sanctions, "the lack of assurance that the United States would participate in anti-Japanese commercial discrimination was a discouragement to League plans for economic sanctions against Japan."[71] Presumably, this "lack of assurance" was also an encouragement to the Japanese in their expansionist policies. Imposing sanctions has its costs, but it may also be costly *not* to impose sanctions in some situations. Some writers, indeed, see a direct chain of events linking failure to impose sanctions in 1931–1932 to the eventual attack on Pearl Harbor.[72] Although appeasement does not deserve the poor reputation as a strategy that it acquired at Munich in 1938, it is a strategy that must be used with caution and with a sense of timing. "Once a government has passed the critical point of policy, after which it evaluates economic opportunity solely as a contribution to military preparedness and evaluates foreign concessions solely as evidence of weakness, there is a danger that conciliatory policies by others may stimulate a government's aggressiveness."[73] Wright seems to believe that Japan passed that critical point in 1931, when "Japanese leadership passed from commercial-minded to mil-

---

[69] Prange, *At Dawn We Slept*, p. 170; Snyder and Diesing, *Conflict Among Nations*, pp. 124-129; and Wright, *A Study of War*, pp. 1466-1491. Renwick's (*Economic Sanctions*, p. 63) depiction of the attack on Pearl Harbor as a "mad dog" act is refuted by Russett's observation that "whatever the nature of the decision to go to war, it was arrived at and reinforced over a long period of time, and was not the result of anyone's possible 'irrational' impulse" ("Pearl Harbor," p. 90).

[70] Cf. Bienen and Gilpin: "In retrospect, the American sanctions policy must be judged as reckless" ("Evaluation," p. IIIb,7).

[71] Benjamin H. Williams, "The Coming of Economic Sanctions into American Practice," *American Journal of International Law* XXXVII (July 1943):386-387.

[72] Maurice Baumont, *The Origins of the Second World War*, trans. Simone de Couvreur Ferguson (New Haven: Yale University Press, 1978), p. 41.

[73] Wright, *A Study of War*, p. 1316.

itary-minded politicians.''[74] If so, it suggests that if U.S. economic sanctions were aimed at deterrence, they should have been applied about ten years earlier.

Some analysts focus on 1937 as a critical point if Japan was to be deterred. With the United States providing oil, scrap iron, and raw materials, the Japanese invaded China. Although Roosevelt's "Quarantine Speech" hinted at the possibility of U.S. economic sanctions, the U.S. protest amounted to little, prompting the British prime minister to observe that "it is always best and safest to count on nothing from the Americans but words."[75] Feis notes ominously that "Japan and Germany, of course, measured the episode." The only way a stable settlement between China and Japan could have been worked out, according to Feis, was by "firm collective action" in 1937 that would have "offered Japan an inducement for peace and met refusal with compulsion. But this lesson was not learned, or even stated boldly, until three years later—too late to prevent tragedy."[76]

It may be that the economic sanctions imposed by the United States in 1941 were the critical straw on the camel's back that affected at least the timing of the U.S. war with Japan. But in a more profound sense the failure to impose sanctions against Japan in 1931 and 1937 was responsible for a large number of straws added before the camel was overburdened. Some may draw the lesson from U.S. sanctions against Japan in 1941 that sanctions are very costly because they may provoke war. Others, however, viewing the U.S. sanctions in historical perspective, may see the lesson as being that the *nonuse* of economic sanctions in some situations can be as costly and dangerous as using them, perhaps more so.

Hardly anyone denies that the U.S. embargo was highly successful in denying war material to a potential enemy, in imposing costs on Japan, or in preserving resources that could—and would—be used by the United States and her allies at a later date.[77] Even the costs were minimal since the United States was able to save war-related resources for her own use. The big question, of course, is whether to consider the onset of war with Japan a cost of U.S. sanctions. To the extent that sanctions are considered a cause of the war, their utility will seem rather low; but to the extent that the war is viewed as having other and more profound causes, such as the

---

[74] Ibid., p. 853n.

[75] Feis, *Road to Pearl Harbor*, pp. 12-13.

[76] Ibid., pp. 12-13, 15-16. Sumner Welles believed that there was "surely good reason to believe that in 1937 a total trade embargo, imposed by a Britain not yet involved in a war for survival, together with the United States and the remaining members of the Nine Powers, and backed if necessary by force, could have compelled the Japanese Army to abandon its plans for aggressive expansion" (*Seven Decisions that Shaped History* [New York: Harper and Row, 1951], p. 92).

[77] Feis lists several ways the embargo affected Japanese capabilities. (*Road to Pearl Harbor*, p. 109.)

lackadaisical response to Japanese aggression in 1931 and 1937, their utility will seem higher since war cannot then be counted as a cost. (Counterfactuals do matter!) Bienen and Gilpin contend that "the *only* purpose served by economic sanctions . . . was to trigger a war with Japan"; and "unless one takes the view that the imposition of economic sanctions in July 1941 was deliberately provocative and was calculated to force the Japanese to initiate war against the isolationist United States, *one must conclude that* economic sanctions . . . were not only ineffective but actually counter-productive in their consequences."[78] However, if one estimates the probability of war as very high in July 1941 and if one drops the unrealistic assumption that the sole objective of the sanctions was to deter, with little or no thought of defense, their conclusion seems not only unnecessary but more than a little overstated.[79]

Did American policy makers have alternative policy options that would have worked better than economic sanctions? Any alternative to an embargo in July 1941 needed to have a high probability of success with respect to deterrence since the probability of successful deterrence had to be weighed against the absolute certainty that continued trade with Japan would strengthen the war-making capabilities of a potential enemy. Desperate hopes that an alternative could be found were not enough; there had to be a reasonable prospect of success in order to offset such costs. Nearly every diplomatic and propagandistic alternative had been exhausted by July 1941. Even limited economic sanctions were not deterring Japan.[80] This left only military statecraft, but what options were likely to work? An attack on Japan was out of the question. The country was not ready to support such a move, and besides, this option was guaranteed to be counterproductive with respect to deterrence. The one way to be absolutely certain of war with a country is to attack it. This left only the *threat* of military force, but threats must be credible in order to work. The United States had spent twenty years creating its image as an isolationist country unwilling to use force. Refusal to join the League of Nations, refusal to support economic sanctions against Japan in 1931 and 1937 and against Italy in 1935–36 had undermined the American ability to make credible threats. Even the Japanese sinking of a U.S. warship in 1937 had elicited a proposal in the House of Representatives to require a national referendum on a declaration

[78] "Evaluation," pp. IIIb,6-7. Italics added. On the revisionist thesis that FDR intended to provoke war, see Prange, *At Dawn We Slept*, pp. 839-850.

[79] The argument of Bienen and Gilpin is weakened more than they seem to realize by their admission that "war was undoubtedly inevitable once the United States decided not to sacrifice China in order to gain time in which to increase America's preparedness for war" ("Evaluation," p. IIIb,6).

[80] See Prange, *At Dawn We Slept*, p. 170; and Feis, *Road to Pearl Harbor*, pp. 153-161.

of war except in case of actual invasion, a proposal only narrowly defeated after strong efforts by the White House.

> In the disturbed realm of diplomacy which the United States and Japan had entered, the language used is in part symbolic, in part spoken. Battleships and economic controls are the symbol of power in reserve, symbols used to give edge to verbal warnings, a way of saying "Do you see what I mean?" without saying it.[81]

But how could the Japanese be expected to know whether the United States really meant it when it said it was unwilling to acquiesce to Japanese desires?

> To yield may be to signal that one can be expected to yield; to yield often or continually indicates acknowledgement that that is one's role. To yield repeatedly up to some limit and then to say "enough" may guarantee that the first show of obduracy loses the game for both sides. . . . If one side yields on a series of issues, when the matters at stake are not critical, it may be difficult to communicate to the other just when a vital issue has been reached. . . . No service is done to the other side by behaving in a way that undermines its belief in one's ultimate firmness. It may be safer in a long run to hew to the center of the road than to yield six inches on successive nights, if one really intends to stop yielding before he is pushed onto the shoulder. It may save both sides a collision.[82]

The United States had yielded to Japanese aggression so many times in the 1930s that it could not in July 1941 suddenly say "enough" and expect to be believed. If, in fact, the United States was unwilling to yield with respect to Japanese desires in China, it should have signaled this sooner, perhaps by using economic sanctions. Indeed, Japanese statesmen could rightly complain that America had misled them by its refusal to impose sanctions earlier. In the long run American appeasement was no favor to the Japanese. America was paying the price for twenty years of isolationism; an image created over two decades could not be changed in a few months. "An undesired image," as Robert Jervis points out, "can involve costs for which almost no amount of the usual kinds of power can compensate and can be a handicap almost impossible to overcome."[83] Prange's judgment that "when the alternatives are examined, it is difficult to see what other course Roosevelt could have taken at this point"[84] is difficult to dispute.

---

[81] Feis, *Road to Pearl Harbor*, p. 159.
[82] Schelling, *Arms and Influence*, pp. 118, 124.
[83] *The Logic of Images*, p. 6.
[84] Prange, *At Dawn We Slept*, p. 171.

"Lessons," as was noted before, can be dangerous and misleading; but for those who are determined to squeeze "lessons" out of single historical cases, it should be noted that there are better candidates than the "economic-sanctions-are-useless-and-counterproductive-lesson" so often derived from the case of U.S. sanctions against Japan. The following are some possibilities:

1. Images matter and can sometimes be very costly to change. (Ask any leopard!)

2. Appeasement can be risky if the limits are not clearly circumscribed. (Ask any degenerate teenager who plays "chicken.") Corollary: appeasement, like rain dancing, always works—if there are no limits on how much you are willing to do.

3. Contrary to the alleged "lesson" of the League experience, economic sanctions can be very potent even when not universally applied. (Ask the Japanese.)

4. Positing a single goal vis-à-vis a single target can be a very misleading way to analyze the capabilities of nation-states. (Ask any foreign policy maker.)

5. In positing the objectives of an influence attempt, the intended changes in the *capabilities* of the target should be considered as well as intended changes in the *intentions* of the target. (Ask a prison warden or the parent of a two-year-old.)

6. In capability analysis small changes in the postulated situation, such as one's assumption about the autonomous probability[85] of war between the United States and Japan in 1941, can make a big difference. (Ask the millionaire accustomed to having his way who finds himself stranded in a small midwestern town without his wallet.)

7. Nonuse of economic sanctions can be a costly policy option. (Ask American foreign policy makers trying to find a way to deter Japan in July 1941.)

United States and Cuba

From July 1960 to July 1963 the United States imposed a series of controls on trade with Cuba culminating in the freezing of Cuban assets. In addition, the United States pressured its European allies, Japan, and Latin American states to support these economic sanctions. The Organization of American States imposed economic sanctions on Cuba in 1964 and maintained them until 1975. The unilateral U.S. embargo on trade

---

[85] The autonomous probability of event "X" is the probability that X would occur in the absence of any attempt to change that probability. See Karl W. Deutsch, *The Analysis of International Relations*, 2d ed. (Englewood Cliffs, N.J.: Prentice-Hall, 1978), pp. 29-31, 159.

with Cuba is still in effect more than twenty years later. Since trade with
the United States constituted about two-thirds of Cuba's foreign trade, the
potential impact of the embargo was great. This economic impact, however,
was partially nullified by the Soviet Union's willingness to step in. By
1961 Cuba's trade with communist countries, especially the Soviet Union,
was as large a proportion of its total trade as trade with the United States
had been prior to the embargo.[86] As with the other "classic cases," there
is a widespread view that sanctions against Cuba have not worked very
well. Abraham F. Lowenthal describes American policy as "forlorn because Cuba has already broken down the blockade"; Knorr lists it among
cases where trade sanctions have "clearly failed", Donald Losman concludes that sanctions "have been economically effective, yet politically
unsuccessful"; the Commission on United States-Latin American Relations, in apparent contrast with Losman, argues that "economically, the
U.S. embargo is ineffective"; Bienen and Gilpin assert that "it is hard to
see that trade sanctions have gained the United States anything on balance";
Gunnar Adler-Karlsson views the embargo as having "shown itself to be
an inefficient policy" in Cuba; and Margaret Doxey notes that "the general
ineffectiveness of the embargoes has long been apparent."[87] Are such
pessimistic conclusions buttressed by cogent argument and persuasive evidence? Let us examine the case more closely.

First, it is important to understand the sense in which Castro's Cuba
constituted a problem for American policy makers. From an economic
standpoint communism in Cuba represented a nuisance but hardly a major
problem. Communist sugar and cigars, after all, are not much different
from their capitalist counterparts. Forgoing economic relations with Cuba
was much easier for the United States than for Cuba, since Cuban trade
was but a small fraction of total U.S. trade, which in turn was small
relative to American GNP. Militarily, it was a more important but still
relatively insignificant problem. There were, of course, some who still did
not understand the full implications of air power and the nuclear age, who
insisted that the Panama Canal was as important as it had been in 1915
and who murmured ominously about the Cuban threat to the "soft un-

---

[86] For an overview of the factual situation, see Schreiber, "Economic Coercion as an
Instrument of Foreign Policy."

[87] Lowenthal, "Cuba: Time For a Change," *Foreign Policy*, no. 20 (Fall 1975), p. 70;
Knorr, *Power of Nations*, p. 152; Losman, *International Economic Sanctions*, p. 44; "A
Report of the Commission on United States-Latin American Relations," in *The Americas in
a Changing World* (New York: Quadrangle, 1975), p. 28; Bienen and Gilpin, "Evaluation,"
pp. IIId,7,10; Adler-Karlsson, *Western Economic Warfare*, p. 213; and Doxey, "Sanctions
Revisited," *International Journal* XXXI (Winter 1975-1976):69. See also Roger Fisher's
description of sanctions against Cuba as "a total failure" in *Newsweek*, January 14, 1980.
Hufbauer and Schott give this case the lowest possible success rating (*Economic Sanctions*,
pp. 51-52).

derbelly" of the United States. But the strategic significance of the Panama
Canal had been greatly diminished by modern technology, and Soviet
submarines did not require a Cuban base in order to operate in the Caribbean. Even the much exaggerated threat of Soviet missiles in Cuba in
1962 was at first minimized by the American secretary of defense, who
advocated "doing nothing" on the grounds that "a missile is a missile."[88]
Military considerations mattered more than economic ones, but they were
not the heart of the matter. The major problem Cuba posed for American
foreign policy was political and psychological. Two pillars of U.S. foreign
policy were simultaneously being challenged. First, for 140 years, the
United States had contended that the Western Hemisphere was its sphere
of influence; and second, since World War II, the containment of communist influence had emerged as the single most important touchstone of
American policy. A successful communist government with ties to the
Soviet Union established "just offshore" of the American mainland by a
charismatic leader with expansive aspirations constituted first and foremost
an important *symbolic* threat to the Monroe Doctrine and American anticommunism. Castro's defiant taunts and dares placed the American reputation for action at stake regardless of the desires of U.S. policy makers.
The game of "chicken" requires cooperation to avoid playing, since declining to play, once publicly asked, is to have played and lost.[89] If the
existence of a communist government in Cuba could have been kept a
secret from the world, it would not have bothered American policy makers
nearly so much.

What then were the goals and targets of American economic sanctions
against Cuba? A statement of objectives by Secretary of State Dean Rusk
in 1964 is often cited in answer to this question. This statement, which is
prefaced by a seldom noted explicit disavowal that the policy is "likely
to bring down the Castro regime," describes "four limited, but nonetheless
substantial, objectives":

> First, to reduce Castro's will and ability to export subversion and
> violence to the other American states;
> Second, to make plain to the people of Cuba that Castro's regime
> cannot serve their interests;
> Third, to demonstrate to the peoples of the American Republics
> that communism has no future in the Western Hemisphere; and
> Fourth, to increase the cost to the Soviet Union of maintaining a
> Communist outpost in the Western Hemisphere.[90]

[88] Graham Allison, *Essence of Decision*, pp. 195-196.
[89] See Schelling, *Arms and Influence*, pp. 116-125, esp. 123. This description of the
situation is intended neither to condone nor condemn American policy. It does, I believe,
capture the values and perceptions of American policy makers in their definition of the
"Cuban problem."
[90] U.S. Senate, Committee on Foreign Relations, *Hearings: East-West Trade*, 88th Cong.,

Although this statement is useful in demonstrating the shallowness of attempts to assess the utility of economic sanctions toward Cuba solely or primarily in terms of their ability to topple Castro or exterminate communism,[91] it still does not capture the complexity of American policy. The structure of goals and targets in the American influence attempt was at least as complex as the following depiction, probably more so:

1. *Soviet Union.*   In addition to imposing costs on the Soviet Union for maintaining a "Communist outpost," the United States was sending a message to the Soviets that it refused to recognize the legitimacy either of communism in the Western Hemisphere or of Soviet influence in that part of the world. A threshold had been crossed, and the United States wanted the Soviets to know that it had not gone unnoticed.

2. *Other Latin American and Caribbean states.*   The U.S. sanctions constituted a reiteration and demonstration of American resolve to oppose communism in the hemisphere in order both to reassure ruling elites and to warn would-be revolutionaries lest there be any misunderstanding about the intensity of U.S. hostility to communism. Also, an important objective of using sanctions to damage the Cuban economy was to reduce the attractiveness of the "Cuban example" to other countries.

3. *European allies and Japan.*   Sanctions were a way of demonstrating the strength of U.S. commitment to oppose communism, a way of saying "we really mean it!"

4. *Third World countries in general.*   If communism and the Soviets in particular could establish a foothold on the very "doorstep" of the United States, Third World countries might understandably begin to doubt the determination of the United States to oppose both. Sanctions were intended to send a message to them also.

5. *Cuba.*   American objectives with respect to Cuba were at least four: First, to reduce Castro's will, i.e., change his intentions, with respect to exporting revolution to other countries in the hemisphere. Second, to reduce Cuban *capabilities* to export revolution. (This deserves to be listed separately since it is often neglected in assessments of the effectiveness of the sanctions.) Third, to impose costs on the Cuban people for continued support

---

2d sess., 1964, p. 13. For other statements that discuss U.S. sanctions against Cuba in the context of overall American foreign policy, see Dean Rusk, "Why We Treat Different Communist Countries Differently," *Department of State Bulletin*, March 16, 1964, pp. 390-396; George Ball, "Principles of Our Policy Toward Cuba," *Department of State Bulletin*, May 11, 1964, pp. 738-744; and Edwin M. Martin, "Cuba, Latin America, and Communism," *Department of State Bulletin*, October 14, 1963, pp. 574-582.

[91] For example, see Losman, *International Economic Sanctions*, pp. 20-46.

of Castro. And fourth, to encourage opponents and potential opponents of Castro by implying U.S. support for their efforts. Despite Rusk's disavowal of the expectation that economic measures alone could bring down Castro, this should probably be counted as one of the goals that was at least hoped for if not "expected," especially during the first two or three years of the influence attempt.

How useful were economic sanctions in pursuing these goals? Almost no one denies the success of the embargo in communicating American views to the Soviet leaders or in imposing costs on them for their support of Castro.[92] A report prepared for Congress estimated economic support for Cuba at 0.4 percent of Soviet GNP in 1979. Dismissing this as a "relatively insignificant" burden on the Soviet economy, the report went on to emphasize what it viewed as a more significant burden, the hard currency cost of supplying oil to Cuba.[93] In evaluating the report's description of the aid burden as "relatively insignificant," however, it would be well to note that this is roughly equal to the total burden of *all* U.S. economic aid programs during 1979.[94]

The impact on other countries in the Caribbean and Latin America is difficult to determine, but there is little evidence of failure. The American hostility to communism in the hemisphere is well understood by all, but perhaps this message was conveyed in other ways as well. What would constitute persuasive evidence of failure with respect to American goals in Latin America and the Caribbean? Any of the following would be relevant indicators of failure: (1) Other countries in the hemisphere continuing to do "business as usual" with Cuba—but in fact the Organization of American States supported the sanctions from 1964 to 1975, and most other countries in the hemisphere did not maintain normal diplomatic and commercial relations with Cuba, at least not during the 1960s. (2) A high degree of Cuban influence outside of intellectual circles throughout the area, but in fact "Cuba's influence and importance in the Americas remain

[92] See, for example, Alfred Stepan, "The United States and Latin America: Vital Interests and the Instruments of Power," *Foreign Affairs* LVIII (1980):686; Knorr, *Power of Nations*, p. 149; Bienen and Gilpin, "Evaluation," p. IIId,1; Doxey, *Economic Sanctions*, 1st ed., p. 41; and Jorge I. Domínguez, "Taming the Cuban Shrew," *Foreign Policy*, no. 10 (Spring 1973), p. 107. Domínguez, however, does not view the imposition of costs on the Soviets as an indicator of success, but rather as a paradoxical indirect side effect resulting from the *failure* of U.S. policy (pp. 106-107).

[93] U.S. Congress, Joint Economic Committee, *Cuba Faces the Economic Realities of the 1980s*, Committee Print, 97th Cong., 2d sess., 1982, p. 18.

[94] This is a conservative estimate in that it includes *all* economic loans and grants by the United States. A proper calculation of the U.S. economic aid burden, such as the OECD does, would result in an even lower estimate. Thus, the burden of Soviet economic aid to Cuba is probably greater than the total burden of U.S. economic aid to all countries.

very modest.''[95] (3) An "economic miracle" in Cuba that demonstrated the superiority of the communist road to development, but in fact one is more likely to find references to Cuba as "the laughingstock of Socialist economics.''[96] (4) A high degree of success by Cuba in achieving its goals of freedom from dependence on foreign countries and on sugar, but in fact Cuba is as dependent on sugar as ever and as dependent on the Soviet Union as it used to be on the United States. Indeed, it now holds "the dubious distinction in Latin America of having both Soviet and U.S. naval facilities on its island.''[97] And (5) the establishment of Cuban-style revolutionary governments elsewhere in the region, but in fact there was none until the Nicaraguan revolution in 1979. No doubt the absence of such indicators is not entirely due to U.S. sanctions against Cuba, but such absence is at least consistent with the proposition that such measures were a contributing factor. The absence of such indicators is less easy to reconcile with the assertion that the embargo "clearly failed" to achieve its goals.

Insofar as the sanctions were intended to reiterate and reinforce perceptions of American commitment to a policy of anticommunism, they were probably moderately successful. The effect on European allies, however, was mitigated by two factors. First, the fact that the United States was simultaneously negotiating to sell wheat to the Soviet Union while admonishing its allies not to trade with communist Cuba impaired the credibility and clarity of the American message. And second, having used the Monroe Doctrine for 140 years to deny the legitimacy of European influence in the Western Hemisphere, there was more than a little irony in the United States request for help in upholding that doctrine with respect to Cuba.

Most of the arguments that the sanctions failed, however, concentrate on the impact on Cuba itself. With respect to the objective of weakening Castro's determination to export revolution to other countries in the hemisphere, the sanctions may well have been counterproductive in that they may have increased Castro's *desire* to export his revolution. This assessment, of course, must contend with the awkward fact that Castro does seem to be much less interested in subverting other Latin American governments than he used to be. The existence of other plausible explanations, however—Soviet pressure, the lack of success, and the exacerbation of Cuban relations with other states—suggests caution about attributing Castro's apparent change of heart to American sanctions. Still, it should also be noted—but rarely is—that a plausible chain of reasoning linking the embargo with the shift in Castro's foreign policy priorities also exists. Domínguez, for example, denies that American sanctions had anything to

---

[95] Jorge I. Domínguez, "Cuban Foreign Policy," *Foreign Affairs* LVII (Fall 1978):92.

[96] Domínguez, "Taming the Cuban Shrew," p. 107.

[97] Edward Gonzalez, "The United States and Castro: Breaking the Deadlock," *Foreign Affairs* L (July 1972):732.

do with Castro's change in policy but admits that the shift coincided with "the rise of more concern with [Cuba's] own development."[98] But why did Cuba need to increase its concern with its domestic economic situation? Presumably because the Cuban economy was not doing so well. And why was the Cuban economy not doing so well? Partially because of the damaging effects of the U.S. embargo. If the embargo damaged the Cuban economy enough to cause Castro to rearrange his priorities so as to give domestic development more attention and foreign adventurism less attention, the sanctions may be said to have reduced his will to export revolution. In sum, it is agreed that sometime in the late sixties or early seventies Castro changed his policy toward other countries in the hemisphere, but it is not clear why this happened. Several plausible hypotheses exist— including at least one that links the change with the effects of the embargo— but none has been clearly established as superior to the others. Perhaps all were contributing factors. Confident assertions that the embargo was "irrelevant" to the shift in Castro's foreign policy priorities, however, do not seem to be warranted by the evidence, at least not until plausible hypotheses linking the embargo with the change have been recognized and refuted.[99]

With respect to the embargo's effect on Cuban *capabilities* for successful promotion of subversion abroad, the evidence is less ambiguous. Assuming that a larger economic base would enhance Cuba's capabilities to support foreign adventurism, it is only necessary to ask whether Cuba's economy was hurt by the embargo. Since there is general agreement that it was, it seems difficult to deny that Cuban capabilities were reduced. At least the burden of proof would seem to rest with those who would purport to have found an exception to the general rule that having more resources usually makes things easier. The proposition that U.S. sanctions helped to "curtail Castro's revolutionary activity in Latin America" is certainly not refuted by Bienen and Gilpin's observation that "Cuban supplies still could be shipped to guerrillas."[100] The relevant questions concern how many supplies could be shipped, how often, and at what cost. Until such questions are addressed, it is reasonable to assume that to the extent that the embargo reduced the amount of economic resources available to Castro below what they otherwise would have been, it helped to curtail his capability to support foreign guerrilla movements.

[98] "Taming the Cuban Shrew," p. 105.

[99] The assertion that the embargo was "irrelevant" is made by Domínguez, ibid., pp. 105, 114. In a later publication Domínguez notes the line of argument attributing the shift in Cuban policy to the effects of the embargo, but it is not clear whether he subscribes to it or is just noting it in passing. (Jorge I. Domínguez, "U.S. Policy Toward Cuba: A Discussion of Options," in *The Americas in a Changing World*, p. 124.)

[100] Bienen and Gilpin, "Evaluation," pp. IIId,8.

Even those who believe that sanctions against Cuba have been a failure often admit that they were at least moderately successful in damaging the Cuban economy, although they usually go on to point out the failure of such measures to "bring the Cuban economy to its knees"—a metaphor that is not particularly helpful in assessing the effectiveness of economic sanctions.[101] During the first decade of the embargo Cuban economic performance was certainly not likely to generate much envy among other countries in the hemisphere. Indeed, Cuban per capita GNP was lower at the end of ten years of communism than it had been before Castro took over. World Bank estimates of average annual rates of growth in per capita GNP from 1960 to 1970 rated Cuba at -0.6 percent, lower than any other developing country in the Western Hemisphere except Haiti and the Netherlands Antilles.[102] And a report prepared for Congress in 1982 drew the following conclusions about the impact of the trade embargo:

> The continued denial of Cuban access to U.S. trade and financial markets has effectively restricted the potential for trade and investment by other Western countries and narrowly circumscribed Havana's options for economic development. . . . Thus, the U.S. embargo has been and continues to be not only a major, but a crucial impediment to Cuba's efforts at diversifying and expanding its hard currency trade, the key to improved economic growth and living standards. Indeed, it is fair to say that the U.S. embargo has condemned and will continue to condemn the Cuban economy to continued stagnation, with occasional temporary blips of modest improvement tied to the sugar price increases.[103]

Assessing the effectiveness of the embargo is tricky. On the one hand, one must guard against exaggerating the impact of the sanctions by attributing the poor performance of the Cuban economy entirely to the effects of the embargo, which was clearly not the case, since poor management, the emigration of skilled laborers, and overcentralization also played a role. On the other hand, it is also a mistake to deny the continuing impact of sanctions just because the Cubans seem to have "adjusted" to them. Such "adjustment"—getting used to being poor?—may make the costs being imposed by the embargo difficult to observe, but it does not necessarily eliminate them.

No aspect of assessing the effectiveness of sanctions against Cuba is more fraught with misunderstanding than interpreting the nature and significance of the costs imposed on the Cuban economy. The major points

---

[101] For examples, see Bienen and Gilpin, "Evaluation," pp. IIId,7-8; Knorr, *Power of Nations*, p. 149; and Losman, *International Economic Sanctions*, pp. 20-46.

[102] International Bank for Reconstruction and Development, *World Bank Atlas*, 1972.

[103] Joint Economic Committee, *Cuba Faces Economic Realities*, p. 11.

in need of clarification are as follows: (1) *Costs, by definition, refer to value forgone.* It makes no sense to deny the economic impact of the embargo on the one hand while admitting on the other that the Cuban economy would be better off without the embargo.[104] If the sanctions are having no impact, lifting the embargo should not affect the Cuban economy at all. (2) *From the standpoint of conventional power analysis, the imposition of costs for noncompliance is a measure of political influence.* Thus, to admit that economic value is being forgone by Cuba because of the U.S. embargo is to admit that political influence is being exercised.[105] (3) *Costs need not be perceived in order to have political effects.* Both the capabilities and the intentions of a target state can be influenced regardless of whether the costs imposed are perceived by anyone. To the extent that preclusive buying of Spanish wolfram by the United States during World War II kept wolfram out of German hands, it succeeded in weakening Hitler's war-making capability regardless of whether he was aware of what was happening. And if economic sanctions can damage an economy enough to cause the government to shift its policy priorities, such measures may affect the intentions of the target state even though the source of the economic hardship may be unperceived by its leaders. And (4) *Costs imposed are by definition benefits that may be conferred.* It is sometimes argued that the United States has "virtually no mechanisms for influencing Cuban behavior";[106] that "the United States has very little leverage on Cuba short of acts of war";[107] or that "a new embargo cannot be imposed on top of the old one."[108] Such views are apparently based on an implicit assumption that power flows only from negative sanctions, and there are few such sanctions short of war left for American policy makers to use. Although this is true, it ignores the vast array of techniques of statecraft based on positive sanctions available to the United States. Indeed, the embargo has expanded the range of positive sanctions at the

[104] Stepan, for example, asserts that "by the mid-1960s Cuba had . . . counterbalanced the U.S. embargo by the Soviet presence"; but in the very next sentence he admits that the sanctions have "contributed to Cuba's sluggish economy" ("United States and Latin America," p. 686). And Lowenthal describes Cuba as having "broken down the blockade" ("Cuba," p. 70) but later asserts that "Cuba would undoubtedly value the increased economic security that improved relations with the United States would afford" (p. 81).

[105] Noting the failure of the sanctions to topple Castro, Weintraub surmises that the primary aim of U.S. policy has become punishment as an end in itself. (*Economic Coercion*, p. 10.) This conclusion is unwarranted, however, since imposing costs on Cuba was related to several other goals of U.S. policy, such as lowering the attractiveness of the Cuban example to others, limiting Castro's capabilities, and imposing costs on the Soviet Union. Pure, unadulterated sadism is rarely a foreign policy goal.

[106] Stepan, "United States and Latin America," p. 686.

[107] Domínguez, "Cuban Foreign Policy," p. 105.

[108] Ibid., p. 108.

disposal of American decision makers. Not only the traditional instruments of aid, trade subsidies (premium prices for sugar?), and so on are available, but also the promise to lift the embargo wholly or partially is now a potentially useful carrot for influencing Cuba. This power resource has literally been created by the embargo, since it was not available in 1960. There is little or no efficacy in offering to stop rocking the boat in exchange for B's compliance if one is not rocking the boat at the time the offer is made, and it is likewise useless to offer to lift an embargo until *after* one has actually imposed one. Clearly, after twenty years, the Cuban "baseline of expectations" has shifted so as to regard lifting the embargo as a positive sanction; the same could not be said in 1960.[109] Lowenthal has suggested that Castro would like the embargo to be lifted and would be willing to compromise in order to achieve this goal.[110] Thus, the costs imposed on Cuba by the U.S. embargo not only constitute a kind of continuing influence on Cuba, they also provide a source of potential leverage in the form of the actual or promised lifting of the embargo. If the impact of the sanctions were as slight as is often asserted, the lifting of the embargo should be a matter of indifference to Castro. Apparently it is not.

The attempt to encourage opposition to Castro through the imposition of economic sanctions is often asserted to have been counterproductive not because opponents were not encouraged but because support for Castro was encouraged even more. This "rally round the flag" effect has been noted before and cannot be denied. With respect to this goal, the sanctions probably were counterproductive. The matter is not quite so simple as is often implied, however; and some qualification is in order. Not all of the enthusiastic domestic support for the Castro regime can be blamed on a reaction to economic sanctions. Some of the support had little to do with the United States but rather was a reaction to the much needed domestic reforms promised by Castro. To the extent that anti-Americanism constituted a unifying force for Castro's supporters, some of this would have occurred regardless of what the United States did—drumming up domestic support by using the "colossus of the North" as a scapegoat is a time-honored and widespread practice in Latin America. The appeal of anti-Americanism and communism to Cubans probably had more to do with the Platt Amendment than with the Soviet Union. Indeed, Wiles suggests that blaming communism and anti-Americanism in Cuba on the *cessation*

[109] On positive sanctions and the "baseline of expectations" see Baldwin, "The Power of Positive Sanctions."

[110] "Cuba," p. 76. See also Roger W. Fontaine, *On Negotiating With Cuba* (Washington, D.C.: American Enterprise Institute, 1975), pp. 58-59; and Enrique A. Baloyra, "Madness of the Method: The United States and Cuba," in *Latin America, the United States, and the Inter-American System,* ed. John D. Martz and Lars Schoultz (Boulder, Colo.: Westview, 1980), pp. 115-144.

of trade gets things backwards: "Who would deny that Cuba would never have gone Communist but for free trade with the United States. . . . That Castro's revolution took an anti-United States turn is beyond question due to the 'close contact with and knowledge of' the United States brought about by free trade."[111] Wiles may be stretching the point a little, but he does help to place events in Cuba in an historical perspective. Furthermore, to the extent that U.S. actions were responsible for stimulating support for Castro, the abortive Bay of Pigs invasion and the Cuban missile crisis probably stirred up more anti-American passions than the embargo. Nothing triggers the "rally round the flag" effect faster than actual or threatened military attack. Thus, although the embargo probably was counterproductive in its attempt to undermine support for the Cuban regime, the importance of this fact can easily be exaggerated. Anti-Americanism would have been an important rallying cry of the Cuban revolution even without the embargo.

Like any other influence attempt, the Cuban embargo entailed costs for the United States. These costs were economic, psychological, and political. The economic costs were in terms of trade forgone and assets lost through expropriation. Although such costs were real, they should not be overestimated. The United States quickly found other places to buy sugar and even rejuvenated its domestic sugar-producing capacity.[112] Since the United States had been paying a premium for Cuban sugar, one could even argue that Americans might have saved money as a result of the embargo. Some writers imply that since the value of the assets seized by Castro was ten times the value of those blocked by the United States, the costs to the latter were not worth it.[113] This cost estimate, however, should be discounted in two ways. In the first place, the United States was probably at least ten times more able than Cuba to afford such costs; and in the second place, Cuba probably would have seized at least some of the U.S. assets regardless of what the United States did. If so, not all the assets seized by Castro are properly attributable as costs of the U.S. influence attempt.

Knorr contends that in addition to such economic costs the United States incurred "a considerable loss of respect and goodwill in western Europe and the underdeveloped world, including much of Latin American public opinion."[114] Although there may be some truth in this charge, several qualifications are in order. First, the intrusion of a "communist outpost"

---

[111] *Communist International Economics*, p. 539.

[112] As a cigar lover who believes that Americans consume too much sugar anyway, I do not necessarily agree with the prevailing opinion that loss of the Cuban sugar was the most important value forgone by the United States; but I yield to the opinion of the marketplace.

[113] Robert Carswell, "Economic Sanctions and the Iranian Experience," *Foreign Affairs* LX (Winter 1981-1982):259.

[114] Knorr, *Power of Nations*, p. 149. See also Bienen and Gilpin, "Evaluation," p. IIId,1.

into the hemisphere threatened the U.S. world image no matter what it did or did not do. Doing nothing would also have entailed costs in terms of the U.S. reputation for action. Second, the sympathy of Third World countries with Cuba was probably more a function of the basic structure of the situation, i.e., a confrontation between a superpower and a small country, than of any particular technique of statecraft used by the United States. Small, weak countries have an understandable concern for the underdog in such circumstances. Third, to the extent that the techniques of statecraft used by American policy makers in dealing with Cuba caused a "loss of respect and goodwill" in the rest of the world, most of the blame belongs to military rather than economic instruments. The maintenance of the unwanted Guantanamo naval base and the Bay of Pigs invasion were probably more important than the embargo in tarnishing the U.S. world image.[115] And a fourth qualification with respect to the implications of the embargo for the U.S. image is that by comparison with the historical American penchant for military intervention in the region, economic measures were a sober and restrained response to a vexing situation. Even by comparison with the policies that immediately preceded it, the embargo was an exercise in restraint, as Domínguez notes: "When it [i.e., the embargo] was instituted, it was, in fact, a de-escalation from the policies of the late Eisenhower and early Kennedy Administrations. It was a sign of flexibility and moderation."[116] On balance, it may well be true that the embargo entailed costs in terms of the U.S. image in other countries, but the foregoing qualifications suggest that such costs were rather modest. The political costs arose mainly from American attempts to pressure other countries into supporting the embargo. Both threatened aid cut-offs and the attempt to make American laws binding on foreign subsidiaries of U.S.-based parent companies were used. The latter raised the thorny issues of extraterritoriality and national sovereignty and was unnecessarily costly to America's relations with Europe. This cost was both the most significant and the least necessary of the costs of the embargo.

Increased Cuban dependence on the Soviet Union is usually cited as a cost of the U.S. embargo, but this may be misleading. Increased costs to the Soviet Union were a definite American goal, and this was tantamount to increased Cuban dependence on the Soviets, i.e., other things being equal, the higher the cost to the Soviets, the greater the Cuban dependence was likely to be. Cuban dependence on the Soviet Union had two additional advantages from the standpoint of U.S. policy makers. Since dependence on the Soviets is not a particularly pleasant experience, other states were

---

[115] Of course, most of the respect and goodwill lost by the United States in the 1960s was caused by the reckless use of military force in Vietnam.

[116] "Taming the Cuban Shrew," p. 113.

unlikely to be anxious to follow the Cuban example. Also, increased Soviet involvement in Cuba made it easier for the United States to demonstrate what it had maintained all along—that communism in Cuba was not an indigenous nationalist movement but rather "the intrusion into this hemisphere of an alien way of life."[117] From this perspective the embargo was a way of forcing the Soviets to become more visible. This willingness to countenance or even encourage dependence on the Soviet Union contrasts with the American approach to Eastern Europe. The secretary of state, however, pointed out that it was one thing to try to woo countries traditionally within the Soviet orbit, but it was quite another to woo a country traditionally in the U.S. sphere of influence in order to coax it not to leave. Such a precedent might give other countries similar ideas. Thus, whereas positive sanctions seemed to be in order with respect to Eastern Europe, negative sanctions were in order with respect to Cuba.[118]

Would noneconomic techniques of statecraft have worked better? Propaganda was used but was a relatively weak instrument in this situation. The credibility of the U.S. commitment to its policy of anticommunism and the validity of the Monroe Doctrine had been challenged—at least in the eyes of American decision makers. A stronger response was needed. Diplomacy, too, had been tried but had many of the same drawbacks as propaganda. Indeed, diplomacy had a particular handicap from the standpoint of U.S. policy. The basic assumption of diplomacy is acceptance of the existence of the target state. Diplomacy may be worse than useless for purposes of denying the legitimacy of the very existence of the other party or, as one State Department official put it, declaring the target to be "a pariah in the Western World."[119] Sweeping moral condemnations are difficult to express through diplomacy, which, of course, is one reason why those who oppose a "moralistic" approach to foreign policy often favor diplomacy. Virtually none of the goals of American policy makers was likely to be attained through diplomacy.

This leaves only military force. Military force, of course, was tried in the disastrous Bay of Pigs invasion of 1961, an undertaking described by Theodore Draper as "one of those rare politico-military events—a perfect failure."[120] Still, a full-scale military invasion could probably have been very effective in demonstrating American resolve, removing Castro, and

[117] Ball, "Our Policy Toward Cuba," p. 744. For another example of this kind of cold war ideology with respect to Cuba, see Mose L. Harvey, *East West Trade and United States Policy* (New York: National Association of Manufacturers, 1966), pp. 114-120.

[118] *East-West Trade Hearings*, pp. 3-22; and Rusk, "Why We Treat Different Communist Countries Differently," pp. 390-396.

[119] Martin, "Cuba, Latin America, and Communism," p. 575. The exception, of course, is a break in diplomatic relations, which the United States tried in January, 1961.

[120] Quoted in Fontaine, *On Negotiating with Cuba*, p. 41.

making the Cuban example unattractive, although it would have cost the Soviet Union very little. The costs to the United States, however, would have been staggering. If the embargo hurt the American image in the Third World, an invasion would have been much more costly. Economically, morally, psychologically, and politically, an invasion would certainly have been more costly than economic sanctions. And after the invasion, the United States would have faced the difficult decision of whether to occupy or pull out, leaving behind a residue of resentment and sympathy with communism that would last for years. As in Vietnam, an American military presence would probably have created more communists than it eliminated. It was precisely in this light that American policy makers viewed the policy of "economic denial."

> To those who urge "stronger action," I can say only, as the President has, that while military action against Cuba sounds like a simple proposition of "going in and getting it over with," this involves awesome risks. The terrible costs that very likely would be involved in such a course of action should be borne in mind when it is lightly proposed that those who bear the full responsibility opt for "action." Neither should it be forgotten that what might ensue from a "tougher policy" against Cuba could not necessarily be limited to a clean-cut military operation in the Caribbean. The interrelation of our global foreign policies practically insures that such an operation could not be delimited but rather could be expected to spill over into other areas, with unpredictable results.[121]

In terms of the goals of American policy makers, the choice was not between a "soft line" based on propaganda and diplomacy and a "hard line" based on economic sanctions, but rather between a "soft line" based on economic sanctions and a "hard line" based on military force. They seem to have chosen the most cost-effective alternative.

Given the goals of U.S. policy makers and given the likely costs and benefits of alternative courses of action, it is difficult to deny that economic sanctions offered the best available combination of costs and benefits. This policy option did not lead to stunning success, but it was partially successful in approximating some of the goals; and it avoided the exorbitant costs associated with a military approach. American policy makers did not naively choose policy instruments doomed to certain failure, but rather chose a rational and prudent course of action that was more successful than is generally recognized.

If criticisms of American policy toward Cuba since 1960 are to be made,

---

[121] Martin, "Cuba, Latin America, and Communism," p. 575. See also Ball, "Our Policy Toward Cuba," p. 741.

they should focus more on the definition of goals and the execution of the influence attempt than on the techniques of statecraft employed. Perhaps the United States should not have been so rigidly anticommunist, perhaps it should have been more ready to allow the Monroe Doctrine to fade away, perhaps it should have been more respectful of Cuba's right to self-determination and of the obligations with respect to nonintervention, and perhaps it should have recognized that it does not own the Western Hemisphere; but these are essentially matters that affected the way American policy makers defined their goals. Once the goals had been chosen, it is difficult to fault their choice of foreign policy instruments. American policy toward Cuba may also have suffered from bad timing. During the period 1969–1974 Cuban foreign policy greatly moderated its subversive activities in the Western Hemisphere, a change recognized and rewarded when the Organization of American States lifted economic sanctions in 1975. Perhaps the United States should have declared the embargo a success and ended it during that period.[122] It was difficult for other countries to understand why the United States continued a hard line toward Cuba while seeking rapprochement with China and détente with the Soviet Union. What had started out as a unified front against global communism seemed to be degenerating into a strictly U.S.–Cuban affair. Small wonder that support for the embargo from other countries was increasingly difficult to come by. But, alas, the American policy makers had little time for Cuba; they were preoccupied with extricating the United States from Vietnam, subverting the elected government of Chile, and wondering what to do about Watergate. By 1975 Cuba had returned to international adventurism, this time in Africa; and a new set of U.S. goals seemed to be emerging.

The purpose of this discussion, however, is not to assess the wisdom of American policy, but rather to determine the utility of economic statecraft in pursuing U.S. foreign policy objectives (primarily from 1960 to 1975). More precisely, it is to judge whether the case provides support for the proposition that economic sanctions are ineffective, counterproductive, and expensive techniques of statecraft. Whatever "lessons" might be learned from the U.S. embargo against Cuba, the lesson that economic sanctions have relatively low utility does not seem to be one of them. If lessons there must be, perhaps the following would suffice:

1. When big powers pick on small weak countries, they are likely to be viewed as bullies.
2. Knowing when to lift sanctions is as important as knowing when to impose them.

[122] Cf. George W. Ball, "Your Evil Embargo: Our Purity of Purpose," *New York Times*, March 21, 1974.

3. Economic sanctions can have a significant economic impact on a target country even when they are not universal.
4. Imposing unilateral sanctions is one thing, but clumsy efforts to twist arms to get other countries to follow suit is another.
5. Military statecraft can be a costly and counterproductive undertaking, as the Bay of Pigs affair demonstrates.
6. Images matter!
7. Geography matters!
8. History matters!
9. It is wise to try to understand the goals of a policy before condemning the means used to implement it. (The ends may not always justify the means, but they at least help in assessing the effectiveness of the means.)
10. The country on whom economic sanctions are imposed may or may not be the primary target of the influence attempt.
11. What looks like a clear-cut failure from one perspective may be a qualified success from another.

THE UNITED NATIONS AND RHODESIA

In November 1965 the government of Rhodesia, a former colony of Great Britain, issued a "Unilateral Declaration of Independence" (UDI) asserting its independence.[123] Rhodesia's political system was controlled by a small minority of white people, and Britain had been trying to make a commitment to eventual majority rule a precondition for independence. The matter involved the most sensitive issue on the African continent, the allocation of political power along racial lines. After a year of diplomacy, propaganda, and a variety of economic sanctions, Britain brought the matter to the United Nations Security Council, which, for the first time in its history, invoked Articles 39 and 41 of the United Nations Charter and imposed mandatory economic sanctions on Rhodesia. These sanctions remained in force until December 1979. Although the sanctions were circumvented to some extent by many countries, including the United States, Britain, Japan, and the Soviet Union, it is generally agreed that South Africa, which shared a common border with this landlocked country, was the primary conduit for evading the sanctions. Despite the eventual establishment of an independent Rhodesia, renamed Zimbabwe, in April 1980 based on majority rule, the case is frequently cited as an example of the

---

[123] The precise legal status of Rhodesia in 1965 is a matter of dispute, but this has little relevance to the argument presented here. On this and other aspects of Rhodesian sanctions see Strack, *Sanctions: The Case of Rhodesia*. See also Margaret Doxey, "The Making of Zimbabwe: From Illegal to Legal Independence," *The Year Book of World Affairs* XXXVI (1982):151-165.

failure of economic sanctions. According to Bienen and Gilpin, "most observers have concluded that sanctions were a great failure in Rhodesia"; Harry Strack contends that the Rhodesian case confirms the general conclusion of others that economic sanctions are "ineffective and may be counterproductive"; Losman views the sanctions as politically ineffective despite some "damaging economic results"; Richard C. Porter denies that there were any significantly damaging economic results; Adler-Karlsson sees the United Nations sanctions as having been "defeated"; Judith Miller refers to them as having "proved unsuccessful"; James Reston cites the case of Rhodesia as evidence that "economic sanctions don't really work"; and Roger Fisher mentions the Rhodesian experience in a similar context. [124] Once it became apparent that Rhodesia was destined to have majority rule, commentators have usually insisted that the primary goal of the sanctions was attained because of factors other than economic sanctions. [125]

In specifying the structure of the influence attempt in terms of goals and targets there is an immediate difficulty since various members of the United Nations had different, and even opposing, objectives. As in the case of the League of Nations, the discussion here will focus on the dominant actors, Great Britain and, to a lesser extent, the United States. This does not matter greatly, however, since many goals, especially insofar as Rhodesia was the target, were shared by much of the international community. The targets and objectives of the sanctions against Rhodesia could be summarized as follows: [126]

Rhodesia

The primary objective was a political system based on majority rule in Rhodesia. Opinions differed, of course, on how soon this change should be implemented; but the basic goal of eventual majority rule was widely shared. Secondary goals with respect to Rhodesia included the following:

---

[124] Bienen and Gilpin, "Evaluation," p. IIIe,16; Strack, *Sanctions*, p. 238; Losman, *International Economic Sanctions*, pp. 80-124; Porter, "Economic Sanctions"; Adler-Karlsson, "The U.S. Embargo," p. 171; Judith Miller, "When Sanctions Worked," *Foreign Policy*, no. 39 (Summer 1980), p. 118; James Reston, "Moscow Uses Muscle," *New York Times*, January 2, 1980; and Fisher, "Sanctions Won't Work," p. 21. See also the testimony in 1969 of Dean Acheson and Charles Burton Marshall that sanctions against Rhodesia had not worked and would not work. (U.S. House of Representatives, Committee on Foreign Affairs, *Hearings: Rhodesia and United States Foreign Policy*, 91st Cong., 1st sess., 1969, pp. 100-168. Cited hereafter as *Hearings on Rhodesia*.) Oddly, Strack immediately follows with the declaration that "this does not suggest, however, that sanctions by themselves have failed to achieve secondary goals or that they have not had any adverse effects on Rhodesia." (p. 238).

[125] See, for example, Milton Friedman, "Economic Sanctions," p. 76.

[126] Strack presents a useful discussion of the objectives of various actors which is more detailed and slightly different from that presented here. (*Sanctions*, pp. 24-40.)

1.   Avoiding the use of force was especially important to Britain but was also a goal for many other states. The Third World states advocating the use of force were probably less interested in the use of force *per se* than in demonstrating the intensity of their commitment to the primary goal.

2.   The isolation of Rhodesia and the moral censure of its policies could be considered either together or separately as secondary goals. No matter what the wording of any particular resolution, the underlying issue was the morality of allocating political power along racial lines. The question of South Africa was never far away.

3.   Encouraging opponents of the Rhodesian regime was another secondary goal.

4.   Imposing costs for noncompliance. This goal is often misunderstood as seeking vengeance or punishment as an end in itself.[127] Without denying the possible influence of such motives, however, it should be noted that this goal was consonant with the idea of maintaining pressure on Rhodesia to comply. There is no reason to believe that sadistic motives were dominant.

African and Other Third World States

Rhodesia was not the only target of this influence attempt, although it was probably the primary target for most states. For Britain and the United States, black Africa and the Third World in general were also targets. The basic dilemma for Britain and, to a lesser extent, the United States was how to demonstrate intense disapproval of the white regime and commitment to eventual majority rule while simultaneously resisting pressure to use military force. Britain's colonial past and America's history of internal racial problems had weakened the credibility of mere words for each nation.

Before examining the effectiveness of economic sanctions in achieving these goals, the extraordinary difficulty of the primary objective should be noted. White supremacy was not merely an incidental characteristic of the Rhodesian polity, it was a fundamental—perhaps *the* fundamental—principle of the whole society. Rhodesian whites believed that their country and their very lives were at stake and compared the situation to that facing Britain in 1939.[128] By 1978 the Rhodesian regime headed by Ian Smith had conceded the principle of majority rule, which a decade earlier had been ruled out in Smith's lifetime.[129] This was a substantial shift in Rhodesian policy with respect to a fundamental issue. *Considering the difficulty of the task,* twelve years was a remarkably short—at least reasonably

---

[127] See testimony by Marshall and Acheson in *Hearings on Rhodesia*, pp. 102-103, 144; and Galtung, "On the Effects of International Economic Sanctions," pp. 379-380.

[128] Strack, *Sanctions*, p. 14.

[129] Doxey, "Zimbabwe," p. 161.

short—period of time for such a change.[130] This should be abundantly apparent to any observer of the speed with which the American government has been able to execute the easier task of implementing the U.S. Supreme Court decision in *Brown vs. Board of Education* (1954).

To say that the primary goal was achieved "with all deliberate speed," however, is not to have said much, if anything, about the effectiveness of economic sanctions in bringing about this result. Was majority rule achieved without regard to sanctions, because of sanctions, or despite sanctions? Although such important questions cannot be avoided, their consideration will be postponed until after the degree of success in achieving secondary goals has been reviewed. For now it suffices to stipulate the existence of majority rule (at least in theory) in Rhodesia and to note that the causes have yet to be identified.

With respect to avoiding the use of military force, sanctions seem to have had a high degree of success. At no time did the United Nations, Britain, or the United States even come close to using force against Rhodesia. What about the possibility of a "mad dog" attack by the target state, which was so feared when the League of Nations had imposed sanctions on Italy? Not only did no such attack occur, but in this case the target state responded by going out of its way to "establish a pattern of conduct in its foreign relations that in no way could be construed as hostile or threatening."[131]

With respect to the goals of isolating Rhodesia and expressing the moral disapproval of the international community, the sanctions also achieved a remarkable degree of success. Not a single state—not even Portugal or South Africa—recognized the Smith regime as the legitimate government of Rhodesia. Rhodesia came to be regarded as a "pariah state," a moral leper in the international community. Rhodesia will always be remembered as the first country against which the United Nations imposed mandatory sanctions. This historic event had a symbolic significance that went beyond any economic inconvenience that might or might not have accompanied the act. Not even South Africa had been so treated. As evidence that this isolation mattered to Rhodesians, Strack observes that "anyone who has read Rhodesian newspapers and parliamentary debates since UDI and has lived in Rhodesia for even a short period of time cannot fail to notice the longing for recognition—the reaching out for any scrap of recognition."[132]

The idea that economic sanctions will provide psychological support

---

[130] British Prime Minister Harold Wilson's ill-considered and ridiculous comment in 1966 that sanctions would work in weeks rather than months was just that and should be so considered. Instead, it seems to have become the basic reference point for assessing the effectiveness of the sanctions for many people. Strack, *Sanctions*, p. 18.

[131] Ibid., pp. 44, 249.

[132] Ibid., p. 83.

and encouragement for internal opponents of the government of the target state has been frequently ridiculed ever since the League of Nations sanctions against Italy. Indeed, one of the most important points in Johan Galtung's frequently cited article is that external negative sanctions are likely to increase rather than decrease internal social cohesion and political integration.[133] This "rally round the flag" effect is the single most common basis for the charge that economic sanctions tend to be counterproductive. Now, obviously, if this proposition is to be given a fair test, *all* the potential or actual internal opponents of the regime must be considered. To ignore the black population (96 percent) while considering the impact of the sanctions on the white population (4 percent) provides very little support for the conclusion that "the theory that economic sanctions would be an act of support for the opposing groups" in the target state is not validated.[134] Although sanctions against Rhodesia did indeed increase support for the Smith regime *within the white community*, there is no evidence that they had similar effects on the black majority. On the contrary, as Doxey points out, "the claims and interests of black Rhodesians were sustained and reinforced" by sanctions because "the majority of the population of Zimbabwe were from the outset, seeking the same outcome as their external supporters"; thus, "the solidarity under pressure which has been characteristic of other cases" of economic sanctions "was restricted in Zimbabwe to the dominant white elite."[135] The conclusion that the sanctions were at least somewhat successful in encouraging internal opposition to the regime is buttressed by the fact that these opponents explicitly objected whenever the lifting of sanctions was being considered. It is ironic that Galtung should have chosen the case of Rhodesia to illustrate his theory of increasing political integration in response to external economic sanctions, for this is one of the few cases that dramatically contradicts his theory.

The tendency to assume that since sanctions against Italy and Cuba had unifying effects on the target state this would always be the case, can transform a plausible hypothesis about probable tendencies into an "iron law." The dangers of this are illustrated by the testimony of Charles Burton Marshall and Dean Acheson three years after sanctions had been implemented by the United Nations. Prefacing his remarks with observations about the difficulties of facing up to the facts of failure and admitting that

---

[133] "International Economic Sanctions," pp. 388-391.

[134] For an example of an argument to this effect, see Wallensteen, "Economic Sanctions," pp. 257-258. See also Losman's testimony in 1980 that "Ian Smith . . . was able to rally the people and power structure around him, snuff out opposition, unite and solidify resistance against the desired goals of the sanctions initiators" (U.S. Senate, Committee on Banking, Housing, and Urban Affairs, *Hearings: U.S. Embargo of Food and Technology*, p. 186).

[135] "Zimbabwe," pp. 161, 165.

one's premises are wrong—an obvious jab at the supporters of sanctions against Rhodesia—Marshall depicted the following scenario:

> The following results were projected in applying sanctions to Rhodesia: deprivation and economic dislocation, compounding of internal difficulties to a degree making it impossible for the regime to go on governing, erosion and destruction of the regime's political base, then either a popular upsurge to supplant the regime or a capitulation on its part, and finally a contrite submission to British terms to insure an end to white domination in the Rhodesian electorate and governing structure.[136]

In context it is clear that this scenario was intended to drive home his point that only the most stubborn and close-minded sanctions supporter could refuse to recognize the failure of the policy. Marshall went on to read part of Galtung's article into the record, citing it as "the best examination of the point" he knew of, adding that it was "based on thorough empirical research done *in the first few weeks after* imposition of sanctions."[137] Acheson testified in a similar vein, confidently asserting the "delusory" nature of sanctions and predicting inevitable failure in the attempt to use economic sanctions "to foment civil disturbance, uprisings, revolution, and violence" within the target state.[138] Avowing that *all* the results to date had been "contraproductive," he declared the sanctions a "manifest failure."[139] Although both Marshall and Acheson implied that the hypothetical sequence of events in their scenarios was wildly improbable, a decade later their descriptions corresponded more closely with what actually happened than almost anything written by serious students of sanctions during that period! Although the extent to which international support expressed through economic sanctions stimulated domestic opposition in Rhodesia is arguable, it is difficult to dispute the fact that internal opposition increased greatly during the sanctions period and that leaders of this opposition tended to regard the economic sanctions as symbolic of external support for their cause.

With respect to the goal of imposing costs for noncompliance on Rhodesia, the sanctions seemed to be moderately successful in imposing psychological and political costs; but, since these were already discussed with

---

[136] *Hearings on Rhodesia*, pp. 101-102.

[137] Ibid. Italics added.

[138] Ibid., pp. 126-127.

[139] Ibid., p. 143. In 1971 Acheson rendered similar testimony referring to Rhodesian sanctions as "an abject failure" that "must continue to fail" and, never afraid of claiming too much, as having failed not only in their major purpose but in "every purpose." (U.S. Senate, Committee on Foreign Relations, *Hearings: U.N. Sanctions Against Rhodesia—Chrome*, 92d Cong., 1st sess., 1971, pp. 38-40. Hereafter cited as *Hearings on Chrome*.)

reference to the goals of isolation and censure, only the economic costs will be considered here. The extent to which sanctions imposed costs on the Rhodesian economy is a matter of dispute. On one extreme are unequivocal assertions of at least some economic impact. Thus, Bienen and Gilpin declare that "all analysts of the impact of sanctions on the Rhodesian economy agree that sanctions increased the costs of trade for Rhodesia, created foreign exchange problems," and led to "bottlenecks in certain areas"; while Robin Renwick concludes that "there can be no doubt that sanctions had a significant economic effect, causing a severe loss of export earnings and foreign exchange difficulties and acting as a brake on economic growth."[140] At the other extreme is Richard Porter's survey of various ways in which sanctions might cause economic hardship, leading him to conclude that "whatever one means by 'succeed', sanctions against Rhodesia clearly did not succeed."[141] In between these two extremes are a number of scholars who acknowledge the likelihood of some economic impact while denying that these effects were great enough to bring about political success.[142] Perhaps the most judicious of these is the following:

> Over the years, sanctions produced an effect, though it was a slow and debilitating, rather than a quick and decisive one. Sanctions-busting was a complicated and expensive business, which raised the cost of living. Rhodesia in 1965 had been poised for speedy growth, particularly in mining. This prospect did not materialize. In time the cumulative impact of restrictions on travel to, and communications with, places other than South Africa became steadily harder to bear.[143]

Since opinion is split with respect to the economic costs imposed on Rhodesia, conservative assumptions suggest that success with respect to this goal should be recorded as minimal. However, two aspects of the economic impact that do not seem to be matters of dispute should be noted. First, whatever the degree of economic impact, the Rhodesian economy was clearly not "crippled," "halted," "brought to its knees," or delivered any "crushing economic blows." Although such metaphors, as noted before, are not especially precise, they do convey the idea that costs to Rhodesia were bearable. Second, it is generally agreed that the adverse economic effects of sanctions, especially in terms of employment, tended

---

[140] Bienen and Gilpin, "Evaluation," p. IIIe,2; Renwick, *Economic Sanctions*, p. 76.

[141] Porter, "Economic Sanctions," p. 107.

[142] Doxey, "Zimbabwe"; Losman, *International Economic Sanctions*, pp. 80-123; Strack, *Sanctions*, pp. 85-166; D. G. Clarke, "Zimbabwe's International Economic Position and Aspects of Sanctions Removal," *Journal of Commonwealth and Comparative Politics* XVIII (March 1980):28-54; and Lord Saint Brides, "The Lessons of Zimbabwe-Rhodesia," *International Security* IV (Spring 1980):177-184.

[143] Saint Brides, "Lessons," p. 180.

to fall disproportionately on black Rhodesians. Although regrettable, the question of whether this should be regarded as irrelevant to, promotive of, or detrimental to the achievement of the primary goal of the influence attempt should not be answered too quickly—a point to be considered later.

With respect to the objective of demonstrating intense commitment to the principle of majority rule in Africa without using force, mandatory economic sanctions were probably moderately successful from the standpoint of Britain, the United States, and the United Nations itself. The significance of the mandatory sanctions was enhanced by the fact that either Britain or the United States could have vetoed such measures, by the fact that they were more costly than propaganda or diplomacy, and by the well understood fact that the lifting of the sanctions would be subject to a Soviet veto. Short of military force, this was about the strongest and most impressive move that could have been made to demonstrate recognition of what G. Mennen Williams had aptly labelled "a kind of African West Berlin" in terms of its symbolic importance to Africans.[144]

The question of the extent to which economic sanctions contributed to the primary goal of establishing majority rule in Rhodesia, the most crucial question of all in assessing the effectiveness of the sanctions, must now be addressed. The common line of argument in judging the efficacy of economic sanctions is to classify an influence attempt as a failure if the primary goal is not completely attained. Although this makes it easy to portray most instances of economic sanctions as "failures," the Rhodesian case is not so easily dismissed. In order to justify the conclusion that sanctions against Rhodesia failed, alternative explanations for the eventual outcome must be offered. The most common alternative explanation is that guerrilla warfare was responsible for the shift in the government's policy. Some of the positions taken on this issue are listed below.

> All analysts agree that . . . it was not economic weakness brought about through trade and investment sanctions but military struggle in Rhodesia that has made the survival of the Smith regime problematic.[145]

Comment: Is it possible that the "military struggle" was in some sense "brought about" by the sanctions? Even if there were no causal links

---

[144] *Hearings on Rhodesia*, p. 169. Of course, not everyone would agree that impressing African states was a desirable goal. Acheson, for instance, answered a question about the possible reaction to lifting sanctions in 1971 as follows: "I suppose it will raise a great deal of commotion among governing regimes in black Africa. This wouldn't worry me a bit, not a bit. It does not impair any national interest of ours. We have been following the wrong course in Africa. I would call it the Soapy Williams hangover that we have, and the sooner we get rid of that nonsense the better off we will be" (*Hearings on Chrome*, p. 41).

[145] Bienen and Gilpin, "Evaluation," p. IIIe,2.

whatever between sanctions and the war, to the extent that "economic weakness" was caused by sanctions, the Rhodesian capability for coping with the war was reduced.

The combined effects of sanctions, Mozambique hostility, and the guerrilla war accomplished what the sanctions program alone could not do.[146]

Comment: Is it possible that Mozambique hostility and/or the guerrilla war were themselves partially results of sanctions? Although Strack sees the war and the attitude of Mozambique as causally related, he regards the relationship between sanctions and the war as "spurious," but he makes no serious attempt to demonstrate the latter point.[147]

The main factors in inducing Mr. Smith to move to this position were the war and strong pressure from South Africa. . . . Sanctions were a secondary factor.[148]

Comment: Is it possible that the war and/or the South African attitude were causally linked with sanctions?

The mounting costs of guerrilla warfare, the greater militancy of surrounding states, the increase in Cuban and Soviet influence, and a number of other factors have forced Smith to accept the principle of majority rule. Sanctions continue, but it is these other factors (coupled with pressure from South Africa) that have brought about this dramatic change in the Rhodesian position. . . . The imminent downfall of the white government in Rhodesia, if it occurs, will be the result of armed conflict rather than sanctions.[149]

Comment: Did economic sanctions have anything to do with the emergence of these "other factors" during the 1970s? The logic of Losman's position is remarkable. In the passages quoted he seems to be denying causal connections between sanctions and majority rule; yet elsewhere he explicitly asserts a causal link between sanctions and the war. Thus, he depicts guerrilla warfare as one of the unintended and undesirable by-products of the imposition of economic sanctions. "Without question," he argues, "growth in African unemployment . . . and frustrations of Africans at the failure of sanctions . . . have contributed to the very substantial rise in terrorism and armed conflict."[150] In the light of this contention that eco-

---

[146] Strack, *Sanctions*, p. 238.

[147] Ibid., pp. 237, xvi.

[148] Renwick, *Economic Sanctions*, p. 54.

[149] Losman, *International Economic Sanctions*, pp. 122–123, 136.

[150] Ibid., p. 120. See also p. 136. Earlier Losman notes that the brunt of the impact of sanctions had fallen on the "Africans," who he describes as "not a group that can place

nomic sanctions triggered a chain of events leading to guerrilla warfare and the downfall of the regime, Losman's denial of the political success of sanctions is puzzling. His basic criterion of success is that the "economic damage inflicted" by sanctions "must be sufficient to unleash domestic political pressures that will either topple an intransigent regime or bring about the adoption of new policies more in accord with the norms of the boycotting nations" (p. 128); yet when confronted with evidence that such domestic political pressures have indeed been unleashed, he fails to make the appropriate inference. Surely guerrilla warfare is one of the most dramatic forms of domestic political pressure imaginable. Ironically, Losman interprets this evidence that sanctions were working as a consequence of the failure of sanctions.[151]

> Armed guerrilla warfare—not economic sanctions—destroyed its [i.e., Rhodesia's] stability.[152]

Comment: None.

> In evaluating the role of UN sanctions against Rhodesia, the first and obvious conclusion must be that for as long as they were the main instrument of pressure they did not achieve the goal of ending UDI.[153]

Comment: Economic sanctions *were* the "main instrument" used by the United Nations from 1966 to 1979. Guerrilla warfare was never an "in-

---

serious political pressure upon the regime," (p. 114) and asserts that "the domestic discontent that was to have been stirred by the dislocations caused by sanctions occurred only on a limited basis and mainly in one year" (p. 115). It is difficult to reconcile such comments with his later assertion of causal links among African unemployment, guerrilla warfare, and the downfall of the white regime.

[151] Both Losman and Strack see a causal connection between the incidence of domestic violence in Rhodesia and the impact of sanctions; yet neither views this as evidence of success. On the contrary, they count such effects as counterproductive. In Strack's case this seems to be based on the fact that sanctions increased the suffering of the very people they were supposed to help. In Losman's case the logic is that nonmilitary techniques of statecraft *must* have nonviolent effects in order to succeed. Strack's position underscores the importance of assessing efficacy in terms of the originally postulated goals. The primary goal of Rhodesian sanctions was not to "help" black Rhodesians in some general way but rather to increase their political power; thus, his concern about human suffering is relevant to assessing costs rather than effectiveness. Losman's argument demonstrates the importance of allowing for multiple bases of power. Nonviolent techniques of statecraft may indeed have violent effects. Nor is there any contradiction here with respect to the goal of avoiding war. That goal concerned the avoidance of armed conflict between the sanctioning powers and Rhodesians; it said nothing about warfare within Rhodesia among Rhodesians. See Losman, *International Economic Sanctions*, p. 136; Strack, *Sanctions*, p. 237; and Strack's testimony in favor of lifting sanctions in 1972 (U.S. House of Representatives, Committee on Foreign Affairs, *Hearings: Sanctions as an Instrumentality of the United Nations—Rhodesia as a Case Study*, 92d Cong., 2d sess., 1972, pp. 110-113).

[152] Friedman, *Newsweek*, January 21, 1980, p. 76.

[153] Doxey, *Economic Sanctions*, 2d ed., p. 73.

strument of pressure" *used by the United Nations* except insofar as it was a consequence of economic sanctions. In fairness to Doxey, however, it should be noted that her treatments of economic sanctions against Rhodesia are the fairest and most judicious available. She tends to view economic sanctions as a significant, if not decisive, factor in undermining the legitimacy of the white regime and even hints at possible causal links between the effects of sanctions and the rise of the guerrilla movement. As early as 1972 she pinpointed the "serious growth in African unemployment" as an effect of sanctions that could be ignored by the regime only "temporarily";[154] and in 1982 she observed that this situation "encouraged enrollment in the guerrilla forces at a later stage."[155]

The questions noted with respect to the above quotations are not intended to be rhetorical but rather to identify topics that should have been—but usually were not—addressed seriously by the authors. The main point is that most writers have failed even to consider, let alone refute, plausible hypotheses establishing causal links between armed insurgency in Rhodesia and economic sanctions. These sanctions were clearly intended to undermine the legitimacy of the white regime and to encourage opposition to that regime. The precise mechanism through which economic sanctions eventually contributed to producing those results may not have been anticipated but, as the testimony of Marshall and Acheson cited earlier suggests, such consequences were not entirely unforeseeable. The tendency of studies of economic statecraft to emphasize detrimental effects that were not specifically anticipated calls to mind the warning of Albert Hirschman regarding the tendency to ignore the other side of this coin:

> Economists have often dwelt upon situations in which a policy is self-defeating, i.e., leads to certain unforeseen repercussions which foil the aim at which the policy was originally directed. It is, however, equally possible that a policy has unforeseen effects which reinforce rather than destroy the result which the policy had tried to bring about.[156]

Are there plausible hypotheses linking the effects of economic sanctions against Rhodesia with guerrilla warfare? Ted Robert Gurr suggests several worthy of at least some consideration:[157]

1. "The potential for collective violence varies strongly with the intensity and scope of relative deprivation (RD) among members of a collectivity."

---

[154] "International Sanctions: A Framework for Analysis with Special Reference to the U.N. and Southern Africa," *International Organization* XXVI (Summer 1972):545.

[155] "Zimbabwe," p. 157.

[156] *National Power*, pp. 39-40.

[157] *Why Men Rebel* (Princeton: Princeton University Press, 1970), pp. 360-366.

Comment: United Nations sanctions were, in effect, a certification by the international community of the relative deprivation of black Rhodesians.

2. "The potential for political violence varies strongly with the intensity and scope of normative justifications for political violence among members of a collectivity."

Comment: Although United Nations sanctions did not specifically endorse violence, they made it easier to justify since they certified the relative deprivation of black Rhodesians to be not only an empirical fact but also a deplorable one.

3. "Any decrease in the average level of value capabilities in a collectivity without an accompanying decrease in value expectations increases the intensity of RD."

Comment: Unemployment is an example *par excellence* of a sudden decrease in value capabilities. "Deprivation-induced discontent is a general spur to action. Psychological theory and group conflict theory both suggest that the greater the intensity of discontent, the more likely is violence" (p. 13). As is frequently noted, the brunt of the deprivational effects of sanctions fell on the black population. It would not be surprising if this increased the discontent of those affected.

4. "In any heterogeneous population, the intensity of RD is greatest with respect to discrepancy affecting economic values."

Comment: It is precisely the economic effects of sanctions that were deflected from the white to the black population of Rhodesia.

5. "The intensity and scope of normative justifications for political violence vary strongly and inversely with the intensity and scope of regime legitimacy."

Comment: During the period that sanctions were in effect the black population moved from acquiescence toward opposition to the regime. The voting of mandatory sanctions—an unprecedented step in United Nations history—constituted the most universal peacetime assault on the legitimacy of a regime in the history of the world.[158] To the extent that sanctions were successful in undermining the legitimacy of the regime, they created conditions in which political violence was more likely.

6. "The intensity of normative justifications for political violence varies strongly with the extent to which symbolic appeals offer plausible explanations of the sources of RD, identify political targets for violence, and provide symbols of group identification."

Comment: The United Nations sanctions implied both an identifiable target and an explanation for deprivation that seemed plausible to black Rho-

---

[158] Perhaps the "peacetime" qualification is unneeded, since the scope of the international condemnation was unprecedented. The revulsion toward Axis regimes during World War II, however, may have made up in intensity what it lacked in universality.

desians—to whit, the white regime and its supporters are responsible for your problems.

7. "The likelihood of internal war varies with the degree of foreign support for dissidents."

Comment: At least at the symbolic level, the amount of foreign support for regime opponents was massive and unprecedented.

Testing the validity of these hypotheses with regard to sanctions against Rhodesia is beyond the scope of this book. They are mentioned here only to illustrate the existence of carefully constructed, plausible hypotheses that suggest possible causal connections between sanctions and guerrilla warfare in Rhodesia. There seems to be ample reason to suspect that sanctions might have contributed to creating conditions in Rhodesia that enhanced the likelihood of political violence. Until such hypotheses have been considered, assertions that economic sanctions failed while guerrilla warfare succeeded in bringing majority rule to Rhodesia seem premature. The fact that the misery of black Rhodesians may have been the causal condition that explains the success of the sanctions may be an ugly and unpleasant possibility to consider, but that is no excuse for ignoring it. Truth and beauty do not always go together.

Other hypotheses suggested to explain the acceptance of majority rule in Rhodesia include the following:

1. The hostility of Mozambique was an important cause.

Comment: Mozambique was an important base of support for the guerrillas. The problem with this hypothesis is not its validity but rather its implied denial that economic sanctions were at least partially responsible for the posture of Mozambique. If the entire international community had been supporting rather than censuring the white regime in Rhodesia, would Mozambique have had the same propensity to intervene? The costs of intervention in a "pariah state" are likely to be lower than those incurred in intervening in a "respectable" state. On an *a priori* basis, the failure even to consider the possibility of causal links between sanctions and the attitude of Mozambique seems unjustified.[159]

2. Pressure from South Africa changed the attitude of the Smith government.

Comment: Again, this is probably true but does not necessarily mean that economic sanctions did not matter. The sanctions kept the issue of white rule in the international and African spotlight, and close association with the Smith regime was becoming more and more costly for South Africa, especially from a political and psychological standpoint. The desire of

---

[159] This is a minimalist argument. If, as Doxey suggests, the sanctions against Rhodesia tended to undermine the legitimacy of white rule in "Southern Africa as a whole," the very existence of Mozambique as an independent political entity was partially caused by sanctions. Doxey, *Economic Sanctions*, 2d ed., p. 79.

South Africa to distance itself from Rhodesian intransigence is more likely to have been an indication that sanctions were working than that they had failed. The possibility is plausible enough, at least, that it cannot simply be ignored. Even if the *desire* of South Africa arose for reasons that had nothing whatever to do with sanctions, the *capability* of South Africa to bring pressure to bear on Rhodesia may have had a great deal to do with sanctions. To the extent that sanctions increased Rhodesian dependence on South Africa, they also gave South Africa more capability to influence Rhodesian policy.

3. Political, diplomatic, and psychological isolation of Rhodesia was more important than the effects of economic sanctions.[160]

Comment: Once again, this is probably true but misleading, since the political, diplomatic, and psychological isolation of Rhodesia *was an effect* of economic sanctions, at least to some extent. The effects of imposing economic sanctions are not—and cannot be—confined to the economic realm; nor was this intended by those who imposed them. The United Nations influence attempt vis-à-vis Rhodesia was spearheaded by mandatory economic sanctions. From 1966 to 1979 every other measure was supplementary to the basic instrument of economic sanctions. Indeed, the primary instrument through which the international community expressed the intensity of its revulsion toward the Smith regime was economic sanctions. This was not mere diplomatic nonrecognition; this was diplomatic nonrecognition with a vengeance; it was nonrecognition expressed in a way that made people understand that there was something extraordinary about this case. To pretend that the effects of economic sanctions against Rhodesia can be—or should be—measured in terms of mere economic statistics is grossly misleading. The imposition of sanctions was a political act that was intended to have political effects. To portray the situation as one in which economic sanctions had little or nothing to do with the psychological, political, and diplomatic isolation of Rhodesia is to misconstrue both the intended and actual effects of the sanctions.

The costs of the United Nations sanctions against Rhodesia appear to have been moderate and bearable for those imposing them. Indeed, the leakiness that impaired their economic impact had the corresponding advantage of moderating the economic costs of the sanctions. Perhaps the most controversial cost was increased American dependence on the Soviet Union for chrome, but the importance of this seems to have been exaggerated.[161] If the guerrilla war is viewed as a consequence of sanctions, of course, the costs loom somewhat larger—including more than 12,000 lives. Although this is certainly a relevant consideration, it must be re-

[160] See, for example, Strack, *Sanctions*, p. 247.
[161] Ibid., pp. 146-164.

membered that the costs of an influence attempt are here defined in terms of the values of the decision makers; and although one might wish that statesmen would value each human life equally, it would be naive to assume that they do. Making sure that their own citizens were not endangered was probably more important for most governments than protecting the lives of Rhodesians. Thus, most governments in the United Nations, rightly or wrongly, probably regarded 12,000 Rhodesian lives as a more acceptable cost than the lives of a much smaller number of their own citizens. A universal ethics that would make each life count the same in the calculus of the world's statesmen has not yet emerged.

Would alternative policy instruments have been more useful? Diplomacy and propaganda would have been less costly but would also have been less effective with respect to every goal except avoiding the use of force. Indeed, it was the comparative costliness of economic sanctions that made them more effective as symbols of condemnation, as encouragement to regime opponents, and as signs of good faith to Third World countries. It is even possible that the use of force would have been more likely in the absence of economic sanctions since pressure from the Third World to use force was to some extent defused by the sanctions. Military force might have achieved the same outcome faster but would have risked the lives of those imposing the military sanctions. This option was thus ruled out as too costly from the start. The assertion that "it is hard to escape the conclusion that the Rhodesian issue has been mishandled"[162] implies the existence of at least one alternative course of action with a demonstrably better combination of costs and effectiveness; it is incumbent on those who draw such conclusions to identify such policy options. The vague assertion that statesmen should have practiced "skillful manipulation of the innumerable factors at play in international politics,"[163] however, does not constitute adequate specification of an alternative course of action.

Overall, the sanctions against Rhodesia were moderately successful in approximating most of the goals of the sanctioning states at an acceptable cost level. If causal links between sanctions and guerrilla warfare in Rhodesia are postulated, the effectiveness in achieving the primary goal of majority rule was probably much better than anyone expected—or had a right to expect. In comparison with other instruments of statecraft, the combination of costs and benefits associated with economic sanctions was probably preferable to that associated with any of the alternatives.

For those who insist on "lessons," the following are probably among the less dangerous and misleading ones:

[162] Grieve, "Economic Sanctions," p. 441.
[163] Ibid., p. 443.

1. In economic statecraft, as in other spheres of life, perseverance sometimes pays.
2. Economic sanctions may have more of an impact than anyone expects.
3. The "rally round the flag" effect is not an "iron law" of politics.
4. The most important effects of economic sanctions may not be economic. (Economic sanctions may move in mysterious ways.)

CONCLUSION

With the exception of the Megarian Decree, the cases examined in this chapter—together with the East-West trade embargo, to be considered in the following chapter—constitute the most frequently cited evidence in support of the alleged ineffectiveness, counterproductivity, relative costliness, and low utility of economic sanctions as techniques of statecraft.[164] It bears repeating that the purpose of this chapter has not been to show that economic sanctions were clearly or completely successful in any of these cases. Rather it has been to assess the adequacy of the evidence and arguments adduced to support the contention that these were cases of clearcut, obvious, indisputable, and overwhelming failure.

Bienen and Gilpin preface consideration of these cases with the following observation:

> Each case was chosen because it is representative of a much larger universe of past efforts to apply economic sanctions to achieve one or another political objective. . . . Moreover, though none proved to be effective, they are not atypical "hard" cases. On the contrary, they are cases where one might have anticipated sanctions to have been successful. For this reason, the analysis of these cases lends support to the nearly unanimous conclusion of scholars that sanctions seldom achieve their purposes and more likely have severe counterproductive consequences.[165]

The representative nature of these cases, however, is questionable; adjectives like "bizarre" and "unique" are as likely to leap to mind as "commonplace" and "typical." The attempt to impose sanctions against Italy was the first—and last—time that the League applied Article 16 of the Covenant. The U.S. sanctions against Japan were imposed two years after the beginning of World War II. The sanctions against Cuba were heavily influenced by the peculiar geographic, historical, and psychological rela-

---

[164] These cases are also an important part of the empirical support for the more sweeping view that economic statecraft in general tends to share these characteristics.

[165] "Evaluation," pp. III,2-3. They include U.S. sanctions against Uganda as an additional case. On this case see Miller, "When Sanctions Worked."

tionship between Cuba and the United States; the Platt Amendment, after all, was a rather unusual historical antecedent even in terms of U.S. relations with Caribbean states. And the sanctions against Rhodesia constituted an unprecedented invocation of Articles 39 and 41 of the United Nations Charter. Every historical case, of course, is unique; and generalization is impossible if one insists on complete comparability. Still, the proposition that these cases are "representative of a much larger universe of past efforts" should be viewed with a certain amount of healthy skepticism.

One thing they all seem to have in common is the immense difficulty of the undertaking. In every case changes in fundamental policy were at stake and compliance was extremely costly for at least one of the target states. None of these cases provides much, if any, support for the general proposition that economic sanctions are likely to be less effective or more counterproductive than alternative techniques of statecraft. On the contrary, studies of these cases tend to be based on selective evidence that ignores relevant plausible hypotheses, oversimplified and inadequate specification of the structure of goals and targets, failure to consider the level of difficulty of the undertaking, the absence of serious consideration of alternative courses of action, failure to consider varying degrees of success, a propensity to overgeneralize, and an overall tendency to underestimate the effectiveness and utility of economic sanctions.

This chapter suggests that evidence with respect to the utility of economic sanctions in these cases is inconclusive in many respects, and there are still many questions worthy of research. The evidence is mixed, ambiguous, and usually consistent with more than one interpretation, which suggests that moderate and qualified conclusions are more appropriate than simple, clear-cut, sweeping generalizations. In each of the "classic cases" examined in this chapter the evidence is compatible with, and in some respects supportive of, the conclusion that economic sanctions were moderately successful in approximating at least some of the intended objectives at acceptable costs. Policy alternatives with clearly discernible higher utility are not easy to identify in any of these cases. When the multiplicity of goals and targets, levels of difficulty, multiple bases of power, and likely utility of alternative policy instruments are considered, these cases provide little in the way of "overwhelming historical evidence" supporting the contention that economic sanctions are ineffective, counterproductive, unusually expensive, or relatively low in utility compared to other techniques of statecraft.

CHAPTER 9

FOREIGN TRADE

*War and commerce are but two different means
of arriving at the same aim which is to possess
what is desired. Trade is nothing but a homage
paid to the strength of the possessor by him who
aspires to the possession; it is an attempt to obtain
by mutual agreement that which one does not hope
any longer to obtain by violence. The idea of
commerce would never occur to a man who would
always be the strongest. It is experience, proving to
him that war, i.e., the use of his force against the
force of others, is exposed to various resistances
and various failures, which makes him have
recourse to commerce, that is, to a means more
subtle and better fitted to induce the interest of
others to consent to what is his own interest.*[1]

Regulation of foreign trade has been used as a technique of statecraft throughout history. This chapter will consider the general nature of trade policy, some theoretical concepts useful for understanding trade controls, and some historical cases of the alleged failure of trade sanctions.

TRADE POLICY

An embargo on trading "strategic goods" to the Soviet Union or a boycott of Iranian oil are front-page news items, but trade policy can be used to promote foreign policy goals in less obvious—and often more successful—ways. Thomas Schelling points out that trade, defined broadly "to include investment, shipping, tourism, and the management of enterprises, . . . is what most of international relations are about." He adds that "trade policies can antagonize governments, generate resentments in populations, hurt economies, influence the tenure of governments, even provoke hostilities."[2] To the extent that policy makers deliberately modify

---

[1] Benjamin Constant, quoted in Hirschman, *National Power*, pp. 14n-15n.

[2] Thomas Schelling, "National Security Considerations Affecting Trade Policy," in *United States International Economic Policy in an Interdependent World*, papers submitted to the Commission on International Trade and Investment Policy, Compendium of Papers, vol. 1, July 1971, p. 737.

trade policy in order to avoid (or ensure) such effects, they are practicing economic statecraft.

Even those sensitive to the relationship between trade and foreign policy sometimes fail to recognize the use of trade policy for purposes of statecraft. Thus, Benjamin Cohen, who views foreign economic policy as "part of a country's total foreign policy," contends that foreign aid has been "just about . . . [the] only instrument of policy" used by the United States to promote economic development in the Third World. "Trade policy," he states, "has not in fact been used much for this purpose at all."[3] And Albert O. Hirschman, who focused on "the possibility of using trade as a means of political pressure and leverage," observes that "during the first two decades of the postwar period, foreign aid and capital flows largely replaced trade as the principal arena for the political element in international economic relations."[4] From the analytical perspective of economic statecraft, both statements are not merely wrong; they are wrong in a way that makes it nearly impossible to grasp the basic dimensions of American economic statecraft after World War II. Foreign aid garnered more publicity, but trade policy—at least from 1944 to 1962—was the principal economic technique of statecraft employed by American policy makers. Official American policy viewed aid as a temporary stopgap measure in promoting European recovery from the war and as a secondary, supplementary measure in promoting economic development in the Third World. The basic American message—reiterated *ad infinitum*—to both Europe and the Third World was that trade liberalization on a nondiscriminatory basis was the key to solving their problems.[5]

The American use of trade policy to construct an international economic order based on nondiscriminatory trade liberalization in the period after World War II was one of the most successful influence attempts using economic policy instruments ever undertaken. The establishment of a liberal international economic order was intended to stimulate higher levels of international trade and prosperity throughout the noncommunist world. Although the lack of economic statistics for periods prior to World War

[3] Cohen, ed., *American Foreign Economic Policy*, p. 32.

[4] *National Power*, p. v.

[5] See Baldwin, *Economic Development*; *Foreign Aid and American Foreign Policy: A Documentary Analysis* (New York: Praeger, 1966), pp. 45-66, 172-185; and Gottfried Haberler, "The Liberal International Economic Order in Historical Perspective," in *Challenges to a Liberal International Economic Order*, ed. Ryan C. Amacher, Gottfried Haberler, and Thomas D. Willett (Washington, D.C.: American Enterprise Institute, 1979), pp. 43-65. Note that the question of whether trade liberalization actually does promote economic growth is irrelevant to deciding whether to treat American trade policy as a technique of statecraft with respect to this goal. It is only necessary to show that policy makers intended American trade policy to further this goal. The attainability of a goal is not a defining characteristic of statecraft.

II prevents a definitive conclusion, few would deny that the first three decades after the war were a period of unprecedented growth and prosperity. Even most Third World countries experienced unprecedented growth, although progress was less spectacular in those countries.[6]

Trade policy, of course, was not the only technique of statecraft used by U.S. policy makers in promoting these goals. Military statecraft was helpful to the extent that it stabilized the international political framework within which international economic relations occur. Propaganda and diplomacy were also useful tools for promoting the new economic order. Other economic techniques, such as aid (especially Marshall Plan aid), currency stabilization, and promotion of private investment, were also important components of American foreign policy. But American trade policy was the key to success. Even at the Bretton Woods Conference in 1944, this was well understood. As one observer put it:

> Commercial policy . . . is held to be the clue to the whole show, for there is practically no one here who has the slightest confidence in the efficacy of any of the machinery in the process of building in the absence of an American trade policy that lowers tariff barriers and makes it possible for the world's greatest creditor nation to perform her proper function of buyer.[7]

The "carrot" that induced other countries to reduce tariffs and to limit discrimination was the offer to reduce American trade barriers on a reciprocal basis. Without this positive inducement, other countries were not willing to make significant changes in their commercial policy. American trade policy was thus the cornerstone of the postwar liberal international economic order.

Although promoting nondiscrimination as the basic organizing principle of international trade was an important goal of American postwar trade policy, the American commitment to this goal is easily exaggerated. Consider the following portrayal of U.S. policy aims:

> A major objective of the United States at the end of the Second World War was to reestablish a liberal and multilateral world economy. . . . If peace, democracy, and world order were to be achieved, President Roosevelt and his advisers reasoned, international economic relations must be depoliticized through the creation of an open world economy based on non-discrimination and free trade.

[6] Haberler, "Liberal International Economic Order," pp. 49-52; Simon Kuznets, *Economic Growth of Nations* (Cambridge: Harvard University Press, 1971); and "Aspects of Post-World War II Growth in Less Developed Countries," in *Evolution, Welfare, and Time in Economics: Essays in Honor of Nicholas Georgescu-Roegen*, ed. A. M. Tang, E. M. Westfield, and James E. Worley (Lexington, Mass.: Lexington Books, 1976), pp. 39-65.

[7] *New York Times*, July 16, 1944, pt. 4, p. 7.

While this separation of international economics and politics (that is, of diplomacy and the market) has frequently been violated by the United States itself, this ideal has correctly remained a goal of American foreign policy. This general commitment on the part of the United States has been embodied in the General Agreement on Tariff [*sic*] and Trade (GATT). The American goal of depoliticized and non-discriminatory trade not only fostered an unprecedented era of world commerce but it greatly reinforced the harmony of interest among the United States and its allies.[8]

The thrust of the argument in this passage can be misleading insofar as it implies that American postwar trade policy has been characterized by unqualified support for the "ideal" of nondiscriminatory trade. Indeed, selective trade discrimination for foreign policy purposes—i.e., not merely to protect domestic agricultural interests—has been an integral part of United States trade policy for most of the postwar period. The most important exceptions to the general rule of nondiscrimination in the Charter of the proposed International Trade Organization (ITO),[9] which were incorporated into GATT, were as follows: (1) Countries with severe balance-of-payments difficulties were permitted to discriminate against American goods. Although the British initiated this idea, the United States acquiesced to it throughout most of the 1950s. (2) Regional customs unions were permitted to discriminate against the United States. The United States encouraged such discrimination in order to promote both the recovery and the integration of Western Europe. Strengthening and unifying Europe were in turn part of the overall American strategy for containment of the Soviet

[8] Bienen and Gilpin, "Evaluation," p. VII,2. The term "politicization" is nearly always applied to actions of which one disapproves. If this term is to be used in a neutral way, the American attempts to reshape the international economic order after World War II through policies of free trade must be considered a political act, and thus, a form of politicization. See Gene M. Lyons, David A. Baldwin, and Donald W. McNemar, "The 'Politicization' Issue in the U.N. Specialized Agencies," *Proceedings of the Academy of Political Science*, XXXII (1977):81-92.

[9] The ITO was supposed to be the trade counterpart of the International Monetary Fund and the International Bank for Reconstruction and Development. The ITO never came into existence because the United States never ratified the charter and other states were unwilling to do so unless the United States did. Most of the GATT agreement was part of the ITO Charter. See Wilcox, *A Charter for World Trade*; William Adams Brown, *The United States and the Restoration of World Trade* (Washington, D.C.: Brookings Institution, 1950); Gardner Patterson, *Discrimination in International Trade: The Policy Issues, 1945-1965* (Princeton: Princeton University Press, 1965); Raymond F. Mikesell, *United States Economic Policy and International Relations* (New York: McGraw-Hill, 1952); Kenneth W. Dam, *The GATT: Law and International Economic Organization* (Chicago: University of Chicago Press, 1970); and Richard N. Gardner, *Sterling-Dollar Diplomacy in Current Perspective*, expanded ed. (New York: Columbia University Press, 1980).

Union.[10] (3) Discriminatory measures were also permitted for the purpose of protecting "essential security interests." These measures, which are defined broadly enough to permit almost anything, were included at the instance of the United States and were prerequisite to its approval of the ITO Charter.[11] Although Bienen and Gilpin rightly assert that the American commitment to nondiscriminatory trade "greatly reinforced the harmony of interest among the United States and its allies," it would also be correct to attribute such harmonizing effects to American willingness to permit its allies to discriminate against it during the 1950s.

Two additional instances of selective discrimination have also been part of American postwar trade policy. At least since 1948, American policy has been to treat trade with communist countries in a discriminatory manner. In addition, discrimination *in favor* of noncommunist less developed countries has been part of American trade policy since 1975. This principle had been incorporated into the ITO Charter despite United States opposition in 1948, but it was not adopted by GATT until the mid-1960s. Although the United States has never been enthusiastic about this kind of discrimination, it is now part of American trade policy. Thus, although promoting the general principle of nondiscriminatory trade among noncommunist countries has been an important element in postwar United States policy, selective discrimination has also been a technique of American statecraft. If one is to appreciate the variety of economic techniques of statecraft employed by the United States, it is better not to characterize such selective discrimination as lapses from orthodoxy, as imperfections in American trade policy, or as examples of failure to live up to the ideal of nondiscrimination.

Basic Concepts

Before discussing particular cases of trade policy, some basic conceptual issues need to be addressed. These include the supply and influence effects and "strategic goods."

Supply and Influence Effects

In *National Power and the Structure of Foreign Trade* Albert O. Hirschman describes and analyzes foreign trade as an instrument of national power. He calls the "two main effects" of foreign trade on "the power position of a country" the "supply effect" and the "influence effect" (pp.

[10] John Lewis Gaddis, *Strategies of Containment* (New York: Oxford University Press, 1982), p. 63.
[11] Wilcox, *A Charter for World Trade*, pp. 182-183.

13ff.). "The first effect is certain to be positive: By providing a more plentiful supply of goods or by replacing goods wanted less by goods wanted more (from the power standpoint), foreign trade enhances the potential military force of a country" (p. 14). Hirschman, however, regards the implications of the supply effect as "obvious" and hardly in need of "further elaboration"; therefore, he devotes the bulk of his attention to the more theoretically interesting and less well understood influence effect. Whereas the first effect derives from the would-be power wielder's "gain from trade,"[12] the second effect derives from the ability to deprive one's trading partners of *their* gains from trade by exercising the right of every sovereign state to interrupt its own export and import trade. Hirschman views the influence effect as more important than the supply effect and asserts "that economic pressure upon a country consists mainly of the threat of severance and ultimately of actual interruption of external economic relations with that country." He further contends that this sovereign right to interrupt commercial or financial relations is "the root cause of the political or power aspect of international economic relations" (pp. 15-16). Hirschman then discusses a number of policies that would make it difficult for the power wielder's trading partners either to dispense with or to substitute for trade with the power-wielding country.

Although Hirschman was writing against the background of Nazi Germany's policies toward Eastern Europe in the 1930s, his discussion of the supply and influence effects is still required reading for any serious student of economic statecraft. The rigor and analytical depth go far beyond that achieved in most treatments of the subject. The two most significant and lasting contributions of his discussion are the demonstration of the inherent political implications of international trade and the elucidation of some less obvious—perhaps even counterintuitive—aspects of the relationship between trade and dependency. At the time Hirschman was writing (as now) it was often asserted that state intervention in international economic affairs and discriminatory commercial policies have the deleterious effect of "politicizing" international trade, the implication being that trade could be "depoliticized" by relying on private enterprise and nondiscrimination. Hirschman demonstrated that trade among sovereign states has potential political ramifications "whether it takes place under a system of free trade or protection, of state trading or private enterprise, of most-favored-nation clause, or of discriminating treatments."[13]

[12] He defines "gain from trade" by quoting Alfred Marshall as follows: "The direct gain which a country derives from her foreign trade is the excess of the value to her of the things which she imports over the value to her of the things which she could have made for herself with the capital and labour devoted to producing the things which she exported in exchange for them" (p. 18).

[13] Ibid., p. 78. Compare with Bienen and Gilpin's depiction of recent American use of

Hirschman's discussion of trade dependence is perhaps more relevant to contemporary issues than it was when he wrote it, since the emergence of the Third World has generated a great deal of debate about the nature, causes, and implications of dependency. Hirschman's cool reason is a useful antidote to the superficial and emotional nature of many contemporary discussions.[14] Whereas much of this debate focuses on the harmful effects of international trade on Third World countries, Hirschman has demonstrated that dependency varies directly—*not inversely*—with the gain from trade. Thus, one cannot simultaneously argue that a given country derives no (or negative) gain from trade and that it is dependent on that trade.[15] Similarly, many of the proposals designed to increase the gains from trade of Third World countries are likely to have the unintended and unacknowledged effect of increasing their dependence on trade.[16] Hirschman's discussion of the relationship between dependency and the gains from trade is certainly not the last word on the subject, but it is difficult to see how intelligent discussion can proceed far without at least taking account of his position.

Although Hirschman's analysis of the supply and influence effects has lasting value, its limitations should also be recognized. For the student of economic statecraft, most of these limitations stem from the assumptions made in order to focus on the basic elements of the effects and from the fact that he was writing prior to the revolution in power analysis which began in 1950 (see chapter 2). Thus, a contemporary reading of Hirschman should be undertaken with the following points in mind.

(1) *Hirschman's conception of national power involves ambiguity and a military bias.* He defines it as the "power of coercion which one nation may bring to bear upon other nations, the method of coercion being military or 'peaceful' " (p. 13). Although this seems to allow for nonmilitary coercion, the quotation marks enclosing "peaceful" arouse suspicion. When the supply effect is discussed immediately after the definition of national power, "war," "military force," "the threat of war," "war machine," and "military pressure" are the terms used; indeed, Hirschman denies that there can be any supply effect in a warless world (p. 14). Although the discussion of the supply effect suggests that national power

---

economic sanctions as the "re-politicization of international economic relations" ("Evaluation," p. VII,2); and with Klaus Knorr's assertion that the "power uses of trade are essentially discriminatory" (*Power of Nations*, p. 160).

[14] On this point see Baldwin, "Interdependence and Power."

[15] This is true, of course, only for the country as a whole. Much of the contemporary literature on dependency focuses not on the effects on the country as a whole but rather on the differential effects on subgroups within the country.

[16] On this point, see David A. Baldwin, "Foreign Aid, Intervention, and Influence," *World Politics* XXI (April 1969):445-446.

is to be equated with military power, such is not the case, since in analyzing the influence effect, Hirschman goes out of his way to show that this effect occurs even in a warless world (p. 15).

(2) *The conception of power is cast primarily in terms of negative sanctions.* Thus, the supply effect is discussed entirely in terms of the would-be power wielder, not in terms of the target country. True, the target country's gain from trade is relevant, but only insofar as it strengthens the influence effect. Hirschman neither considers nor allows for the possibility that country A may want to enhance the supply effect in country B as a direct means of influence. Thus trade in order to strengthen a military ally, to decrease the dependence of the target country on a third country, or to lessen the dependence of a hostile target country on imported oil all involve the use of trade as a positive sanction, i.e. deliberate effort to strengthen the supply effect, in the target country. American toleration of adverse trade discrimination by European allies in 1947–1957, the American willingness to trade with Eastern European satellite countries, and the recent proposal that the United States sell specialized oil recovery technology to the Soviet Union in order to allow it to increase domestic production and lessen its potential interest in Persian Gulf oil are all examples of influence attempts based on enhancing the supply effect in the target country. The only reason Hirschman allows for strengthening the target country's gain from trade is to increase dependency. The possibility of a direct exercise of power through the positive sanction of increasing another country's gain from trade is not considered.

(3) *The noneconomic bases of power exercised by trade policy are explicitly ruled out of consideration* (p. 13). Indeed, since Hirschman does not draw a clear distinction between the instruments of policy and the bases of power, his position is a bit murky on this matter. He clearly does not address—and did not intend to address—such questions as how foreign trade can be used to send signals to other countries. Many of the ways in which foreign trade can serve as an instrument of national power are thus outside the scope of Hirschman's book. His book is necessary to an understanding of the relationship between trade and power, but it is surely not sufficient.

(4) *The most important contribution of postwar power analysis has been to emphasize the importance of the policy-contingency framework within which capabilities are assessed; thus it is not surprising that a book written during World War II should be relatively weak with respect to this aspect of power analysis.* For example, the questions of *whom* one trades with and *why* could be usefully elaborated. Although Hirschman considers the implications of trading with poor, small, friendly, and/or "subject" countries (pp. 34-35), he barely scratches the surface of this important topic. With respect to the supply effect, he considers measures designed

to protect one's own gain from trade, but measures intended to diminish a potential enemy's gain from trade, such as preclusive buying, or measures designed to promote the gain from trade of an ally are ignored. With respect to the influence effect, measures intended to diminish the dependence of a second country on a third country are not considered. For example, if the United States wanted to reduce Yugoslavia's dependence on trade with the Soviet Union, it could merely announce its willingness to trade with Yugoslavia. Since dependency is a function not only of the amount of trade but also of the availability of alternatives, such an announcement would tend to reduce Yugoslavian dependence on the Soviet Union *even in the absence of any actual trade with the United States*.[17] Perhaps the most obvious and least justifiable shortcoming of Hirschman's treatment of policy-contingency frameworks is his insistence that the supply effect "requires at least the possibility of war" (p. 14). Since the supply effect can enhance the *nonmilitary* capabilities of a state—the ability to provide foreign aid, for example—Hirschman's statement is clearly false. In sum, although Hirschman's discussion of foreign trade as an instrument of national power is a useful and necessary contribution to understanding this topic, his analysis should be supplemented with insights and analytical techniques drawn from modern power analysis.

"Strategic Goods"

Widespread misunderstanding of the concept of "strategic goods" is one of the biggest impediments to intelligent discussion of economic statecraft, especially when issues of East-West trade are considered. Understanding this concept requires both political and economic analysis, but not beyond the level of an introductory college course in each subject. The essential points can be stated succinctly:

1. *Some things—goods, services, ideas, people, or whatever—have*

[17] Franklyn D. Holzman's observation that "two nations must be economically interdependent before one can directly practice economic warfare against the other" is either false or tautological. If it implies that direct economic intercourse between two nations is necessary for one of them to practice economic warfare on the other, the proposition is surely false. The example of Yugoslavia cited above and the Allies' preclusive buying of wolfram to keep it out of German hands during World War II demonstrate this. If, on the other hand, "interdependence" simply implies the ability of each country to affect the economic welfare of the other, the statement is tautological. (*International Trade Under Communism—Politics and Economics* [New York: Basic Books, 1976], p. 55.) Murray C. Kemp's assertion that "in an interdependent world trading system, the trading pattern of each country, and the level of its welfare, depend on the production and consumption decisions of every other country, even of those countries with whom the first country has no direct trading contacts" is probably also tautological; but it has the redeeming quality of making it clear that direct trade is not a requisite for either interdependence or economic warfare. (*The Pure Theory of International Trade*, p. 208.) On the tautological nature of statements about dependency, see Baldwin, "Interdependence and Power," pp. 500-503.

more strategic value than others. That is, for any *given* strategy, some things have more utility than others; this is the basic intuitive notion underlying the concept of "strategic goods." More precisely, a "strategic good" is "an item for which the marginal elasticity of demand is very low and for which there is no readily available substitute."[18]

2. *In practice it is often difficult to identify such goods.* This does not, however, mean that one person's guess is as good as another's or that coin flipping is an appropriate way to determine which goods are strategic.

3. *The "strategic" quality of a good is a function of the situation; it is not intrinsic to the good itself.* Thus, the question of how strategic an item is cannot be determined by examining the item itself; nor can it be determined by analyzing all the possible uses to which the item may be put. What is highly "strategic" with respect to one target country may not be very "strategic" at all with respect to another. Wheat, for example, might be highly strategic if the Soviet Union is the target country; but it is unlikely to have much strategic value if Argentina is the target.

From the standpoint of international trade a "strategic" item is anything that is needed to pursue a given strategy and that is relatively inefficient to produce at home. The doctrine of comparative costs suggests that the appropriate policy is to produce at home what can be produced relatively efficiently and to buy abroad what is relatively inefficient to produce at home. Thomas Schelling constructs a hypothetical situation in which a war-like country trying to build up its military capability would be wise to purchase bicycles abroad instead of jet planes, thus proving that bicycles are not *necessarily* of less strategic value than jet planes![19] Schelling sums up the point as follows:

> It is not . . . a purely rhetorical question whether the Russians would rather . . . [import] jet aircraft or suits of clothing with their foreign-exchange earnings. . . . If the Russians are determined to consume clothes as well as aircraft, the strategic question is whether they get more planes by producing them at home and buying clothes abroad or by purchasing planes abroad and producing clothes. To put it differently, the question of how many planes and how much clothing to budget for is quite separate from the question of which to produce domestically and which to procure with exports.
>
> The inadequacy—even illogic—of . . . [the conventional view that some goods are intrinsically more strategic than others stems from the assumption] that items are only strategic if they can be used for

[18] Theodore Kent Osgood, "East-West Trade Controls and Economic Warfare" (Ph.D. dissertation, Yale University, 1957), p. 89.

[19] *International Economics*, pp. 498-504. For teaching purposes I use an even more extreme example, showing that hula hoops may be more strategic than jet planes, to make the same point.

war, or converted for war, or processed into war-type goods. This view ignores the fact that a nation's resources can be used to produce alternative goods. The most peace-like of civilian goods will be "strategic imports" to the Russians, if the Russians plan to consume some of them and find them difficult to produce. For in that case any saving that accrues to the Russian economy through the gains from trade, is a saving in resources that can be applied to military or other use.[20]

The reason it is difficult in practice to know how strategic an item is stems from the need to know the comparative cost position of the target country. Since the Soviet Union has a large and complex economy, such judgments may require a detailed knowledge of the Soviet economy. This is not always the case, however; one need not be a Soviet expert or an economic genius to conclude that the agricultural sector of that economy is one of the less efficient. The obvious inference is that agricultural products are likely to be among the more strategic items that could be exported to that country.

Before examining some examples of statements about "strategic goods," some implications of the above discussion should be noted: First, *a priori*, there is nothing absurd or ridiculous about suggesting that toys, buttons, combs, wheat, breakfast food, tractors, or clothing might be "strategic goods." The popular tendency to ridicule such arguments merely exemplifies the "strategic goods fallacy." Second, tanks, jet engines, munitions, and submarines are not *obviously*, *self-evidently*, or *necessarily* more strategic or of more military value than so-called civilian items. The military significance or utility of a tank is not an intrinsic quality of the tank. Third, a policy maker's desire to expand lists of embargoed items is not necessarily a sign of bureaucratic timidity, emotionalism, or stupidity. It is a rational strategy for decision making under conditions of uncertainty. And fourth, to the extent that resources in the target country are fungible, neither the type of good exported nor the end-user matters much; what really matters is the amount of resources in the target country freed for other uses.[21] Let us now examine some examples of statements about "strategic goods."

EXAMPLE NO. 1

A crucial question in designing and evaluating such a policy concerns the meaning of "strategic goods." Military systems, such as warships, tanks, and guided missiles, create no problem of identification. . . .[22]

---

[20] Ibid., p. 500. For similar treatments of the concept of "strategic goods," see Wu, *Economic Warfare*, pp. 10-13; Wiles, *Communist International Economics*, pp. 463-466; and Robert E. Klitgaard, *National Security and Export Controls*, Rand Corporation Report, R-1432-1-ARPA/CIEP (April 1974).

[21] See Klitgaard, "National Security," pp. v-54.

[22] Knorr, *Power of Nations*, p. 143.

Comment: This statement illustrates how easily even the experts can fall into the trap of the strategic goods fallacy. As a leading authority—perhaps *the* leading authority—on the economic bases of military power, Knorr understands full well that "military systems" may not be strategic goods. Indeed, later in the same paragraph he suggests that "the import of type-writers and toys" may release labor for armament industries; the same logic in reverse could be used to suggest that imports of military systems may release labor *from* armament industries!

EXAMPLE NO. 2

Being equally anti-Communist, our allies join us in refusing to sell to Communist countries items which contribute significantly to Communist military potential. But, going far beyond this agreement with our allies, we have isolated ourselves as the only country in the Free World which legally restricts sales of *nonmilitary* goods to Communist countries.[23]

Comment: This is an excellent example of the strategic goods fallacy (i.e., the idea that strategic qualities are inherent). There is no reason whatever to believe, *a priori*, that wheat, plastic combs, or buttons will contribute less "significantly to Communist military potential" than tanks, jets, and jeeps. Indeed, there is reason to suspect that the military sector of the Soviet economy is relatively efficient and that the agricultural sector is relatively inefficient, thus making it plausible to suggest that wheat might add more to Soviet military potential than arms shipments. The relationship between "anticommunism" and views on "strategic goods" is significant and should be noted. If two parties are equally rational, how can they share the same view of the communist "threat" ("challenge," "dispute," "opportunity," or whatever) and still disagree on the length of the list of "strategic goods"? Three hypotheses might be considered: (1) One party does not understand the implications of fungibility and/or the logic of comparative costs. European economists, however, surely understand fungibility and comparative costs as well as American economists. One should always be wary of explanations that attribute stupidity to those holding opinions contrary to one's own. (2) One party has reason to believe that resources are not in fact fungible in the Soviet Union in the relevant time period or to believe that it has such superior knowledge of the Soviet economy that it can be relatively certain of its ability to identify strategic goods. One problem with this hypothesis is that the Europeans claim no such superior knowledge. Another problem is that the time period in which resources are likely to be nonfungible is the short run, which is precisely

[23] Jay H. Cerf, "We Should Do More Business with the Communists," in *American Foreign Economic Policy*, ed. Benjamin J. Cohen (New York: Harper and Row, 1968), p. 306. (Italics in original.)

the kind of outlook for which the Europeans criticize American policy. There is a "catch-22" in the long-run versus short-run assumption: If, on the one hand, one assumes that the Soviet threat is short run, i.e., that war is imminent, then an embargo on all trade would seem appropriate in order to keep resources out of the grasp of a potential enemy. If, on the other hand, one assumes that the Soviet threat is long term, then the fungibility of resources increases, thus making any export that enhances the Soviet gain from trade of potential military significance. The difference between long- and short-run outlooks does not seem to be the key to understanding this puzzlement. (3) One party may not, in fact, share the other party's view of the nature or magnitude of the communist threat and may be less "anticommunist" in the sense that they believe that the benefits of providing strategic goods to the Soviet Union are likely to outweigh the costs. This hypothesis suggests a flaw in the initial assumption that both parties were equally "anticommunist." This would go a long way toward explaining the difference between European and American views of "strategic goods," but it raises the question of why either or both sides might want to disguise disagreement with respect to the nature and/or magnitude of the Soviet threat as a relatively minor technical dispute over the nature of "strategic goods." For now, it suffices to have raised this question; we shall return to it in the discussion of East-West trade later in this chapter.

EXAMPLE NO. 3

Of course, anything one pleases can be regarded as strategic material, even a button, because it can be sewn onto a soldier's pants. A soldier will not wear pants without buttons, since otherwise he would have to hold them up with his hands. And then what can he do with his weapon? If one reasons thus, then buttons also are a particularly strategic material.[24]

Comment: This comment by Khrushchev is widely quoted, usually in a context suggesting that only extremists could possibly believe that buttons are strategic items. There is, of course, nothing funny or extreme about considering buttons as a strategic item. It might be helpful if those who quote this would pause to consider *why* Khrushchev finds it useful to ridicule the concept of strategic goods.

EXAMPLE NO. 4

The concept of what is "strategic" defies a clear-cut and universally acceptable definition. In the narrowest sense, it covers items of direct military use and such items are reasonably easy to identify and define. On the other hand, extremists . . . would regard any item as being

[24] Quoted from a speech by Nikita S. Khrushchev in 1963 by Angela Stent, *From Embargo to Ostpolitik*, p. 93.

of strategic value because if the opponent country wants it it must strengthen that country in one way or another; a similar attitude was entertained by Dr. Adenauer, who at one stage considered wheat as a strategic item. Others would take a stand somewhere between the two views. A general non-committal definition may be taken as: "strategic items are those raw materials and manufactures (including munitions) which would increase the military strength of the Soviet bloc."[25]

Comment: This passage is a typical example of the style of reasoning that pervades discussions of export controls on trade with communist countries. First, it is asserted that "everyone agrees" that items of "obvious" or "direct" military utility, presumably munitions, should be restricted. Second, an "extremist" position maintaining that goods that are "obviously" "peaceful" or "civilian" in nature, such as buttons, plastic combs, and wheat, might be strategic is acknowledged. Third, it is suggested or implied that most "reasonable people" focus their attention on the gray area between goods that "obviously" are strategic and goods that "obviously" are not. Thus, the debate is depicted as one over borderline cases in which everyone agrees that strategic qualities inhere in a good, but in which reasonable people may disagree with respect to goods that have more than one use. A moderate and reasonable person, it is implied, would neither question the strategic nature of munitions nor give serious consideration to the proposition that wheat might be a strategic good. The main argument, however, is not between extremists and moderates who share a common concept of "strategic goods"; the main argument is between those who understand the concept of strategic goods and those holding a fallacious view of strategic goods. Munitions and/or wheat may or may not be strategic in any given situation, but one thing is certain: No sensible judgment one way or the other can be rendered on an *a priori* basis. The debate over "strategic goods," if taken at face value, is between those who understand this and those who do not. The latter, unfortunately, seem to outnumber the former.

EXAMPLE NO. 5

The subject of this book is the Western economic warfare against the communist nations in the form of an embargo policy on so-called "strategic" goods. . . . The central key to an understanding of the policy is to understand the meaning of the concept of a "strategic" commodity. . . . The fact is that no simple definition of a "strategic" commodity exists. Definitions which are to be found in the literature, such as "goods that were directly related to military strength," or

---

[25] Jozef Wilczynski, *The Economics and Politics of East-West Trade* (New York: Praeger, 1969), p. 275.

goods, "the delivery of which would bring the Eastern parties in a strategically unfavourable position," are tautological. . . . A sharp or precise definition has never been presented in the embargo literature. Leon Herman has spoken about a "strategic good" as "an illusionary concept" and Osgood has complained about its "ambiguity, if not outright absurdity."[26]

Comment: Having asserted an understanding of the concept of "strategic goods" to be "the central key" to understanding his topic, Adler-Karlsson furnishes little evidence of such understanding. In the first place, there is nothing particularly difficult or obscure about the concept as explicated by Schelling, Osgood, or Wu, although each notes the widespread popular misunderstanding of it.[27] In the second place, the first definition supposedly "found in the literature" is drawn from a passage in which Schelling is summarizing concepts found in legislation, congressional discussions, and official policy pronouncements as a prelude to his devastating attack on such conceptions.[28] The ten pages following the passage cited by Adler-Karlsson contain the clearest and most precise definition of the concept of strategic goods available then or now. In the third place, the assertion that definitions of strategic goods "are tautological" is puzzling. For most social scientists *propositions* are not supposed to be tautological but *definitions* are.[29] And in the fourth place, the quotation from Osgood is quite misleading. It is drawn from a chapter in which he is surveying various examples of misusage of the term. Osgood refers to the "ambiguity, if not the outright absurdity of the concept of 'strategic goods' *as that phrase is currently used*."[30] The omission of the italicized words makes a difference. Since Osgood has provided a precise definition of the concept in the chapter immediately preceding the one cited by Adler-Karlsson, he is

---

[26] Adler-Karlsson, *Western Economic Warfare*, pp. 1-2. Knorr bases his discussion of the anticommunist embargo on this book, describing it as "the best treatment of the subject" (*Power of Nations*, p. 335). Bienen and Gilpin, in turn, base their discussion on Knorr but declare Adler-Karlsson's book to be "the authoritative study of the Western economic boycott of the Soviet bloc" ("Evaluation," p. IIIc,6). Wilczynski labels Adler-Karlsson's study "comprehensive and authoritative" (*East-West Trade*, p. 288).

[27] Schelling, *International Economics*, pp. 498-504; Osgood, "East-West Trade Controls," pp. 89-102; and Wu, *Economic Warfare*, pp. 10-14. Although all of these sources were available at the time Adler-Karlsson was writing, he cites only the first two. Although one might expect to find references to Hirschman, Wu's *Economic Warfare*, and Jacob Viner's *Trade Relations Between Free Market and Controlled Economies* (League of Nations Pub. II. Economic and Financial, 1943. II.A.4) in a "comprehensive and authoritative" study of the East-West trade embargo, there is none.

[28] Cf. Schelling, *International Economics*, p. 493.

[29] On definitions see Dahl, *Modern Political Analysis*, 3d ed., pp. 17-19.

[30] Osgood, "East-West Trade Controls," p. 102. Italics added.

obviously referring to popular usage rather than to inherent or necessary defects in the concept.

EXAMPLE NO. 6

The embargo policy is a combination of export restrictions on both military and non-military commodities. To make a firm distinction between these two groups is impossible. The description below will, however, follow a distinction which has been made by the American policy makers, and which excludes from treatment the purely military items of arms, ammunition and implements of war. . . . What is treated is thus the embargo on what conventionally is considered to be civilian goods. It is, however, evident that these goods often have a potential military use.[31]

Comment: It is difficult to see how a study delimited this way could get to the heart of the controversy over "strategic goods." One of the most important implications of the fungibility of resources is that the distinction between "civilian" and "military" exports is irrelevant to assessing the net impact of trade on the military (or nonmilitary) capabilities of the target country. It is precisely the conventional view of "civilian goods" as inherently "peaceful" that is the source of confusion.

EXAMPLE NO. 7

In economics everything is related to everything else. A Western export embargo on selected non-military items, preferably those of great domestic necessity but relatively expensive to produce internally in the Soviet Union, could force the resource allocation of the adversary from military to non-military production. The logic of this reasoning, when drawn out to its end, has been given in the muzhik-language of the Soviet Prime Minister, Khrushchev, who said that the most strategic of all commodities was buttons, because without them the soldiers could only fight with one hand as the other one would be occupied in holding up their trousers. Some American strategists have not come very far from this ridiculousness when they included plastic combs in the strategic lists and even reportedly wanted to include brassières and shirt buttons.[32]

Comment: Having set forth a reasonable summary of the theory and policy implications of comparative costs, Adler-Karlsson dismisses such reasoning as ridiculous.

[31] Adler-Karlsson, *Western Economic Warfare*, p. 3.
[32] Ibid., p. 32.

EXAMPLE NO. 8

> Our "semi-economic warfare" . . . does not really hurt the Communist countries . . . since they can simply trade elsewhere or produce themselves what we withhold. . . . It should be borne in mind that the more resources which the Soviets allocate to production of goods for export, the fewer, relatively, they can allocate to production of military goods.[33]

Comment: The fact that the Soviets can produce themselves or buy elsewhere "what we withhold" does not prove that an embargo does not "hurt the Communist countries." The question is whether they can buy it or make it *as efficiently* as if they had purchased it from us. The logic of this passage seems to deny the fundamental fact that trade enhances the productivity of the economy of the trading country. That, after all, is why countries engage in foreign trade. Knorr puts the point clearly and succinctly as follows:

> Foreign trade permits states to emphasize those patterns of production for which their productive resources are comparatively most suited and to obtain through exchange those goods and services which they themselves can produce only at relatively great cost or cannot produce at all. By specialization, nations obtain a larger output from their productive capacity than they would if they had to be self-sufficient. Military potential is enhanced as GNP and GNP per capita are increased whether military equipment and supplies enter a nation's foreign trade or not. The effect is simply one of increasing productivity.[34]

If one wants to understand the effects of trade embargoes, it helps to understand how and why nations gain from engaging in trade.

The controversy over what constitutes a "strategic good" has been going on for thirty years. Is there evidence of learning? Have the logical and policy implications of the fungibility of resources and the doctrine of comparative costs been absorbed into American foreign policy with respect to export controls? If so, such changes are hard to detect. The one-case-at-a-time approach based on scrutinizing a given item in order to determine its intrinsic military significance still seems to be firmly ensconced in the policy-making process. True, terms like "military significance" or "military utility" have to some extent replaced "strategic"; but the basic issues remain unchanged. True, "technology" is now the item most in the spot-

---

[33] Harold J. Berman, "A Reappraisal of U.S.–U.S.S.R. Trade Policy," *Harvard Business Review* XLII (July-August 1964):141, 151.

[34] Klaus Knorr, *Military Power and Potential* (Lexington, Mass.: D. C. Heath, 1970), p. 106.

light when East-West trade is discussed; but the basic analytical principles applicable to determining the strategic qualities of a given technology are really the same as those explicated by Schelling twenty-five years ago. In 1958 Schelling listed five criteria used by the executive branch to determine strategic importance:

1. How an item can be used in war;
2. How it can be converted to war use;
3. How it contributes to military production;
4. Whether its control would cause a critical deficiency in the Soviet war economy; and
5. Whether the item embodies information useful to the Soviets in war production.[35]

Schelling proceeded to demonstrate the "inadequacy—even illogic—of the five criteria" stemming from the assumption that "items are only strategic if they can be used for war, or converted for war, or processed into war-type goods" (p. 500).

In 1979 a report by the Office of Technology Assessment listed the following criteria used by the Department of Defense to determine the degree to which a good makes "a significant contribution to the military potential of any other nation or nations which would prove detrimental to the national security of the United States":

1. Is the item appropriate in quantity, quality, demonstrable need, design, etc. to the stated civilian end use?
2. Is there any evidence that the stated end user is engaged in military or military support activities to which this item could be applied?
3. How difficult would it be to divert this item to military purposes?
4. Could such diversion be carried out without detection?
5. Is there evidence of a serious deficiency in the military sector which this item, if diverted, would fill?
6. Is technology of military significance which is not already available, extractable from this item?[36]

Although the wording may have changed, the underlying assumption still seems to be that "items are only strategic if they can be used for war, or converted for war, or processed into war-type goods."

In 1983 an updated version of the report by the Office of Technology Assessment entitled one section "Towards a Definition of Military Sig-

---

[35] *International Economics*, p. 498.

[36] U.S. Congress, Office of Technology Assessment, *Technology and East-West Trade*, November 1979, pp. 90-91. (Hereafter cited as OTA, *Technology and E-W Trade*.)

nificance."[37] It uses the style of reasoning by now familiar to anyone who has followed the postwar debate on "strategic goods." First, "items of potential military value which the U.S.S.R. might wish to purchase from the United States" are arranged on a continuum, with goods "which have a direct military utility" at one end and "items which are unarguably destined for civilian" use, such as grain, at the other end. Second, it is observed that "there is little dispute" about the wisdom of restricting exports of items on the "direct military utility" end of the spectrum. It is noted that "some" (extremists?) would even argue for the "extension of export controls" to "civilian" goods like grain or pipelayers on the grounds that "such exports generally strengthen the Soviet economy" and thus Soviet military capabilities, or that "exports 'free' resources for the military sector which the U.S.S.R. would otherwise have to devote to nonmilitary uses." Third, having noted such arguments, the report proceeds to ignore them, declaring the gray area between the two ends of the spectrum to be the primary "battleground" of the debate, which will be "fought out case by case." The view of "military utility" as an inherent trait to be determined by consideration of the possible military uses of a given item is still embedded in American export control policy. The law of diminishing marginal utility, the doctrine of comparative costs, and the fungibility of resources seem to be ignored by such an approach. What Wu labeled the "strategic materials fallacy" in 1952 appears to be alive and well thirty years later.[38]

That this fallacy is found in legislation, official reports, or congressional speeches is not particularly worrisome. There has never been any wording in American export control legislation that would prevent sensible implementation by administrators who understood the nature and implications of the "strategic materials fallacy." The frequency with which this fallacy appears in the scholarly literature, even in purportedly "authoritative studies," however, should be cause for concern. A policy maker can legitimately argue that for "appearances' sake" he must treat munitions as if they were intrinsically highly strategic while assuring us that he really understands that they are not; but a scholar can claim no such extenuating circumstance.

KNORR'S CASES OF TRADE SANCTIONS

In treating "trade restrictions as economic pressure" Knorr bases his discussion largely on the "detailed study" of twenty-two cases, most of

---

[37] U.S. Congress, Office of Technology Assessment, *Technology and East-West Trade: An Update*, May 1983, pp. 83-84.
[38] Wu, *Economic Warfare*, p. 11.

which occurred after World War II and all of which attracted "considerable diplomatic attention."[39] Although the American sanctions against Cuba and the Soviet sanctions against Albania are discussed briefly, few details are provided concerning the other twenty cases. The country imposing the trade restrictions, the primary target (a single country in all but one case), the date, the form of trade restriction, the general issue involved, and a characterization of the outcome as successful, compromise settlement, ambiguous, or clear failure are the details provided for most cases. Those desiring more details are referred to two books for cases involving the Soviet Union and to "numerous sources" for the other cases.[40] Knorr concludes that four of the twenty-two influence attempts were successes, three ended in compromise settlements, two had ambiguous outcomes, and thirteen clearly failed. Moreover, Knorr adds, "exceptional circumstances account for the four successful cases" (p. 152). Knorr says nothing about the possibility that "exceptional circumstances" may have accounted for any of the cases that "clearly failed." The overall conclusion is that "the dramatic use of economic power in the form of trade restrictions [is] apt to fail in the large majority of instances" (p. 152).

The case against the likely effectiveness of such measures on theoretical grounds seems almost overwhelming when buttressed by these twenty-two cases. As a preliminary test of the significance of these cases, they will be examined in terms of the nine questions to be asked when evaluating case studies in economic statecraft.[41]

1. *Have the policy-contingency frameworks for each case been carefully established?* Knorr admits that the "identification of the objectives is important, because . . . effectiveness . . . can obviously be assessed only in terms of whether or not, or the degree to which, the objective was achieved" (p. 150). Having noted this, however, he devotes little attention to specifying the particular goals and targets of each influence attempt. For the most part, the secondary and tertiary goals and/or targets are ignored. In some cases no information whatsoever about objectives is supplied (e.g., the cases involving Austria-Hungary). Although noting his suspicion that "not rarely" one objective may have been "to deter third states from following the example set by the punished actor" (p. 151), this does not seem to have been one of the criteria used in judging effectiveness. Knorr distinguishes between attempts to affect the intentions of the target and attempting to affect the capabilities of the target and notes

---

[39] Knorr, *Power of Nations*, pp. 147-160.

[40] Ibid., p. 336. The books on the Soviet Union are Wiles, *Communist International Economics*, and Robert Owen Freedman, *Economic Warfare in the Communist Bloc: A Study of Economic Pressure Against Yugoslavia, Albania, and Communist China* (New York: Praeger, 1970).

[41] See chapter 8.

that it is often unclear whether trade restrictions are "designed to influence or to weaken the target state" (p. 151). Without offering any justification, Knorr then states that regardless of "whatever other purposes may have been involved" in the twenty-two cases, "it is assumed as a matter of judgment that coercion was the major, if not the exclusive, intention" (p. 151). It is, of course, possible to focus an influence attempt on the target's intentions, its capabilities, or both; but arbitrarily ruling out the last two possibilities is not very helpful.[42]

2.   *Is the level of difficulty taken into account?* Knorr recognizes that all of the cases generated considerable publicity and admits that such conditions may make compliance difficult for the target country (pp. 155-156). It is not clear, however, that he makes appropriate adjustments in assessing effectiveness to take account of this condition.

3.   *Is utility discussed in terms of alternative policy options?* For the most part, Knorr focuses on effectiveness rather than utility in discussing these cases. He does discuss both the political and economic costs of such trade restrictions, but he gives little or no attention to identifying or evaluating alternative policy instruments in each case.

4.   *Is success treated as a matter of degree?* Ostensibly, yes, but the classification of thirteen cases as *clear* failure is disconcerting. In assessing the effectiveness of U.S. trade restrictions on Cuba, for example, Knorr notes five possible goals of American policy, punishment plus four goals enumerated by Dean Rusk (p. 149). He estimates that the United States "probably succeeded" with respect to punishing Cuba and "certainly succeeded" with respect to imposing costs on the Soviet Union, but he regards success with respect to the other three goals as "doubtful." One might expect, therefore, that Knorr would classify this influence attempt as "partially effective" or as "ambiguous" in order to indicate some degree of success. Not so; the case is labeled among those that "clearly failed" (p. 152).

5.   *Does the author allow for multiple bases of power?* Knorr does note the possibility that economic sanctions might be interpreted by the target state as an implied threat of military action if compliance is not forthcoming (p. 151). It is not clear, however, that he would view this in terms of the economic sanction working through a military power base, as the following comment indicates: "If this were so, success might have resulted from such expectation [i.e., of military action] rather than from the economic sanction" (p. 151). This comment suggests that Knorr might explain such a situation as one in which economic sanctions only *seemed to be effective*, rather than as a situation in which they succeeded by working through a military power base. Still, Knorr elsewhere (pp. 93-96) explicitly ac-

---

[42] Knorr's conception of "coercion," discussed in chapter 2, is part of the difficulty here.

knowledges the possibility of noneconomic bases of economic power; so this question deserves an affirmative answer even though little attention is devoted to this possibility in the discussion of trade restrictions.[43]

6. *Are certain foreign policy goals treated as inherently inferior?* Since Knorr's general position is that such measures can be used to pursue "a wide spectrum of national ends" (p. 134), one must assume a negative answer. The use of economic techniques for symbolic purposes, i.e., signaling, does not, however, receive a great deal of attention from Knorr.

7. *Are the costs of noncompliance treated as a measure of effectiveness?* It is difficult to reconcile Knorr's general theoretical position on this issue with his treatment of the case studies of trade restrictions. In his general analytical framework, costs of noncompliance are clearly labeled as a measure of power (p. 13). In treating the case studies, however, some cases classified as clear failures are viewed as having incurred significant costs for noncompliance (e.g., Albania and Cuba). Moreover, the following passage is difficult to interpret: "There is a second common, although usually subsidiary, factor that militates against the successful application of coercive trade restrictions. The target state will usually suffer economic distress" (p. 154). Contrary to the view that costs of noncompliance are a measure of the effectiveness of an influence attempt, this passage *seems* to suggest that such costs are evidence of failure. Such an interpretation, however, would be a complete reversal of Knorr's earlier position. Knorr's intended meaning in this confusing paragraph is presumably something like the following: *Despite* the fact that the target state will usually suffer economic distress when trade restrictions are applied, the amount of economic deprivation is likely to be bearable; and compliance is unlikely to be forthcoming. Nevertheless, the generalization that "the target state will usually suffer economic distress" is difficult to reconcile with the proposition that "the dramatic use of economic power in the form of trade restrictions [is] apt to fail in the large majority of instances" (p. 152). If, indeed, the imposition of costs for noncompliance is a criterion for judging the effectiveness of an influence attempt, and if one assumes that such trade restrictions usually cause "economic distress" in target countries, the appropriate conclusion would appear to be as follows: "The dramatic use of economic power in the form of trade restrictions is apt to be at least

[43] It is not entirely clear that Knorr's conception of a "power base" is the same as that used by Lasswell and Kaplan. Since they use it to refer to the causal condition of success, the term is partially a function of the value system of the target of the influence attempt. For Knorr, however, the term seems to refer to the causal conditions that explain the availability of policy instruments to statesmen. In short, whereas Lasswell and Kaplan view "power base" as a "relational" term, Knorr seems, at least at times, to treat it as a "property" term. See Lasswell and Kaplan, *Power and Society*, pp. 83-84; and Baldwin, "Power Analysis," pp. 170-171.

partially successful with respect to imposing costs for noncompliance in the large majority of cases.''

8. *Is the relevance of counterfactual conditions acknowledged?* Some attention is given to this analytical problem, e.g., in considering relations between the Soviet Union and Yugoslavia (p. 152).

9. *Are the generalizations commensurate with the evidence?* This question deserves more attention than can be given here, but anytime the outcome of an influence attempt is characterized as ''clear failure,'' caution is in order. The outcomes of influence attempts are rarely clear-cut. Without any intention of giving Knorr's cases the serious and detailed examination they deserve, we might, however, note questions that have been raised by a preliminary and cursory inspection. In each case listed below, there is reason to suspect that the outcome of the influence attempt might not have been so clear as Knorr contends.

United States vs. Cuba

This case was discussed in the preceding chapter, and, for reasons presented there, ''clear failure'' does not seem to be an adequate characterization of the outcome. Everyone seems to agree, for example, that the United States *at least* succeeded in imposing costs on the Soviet Union.

United States vs. Japan (1940)

Again, for reasons discussed in the consideration of this case in the previous chapter, classification of the outcome as ''clear failure'' is questionable.

Great Britain vs. Iran (1951)

Knorr classifies the outcome of this case as a ''compromise settlement,'' but Peter Wallensteen, who shares Knorr's pessimistic view of the efficacy of economic sanctions, calls it a success, a category containing only two of Wallensteen's eighteen cases.[44] Gary Clyde Hufbauer and Jeffrey J. Schott also classify this case as successful.[45] Knorr, of course, may be right; but the outcome is at least one on which reasonable people—even those who take a dim view of economic sanctions—may differ.

United States vs. Dominican Republic (1960)

Although Knorr labels the outcome of this influence attempt as ''ambiguous,'' this is the second of Wallensteen's two cases of ''success.'' Again, Hufbauer and Schott agree with Wallensteen.

[44] ''Characteristics of Economic Sanctions,'' pp. 249-251.
[45] *Economic Sanctions.*

Soviet Union vs. Australia (1954)

In this case the Soviet Union broke diplomatic relations and cut off virtually all trade with Australia to protest Australian interference with Soviet attempts to recover a spy who had defected. Australian refusal to extradite the spy is the apparent basis for Knorr's classification of this case as clear failure. Wiles, however, suggests several points that should be considered in evaluating the effectiveness and utility of this influence attempt.[46] In the first place, secondary objectives and targets probably were significant. Noting that "the right to kidnap one's own diplomats is absolutely vital to a totalitarian country," Wiles suggests that the Soviets may have used the boycott/embargo to deter "*other* governments" from similar actions. Wiles even goes on to speculate that "this example may indeed have been salutary to states in a weaker economic position" than Australia. In other words, the trade sanctions were being used to add credibility to the signal sent by the break in diplomatic relations. In this case some consideration should also be given to the possibility that the deterrent effect was the *primary* objective while the immediate issue at hand may have been of secondary importance. Wiles mentions two other factors that are relevant to assessing the utility of the Soviet measures. One is the low cost to the Soviet Union stemming from its ability to switch wool purchases from Australia to South Africa, and the other is the absence of viable alternatives: "What else could the USSR have done?" Although Wiles concludes that "from the narrow economic point of view, . . . the whole thing was a farce," he implies the existence of another perspective— such as the one developed in this book—which might yield a different conclusion.[47]

Soviet Union vs. Yugoslavia (1948)

Knorr describes this case as an attempt to coerce a "disloyal ally" that clearly failed. A number of points, however, should be considered before accepting this judgment. First, the fact that this was the first open dispute between two communist countries is an important—perhaps even the most important—dimension of the situation. First impressions matter; precedents tend to be set. One important incentive, after all, for punishing "disloyal allies" is likely to be to discourage other allies from following suit. This was the first public challenge to Soviet domination of the communist bloc, and the costs to the Soviets of ignoring it would have been significant. It is difficult to believe that the symbolic importance of Tito's challenge was lost on Stalin. If, as Knorr suggests, the purpose of punitive trade restrictions is "not rarely" to "deter third parties from following the example

[46] Wiles, *Communist International Economics*, pp. 501-502.
[47] Ibid. Italics in original.

set by the punished actor'' (p. 151), then the Yugoslavian ''heresy'' would seem to be an example *par excellence* of such a situation. Not only was Yugoslavia not the *sole* target Stalin had in mind, it may not even have been the *primary* target. Indeed, Yugoslavia provided Stalin with a particularly inviting opportunity to send a message to other communist countries. After all, Tito did not owe his job to Stalin, and Yugoslavia was never firmly under Soviet control. If *even* a fringe country like Yugoslavia could incur such wrath, just imagine what could happen to other Eastern European countries. The symbolic aspects of this influence attempt may not have been of primary importance—although this point should not be conceded too quickly—but it is difficult to imagine an adequate overall assessment of its effectiveness that ignores such considerations completely. Second, the costs imposed on Yugoslavia were severe enough to make others think twice before following Tito's example. Wiles refers to a ''very unpleasant period of readjustment,''[48] and Freedman notes the severe damage done to the Yugoslavian economy.[49] Such costs are relevant to judging effectiveness not only as costs for Yugoslavian noncompliance but also in terms of their deterrent effects on other communist countries. Third, there were few alternatives available to Stalin. Propaganda, military threats, and diplomatic pressure had already been applied. About the only unused techniques were breaking diplomatic relations, which probably would have been less effective than trade sanctions, and military force, which was too risky because of uncertainty about what the Western countries might do.[50]

Soviet Union vs. Yugoslavia (1956)

After the rapprochement between the Soviet Union and Yugoslavia in 1955, Tito again irritated the Soviets by publicly supporting the Hungarian Revolution and by his refusal in 1957 to attend the fortieth anniversary conference of ruling parties in Moscow.[51] Once again the Soviets imposed trade restrictions, and once again Knorr declared them to be a clear failure. Two extenuating circumstances should be considered, however, before this judgment is accepted. First, unlike 1948, the trade restrictions were rather mild. As Wiles observes: ''It could hardly be said that [the] USSR declared economic war on Yugoslavia, when their inter-trade turnover dropped, in 1957-58, by a mere 20% in current prices.'' It would appear that this was intended as a light reprimand rather than a Stalinesque attempt to crush Tito. A second extenuating circumstance is the China factor. The Sino-Soviet rift was beginning at about this time, and Mao Tse-tung reportedly viewed Tito as ''the arch enemy.'' The Soviets could hardly allow them-

---

[48] Ibid., p. 500.
[49] *Economic Warfare*, p. 48.
[50] Cf. ibid., p. 47.
[51] Wiles, *Communist International Economics*, p. 507.

selves to be perceived as "soft on Titoism"; therefore they "reluctantly followed suit."[52] This suggests that any assessment of the effectiveness of this influence attempt should allow for the restrained nature of the restrictions imposed, the importance of symbolic goals, and the probable existence of targets other than Yugoslavia, such as China and other communist states. It should also consider the costs the Soviet Union would have incurred if it had allowed itself to be perceived as letting Tito's defiance go totally unpunished.

Soviet Union vs. Albania (1960)

This case was also intimately tied to the battle between the Soviet Union and China for leadership of the communist movement. In 1960 Albania openly sided with the Chinese at an international conference of communist countries. Although this is another of Knorr's clear failures, the case was not simply a matter of Albania's failure to give in to Moscow. Both the Chinese and other communist states were probably among the intended targets. Moreover, Knorr admits that "Albania suffered acute economic distress" as a result of the Soviet sanctions. This suggests that the influence attempt was at least partially successful in imposing costs for noncompliance.

Soviet Union vs. China (1960)

The Chinese ideological attack on the Soviet Union in 1960 led to a rather abrupt withdrawal of Soviet technicians from China, followed by a gradual falling off in trade over the next few years; but there was no embargo. Wiles suggests that trade levels between the two countries were "irrationally" high in 1960 and that some of the cutback was in order anyway. He further notes that "so little real Sino-Soviet economic war was there that non-machinery imports kept up very well" and "the all-important oil item kept up."[53] Precisely what the Soviet Union hoped to achieve with such measures is not entirely clear. Imposing costs on China was probably a goal, one with some success. Third parties, including India and other communist states, were probably intended targets. Knorr's characterization of the case as a clear failure is puzzling. It is difficult to believe that the Soviets really expected such mild measures to bring drastic changes in Chinese policy. The appropriate question would seem to be, what then were the more modest and less obvious objectives of this influence attempt?

Turkey vs. Austria-Hungary (1908)

This case concerns a Turkish boycott protesting the annexation of Bosnia-Herzegovina by Austria-Hungary in 1908. Although Knorr provides no

---

[52] Ibid.
[53] Ibid., pp. 509-513.

details about this case, his characterization of it as a clear failure probably rests on the assumption that the primary Turkish goal was the return of the territory. This is not a very helpful assumption in understanding this case, and few, if any, seem to agree with it.[54] The Treaty of Berlin (1878) had given Austria-Hungary the right to "occupy and administer" this area, which it had been doing for thirty years before the annexation proclamation. The chief reason for not annexing the territory outright in 1878 stemmed more from the internal politics of Austria-Hungary than from any objections by other powers; indeed, there was a general understanding that formal annexation would follow within a few years.[55] Thus, after an initial outraged reaction, sentiment in Turkey focused on compelling Austria-Hungary to pay compensation. The latter firmly opposed any such payment, maintaining that this would sully its national honor.

Shortly after the annexation announcement, the Young Turks organized a boycott. Since the boycott was not organized by the government, this case does not, strictly speaking, constitute economic statecraft as defined here. The boycott did, however, provide the government with a bargaining chip, which it used adroitly. The boycott is widely viewed as a significant factor determining the ultimate settlement, in which Austria-Hungary had to pay a humiliating indemnity of more than two million pounds. One writer refers to the boycott as "devastating" and as generating pressure on the Austro-Hungarian government both from internal commercial interests and from Germany, who feared the "terrible boycott" would be extended to include German goods.[56] And in January, 1909 the First Dragoman of the British Embassy wrote that Austria-Hungary "has yielded to the gentle pressure which takes its name from Captain Boycott."[57] Another writer concludes that Turkey "outplayed" Austria-Hungary at every turn, that there was no way the boycott could have been broken except by the humiliating indemnity to which Austria-Hungary was ultimately driven, and that "in the end, the Turks got nearly everything they desired."[58]

West Germany vs. Soviet Union (1962)

Although it is not entirely clear what Knorr is referring to here, he apparently has in mind the embargo on shipment of large-diameter steel

[54] The discussion here is based on the following sources: Frank Maloy Anderson and Amos Shartle Hershey, eds., *Handbook for the Diplomatic History of Europe, Asia, and Africa, 1870-1914* (Washington, D.C.: Government Printing Office, 1918); Bernadotte E. Schmitt, *The Annexation of Bosnia, 1908-1909* (Cambridge: Cambridge University Press, 1937); and Wade Dewood David, *European Diplomacy in the Near Eastern Question, 1906-1909* (Urbana: University of Illinois Press, 1940).

[55] See Anderson and Hershey, eds., *Handbook*, pp. 87, 374.

[56] David, *European Diplomacy*, pp. 101-103.

[57] Ibid., p. 102n.

[58] Schmitt, *Annexation*, pp. 123-124.

pipes to the Soviet Union imposed in 1962. This case illustrates the importance of careful specification of who is trying to get whom to do what in capability analysis. Although Knorr indicates that the West German trade restrictions were a reprisal against the erection of the Berlin Wall (p. 150), neither Adler-Karlsson nor Stent even mentions this objective.[59] Both portray the United States as the prime mover behind the embargo rather than West Germany, who seems to have reluctantly acquiesced to the embargo in order to placate her powerful ally. Since the embargo was technically grounded in a secret NATO resolution adopted in November 1962, the influence attempt could also be viewed from that organization's perspective.[60] American objectives were complex and involved both the Soviet Union and the NATO allies as targets. The objectives included weakening Soviet military capabilities, slowing the expansion of Soviet oil-exporting capabilities, and asserting American "predominance in the Western alliance in matters of East-West trade."[61] Although it is not clear how much the United States thought that such measures might retard the construction of Soviet pipelines, the consensus seems to be that a delay of about one year was achieved.[62] Stent describes this as only a marginal and temporary success, but, then, that may be about what U.S. policy makers were after. Depicting the American attempt to "reimpose" its "control over its policy on East-West trade" as "only partly successful," Stent judges the overall results to have been "mixed" from the standpoint of the United States.[63]

If this case is considered from the West German point of view, as Knorr suggests, the primary objective was demonstrating loyalty to and support for its American ally; "by contrast, the perceived need to prevent the building of the Friendship Pipeline was only a secondary goal."[64] The German effort to comply with American demands was so manifestly costly to Bonn in terms of domestic politics that the United States was probably very impressed with this demonstration of loyalty. Thus, West Germany was probably relatively successful with respect to her primary goal. Whether a delay of one year in the construction of the Soviet pipeline constituted a partial success or a partial failure with respect to the second

---

[59] Adler-Karlsson, *Western Economic Warfare*, pp. 129-132; and Stent, *From Embargo to Ostpolitik*, pp. 93-126.

[60] Unless otherwise specified, the details of this case are drawn from Stent, *From Embargo to Ostpolitik*, pp. 93-126.

[61] Ibid., p. 103.

[62] Cf. Ibid., pp. 103-104; and OTA, *Technology and E-W Trade*, p. 168. The Soviet establishment of its own pipe-making facility in response to the embargo is often cited as an example of the undesirable side effects of embargoes, but the inferior quality of the pipe thereby produced is seldom noted.

[63] Stent, *From Embargo to Ostpolitik*, p. 125.

[64] Ibid.

objective is, of course, an arguable question. "Clear failure," however, does not quite capture the many complexities of this case.

Arab Boycott of Foreign Companies Operating in Israel
(since 1955)

In 1955 the Arab League extended its boycott on trade with Israel to include the blacklisting of any company that operated in Israel. Knorr portrays this as an act "designed to weaken Israel" (p. 151) and includes it in his list of cases that have "clearly failed." Since there are many who maintain that the Arab boycott has indeed weakened Israel, the basis for Knorr's assessment is not obvious. Writing on the first decade of Israeli statehood, Marver H. Bernstein contends that the boycott "directly cost Israel about $40 million a year" and "slowed down the pace of economic development by closing nearby markets to Israel."[65] Another writer argues that "short of war the boycott has proved to be the most effective weapon" the Arabs have for "combatting Israel."[66] Asserting that the boycott has had "a certain degree of success" when directed against "small and medium-sized corporations," Dan S. Chill concludes that it has had "an inestimably adverse effect on Israel's economy."[67] Even those who are rather contemptuous of the boycott's pre-1973 effects on Israel often express concern about its actual or potential effects after the Arab demonstration of its oil power.[68]

It is doubtful that the Arab boycott can be adequately assessed without consideration of objectives other than merely weakening Israel. For many Arab states participation in the boycott is a way of demonstrating support for the Arab cause. It is also a symbolic way simultaneously to condemn Israel and to demonstrate Arab unity to the Western powers. Although the Arab boycott has not—and will not—destroy Israel, it has been partially successful. It is worth noting, also, that military statecraft, which has cost the Arabs far more, has not been especially effective either.

The twelve cases mentioned above deserve detailed investigation that goes beyond the preliminary probing underlying the discussion here. In each case there is reason to suspect that thorough study using the analytical framework developed here might lead to conclusions somewhat different

[65] *The Politics of Israel: The First Decade of Statehood* (Princeton: Princeton University Press, 1957), p. 187.

[66] Marwan Iskander, "Arab Boycott of Israel," *Middle East Forum*, October 1960, p. 30.

[67] *The Arab Boycott of Israel* (New York: Praeger, 1976), pp. xi, 22-29.

[68] See Walter Henry Nelson and Terence C. F. Prittie, *The Economic War Against the Jews* (New York: Random House, 1977); and U.S. House of Representatives, Committee on International Relations, *Hearings: Extension of the Export Administration Act of 1969*, part I, 94th Cong., 2d sess., 1976. *The Encyclopedia of Zionism and Israel* (New York: McGraw-Hill, 1971) describes the Arab boycott as "partly successful" (p. 56).

from Knorr's. Suppose that the differences between Knorr and Wallensteen, noted in the cases of Great Britain versus Iran and the United States versus the Dominican Republic, are resolved in favor of Knorr and that half of the remaining ten cases turn out to be clear failures, as Knorr maintains. If the five cases remaining—say, United States versus Cuba, United States versus Japan, Turkey versus Austria-Hungary, and two others—are moved from the category of clear failure to the category of "ambiguous outcome," the overall results of the twenty-two cases would be four classified as successes, seven as ambiguous, three as compromises, and eight as clear failures. This modest reclassification provides grounds for caution with respect to the conclusion that "the dramatic use of economic power in the form of trade restrictions [is] apt to fail in the large majority of instances."[69]

EAST-WEST TRADE EMBARGO

Restrictions on trade with communist countries have been part of American foreign policy since 1948. Any attempt to generalize about a policy that has evolved for over thirty years, of course, is bound to neglect many important details. The discussion here can only touch on a number of points that deserve lengthy exposition, but the purpose is merely to test the applicability of the analytical approach, not to render a definitive case study. The embargo on trade with communist countries, as Secretary of State Dean Rusk testified in 1964, "is an integral part of our overall policy toward international communism, and we must view it in this broad framework."[70] Four stages in the evolution of the American embargo policy may be roughly identified: In the first, extending from 1948 to 1958, the United States was dealing from a position of relative strength and tended to take a strongly anticommunist position. During this period the United States applied pressure to its European allies to support the longer lists of embargoed "strategic items," which it preferred, as opposed to the shorter lists preferred by the Europeans. As the European countries regained their economic strength, they became less responsive to such pressure from the Americans and began to increase trade with communist countries. The second period, 1959–1969, was one in which U.S. policy makers became increasingly aware of the limits of American power—with considerable help from the Vietnamese—and in which a more complex and differentiated strategy toward dealing with communist countries was beginning to emerge. A third period, extending from 1970 to 1978 might be described as the era of détente, a period in which the United States seemed prepared

---

[69] Knorr, *Power of Nations*, p. 152.
[70] *East-West Trade Hearings*, p. 4.

to accept Soviet power as a fact of international life and to try to work out arrangements for "peaceful coexistence." During this period increased trade with the Soviet Union was viewed as an inducement for political cooperation in the short run and as a means of increasing Soviet dependence on the international economy in the longer run. The emphasis during this period was on when and how to use relaxation of trade controls as a positive sanction to influence communist countries. The fourth period dates from 1979, when American policy makers backed away from the policy of détente after the Soviet invasion of Afghanistan and the deterioration of the situation in Poland. During the whole thirty-year period American trade policy with respect to communist countries has varied in accordance with the overall policy toward East-West relations. Disagreement between the United States and its European allies with respect to the length of the lists of embargoed items has also been a more or less constant characteristic of the period.

The importance of evaluating the utility of techniques of statecraft in terms of the goals of those using such techniques has been reiterated many times in previous chapters. Nowhere is this better illustrated than in East-West relations. To assess the utility of the trade embargo, one must first understand how policy makers perceived the nature of the problem. At no time since 1946 has there been unanimity with respect to the nature of the problem either among NATO members or within the American foreign-policy-making establishment. For the sake of economy of discussion, these viewpoints will be grouped into two categories, labeled "hard-line" and "soft-line." The two perspectives may be distinguished in terms of the following criteria:

1. *Nature and magnitude of the communist threat.* The hard-line perspective emphasizes the great magnitude and multidimensional nature of the threat. Thus, the threat is viewed as economic and ideological as well as political and military. The soft line views the threat as less serious and emphasizes its political and military dimensions.

2. *Time horizon.* Hard-liners are more likely to emphasize the immediacy of the threat and the urgency of responding to it, while soft-liners tend to emphasize the long-term nature of the problem and the need to avoid short-term overreaction.

3. *Relationship between nationalism and communism.* Hard-liners emphasize the monolithic and conspiratorial nature of the international communist movement, while soft-liners are more likely to emphasize nationalistic forces and the polycentric tendencies among communist states.

4. *Wellsprings of Soviet behavior.* Whereas hard-liners tend to view Soviet foreign policy as expansionist and stemming from com-

munist ideology, soft-liners are likely to emphasize the goal of national security and Soviet reactions to Western actions they perceive as threatening.

5. *Ultimate Western goal.* Hard-liners tend to view East-West relations in terms of a zero-sum game in which one side must eventually emerge victorious, while soft-liners emphasize the mixed-motive game and the goals of mutual accommodation and coexistence.

The actual policy position of any given statesman, of course, is likely to be more complex; but these criteria can be helpful in giving rough approximations of different viewpoints. Daniel Yergin has recently described these two viewpoints in terms of what he calls the "Riga" and "Yalta" axioms, corresponding roughly to the hard- and soft-line positions respectively:

> Two interpretations . . . competed for hegemony in the American policy elite in the middle 1940s. At the heart of the first set was an image of the Soviet Union as a world revolutionary state, denying the possibilities of coexistence, committed to unrelenting ideological warfare, powered by a messianic drive for world mastery. The second . . . [image] downplayed the role of ideology and the foreign policy consequences of authoritarian domestic practices, and instead saw the Soviet Union behaving like a traditional Great Power within the international system, rather than trying to overthrow it. The first set I call, for shorthand, the Riga axioms; the second, the Yalta axioms.[71]

Yergin goes on to note that the "Riga axioms" provided the basis for postwar American policy with respect to East-West relations and that even today these two sets of axioms "provide the points of reference for the continuing debate about how to organize U.S. relations with the Soviet Union"—the Riga axioms defining a cold war outlook and the Yalta axioms underlying détente.[72] Since the hard-line, or Riga, axioms have been the dominant rationale for most of the postwar period, this position will be the basic point of reference for evaluating the utility of the strategic trade embargo.[73]

As with most foreign policy undertakings, the goals and targets of U.S. trade restrictions included a variety of objectives and actors.

[71] Daniel Yergin, *The Shattered Peace: The Origins of the Cold War and the National Security State* (Boston: Houghton Mifflin, 1978), p. 11.

[72] Ibid. For a similar study of the evolution of thinking about East-West relations, which uses slightly different terminology, see Gaddis, *Strategies of Containment*. See also William Welch, *American Images of Soviet Foreign Policy* (New Haven: Yale University Press, 1970).

[73] For two discussions of East-West trade from a clearly defined hard-line–cold-war perspective, see Wu, *Economic Warfare*, pp. 57, 311-335, 366-388; and Harvey, *East West Trade*.

Soviet Union

The Soviet Union was the primary target of American trade restrictions. The overall primary objective was to contain and minimize Soviet influence of any kind everywhere in the world. Secondary goals viewed as contributing to this overall objective were as follows:

1. Inhibiting the growth of Soviet military capabilities.
2. Inhibiting the development of the Soviet economy in order to weaken the economic base on which military potential rests and to discourage Third World states from following the Soviet path to development.
3. Intensifying internal Soviet political difficulties.
4. Weakening the ideological appeal of communism by symbolic condemnation and moral stigmatization.
5. Deterring Soviet expansionism by demonstrating the intensity of American resolve to resist such moves.

United States Allies

With respect to America's allies the trade restrictions were intended to demonstrate the strength of American resolve to resist communism and dramatize the importance of the split between communist and noncommunist countries.

Third World States

With respect to uncommitted states in what is now called the Third World, the goals were:

1. To demonstrate U.S. commitment to resist communism.
2. To weaken the attractiveness of the Soviet approach to economic development by inhibiting Soviet economic growth.
3. To weaken the moral and political attractiveness of the communist example by making American repugnance for communism unmistakably clear.

Other Communist States

To the extent that the embargo was applied to them the goal was primarily to inhibit their ability to support the communist cause in general. To the extent that trade restrictions were applied more leniently to them—e.g., Yugoslavia, Poland, and Hungary—the goal was to undermine the cohesion of the communist bloc by reducing economic dependence on the Soviet Union. Devising a strategy with respect to these states was the most difficult aspect of the hard-line approach. Hard-liners tended to be more comfortable with treating all communist countries alike, in accordance with the belief that communism, *per se*, rather than the Soviet state, was the real enemy. Ambivalence on this point has troubled hard-liners throughout the postwar period.

In contrast, the soft-line approach tended to differ from the hard-line approach in the following ways:

1.   Whereas hard-liners emphasized minimizing communist influence of all kinds in all parts of the world, soft-liners were more likely to focus on containing the territorial expansion of the Soviet Union with special reference to Europe and Japan. Their goals were more limited and pragmatic, less ideological and universal.

2.   Whereas hard-liners were interested in isolating and condemning communist states, soft-liners were more likely to emphasize puncturing the "iron curtain" by the integrating effects of trade. This idea, drawn from the theory of "functionalism," was the mainstay of the policy of détente.

3.   Whereas hard-liners emphasized the importance of demonstrating resolve in order to impress allies and neutrals, soft-liners were likely to argue that the rigid and doctrinaire image of the United States thereby created was more a cost to be avoided than a benefit to be sought.

4.   Whereas hard-liners were ambivalent about treatment of Eastern European communist states, soft-liners found differential treatment easy to reconcile with their worldview. They consistently and effectively argued for treating Eastern European communist states more leniently in order to encourage polycentrism in the communist bloc.

5.   The greatest difficulties in the soft-liner's position arose from their desire to combine an image of anticommunism with a policy of building bridges to the East through trade. This has led them to downplay or ignore the importance of the symbolic aspects of the embargo with respect to demonstrating anticommunist commitment and to advocating ever shorter lists of embargoed "strategic" goods while proclaiming their desire to avoid contributing to Soviet military potential.

The strategic embargo policy has been pronounced a "serious failure" by Adler-Karlsson and has been labeled an "expensive mistake" by Knorr.[74] As with the other "classic cases" discussed in the previous chapter, the alleged failure is somewhat less obvious when judged in terms of a policy-contingency framework based on multiple goals and targets. Consider the following estimates of effectiveness.

The primary goals of containing and minimizing Soviet influence may be considered separately. Extensive expansion of Soviet territorial control since 1950 would constitute clear evidence of the failure of American

[74] Adler-Karlsson, "The U.S. Embargo," p. 170; cf. Adler-Karlsson, *Western Economic Warfare*, p. 9; Knorr, *Power of Nations*, p. 146.

containment policy. With the exception of the Soviet invasion of Afghanistan in December 1979, however, the territorial boundaries of Soviet power have remained remarkably stable. This is not to say that the policy of containment succeeded *because* of the embargo; it is only to point to the absence of evidence of clear failure. The containment and/or minimization of communist influence other than direct territorial control is difficult to estimate. Those who pursue unlimited goals—such as the eradication of *all* communist influence—rarely achieve more than partial success. Clearly, both Soviet and communist influence have grown. The examples of Vietnam and Cuba are perhaps most commonly cited; but neither was primarily Soviet induced. In Vietnam, communists had been the primary custodians of nationalist sentiment since the 1930s; and in Cuba, the peculiarities of relations with the United States were more important than Soviet influence.

The efficacy of the embargo with respect to inhibiting Soviet military potential is often challenged in two ways. First, it is pointed out that the Soviet Union gives such high priority to military capability that shortages in the military sector tend to be made up from other sectors of the economy.[75] Even if this is an accurate observation, it should not be viewed as evidence of failure to inhibit the build-up of Soviet military capability. Rather, it should be portrayed as a situation in which the embargo succeeded in imposing costs on the Soviet Union for the maintenance of its military priorities. The most appropriate response to Knorr's denial that there is "any evidence that the Soviet military sector suffered"[76] as a result of the embargo is Knorr's own earlier argument that in a world of scarce resources "the overall availability of resources limits the ability of governments to develop, maintain, and employ military strength."[77] The effectiveness of the embargo is also challenged as having "insufficiently" held back the growth of Soviet military power.[78] The growth of Soviet military capabilities relative to those of the United States is often cited in support of this viewpoint. Such evidence, however, is beside the point unless it is stated or implied that Soviet military capability would *not* have grown still faster in the absence of the embargo. The test of the efficacy of the embargo is not whether Soviet military power increased, *but whether it increased as much (or as cheaply) as it otherwise would have.* (Counterfactual conditions matter!)

With respect to the goal of inhibiting Soviet economic growth, similar arguments are often used to show the futility of the embargo. Thus, the fact that the Soviet growth rate was higher than that of the United States during the 1950s is beside the point. The appropriate reference point is

[75] See, for example, Adler-Karlsson, *Western Economic Warfare*, p. 9.
[76] *Power of Nations*, p. 145.
[77] *Military Power and Potential*, p. 47.
[78] See, for example, Bienen and Gilpin, "Evaluation," pp. IIIc,4-5.

what the Soviet rate of growth *would have been* in the absence of the embargo. While this is difficult to estimate precisely, the theory of comparative costs allows a deductive inference that the rate was probably lower without trade than it would have been with trade. Even Adler-Karlsson and Knorr admit that the embargo imposed some costs on the Soviet economy.

The goal of imposing costs on the Soviet Union great enough to cause severe domestic political difficulties for the regime had little chance of success, and there is little evidence that it has had much. The hard-line view probably underestimates the degree of stability of the Soviet regime.

As a means of symbolic moral condemnation of communism the embargo has probably achieved a moderate degree of success. This is not a matter of mere "expressive behavior" as the following passage implies: "By emotionalism is here meant that the policy can be considered as a way of giving vent to a deep psychological animosity to the communist system, a demonstration of disapproval, . . . having a value in itself, divorced from any desire to achieve a concrete political result."[79] While such "emotionalism" may well have played a role, American policy can also be viewed in instrumentalist terms. Psychological warfare was an important part of American cold war strategy for John Foster Dulles. Denying the relevance of "neutralism," Dulles portrayed the East-West split in moral terms emphasizing the complete moral and spiritual incompatibility between the communist way of life and that of the "Free World."[80] American policy was thus intended not only to contain expansion of the Soviet state but also to alert the rest of the world to what he saw as the most dangerous threat to civilization—the evil of communism. In the context of such a foreign policy, the conduct of normal commercial relations with communist countries made little or no sense. How could American foreign policy makers have expected other countries to take their warnings about the evils of communism seriously if the United States were conducting "business as usual" with such countries? The embargo thus reinforced the credibility of the American view that communism was an immense economic, political, military, and ideological threat to all noncommunist nations. Within the framework of assumptions and goals of the hard-line cold warriors, it is difficult to deny the beneficial symbolic effects of the embargo. Depicting other countries as the devil incarnate may or may not be wise foreign

[79] Adler-Karlsson, *Western Economic Warfare*, p. 33.

[80] On the outlook of Dulles and other American policy makers, see Gaddis, *Strategies of Containment*, esp. pp. 127-198. See also David J. Finlay, Ole R. Holsti, and Richard R. Fagan, *Enemies in Politics* (Chicago: Rand McNally, 1967), pp. 25-96. Gaddis (p. 223) notes that W. W. Rostow, advisor to both presidents Kennedy and Johnson, tended to view communism as a "disease." The policy implications of this metaphor are about the same as the more theological perspective of Dulles.

policy, but once one accepts such a goal as given, it is difficult to justify normal commercial relations with such countries. If one assumes that American foreign policy makers were embarked on an ideological crusade against communism during the 1950s and early 1960s, then the effectiveness of the embargo must be judged in terms of its compatability with, and contribution to, that undertaking.

The last goal with respect to the Soviet Union was to impress the Soviets with the degree of American resolve and thereby strengthen the deterrence posture of the United States. Although it is doubtful that the Soviets needed convincing on this point or that the embargo contributed much to the credibility of the overall American deterrent threat, when one is threatening to blow up the world in order to save it from the scourge of communism, it is wise to avoid misunderstanding by making the threat as clear as possible. Under such circumstances, even a tiny additional increment of credibility may be well worth its cost. Willingness to carry on business as usual might have caused doubts in some Soviet minds as to whether the Americans "really meant it."

Insofar as the European allies were concerned, the goal of the embargo was not merely to reassure them of the credibility of the American commitment to save them from Soviet expansionism but also to impress upon them the American view that resisting communism, especially outside of Europe, was more important than they might think. Whereas the first impression was intended to be reassuring, the unsettling effect of the second on the Europeans was probably not accidental.

With respect to Third World countries, the embargo must also be evaluated in terms of the overall American policy of convincing such countries to have as little to do with communism or communist states as possible. Although the embargo itself may have been much less important in conveying this message than American aid programs, consider what the U.S. image would have been if it had been carrying on business as usual with communist countries while admonishing Third World countries to "do as I say, not as I do." Clergymen are more effective if they practice what they preach.

No aspect of the embargo has been so misunderstood as the symbolic dimension. A memo from W. W. Rostow to the State Department's Policy Planning Council in 1963 pointed out that the embargo "has been intricately interwoven" into the overall American "cold war posture" and depicted trade denial as "an important symbol of our cold war resolve and purpose and of our moral disapproval of the USSR."[81] Adler-Karlsson quotes a similar statement in which Mose Harvey contends that "the restrictive trade policy, perhaps more than anything else, has served to signify United

---

[81] Quoted in Stent, *From Embargo to Ostpolitik*, p. 93.

States' concern that all free countries of the world maintain every possible safeguard against the grave dangers engendered by the Soviet-led communist drive.''[82] Seizing on the phrase "more than anything else," Adler-Karlsson disputes Harvey's assertion on the grounds that other measures, such as "U.S. determination to maintain a military superiority, the building up of the system of alliances," and economic aid programs, have been more important (p. 128). Actions, however, are more effective in "signifying concern" if they are unambiguously extraordinary. Maintaining military superiority, forming alliances, and giving aid are all things that the United States and other countries have done for reasons other than anticommunism. In short, they lend themselves to more than one interpretation. The anticommunist trade restrictions, however, were obviously and solely an anticommunist measure. Adler-Karlsson goes on to point out that what Harvey views as "praiseworthy steadfastness" is likely to be seen by Europeans as "a rigid die-hardness" (p. 128). This, of course, is true; one person's "binding commitment" is another person's "pigheadedness." What is objectionable is that Adler-Karlsson makes this point in the context of an evaluation of the "rationality" of the U.S. embargo policy. Far from being the evidence of irrationality or failure that Adler-Karlsson supposes it to be, perception of the U.S. policy stance as "rigid die-hardness" is a sign that American policy has successfully projected an image of a binding commitment. The fact that those who disapprove of this binding commitment may pin pejorative labels on it is quite beside the point. The rationality and/or effectiveness of U.S. policy must be judged in terms of the goals of American policy makers rather than in terms of the goals others might wish America would pursue.

The effectiveness of the embargo with respect to the Eastern European communist states is awkward because of the ambivalence of hard-liners on this issue. For the most part, actual practice has deviated from the purist hard-line position with respect to Eastern Europe; and the policy of treating countries like Poland, Hungary, Yugoslavia, and Romania more leniently appears to have been successful in reinforcing polycentric tendencies in the communist bloc. Dean Rusk defended this policy in 1964 on the grounds that "since the Communist countries no longer form a completely monolithic bloc in political terms, it follows that we should not treat them as a monolith in trade terms."[83] The difficulty of reconciling such a policy with hard-line purism was illustrated by Senator Frank Lausche's questioning of Rusk with respect to whether such trade might undermine the credibility of America's commitment to the liberation of Eastern European

[82] Harvey, *East West Trade*, p. 124, quoted in Adler-Karlsson, *Western Economic Warfare*, p. 128.

[83] *East-West Trade Hearings*, p. 5. See also Rusk, "Why We Treat Different Communist Countries Differently," pp. 390-396.

countries from communist rule. Although the answer was obviously that it did indeed have such side effects, the secretary of state was understandably reluctant to admit this.[84]

The case against the anticommunist trade restrictions rests at least as much on the magnitude of the alleged costs of such a policy as on belittling the benefits. Six of the more important costs that have been attributed to the embargo will be examined.

Cost No. 1: Exacerbation of East-West Tension[85]

The embargo was clearly part of an overall strategy of confronting and resisting communism. In this context the observation that it irritated the Soviet policy makers is not necessarily evidence of failure or of an unintended side effect. In any case it is easy to get causal arrows reversed when discussing this alleged cost. As Wiles points out, "political hostility, entirely mutual, preceded the embargo."[86] It is also easy to overlook alternative explanations of East-West tension. Gaddis, for example, mentions the formation of NATO, the rearming of Germany, the retention of American forces in postoccupation Japan, and the decision to build the hydrogen bomb as actions that were particularly irritating to the Soviets in the early cold war period.[87] Thus, if one discounts the *intended* increase in tensions caused by the embargo and takes account of all the other reasons for East-West tension, the amount that can fairly be attributed to the embargo is likely to be rather small.

Cost No. 2: Exacerbation of U.S. Relations with European Allies[88]

This alleged cost is so widely accepted that it has become part of the seldom questioned "conventional wisdom" regarding trade sanctions. In every decade since the embargo was implemented in 1948, including recent debates with respect to Afghanistan and Poland, the basic elements of the argument have been the same. The dispute, it is said, is merely tactical; it concerns means rather than ends. How could it be otherwise? The Europeans, after all, share American security interests and are as much op-

---

[84] *East-West Trade Hearings*, p. 25.

[85] Adler-Karlsson, *Western Economic Warfare*, pp. 9, 88-89, 112-114; Knorr, *Power of Nations*, p. 146.

[86] Wiles, *Communist International Economics*, p. 555.

[87] Gaddis, *Strategies of Containment*, p. 71.

[88] Knorr, *Power of Nations*, p. 145; Adler-Karlsson, *Western Economic Warfare*, pp. 9, 36-49, 89, 129-137; OTA, *Technology and E-W Trade*, pp. 173-202; and U.S. House of Representatives, Committee on Foreign Affairs, *Hearings: United States–Western European Relations in 1980*, 96th Cong., 2d sess., 1980 (hereafter cited as *Hearings on U.S.–W. European Relations*).

posed to communism as the United States. European resistance to American pressure for more stringent restrictions on trade is not based on differing perceptions of the problems, but rather stems from Europe's relatively greater dependence on trade with the East and on the European view that economic sanctions do not work. The problem arises from American intransigence with respect to the "minor tactical" question of how long the list of embargoed items should be. To drive this point home, it is usually pointed out that "America's allies do not deny the basic necessity of withholding items of direct military relevance from the Communist world";[89] or, as Adler-Karlsson put it with respect to the early 1950s, "there was never any real dispute over the fact that 'goods of real military value', as conventionally understood, should be prevented from reaching the communist orbit."[90]

Before accepting this conventional view of the manner in which trade sanctions exacerbate relations among the Western allies, some critical questions are in order: (1) Do Europeans object to economic sanctions either as a matter of principle or because they never work? Their use of such measures during both world wars, during the British imbroglio with Argentina in 1982, and their apparent readiness to use them if the Soviet Union had used its own troops to pacify Poland in 1981, suggest that across-the-board reluctance to use economic sanctions is not really the root of the problem.

(2) Do Europeans basically agree with the American definition of the "communist problem" and how to approach it? The root cause of friction within NATO with respect to East-West economic relations is fundamental European disagreement with the hard-line outlook that has dominated American foreign policy during most of the postwar period.[91] Whereas the hard line emphasizes the global implications of the threat, Europe emphasizes its regional aspects; whereas the hard line depicts the threat as large, the Europeans see it as small; whereas the hard line emphasizes international communism as the threat, the Europeans emphasize the traditional interests of the Soviet state as a European power; whereas the hard line stresses the symbolic and ideological aspects of the problem, the Europeans see it in more concrete pragmatic terms; and whereas the hard line questions the legitimacy of the Soviet regime and implies an ultimate

[89] OTA, *Technology and E-W Trade*, p. 12.

[90] *Western Economic Warfare*, pp. 40-41.

[91] At a conference in December 1982 on East-West commercial relations, Angela Stent repeatedly pointed out that "Europeans do not share our definition of security." (U.S. Senate, Committee on Foreign Relations, *The Premises of East-West Commercial Relations: A Workshop Sponsored by the Committee on Foreign Relations and Congressional Research Service*, Committee Print, 97th Cong., 2d sess., 1982, pp. 154, 181, 183, 193. Cited hereafter as *Premises Workshop*.)

goal of eradicating communism, the Europeans accept the Soviet regime and imply an ultimate goal of coexistence. In short, during most of the postwar period, the Europeans have tended to share the soft-liners' view of the nature and magnitude of the East-West problem.[92]

(3) Does European agreement that "goods of real military value as conventionally understood" signify basic agreement with the United States position? Not in the least. As was noted in discussing the concept of "strategic goods," the conventional understanding of "goods of real military value" is almost completely fallacious. Assuming that Europeans understand the implications of resource fungibility as well as American policy makers, how does one explain their insistence on relatively short lists? The logic of fungibility indicates that, other things being equal, the longer the list, the more Soviet military potential is limited. Assuming that the Europeans understand this as well as the Americans, the only alternative seems to be that Europeans view the costs and/or benefits of limiting Soviet military potential differently than the Americans. If this is indeed the case, why disguise the real issue as a mere tactical disagreement over the utility of economic sanctions? Why describe a disagreement over ends as one concerning means? The answer from the policy makers' perspective is clear enough. The single most important assumption underlying NATO is that members share a fundamental view of the nature and magnitude of the communist threat. In the interests of NATO unity and viability, there are strong incentives to conceal disagreements with respect to this matter. Although it is understandable, perhaps even justifiable, that policy makers would try to disguise such fundamental differences as minor disagreements about the utility of sanctions, it is difficult to understand or justify the tendency of scholars to adopt the same viewpoint.

The arguments that sanctions generate ill will within the Western alliance and/or that "later polycentrism" in NATO may "in part be traced back to the intra-Western quarrel over the embargo policy"[93] are greatly weakened by the availability of plausible alternative explanations for such phenomena. Such explanations of friction between America and Europe are rooted in culture and power. Traditional European attitudes have portrayed European diplomacy as subtle, adept, and sophisticated, while American diplomacy has been viewed as clumsy, inept, primitive, and moralistic. Following the Second World War, however, the former European Great Powers found themselves dependent on the United States for both military

---

[92] A possible exception to the European tendency to adopt the soft-line view is the period 1947–1950, during which the Europeans took the initiative in forming NATO and in which they tended to emphasize the military threat, while the United States stressed the importance of economic recovery. On this point see Gaddis, *Strategies of Containment*, pp. 25-88, esp. pp. 72-74.

[93] Adler-Karlsson, *Western Economic Warfare*, p. 89.

security and economic recovery. That they simultaneously recognized and resented this dependency and the accompanying loss of status is not surprising. What is surprising is how seldom it is recognized that the tendency of American actions to generate European resentment is embedded in the structure of the Western alliance. In testimony before a congressional committee a former British ambassador to the United States explained the relevance of the "old unwritten convention that America decides and the Europeans complain" and pointed out the necessity for American policy makers to bear in mind that "whatever the United States does, it will tend to be damned if it does, and damned if it does not. If you consult, you will be accused of failing to show leadership. If you show leadership, you will be complained at for failing to consult."[94] Given traditional European attitudes toward American diplomacy, it was inevitable—well, highly probable anyway—that the recovery of European economic and political strength would lead to polycentric tendencies in NATO. By comparison, the effects of friction generated by the embargo were probably trivial at best. It is true that the economic cost of an embargo is greater for Europe than for the United States, but the amounts are small enough to be bearable if the stakes were perceived as important.

Indeed, if NATO cohesion is a criterion, it is not clear that détente and increased levels of East-West trade would lead to greater cohesion. The glue that holds NATO together is the perception of the communist threat, and the embargo is a symbolic reminder of that threat. "Business as usual" with communist states is likely to dim Western awareness of this threat, thus weakening the single most important determinant of NATO unity. Of course, many who favor détente and more East-West trade believe that the communist threat has been exaggerated by the West, thereby making diminished awareness of the alleged threat desirable. This may well be, but such arguments should stand on their own merits and not be hidden behind arguments implying that abandoning the anticommunist embargo would increase unity within the Western alliance. In this case, other things are unlikely to remain equal.

Cost No. 3: Enhancing Bloc Unity

The embargo probably did strengthen Soviet control of the bloc countries, especially in the early years. Whether the later policy of more lenient

---

[94] *Hearings on U.S.–W. European Relations*, pp. 141-164, 293-303. See also the testimony of Simon H. Serfaty in the same hearings, pp. 2-45; and testimony of Richard Cooper in U.S. Senate, Committee on Foreign Relations, *Hearings: Economic Relations with the Soviet Union*, 97th Cong., 2d sess., 1982, pp. 153-179 (cited hereafter as *Hearings on Economic Relations with Soviet Union.*)

treatment for some countries has offset this tendency is difficult to judge. In general, this cost must be viewed as a serious drawback of the embargo.

Cost No. 4: Gains from Trade

As the level of East-West trade grew in the 1970s, the perceived loss in terms of gains from trade that would be incurred from a complete embargo also grew. In 1977 trade with communist countries accounted for about 5 percent of Western European imports and exports as compared with a corresponding figure of only 1-2 percent for the United States.[95] Since trade is a bigger percentage of GNP in European countries than in the United States, the prospective loss implied by a trade cutoff, although not devastating, is large enough to be viewed as a significant cost at least by European policy makers. Sluggish economies intensify such concerns.

Cost No. 5: Increased Self-Sufficiency in USSR

It is difficult to know how to evaluate this alleged cost. Obviously, depriving the Soviet Union of gains from trade increases Soviet self-sufficiency. This, in a sense, is what an embargo is supposed to do. Since self-sufficient economies are less efficient, it is not clear whether this is a benefit or a cost. It could just as well be argued that forcing the Soviet Union to be self-sufficient is just another way of saying that the embargo reduces the productivity of the Soviet economy. Whether this should count as a cost or a sign of success, of course, depends on the goals of the embargo.

Cost No. 6: Weakening of Western Institutions

This cost consists of charges made by Adler-Karlsson that have not been taken very seriously by other scholars. Even Knorr, who compiles a formidable list of costs drawing largely on Adler-Karlsson's work, ignores this category of costs.[96] Adler-Karlsson identifies five ways in which the embargo policy allegedly endangered Western institutions:[97]

(1)   U.S. trade policy toward communist countries has been based on political considerations, a charge often leveled against communist countries.

Comment: While undoubtedly true, it is rather beside the point. All trade policy can be shown to have some political dimension. This hardly means that there are not important differences in the *degree* and *kind* of political

[95] OTA, *Technology and E-W Trade*, p. 38.
[96] *Power of Nations*, pp. 145-146.
[97] *Western Economic Warfare*, p. 10.

involvement in trade manifest in the limited American trade restrictions with respect to communist countries and the state trading conducted by communist countries.

(2)   The embargo lists have been shrouded in secrecy.

Comment: Although this is true, it is hardly as sinister in its implications as Adler-Karlsson implies. The fact of the embargo has been well known for a long time. The suggestion that keeping the specific composition of the embargo lists secret threatens the foundations of Western institutions is a bit overdrawn.

(3)   In implementing the policy "doubtful legal practices have been used."

Comment: In a discussion that barely scratches the surface of the legal questions involved, Adler-Karlsson implies that the Battle Act, requiring U.S. aid recipients to support the embargo or forgo aid, was a violation of international law (p. 43). No extenuating circumstances or competing legal principles are considered; nor does he point out that any European state that believed its legal obligations prevented it from supporting the embargo was free to forgo American aid.

(4)   In implementing the embargo the United States has gathered economic intelligence in allied countries.

Comment: Adler-Karlsson seems to be appalled that the United States would engage in checking up on the activities of foreign firms in order to determine whether U.S. export licenses, U.S. loans, and U.S. procurement contracts should be given to such firms. In general, Adler-Karlsson does not seem to distinguish between rights guaranteed by law and privileges bestowed by policy decisions. He thus compares denying an export license or withholding a loan with the punishment of criminal actions and describes U.S. officials who gather information about the activities of foreign business firms as "an American secret police" operating in Europe.

(5)   "Power pressure has been put on reluctant allied nations in a way which should be alien to a voluntary alliance" (p. 10).

Comment: Adler-Karlsson discusses this in terms of an alleged "fundamental principle" that makes it illegitimate for members of a "voluntary alliance" to bring pressure to bear on one another (pp. 42-43). This idea is novel indeed; if there has ever been an alliance in which this so-called basic principle was observed, it has escaped the attention of most other students of international politics.[98] Precisely how American attempts to

---

[98] Most students of international politics would probably agree with Michael Mandelbaum that "dissension among the allies is a feature of all alliances" and that "there is always tugging and pulling, or, to use the language of politics, threatening and negotiating between and among allies." (*The Nuclear Revolution: International Politics Before and After Hiroshima* [Cambridge: Cambridge University Press, 1981], p. 151.) See also Glenn H. Snyder, "The Security Dilemma in Alliance Politics," *World Politics* XXXVI (July 1984):461-495.

influence its Western allies constituted a threat to Western institutions is not spelled out.

When alternative techniques of statecraft are considered, the anticommunist trade restrictions seem to have been well nigh unavoidable. The hard-line approach, after all, envisioned the communist threat as immense, immediate, and multidimensional. It called for combatting communism on many levels in all parts of the world. Propaganda was used extensively; diplomacy—short of actually breaking relations—was also used; and military alliances were formed with every willing country. The hard line was simply incompatible with either doing nothing or "business as usual" with the communists. The period from 1948 to 1962 included such events as the coup in Czechoslovakia, the Berlin blockade, the Korean War, brutal repression of uprisings in Poland and Hungary, the Soviet refusal to evacuate Eastern Europe, the Berlin Wall, and the Cuban missile crisis—all of which were perceived by American policy makers as provocative actions by communist states. How was the United States to respond? Diplomatic protest and propaganda seemed weak and inappropriate by themselves; yet military threats or intervention seemed too risky in a nuclear world. In sum, it is difficult to identify an alternative to trade restrictions that would have involved a combination of costs and benefits that was clearly superior to the chosen policy.

A Postscript on Rationality

Whereas Adler-Karlsson depicts the embargo as highly irrational,[99] the discussion here suggests that it was not so irrational *given the policy-contingency framework of the hard-liners*. The discussion here also implies that the soft-liners' case has had less logical cohesion than that of the hard-liners. Especially with respect to the treatment of "strategic goods," this is probably true. The utility of techniques of statecraft, as has been stated many times in this book, should be judged in terms of the goals of the policy makers, not in terms of the policy preferences of the analyst. For the record, however, it should be noted that the author's own views are closer to the soft- than to the hard-line approach. How, it may be asked, can this same author contend that the views of the latter display more logic than the views of the former? The internal logical cohesion of an argument is only one of several criteria relevant to policy analysis. The assumptions underlying that argument are equally important. Although comparing the assumptions underlying the hard- and soft-line approaches is beyond the scope of this book, the assumptions of the hard-liners appear to be fewer and simpler than those of the soft-liners. Since it is usually easier to construct a logically cohesive argument on the basis of a few simple

[99] *Western Economic Warfare*, pp. 111-129 et passim.

assumptions than to construct a similarly rigorous argument on the basis of a large number of complex assumptions, it should not be surprising that the hard-liners' case is more rational.

AMERICA AND IRAN: 1979–1981

On November 4, 1979 Iranian militants seized the United States embassy in Tehran and took sixty-six Americans hostage, demanding the return of the deposed shah. During the ensuing fourteen months American policy makers employed several means, including economic sanctions, in response to this situation. Strictly speaking, trade sanctions were not the primary economic technique in this case: although exports of military spare parts and imports of Iranian oil were cut off about a week after the takeover, the most important sanction was the freezing of more than twelve billion dollars of Iranian assets on November 14. Still, the case is instructive with regard to the uses of economic statecraft.

What were the goals and targets of this influence attempt? As with the previously considered cases, they were more complex than first appearances would indicate and probably looked something like the following:

Iran

The two primary objectives were to demonstrate American resolve to resist blackmail and the safe return of the hostages. American foreign policy makers disagreed as to which goal should be given priority, but both were clearly important in their eyes. Whereas presidential advisor Zbigniew Brzezinski argued that the nation's honor and credibility should come first, Secretary of State Cyrus Vance cautioned that "this nation will ultimately be judged by our restraint in the face of provocation, and on the safe return of our hostages."[100] "This crisis," as President Carter observed on November 16, 1979, "calls for firmness and it calls for restraint."[101] The Iranian leaders needed to be brought "to their senses," the president said later, "I thought depriving them of about twelve billion dollars in ready assets was a good way to get their attention."[102] Economic sanctions, then, were intended to send a message to Iran to the effect that

[100] Hamilton Jordan, *Crisis: The Last Year of the Carter Presidency* (New York: G. P. Putnam's Sons, 1982), pp. 44–45; and Zbigniew Brzezinski, *Power and Principle: Memoirs of the National Security Adviser, 1977-1981* (New York: Farrar, Straus, Giroux, 1983), pp. 480–481.

[101] *New York Times*, November 16, 1979.

[102] Jimmy Carter, *Keeping Faith: Memoirs of a President* (New York: Bantam, 1982), pp. 464–465. A series of articles in the *New York Times* captured the signaling aspects of the sanctions remarkably well: Hedrick Smith, "A Symbolic Oil Cutoff," November 13, 1979; Terence Smith, "Carter's Strategy on Iran: U.S. Seeks to Project Tough Image Without Risking Lives of Hostages," November 15, 1979; and Steven Rattner, "The Economic Warfare Was Also Psychological," November 18, 1979.

although the United States was unwilling to give in to Iranian demands, it was also amenable to seeking a peaceful settlement of the dispute.

Secondary goals with respect to Iran included imposing economic costs on Iran and depriving Iran of certain policy options. Because the crisis was not expected to drag on as long as it ultimately did and because the economic costs would obviously not immediately hurt Iran, these goals were probably viewed as less important than the signaling aspects of the sanctions. It is also worth noting that there was some concern that overly severe economic or military sanctions might so weaken Iranian institutions as to risk chaos and/or inability to resist undue Soviet pressures in the future.[103] Both the boycott of Iranian oil (November 12) and the freezing of Iranian assets (November 14) were preemptive moves designed in part to head off Iranian attempts to cut off oil and withdraw assets.

Robert Carswell, a Treasury official involved in implementing the freeze order, suggests that forestalling a threat to the dollar and protecting the property claims of American citizens against Iran were also objectives of the influence attempt.[104] Since accounts by Jordan, Brzezinski, and Carter pay little or no attention to such goals, it may be assumed that they were of tertiary importance at best.

Third Parties

The Iranians were not the only targets of American sanctions. America's allies, the Third World in general and Islamic countries in the Middle East in particular, and even communist countries, especially the Soviet Union, were targets. Three objectives, unranked in terms of importance, were as follows:

(1) Maintain—and perhaps even strengthen—the credibility of the American image by demonstrating firm resolve. Aside from the immediate desire to discourage similar assaults on American embassies in other countries, Brzezinski reportedly saw the crisis as "an opportunity, a chance for the President to show the world that he is capable of handling a crisis with international implications . . . a chance to show American resolve!"[105]

(2) Generate international pressure on Iran. Although the United States took the matter to the United Nations Security Council almost immediately, the economic sanctions were a way of signaling other countries that American patience was limited and that help was expected. As Carter put it, "I wanted our message to Khomeini to go to our major trading partners as

---

[103] Cf. Robert Carswell, "Economic Sanctions," p. 253; and Cyrus Vance, *Hard Choices: Critical Years in America's Foreign Policy* (New York: Simon and Schuster, 1983), pp. 387, 398.

[104] Carswell, "Economic Sanctions," pp. 249-258.

[105] Jordan, *Crisis*, p. 53. Cf. Brzezinski, *Power and Principle*, pp. 480-481.

well, so that they would be more eager to discourage Iran from Khomeini's oft-repeated threat to punish our people.''[106] The sanctions were thus intended partly as a way to intensify the diplomatic isolation and censure of Iran.

(3)   Preserve Islamic support in resisting Soviet moves in the Middle East. Although not an objective of the sanctions in the beginning, it emerged as one in the aftermath of the Soviet invasion of Afghanistan in December. Brzezinski summarizes the impact of that event on the thinking of American policy makers as follows:

> The Soviet invasion of Afghanistan meant that henceforth any action taken by us toward Iran had to be guided, to a much larger extent than heretofore, by its likely consequences for regional containment of Soviet ambitions. More specifically, the Soviet invasion of Afghanistan made it more important to mobilize Islamic resistance against the Soviets—and that dictated avoiding anything which might split Islamic opposition to Soviet expansionism. In turn, it was more important than before to avoid an Iranian-American military confrontation.
>
> In other words, until the Soviet invasion . . . the trend was toward more and more serious consideration of military action. The Soviet aggression . . . arrested this trend, and our strategy increasingly became that of saving the hostages' lives *and* of promoting our national interest by exercising military restraint.[107]

Before assessing the effectiveness of this influence attempt, the level of difficulty should be noted. Three factors complicated what might otherwise have been accomplished by a mere diplomatic protest. The sanctity of diplomats and embassies, after all, is one of the most fundamental and widely accepted norms in the international community. Such problems with unruly behavior are usually settled quickly. The Iranian situation, however, was not ordinary. Anti-American feelings, reflecting Iranian anger over American support for the deposed shah, were strong throughout the crisis; and any Iranian leader who seemed willing to negotiate seriously with the United States risked being vilified as a collaborator with the devil. In addition, the political instability—indeed, near chaos—in Iran during most of the period enhanced the difficulty of dealing with the crisis. For nine months, for example, Iran had no prime minister.[108] Yet another complicating factor was the conflict between the American goals of dem-

---

[106] Carter, *Keeping Faith*, p. 466. See also Jordan, *Crisis*, p. 55; Brzezinski, *Power and Principle*, p. 479; and Vance, *Hard Choices*, p. 377.

[107] Brzezinski, *Power and Principle*, p. 485.

[108] See J. C. Hurewitz, ''The Middle East: A Year of Turmoil,'' *Foreign Affairs* LIX (1981):546-547.

onstrating resolve on the one hand and safeguarding the lives of the hostages on the other. Either objective would have been much easier to attain in the absence of the other.[109]

In terms of effectiveness, the attempt to demonstrate both resolve and restraint probably had little or no impact on Iran. In the political turmoil in Iran there was simply no one who could speak with authority to be impressed by American actions, no one to receive Carter's message. Rudderless states are difficult to influence. In the early part of the crisis, Khomeini himself may have been powerless to deliver the hostages unharmed, even if he had been impressed with American resolve or restraint, which he probably was not. The miracle is that the hostages were eventually returned unharmed. Although not clearly foreseen as such, the frozen Iranian assets evolved into a valuable bargaining chip that could be exchanged for the hostages without sullying American national honor. The importance of this bargaining chip should not be underestimated. The basic problem from the beginning was that the United States had nothing that could be honorably offered to Iran. From the U.S. perspective, it was the victim of a blatantly illegal blackmail attempt. Everything that Iran demanded was anathema to American policy makers. Seizing the blackmailer's own assets, however, provided the United States with a *usable* bargaining chip. Once Iran came to view the return of its assets as an American concession, the biggest obstacle to settlement had been overcome. On the one hand, the Iranians needed to be able to claim that they had forced the United States to grant concessions; while on the other hand, American policy makers needed to be able to plausibly deny that any such concessions had been made. Unfreezing the Iranian assets provided both sides with a way out of this dilemma.[110]

With respect to imposing economic costs on Iran, the sanctions eventually proved rather effective. Although sanctions were not responsible for either the poor state of the Iranian economy in the fall of 1980 or the war with Iraq, they "deprived Iran of critical supplies and spare parts and forced it into expensive deals with unreliable middlemen." By late fall Iran was at war with Iraq, its receipts from oil sales had dropped to "virtually nothing," and its financial reserves were rapidly being depleted.[111] In such a situation, the costs imposed by sanctions probably

[109] For an argument that Carter may have exacerbated this difficulty by continual public reiteration of the high value he placed on the hostages' lives, see Betty Glad, "Jimmy Carter's Management of the Hostage Conflict: A Bargaining Perspective," paper presented at the American Political Science Association Meeting, New York, 1981 (mimeo).

[110] On the use of the frozen assets as a bargaining chip, see Glad, "Carter's Management," pp. 14, 53, 66; Carswell, "Economic Sanctions," p. 259; and Vance, *Hard Choices*, pp. 377-378.

[111] Carswell, "Economic Sanctions," p. 247.

appeared more significant to Iranian policy makers than they had six months earlier.

Carter's attempt to disarm Iran with respect to an actual or threatened oil embargo was highly effective. Adler-Karlsson's depiction of this is less than generous. He asserts that "the Carter administration *tried* to preempt the Iranian use of one potential weapon of blackmail, an oil embargo," and noting that "the action . . . [was] probably doomed from the beginning," concludes that the "U.S. action should, at the maximum, be interpreted as a demonstration that the United States could manage its own oil supply without help from Iran."[112] It is unclear why Adler-Karlsson uses the word "tried," since the success of the preemption was nearly instantaneous. Once oil imports from Iran were forbidden, any Iranian embargo against the United States, actual or threatened, was pointless. Adler-Karlsson implies that the influence attempt was doomed to fail unless the United States could get other nations to join in the boycott, but this was not the goal. Just as Pericles had entreated the Athenians to destroy their own houses to show the Peloponnesians that threats to destroy Athenian property were unlikely to work,[113] so Carter wanted to "eliminate any suggestion that economic pressure can weaken our stand on basic issues of principle."[114] Similarly, the freezing of Iranian assets neutralized Iranian threats of precipitous withdrawal and denied Iran even the propaganda victory that would ensue from such a sudden outflow of money from American banks.[115]

With respect to the tertiary goal of protecting the dollar, little need be said. Even if the Iranians had withdrawn the money, the threat to the dollar would probably have been minimal. The goal of protecting property claims against Iran, insofar as it was a goal at all, was probably "overachieved" in the sense that the final settlement "put virtually all U.S. lenders and claimants against Iran in a much more favorable position than they had been prior to the seizure of the hostages."[116]

The handling of the hostage situation was unlikely to encourage others to seize American embassies, but the broader bolstering of American credibility that Brzezinski hoped for probably evaporated as the crisis dragged on. With respect to generating international pressure on Iran, the sanctions were probably helpful. Many states that rarely side with the United States in the United Nations supported her on this issue, something many would have found it harder to do if the United States had used force against Iran.

[112] "U.S. Embargo," p. 179. Italics added.
[113] Thucydides, *History of the Peloponnesian War* (Modern Library), p. 82.
[114] *Wall Street Journal*, November 12, 1979. See also *New York Times*, November 13, 1979.
[115] *New York Times*, November 15, 1979.
[116] Carswell, "Economic Sanctions," p. 259.

The European allies were reluctant to join in the sanctions but they provided diplomatic support and, more importantly, acquiesced to American exercise of extraterritoriality with respect to freezing Iranian assets in overseas branches of American banks. "This exercise of extraterritorial power meant the difference between depriving Iran of $6 billion and $12 billion."[117]

With respect to avoiding military confrontation with Iran in order to avoid alienating other Muslim countries, the sanctions were quite successful. The same could not be said of the abortive military rescue attempt.

In January 1981 *The Economist* provided the following overall assessment of the effectiveness of American policy toward Iran during the crisis:

> Dignity and temper almost intact, the United States had succeeded in peacefully prying its embassy staff from the hands of a government-turned-gangster for a ransom siphoned from Iran's own bank account. That was no small achievement for a giant which had found its strength unusable against a petulant pygmy. . . .
>
> Mr. Carter can . . . take credit for having grabbed the bargaining chip—Iran's assets in American banks—for which the hostages were eventually exchanged. He avoided making a settlement with blackmailers which might have encouraged further blackmail. . . . The Iranians first sought the extradition of the Shah; he never returned. They sought an American admission of past responsibility for meddling in Iran; none was forthcoming. They sought the return of the Shah's wealth; it has not come, and almost certainly very little will. They had sought the cancellation of all existing American claims on Iran. Instead, the American government cancelled its own claims and agreed to sit on any claims arising from the detention of the hostages. . . . The Iranians secured an end to the freeze on their assets and to western economic sanctions. But there would have been no freeze, or sanctions, had the hostages never been taken. . . . But the main test for any hostage deal was whether it might encourage another government of would-be America-bashers to grab another embassy. The answer, almost certainly, is no.[118]

The costs of economic sanctions against Iran were remarkably small. U.S. pressure on Europe to apply economic sanctions in April was used as a smokescreen to divert attention from the military rescue mission planned for May. The United States even argued that Europe should do this in order to head off the use of force by the Americans. When it later became known that this was a ruse, the Europeans were justifiably irritated.

---

[117] Ibid., p. 261.
[118] "Our People, Your Money," *The Economist*, January 24, 1981, p. 11.

Most of this ill will, however, should be charged as a cost of the rescue mission, not economic sanctions.

Many viewed the most significant cost of the sanctions as the precedent of American willingness to use foreign-owned funds in American banks as tools of foreign policy.[119] The Treasury and the banking community in general were particularly concerned about the effect on the future willingness of foreigners to maintain deposits with American banks. The *Wall Street Journal*, for example, suggested that the quickness with which the freeze was imposed "reinforced a widely held opinion around the world that this administration is not as serious as it should be about the integrity of the U.S. dollar and the sanctity of private property."[120] And former Treasury official Robert Carswell argued that the cost was so large that such measures should be used in the future only after exhausting "every possible avenue of multilateral cooperation," even if this means "substantial modification" in U.S. objectives. Depicting "leadership when our allies do not follow" as a luxury the United States can no longer afford, Carswell implies that making "ideological points" or demonstrating resolve is not worth endangering the value of the dollar.[121]

While such arguments cannot be dismissed, there are five reasons to partially discount them. First, while concern for the "integrity of the dollar" and the "sanctity of private property" are of some importance, the implication that they should take priority over the credibility of the U.S. reputation for action or the sanctity of American embassies is likely to strike foreign policy makers as reflecting a banker's view of the world. Refusal to take unilateral action may be a fine way to protect the dollar, but it would not have been a very effective way to demonstrate resolve in the hostage crisis. Second, since several of the goals concerned impressing other countries with the intensity of American concern, the risk to the dollar was actually beneficial insofar as it added credibility to the signal. Third, the unusual circumstances surrounding American use of such measures are easily perceived by would-be depositors in U.S. banks. Aside from communist countries, the only American use of such techniques has been with respect to Iran and Rhodesia. In the latter two cases American action was backed up by nearly universal international condemnation of the target country. The United Nations Security Council imposed mandatory sanctions on the one and threatened sanctions against the other. Such usage hardly indicates an American commitment to promiscuous asset freezing. Fourth, the freeze order against Iran was issued only after an Iranian announcement of its intention to withdraw the funds. Thus, the

[119] See Carswell, "Economic Sanctions," p. 248ff.
[120] Editorial, December, 4, 1979.
[121] "Economic Sanctions," pp. 264-265.

freezing action could be at least partially justified as an attempt to defend the dollar rather than as a willingness to see it weakened. And fifth, even if the precedent does strengthen fears that the United States might again freeze the assets of a country that flagrantly provokes it, this is not an unmitigated evil. Such fears may discourage others from such provocations in the future.

Another cost that is often implied or stated in private but rarely in public is the possible loss of confidence in American resolve stemming from reluctance to use force in the face of intense provocation. In the eyes of many, great powers are supposed to be prepared to sacrifice lives to protect national honor, credibility, and so on. Carter's emphasis on putting the lives of the hostages first virtually ruled out military action and indicated a lack of toughness to some.[122] To the extent that this occurred, however, the cost was more a function of the goals pursued rather than of the means chosen. Once preserving the hostages' lives was defined as a primary goal, it was unfair to blame economic sanctions for their failure to place those lives at risk. They were, after all, intended to avoid that very risk.

Were there alternatives to economic sanctions that would likely have had more utility in approximating the goals of the Carter administration? Propaganda and diplomacy were used, and the latter, at least, would probably have brought the hostages home eventually. By themselves, however, such techniques seemed a weak response to such a flagrant provocation and would have done little or nothing to demonstrate American resolve. The military option was almost certain to endanger the lives of at least some, and probably all, of the hostages. The Iranian militants threatened to kill the hostages if military force were used, and there was no reason to doubt the credibility of this threat. *Given the primary goal of safe return of the hostages*, military force was virtually useless throughout the crisis. After the Soviet invasion of Afghanistan, the need to avoid alienating Islamic countries curtailed the utility of military force still further. The military rescue mission would almost certainly have involved casualties among the hostages if it had not aborted in the early stages. The costs of this effort turned out to be—and should have been foreseen to be—enormous by comparison with the probable effectiveness.[123] The European allies resented being used as a smokescreen; the U.S. reputation for effective action suffered; lives were lost; Iran became less isolated in terms

---

[122] See Terence Smith, "Putting the Hostages' Lives First," *New York Times Magazine*, May 17, 1981; Eugene V. Rostow, "Letter to the Editor," *New York Times*, May 23, 1980; and Glad, "Carter's Management," pp. 16-17. Vance (*Hard Choices*, p. 380) states his belief that it was a mistake for the United States to place so much public emphasis on the safe return of the hostages.

[123] On the drawbacks of military statecraft in this case, see Vance, *Hard Choices*, pp. 377, 387, 398, 408.

of world opinion; and, according to the secretary general of NATO, the raid "further complicated the already delicate situation in the Middle East."[124] It is difficult to avoid the conclusion that military force was immensely counterproductive in the Iranian crisis. Nor is there any reason to believe that threats would have helped the situation. As Leslie Gelb observed, the Iranians were "going through a national nervous breakdown, and . . . you [could not] deal with them by threats of force."[125]

In January 1980 Roger Fisher suggested an alternative approach to the hostage crisis that is instructive to review with the benefit of hindsight for two reasons. First, it shows the difficulty of identifying useful alternatives; and second, it illustrates the dangers of generalizing on the basis of the conventional wisdom about economic sanctions.[126] Entitling the article "Sanctions Won't Work," Fisher advocated a diplomatic approach based on finding "measures that will solve their problem in a way that solves ours." This, of course, is sensible advice in many situations; but in this one, such measures were hard to come by. The Iranians wanted to humiliate the United States, and the United States wanted to prevent them from doing it. To agree to cooperate with an "impartial international investigation of the past conduct of the United States" in Iran while under duress might appeal to Iran, but it was unlikely to appeal to the United States. Fisher suggested that American policy should be to "give the Iranians no more and no less than that to which they would have been entitled without seizing the embassy." The trouble with this proposal is that by seizing the embassy, the Iranians changed the situation to one in which the United States was under duress. Just as President Kennedy refused to withdraw Jupiter missiles from Turkey—something he had actually ordered done earlier—in the midst of the Cuban missile crisis, so the Carter administration was reluctant to establish the precedent that it could be blackmailed into negotiation.

Fisher bolstered the case for his proposal by asserting that "we can safely predict that sanctions against Iran will tend" to have a number of effects. These predicted effects were as follows:

1. *Unite Iranians behind Khomeini.*

Comment: If this refers to the likelihood of stirring up Khomeini's supporters, sanctions would seem to be redundant, since Khomeini seemed to have no trouble inflaming their passions. If it refers to anti-Khomeini factions, it is doubtful that the sanctions had much effect on their attitude toward Khomeini.

2. *Make it politically difficult for the Iranians to back down.*

[124] See Glad, "Carter's Management," pp. 40-48; and *The Economist*, May 3, 1980.
[125] *Hearings on U.S.–W. European Relations*, p. 60.
[126] Fisher, "Sanctions Won't Work," *Newsweek*, January 14, 1980, p. 21.

Comment: As it turned out, the reverse of this proposition is closer to the truth. The seizure of Iranian assets gave both sides something to bargain about later on and allowed the Iranians to claim that they had acquired a quid pro quo for the hostages rather than having backed down. By creating a new problem for the Iranians, the freezing of the assets had actually created the possibility of following Fisher's advice to find measures that would solve their problem, i.e., return of the assets, in a way that solved ours, i.e., return of the hostages on honorable terms.

3.   *Divert their attention from internal difficulties to the foreign foe.*
Comment: This, of course, happened; but probably not because of the sanctions. The militants in the embassy, the parades, television harangues, and memories of American support for the shah sufficed to produce this effect.

4.   *Be economically insignificant amidst the current chaos in Iran.*
Comment: But as the economic situation in Iran continued to deteriorate and the war with Iraq began, effects that may have seemed insignificant early in the crisis may have loomed larger in Iranian calculations. By fall both the frozen assets and the access to spare parts were of growing significance.

5.   *Increase the Soviet role in Iran.*
Comment: The sanctions could be viewed as having the opposite effect insofar as they provided an alternative permitting the United States to avoid the use of military force. As was noted above, this is precisely how Brzezinski portrayed the situation after the Soviet invasion of Afghanistan, i.e., in order to preserve Islamic unity in resisting Soviet influence, military action—*the main alternative to sanctions being considered*—had to be ruled out.[127]

6.   *Cause the United States to be held responsible for the serious difficulties Iran faces.*
Comment: The United States was already being used as the scapegoat for Iranian difficulties even before the seizure of the hostages. This effect was bound to occur, sanctions or no sanctions.

7.   *Divide international support for the United States.*
Comment: The United States could hardly expect other countries to be more indignant about the embassy takeover than it showed itself to be. Mere propaganda and diplomacy might have led others to perceive the United States as indifferent, impotent, or both. International support, after all, was not motivated entirely by the sympathy of other states; it was also offered partly as an implicit quid pro quo to keep the United States from using military force.[128] In the context of what was generally agreed to be

---

[127] Brzezinski, *Power and Principle*, p. 485.
[128] At times the exchange of foreign support for American restraint was explicit, as when the United States asked the Europeans to join in the sanctions as a way of heading off U.S.

flagrant provocation, other states viewed economic sanctions as a moderate rather than a reckless response. In April 1980 United Nations delegates, who had often criticized the United States for "hasty overreaction," reportedly viewed the American response to Iran as demonstrating "remarkable restraint."[129] In any event, it is difficult to think of any American foreign policy since World War II that has received more widespread international support than the handling of the hostage crisis. Even the Soviet Union withheld its veto of the early Security Council denunciations of Iran. The sanctions probably maximized international support by demonstrating *both* impatience and restraint.

8.   *Change the issue from our sure success in resisting Iranian coercion to our probable failure in coercing them.*

Comment: When someone throws down the gauntlet, Fisher seems to suggest that one should either walk away claiming to have successfully resisted the attempt to coerce one into a duel or offer a polite "excuse me, but I think you might have dropped your glove." Unfortunately, when gauntlets are thrown down in public, there are limits to one's ability to plausibly redefine the situation. In Iran the gauntlet had been flamboyantly thrown down; the United States had been successfully coerced in the sense that the embassy takeover and the hostage seizure had succeeded. The overriding question was not whether the United States would submit to further coercion by returning the shah but rather what the United States would do in response to the coercion already inflicted upon it. The American reputation for action was at stake whether U.S. policy makers wanted it that way or not; the world was watching.

It is always easier to view a situation with the benefit of hindsight. Predictions in international politics are always tricky, but assertions that one can "safely predict" the effects of economic sanctions on the basis of the conventional wisdom about sanctions can be especially so. Considering the objectives of American policy, the difficulty of the situation, and the lack of alternatives likely to have had higher utility, the sanctions against Iran do not provide support for the conventional view of such measures as ineffective and counterproductive.

THE AFGHANISTAN EMBARGO

When Soviet troops invaded Afghanistan on December 25, 1979, the Carter administration responded in a number of ways, including stepped up military spending, proposed legislation to reinstitute draft registration, recall of the American ambassador from Moscow, vigorous denunciation,

---

military action. See *Hearings on U.S.–W. European Relations*, p. 73; and Vance, *Hard Choices*, p. 381.

[129] *New York Times*, April 8, 1980.

withdrawal of the SALT II treaty from the Senate, a threat to boycott the Olympics (which was eventually carried out), a cutback in Soviet fishing privileges, tightening of restrictions on high technology exports to the Soviet Union, an explicit threat to repel "by any means necessary, including military force," any attempt by an "outside force to gain control of the Persian Gulf region" (the "Carter Doctrine"), and a partial embargo on grain shipments to the Soviet Union.[130] The most dramatic of these actions was the embargo on seventeen million metric tons of grain that the U.S. government had agreed only months earlier to allow the Soviets to buy.[131] The embargo did not affect exports of eight million metric tons agreed to as part of a five-year deal with the Soviet Union and to which the American government had specifically pledged not to apply export controls. The grain embargo was eventually lifted in April 1981, in fulfillment of a campaign promise by President Reagan.

The key to understanding this influence attempt by the United States is the realization that it had very little to do with Afghanistan *per se* and a great deal to do with America's reputation for action in Southwest Asia and elsewhere. "The stakes involved today in many specific conflicts," observes Robert Jervis, "are less concrete possessions, such as money and territory (e.g. Berlin), than images of resolve and intention."[132] Nowhere is this better illustrated than in the American response to the Soviet invasion of Afghanistan. The issue was not so much why the Soviets had gone into Afghanistan in the first place, but rather how reactions to their having gone in might affect possible *future* Soviet intentions elsewhere in the world, especially in Southwest Asia. The overriding concerns were American perceptions of future Soviet intentions and Soviet perceptions of future American intentions. The dangers associated with Soviet underestimation of the strength of American resolve to resist Soviet threats to Persian Gulf oil were incalculable. The fundamental issue was not the freedom of a few valiant Afghans, but rather the avoidance of nuclear war at some future

---

[130] For a useful review of this case see U.S. House of Representatives, Committee on Foreign Affairs, *An Assessment of the Afghanistan Sanctions: Implications for Trade and Diplomacy in the 1980's*, report prepared by the Congressional Research Service (Committee Print), 97th Cong., 1st sess., 1981 (hereafter cited as *Assessment of Afghanistan Sanctions*). The "Carter Doctrine" was announced in "The State of the Union Address," January 23, 1980.

[131] Contrary to the view stated here, Hurewitz contends that the "Carter Doctrine" constituted the "most dramatic single act" taken in response to the invasion. ("The Middle East," p. 557.) The validity of this contention can be readily tested by readers. Simply ask a few friends how Carter responded to the Soviet invasion of Afghanistan. The most likely responses are the grain embargo and the Olympic boycott. Indeed, few will probably even remember the name of the "Carter Doctrine," let alone its content. Dramatic acts, after all, exist in the mind of the beholder.

[132] *Logic of Images*, p. 20.

date. Afghanistan is not an area of vital interest to the United States, but the Soviet image of America's intentions and capabilities is as vital as any interest the United States has.

What then were the goals and targets of the Carter grain embargo? The primary target was the Soviet Union; secondary targets were the European allies; and tertiary targets included the Third World in general, Pakistan, and Moscow's Eastern European allies. The goals with respect to each target were probably structured along the following lines:

U.S. Goals: Soviet Union

The primary American objective was to send a three-part message to the Kremlin. First, "the Soviets," as Carter put it, "must understand our deep concern."[133] The first forceful use of Soviet troops outside of Eastern Europe since World War II was a serious matter in the eyes of American policy makers, and they wanted the Soviets to know it. Brzezinski describes the event as "a major watershed in the Soviet-American relationship";[134] and Carter's State of the Union address asserted that "the implications of the Soviet invasion of Afghanistan could pose the most serious threat to the peace since the Second World War."[135] And Marshall Shulman characterized the sanctions as "largely by way of indicating the seriousness with which we take the Soviet action in Afghanistan and the indication that it is not a case of business as usual."[136] The second part of the message was that although the Soviet move into Afghanistan was serious, any attempt to move beyond Afghanistan would be *much more* unacceptable to the United States, thus implying a threat to respond even more vigorously, possibly with military force. (This threat was later made explicit in the "Carter Doctrine.") The presidential address announcing the grain embargo emphasized the ominous implications of the Soviet move for Iran, Pakistan, world oil supplies, the United States and its allies, and world peace and stability in general. Carter, Vance, and Brzezinski *all* viewed the invasion as caused in part by Soviet "miscalculation" of America's vital interests and its determination to defend them.[137]

The third part of the message concerned the credibility of the first two

[133] Address to the Nation, "Soviet Invasion of Afghanistan," *Weekly Compilation of President Documents* 16, 1 (January 4, 1980):26.

[134] Brzezinski, *Power and Principle*, p. 429.

[135] *Weekly Compilation of Presidential Documents* 16, 4 (January 23, 1980):196. Note that he did not say the invasion itself constituted such a threat, but rather the possible implications thereof.

[136] U.S. House of Representatives, Committee on Foreign Affairs, *Hearings: East-West Relations in the Aftermath of Soviet Invasion of Afghanistan*, 96th Cong., 2d sess., 1980, p. 28.

[137] Carter, *Keeping Faith*, p. 472; Brzezinski, *Power and Principle*, p. 432; and Vance, *Hard Choices*, p. 389.

parts. In effect, it said, "How do you know that we really mean it when we say that we are upset and when we threaten to escalate if you go further?" The answer lay in the vehicle used to communicate the message, i.e., the grain embargo. From this perspective, the most important costs were not those imposed on the Soviet Union but rather those the United States was willing to impose on itself, for it is these costs that bolster the credibility of the message. Taken together, this three-part message was an attempt to deter the Soviet Union from further actions. The *New York Times*, which provided excellent interpretive reporting of the significance of the grain embargo, recognized the primary goal of the embargo in an editorial worthy of Jervis or Schelling. Noting that Moscow may have underestimated the degree to which American policy makers perceive the invasion as threatening the Persian Gulf and pointing out that "such misperceptions can cause powerful nations to stumble into conflict," the *Times* endorsed Carter's use of "clear and even self-injuring demonstrations of alarm" in the form of "trade embargoes and diplomatic disruptions" in order to "declare America's interests and determination to defend them in western Asia."[138]

The secondary goal with respect to the Soviet Union was to impose costs on the Soviets for refusal to withdraw. "Verbal condemnation is not enough," the president said in his State of the Union Address, "the Soviet Union must pay a concrete price for their aggression." Not everyone would agree that this purpose was of secondary importance. A study prepared for Congress, for example, depicts imposing costs on the Soviets as the primary goal, while communicating the "seriousness with which the United States viewed the invasion" is portrayed as "another, albeit implicit, purpose."[139] How can one be sure that signaling was primary, while punishment was secondary? Although certainty is impossible, the following factors support such an interpretation:

(1) The important question is whether deterring further Soviet acts of aggression was more important than punishing the Soviets for refusal to withdraw. Nearly all of Carter's public statements indicate that this was indeed the case. Testimony by the secretary of state in March 1980 supports the interpretation of deterrence as primary and punishment as secondary in importance.[140] Even the report to Congress seems to accept the priority of deterrence over punishment when it states that "by punishing the U.S.S.R., the administration sought to deter it from further aggression."[141]

---

[138] *New York Times*, January 13, 1980. See also various articles appearing on January 5, 1980; and Vance, *Hard Choices*, p. 389.

[139] *Assessment of Afghanistan Sanctions*, p. 22.

[140] U.S. Senate, Committee on Foreign Relations, *Hearing: U.S. Foreign Policy Objectives*, 96th Cong., 2d sess., 1980, p. 27. See also OTA, *Technology and E-W Trade: An Update*, p. 28.

[141] *Assessment of Afghanistan Sanctions*, p. 22.

(2) Once the priority of deterrence is admitted, it is easy to show that punishment was of lesser importance. This follows from the logic of deterrence, i.e., *punishment does not deter, threats do*.[142] The only practical relevance punishing the Soviet Union could have for deterring it would be if such punishment served as a signal implying that similar—or more severe—punishments would follow further aggression in the future and/or if punishment were being used to add credibility to explicit or implicit threats with respect to future Soviet actions. Thus, to say that the punishment was intended to deter is, in effect, to admit that the symbolic functions of the punishment were more important than the cost-imposing functions.

(3) Since deterrence is a matter of threat communication rather than of punishment *per se*, it can be assumed that if deterring future Soviet moves was more important to American policy makers than getting them to withdraw, then communicating "the seriousness with which the United States viewed the invasion to the Soviet leadership" was more important than making them pay a price. The point of communicating serious concern, after all, was to imply a deterrent threat. Apart from implications for future American behavior, the seriousness of American concern about the invasion would be a matter of little or no concern for Soviet decision makers.

At least one writer goes beyond merely asserting the primacy of imposing costs on the Soviet Union and explicitly denies that deterring further Soviet aggression was a goal at all.[143] Although initially implying that the embargo was an attempt to "teach someone a lesson," Robert Paarlberg proceeds to pay little or no attention to the content of the intended "lesson" and, in fact, never considers what signal, if any, the embargo was supposed to convey to the Soviets. Instead he describes the purpose of the embargo as follows:

> Accepting the President's language, the embargo had a highly limited but clearly stated purpose. The announced objective was not to force the Soviet Union to remove any or all of its occupying troops from Afghanistan. The objective was not to deter a further act of Soviet aggression. If it had been, it would have made greater sense to continue grain exports on a conditional basis. . . . The purpose of the grain embargo, as stated by the President, was simply to punish the Soviet Union for its invasion of Afghanistan. (p. 155)

Even accepting the assumption that the president's public statements should be taken at face value, this interpretation is difficult to accept. In announcing the embargo the president had made it clear that the invasion was "an extremely serious threat to peace *because* of the threat of further Soviet

---

[142] Baldwin, "Thinking About Threats," pp. 76-77.

[143] Robert L. Paarlberg, "Lessons of the Grain Embargo," *Foreign Affairs* LIX (Fall 1980):155.

expansion,'' had emphasized the threat to Iran, Pakistan, and ''the world's oil supplies,'' had asserted the need for the Soviets to ''understand our deep concern'' (presumably not just for educational purposes), had noted the importance of removing any doubt from the minds of ''our potential adversaries'' about American willingness, determination, and capacity to take such measures, and had ended with a specific assertion of determination to ''deter aggression.''[144] Subsequent public statements by the president underscored the importance of deterring future Soviet aggression. In the ''State of the Union Address'' the president made the deterrent threat ''absolutely clear'' in the ''Carter Doctrine.'' And in an address to the American Society of Newspaper Editors in April, he noted that American failure to respond to the invasion would have constituted ''a cynical signal to the world that could only encourage further aggression'' and stated that ''a very clear signal has been sent to the Soviet Union'' condemning their actions and conveying the threat of possible responses ''beyond economic and political actions'' in the event of ''further aggression.''[145] Thus, even if analysis is confined to public presidential statements, the denial that deterrence was an objective of the embargo is difficult to support.[146]

A third objective with respect to the Soviet Union, probably of tertiary importance, was to signal a desire to preserve the framework of East-West cooperation built up over the preceding decade. This goal, which could be inferred from the partial nature of the grain embargo, was spelled out by both Secretary of State Vance and Undersecretary of State for Economic Affairs Richard Cooper in testimony before Congress.[147] Cooper depicted the sanctions as ''firm enough to get their attention'' but at the same time limited enough to ''preserve a base whereby we can restore . . . the potentially cooperative aspects of our relationship.''[148]

[144] Carter, ''Soviet Invasion of Afghanistan,'' January 4, 1980. Italics added.

[145] Weekly Compilation of Presidential Documents 16, 15 (April 10, 1980):635, 643.

[146] Paarlberg's observation that continuing grain exports ''on a conditional basis'' would have ''made more sense'' if deterrence were the goal is apparently rooted in the assumption that a threat to cut grain exports again would thereby be more potent as a deterrent. If grain exports were the only tool available for making deterrent threats, of course, Paarlberg's point would be well taken. Such a threat, however, would have failed to convey the seriousness of Carter's purpose. The cut in grain exports both implied a threat of future action—possibly military—and strengthened the credibility of that implied threat, a threat which was later made explicit. The implied deterrent threat was not necessarily—or even probably—economic; it was military. The message was something like the following: ''You have entered dangerous territory. The restrained nature of my response indicates that my vital interests are not at stake, but the costliness of this message (to me) should also make it clear to you that there are other interests nearby which I do regard as vital. Beware!''

[147] Hearing on U.S. Foreign Policy Objectives, pp. 30-31; and U.S. Senate, Committee on Banking, Housing, and Urban Affairs, Hearings: U.S. Embargo of Food and Technology to the Soviet Union, 96th Cong., 2d sess., 1980, pp. 124-125 (hereafter cited as Hearings on U.S. Embargo).

[148] Hearings on U.S. Embargo, p. 124.

U.S. Goals: European Allies

Although rarely treated as such, the allies were also targets of the grain embargo.[149] The main objective with respect to the allies was to assert leadership through demonstrating American willingness to incur costs. Brzezinski, as he had in the Iranian crisis, saw the Afghanistan invasion as "an opportunity" for Carter to "demonstrate his genuine toughness."[150] Carter himself refers to Afghanistan in terms of the need to "demonstrate our resolve" and to "remind the rest of the world how vital our stakes were in the Persian Gulf region."[151] Hamilton Jordan observes that "to our allies, the real test of American resolve in the face of Soviet aggression was whether or not a President, in the middle of a tough re-election campaign, would embargo grain sales from the United States and possibly alienate farmers." He quotes the president on the day the decision was made as follows: "How am I going to lead the West and persuade our allies to impose sanctions against the Russians if we aren't willing to make some sacrifices ourselves? What can I say to Margaret Thatcher or Helmut Schmidt if we fail to exercise the single option that hurts the Russians most?"[152]

U.S. Goals: Other Countries

The embargo was a way for the United States both to call attention to the outrageous Soviet actions and to demonstrate its resolve to resist further Soviet advances.

How effective was the grain embargo in approximating its goals? Although Brzezinski lists the sanctions against the Soviet Union after the invasion of Afghanistan among Carter's foremost accomplishments in the foreign policy area and Carter himself maintains that the embargo was "very effective," others have been less kind.[153] After endorsing the embargo in January 1980, because "it was high time for the United States to do something firm and show our resistance in a manner they could understand" (a view that emphasizes signaling), former Agriculture Secretary Earl Butz declared it "totally ineffective" in October 1982, because the Soviets bought grain elsewhere (a view that has little to do with signaling and a lot to do with imposing costs).[154] Robert Gilpin testified in March 1980, describing the sanctions as a "knee-jerk reaction," and pro-

---

[149] The otherwise useful study by the Congressional Research Service, *Assessment of the Afghanistan Sanctions*, for example, does not portray the allies as targets. Oddly enough, although Paarlberg ignores signals directed at the Soviet Union, he does note the use of the embargo to signal the allies. ("Lessons," p. 160).

[150] *Power and Principle*, p. 429.

[151] *Keeping Faith*, p. 482.

[152] *Crisis*, p. 100.

[153] Brzezinski, *Power and Principle*, pp. 528-529; Carter, *Keeping Faith*, p. 477.

[154] *New York Times*, January 24, 1980; and *Los Angeles Times*, October 22, 1982.

ceeded to summarize the study he and Bienen had done in 1979 emphasizing the tendency of economic sanctions to be ineffective, expensive, and counterproductive. Noting the symbolic uses of sanctions, Gilpin denied their utility in sending deterrent signals—"If by effectiveness one means a capacity to deter or compel other countries, then, what economic sanctions ultimately symbolize is our weakness and impotence."[155] Following Gilpin, Donald Losman testified that "economic sanctions have been *totally* ineffective in obtaining the political goals of those nations imposing them" and concluded that the Carter administration's sanctions against the Soviet Union were "bad politics, bad economics, and poor diplomacy" since "in almost every case, sanctions have been unsuccessful, masochistic, and counterproductive."[156] J. C. Hurewitz, in the *Foreign Affairs* review of events in 1980, asserted that the embargo could "only be described as an overall failure with at most spotty and uncertain impact."[157] *U.S. News and World Report* declared the sanctions "a flop" on the grounds that they were "hurting Americans more than Russians" and had not induced Soviet withdrawal from Afghanistan, which, the magazine alleged, was the president's "basic objective."[158] Richard Gilmore, emphasizing Soviet withdrawal, cost imposition with respect to the USSR, and cost minimization with respect to the United States, concluded that "the overall effects of the embargo proved damaging to the United States on all fronts."[159] And a recent study by the Office of Technology Assessment describes the results of the grain embargo as "inconclusive at best" and notes that "many argue" that it was a failure.[160] Clearly, the Carter grain embargo is not universally regarded as a smashing success. Let us review the effectiveness with respect to the policy-contingency framework constructed earlier.

Sanctions Effectiveness: Soviet Union

There is little reason to doubt that the political message the embargo was intended to convey reached Moscow. The Congressional Research Service uses stronger language in asserting that "undoubtedly, the political message that the sanctions were intended to convey got through to the Soviet leadership."[161] Robert Kaiser notes that "President Carter's demonstration of American willingness to link grain sales to general diplomacy must have had a deep impact on Soviet leaders, who had previously as-

---

[155] *Hearings on U.S. Embargo*, pp. 165-184.
[156] Ibid., pp. 184-205. Italics added.
[157] Hurewitz, "The Middle East," p. 553.
[158] *U.S. News and World Report*, June 16, 1980.
[159] *A Poor Harvest: The Clash of Policies and Interests in the Grain Trade* (New York: Longman, 1982), pp. 166-168.
[160] OTA, *Technology and E-W Trade Update*, p. 70.
[161] *Assessment of Afghanistan Sanctions*, p. 1.

sumed that the laws of capitalism required Americans to sell them grain regardless of political considerations.''[162] Of course, communicating a deterrent threat in a credible way is one thing; actually deterring is another. Whether the Soviets were actually deterred is difficult to judge, but Brzezinski suggests that the credibility gained by the American firm response to the invasion of Afghanistan helped to head off a probable Soviet intervention in Poland in December 1980.[163]

With respect to the goal of imposing costs for refusal to withdraw, the embargo was less successful. The Soviet Union was able to replace most of the grain embargoed by the United States from other suppliers, such as Canada, Australia, and especially Argentina.[164] This is not to say that no costs were inflicted on the Soviets, but rather that the costs were mostly in the form of increased uncertainty among Soviet planners, disrupted shipping schedules, and higher prices. These effects certainly fell far short of the original expectations of the Carter administration. One indirect measure of the impact of the grain embargo on the Soviet Union, however, is seldom noted. If the opportunity costs of forgoing American grain were indeed as low as is often implied, one would have expected the Soviets to show their disdain for American actions and their lack of dependence on American grain by boycotting such grain at least for a while. It is humiliating enough for the Soviets to buy American grain under the best of circumstances, but to continue buying it after the effrontery of the American embargo must have been difficult to take. Instead of boycotting, however, the Soviets swallowed their pride and purchased the maximum amount authorized by the five-year Soviet-American grain deal.[165] When adding up the costs imposed on the Soviet Union by the embargo, this psychological cost is usually omitted. Soviet willingness to incur this cost suggests that forgoing American wheat earlier in the year may have inconvenienced them more than is generally realized. Although the costs imposed on the Soviet Union were not negligible, the effectiveness of the embargo with respect to this goal should probably be judged as very low.

The goal of preserving the framework of East-West cooperation worked out in the era of détente was in conflict with the goal of expressing outrage. Obviously, more serious concern would have been communicated if the grain embargo had been total rather than partial. Perhaps the continued Soviet interest in trade with the United States is some evidence of success in approximating this goal.

[162] Robert G. Kaiser, "U.S.-Soviet Relations: Goodbye to Détente," *Foreign Affairs* LIX (1981):511-512.

[163] *Power and Principle*, pp. 463, 468.

[164] See *Assessment of Afghanistan Sanctions*, pp. 39-44; Paarlberg, "Lessons," pp. 149-155; and Gilmore, *Poor Harvest*, pp. 166-168.

[165] *Assessment of Afghanistan Sanctions*, p. 34.

Sanctions Effectiveness: European Allies

The best test of the effectiveness of the grain embargo in demonstrating American resolve to the allies is not their willingness to follow suit, but rather their recognition of the costliness of the embargo to the Carter administration.[166] That a grain embargo was something Carter had specifically pledged to avoid could hardly fail to impress leaders of democratic countries. A *New York Times* report the day after the grain embargo was announced captures the basic elements of the situation:

> All week . . . allied diplomats watched to see whether the President would take the domestic political risks and accept the economic costs of a grain embargo against Moscow. . . . "Our judgment is that we have greater credibility with the allies today," said a senior official. "They needed a sign that we were going to do something big and now they have it. Both we and the Europeans have technology sales to the Soviets, but stopping grain shipments costs us something immediately. We felt if this was going to go further, we had to lay our marker down."[167]

Former British Ambassador to the United States Peter Jay testified to the effectiveness of the American attempt to demonstrate resolve as follows:

> There was a momentum in the early moments of this year when the firmness and leadership coming from the United States was rather dramatic and visibly increased. A very firm line was taken by the United States and, in my observation, had a visibly salutary effect that cooperation increased rather dramatically.[168]

Sanctions Effectiveness: Other Countries

As a means of condemning Soviet actions and demonstrating American resolve in a firm yet responsible manner, the embargo seems to have been moderately effective. As the Congressional Research Service put it:

---

[166] With respect to the success of the grain embargo, the relevant costs are *not* those that were ultimately incurred, but rather those that were *expected* at the time the embargo was announced. That the *actual* costs, both political and economic, turned out to be lower than anyone expected did not impair the effectiveness of the embargo in bolstering the credibility of American signals.

[167] *New York Times*, January 5, 1980. The phrase "lay down a marker" was also used by the president with respect to the credibility of the deterrent threat sent to the Soviets. (*Weekly Compilation of Presidential Documents*, January 8, 1980, p. 43.) It refers to the size of the bet one is willing to make, *ergo*, the magnitude of the costs one is willing to incur. The Carter administration understood the relationship between incurring costs and demonstrating resolve.

[168] *Hearings on U.S.–W. European Relations*, p. 147. See also Peter Jay "Europe's Ostrich and America's Eagle," *Economist*, March 8, 1980.

Generally, the reaction of Western and developing—especially Is-lamic—nations was negative to the Soviet invasion and positive to U.S. political-economic response. Many favoring the U.S. response especially preferred the form of response. Military action was opposed as it might unsettle the volatile region of South Asia or escalate into a global U.S.-USSR confrontation.[169]

Overall, the grain embargo was probably highly effective in impressing the Soviets with the grave implications of the invasion, minimally effective in imposing significant costs for refusal to withdraw, and moderately effective in demonstrating its commitment to resist further Soviet moves to the allies and other countries.

The embargo was costly, but then it would have been worthless as a means of demonstrating resolve if it had been costless. It was precisely the easily perceived costliness of the embargo, especially in terms of Carter's political career, that made the grain embargo such an effective way to say "We really mean it" to the Soviet Union and other countries. This unusual importance of the costliness of the embargo makes it all the more ironic that many attempts to assess the effectiveness of the embargo use the criterion of comparing the costs inflicted upon the Soviet Union with the costs incurred by the United States, a misleading measure of effectiveness even when demonstrating resolve is not one of the goals of the influence attempt.[170]

Aside from the domestic political costs to the Carter administration during the presidential campaign, three types of costs are often mentioned with respect to the grain embargo. First are the economic costs to the United States as a grain exporter and to farmers in particular. These costs actually turned out to be much less than anyone expected. In a sense, the fungibility of grain that made enforcement of the embargo difficult also softened the economic impact on the United States. The grain trade simply rearranged itself so that everyone ended up about where they would have been anyway. Indeed, U.S. grain exports increased by 22 percent during the first year of the embargo; and the American share of international sales of wheat and coarse grain increased from 55 percent to 57 percent during the same period.[171] Farm groups and congressmen from farm states have

---

[169] *Assessment of Afghanistan Sanctions*, p. 8.

[170] See ibid., pp. 6, 38; and U.S. Senate, Committee on Agriculture, *Hearings: Economic Impact of Agricultural Embargoes*, 97th Cong., 2d sess., 1982, p. 101. For two unusually incisive comments, the first noting the relationship between costs and credibility and the second challenging the criterion of comparing our costs with theirs, see testimony by Charles Wolf, *Hearings on Economic Relations with Soviet Union*, pp. 132-134; and testimony by Peter Kenen, *Hearings on U.S.–W. European Relations*, p. 108.

[171] *Hearings on Economic Impact of Agricultural Embargoes*, p. 24; and *Assessment of Afghanistan Sanctions*, p. 47.

grossly exaggerated the effects of the embargo on farmers. As Paarlberg and others have pointed out, however, a 20-percent decrease in farm income was forecast even *before* the embargo was imposed. Other problems of farmers are accounted for largely by inflation, high fuel costs, high interest rates, drought, and sluggish economic growth in general.[172] Overall, the economic cost to the United States as a whole and to farmers in particular has been moderate at best.

Another cost attributed to the grain embargo is the abandoning of "free market principles" implied by such actions.[173] This cost, however, is one the United States can easily afford. Just as Richard Nixon's reputation as a comitted anticommunist allowed him to pursue détente with the Soviet Union and rapprochement with China without fear of charges that he was "soft on communism," so the United States reputation as the standard bearer of free enterprise permits it to use trade restrictions occasionally without fear of charges that it has abandoned free market principles. Sanctions against communist states can even be portrayed as defending such principles.

As with the question of East-West trade since 1948, another cost that is inevitably mentioned is the alleged damage to the unity of the Western alliance. Once again, however, it is necessary to distinguish between weaknesses in the alliance that are *caused by* differences of opinion about the wisdom of imposing economic sanctions in a given situation and the preexisting weaknesses which merely become harder to cover up during such arguments. Former U.S. Ambassador to NATO Robert Ellsworth has pointed out that if the problem had been a massing of Soviet troops around Berlin rather than an invasion of Afghanistan, "there would not have been any problem" because "everybody would have seen it exactly the same." The fundamental difficulty, as the ambassador notes, is "a very basic geopolitical difference of perception." Whereas American policy makers tended to view the invasion as "almost destroying the basis for détente," the Europeans have tended to see it as "a regional problem, a peripheral problem that would leave détente—at least in Europe—unaffected."[174] If there would have been no quibbling over the utility of economic sanctions had the crisis concerned Berlin rather than Kabul, it is difficult to justify

[172] Paarlberg, "Lessons," p. 149; testimony by Paarlberg, *Hearings on Economic Impact of Agricultural Embargoes*, p. 24; and *Assessment of Afghanistan Sanctions*, pp. 45-46.

[173] See, for example, Gilmore, *Poor Harvest*, p. 174. Gilmore's general view that "government interventions in the marketplace for foreign policy purposes have done nothing to strengthen the U.S. agricultural economy" is puzzling. Such measures, it would seem, should be judged in terms of their intended objectives. If they were not intended to strengthen the U.S. agricultural economy, then failure to do so is not very persuasive evidence that such measures are ineffective.

[174] *Hearings on U.S.–W. European Relations*, p. 72. See also similar comments by Angela Stent, *Premises Workshop*, pp. 154, 181, 183, 193.

blaming economic sanctions for the strains on the Western alliance arising from efforts to coordinate a response to the invasion of Afghanistan. The root cause of the strains on the alliance was not differing views of the utility of economic sanctions; it was differing views of the nature, magnitude, and implications of the threat to Western security implied by the Soviet invasion. To depict these strains as caused by tactical disagreements with respect to particular techniques of statecraft does not facilitate clear thinking about either economic sanctions or the problems of the NATO alliance.

Given the objectives of the Carter administration, what were the alternatives to the grain embargo?[175] First, the implications of *not* imposing a grain embargo should be considered. Since the United States had agreed in the previous October to sell a total of twenty-five million tons of grain to the Soviet Union during 1980, "without an embargo of some kind, the President would have found himself presiding over the largest 'Russian grain deal' on record."[176] The alternative to a grain embargo was "business as usual"—perhaps even better than usual—with respect to the grain trade. This too would have sent a signal to the Soviets and other countries, but not the signal that the Carter administration wanted sent! As Marshall Goldman has pointed out, the United States had "economic levers" to pull in 1980 that were unavailable to protest events in Hungary in 1956 and Czechoslovakia in 1968.[177] The option to "pull the economic lever" existed in 1980, and, more importantly, *the whole world knew it.* Failure to impose a grain embargo might have been extremely costly to America's image. By comparison, the costs of the embargo to the American farmer were trivial at best.

Propaganda and diplomacy were possible alternatives, but short of a break in diplomatic relations, neither was likely to convey the intensity of American concern as well as the grain embargo. Doubling the broadcasts on Radio Liberty or Radio Free Europe, as one critic suggested, would probably have impressed the Soviets much less than the embargo.[178]

Most critics of the embargo, to the extent that they proposed any alternatives at all, favored some kind of military statecraft. The *Wall Street Journal*, for example, criticized the administration for using economic

[175] As is often the case, this question tends to be ignored by critics of the embargo. Richard D. Erb, for example, testified against the use of economic sanctions in 1980; but when asked what he would do "when the Soviets do something you don't like, to show your displeasure," he ignored the question and replied that the Soviets would never have gone into Afghanistan in the first place if the wrong signals had not been sent to the Soviet Union during the preceding two years. *Hearings on U.S.–W. European Relations*, pp. 113-114.

[176] Paarlberg, "Lessons," p. 160.

[177] *Hearings on U.S. Embargo*, pp. 224-225.

[178] See comments by former Kissinger aide Kempton B. Jenkins, *Premises Workshop*, p. 117.

measures "to respond to a military operation," accused it of being "prejudiced against and perhaps even afraid of military power," and suggested the following alternatives: increased military spending; stationing U.S. troops in the Middle East; relaxing restrictions on U.S. intelligence organizations; reinstatement of draft registration; "new faces at the White House and State Department"; and a crash program to develop the sealaunched cruise missile.[179] Several of these measures, of course, were part of the administration's overall response to the Soviet invasion. But with the possible exception of "new faces" in the administration, none had immediate effects dramatic enough to convey Carter's message in an unambiguous way. Most of them involved uncertain future costs rather than certain present costs, and each could be interpreted as something the administration intended to do anyway. Jenkins complained that the American response lacked "symmetry and proportionality," suggesting that "a move of potential strategic and even historic significance" in the "military field" would have been more appropriate.[180] Although invasion of Mexico would seem to be the nearest counterpart move available to the United States, Jenkins did not suggest that—although he did indicate that blockading Cuba was the "kind of thinking" he was "not opposed to."[181] The basic difficulty with military responses was finding one that would convey the intended message in an unambiguous way, that was likely to be viewed as "connected" to the Soviet action (something that could not be said of blockading Cuba), and that was immediately costly to the United States— but not so costly as to risk war. Indeed, since one of the objectives was to demonstrate the "toughness" not only of the United States in general, but of the Carter administration in particular, the costs needed to be easily perceivable as attributable to the administration. Carter's well-known pledge to avoid agricultural embargoes made a grain embargo an especially effective way for him to demonstrate *his* anger and *his* resolve. The same could not be said for any of the proposed alternatives.

If appropriate criteria are applied, the Carter grain embargo does not appear to be the ill-considered, inappropriate, ineffective, and relatively expensive undertaking that it is often implied to be. The prime objective was neither to get Soviet troops out of Kabul nor to produce hungry Russians; it was to send a clear signal to the Soviet Union. Once that is understood and the costs and benefits of alternative courses of action are considered, it is difficult to see what other course of action would have yielded a clearly superior combination of cost and effectiveness.[182] Perhaps

---

[179] *Wall Street Journal*, January 7 and 8, 1980.

[180] *Premises Workshop*, p. 116.

[181] Ibid., p. 132.

[182] Even Paarlberg's pessimistic assessment of the utility of the embargo concludes that when viewed against the alternatives, it was "not so much a serious mistake as an unhappy necessity" (p. 161).

Carter was wrong to respond at all. Perhaps the first use of Soviet troops outside the communist bloc since 1945 should have been allowed to go unnoticed. But such considerations are irrelevant to assessing the utility of the grain embargo as a technique of statecraft, for the capability analyst must accept the perceptions and goals of the policy maker as given and proceed from there.

The "lessons" of the Carter grain embargo for the student of economic statecraft derive less from the case itself than from the way the case has been analyzed. The treatments by Paarlberg and Adler-Karlsson are especially instructive.

Paarlberg's article illustrates three common pitfalls in analyzing economic statecraft: (1) inadequate specification of the policy-contingency framework; (2) failure to allow for multiple bases of power; and (3) a dichotomous conception of success and failure. With respect to the first pitfall, as has already been noted, Paarlberg's analysis ignores the objective of signaling the Soviet Union and denies that deterrence was an objective of the embargo. With respect to the second pitfall, concerning the bases of power, Paarlberg identifies three requisites for "any effective exercise of food power" (p. 145). These include maintenance of control over food exports by foreign policy officials in the embargoing state, prevention of transshipment and redirection of trade by other countries, and actual reduction in the food imports of the target country. He compares these requirements to a "three-linked chain" which must "hold at each of these points," for "an embargo that fails at any one of the three will fail altogether." This model, of course, is suitable only for analyzing the effectiveness of an embargo with respect to the goal of imposing costs on the target country. It is likely to be unsuitable for assessing the effectiveness of an embargo imposed for any other purpose, such as demonstrating resolve or expressing condemnation. If Paarlberg's postulated policy-contingency framework had included the goal of sending a signal to the Soviets, the inadequacies of these causal conditions of success (i.e., bases of power) would have become readily apparent, since none is necessary for an embargo to be effective in sending a signal to the target. Indeed, it would be difficult to find an instance in which an embargo was imposed *solely* for the purpose of imposing costs on an adversary. With respect to the third pitfall, concerning a dichotomous conception of success and failure, the analogy of the "three-linked chain" implies that embargoes either succeed or fail without allowing for intermediate degrees of success or failure. Chains either hold—and therefore succeed—or they break—and therefore "fail altogether." Comparing the determinants of success of an embargo to the links of a chain makes it difficult to think of success as a matter of degree.

Adler-Karlsson's analysis of economic sanctions with respect to both the Iranian hostage crisis and the Soviet invasion of Afghanistan is similar to Paarlberg's treatment in its inadequate specification of the objectives and targets of the influence attempts and in the "three preconditions for a successful embargo."[183] Indeed, the similarities are so great that the comments made with respect to Paarlberg's analysis are applicable, *mutatis mutandis*, to Adler-Karlsson's article. Adler-Karlsson's treatment, however, illustrates two additional pitfalls in the analysis of economic statecraft: (1) the dangers of uncritical acceptance of the conventional wisdom; and (2) underestimation of the importance of the symbolic aspects of international politics. Adler-Karlsson is so firmly convinced of the futility of embargoes that he accuses the Carter administration of "bad faith" for even suggesting that the economic sanctions undertaken in the context of the Iranian situation or the Afghanistan invasion were intended to promote foreign policy goals (pp. 183ff). Four arguments are advanced to support this view: First, "almost all analysts" agree that the Western embargo against the communist countries "has been a failure," and this "general knowledge must have been available to most Carter specialists." Second, as "good scholars," Zbigniew Brzezinski and Marshall Shulman in particular must have been "very well aware of the futility of trying to change major foreign policies of adversaries with the help of embargoes." Third, the members of Carter's cabinet "most concerned," i.e., representatives from the departments of Agriculture, Commerce, and Treasury, were reportedly "not favourable" to the embargo, but were overruled. And fourth, it must have been apparent to the United States that allied support would not be forthcoming.

> These four arguments, taken together, indicate that the Carter administration *could not in good faith* believe that the embargo actions undertaken would really help to release the hostages in Iran or "roll back" the Russians from Afghanistan. These actions *must have been* undertaken for some other reason. (p. 184; italics added)

Adler-Karlsson concludes that the embargoes were not really foreign policy instruments at all but rather instruments of domestic policy. He then castigates the Carter administration for disrupting the Western alliance by asking the allies to legitimize what are in fact domestic policy actions rather than foreign policy actions.

Although a number of the points in this rather breathtaking chain of reasoning are disputable, it is the style rather than the substance of the argument that is most instructive. Therefore, only Adler-Karlsson's contention that the cabinet members "most concerned" with the proposed anti-Soviet embargo were from the departments of Agriculture, Commerce, and Treasury will be questioned. Inasmuch as the primary issue was dip-

---

[183] Adler-Karlsson, "U.S. Embargo."

lomatic and strategic, one would have thought that foreign policy specialists such as National Security Adviser Brzezinski, Secretary of State Vance, and Secretary of Defense Harold Brown would have been those "most concerned" with the decision. In fact, both Brzezinski and Vance strongly favored the grain embargo—apparently one of the few times they agreed on anything![184]

As already noted, however, the style of Adler-Karlsson's reasoning is more significant than the content. He is so utterly confident that embargoes are always inefficient and counterproductive techniques of statecraft that he is unwilling even to consider the possibility that knowledgeable, sincere, well-intentioned foreign policy makers could actually believe that such measures would be helpful in promoting American foreign policy goals in either the Iranian or the Afghanistan situation. Since American policy makers *must have* known this, they *must have had* ulterior motives, motives that had nothing to do with foreign policy. Note that Adler-Karlsson's argument is *not* merely that the embargoes were unlikely to succeed or that they were likely to be counterproductive. Nor is it that alternative policy options were more likely to succeed. His argument is that the inevitable failure and counterproductivity of the economic sanctions were so *obvious* that no reasonable policy maker could possibly have chosen them in good faith.

Another common pitfall in analyzing economic statecraft illustrated by Adler-Karlsson's article is the tendency to underestimate the importance of the symbolic aspects of international politics. In the first place, symbolic actions are depicted as primarily, if not entirely, directed at the domestic audience. Symbolic acts are primarily intended to "soothe" American public opinion—the opinion of "the moralistic and unenlightened masses" (p. 185). The question raised, of course, is not whether symbolic acts are often directed at domestic public opinion, because this is undoubtedly true. Rather, the question is whether symbolic acts may be performed for legitimate and important reasons other than concern for domestic public opinion. Adler-Karlsson apparently thinks not, at least so his distinction between "symbolic actions" and "serious foreign economic policy actions" would seem to suggest (p. 183).

Adler-Karlsson's treatment of symbolic acts as relatively unimportant and as primarily for domestic consumption is not unusual in the literature of economic statecraft. He simply makes explicit the assumptions that many leave implicit. Gilpin's depiction of economic sanctions as means to "appease domestic opinion" by appearing to be "doing something" and his denial of the instrumental, as opposed to the expressive, functions

---

[184] Brzezinski, *Power and Principle*, p. 431; and Vance, *Hard Choices*, pp. 389-390.

of symbolic acts is, after all, not much different from the positions of Adler-Karlsson.[185]

POLAND AND THE PIPELINE

In 1981 and 1982 the Reagan administration's use of economic sanctions was one of the most controversial foreign policy actions the administration had undertaken. This study has reiterated the importance of establishing the goals and targets of an influence attempt *prior* to assessing the utility of the techniques of statecraft used in that influence attempt. Since the goals and targets of this particular influence attempt, or series of influence attempts, are extraordinarily complex, confused, and confusing, any generalization about the utility of economic sanctions on the basis of this case is likely to be misleading. Still, those who are convinced that such measures are always or usually ineffective, costly, and counterproductive have pointed to this case as supporting their position; therefore, some attempt to sort out the various dimensions of the case is in order.

The key to understanding this case lies in the distinction between the two fundamentally different approaches to East-West relations reflected in the hard-line/soft-line viewpoints discussed in connection with the anticommunist strategic trade restrictions.[186] Although Western European views have usually been softer than the American approach, the differences between the European and American viewpoints were less salient as the soft-line view gradually became dominant among American foreign policy makers during the late 1960s and the 1970s. Thus, whereas American policy in the 1970s might be described as soft-line, the European position was usually even softer. During the last two years of the Carter administration, however, the hard-line approach began to reassert itself among American policy makers. The Reagan administration contained many who favored a return to the hard-line approach. This shift in outlook widened the gap between the Europeans and Americans, a fact likely to become apparent the first time a crisis in East-West relations occurred. If this interpretation is correct, the imbroglio in 1982 was not primarily about economic sanctions, martial law in Poland, or the pipeline; it was about the overall strategy in terms of which East-West relations should be guided. Specific issues, such as sanctions, the Polish situation, and the pipeline, appear to have been mere catalysts rather than basic causes of tension.

[185] *Hearings on U.S. Embargo*, pp. 165-184, esp. pp. 166-167, 173, 183-184.

[186] For a suggestion that the pipeline embargo should be viewed as an attempt to develop and implement "a new, more comprehensive defense strategy," see Louis J. Walinsky, "Coherent Defense Strategy: On the Case for Economic Denial," *Foreign Affairs* LXI (Winter 1982-1983):272.

With this perspective in mind, the salient aspects of the case will be reviewed.

The case may be divided into three stages as follows: stage one, December 1980–December 1981; stage two, January 1982–June 1982; and stage three, July 1982–November 1982. During the first stage there seems to have been general agreement among the NATO countries that deterring Soviet military intervention in Poland was the main goal. Furthermore, they were reportedly agreed that economic sanctions would be imposed on the Soviet Union in the event of such a move.[187] Difficulties arose, however, when the crackdown in Poland was conducted by Poles rather than by Soviet troops. Although some consideration had reportedly been given to such a contingency, no agreement had been reached as to how or whether to respond to it.[188] The events in this first stage lend themselves to several plausible interpretations. For example, it could be argued that the Soviet Union adroitly circumvented the NATO deterrent threat. It could also be maintained that the threatened economic sanctions were successful in deterring Soviet military intervention. (Indeed, both arguments may be true.) Many factors probably influenced Soviet decision making, but the possibility that the threat of Western economic retaliation was among them at least deserves serious consideration. If the threat of sanctions did influence the Soviet decision, this would have been no small accomplishment. As George Kennan observed in February 1982, "one of the most significant things that has happened and perhaps *the* most significant is the very fact that despite all that has occurred in Poland in the last year and one-half, the Soviet Union has not intervened actively with its own forces."[189] If, indeed, threatened economic sanctions were partially responsible for this significant event, they are unlikely to get any credit for it.

The Western allies could, of course, have congratulated themselves on having successfully deterred Soviet armed intervention and proceeded with business as usual. The gauntlet had *not* been thrown down; their reputations for action were *not* unambiguously threatened by Polish martial law. The Reagan administration, however, chose to interpret the situation as calling

[187] The *New York Times* (April 26, 1981; December 30, 1981) asserted that NATO had agreed in December 1980 to "halt all trade with Moscow in the event of Soviet military intervention." Raymond Aron notes merely that "they had agreed on the measures they would take together" without specifying the nature of those measures. ("Ideology in Search of a Policy," *Foreign Affairs* LX [1982]:514.) Brzezinski (*Power and Principle*, p. 466) claims to have received assurance in December 1980 that even West Germany would join in economic sanctions in the event of Soviet military intervention in Poland. William G. Hyland, however, contends that "the use of economic relations as a retaliatory measure was far from agreed Western policy" when martial law was imposed in Poland in December 1981. ("U.S.-Soviet Relations: The Long Road Back," *Foreign Affairs* LX (1982):543.)

[188] *New York Times*, December 30, 1981.

[189] *New York Times*, February 14, 1982.

for a Western response; and this led to the second stage of the Polish crisis, roughly the first six months of 1982. On December 29, 1981, President Reagan announced an embargo on the export of American oil and gas technologies and equipment to the Soviet Union. This relatively modest step was justified by administration officials on the grounds that "the United States must take the lead in demonstrating more than verbal opposition to the military crackdown in Poland."[190] This, of course, sounded very much like the justification of the Carter grain embargo. The difference was that whereas Carter had chosen an option that was clearly expected to be economically costly to the United States as a whole and likely to be politically costly to his administration, Reagan chose a relatively costless policy option. The relationship between demonstrating resolve and willingness to incur costs did not seem to be so well understood by Reagan as by Carter.

The failure to embargo grain did not escape the notice of either the allies or the Soviets. Early in January the United States began to apply pressure to the European allies to stop supplying parts for the construction of a Soviet pipeline which would supply natural gas to Western Europe. From January to June this issue steadily acquired prominence and became broadened. Reagan administration officials objected not only to the supply of construction materials for the pipeline, but also to credits advanced to the Soviets for its construction, and to the European dependence on the Soviet Union that was likely to result from purchasing the gas after it was built. As emphasis on the Polish situation receded, the controversy over the pipeline emerged as an issue in its own right. Indeed, since from the time it took office the Reagan administration had been objecting to the pipeline, Europeans began to suspect that the Polish situation was merely an excuse for the United States to intensify pressure on this issue. To them it seemed that the United States was urging costly sacrifices on their part without making comparable sacrifices itself. The United States, for example, was unwilling to cut back its lucrative grain trade with the Soviets or to consider easing the European energy problem by reducing its own energy consumption—say, by charging as much for gasoline as European countries do. At least the Carter administration seemed to understand what it meant to "lay down a marker." It is small wonder that European irritation grew as United States pressure continued.[191]

After Reagan was unable to secure allied agreement to increased re-

---

[190] *New York Times*, December 29, 1981.

[191] On the evolution of the American pressure with respect to the pipeline, see *New York Times*, January 11, 1982; January 12, 1982; January 13, 1982; January 22, 1982; February 12, 1982; February 21, 1982; February 26, 1982; Stephen S. Rosenfeld, "Testing the Hard Line," *Foreign Affairs* LXI (1983):489-510; and Josef Joffe, "Europe and America: The Politics of Resentment (cont'd)," *Foreign Affairs* LXI (1983):569-590.

strictions on trade and credit for the Soviet Union at a summit meeting in June, he extended the embargo on oil and gas equipment to apply to foreign susidiaries of American companies, thus entering the third stage of what had started out as a dispute over Soviet actions in Poland but which was evolving into one over European trade policy, extraterritorial application of American export controls, and the relative merits of the hard- versus the soft-line approach to East-West relations in general. In a sense, the heart of the issue—the basic underlying source of the disagreement— emerged only during this third stage.

The extension of the embargo to foreign subsidiaries of American parent companies set off a furor within the alliance that lasted until the Reagan administration backed down in November 1982. Poland was all but ignored as the dispute focused on U.S. relations with Western Europe. The rhetoric about "toughness" and "demonstrating resolve" was reminiscent of the Carter grain embargo except that Carter made costly sacrifices in order to demonstrate toughness and seemed to understand that leaders were expected to pay higher costs. The Reagan administration, by contrast, seemed more interested in demonstrating toughness toward its allies than toward the Soviet Union and was advocating costly sacrifices for others while steadfastly refusing to reduce grain exports to the Soviets. The *Wall Street Journal*, having ridiculed the Carter grain embargo, effusively supported the twists and turns of Reagan on the pipeline sanctions. Hailing the arrival of a "welcome turning point" in American foreign policy, the *Journal* praised Reagan's willingness to "risk confrontations" with the allies as demonstrating that he "can take the heat." "This is what leadership of an alliance is all about." The president "should hang tough" and not allow "himself to be backed down by François Mitterrand."[192] Whereas Carter had imposed costs on himself to demonstrate resolve, the Reagan administration seemed determined to do this by imposing costs on others.

As the arguments against the pipeline changed almost weekly, it became increasingly apparent that the fundamental source of the friction was the general issue of whether to pursue a hard or soft line in relations with the Soviet Union. Describing the crackdown in Poland as "nothing but a pretext" for implementing a hard-line approach, Michel Tatu noted that the question was no longer one of "punishing Moscow for this or that aggression, but of applying global and strategic pressure intended to destabilize the entire Soviet system."[193] This, of course, is the traditional hard-line approach. Pragmatic coping with specific Soviet actions in an attempt to promote coexistence in a complex relationship involving both conflicting and common interests is replaced by a general policy orientation

[192] *Wall Street Journal*, June 23, 1982; July 23, 1982; and August 20, 1982.
[193] "U.S.-Soviet Relations: A Turning Point?" *Foreign Affairs* LXI (1983):600.

of hostility to communism in general with the ultimate goal of victory rather than coexistence. Even Richard Nixon complained in the midst of the pipeline imbroglio about those who "tend to regard United States-Soviet relations as a zero-sum exercise" and who think that "if we just squeeze the Russians economically the regime will collapse."[194] The difficulty with trying to assess the utility of the pipeline embargo is that the goals and targets of the Reagan administration are nearly impossible to determine. Throughout the controversy, the debate between hard- and soft-liners was going on *within* the administration, with the State Department emphasizing the soft line and the White House and Defense Department pushing the hard line. "For some people in the Reagan entourage, the long-range objective is nothing less than to effect a gradual transformation or a collapse of the Soviet system of government—to sweep it into the 'dustbin of history.' "[195]

Judged from the perspective of the soft-liners, the pipeline sanctions were disastrous—"a blunder of historic proportions."[196] The Polish situation did not seem to be much affected; the unity of the alliance was severely strained; construction of the pipeline continued; Soviet-American relations deteriorated; and instead of projecting an image of firm and legitimate leadership of the alliance, the Reagan administration's actions seemed high-handed, dictatorial, and doctrinaire. If it could be established that the administration was pursuing soft-line policy objectives, the case would seem to bolster the conventional wisdom with respect to the utility of economic sanctions.

But is the soft-line viewpoint appropriate for assessing the success of the sanctions in this case? If one assumes that an important goal of the Reagan administration was to use the occasion of the pipeline/Polish issue to raise more fundamental issues with its allies—to trigger an agonizing reappraisal of the underlying premises of the whole Western approach to relations with the Soviet Union—the influence attempt may have been more successful than appearances would indicate. As Angela Stent has pointed out, "the pipeline sanctions have already had one beneficial effect. They have made the Europeans realize that they must reevaluate their East-West commercial policies."[197] No overall attempt to assess the utility of the pipeline sanctions will be made here. If such an attempt were to be made, it might be desirable to treat it as several cases rather than as one. For example, each of the following could be analyzed separately: (1)

[194] *New York Times*, August 18, 1982. See also the similar argument by George W. Ball, "The Case Against Sanctions," *New York Times Magazine*, September 19, 1982.
[195] Seweryn Bialer and Joan Afferica, "Reagan and Russia," *Foreign Affairs* LXI (Winter 1982-1983):261.
[196] Joffe, "Europe and America," p. 575.
[197] *Premises Workshop*, p. 164.

threatened sanctions against the Soviet Union in case of military intervention in Poland; (2) actual sanctions against Poland and the Soviet Union after the imposition of martial law in Poland; (3) sanctions by the United States against companies in Europe, ostensibly intended to slow construction on the pipeline.

Although the pipeline/Polish crisis was divided into three stages previously, it might be helpful to add a fourth—the most critical stage of all. This is the stage in which "lessons" are drawn from the case. Two such efforts to draw "lessons" from this experience are instructive. The first is a report issued in May 1983 by the Office of Technology Assessment.[198] Two aspects of this report, concerning the symbolic functions of sanctions and the goals of the pipeline sanctions, are of special interest. Noting that "it has been argued that" the utility of economic sanctions "should be judged," at least in some cases, "according to their symbolic value," the report asserts that such criteria raise "several difficult questions" (p. 71):

Are trade sanctions appropriate means through which to show concern?
Comment: Obviously, this depends on the particular situation at hand and should not be answered in a general way. It depends on the goals and targets of the influence attempt, the probable costs and benefits, and the costs and benefits associated with alternative policy options.

Should they be imposed even if there exists a danger that they will hurt the United States as much or more than they hurt the USSR?
Comment: As has already been noted, the criterion of comparing our costs with theirs can be quite misleading. The appropriate comparison is between our costs and our benefits with respect to various policy options. The situation in which our benefits correspond precisely with their costs is a very special case. Also, for some symbolic purposes, such as demonstrating resolve, self-inflicted costs may be necessary. The ability to incur costs is inextricably linked with the ability to make binding commitments.[199] In a cost-free world, no one could ever demonstrate resolve.

Should they be imposed even if they risk damage to alliance relationships?
Comment: This question can only be sensibly answered in the context of a postulated or actual situation. Once again, it depends on the stakes involved, the costs and benefits of various options, and so on. The idea that "endangering the alliance" is never justified is indefensible. The purpose of the alliance is obviously prior to preserving its unity. There may be occasions when it is desirable to rock the boat a little in order to get the attention of other passengers so that one can call their attention to an even greater danger, e.g., "We're sinking!" or "There's a reef ahead!"

---

[198] OTA, *Technology and E-W Trade Update.*
[199] See Schelling, *Strategy of Conflict*, pp. 3-52, esp. p. 43.

It would not be too farfetched to depict the perceptions of the pipeline sanctions by some members of the Reagan administration in such terms. For example, perhaps the Reagan administration was disrupting the alliance a little in order to impress upon the Europeans its views of the dangers of a soft-line approach.[200] In other words, disrupting the alliance in order to force a reevaluation of the basic underlying purposes of the alliance may be justifiable. Unity at any price is a difficult position to defend.

In sum, the questions posed by the report are loaded and misleading. None is likely to stimulate fruitful thinking about the utility of economic sanctions as techniques of statecraft.

The report points out that when economic sanctions are used to send political messages, effectiveness is impaired if the content of the message is unclear (p. 71). This, of course, is true; but the report gives a misleading impression of the likelihood of this. Thus, although the report is evaluating *both* the Carter grain embargo and the Reagan pipeline sanctions, the former is conveniently ignored in making this point. The report points to the many justifications put forth by the administration in support of the pipeline sanctions as evidence of the lack of clarity in political messages sent via economic sanctions, thus leaving the impression that this is an inherent problem of economic sanctions. If the Carter grain embargo had been examined, however, a different impression would be conveyed, because in that instance the message was loud and clear. Even the message of the Reagan pipeline sanctions may have been clearer than the report implies. Indeed, the Europeans seem to have had no trouble at all reading the message. As Tatu points out, most Europeans interpreted the pipeline sanctions as a "pretext" for the Reagan administration to try to get them to shift from a soft- to a hard-line approach in dealing with the Soviet Union.[201] To describe this as yet "another example of the basic lack of communication between the United States and its closest allies"[202] is quite misleading. They understood the message; they simply did not like what it said!

The second aspect of the report that is instructive for the student of economic statecraft involves the treatment of the goals of hard- and soft-liners. Thus, the section on "costs and benefits" concludes as follows:

> In the final analysis, each of the positions described here rests as much on fundamental beliefs as it does on empirical evidence. Each is shaped as much by the world view of its holders as by objective

---

[200] The question of whether such concerns accurately reflect the views of the administration in this instance is beside the point. The point is simply that such an interpretation is among those plausible enough to deserve consideration.

[201] "U.S.-Soviet Relations," p. 600.

[202] OTA, *Technology and E-W Trade Update*, p. 66.

weighing of the economic, political, military costs, and benefits of alternative policies. Those who believe that the United States and Soviet Union are destined to remain implacable enemies, that military conflict is probably inevitable, and/or that it is primarily the threat of retaliatory force which restrains Soviet aggression are likely to judge that the benefits of U.S. policies outweighed the costs. Those who believe that the United States can and must learn to live with a strong Soviet Union, and that the USSR is best restrained by being drawn into normal relations with the Western world are more likely to look askance at the utility of trade sanctions in moderating Soviet behavior. (p. 72)

At first, this passage seems similar to the approach in this book, i.e., it relates the hard and soft lines to differing estimates of the utility of economic sanctions. Closer inspection, however, reveals a potential fundamental difference. The approach in this book stresses the importance of specifying the policy-contingency framework of an influence attempt *before* attempting to assess the utility of techniques of statecraft used in that influence attempt. Although this approach does not permit precise measurement of the costs and benefits associated with a given technique, it does presume that objectivity is possible in the sense that the analyst need not share the perceptions or values of the decision makers being studied. That is, one need not *be* a hard-liner in order to make reasonably objective judgments about the utility of economic sanctions in promoting hard-line goals in a particular situation. Although it is important—nay, essential— to *understand* the decision makers' goals and perceptions, it is not necessary to *agree* with them. This passage, however, gives the impression that judgments of the utility of economic sanctions are inseparable from the "world view" of the analyst. If the authors of the report are merely offering the *empirical* observation that participants in the debate over the utility of economic sanctions are not always objective, their point is well taken; but if they are implying that objective assessment of the utility of economic sanctions is impossible, then this book is an exercise in futility.

Another effort to extract "lessons" from the Reagan administration's experience with economic sanctions is that of E. A. Hewett, a Brookings Institution economist.[203]

The clearest and most important illustration of economic sanctions for foreign policy reasons is the U.S. embargo on oil and gas technology exports to the Soviet Union imposed on December 29, extended on June 18 to West European firms and to U.S. affiliates in any country, and removed on November 13 of this year. Our expe-

[203] *Premises Workshop*, pp. 77-83.

rience with that embargo is rich with lessons that future policy-makers should contemplate if they decide at some point once again to set off down this road. (p. 78)

Comment: In assessing the utility of techniques of statecraft, the single most important requirement is clear specification of the policy-contingency framework within which the influence attempt takes place. One cannot even begin to identify costs and benefits until this step is taken. Although determination of the goals and targets of an influence attempt is never easy, it is harder in some cases than in others. If there is a case in which it is more difficult to establish the relevant goals and targets than the case of the Reagan pipeline embargo, it has not yet come to this writer's attention. During the first six months of the embargo the disagreement within the administration with respect to appropriate goals and targets was especially intense. There is reason to suspect that the "hidden agenda" of the Reagan administration was different from the ever-changing policy objectives specified by administrative spokesmen. Far from being "the clearest . . . illustration of economic sanctions for foreign policy reasons," this case is one of the most complex and least clear cases on record. It would be difficult to imagine a less useful case from which to draw "lessons that future policy-makers should contemplate."

Lesson No. 1A: The costs and benefits of economic sanctions are in different currencies and are therefore difficult to compare.[204]
Comment: Basically, Hewett suggests that whereas costs tend to be measurable in terms of money, benefits do not.[205] Although he admits the possibility of political costs, he asserts that they "will probably be secondary and will flow from the economic costs" (p. 78). This is a common but quite misleading way to think about economic sanctions. No general rule on this point is in order. Although it is true that economic costs and benefits tend to be easier to measure than political costs and benefits, no *a priori* statement about the relative distribution of each category of cost or benefit should be made.[206] The question of whether the costs of a particular influence attempt are mostly economic or mostly political depends on the situation. Economic costs are likely to *seem* larger only because they are easier to measure, but optical illusions should not be confused with reality. Hewett is certainly right about the difficulty of comparing the costs and benefits of influence attempts—power analysis is hard. This is not, however, a peculiarity of influence attempts based on economic sanctions.

[204] Hewett's "lessons" will be paraphrased rather than directly quoted.

[205] For a similar view, see Hufbauer and Schott, *Economic Sanctions*, esp. p. 63.

[206] For a detailed comparison of political and economic "currencies," see Baldwin, "Money and Power."

Lesson No. 1B: The benefits of an embargo policy are far less certain than the costs. When an embargo is undertaken, the costs are fairly immediate and easy to see. But the foreign policy benefits of an embargo, if they occur at all, will only come at the end of a very long, fragile, and uncertain chain of events.

Comment: Although Hewett includes this as part of the first lesson, there seems to be no logical or empirical relationship between this lesson and the previous one; therefore, it is treated here as a separate point. Although the question of the relative certainty of the costs and benefits of an embargo might be treated as a hypothesis to be tested, there seems to be no reason to accept Hewett's *a priori* assertion. The relative certainty of the costs and benefits is likely to depend greatly on who is trying to get whom to do what in a given situation. Although economic sanctions are sometimes used to produce indirect effects, e.g., a wheat embargo intended to reduce Soviet military potential, this is not always the case. The contention that foreign policy benefits will *only* come at the end of a very long and uncertain chain of events is surely false. Examples of "fairly immediate" goal approximation as a result of economic sanctions include the following: expression of international condemnation of Rhodesia through mandatory United Nations sanctions; demonstration of serious concern and resolve by the Carter grain embargo; neutralization of the Iranian threat to cut off oil shipments to the United States by Carter's announcement of a boycott of Iranian oil; neutralization of the Iranian threat to make huge withdrawals from American banks by Carter's order to freeze Iranian assets; signaling American opposition to and commitment to resist communism in the Western Hemisphere through sanctions against Cuba; and so on. Many of these more immediate effects, of course, involve using economic sanctions to send signals; but successfully transmitted signals can be—and often are— very important foreign policy benefits. In short, sometimes the benefits of economic sanctions are immediately realized; sometimes they are not. Likewise, sometimes the costs are immediate; sometimes they are not. The lesson that Hewett derives from the pipeline embargo is quite misleading.

Lesson No. 2: Whereas the benefits of economic sanctions tend to be diffused throughout the whole society, the costs tend to fall unevenly on a few.

Comment: Although this is probably true, it does not seem to be a peculiar characteristic of economic sanctions. This "public goods" argument applies to many public policies. Hewett notes the similarity with national defense policies with respect to the diffuse distribution of benefits but implies that defense is different since the tax burden of defense is distributed more evenly than the costs of economic sanctions. Two comments are in order: First, even if this is a characteristic of embargoes, it is not, in principle, a necessary one. Measures can be taken to equalize the costs of embargoes if the political will to do so exists. And second, while Hewett's point about the costs of defense is telling if one thinks in terms of the burden of supporting the defense establishment during peacetime, it is less so under wartime conditions. Ask any veteran of Vietnam, World War II, or Korea about this. During wartime, the costs of defense fall unevenly on the young, the male, the less well educated, and the poor.

Lesson No. 3: The costs of an embargo may linger far beyond when the benefits dissipate.
Comment: Hewett seems to be thinking only of benefits such as short-term policy changes in the target country. When embargoes are used to change the image of one's country, the benefits may be quite long lasting. There is simply no reason to accept the *a priori* assertion that costs will be more long lasting than benefits. It depends on the situation. Indeed, if demonstrating resolve through economic sanctions helps countries understand each other's vital interests, such measures can be helpful in preventing war. The benefits of avoiding war may be very long lasting.

Lesson No. 4: Embargoes may have unintended side effects on countries other than the target.
Comment: Although true in some cases, it is not clear that this distinguishes economic sanctions from other techniques of statecraft. War, propaganda, and diplomacy can also have such unintended side effects. In context Hewett seems to have in mind the effects of the United States embargo on the Soviet Union on the Western European allies. For reasons that should be obvious from the above discussion of the pipeline sanctions, however, this may not be a good example. It is not at all clear that the allies were not intended to be targets of the Reagan sanctions. Indeed, they may well have been the primary targets!

Hewett concludes that if the "lessons" of the pipeline embargo are considered by future policy makers contemplating similar measures, "an embargo would rarely pass muster as a foreign policy tool" (p. 83). He notes that a situation in which "an embargo was the only tool available to protest a particularly distasteful policy of another government" might be an exception, but observes that since the United States is "a great world power," it will rarely be "in such a single-option situation" (p. 83).[207] This, of course, is a rather significant exception, one that makes it clear

[207] Only at the end of his discussion does Hewett make this comment on the possible exception to his "lessons" represented by a case in which protesting a particularly distasteful policy of another government was the goal. The pipeline embargo, of course, began as precisely that kind of a case, i.e., a protest of the crackdown in Poland. It seems odd to draw lessons from a case and then note that cases like this one might be exceptions to those lessons.

that his "lessons" were not constructed with symbolic functions in mind. It should also be noted that protesting distasteful action by another government is only one of many instrumental and symbolic uses of embargoes. The suggestion that "great powers" like the United States usually have preferable alternatives to embargoes may overestimate the advantages of being a so-called great power. It is precisely because of its fantastic military arsenal that the United States must be cautious about using it. Small and weak countries can afford to make mistakes in choosing instruments of statecraft; America cannot. It may well be that no country in the world has a greater need for alternatives to military statecraft than the United States.

In sum, the Reagan administration's experience with the pipeline embargo is not apt to yield useful "lessons." It may never be clear just who was trying to influence whom with respect to what. By the fall of 1982, the relationship between Polish martial law and the embargo became increasingly obscure, as the preexisting differences of opinion about the hard and soft lines among NATO members became ever more apparent.

CHAPTER 10

FOREIGN AID

Man has almost constant occasion for the help of his brethren, and it is in vain for him to expect it from their benevolence only. He will be more likely to prevail if he can interest their self-love in his favour, and shew them that it is for their own advantage to do for him what he requires of them. Whoever offers to another a bargain of any kind, proposes to do this. Give me that which I want, and you shall have this which you want, is the meaning of every such offer; and it is in this manner that we obtain from one another the far greater part of those good offices which we stand in need of.[1]

Foreign aid has received a great deal of attention since World War II. The conventional wisdom depicts it as emerging in the aftermath of the war as a tool for alleviating the miseries of war and promoting European recovery. After the spectacular success of the Marshall Plan, so the story goes, a similar approach was tried with respect to stimulating economic development in the Third World, but the results were disappointing. "By now," observes Robert Packenham, "it is almost a cliché to assert that Marshall Plan concepts were transferred inappropriately to the Third World."[2] The "massive aid" approach that had worked so well in Europe was a failure when applied to poor countries elsewhere in the world. As with the conventional wisdom regarding other economic techniques of statecraft, however, healthy skepticism is in order.

No full-scale review of the use of foreign aid since World War II or of the host of analytical problems involved in such an undertaking will be attempted here.[3] Instead, this chapter will address only a few of the more important conceptual and theoretical problems associated with the study

[1] Adam Smith, *Wealth of Nations*, p. 14.

[2] *Liberal America and the Third World: Political Development Ideas in Foreign Aid and Social Science* (Princeton: Princeton University Press, 1973), p. 38.

[3] For discussion of some of these problems, see David A. Baldwin, "Analytical Notes on Foreign Aid and Politics," *Background* X (May 1966):66-90; *Economic Development; Foreign Aid*; "International Aid and International Politics," *Public Administration Review* XXIX (January-February 1969):94-99; and "Foreign Aid."

of foreign aid, examine some of Klaus Knorr's cases of aid failure,[4] and briefly survey the American experience with this technique of statecraft with special reference to the Third World.

THEORETICAL PROBLEMS

Three categories of theoretical problems with respect to foreign aid will be discussed: (1) definition and measurement; (2) not giving aid; and (3) measuring effectiveness.

Definition and Measurement

Debate on how to conceptualize foreign aid has been carried on at a highly politicized level. Defenders of foreign aid have described this label as a "millstone of imponderable weight"[5] that gives the misleading impression that American policy makers are disbursing money to foreigners without reference to American foreign policy goals. This label makes it easy for the opponents of aid programs to depict such actions as "throwing money down a rathole" or "international do-goodism." Defenders often assert that what is called foreign aid is neither "foreign" nor "aid," thereby implying that the money is being used to promote American "national interests." Indeed the distinction between aid as a unilateral international transfer of resources and aid as a reciprocal exchange of benefits has pervaded the debate over foreign aid throughout the entire postwar period. Sometimes it is framed in terms of humanitarianism versus the donors' self-interest; at other times it is depicted as a debate between those who view aid as "an end in itself" versus those who see aid as an instrument of foreign policy.[6] But the underlying conceptual issue is always the same—is aid a gift or not?

Both the nature and longevity of this issue are illustrated by comparing a 1955 report on the political economy of American foreign policy[7] with Knorr's *The Power of Nations*, published twenty years later. The former refers to "two distinct meanings which are often confused, not only in

---

[4] *Power of Nations*, pp. 180-183, 337-339.

[5] Frank M. Coffin, *Witness for Aid* (Boston: Houghton Mifflin, 1964), p. 63.

[6] For examples, see George Liska, *The New Statecraft: Foreign Aid in American Foreign Policy* (Chicago: University of Chicago Press, 1960); R. D. McKinlay and R. Little, "A Foreign Policy Model of U.S. Bilateral Aid Allocation," *World Politics* XXX (October 1977):58-86; Goran Ohlin, *Foreign Aid Policies Reconsidered* (Paris: Organization for Economic Cooperation and Development, 1966), pp. 13-54; Hans Morgenthau, "A Political Theory of Foreign Aid," *American Political Science Review* LVI (June 1962):301-309; and Gunnar Myrdal, *Against the Stream: Critical Essays on Economics* (New York: Pantheon, 1973).

[7] *The Political Economy of American Foreign Policy* (New York: Henry Holt, 1955).

ordinary discourse but also in policy-making.'' In the first meaning ''aid'' is ''any transfer of economic resources by the United States Government to other countries for any purpose other than payment of an obligation.'' In the second meaning ''a transfer of resources is 'aid' only if it is strictly unilateral and nothing material or specific is received in return—that is, only if it involves no element of mutuality, bargain or *quid pro quo*. In this second sense, a loan would not be 'aid,' but a grant would be considered 'aid' unless it were given in exchange for some specific benefit to the United States, or as part of some mutually beneficial arrangement'' (p. 315). The second meaning raises a question. Many valuable things are neither material nor specific, e.g., friendship, respect, status, deference, and so on. Thus, the quid pro quo may be real and important yet unmeasurable in terms of money. How should such a transaction be classified? Since most foreign policy goals are not measurable in monetary terms, this is an especially important consideration for the student of economic statecraft.

Knorr's treatment of the concept of aid is remarkably similar to the second meaning of the 1955 report. Aid is defined as a ''concessionary transfer of resources''; loans at commercial interest rates are ruled out; and ''so-called aid that is given and received strictly as a quid pro quo, as a payment for something specific, whether it is an air base or a vote on an issue in the United Nations,'' is disregarded on the grounds that in such cases aid is ''simply a disguise for a purchase price, or a bribe, a fact understood by both parties'' (pp. 168-171). Although Knorr does not rule out the possibility of mutually beneficial aid relationships (indeed he maintains that ''international aid transactions are always motivated by government interests on both sides''), the extent to which the relationship ''reflects a voluntarily cooperative mutuality of interest'' is crucial to his analysis of aid and influence. For Knorr, there is a ''clear difference in principle'' between compliance that is ''bought'' and that which is ''freely given.'' This distinction leads him to describe ''aid given for some advantage to be received by the donor'' as a ''pseudogift'' (pp. 172-175).

Critical analysis of this position is useful in identifying the conceptual difficulties in thinking about foreign aid as a technique of statecraft. The fundamental difficulty is the reluctance to treat mutually beneficial exchange relations in terms of power. Foreign aid is very much like an ordinary commercial exchange transaction in that one party uses economic resources to get another party to change his behavior. Thus, instead of, say, threatening B with military attack in order to get B to do X, A offers B an economic inducement to do X. The result could be viewed as A's buying of B's compliance. Although Knorr is correct in asserting that this is different from ''a consumer buying a bicycle'' (p. 175), it is also correct to say that there are many similarities between the two situations. The question, then, is whether economic statecraft can be understood better by emphasizing the differences or by emphasizing the similarities.[8]

Social exchange theory provides an alternative way to think about foreign aid transactions.[9] This approach depicts ordinary economic exchange as merely a subcategory of a broader range of social phenomena in which people reward others in the expectation that the favor will be reciprocated. This theoretical stance is compatible with the statecraft perspective in that both exclude expressive behavior and irrational behavior. Thus, giving aid because it is the right thing to do or because it makes you feel good is expressive behavior since it is an end in itself. Similarly, irrational aid giving, i.e., aid giving in which there is no attempt to adapt means to ends, would be ruled out. Indeed, aid that is completely unilateral cannot be an instrument of statecraft at all, since the statecraft perspective implies that aid is a means to an end.

Adoption of a social exchange perspective is especially helpful in dealing with the thorny question of the actual or alleged "gift-like" nature of foreign aid. In common parlance, gifts are freely given with no expectation of anything in return. It is considered bad taste to insist on a quid pro quo for what is supposed to be a gift. Indeed, if the quid pro quo is *obviously* expected, the recipient and onlookers are likely to deny that the original "gift" should be so labeled. They may try to relabel it as a "pseudogift," a bribe, or a purchase. Common parlance is quite misleading with respect to gifts since social deception is deeply embedded in the social process of giving and receiving gifts. Marcel Mauss identifies a set of social phenomena "which are in theory voluntary, disinterested and spontaneous; but are in fact obligatory and interested." Noting that such phenomena usually take the form of generously offered gifts, he asserts that the behavior associated with such actions is "formal pretense and social deception."[10] Thus, while people *pretend* not to expect a quid pro quo in return for a gift, they actually do expect gifts to be reciprocated and are likely to inflict social disapproval on those who fail to reciprocate. Gift giving generates

---

[8] For further discussion, see Baldwin, "Power and Social Exchange."

[9] The best introduction to social exchange theory is Blau, *Exchange and Power in Social Life*.

[10] *The Gift* [1925], trans. Ian Cunnison (Glencoe, Ill.: Free Press, 1954), p. 1. For an application of this perspective to the Marshall Plan, see Wilton S. Dillon, *Gifts and Nations* (The Hague: Mouton, 1968). See also Claude Lévi-Strauss, "The Principle of Reciprocity," in *Sociological Theory*, ed. Lewis A. Coser and Bernard Rosenberg (New York: Macmillan, 1957), pp. 84-94; François Perroux, "The Gift: Its Economic Meaning in Contemporary Capitalism," *Diogenes*, no. 6 (Spring 1954), pp. 1-19; Alvin W. Gouldner, "The Norm of Reciprocity," *American Sociological Review* XXV (April 1960):161-178; H. Newell Wardle, "Gifts," *Encyclopedia of the Social Sciences*, vol. 3 (New York: Macmillan, 1937), pp. 657-658; and Peter M. Blau, "Interaction: Social Exchange," *International Encyclopedia of the Social Sciences*, vol. 7 (New York: Free Press, 1968), pp. 452-457.

an obligation to reciprocate regardless of whether any specific quid pro quo is agreed upon at the time the gift is given. Indeed, the giver is likely to—nay, is expected to—deny, explicitly or implicitly, that any quid pro quo is expected. This, however, is a social lie and is tacitly understood to be such by both giver and receiver.

From this analytical perspective, much of what has been written about foreign aid is beside the point. The question is *not* whether foreign aid should be viewed as a gift, but whether one understands the true role of gifts in social processes. Once the socially deceptive rhetoric associated with gift giving is recognized for what it is, treating foreign aid as an instrument of statecraft is easier. Indeed, the distinction between aid and trade becomes blurred as the reciprocal nature of aid is recognized.[11] As the study of economic statecraft progresses, the categories of "aid" and "trade" may be replaced by categories more directly related to the study of statecraft. For now, however, this conventional distinction will be retained.

The above discussion does not imply that conventional conceptions of foreign aid as concessionary and unilateral transfers of resources are useless. Such conceptions have been developed by those interested in measuring the cost (burden or degree of sacrifice) of aid donors and/or the benefits (i.e., net resource transfer) to aid recipients. Conventional conceptions of aid useful for such purposes may be less useful in determining the effectiveness of aid in promoting foreign policy goals. Thus, from the standpoint of estimating the strictly economic costs to donors and benefits to recipients of aid, it makes sense to discount loans and tied aid in order to determine the "grant equivalent" of such aid.[12] It is not clear, however, that this is the best approach for the student of economic statecraft. From the statesman's point of view, the political costs of aid giving are likely to matter as much as the economic costs, and short-term costs are likely to matter more than long-term costs. Thus, while lumping loans and grants together may be undesirable for some purposes, it may be useful if the purpose is to get an overview of how foreign policy makers are combining various economic and noneconomic tools of statecraft over time.

How one measures foreign aid, of course, depends on how one defines

[11] Charles Kindleberger recognizes the similarities between aid and trade, noting that aid may be used to buy "peace and quiet," foreign policy support, or other "intangibles" not measurable in monetary terms. But he implies that these are elements of impurity in an aid relationship by asserting that "in pure aid, there is no payment, either in money or in support for the donor's foreign policy." (*Power and Money*, pp. 133-135.)

[12] Indeed, a definition of aid useful for measuring the donor's economic costs may differ from one useful in measuring value to the recipient. On this point, see John Pincus, *Trade, Aid, and Development* (New York: McGraw-Hill, 1967), pp. 308-342; and *Economic Aid and International Cost Sharing* (Baltimore: Johns Hopkins Press, 1965), pp. 113-145.

it. There is no single "right way" to do it as long as the standard of measurement can be justified in terms of one's analytical purposes. There is another type of measurement, however, that often goes unnoticed. It might be called tacit, implicit, casual, or even unconscious measurement. This occurs when aid programs are described as "massive," "huge," "large-scale," or "substantial" without reference to any apparent standard of measurement.[13] Precisely because this type of measurement attracts little attention, it is apt to creep into thinking about foreign aid without notice. The United States, after all, has spent more than two hundred billion dollars on foreign aid since World War II, and "everyone agrees" that such a figure is "massive"—but compared to what? How can the average person comprehend the significance of such a figure?

Comparing it with amounts spent on cosmetics, tobacco, liquor, or tourism[14] may be helpful to the average citizen; but such comparisons are less useful to statesmen or foreign policy analysts. The latter two groups are likely to find criteria such as the following more helpful: (1) aid levels compared with military spending; (2) aid levels compared to estimates of amounts required to accomplish given foreign policy objectives; (3) aid levels compared to what the donors could reasonably afford; (4) aid levels compared to what has become politically acceptable in the donor country; and (5) aid levels compared to amounts that have been seriously suggested by responsible scholars and political leaders.

Comparing aid allocations with military spending is especially helpful in providing a rough indicator of the relative emphasis policy makers place on various techniques of statecraft. It is also useful for another reason. Although today there is a tendency to regard as "natural" a situation in which military spending is more than ten times as big as that for foreign aid, this has not always been the case. As table 4 shows, there have been years since World War II in which the aid budget was about one-third of the military budget. In 1982, even the most generous possible estimate of aid levels indicates that the disparity between aid and military statecraft has greatly declined since the early postwar period.[15] Table 4 suggests that the terms "huge," "massive," "gigantic," and so on are more applicable

---

[13] For examples, see Knorr, *Power of Nations*, pp. 167, 192; Kaplan, *The Challenge of Foreign Aid*, pp. 160-161; Bienen and Gilpin, "Evaluation," p. V,4; and Klaus Knorr and Gardner Patterson, eds., *A Critique of the Randall Commission Report on United States Foreign Economic Policy* (Princeton: International Finance Section and Center of International Studies, 1954), p. 34.

[14] For example, Coffin, *Witness for Aid*, p. 136.

[15] As the notes to table 4 indicate, "aid" is used in a more inclusive sense here than in other studies. This obviously exaggerates the magnitude of American aid. Such "maximalist" figures, however, function as conservative assumptions for the argument that follows. The point is that *even* maximalist estimates of aid levels do not change the general orders of magnitude of interest here.

Table 4

U.S. Allocations for Foreign Aid and Defense, 1946-1982 (as percentage of GNP)

Fiscal Years	*Defense*[a]	*Foreign Aid*[b]
1946-48	10.2	2.2
1949-52	7.6	2.4
1953-61	10.3	1.2
1962	9.1	1.3
1963	8.9	1.3
1964	8.5	.9
1965	7.2	.8
1966	7.6	1.0
1967	8.8	1.0
1968	9.3	1.0
1969	8.7	.8
1970	8.1	.8
1971	7.3	.9
1972	6.8	1.0
1973	6.0	1.0
1974	5.6	.9
1975	5.8	.6
1976	5.3	.5
1977	5.2	.5
1978	5.0	.6
1979	5.0	.8
1980	5.3	.5
1981	5.6	.5
1982	6.1	.5

SOURCES: U.S. Bureau of the Census, *Historical Statistics of the United States, Colonial Times to 1970* (Washington, D.C.: G.P.O., 1975), p. 1116; U.S. Bureau of the Census, *Statistical Abstract of the United States, 1982-83* (Washington, D.C.: G.P.O., 1982), p. 350; and Agency for International Development, *U.S. Overseas Loans and Grants and Assistance from International Organizations, Obligations and Loan Authorizations*, annual editions since 1975.

[a] Excluding veterans' benefits.

[b] Aid includes military assistance, Export-Import Bank long-term loans, capital subscriptions to international organizations, Peace Corps, Food for Peace, and loans and grants for A.I.D. and predecessor agencies.

to the military budget than the aid budget, at least as far as the United States is concerned. If such terms are used to describe aid, what is left in the vocabulary of statecraft for describing the much higher order of magnitude of military spending?

The question of the size of aid relative to the foreign policy goals it is supposed to accomplish will be considered later in this chapter. The criteria of affordability, political acceptability, and discussability may be considered together. The current conventional wisdom on aid depicts it as "large" but not necessarily as "large enough." A proposed increase in American aid levels of, say, 20 to 50 percent *might* be considered "plausible" and "responsible." A proposal to quadruple the aid program, however, would probably be viewed as "radical, wildly unrealistic, and irresponsible"— even by aid officials themselves. Yet, it is worth remembering that aid levels of more than 2 percent of GNP per annum are not unknown in the postwar history of American statecraft. The framework within which the debate over the size of the American aid program occurs is so firmly embedded in the national psyche that it is difficult to place in perspective. Opponents of foreign aid, however, have worked steadily since 1949 to establish a framework for debate in which small and affordable aid levels are depicted as large and unaffordable.[16] It is therefore helpful in gaining perspective to review some of the proposals actually made in the 1950s. In July 1950, Walter Reuther proposed that the United States pledge thirteen billion dollars per year—more than 4 percent of GNP in 1950—for the next one hundred years to promote world economic development through the United Nations.[17] A year later Jacob Javits suggested that the United States should invest 2 percent of its GNP per year in the underdeveloped areas of the world through the United Nations.[18] In September 1951, the distinguished economist Sumner H. Slichter argued that the American economy could easily afford the eight and one-half billion dollar aid package then proposed—representing 2.5 percent of the GNP at the time. He noted that this could be done without inflation, without incentive-robbing taxes, without reducing the amount of domestic capital per worker, and without reducing per capita consumption levels.[19] And in 1956 Reuther advanced a scaled down proposal for the United States to commit 2 percent of GNP for the next twenty-five years to aid programs.[20]

The proposals above are mentioned merely to illustrate the shrinkage in the terms of "responsible" public debate about the size of the American aid program. There has always been substantial support for zero aid levels, but the upward limit has declined from a high point of perhaps 5 percent to the present level of about 1 percent of GNP. The imposition of limits on the range of responsible discussion of foreign aid is an excellent example of the ability of some groups to exercise power by "confining the scope of decision-making to relatively 'safe' issues." As Peter Bachrach and

---

[16] On the evolution of the views of Congress, the business elite, and others, see Baldwin, *Economic Development*.

[17] *New York Times*, July 19, 1950.

[18] *New York Times*, June 15, 1951.

[19] "A Balance Sheet on Foreign Aid," *New York Times Magazine*, September 9, 1951.

[20] *New York Times*, March 25, 1956.

Morton S. Baratz pointed out, "to the extent that a person or group—consciously or unconsciously—creates or reinforces barriers to the public airing of policy conflicts, that person or group has power."[21] With respect to the foreign aid debate, there are no serious arguments as to whether or not the United States aid program should be, say, 10 percent of the GNP; such arguments are "unthinkable," beyond the bounds of responsible discussion. Why? Not because the United States cannot afford it, not because it is a self-evidently ridiculous idea, but rather for three reasons: First, opponents of aid programs have campaigned effectively to make small amounts of aid seem large. Second, the slippery and misleading concept of "absorptive capacity"—allegedly limiting the amount of capital a country can "absorb"—has gained currency. This concept gives the erroneous impression that the amount of capital a country can "absorb" is a technical economic matter rather than a political and social matter.[22] And third, the casual and implicit idea that aid programs have been "massive" has colored thinking about foreign aid as a technique of statecraft. The first step toward objective analysis of foreign aid is to purge one's thoughts of preconceived ideas about the "huge" size of postwar aid programs. Table 5 represents only the personal judgments of the author, but I submit that the outlook represented there constitutes a better starting point for objective analysis of foreign aid than the conventional wisdom on this topic.

Nothing has hampered objective discussion of foreign aid as a technique of statecraft more than the implicit assumption that aid magnitudes have

Table 5

Aid Magnitudes Judged by Various Criteria (1946-1982)

Criterion	Estimate of Comparative Aid Magnitude
Military budget	Small
Amount required to accomplish goals	Trivial
Amount U.S. economy could afford	Trivial
Amount that has become politically acceptable in U.S.	Moderate
Amount suggested by responsible scholars and political leaders	Small

[21] "Two Faces of Power," *American Political Science Review* LVI (December 1962):948-949.

[22] On this point see Pincus, *Trade, Aid and Development*, pp. 297-304; Baldwin, *Economic Development*, p. 193; and Frederic Benham, *Economic Aid to Underdeveloped Countries* (New York: Oxford University Press, 1961), p. 116.

been "huge" or "massive" since World War II. Whenever one encounters such statements, the appropriate question is—"compared to what?"

Not Giving Aid: A Technique of Statecraft?

In order to assess the impact of foreign aid—say, from the World Bank—the first and most important step is perusal of a list of projects financed by the bank, or at least this is the common assertion. Although the common-sense appeal of this approach is strong, it may be neither the first nor the most important step in determining the impact of aid. It may be at least as instructive to examine a list of rejected proposals and even a list of proposals that were not submitted but which would have been submitted if the aid criteria promulgated by the bank had been different. In the past I have sometimes referred to such an approach as the study of "non-aid" or "strategic nonlending."[23] There is nothing either particularly insightful or unusually obscure about such labels. They were simply intended to call attention to an obvious but often neglected aspect of aid giving. Any specification of the conditions under which aid will be provided implies, ipso facto, a set of conditions under which aid will not be given. Indeed, some conditions for aid giving do not even have to be (and seldom are) spelled out. The implications of "biting the hand that feeds you" are tacitly understood by both donor and recipient. For example, international aid agreements are unlikely to contain a clause indicating that aid will be cut off if the recipient launches a full-scale military attack on the donor, but this does not mean that such a condition is nonexistent. Some conditions go without saying.

One advantage of thinking about aid this way is that it helps in demonstrating the irrelevance of that will-o'-the-wisp often called "stringless aid." The concept of aid without strings implies both that aid would be distributed randomly and that aid would continue to be so allocated regardless of the behavior of the recipient states. This is useful since the sooner the preposterous requirements of stringless aid are understood, the sooner one can get on with examining the important problems of the number and kind of strings on aid that are desirable from various points of view. Strings versus no strings is an intellectual dead end.

Another advantage of emphasizing non-aid is that it facilitates understanding how aid relates to the goals of United States foreign policy. One of the important postwar American foreign policy goals has been to promote the flow of private foreign investment. Since capital provided by public

---

[23] See Baldwin, *Economic Development*, pp. 37-42; "Foreign Aid," pp. 429-432; and "The International Bank in Political Perspective," *World Politics* XVIII (October 1965):75-79.

sources, i.e., governments and international organizations, always competes in some sense with private capital, the United States has always been wary of large-scale governmental aid programs. This wariness has been consistently reflected not only in American policy statements but also in international aid agencies such as the International Bank for Reconstruction and Development. The average well-informed citizen who views the International Bank as a development lending agency would probably not be able to identify the source if the purposes of the bank were excerpted from the Articles of Agreement and presented to him. The five purposes commit the bank to "facilitating the investment of capital for productive purposes," promoting "private foreign investment," promoting trade and balance-of-payments equilibrium, coordinating its activities with "other channels" so as to ensure that "urgent projects" are given priority, and conducting "its operations with due regard to the effect of international investment on business conditions in the territories of members." The activity most visibly associated with the image of the World Bank, i.e., making loans, is mentioned only as a subsidiary element in the section on promoting private foreign investment. Here the bank is authorized to make its own loans with the provisos that such loans would "supplement private investment" and that they would be made only when private capital was "not available on reasonable terms." The purposes embodied in the Articles of Agreement, of course, do not necessarily describe the actual operations of the World Bank today, but they do provide a dramatic illustration of the way American foreign policy makers envisioned the role of the bank in 1944.

There is nothing unusual about the purposes of the International Bank described in the Articles of Agreement. Time and again since 1944 American foreign policy makers have gone out of their way to emphasize what aid should *not* be given for.[24] The "General Policy Statement of the Export-Import Bank of Washington" in 1945 contained a special section devoted to outlining what the bank would *not* do.[25] The Randall Commission Report in 1954 exhorted the government to make it "abundantly clear to prospective borrowers" that American public lending would not be a substitute for private investment.[26] And the Clay Report in 1963 advocated "judicious withholding of funds" in order to encourage "internal reform" in developing nations.[27]

---

[24] For documentation and further discussion, see Baldwin, *Economic Development*.

[25] *Department of State Bulletin*, September 27, 1945, p. 443.

[26] Commission on Foreign Economic Policy, *Report to the President and the Congress* (Washington, D.C.: G.P.O., 1954), p. 23.

[27] Committee to Strengthen the Security of the Free World, *The Scope and Distribution of United States Military and Economic Assistance Programs* (Washington, D.C.: G.P.O., 1963), p. 13.

American policy toward foreign aid and private foreign investment has often confounded attempts to discern the rationale of American foreign aid policy. In each of the following examples the concept of non-aid would have been helpful in understanding American policy:

> With respect to the underdeveloped Third World, . . . just about our only instrument of policy . . . has been the foreign-aid program. . . . Trade policy has not in fact been used much for this purpose at all, and private investors have never really received much special encouragement to seek out investment opportunities in the less developed countries. And, for that matter, the foreign-aid program itself has never been very large relative to our potential.[28]

Comment: The most important "special encouragement" that private investors were interested in was assurance that American foreign aid programs would be kept small. They believed that "hopes of receiving large-scale grant aid" tended "to induce foreign governments to be less receptive to private capital."[29] Thus, they continually demanded reassurance that the overall size of the aid program would be kept small and that scrupulous efforts would be made to avoid providing aid for projects potentially attractive to private foreign investors. It was precisely the "non-aid" referred to in the last sentence of this passage that constituted the single most important type of "special encouragement" to potential investors. It was the relatively small size of the American aid program that was supposed to provide the critical incentive for other countries to "create favorable climates" for foreign private investment.[30]

> Measures taken to stimulate private investment in underdeveloped countries were regarded favourably, especially as a means of transferring technology and skills, but it was never suggested that the promotion of U.S. investment could constitute an objective of assistance policy.[31]

Comment: Not only was it "suggested" that promoting private foreign investment was an objective of American aid policy, it was hardly ever portrayed in any other way. Not only was promoting private foreign investment one of the fundamental purposes of the International Bank, but almost every other vehicle of American aid also contained a prohibition

[28] Cohen, ed., *American Foreign Economic Policy*, pp. 32-33.

[29] American Enterprise Association, "American Private Enterprise, Foreign Economic Development, and the Aid Program," *Foreign Aid Program: Compilation of Studies and Surveys*, 85th Cong., 1st sess., S. Doc. 52, 1957, p. 548.

[30] For further discussion and documentation, see Baldwin, *Economic Development*; *Foreign Aid*; and "Foreign Aid."

[31] Ohlin, *Foreign Aid Policies Reconsidered*, p. 19.

on competition with private capital. American foreign policy makers proclaimed again and again their desire for less developed countries to rely primarily on private capital, and U.S. assistance policy was formulated so as to encourage such reliance. "Assistance policy" includes not only what is funded but also what is *not* to be funded. Once this is considered, it is difficult to deny that promoting private foreign investment was one of the goals of American "assistance policy."[32]

> During the 1950's, U.S. aid policy was dominated by the curious notion that aid should be denied countries that are potentially attractive to U.S. investors. Latin America was considered capable of attracting all the foreign capital it needed from private sources; aid was considered to be a palliative that discouraged countries from creating appropriate conditions to attract foreign investors.[33]

Comment: Why should this be regarded as a "curious" situation? It is precisely the kind of behavior we should expect from a nation for which avoidance of competition with private capital is one of the basic guiding principles of its aid program. After we grow accustomed to thinking of non-aid as a technique of statecraft, there is nothing at all puzzling about the situation described. It was clearly United States policy to withhold aid from certain countries in order to force (encourage?) them to rely on foreign private investment. The same author notes that since the ten states that harbor two-thirds of all U.S. private investment in developing areas have received less than 7 percent of American postwar economic aid, the United States cannot be accused of allocating its aid funds so as to further the interests of its private investors.[34] Precisely the opposite conclusion can be drawn. At the time this passage was written (1967), American private investors had been exhorting the government for twenty years to withhold aid funds from areas where they might compete with private capital. Official policy statements had repeatedly committed the government to comply with this exhortation. The empirical evidence is consistent with an American aid policy designed to help private investors by using non-aid to influence foreign investment climates.[35]

A study of American aid allocation found an inverse relationship between the amount of aid provided and the income from private investments in the recipient countries. The study concludes that "the results unequivocally demonstrate that the absolute commitment displayed through aid is not

[32] For further discussion and documentation, see references in footnote 30.
[33] Kaplan, *Challenge of Foreign Aid*, p. 179.
[34] Ibid., pp. 179, 185.
[35] Baldwin, "Foreign Aid," p. 432.

used to reinforce investment patterns.''[36] No such conclusion is justified. Indeed, this is precisely the pattern of aid allocation that one would predict if avoiding competition with private capital were an important principle of aid distribution. American aid allocation strategy is difficult to comprehend without an understanding of how non-aid can be used to ''reinforce investment patterns.''

The negative correlation between American aid and private foreign investment is not so pronounced as one might expect. This is probably because of two potentially conflicting non-aid principles embedded in American foreign aid strategy. The first, and most important, is the commitment to a relatively small aid total. Thus, at no time since World War II has serious consideration been given to aid levels on the order of magnitude of 10 percent of the GNP. This has been the most important technique by which United States foreign policy makers have sought to influence international investment patterns. A second principle, however, operated in partial conflict with the first. The second principle governed the allocation of aid rather than the total amount. In distributing aid American policy makers were supposed to ensure that aid was not given under circumstances in which private capital might be available on reasonable terms. This meant that aid was more likely to go to countries with relatively poor ''climates for foreign investment.'' The conflict between the two principles arose because the primary incentive for countries to improve their ''climate of foreign investment'' was supposed to be the lack of availability of capital; therefore, providing aid to countries with poor investment climates was likely to weaken their incentive to improve. Regardless of the actual effects of these two principles, the important point to recognize is that a negative or zero correlation between American aid and private investment levels does not necessarily mean that aid was being allocated without reference to the interests of private investors. The hypothesis that a deliberate policy of non-aid for certain purposes was being followed must at least be considered.[37]

Measuring Effectiveness

Estimating the efficacy of foreign aid involves many of the same analytical problems already discussed with reference to other economic instruments of statecraft;[38] therefore the following discussion will be cast in terms of eight principles to be considered in assessing the effectiveness of

[36] McKinlay and Little, ''Foreign Policy Model,'' p. 75. In this study the ''absolute commitment displayed through aid'' simply means the volume of aid.

[37] On the evolution of American policies regarding aid, non-aid, investment, and trade after World War II, see Baldwin, *Economic Development*; and *Foreign Aid*.

[38] See chapter 7.

an influence attempt based on foreign aid. Although these principles are not the only ones relevant to such an undertaking, they are some of the more important ones.

1. *Fungibility matters.*

The fungibility of economic resources that makes the concept of "strategic goods" so slippery in discussing export controls also complicates assessments of the efficacy of foreign aid. When one encounters the assertion that "it is fairly simple to calculate the direct effects of the use of economic instruments" of statecraft because "one can see a bridge or a school that has been built,"[39] or when one is told that "measuring the short-term accomplishments of American aid is deceptively simple" since "when aid is used for humanitarian purposes, . . . its value is already achieved when relief is rendered to those in need,"[40] caution is in order. Such situations may be deceptive, but they are rarely simple. If the bridge would have been built anyway or if the humanitarian disaster relief would have been rendered anyway, the actual net impact is to free resources in the recipient country for other uses. Thus food aid may actually bolster military forces in the recipient state, and military aid may actually result in more houses being built or fewer people going hungry. The only way to make a sensible estimate of the actual impact of the aid is to estimate the difference between the way resources are allocated in the recipient country after receiving aid and the way resources would have been allocated in the absence of aid.[41]

Actually, disaster relief programs are especially poor examples of aid impact that is easy to estimate. These are likely to be situations for which resources would be diverted from other uses if aid were not forthcoming from foreign governments or international organizations. Although the symbolic effects of aid for disaster relief may indeed be immediate and direct, the economic effects are almost sure to lie elsewhere. The relevant question then becomes one of estimating which sectors of the economy would have suffered if foreign aid had not been given.

2. *Forms of aid matter, but. . . .*

The implication of the fungibility of aid resources is that the commodity content of aid indicates little about the ultimate use of such aid. If military aid can masquerade as economic aid and capital assistance can be disguised as technical assistance, it would seem that the forms of aid matter very little. Not so. They matter, but not the way most people think they do.

[39] Howard H. Lentner, *Foreign Policy Analysis: A Comparative and Conceptual Approach* (Columbus, Ohio: Charles E. Merrill, 1974), p. 240.

[40] Montgomery, *Foreign Aid*, p. 72.

[41] For excellent discussions, see Schelling, *International Economics*, pp. 438-445; and Charles Wolf, Jr., *Foreign Aid: Theory and Practice in Southern Asia* (Princeton: Princeton University Press, 1960), pp. 159-162, 187-189, 258, 417-419.

Forms matter, as Thomas Schelling points out, because appearances matter.[42] The form in which aid is given sends a signal—accurate or deceptive—about the intentions of the donor. The symbolic effects of military aid and disaster relief are quite different even though the actual economic impact may be the same. The forms of aid matter because symbols matter.

3. *Concepts matter.*

How one conceives of aid has important implications for assessing the effectiveness of aid as a technique of statecraft. If aid given in return for a relatively specific quid pro quo, such as military base rights or support on a particular vote in the United Nations, is conceptually disregarded, estimates of the efficacy of aid are likely to be lower than if such activities are included in the concept of aid. At first glance this seems to be because aid given in return for a relatively specific quid pro quo is more likely to produce the intended effect on the target state's behavior. Although this may indeed be true, the proposition should not be accepted uncritically. Since specific and explicit quid pro quos are easier to observe than vague and implicit ones, the impression that the former work better than the latter may be merely an optical illusion. That which is easy to perceive is not necessarily truer than that which is difficult to perceive. In any case, the effect of ruling out aid transactions in which the terms of the exchange are relatively easy to perceive is likely to be a systematic tendency to underestimate the effectiveness of foreign aid as a technique of statecraft.[43]

4. *Conflict matters.*

Few would deny that the degree of conflict between the donor's goals and the recipient's goals is an important determinant of the effectiveness of foreign aid as a foreign policy tool. The nature of the relationship between goal conflict and effectiveness, however, is less obvious than it seems to be. This is illustrated by two examples: (1) the relationship between "common interests" and influence; and (2) the relationship between "common interests" and dependency.

Aid relationships, like most other social relationships, involve both

---

[42] Schelling, *International Economics*, pp. 452-457. See also Thomas C. Schelling, "American Foreign Assistance," *World Politics* VII (July 1955):606-626; and Thomas C. Schelling, "American Aid and Economic Development: Some Critical Issues," in *International Stability and Progress* (New York: American Assembly, 1957), pp. 121-169. These three works by Schelling overlap and are somewhat dated, but they still constitute the best discussion of foreign aid analysis available.

[43] Ignoring explicit aid in which there is an explicit quid pro quo can lead to conclusions that are difficult to reconcile with common-sense terminology. Thus, Knorr notes an exchange of U.S. economic aid for the use of Spanish military bases, but excludes such transactions from his conception of economic power, influence, or leverage. ("International Economic Leverage," p. 101.) In effect, Knorr's position implies that large and explicit strings on aid do not constitute leverage at all.

conflicting and common interests. Even when many goals are shared, there is likely to be disagreement between donor and recipient with respect to the amount, timing, and terms of aid. (Usually, recipients would like more, sooner, and with fewer strings.) The best way to approach aid transactions is also the best way to think about social relations in general, i.e., as mixed-motive games rather than as zero-sum or purely cooperative games. It is often stated or implied that foreign aid is more likely to "succeed" if the donor and the recipient share the same or at least compatible goals.[44] One problem with this viewpoint is the risk of confusing goal approximation with influence. If A is trying to get B to do X, B's compliance is one— but only one—indicator of A's influence over B with respect to X. Other important measures of the degree of A's influence concern the probability that B would have done X anyway and the costs to B of complying with A's preferences. Thus, a foreign aid transaction in which A and B share the same goals is likely to involve A getting B to do something that B wanted to do and was likely to have done anyway. To the extent that A's aid makes it possible for B to do X, it is correct to attribute influence to A—but not so much as outward appearances would seem to suggest. The person who commands others to "breathe" or the sun to "rise once a day" is likely to have an impressive record of "goal attainment"; this is not to say that he is exercising much influence.

Influence derives not only from the giving of aid but also from promising to give it, cutting it off, and threatening to cut it off. Dependency on aid, like dependency on trade, stems from the opportunity costs of forgoing the relationship. Thus, the larger the gains from aid, the larger the costs of forgoing aid, and the greater the dependency on aid. The most asymmetrical case of aid dependency would be one in which one party (probably the recipient) values the relationship very highly (i.e., experiences large gains from aid) and the other party (most likely the donor) places little or no value on the relationship. Such a situation maximizes the potential influence of the indifferent party with respect to the dependent party since the former can make costless and credible threats to end the relationship.[45] Recognition of this fact underlies George Liska's contention that "for the donor to remain in control, he must be visibly ready to accept the costs of terminating or reshaping the relationship."[46]

The relationship between aid and dependency leads to the following seldom recognized conclusion: *Other things being equal, the greater the donor's gain from the aid relationship, the more dependent he is on main-*

[44] See, for example, Joan M. Nelson, *Aid, Influence, and Foreign Policy* (New York: Macmillan, 1968), p. 74.
[45] The logic here is precisely the same as that used in determining trade dependency. See Baldwin, "Interdependence and Power."
[46] Liska, *New Statecraft*, p. 69. See also p. 33.

taining the relationship and the less able he is to make credible threats to forgo it. If the donor's gains from aid are a function of the number and importance of the interests he shares with the recipient, then his ability to derive influence from the recipient's dependency on aid is likely to vary *inversely* with such interests. Schelling notes the difficulty of making credible threats when the threatened punishment is likely to hurt the threatener as much or more than the one threatened and points to the "analogy between a parent's threat to a child and the threat that a wealthy paternalistic nation makes to the weak . . . government of a poor nation in, say, extending foreign aid and demanding 'sound' economic policies or cooperative military policies in return."[47] In each case the existence and strength of common interests weakens the credibility of the threat.

Not only is the relationship between aid and dependency seldom acknowledged, it is sometimes explicitly or implicitly denied. Consider the following examples:

> As an instrument of foreign policy, . . . aid is a useless tool unless it can be assumed that there is a strong community of interest between the aid-giving and aid-receiving countries.[48]

Comment: This proposition is difficult to accept. Since aid giving—or receiving—would be unwise in a zero-sum conflict situation, it is probably true that aid implies some common interests; but it does not follow that "a strong community of interest" is either necessary or desirable from the standpoint of the utility of aid as a tool of statecraft. Indeed, the stronger the community of interest, the harder it is for the donor credibly to threaten to cut off aid.

> The presence of conflicting goals makes blanket threats and promises ("if they don't devalue, we'll cut off the aid") entirely incredible. . . .[49]

Comment: It is the presence of *shared* goals that undermines the credibility of threats to cut off aid. Threats to disown one's children unless they keep their rooms tidier are rarely taken seriously.

> The level of . . . dependency established through aid is a function of the degree of interest that the donor has in low-income recipients.[50]

Comment: If this passage referred to the *donor's* dependency on the aid relationship, it would be plausible. Unfortunately, it refers to the *recipient's*

---

[47] *Strategy of Conflict*, p. 11. Cf. Yuan-Li Wu, *Economic Warfare*, pp. 205-207.

[48] Edward S. Mason, *Foreign Aid and Foreign Policy* (New York: Harper and Row, 1964), p. 4.

[49] Pincus, *Trade, Aid and Development*, p. 346.

[50] McKinlay and Little, "Foreign Policy Model," p. 64.

dependency, thus reversing the relationship between donor interest and the donor's ability to derive influence from the recipient's dependency. As the degree of donor interest in the recipient increases, the relationship at first becomes more symmetrical and eventually even becomes asymmetrical as the donor's interest surpasses that of the recipient.

Since critics of aid programs often assert that donors have a strong interest in using aid to create dependency on the part of the recipient, it should be noted that the logic of the aid-dependency relationship mitigates the effects of such influence attempts. Other things being equal, the stronger the donor's interest in creating an asymmetrical dependency relationship, the harder it is to do so, since it is precisely the strength of the donor's interest that creates his own dependency and thereby tends to equalize the dependency relationship. It is only the donor who is relatively indifferent to the dependency relationship created by aid who can credibly threaten to exploit that relationship. (Underdogs take heart; not all the cards are stacked against you!) The implications of the foregoing discussion might be summarized in terms of the following paradoxes: If the World Bank cared less about poor people, it might be able to use threatened aid cut-offs more effectively to improve their lot. If the United States cared less about whether aid recipients went communist, it might be able to use threatened aid cut-offs more effectively to keep them from going communist. If the United States cared less about Israel's survival, it might be able to use threatened aid cut-offs more effectively to ensure Israel's survival. Lesson: Mutual interests are often helpful in promoting peace and welfare, but this is not always the case; conflict can be a healthy thing for all concerned.

5. *Threats matter.*

Estimating the effectiveness of threats can be tricky business. Treatment of the Hickenlooper Amendment in American foreign aid legislation provides an example. This amendment required the president to suspend foreign aid to countries that expropriated American property without taking steps that were in his judgment adequate to ensure just compensation. In effect, the amendment was a standing threat to cut off aid to countries under the specified conditions. Sidney Weintraub notes that it was "invoked only once, . . . but otherwise it helped solve no expropriation problems."[51] The interesting question here is not so much whether Weintraub is correct, but rather how one would go about testing the proposition that it "helped solve no expropriation problems." Suppose that the threat embodied in the Hickenlooper Amendment had been perfectly effective. What would the empirical researcher find? Since threats are implemented only when they fail, no instances of invocation of the amendment would be found.

---

[51] *Economic Coercion*, p. 10.

When deterrence works, success is hard to measure. This is not to suggest anything about the effectiveness of the Hickenlooper Amendment; it is, however, to suggest that the fact that it was only invoked once provides little or no evidence as to whether it "helped solve" expropriation problems. Indeed, frequent invocation would have been evidence that the threat embodied in the legislation was not working very well.

6. *Amounts matter.*

Does foreign aid work? Does eating apples make one ill? While one apple a day is unlikely to produce illness (and may even help fend off doctors!), eating a thousand apples in one day is likely to have a different effect. Likewise, no useful estimate of the efficacy of foreign aid is possible without specifying how much aid one has in mind. When comparing one aid program with another or when comparing foreign aid with military statecraft, the amount of money spent in each case should be taken into account. The appropriate question is not whether military techniques work better than foreign aid; it is whether ten billion dollars worth of aid will do more or less to promote a given set of policy goals than an equivalent amount of military spending. This is not to say that big aid programs always work better than small ones, but the possibility that this is the case must at least be considered.

7. *The future matters.*

Influence attempts are future oriented—the past cannot be changed. This simple and obvious fact has implications for assessing the efficacy of foreign aid as an instrument of statecraft. Just as the prime incentive for states to obey international law is the knowledge that their ability to make binding commitments in the future is affected by their past record of honoring such commitments, the prime incentive of aid recipients to repay loans or to comply with the donor's wishes is the knowledge that their future eligibility for aid depends on their past record. Thus, aid programs with a specific and well-known termination date are likely to provide donors with less leverage as the expected termination date draws nearer. To the extent that Marshall Plan aid gave the United States declining leverage with respect to aid recipients toward the end of the program, this is precisely what should have been expected. Indeed, to the extent that this did not happen, there is reason to suspect that the degree of American influence via the Marshall Plan has been exaggerated. It is grounds for suspecting that Marshall Plan aid helped European states to do things they wanted to do and probably would eventually have done anyway. American aid probably speeded up European economic recovery, but this recovery cannot be attributed entirely to such aid. As noted earlier, influence and goal approximation are not necessarily the same thing.

Expectations about the future are especially important in estimating the relationship between loans and influence. Once a loan has been transferred, the debtor's main incentive to repay is to protect his credit rating so that he can borrow again in the future. The debtor even gains some potential influence with respect to the lender "since the withholding of repayment can be made to exercise the same manner of influence as the withholding of loans."[52] This has special relevance to the huge increases in debts of Third World countries during the 1970s. Since 1945 poor countries have been searching for a way to get rich countries to pay more attention to their problems. They have tried United Nations resolutions, new international organizations such as the United Nations Conference on Trade and Development, exhortation, diplomatic pressure, and economic pressure—all to little or no avail. Ironically, the so-called handicap, the "burden," the "problem" of Third World debt may prove to be just the bargaining chip the Third World has been seeking for forty years. The intertwining of the interests of the Western banking system with the viability of Third World economies may force Western governments and banks to take a more sympathetic view of Third World problems. The very size of the debt means that threatening to default may be an effective way for many Third World countries to keep governmental aid and commercial loans coming their way.

8. *Difficulty matters.*

If a fair test were to be devised for the proposition that foreign aid can be just as useful in promoting Third World development as it was in stimulating European recovery from World War II, allowances would have to be made for the level of effort (measured either in terms of aid per capita or aid as a percentage of recipient GNP) and for the level of difficulty of the undertaking. Thus, if promoting economic development in Third World countries is, say, five times as difficult as stimulating European recovery, then a fair test would be to ask how useful foreign aid would be if five times the effort were to be made during the same period or, alternatively, if the same effort were to be made over a period five times as long. Unfortunately, generalizations about the utility of foreign aid for promoting Third World development rarely make such allowances.

One thing is certain. Any attempt to determine the utility of foreign aid as an instrument of statecraft must be based on a clear distinction between the feasibility of the goals on the one hand and the utility of aid on the other. If the goals are judged to be very low in feasibility to begin with, then it seems unfair to attribute low utility to foreign aid because of failure to approximate such goals. Indeed, if one believes the goals are low in feasibility, then even a small amount of goal approximation should be counted as indicating a high degree of utility of aid.[53]

[52] Viner, *International Economics*, p. 343.

[53] For an example of a study that attributes low utility to foreign aid on the basis of failure to achieve goals that the author judges to have been low in feasibility to begin with, see Packenham, *Liberal America*, esp. pp. 3-18, 178-192.

KNORR'S CASES OF AID SANCTIONS

Knorr bases his analysis of coercive uses of foreign aid on twenty-five "notorious cases" of actual or threatened aid cut-offs that have occurred since World War II.[54] He classifies the outcomes of these influence attempts as follows: success, two; initial success, eventual failure, one; indeterminate, three; failure, nineteen. Knorr concludes that "the historical record does not establish the coercive use of foreign economic or military aid as a generally effective measure" (p. 181). Observing that "overwhelming failure" (p. 181) characterizes such cases, he wonders "whether or not coercion by means of aid cuts can ever be the rational objective of government in any but exceptionally favorable circumstances" (p. 183). Even accepting the apparent equating of twenty-five "notorious" and "unselected" cases with "the historical record," there are reasons to question the characterization of these cases in terms of "overwhelming failure." No attempt will be made to study Knorr's cases in detail, but rather reasons for questioning the "overwhelming" nature of the evidence will be suggested. The purpose is not to refute Knorr's judgments as to the outcome of any of the cases, but rather to suggest the wisdom of suspending judgment about the validity of Knorr's classifications until these cases can be investigated using the analytical framework developed here. Since many of Knorr's cases are included in the 126 cases of foreign aid suspensions considered by James A. Blessing,[55] any case in which Blessing's assessment of the outcome is more favorable than Knorr's will be identified as one deserving further study. This is not to imply that Blessing's estimates are to be preferred to Knorr's, but merely to suggest that when experts differ, more research is needed before definitive judgments are made.

1. *Soviet Union vs. Yugoslavia (1948)*

This was a joint aid and trade cut-off by the Soviet Union and is classified as a failure by Knorr. Since reasons for questioning the characterization of this case as a "failure" were presented in chapter 9, the discussion will not be repeated here.

2. *United States vs. West European Allies (beginning 1953?)*

The United States threatened to cut off aid to Western European countries that failed to cooperate with respect to the embargo on strategic exports to the Soviet Union. Knorr characterizes the outcome as "initial success, final failure" (p. 338). It is not clear what Knorr has in mind here because of an apparent misprint. Although the description of the case (p. 338) states that the United States threats began in 1953, Knorr is fully aware that this is not true. In discussing the anticommunist trade embargo, he

---

[54] *Power of Nations*, pp. 180-183, 337-339.

[55] "The Suspension of Foreign Aid: Macro-Analysis"; and "The Suspension of Foreign Aid by the United States, 1948-1972" (Ph.D. dissertation, State University of New York at Albany, 1975). The latter is cited hereafter as "Suspension of U.S. Foreign Aid."

dates this threat from the late 1940s (pp. 142-143). Indeed, it would be most unfair to date this case from 1953 because that is the approximate date that the efficacy of the threat began to wane. Gunnar Adler-Karlsson agrees with Knorr's contention that the threat began in the late 1940s. Although the threat was never actually implemented, Adler-Karlsson argues that it was very effective in securing European support for restrictions on East-West trade during the Marshall Plan period. He suggests that European support for the embargo declined as the Marshall Plan ended and American aid was reduced.[56] Ignoring the apparent misprint, there seems to be no disagreement between Knorr and Adler-Karlsson with respect to the facts of the case.

The significance of this case—or *cases*—for an overall assessment of the utility of threatened aid cut-offs as techniques of statecraft, however, is not brought out by Knorr's treatment. If the threat was as successful as Adler-Karlsson contends during the Marshall Plan years, this single case could be viewed as separate threats aimed at sixteen countries in each of four years, thus providing sixty-four cases of impressively successful influence attempts. The fact that the decline in the degree of success coincided with the decline in American aid provides no support whatever for the proposition that influence attempts based on threatened aid cut-offs are characterized by "overwhelming failure." Indeed, the evidence from the period 1948-1958 is consistent with the proposition that threatened aid cut-offs can be extremely effective instruments of statecraft, assuming that the efficacy of the threat varies directly with the amount of aid (and/or the value of the aid to the recipient) that one is threatening to cut off—an eminently plausible assumption. This is not to say that the evidence *supports* the proposition that aid is effective, but only to suggest that it is easier to reconcile the evidence with this proposition than with the contrary one. So many other factors were obviously at work that this case—or set of cases—cannot be regarded as an adequate test of either proposition.

3.   *Soviet Union vs. Yugoslavia (1958)*
This is one of the cases of alleged failure discussed in chapter 9.

4.   *Soviet Union vs. China (1960)*
This case of alleged failure is discussed in chapter 9.

5.   *Soviet Union vs. Albania (1961)*
This case of alleged failure is discussed in chapter 9.

6.   *United States vs. Ceylon (1962-1965)*
This case is singled out for more detailed discussion by Knorr in order to "indicate the difficulty of interpretation" (pp. 180-181). The case constituted the first invocation of the Hickenlooper Amendment to cut off aid of about fifteen million dollars per year after American oil refineries were

---

[56] *Western Economic Warfare*, pp. 5-7, 23-30, 36-49, 84, et passim.

nationalized.[57] Eventually, the government fell and the new government "quickly concluded an agreement acceptable to the oil companies" (p. 181). Although Knorr admits that "the outcome seems to indicate a successful attempt to exert economic pressure" (p. 181), he rather ungenerously classifies the outcome as "indeterminate" on the grounds that the causal links between the aid cut-off and eventual compliance are not unequivocally clear. Blessing classifies the case as a success; Richard Stuart Olson implies that the aid cut-off was an important factor in inducing Ceylonese compliance; and Hufbauer and Schott give the case a success rating of sixteen on a sixteen-point scale.[58] More importantly, Olson suggests that an adequate specification of the policy-contingency framework of this influence attempt should take account of Brazil as an important target and the desire of American decision makers to find a salient yet low-cost opportunity to demonstrate the credibility of the threat to implement the Hickenlooper Amendment. Considering the trivial amount of aid cut off and the other goals and targets of the influence attempt, there is reason to suspect that this may have been a rather cost-effective undertaking from the American point of view.

7. *United States vs. Indonesia (1963)*

Knorr describes this simply as an "aid cutoff over President Sukarno's policies" (p. 338) that failed. Blessing classifies it as a success;[59] and Hufbauer and Schott give it a rating of eight on a scale on which a score of nine or more is considered successful.

8. *United States vs. West European Allies (1963-64)*

Knorr describes this case as a threatened military aid cut-off in order to secure support for the embargo against Cuba (p. 338). It is not clear precisely which "allies" Knorr has in mind here. Blessing notes military aid cut-offs of $100,000 to France and the United Kingdom in 1964 and agrees with Knorr in classifying these as failures. But Blessing assesses

---

[57] Knorr's figure of $15 million annually seems high. According to A.I.D. statistics, Ceylon received aid of $20.5 million in 1958; $16.4 million in 1959; $9.4 million in 1960; $5.6 million in 1962; and $4.3 million in 1963. The only aid that appears to have been suspended is that from A.I.D., which amounted to $4.8 million in 1958; $1.9 million in 1959; $6.2 million in 1960; $0.1 million in 1961; $1.2 million in 1962; and $-3.0 million in 1963 (loan repayments). Aid under the Food for Peace program, which accounted for three-quarters of the total aid to Ceylon in the 1958-1962 period, was not suspended. Indeed, it increased from $4.2 million in 1962 to $7.1 million in 1963. Thus, the magnitude of the aid cut-off is greatly exaggerated by Knorr's figure. See Agency for International Development, Statistics and Reports Division, *U.S. Overseas Loans and Grants and Assistance from International Organizations*, special report prepared for the House Foreign Affairs Committee, March 17, 1967, p. 8.

[58] Blessing, "Suspension of U.S. Foreign Aid," pp. 136, 212-213; Olson, "Expropriation and International Economic Coercion: Ceylon and the 'West' 1961-65," *Journal of Developing Areas* XI (January 1977):205-225; and Hufbauer and Schott, *Economic Sanctions*.

[59] "Suspension of U.S. Foreign Aid," pp. 136, 217-218.

the suspension of military aid to Spain with respect to the same issue as a success.[60]

9. *United States vs. Peru (1965)*

This case involved the suspension of some economic aid to Peru in connection with a dispute over properties of Standard Oil of New Jersey in Peru. Although Knorr classifies it as a failure, Blessing views it as a success.[61]

10. *United States vs. Peru (1966)*

Knorr depicts this as an "aid cutoff over [the] same issue" (p. 338) as in 1965. Although he again classifies it as a failure, Olson suggests that such a judgment may be an oversimplification.[62]

11. *United States vs. Israel (1967)*

This refusal to deliver military aircraft in order to induce Israel to work toward a Middle East settlement is classified as indeterminate by Knorr, but Blessing considers it a success.[63]

12. *United States vs. Ecuador and Peru (1969)*

This military aid cut-off over a fisheries dispute is classified as a failure by Knorr, but Blessing views it as a success.[64] This dispute cannot be adequately understood merely as a "fisheries dispute." The dispute concerned the extension of territorial jurisdiction two hundred miles offshore, a position then being opposed by the United States in international negotiations on the Law of the Sea. The significance of the dispute from the United States' point of view concerned the precedent being set, the military implications of the precedent, and the possible effects on its bargaining position in the Law of the Sea negotiations.[65]

13. *United States vs. Chile (1971-72)*

Knorr describes this case as an "aid cutoff in [a] dispute over proper compensation for nationalized properties of American firms" and labels it a "failure" (p. 338). Background on the nature and context of this influence attempt was just beginning to become available when Knorr was writing *The Power of Nations*.[66] With the benefit of hindsight it seems clear that

[60] Ibid., pp. 136, 230-234.

[61] Ibid., pp. 136, 186.

[62] See Olson, "Economic Coercion in World Politics," p. 488; and "Economic Coercion in International Disputes." Hufbauer and Schott give their highest success rating to a case of U.S. sanctions against Peru in 1968, but it is unclear whether this is the same case Knorr cites.

[63] "Suspension of Foreign U.S. Aid," pp. 136, 202.

[64] Ibid., pp. 136, 177, 187-188.

[65] For background, see David C. Loring, "The Fisheries Dispute," in *U.S. Foreign Policy and Peru*, ed. Daniel A. Sharp (Austin: University of Texas Press, 1972), pp. 57-118.

[66] See, for example, Theodore H. Moran, *Multinational Corporations and the Politics of Dependence: Copper in Chile* (Princeton: Princeton University Press, 1974); Paul E. Sigmund, *The Overthrow of Allende and the Politics of Chile, 1964-1976* (Pittsburgh: University of Pittsburgh Press, 1977); Robert J. Alexander, *The Tragedy of Chile* (Westport, Conn.: Green-

American actions cannot be adequately characterized in terms of an "aid cutoff" having to do with a dispute over compensation for nationalized properties. Any investigation of the effectiveness of this influence attempt would have to take into account the following facts:

(a) The so-called aid cutoff was at best a "cutback," since substantial amounts of American aid continued to flow into Chile.

(b) With respect to the goal of improved terms of compensation for nationalized American property, "failure" does not adequately characterize the outcome. Although his party had pledged "*Ni un centavo!*" in compensation, in February 1972, the Allende government agreed to pay a substantial amount to the Kennecott copper mining company as compensation for nationalization.[67] When A gets B to do something he would not otherwise have done, clearly did not want to do, and was publicly pledged not to do, "failure" is not the right label for the outcome of the influence attempt.

(c) The dispute over compensation for the nationalization of American properties had little to do with this influence attempt. As with Cuba in 1960, the immediate and specific economic issues were overshadowed by the larger symbolic and political issues. The second communist country in the hemisphere—the first communist government ever to come to power through democratic constitutional processes—was a matter of concern to American policy makers for reasons far more important than the fate of a few American investments in Chile. "Nationalization of American-owned property was not the issue," states Henry Kissinger, "our concern with Allende was based on national security, not economics."[68] It seems clear from Kissinger's discussion that the compensation issue was more a convenient pretext than a fundamental reason for the aid cutback.[69]

(d) The 1971–72 aid "cutoff," such as it was, was part of a coordinated attempt to "destabilize" the Chilean government, and its efficacy must be assessed in that context. Although few would credit the aid squeeze as a decisive factor, few would deny that it was one of the contributing factors to Allende's eventual downfall.

14.   *United States vs. India (1971)*

This case, classified as a failure by Knorr, concerned an "aid cutoff

---

wood Press, 1978); Henry Kissinger, *The White House Years* (Boston: Little, Brown, 1979), pp. 653-683; James Petras and Morris Morley, "Chilean Destabilization and Its Aftermath: An Analysis and a Critique," *Politics* XI (November 1976):140-148; U.S. House of Representatives, Committee on Foreign Affairs, *Hearings: United States and Chile During the Allende Years, 1970-1973*, 93d Cong., 2d sess., 1975; and Stephen D. Krasner, *Defending the National Interest* (Princeton: Princeton University Press, 1978), pp. 298-312.

[67] Moran, *Multinational Corporations*, pp. 147-152.

[68] Kissinger, *White House Years*, p. 656.

[69] Ibid., pp. 653-683, esp. pp. 681-682.

over India's invasion of East Pakistan'' (p. 338). Blessing, however, describes this as a ''success.''[70]

15.   *United States vs. South Vietnam (1972)*

Knorr describes this as ''hints of aid reductions unless [the] Saigon government heeded United States policy'' and classifies it as an ''apparent failure'' (p. 339). Without denying Knorr's classification of this case, one might well question whether this case typified the outcome of threatened aid cuts toward South Vietnam. Not only could many similar cases be found with different outcomes—Blessing, for example, cites four cases of success[71]—but the whole relationship between the United States and South Vietnam was infused with standing implicit threats to cut off aid unless Saigon heeded American policies. Singling out one case of ''apparent failure'' begs many questions.

Questions similar to those asked with respect to case studies of trade sanctions may be used to evaluate Knorr's cases of actual or threatened aid cut-offs.

1.   *Are policy-contingency frameworks adequately specified?*

The most important shortcoming of Knorr's twenty-five cases is the tendency to describe most cases in terms of a single target and a single goal. Sometimes the goal specified is not even the primary one, e.g., Chile (1971–72) and Peru and Ecuador (1969). Furthermore, the cases are not defined in comparable terms. Thus an influence attempt involving a small aid cut-off during a single year with respect to a single target state weighs as heavily in Knorr's statistics as a threat to cut off a large amount of aid (e.g., the Marshall Plan) to several target states (e.g., Marshall Plan recipients) over several years. A threatened aid cut-off that lasts for four years, *ceterus paribus*, ought to count four times as heavily as one that lasts only one year; and a threat with respect to sixteen targets, *ceterus paribus*, ought to count sixteen times as heavily as a threat aimed at a single country. The means used should also be treated in comparable terms insofar as possible. Thus, a threat to cut off a billion dollars worth of aid should not be counted as comparable to a threat to cut off one-tenth as much. *Ceterus paribus*, only one-tenth as much influence should be expected in the latter case as in the former.

2.   *Are adjustments made for varying levels of difficulty?*

There is no evidence that Knorr includes allowances for differing levels of difficulty in assessing effectiveness in these cases. One way this could be done, for example, would be to measure the actual or threatened aid cut-off as a percentage of the recipient state's GNP. Presumably, a threat

---

[70] ''Suspension of U.S. Foreign Aid,'' pp. 136, 215-216.
[71] Ibid., pp. 136, 223-224.

to cut off aid equivalent to 1 percent of a state's GNP will be only one-tenth as effective (i.e., have only one-tenth the probability of success) as a threat to cut off aid amounting to 10 percent of the recipient's GNP (*ceterus paribus*).

3. *Is success treated as a matter of degree?*

Although three cases are classified as neither success nor failure, the category of "indeterminate" suggests that more information might allow a more definitive classification. Whereas Knorr's assessment of trade sanctions at least allows for "mixed" results, his treatment of aid cut-offs seems less willing to allow for such outcomes. In any case, one gets the impression that most cases (twenty-two out of twenty-five) fall into the categories of either success or failure. The vast middle ground in which influence attempts are partially successful with respect to at least some of their goals and targets receives scant attention from Knorr.

4. *Are alternative policy options considered?*

With the exception of Knorr's observation that low-salience, "undramatic" threats are likely to be more effective (pp. 182-183), little consideration is given to the comparative effectiveness of other policy instruments with respect to the twenty-five cases.

5. *Are costs of noncompliance treated as measures of effectiveness?*

This is an especially important omission in Knorr's analysis. Unless equivalent aid is immediately found from other sources, aid cut-offs nearly always impose some costs on the target state. To the extent that this is true, aid cut-offs are usually at least partially successful in influencing the target state.

6. *Are the generalizations commensurate with the evidence?*

The equation of twenty-five "notorious" and "unselected" cases with "the historical record" is rather disconcerting, especially since the cases are so different. Preliminary, and admittedly cursory, investigation of fifteen of Knorr's cases suggests the need for further study of at least twelve of the nineteen cases of "failure," two of the three "indeterminate" cases, and the case of "initial success, final failure." Acceptance of Knorr's characterization of these cases in terms of "overwhelming failure" should be held in abeyance until further research, using the analytical framework developed here, confirms his conclusions.

Although Blessing's study of cases of aid suspension has been used here as a point of reference for a preliminary check on Knorr's classification of outcomes, I do not intend to imply that Blessing's judgments are to be preferred to Knorr's. Nor should it be inferred that Blessing is more optimistic than Knorr about the likely efficacy of aid cut-offs as techniques of statecraft. Indeed, Blessing views his conclusion that "the suspension of aid does not appear to have been a very effective means of inducing change in recipient behavior" as in "general agreement with the conclusions of numerous other studies which show that neither the granting of aid nor the use of economic sanctions have been effective mechanisms of inducing behavior change in recipient countries."[72]

Blessing defines success in terms of changes in the behavior or policy of the target state so as to be "more in accord with the stated desires of the United States."[73] Although this is a less stringent definition of success than Knorr uses, it is considerably more stringent than that employed here. Overt changes in policy or behavior are the most difficult effects to produce in an influence attempt. Blessing ignores the unstated goals of the United States, secondary goals and targets, costs inflicted on the target, the difficulty of the undertaking, and changes in the attitude of the target country not manifested in overt changes in behavior or policy. Still, Blessing concludes that 69 (55 percent!) of the 126 cases showed some sign of overt change in policy or behavior. Blessing then proceeds to throw out 21 cases involving civil or international war on the grounds that "the suspension of aid was not a major factor in bringing a halt to the hostilities"[74] and 8 cases in which the policy alteration was only nominal. He concludes that "no more than 40 of 126 cases of aid suspension appear to have been directly related to a successful and substantive resolution of the issue or issues involved." This leads to his overall assessment that aid suspension has not been very effective.[75] But is this the appropriate interpretation of his findings? Is a baseball batting average of .320 impressive or not? Is a foreign aid suspension success rate of 32 percent impressive or not? The answer in both cases obviously depends on comparison with some reference point. In baseball a .320 batting average is considered very good—comparatively speaking. Unfortunately, there is no comparable point of reference for determining whether .320 is a good "batting average" for a technique of statecraft.

Although I suspect that a .320 success rate is about as good as can be expected of most techniques of statecraft, I have no way of proving it. One study of the political uses of military force using criteria roughly equivalent to Blessing's found that the outcome of an influence attempt varied greatly in terms of short- and long-run effects and in terms of whether the goal was to "assure," "deter," "compel," or "induce."[76] Whereas

[72] "Suspension of Foreign Aid: Macro-Analysis," p. 533.

[73] Ibid., p. 531.

[74] In at least some of these cases it is plausible to assume that the United States' goal was to avoid involvement in the war. To the extent that this was true, the success of the aid suspension should be judged by this criterion rather than in terms of its impact on "bringing a halt to the hostilities."

[75] "Suspension of Foreign Aid: Macro-Analysis," pp. 532-533. Hufbauer and Schott's study of aid and trade sanctions rates 40 percent of the cases as successful (*Economic Sanctions*, p. 74).

[76] Blechman and Kaplan, eds., *Force Without War*, pp. 88-93.

some modes of using force yielded "positive outcomes" more than 90 percent of the time, other modes did so less than 20 percent of the time. Blessing's cases of aid suspension would have to be categorized in a comparable way before a useful comparison of the two studies could be made. Since the study of military force makes no attempt to allow for counterfactual conditions, both deterrence and assurance tend to receive very high ratings for "positive outcomes." This reflects the fact that the goal in such cases is simply to reinforce existing behavior patterns rather than to change them. If one looks only at the two modes of influence that attempt to *change* target behavior—compellence and inducement—the former yields positive outcomes in 68 percent of the cases in the short term (after six months) but in only 18 percent of the cases after three years. Inducement is associated with positive outcomes in 33 percent of the cases in the short term and in 22 percent of the cases in the longer term.[77] Although such a reference point leaves much to be desired, this comparison suggests that an effectiveness rate of 32 percent may not be so bad after all.

Lack of systematic studies establishing a "normal" success rate for various kinds of international influence attempts makes it difficult to judge the significance of Blessing's assessment that 32 percent of his cases were successful. Blessing's inference that his findings support prevailing beliefs that aid suspension is not very effective as a tool of statecraft is no more warranted than the conclusion that a baseball player is not a very effective batter because his batting average is only .320. Until studies similar to Blessing's have been done for other policy instruments, it is difficult to determine the significance of his results.

FOREIGN AID IN U.S. FOREIGN POLICY

Foreign aid has been disbursed by many different governments for a variety of purposes. A fair assessment of the utility of foreign aid as an instrument of statecraft would have to take account of this wide array of purposes. No such assessment will be attempted here. Instead, some aspects of the conventional wisdom about the role of aid in American foreign policy will be examined. Since the United States is the world's leading aid donor, most discussions of aid eventually center on American policy. In thinking clearly about foreign aid, as in thinking about other forms of economic statecraft, an attitude of healthy skepticism toward conventional wisdom is likely to be helpful. The four aspects of conventional wisdom to be considered concern the lessons of the Marshall Plan, development in the Third World, the role of aid in American policy, the expectations

[77] Ibid., p. 89.

of policy makers and others as to both the efficacy of aid and the political goals of aid.

1. *During the 1950s and 1960s Marshall Plan concepts were transferred from Europe to the Third World.*[78]

The success of the European Recovery Program, popularly known as the Marshall Plan, is rarely questioned even by the severest critics of foreign aid. By 1950, Marshall Plan participants—Germany excepted—were producing more industrial and agricultural products than they had before the war; and the volume of both intra-European trade and European trade with the rest of the world had passed the prewar mark. Even secondary goals such as promoting European integration and eliciting European support for restrictions on trade with communist countries were approximated to a significant extent. More importantly, all this was accomplished with less money than had originally been anticipated. This heady success, according to popular belief, led American policy makers to the erroneous assumption that similar measures would be equally effective with respect to the Third World.

There is undoubtedly some truth in the supposition that some "concepts" of the Marshall Plan era were transferred to later aid programs. As Schelling points out, many of the problems of administering the Marshall Plan were encountered subsequently, including questions regarding the forms of aid, mechanisms for controlling the impact of aid, criteria for allocating aid, and charges of intervention by aid recipients.[79] Not all dimensions of an aid program, however, are of equal importance. Although *size* is not the only important aspect of an aid program, it is usually the single most important one. And any suggestion that this vital concept of the Marshall Plan was transferred to American policies toward Asia, Africa, or Latin America is likely to be seriously misleading.

The most salient characteristic of the Marshall Plan—and probably the one most directly related to its success—is its large size. As table 6 shows, Marshall Plan participants received an annual average of more than twenty dollars per person during the period 1948–1952; and some states received much more than that. By comparison, American aid recipients in Asia, Latin America, and Africa have rarely received aid at an annual rate of more than one or two dollars per person, if that.[80] The magnitude of

---

[78] For examples see Packenham, *Liberal America*, pp. 35-42; Thomas A. Bailey, *The Art of Diplomacy: The American Experience* (New York: Appleton-Century-Crofts, 1968), p. 201; and John Lewis Gaddis, "The Rise and Fall of Détente," *Foreign Affairs* LXII (Winter 1983-1984):359.

[79] Schelling, "American Foreign Assistance" and "American Aid and Economic Development."

[80] Possible exceptions include Israel, Jordan, Laos, Vietnam, Taiwan, and South Korea. Israel, with a thirty-year annual average of nearly two hundred dollars per capita aid, is clearly in a class by itself.

Table 6

U.S. Aid to Marshall Plan Participants, 1948-1952

Country	Average Annual Economic Aid Per Capita	Average Annual Military[a] and Economic Aid Per Capita
Austria	$25	$27
Belgium and Luxembourg	$16	$36
Denmark	$16	$29
France	$16	$35
W. Germany	$12	$15
Greece	$24	$44
Iceland	$72	$72
Ireland	$12	$12
Italy	$ 8	$13
Netherlands	$25	$45
Norway	$19	$50
Portugal	$ 2	$ 5
Sweden	$ 4	$ 4
United Kingdom	$16	$19
Turkey	$ 3	$ 9
Total	$13	$21

SOURCES: U.S. Agency for International Development, *U.S. Overseas Loans and Grants and Assistance from International Organizations*, 1982. Economic aid includes loans from the Export-Import Bank. Population figures for 1950 are from U.S. Bureau of the Census, *World Population 1979—Summary—Recent Demographic Estimates for the Countries and Regions of the World* (Washington, D.C.: G.P.O., 1980).

[a] Since 1978 military assistance figures have reflected the original acquisition value of equipment and supplies. Prior to 1978 excess defense equipment was valued at one-third of its original acquisition value.

Marshall Plan aid in comparison with subsequent aid programs is reflected in the fact that twelve of the thirty-six leading recipients of American aid between 1946 and 1981 are former Marshall Plan participants *despite the fact that most of these countries received little or no American aid during the 1960s and 1970s.*[81] And fourteen former Marshall Plan participants still rank among the forty-one leading postwar American aid recipients on a per capita basis.

Even though the Marshall Plan looms very large in American aid statistics, its size is probably understated. In the first place, most Marshall Plan aid was on a grant basis, whereas a higher percentage of aid to the Third World has been in the form of loans. In the second place, the true

[81] Japan ranks fourteenth but was not a Marshall Plan participant.

value of Marshall Plan aid to its recipients was greater than the distorted exchange rates at the time would imply. Schelling estimates that if exchange rates in the 1948–1952 period had truly reflected the market value of the aid, Marshall Plan aid might have amounted to "more like 5 or 10 percent, rather than 3 or 4 percent, of Europe's own production."[82] And in the third place, adjustments for inflation would make Marshall Plan aid seem even larger by today's standards. Marshall Plan aid levels of twenty dollars per capita would be roughly equivalent to aid levels of sixty dollars per capita in 1980 dollars.

The idea that Marshall Plan concepts were transferred to American policy toward the Third World is a misleading half-truth at best. Indeed, assuming that promoting economic development in the Third World is, say, five times as difficult as stimulating European war recovery—a conservative assumption—adaptation of the Marshall Plan approach to promoting Third World development would have required five times the effort—say, twenty dollars per person per year for twenty years with appropriate adjustments for inflation. Instead, the American aid program with respect to most Third World countries involved per capita aid levels about one-tenth the size of the Marshall Plan effort. The Marshall Plan approach may or may not have worked with respect to promoting Third World development, but the suggestion that it was tried and found wanting is difficult to reconcile with the facts. This judgment is supported by an experienced administrator of American aid programs:

> [The Marshall Plan] experience in re-establishing viable societies in the industrialized world is relevant in many respects to the less developed countries. It is common to explain their poorer record of progress by stressing that conditions are different and less favorable. It is sometimes suggested that failures are attributable to an uncritical application of Marshall Plan ideas and methods to the less responsive problems of the poorer nations. The latter charge is difficult to substantiate, and indeed the opposite may be closer to the truth. The United States was so preoccupied with the difficulties and different circumstances that it assumed only minimal results could be expected. It therefore hesitated to attack the problems as aggressively as it had in Europe. The very assumption helped to assure modest results.[83]

[82] *International Economics*, pp. 432-433.

[83] Kaplan, *Challenge of Foreign Aid*, pp. 122-123. For an argument contrasting the Marshall Plan with American aid to India, see Robert C. Johansen, *The National Interest and the Human Interest* (Princeton: Princeton University Press, 1980), pp. 126-195. Cf. Bienen and Gilpin, "Evaluation," p. V,4, with respect to the failure of "massive" American aid to India.

2. *Economic growth rates in the Third World since 1950 have been lower than was expected.*

"Discouragement with foreign aid set in during the 1960s," observes Charles Kindleberger, "economic development was stubbornly slow." Robert W. Tucker refers to "the disappointment bordering on despair over the results of development strategies and projections confidently set forth in the 1950s and early 1960s." And Packenham uses the fact that "economic development proceeded more slowly than most people had expected" as evidence of the limited effectiveness of foreign aid.[84]

The examples cited here are typical in their vague references to the allegedly overly optimistic expectations of the 1950s and 1960s. Such assertions are almost never buttressed by specific citations; and small wonder, since supportive evidence is difficult to find. In fact, studies of economic development in the 1950s and 1960s were almost all overly pessimistic about the prospects for growth in the Third World. In 1955 W. Arthur Lewis observed that "raising total output by 2 percent per annum is no mean feat." Noting that a "4 percent per annum increase in output is all that the United States achieved from 1870 to 1930," he lamented the fact that "there is no sign of the less developed countries this side of the Iron Curtain beginning to adopt the sort of heroic measures which a 2 to 3 percent per annum increase in output would demand."[85] Another study, published by the Twentieth Century Fund, was slightly more optimistic in observing that a sustained rate of increase in total output "as high as 3 to 5 per cent per year would not be surprising" but was "moderately pessimistic" about the extent to which such gains would be offset by population growth.[86] And Max F. Millikan and W. W. Rostow estimated that "under the most favorable conditions the maximum rate of growth of physical output likely to be achievable by countries in the early stages of development is 3 to 5 per cent per year."[87] In each case these projections proved to be unduly pessimistic with respect to the economic performance of the less developed countries. Studies published in the early 1960s also underestimated the growth rates actually achieved by these countries in the 1960s and 1970s.[88] A study sponsored by the World Bank in 1977

[84] Kindleberger, "U. S. Foreign Economic Policy," p. 410; Tucker, *Inequality of Nations*, p. 53, also p. 162; and Packenham, *Liberal America*, p. 8.

[85] *The Theory of Economic Growth* (Homewood, Ill.: Richard P. Irwin, 1955), pp. 314-315.

[86] Norman S. Buchanan and Norman S. Ellis, *Approaches to Economic Development* (New York: Twentieth Century Fund, 1955), pp. 115-116.

[87] *A Proposal: Key to an Effective Foreign Policy* (New York: Harper, 1957), pp. 20-21.

[88] E.g., Paul Rosenstein-Rodan, "International Aid for Underdeveloped Countries," *Review of Economics and Statistics* XLIII (May 1961):107-138; and Hollis Chenery and Alan Strout, "Foreign Assistance and Economic Development," *American Economic Review* LVI (September 1966):679-733.

concluded that "the GNP per capita in the developing countries as a group grew at an average rate of 3.4 percent a year during 1950–75. . . . This was faster than either the developing countries . . . or the developed nations . . . had grown in any comparable period before 1950 *and exceeded both official goals and private expectations*.[89] Growth could have and should have been faster; distribution was not equitable; and many problems remained unsolved; but the contention that growth rates failed to meet the projections made in the 1950s and early 1960s has little supporting evidence. Pointing to allegedly "disappointing" Third World growth rates in the postwar world is not a very impressive way to prove that foreign aid does not work. These growth rates may or may not have been caused by aid, but it is difficult to deny that impressive growth did in fact occur.

3. *The main instrument of U.S. foreign policy for promoting Third World development was foreign aid.*[90]

The salience of America's foreign aid program can give a misleading impression of its importance relative to other techniques of statecraft in promoting Third World development. The basic American approach to economic development has been remarkably stable and consistent since the end of the Second World War.[91] The following three principles have underlain American policy throughout this period: First, reliance on self-help is the basic technique for promoting economic growth. American policy makers have repeatedly gone to great lengths to emphasize that economic development is primarily a matter of domestic effort and that external assistance can merely supplement such efforts. Both explicitly and implicitly American policy has reflected the belief that development must come from within and cannot be imposed from outside. Second, free trade promotes development. Since international trade is a partial substitute for movement of the factors of production, poor countries will require less external capital if they participate in the liberal trading system. Despite reluctant American acquiescence to Third World demands for trade preferences, the fundamental belief in trade as an "engine of growth" for poor countries has not disappeared. The third principle is that insofar as domestic effort and free trade do not suffice as stimulators of development, devel-

[89] David Morawetz, *Twenty-Five Years of Economic Development, 1950 to 1975* (Baltimore: Johns Hopkins Press, 1977), p. 12. Italics added. See also Ian M. D. Little, *Economic Development: Theory, Policy, and International Relations* (New York: Basic Books, 1982), pp. 108, 120, 210, 269-282; International Bank for Reconstruction and Development, *World Development Report, 1982* (New York: Oxford University Press, 1982); and Herman Kahn, *World Economic Development, 1979 and Beyond* (Boulder, Colo.: Westview, 1979).

[90] Cf. Cohen, *American Foreign Economic Policy*, p. 32; and Packenham, *Liberal America*, p. 318. Although Packenham is primarily interested in political development goals, he depicts economic development goals as intermediate goals to this end.

[91] The discussion here is based on the more thorough and documented treatment of this topic in my *Economic Development and American Foreign Policy*.

oping countries should rely primarily on private rather than public sources for foreign capital. Thus, not only is external assistance of any kind secondary in importance, but governmental foreign aid is merely supplementary to the most important form of this external assistance—private foreign investment. From this perspective, foreign aid appears as only a tertiary instrument for promoting Third World development. Insofar as foreign aid was to be given at all, American policy has consistently reflected a desire to keep the total amount small relative to private capital flows and to avoid competition with private investment as much as possible.

The importance of understanding how foreign aid fits into overall American foreign policy stems from the need to establish criteria for judging the efficacy of aid as a technique of statecraft. Before assessing the effectiveness of aid one must know what it was supposed to accomplish. Packenham's observation that "the magnitude of manageable influence wielded by the U.S. government through its aid programs on Third World economic development has probably been marginal in most cases most of the time" seems to be a pessimistic assessment of the efficacy of foreign aid—at least in the context of Packenham's discussion.[92] If, however, American foreign aid was never intended to play more than a marginal role in promoting economic development in poor countries, Packenham's conclusion could be read as a ringing endorsement of the efficacy of the foreign aid instrument. In judging the effectiveness of an influence attempt, it is well to ask precisely what goals policy makers were seeking to approximate. If marginal influence is all that was sought, then the influence attempt should be judged in that light.

4. *American policy makers were naive about the efficacy of foreign aid and the ease of promoting Third World development.*

The American system of separation of powers and democracy provides an incentive for policy makers to exaggerate the potential benefits of a proposed policy and to downplay its potential costs. Thus, political rhetoric must usually be discounted somewhat in order to get an accurate picture of how policy makers really assess a given policy. Despite the systemic incentives to exaggerate benefits and downplay costs, American foreign policy makers have usually been remarkably restrained in describing the benefits likely to accrue from foreign aid and remarkably frank about the costs. Despite their candor, they have frequently been accused of pedaling a host of assumptions that hindsight readily reveals as having been exceedingly naive.

The most systematic allegation of naivete has been developed by Packenham, who charges policy makers with exaggerating the speed and ease with which economic development could be achieved and both the prob-

---

[92] Packenham, *Liberal America*, p. 182.

ability and desirability of the political effects likely to follow from such development. Indeed, a major part of Packenham's overall argument turns on the validity of the allegation that American policy makers accepted the assumption that "change and development are easy," which he traces to the "liberal tradition in America."[93]

With some writers it is difficult to tell whether a particular naive belief is being attributed to policy makers or to more general "schools of thought" about foreign aid. Edward C. Banfield, for example, asserts the existence of "a widely accepted doctrine" that views "democracy and peace" as following "automatically" from rapid economic development. He also maintains that "American aid doctrine certainly exaggerates greatly the importance of both technical assistance and foreign capital in the development process."[94] George Liska joins Banfield in criticizing those who "assert necessary connections between foreign aid, economic development, and this or that political order, economic order, and international order."[95]

These charges are typical of such allegations in that specific citations are rarely used to support them. Vague references to "widely supported doctrines," "schools of thought," and other unnamed persons are the order of the day. Examination of the historical record with respect to both the statements by policy makers (and policy advisors) and the evidence of aid failure is worthwhile.

One of the most—if not the most—important objectives of postwar American foreign policy, including American foreign aid programs, has been to limit the expansion of communist, especially Soviet, influence. If the sphere of communist influence has increased significantly since 1950, this would constitute impressive evidence of the failure of foreign aid. Writing in 1973, Packenham admits that "the one political development goal of the aid program that was substantially realized in the Third World

[93] Ibid., pp. 3-123, 174-183.

[94] *American Aid Doctrines*, pp. 4-5, 11. Banfield adds that "only in the most backward countries can either kind of aid make a crucial difference, or perhaps even an important one" (p. 11). This illustrates the importance of relating judgments about efficacy to the amount of aid provided. If there are no limits on the size of aid, Banfield's statement is surely false. Banfield explicitly denies this in observing that "if cultural conditions do not favor development, no amount of aid will bring it about." He notes that Cuba and Haiti "have received large amounts of both technical assistance and foreign capital without development taking place" (p. 10). The statement about cultural conditions and development is either a truism or a falsehood. Although it is true that Haiti has received large amounts of aid compared to other countries, there are no grounds whatever for concluding that Haiti's level of development could not be dramatically increased by a hundredfold (thousandfold?) increase in the aid level. Banfield's reference to Cuba is baffling. At the time he was writing, it had received relatively little aid and had the fourth highest GNP per capita in Latin America. (Rosenstein-Rodan, "International Aid," p. 126).

[95] Liska, *New Statecraft*, p. 6.

was the anti-communist one,''[96] which, considering the importance of this goal, is a significant admission. Has the situation changed since 1973? Even the most generous interpretation of "communist influence" does not reveal significant change in the size of the communist sphere. Counting such countries as Cuba, Vietnam, Angola, Mozambique, South Yemen, Ethiopia, Afghanistan, Benin, Congo, Madagascar, Guyana, and Nicaragua, in addition to Eastern Europe, China, Mongolia, and North Korea, the percentage of the world's population living in "communist" countries increased only from 33 percent in 1950 to 39 percent in 1979. In terms of voting members of the United Nations, "communist" states declined from 23 percent in 1950 to 17 percent in 1979.[97] While one cannot necessarily attribute this result to foreign aid—or to any other American technique of statecraft—there does not seem to be much evidence that containment has failed.

A similar conclusion is warranted with respect to the goal of promoting economic development in Asia, Latin America, and Africa. As was noted earlier, the economic growth rates—in terms of both GNP and GNP per capita—in less developed countries between 1950 and 1980 have exceeded most of the expectations and projections of the 1950s and 1960s. Never before have so many people experienced so much economic growth in so short a time span. By any reasonable set of criteria, this growth must be judged as impressive. Some would say that this growth occurred *despite* aid, while others would say that it occurred *because* of aid;[98] but either way the historical record does not provide convincing evidence that aid *failed* to spark economic development.

Have American policy makers tended to portray development as easy, to make exaggerated claims about the efficacy of foreign aid, and to view democracy and peace as an automatic consequence of rapid economic development? If so, it is difficult to document from the public record. As early as 1945 President Roosevelt made it abundantly clear that he considered economic development a domestic matter: "The main job of restoration is not one of relief," he emphasized, "it is one of reconstruction

---

[96] Packenham, *Liberal America*, p. 16. See also pp. 183-184.

[97] Including three votes for the Soviet Union. K. J. Holsti's contention that "foreign aid has not accomplished many of the political purposes for which it was originally designed" is puzzling. He observes that "in the early days of the cold war, many assumed that aid could 'buy' allies, or at least keep them from joining the opposite camp" (*International Politics* 4th ed., pp. 237-238). I have never found an instance of a policy maker stating that allies could be "bought" with aid. The evidence suggests that not many aid recipients have joined "the opposite camp."

[98] For a review of the debate over the causal relationship between aid and growth, see Michael Lipton, "Aid Allocation When Aid is Inadequate: Problems of the Non-Implementation of the Pearson Report," in *Foreign Resources and Economic Development*, ed. T. J. Byres (London: Frank Cass, 1972), pp. 155-182.

which must be largely done by local people and their governments. They will provide the labor, the local money, and most of the materials. The same is true for all the many plans for the improvement of transportation, agriculture, industry, and housing, that are essential to the development of the economically backward areas of the world."[99] In 1949 Secretary of State Dean Acheson declared that "material well-being is no guaranty that democracy will flourish" and noted that "loans of public funds . . . can only be supplementary to the efforts of private capital."[100] In 1950 a report to the president warned that "the process of stimulating development is more complicated and slow than that of assisting recovery in developed countries" and that "obstacles to an acceleration of development, even with outside assistance, are substantial."[101] A similar report in 1951 depicted the needs of the underdeveloped areas as "truly staggering."[102] In 1953 a State Department official observed that it would be "quite unrealistic" to "expect 100 percent success in the sense that all nations aided directly or indirectly by the United States will adopt our brand of politics or economics, or will agree with us in the United Nations or elsewhere" and pointed out that "even the most skillful actions cannot guarantee that those areas will stay on our side."[103] In 1957 President Eisenhower stated that he knew "of no precise relation between economic well-being and responsible political development."[104] And in the same year Secretary of State Dulles insisted that American aid could not "be more than a marginal addition to any country's development efforts."[105] A report to the president in 1957 declared that "we are under no illusion that economic development is a panacea. On the contrary, we know that economic growth will create many problems in the countries undergoing the process."[106] And the report of the Senate Special Committee to Study the Foreign Aid Program in the same year stated its belief that "there are severe limits on the extent to which foreign aid can be used to influence either short-range or long-range developments elsewhere."[107] In 1959 another report for the president,

[99] Cited in Baldwin, *Economic Development*, p. 16.

[100] "Waging Peace in the Americas," *Department of State Bulletin*, September 26, 1949, pp. 464-465. See also Baldwin, *Economic Development*, p. 76.

[101] Gordon Gray, *Report to the President on Foreign Economic Policies* (Washington: G.P.O., 1950), pp. 12, 57.

[102] International Development Advisory Board, *Partners in Progress*, A Report to the President, March 1951, pp. 63-64.

[103] Robert E. Asher, "The Economics of U.S. Foreign Policy," *Department of State Bulletin*, July 6, 1953, p. 8. See also Baldwin, *Economic Development*, pp. 73-74.

[104] Quoted in Baldwin, *Economic Development*, p. 118.

[105] Quoted in ibid., pp. 119-120.

[106] International Development Advisory Board, *A New Emphasis on Economic Development Abroad: A Report to the President of the United States on Ways, Means and Reasons for U.S. Assistance to International Development*, March 1957, p. 8.

[107] U.S. Senate, Special Committee to Study the Foreign Aid Program, *Foreign Aid*, report no. 300, 85th Cong., 1st sess., 1957, p. 9.

popularly known as the "Draper Report," observed that "there is no more difficult administrative undertaking in the United States Government than that posed by the management of the various economic assistance programs and the necessity for assuring their conformity to foreign policy objectives."[108] In his last State of the Union Address President Eisenhower gave the following analysis of the situation:

> All of us must realize, of course, that development in freedom by the newly emerging nations is no mere matter of obtaining outside financial assistance. An indispensable element in this process is a strong and continuing determination on the part of these nations to exercise the national discipline necessary for any sustained development period. These qualities of determination are particularly essential because of the fact that the process of improvement will necessarily be gradual and laborious rather than revolutionary. Moreover, everyone should be aware that the development process is no short-term phenomenon. Many years are required for even the most favorably situated countries.[109]

A month after this presidential statement on the difficulties of economic growth, a State Department spokesman addressed the relationship between economic growth and political developments as follows:

> It takes no special act of imagination or sympathy to grasp the human meaning of economic growth, to appreciate the tyranny that poverty and disease can exercise over man. But the relationship of economic growth to political developments is less direct and obvious. Political developments have a momentum of their own, and it would be unduly optimistic to believe that just so long as our aid is large and our trade free all will be well, or just so long as the less developed countries achieve an increase in income of 2 percent or 4 percent or 6 percent a year they will establish and maintain democratic governments and respect for international law. The relationship of economic growth to political development is not so simple as that.[110]

Spokesmen for the Kennedy administration also pointed out the complicated nature of the development process and the limited impact that aid could be expected to have. Chester Bowles, often depicted as one of the more "naive" members of the Kennedy administration, pointed out that "the process of nation building is inevitably long and tedious and that

[108] *Composite Report of the President's Committee to Study the United States Military Assistance Program*, vol. 1, August 17, 1959, p. 98.

[109] "The State of the Union," address reprinted in *Department of State Bulletin*, January 25, 1960, p. 113.

[110] Edwin M. Martin, "Aspects of U.S. Foreign Economic Policy," *Department of State Bulletin*, February 22, 1960, p. 341.

dramatic results cannot be achieved quickly." "Ten years of experience,"
he noted, "have now taught us that economic development is necessarily
linked to social development, that both are incredibly complex, and that
indigenous built-in factors over which we have no control may profoundly
affect the result." Far from portraying political development as following
automatically from economic development, Bowles explicitly denied that
"economic growth by itself" would achieve free, independent, stable,
peaceful, or happy societies.[111] And Secretary of State Dean Rusk emphasized that economic development was fundamentally a function of
domestic effort, noting that "the aid we can supply will be only a small
portion of the total national effort needed."[112]

The examples in the previous paragraph do not constitute the historical
record, of course; and contravening examples may exist. Those who charge
American officials with naivete, however, rarely cite such specific examples. No instance of an American foreign policy maker stating publicly
and explicitly that economic development is easy, that foreign aid can be
expected to have a massive impact, or that stable, democratic, and peaceful
societies will necessarily be the result of economic growth has ever come
to this writer's attention. Although such statements may exist, the examples
cited above are indicative of the more common tendency to stress the
enormous difficulties, the marginal impact of aid, and the uncertain political
ramifications of economic growth. Interestingly enough, this evidence corresponds with Packenham's findings in interviews with aid officials in
1962–1963. He notes that they "repeatedly stressed the marginality of
American influence on world affairs generally and particularly on internal
change in recipient countries. They stated that it is hard to bring about
economic development and even harder to effect social and political development."[113] Although such evidence would seem to call into question
Packenham's assertion that aid officials believed development was easy,
he sees it as confirming his position since in saying they had "learned"
that development was hard, aid officials were implicitly admitting that they
had previously thought it was easy. Although Packenham may well be
correct, his argument would be more persuasive if there were some independent evidence to support it. Packenham also notes that the American
doctrine that development was a matter of self help "seems to rebut" his
thesis; but once again he saves the hypothesis by asserting that "*verbal
affirmations of the principle of self-help would be more convincing if the*

---

[111] Chester Bowles, "Basic Principles of Foreign Aid," *Department of State Bulletin*,
August 6, 1962, pp. 207-209.

[112] Dean Rusk, "The Foreign Aid Program for Fiscal Year 1963," *Department of State
Bulletin*, April 23, 1962, p. 659.

[113] *Liberal America*, p. 120. See also Packenham, "Political-Development Doctrines in
the American Foreign Aid Program," *World Politics* XVIII (January 1966):227-229.

principle were not so often violated in practice."[114] This interpretation, however, overlooks the primary manifestation of the self-help principle in American policy—i.e., the small size of the American aid program relative either to the size of the problem or to American capacity to provide aid.[115]

The study by Millikan and Rostow in the 1950s received so much public attention that it is sometimes treated as reflective of American aid doctrine.[116] Packenham describes this as "perhaps the best known and probably the most influential" of a series of "government-commissioned studies and research reports on the aid program in 1956 and 1957." He asserts that Millikan and Rostow "explicitly predicted that stable, democratic, and effective governments would result from the economic development which . . . aid would presumably promote."[117] Packenham does not cite a specific passage to support this contention, and it is not clear to which version of the report he is referring.[118] In any case, I have found no passage in either source that would support Packenham's contention. There are, however, several passages explicitly disavowing the view that development is easy and that the political consequences are either automatic or desirable. Consider the following examples:

> It cannot be too strongly emphasized that this program is only one of many instruments which must be used in a co-ordinated way if we are to maximize our influence to promote the development of stable, effective, and democratic societies elsewhere in the world. . . . Economic policy by itself will not achieve the desired result.[119]

> None of the above effects is an automatic consequence of aid or of growth in the level of output. Nor do any of the effects necessarily associate with stability. Political and social change inevitably involve

[114] *Liberal America*, p. 122. Italics in original.

[115] On this point, see Baldwin, *Economic Development*, pp. 16-24, 75-85, 119-134, 192-207, 247-250.

[116] See Ohlin, *Foreign Aid Policies Reconsidered*, p. 18.

[117] *Liberal America*, pp. 56-57.

[118] Although Packenham refers to the government-commissioned study by the Center for International Studies at MIT, he cites only Millikan and Rostow, *A Proposal*, describing it as a "revised version of the MIT study" (p. 57n). Actually, the reverse is true; although both were published in 1957, the preface to *A Proposal* is dated August 27, 1956, while the government contract with MIT was not signed until October 1956. As is true of most "revised versions," the MIT study is more highly qualified and tightly argued than the more widely cited earlier version. See Massachusetts Institute of Technology, Center for International Studies, "The Objectives of United States Economic Assistance Programs," *Foreign Aid Program: Compilation of Studies and Surveys*, prepared under the direction of the Special Committee to Study the Foreign Aid Program, 85th Cong., 1st sess., 1957, Senate Doc. No. 52, pp. 1-73. Cited hereafter as *MIT Study*.

[119] Millikan and Rostow, *A Proposal*, p. 7.

turbulence. . . . [Our] influence is limited and success hardly certain. . . .[120]

The primary objective of economic aid programs as envisaged in this report is the preservation and strengthening of free democratic institutions through holding up the prospect of economic betterment. It is recognized that at certain very low levels of income an improvement in the level of living may be accompanied by political unrest on the part of people who had previously been too close to the margin of subsistence to have the energy for political agitation. It is also true in some circumstances that initial improvement in standards of living brings about an increase in the appetite for further improvement which cannot quickly be satisfied and so is accompanied by unrest. Finally, it may happen that social and political institutions blocking economic development are destroyed without the creation of new institutions which effectively harness the social energy; where this happens, the society may be particularly responsive to demogogic appeals of a nationalist or Communist nature. The correlation between levels of living and free institutions is therefore by no means one for one.[121]

The tasks of fostering self-sustaining growth are difficult and complex.[122]

The closest that Millikan and Rostow come to asserting something like the view Packenham attributes to them is in stating "that American assistance and consequent economic growth can be made to lead to politically mature and stable democratic societies."[123] Even out of context there is a significant difference between saying economic aid "can" lead to stable democratic societies and saying that it "would" have such results. In context, the statement is qualified in a number of additional ways. The section elaborating the above statement specifically notes that "given the unsettling effects on institutions and habit patterns of economic development efforts, a little extra food in the stomach can hardly be expected to insure stable and harmonious political development."[124]

It should also be noted—but seldom is—that the whole MIT argument was qualified by the assertion of five essential conditions that would affect the success of their recommendations. They were as follows:[125]

[120] *MIT Study*, p. 23.
[121] Ibid., p. 68.
[122] Ibid., p. 38.
[123] Ibid., p. 20.
[124] Ibid., pp. 20-21.
[125] Ibid., p. 3. Cf. pp. 70-71.

(1) The United States must make it clear that its aid program will continue for a number of years and will not be affected by fluctuations in the international or the domestic political climate.

Comment: The heart of the matter here was whether aid could be freed from the annual cycle of congressional authorizations and appropriations. This was the single most important part of their argument, and both the Eisenhower and Kennedy administrations suffered defeats in trying to satisfy this condition.

(2) If our aid program is to be effective, it must stand ready to provide sufficient additional resources to launch the underdeveloped countries into self-sustaining growth.

Comment: This implied large increases in U.S. aid levels. Opinions may differ, of course, as to what constitutes a large increase; but aid levels actually decreased as a percentage of GNP after 1957, and absolute increases in aid levels were small.

(3) A development program should concentrate on promoting economic growth, not attempt to serve other peripheral objectives.

Comment: This recommendation that political and/or military considerations be divorced from economic aid allocation decisions was implemented in form but not in practice. Short-term military and political considerations continued to play a role in American aid allocations.

(4) International cooperation in channeling aid to underdeveloped countries will increase its effectiveness.

Comment: This recommendation referred to channeling American aid through international organizations, perhaps even with Soviet participation. The great bulk of American aid, however, continued to be bilateral.

(5) If the rationale for development assistance outlined in this paper is valid for one underdeveloped country in the free world, it is valid for all.[126]

Comment: The idea of making no political or military distinctions among aid recipients was not well received by American foreign policy makers and was never implemented to any significant degree.

In sum, none of the five essential conditions for success of the MIT approach was ever incorporated into American policy to any great extent. Later shortcomings of American foreign aid policy cannot fairly be blamed on the MIT study.

[126] Although the previous four conditions are from p. 3, this one is more clearly stated on p. 71.

Citing examples of American policy makers explicitly disavowing the idea that change and development are easy may raise questions about Packenham's line of argument, but it does not constitute a direct rebuttal of his position, since he argues that such beliefs were the implicit and inarticulate premises underlying American aid policies. It is possible, of course, that policy makers were articulating one set of assumptions while acting on the basis of another set. If the assumptions Packenham attributes to American policy makers were the only ones consistent with the policies actually formulated, Packenham's argument would be greatly strengthened. If, however, an alternative set of equally plausible premises can be identified, his argument is less persuasive. The premises listed below are just as plausible as those suggested by Packenham, just as consistent with actual American policy, and *more* consistent with the explicit statements by policy makers:

(1) *Emergence of the Third World is in the long run an important change in the international system.*

Comment: Although one could argue that American policy makers did not give enough attention to this emerging trend or that they failed to anticipate its precise nature, the assumption that the emergence of the Third World was a matter of no great significance in either the short or long run would probably have been an even more naive assumption than that adopted by the policy makers.

(2) *First impressions matter; the response of the United States to these emergent countries in the early stages of their independence is likely to create an image of the United States that could be difficult to change.*

Comment: Of course, those who do not think images matter would see this as naive. Would it have been more desirable to project an image of the United States as indifferent to the problem of Third World development or as a country that believes that military force is the only thing that matters?

(3) *The status quo is not viable in most Third World states in the long run.*

Comment: Time and again, American foreign policy makers referred to the high probability of social turbulence and political change in the Third World as a result of strong nationalistic forces and the aptly labeled "revolution of rising expectations." American foreign aid policy during the 1950s and early 1960s was based more on the realistic assumption that powerful forces of change were going to reshape the social and political order in the Third World *no matter what the United States did* than on the naive and unrealistic assumption that the status quo was viable so long as the United States refrained from inevitably disruptive aid programs.

(4) *Economic change and political change are related.*

Comment: Of course it would be presumptuous to claim precise knowledge of the nature of the relationship between the political and economic orders, but this was rarely, if ever, done by American policy makers. No matter how unsatisfactory one finds this vague and general assumption to be, it is surely preferable to the unrealistic assumption that politics and economics have little or nothing to do with one another.

(5) *Fundamental changes in the international environment have implications for the utility of various techniques of statecraft.*
Comment: Both military force and diplomacy continued as important techniques of statecraft after World War II, but it became increasingly apparent that they were not enough. The revolution in military technology, especially—but not only—the development of nuclear weaponry, increased the risks of military statecraft. The revolution in the technology of communication and transportation increased interaction among different societies and made the disparity of living standards obvious to many who had been oblivious to it. The process of decolonization gave rise to hopes for rapid improvement in material well-being in Asia and Africa. Mass participation in the political process meant that secret diplomatic agreements were not likely to be as useful as they were in the seventeenth and eighteenth centuries. These changes increased the importance of the economic and psychological dimensions of international politics, thus encouraging more reliance on economic statecraft and propaganda. In a world fraught with revolutionary change, the naive and unrealistic approach would have been to assume that such changes had no implications for statecraft and that diplomacy and military force could be relied upon to deal with any and all problems.[127]

With the benefit of hindsight, it is all too easy to berate foreign policy makers for not being more prescient or for not recognizing changed circumstances sooner; but it is also important to give policy makers credit when they reject even less defensible approaches. The working assumptions of American policy makers with respect to the emergence of the Third World, the prospects for change and stability in poor countries, and the utility of various techniques of statecraft for dealing with these matters could no doubt have been improved upon; but it is well to remember that they could also have been much less realistic than they were. Given the large number of revolutionary changes that have occurred in the postwar international environment, the surprising thing is not the naivete of American policy makers but rather the degree to which they were able to recognize and adapt to so many of these changes. In any case, it is not necessary to assume that policy makers believed that change and development were easy in order to explain American foreign aid policy in the 1950s and 1960s.

[127] For further discussion of the premises underlying American aid policy in the 1950s and 1960s, see Baldwin, *Economic Development and American Foreign Policy.*

CHAPTER 11

THE LEGALITY AND MORALITY OF ECONOMIC STATECRAFT

The will to escape the anarchical consequences of power politics is one thing, the dream that somehow power can be abolished from that area of human life denoted as politics, is quite another. The control of power, that is of men's ability to act, whether by law or morality, is still a function of power in the same sense, as well as of ethics; just as power itself is in important part a function of the ethical convictions of those who act and of those affected by the action. . . . [We] should resist the fashion, modelled on the dream work of our own age, of assuming that the operations of power for good or ill can be abolished by drafting the constitution of a world security organisation. Philosophically speaking, the concept of power is ethically neutral, and it remains in any kind of society a basic principle of social cohesion.[1]

According to Klaus Knorr, "there are no international norms prohibiting monopolist profiteering, just as there are none prohibiting other exercises of economic power."[2] Not everyone would agree, however; questions about which norms are relevant to which forms of economic statecraft have been a continuing source of international controversy since the Second World War. Are strings on foreign aid illegal or immoral intervention in the recipient state? Can aid be given without intervening? Are rich states morally obligated to give aid to poor states? Was the Arab oil embargo legal? Did the United States commit "economic aggression" when it eliminated the subsidy to Cuban sugar prices? Can one state legally or morally apply economic pressure to another state? These questions and others like them have been debated frequently, and no generally accepted answers have yet emerged. This chapter will certainly not settle these

---

[1] Julius Stone, *Aggression and World Order* (Berkeley: University of California Press, 1958), p. 105.

[2] *Power of Nations*, p. 101.

questions, but rather will attempt to clarify some of the issues with respect to both legal and moral norms.

INTERNATIONAL LAW AND ECONOMIC STATECRAFT

In considering the legality of economic statecraft, it is useful to distinguish questions about what the law is from questions about what it ought to be. These two sets of questions will be considered in turn.

What Is the Law?

International law with respect to economic techniques of statecraft is murky. Traditional international law has treated the regulation of foreign trade as one of the "sovereign prerogatives of an independent country"; therefore, in the absence of treaty obligations, states have been free to use trade to pursue a wide variety of foreign policy goals.[3] With respect to the settlement of international differences, traditional international law divided techniques of statecraft into amicable and nonamicable (or compulsive) means of settlement. The former group included negotiation, mediation, conciliation, arbitration, and adjudication; the latter group included such measures as severing diplomatic relations, embargoes, boycotts, "pacific blockades," and war.[4] Because determination of the existence of a legal state of war was very important in traditional international law, an attempt was made to draw a clear distinction between war itself and "measures short of war," such as embargoes, boycotts, and so on. The effort to clarify the legal principles governing the use of "measures short of war," however, was not very successful. Such principles never became well recognized or well established in the traditional law or practice of international relations.[5] The strong legal prohibitions on the use of military force as an instrument of statecraft embodied in the United Nations Charter have made formal states of war almost unknown in the postwar world. This state of affairs

[3] J. Dapray Muir, "The Boycott in International Law," in *Economic Coercion and the New International Economic Order*, ed. Richard B. Lillich (Charlottesville, Va.: Michie, 1976), pp. 22-23, 26; H. Lauterpacht, "Boycott in International Relations," *British Yearbook of International Law* XIV (1933):130; Clyde Eagleton, *International Government*, rev. ed. (New York: Ronald Press, 1948), pp. 90-91; and Charles Cheney Hyde and Louis B. Wehle, "The Boycott in Foreign Affairs," *American Journal of International Law* XXVII (January 1933):2, 4.

[4] L. Oppenheim, *International Law: A Treatise*, 7th ed., vol. 2, ed. H. Lauterpacht (London: Longmans, Green, 1952), pp. 3-176; Julius Stone, *Legal Controls of International Conflict* (New York: Rinehart, 1954), pp. 67-293; and Albert E. Hindmarsh, *Force in Peace* (Cambridge: Harvard University Press, 1933).

[5] Stone, *Legal Controls*, p. 285; and Charles G. Fenwick, *International Law*, 4th ed. (New York: Appleton-Century-Crofts, 1965), p. 634.

has virtually eliminated the rationale for formulating clear rules with respect to "measures short of war"; indeed, it could be argued that this category has little or no significance in terms of the United Nations Charter. The Charter bans the use of "force" in most instances and encourages the settlement of international differences by "peaceful means"; but there is no mention of the middle ground of "measures short of war." Thus, some writers view such measures as "forceful means," and therefore subject to the prohibitions on the use of force, while other writers view them as "peaceful means" and permissible under the Charter.[6]

The period since 1945 has been marked by controversy with respect to the legal status of economic statecraft. In general two schools of thought, one seeking to inhibit (and perhaps prohibit) the use of economic techniques of statecraft and the other seeking to defend such techniques, are identifiable. The first position tends to be supported by the Soviet Union and Third World states, while the second position tends to be supported by Western states, especially the United States and Great Britain. Writers who agree on little else often concur that the legal situation is unclear and that drawing a line between permissible and impermissible forms of economic statecraft is exceedingly difficult.[7] In the following discussion these two contending approaches will be examined with reference to the United Nations Charter, the Charter of the Organization of American States, and the General Agreement on Tariffs and Trade (GATT). It would be highly misleading to label one of these approaches as "modern," "contemporary," or "progressive," while depicting the other as "old-fashioned," "traditional," or "regressive." The debate is about what contemporary international law is and/or should be.

Both schools of thought agree that economic sanctions may be authorized

[6] See, for example, Charles de Visscher, *Theory and Reality in Public International Law*, trans P. E. Corbett (Princeton: Princeton University Press, 1957), p. 289; Stone, *Legal Controls*, pp. 286-288; Fenwick, *International Law*, p. 634; McDougal and Feliciano, *Law and Minimum World Public Order*, pp. 142-143; and Wolfgang Friedmann, *The Changing Structure of International Law* (New York: Columbia University Press, 1964), pp. 253-274. It should be noted that "embargo" in traditional international law usually referred to the forcible retention of vessels belonging to the target state. Such usage, as Stone points out, is "more or less a relic of the past" (p. 291).

[7] See, for example: Paul A. Shneyer and Virginia Barta, "The Legality of the U.S. Economic Blockade Under International Law," *Case Western Reserve Journal of International Law* XIII (Summer 1981):455; Werner Levi, *Law and Politics in the International Society* (Beverly Hills, Calif.: Sage, 1976), p. 79; Lee C. Buchheit, "The Use of Nonviolent Coercion: A Study in Legality Under Article 2(4) of the Charter of the United Nations," in *Economic Coercion and the New International Economic Order*, ed. Richard B. Lillich (Charlottesville, Va.: Michie, 1976), p. 67; James A. Boorman III, "Economic Coercion in International Law: The Arab Oil Weapon and the Ensuing Juridical Issues," in *Economic Coercion and the New International Economic Order*, pp. 280-281; and Georg Schwarzenberger, *Economic World Order?* (Dobbs Ferry, N.Y.: Oceana, 1970), pp. 68-69.

by the United Nations itself. Article 41 of the Charter specifically mentions such measures as among those available to the Security Council. Most of the disagreement focuses on Charter provisions concerning aggression, force, intervention, and peaceful settlement.

AGGRESSION

Although aggression is usually thought of in a military context, considerable pressure has been exerted to expand the definition to include "indirect" aggression through economic measures.[8] The Soviet Union and various Third World countries have led this effort. The primary rationale for broadening the concept of aggression is the assertion that the coercive *effects* of economic statecraft can be as intense as those produced by armed force. As one observer put it:

> The problem is really that of the intensity of coercion mounted by one State against another; and that, while armed force will normally be the most intense form of coercion, and the only form justifying armed response, other forms of coercion, such as economic coercion, could be so intense that, if they were unlawfully applied, they could amount to aggression.[9]

Opposition to expanding the concept of aggression came mainly from Western states, who argued that this not only was a tortured interpretation of the United Nations Charter but also might "weaken the whole concept of aggression" with respect to the primary goal of limiting the use of armed force.[10]

The question of "economic aggression" seems to have been defused, at least for the time being, by agreement in 1974 on a resolution by the United Nations General Assembly defining aggression in terms of the use of "armed force."[11] There was a certain irony, of course, in the timing of this resolution to coincide with the Arab oil embargo. At least one writer has argued that Western statesmen committed a major strategic blunder in sticking to their traditional opposition to the concept of "economic aggression" in the changed circumstances of the 1970s.[12]

[8] See Stone, *Aggression and World Order; Conflict Through Consensus: United Nations Approaches to Aggression* (Baltimore: Johns Hopkins Press, 1977), pp. 87-104; Boorman, "Economic Coercion," pp. 269-279; and Buchheit, "Nonviolent Coercion," pp. 58-61.

[9] S. M. Schwebel, "Aggression, Intervention and Self-Defense in Modern International Law," *Recueil des Cours* (1972-II), pp. 451-452. See also McDougal and Feliciano, *Law,* pp. 194-202.

[10] Stone, *Aggression,* p. 59.

[11] United Nations, General Assembly, 29th Session, December 14, 1974, Resolution 3314, "Definition of Aggression" (A/9631).

[12] Stone, *Conflict Through Consensus,* pp. 101-102.

FORCE

The United Nations Charter, Article 2(4), proscribes the "threat or use of force against the territorial integrity or political independence of any state, or in any manner inconsistent with the Purposes of the United Nations." Does "force" in this context refer only to military force or does it subsume other techniques of statecraft, such as economic measures? The case for interpreting Article 2(4) to apply to nonmilitary policy instruments rests on two kinds of arguments. First, since the Charter explicitly refers to "armed force" elsewhere, it is argued that the absence of a modifier indicates that "force" in Article 2(4) was intended to allow for nonmilitary modes of coercion. The moderate form of this argument usually asserts that "examination of the language and historical background of article 2(4) provides no clear indication of its intended meaning,"[13] thus implying that it is as reasonable to read it one way as another. Once it has been established that Article 2(4) is vague, the way is cleared for arguing that subsequent resolutions passed by the General Assembly provide "clarification" of this allegedly ambiguous section of the Charter. (Some writers, however, go beyond merely asserting the reasonableness of a broad interpretation of Article 2(4) and dismiss the view that it was intended to refer only to armed force as a "myopic and restrictive approach to the regulation of coercion."[14]) The second line of argument used to support a broad interpretation of Article 2(4) points to other international documents that are presumed to be indicative of the attitude of the international community toward the permissible uses of economic coercion.[15] Although such documents do not usually refer directly to Article 2(4), they make it clear that some, if not all, forms of economic coercion are impermissible.[16]

Despite such arguments, most writers agree that Article 2(4) was intended to apply to armed force and does not apply to economic pressure.[17]

[13] Buchheit, "Nonviolent Coercion," p. 68. See also McDougal and Feliciano, Law, pp. 124-125.

[14] Jordan J. Paust and Albert P. Blaustein, "The Arab Oil Weapon—A Threat To International Peace," in Economic Coercion and the New International Economic Order, pp. 128-132.

[15] Documents commonly cited include the following: The Charter of the Organization of American States (OAS); United Nations, General Assembly, 20th Session, December 21, 1965, Resolution 2131, "Declaration on the Admissability of Intervention into the Domestic Affairs of States" (A/6014); and United Nations, General Assembly, 25th Session, October 24, 1970, Resolution 2625, "Declaration on Principles of International Law Concerning Friendly Relations and Cooperation Among States in Accordance with the Charter of the United Nations" (A/8028). For further references see Lillich, Economic Coercion, pp. 369-376.

[16] Cf. Paust and Blaustein, "Arab Oil Weapon," pp. 130-132; and Buchheit, "Nonviolent Coercion," pp. 57-63.

[17] Oppenheim, International Law, vol. 2, p. 153; Derek W. Bowett, "International Law and Economic Coercion," in Economic Coercion and the New International Economic Order,

Among the arguments that may be adduced in support of this position are the following: (1) The ordinary meaning of "force" in the context of discussions of international relations refers to military statecraft. In the absence of qualifying words or phrases, the normal expectation is that a book on "force in international relations" focuses on military force.[18] (2) In the general atmosphere of San Francisco during the drafting of the Charter, military force was the predominant concern. World War II, after all, was still in progress; and any doubts as to the meaning of "force" should be resolved with this in mind. War, not economic pressure, was the problem that infused the atmosphere of the San Francisco conference. (3) The whole international organization movement in the twentieth century has been "fundamentally, even though not exclusively, a reaction to the problem of war."[19] In the absence of clear guidance, it is reasonable to interpret the United Nations Charter in terms of this primary concern with armed warfare. (4) A proposal by Brazil to include economic measures in Article 2(4) was decisively defeated at San Francisco. Thus, it cannot be argued that failure to include economic measures was an oversight; this alternative was specifically rejected. (5) Suggestions that the content of Article 2(4) can be changed by General Assembly resolutions are not persuasive. Such resolutions are merely recommendations and do not constitute binding legal obligations. Furthermore, the procedures for revising the Charter are clearly spelled out in Article 108; and any attempt to modify the meaning of Article 2(4) should use such procedures.[20] In short, both the assertion that the intended meaning of Article 2(4) is unclear and the contention that subsequent resolutions by the General Assembly have modified the meaning of this part of the Charter rest on dubious evidence and argument.

---

p. 89; Leland M. Goodrich, Edvard Hambro, and Anne Patricia Simons, *Charter of the United Nations: Commentary and Documents*, 3d and rev. ed. (New York: Columbia University Press, 1969), pp. 48-49; and Ian Brownlie, *International Law and the Use of Force* (London: Oxford University Press, 1963), p. 362.

[18] See, for example, Northedge, ed., *The Use of Force in International Relations*; and Osgood and Tucker, *Force, Order, and Justice*. Lauterpacht observed in 1933 that "the view that a boycott is an act of economic force identical or comparable with military force in the shape of war is based on a mere manner of speech" ("Boycott," p. 139).

[19] Inis L. Claude, Jr., *Swords into Plowshares*, 4th ed. (New York: Random House, 1971), pp. 215-216. On the preoccupation with war in international thought for the last twenty-five centuries, see Russell, *Theories of International Relations*.

[20] Even Richard A. Falk, who attributes "quasi-legislative" functions to the General Assembly, admits that "if Charter intent is decisive and strictly construed, it becomes impossible to attribute binding legal force to resolutions of the General Assembly or to consider that the Assembly is in any sense an active, potential, or partial legislative organ." (Richard A. Falk, *The Status of Law in International Society* [Princeton: Princeton University Press, 1970], p. 175.)

INTERVENTION

The question of whether economic statecraft is compatible with the principle of nonintervention is less clear-cut. In 1964 Wolfgang Friedmann described the rules with respect to intervention as "one of the least precise parts of international law," noting that "almost the only agreement among writers is that this term covers an area of great confusion."[21] And Talleyrand is said to have described "non-intervention" as "a metaphysical term, which means about the same as intervention."[22] This lack of consensus allows for a wide range of interpretations. On the one hand is a broad concept of intervention as any type of pressure exerted by any means among states, while on the other hand is the narrow view that only "dictatorial interference" which impairs the independence of the target state constitutes intervention.[23] Whereas the narrow view could be interpreted to apply to few, if any, forms of economic statecraft, the broad view could be applied to nearly any use of economic techniques.

The duty of states to refrain from intervening in the affairs of other states is not specifically mentioned in the United Nations Charter, but it is often inferred from such Charter "principles" as respect for "equal rights and self-determination of peoples," the "sovereign equality" of states, and respect for the personality, territorial integrity, and political independence of states.[24] In 1965 the General Assembly's "Declaration on the Admissibility of Intervention into the Domestic Affairs of States" expressed the following view of intervention:

> 1. No State has the right to intervene, directly or indirectly, for any reason whatever, in the internal or external affairs of any other state. Consequently, armed intervention and all other forms of interference or attempted threats against the personality of the state or against its political, economic and cultural elements, are condemned;
>
> 2. No state may use or encourage the use of economic, political, or any other type of measures to coerce another state in order to obtain from it the subordination of the exercise of its sovereign rights or to secure from it advantages of any kind. . . .

[21] Friedmann, *Changing Structure*, pp. 304, 267n.

[22] Quoted in Adrian Guelke, "Force, Intervention and Internal Conflict," in Northedge, ed., *The Use of Force in International Relations*, p. 101.

[23] Wolfgang Friedmann, "Intervention and International Law," in *Intervention in International Politics*, ed. Louis G. M. Jaquet (The Hague: Netherlands Institute of International Affairs, 1971), p. 40; and J. L. Brierly, *The Law of Nations*, ed. Humphrey Waldock, 6th ed. (Oxford: Oxford University Press, 1963), p. 402.

[24] See Hartmut Brosche, "The Arab Oil Embargo and United States Pressure Against Chile: Economic and Political Coercion and the Charter of the United Nations," in *Economic Coercion and the New International Economic Order*, p. 308; and Goodrich, Hambro, and Simons, *Charter*, pp. 25-40.

6. All states shall respect the right of self-determination and independence of peoples and nations, to be freely exercised without any foreign pressure. . . .

Similar wording is contained in the General Assembly's "Declaration on Principles of International Law Concerning Friendly Relations and Cooperation Among States in Accordance with the Charter of the United Nations" (1970).

If taken literally, such sweeping language prohibits any form of pressure among states. Such broad interpretations make compliance by powerful countries like the United States virtually impossible since almost any action of the United States could be viewed as interference or pressure. An increase in American domestic interest rates, for example, may reverberate throughout the international economic system, thus "interfering" with the "economic elements" in other states and exerting pressure on them. Expressing doubts as to whether such a sweeping view of intervention "comports with the realities and current necessities of contemporary international life," one writer suggests that "the appropriate course may be to take these extreme asseverations no more seriously than the Members of the United Nations demonstrate by their actions that they do."[25] Written in 1972, the wisdom of this admonition was starkly illustrated during the 1973 Arab oil embargo, which prompted the following comment by Richard Gardner:

> It was the Afro-Asian group in the United Nations, including the Arab countries, that pressed hardest for this principle and for the proposition that it was already part of international law. Of course, their motive was to prevent the United States and other industrialized countries from using economic power as an instrument of political pressure. Not a single voice has been raised in the United Nations to cite the relevance of this authoritative declaration to the Arab oil embargo—which is typical of the "double standard" that currently prevails in the world organization and accounts for much of the skepticism about the integrity of its decision-making process.[26]

If General Assembly resolutions are regarded as a source of binding legal obligations for states, the constraints on intervention are broad enough to make most forms of statecraft unlawful. If, however, this rather dubious interpretation of the General Assembly's authority is rejected and the traditional narrow view of intervention is retained, the following conclusion by Friedmann is compelling:

[25] Schwebel, "Aggression," pp. 453-454.
[26] Richard N. Gardner, "The Hard Road to World Order," *Foreign Affairs* LII (April 1974):567.

In the present state of international law, it would seem that only physical coercion, lack of legal or political freedom of decision-making, and perhaps exceptional situations where an economic emergency, such as a national famine or disease, would be exploited by the donor for the imposition of oppressive conditions, could be characterized as illegal forms of economic intervention.[27]

Friedmann's conclusion, of course, does not refer to specific treaty obligations incurred by various countries such as those associated with GATT and the OAS. The latter is especially relevant to a discussion of intervention, since much of the wording in the General Assembly resolutions on this topic is based on the following articles in the OAS Charter:

Article 18

No state or group of states has the right to intervene, directly or indirectly, for any reason whatever, in the internal or external affairs of any other state. The foregoing principle prohibits not only armed force but also any other form of interference or attempted threat against the personality of the state or against its political economic and cultural elements.

Article 19

No state may use or encourage the use of coercive measures of an economic or political character in order to force the sovereign will of another state and obtain from it advantages of any kind.[28]

Thus, the United States may dismiss the broad prohibitions on intervention contained in resolutions of the United Nations General Assembly as not legally binding; but the similar provisions of the OAS Charter cannot be so easily ignored. Treaty obligations are to be honored, but what if the treaty provisions are so broad and sweeping that compliance is impossible? Some writers have suggested that such broad prohibitions have little or no meaning, as, for example, in the following comment on Article 15 (now 18):

It is quite apparent that this provision is so broad as to be meaningless. Almost any action of a country in international affairs, particularly that of a large and powerful country like the United States, can be found under this definition to infringe upon the affairs of another country. Trade practices, immigration laws, preclusive or even negotiated purchases, general pronouncements on freedom—in short almost anything the United States does or does not do in its Latin-

[27] "Intervention and International Law," p. 55. Cf. Friedmann, *Changing Structure*, pp. 270-272.

[28] The OAS Charter was revised in 1970. These articles remained unchanged but were renumbered from 15 and 16 to 18 and 19.

American relations could, by applying the yardstick of Article 15 [now 18], be construed as intervention.[29]

In any case, the legal bases of the OAS prohibitions on intervention are quite different from those embodied in United Nations General Assembly resolutions. From this standpoint, it could be argued that the United States has less freedom to use economic statecraft in Latin America than elsewhere in the world.

PACIFIC SETTLEMENT

The United Nations Charter obligates members to "settle their international disputes by peaceful means in such a manner that international peace and security, and justice, are not endangered" (Article 2[3]). Article 33 requires "the parties to any dispute, the continuance of which is likely to endanger the maintenance of international peace and security" to "first of all, seek a resolution by negotiation, inquiry, mediation, conciliation, arbitration, judicial settlement, resort to regional agencies or arrangements, or other peaceful means of their own choice." Although arguments to the effect that economic pressure is forbidden by the Charter have focused mostly on the concepts of aggression, force, and intervention, it has occasionally been suggested that such measures are incompatible with the peaceful settlement provisions of the Charter. Indeed, some proponents of this point of view exhibit remarkable confidence, as evidenced in the following passages:

> As far as Article 2(3) and Chapter VI of the Charter are concerned, *it is beyond doubt* that *any* kind of pressure is contrary to the principle of pacific settlement of disputes.[30]
>
> They [i.e., boycotts] are . . . *unquestionably* incompatible with the duty of states, under article 2(3) of the Charter, to settle their international disputes by peaceful means. . . .[31]

These strong assertions rest on the assumption that embargoes, boycotts, and other kinds of economic pressure "are not peaceful means and not appropriate for the solution of disputes."[32]

---

[29] Richard C. Snyder and Edgar S. Furniss, *American Foreign Policy: Formulation, Principles, and Programs* (New York: Rinehart, 1954), p. 777. Compare with the comment by Lillich that the "prohibitions found in the various UN resolutions are pitched on such a high level of abstraction as to be virtually meaningless" ("Economic Coercion and the 'New International Economic Order': A Second Look at Some First Impressions," in *Economic Coercion and the New International Economic Order*, p. 112).

[30] Brosche, "Arab Oil Embargo," p. 316. Italics added.

[31] Yehuda Z. Blum, "Economic Boycotts in International Law," in *Conference on Transnational Economic Boycotts and Coercion*, ed. Roy M. Mersky, vol. 1 (Dobbs Ferry, N.Y.: Oceana, 1978), p. 99. Italics added.

[32] Brosche, "Arab Oil Embargo," p. 314.

There are, however, several grounds for questioning such an interpretation of the UN Charter. First, the assertion that economic pressure is "not appropriate for the solution of disputes" suggests that disputes cannot be settled by such measures, in other words, that coercive settlement of disputes is a paradox, perhaps even a contradiction in terms. This is a difficult position to defend. Apart from the fact that every parent knows that disputes can often be settled by compulsion, both the logic of the pacific settlement approach and traditional international law have assumed that war itself is one way to settle disputes.[33] If even war can be so considered, it is difficult to deny that milder measures, such as boycotts and embargoes, may also serve as dispute-settling mechanisms. Second, the peaceful settlement principle expressed in Article 2(3) is the logical corollary of the principle set forth in Article 2(4) that states should refrain from the "threat or use of force."[34] The logic of the Charter does not recognize three categories of means for settling disputes—e.g., peaceful, nonpeaceful measures other than force, and force. Rather, it implies that all dispute-settling means that do not involve force are to be considered peaceful. The question, then, is whether "force" as used in Article 2(4) subsumes economic pressure or not. Since it has already been argued that Article 2(4) was not intended to include economic means, it would seem that such measures are subsumed by the peaceful means referred to in Article 2(3); at least, they are not proscribed by that article.

Third, the implication that coercion or pressure cannot be peaceful is questionable. "Pacific," Inis Claude points out, "is a relative term."[35] In the context of the overriding concern with ridding the world of the "scourge of war" that marked not only the San Francisco conference but also the whole international organization movement in the preceding three decades, economic measures were regarded as a peaceful alternative to war rather than as a subcategory of war. John Foster Dulles and Sir Anton Bertram captured the mood of the interwar period in the following words:

> The great advantage of economic sanctions is that on the one hand they can be very potent, while on the other hand, they do not involve that resort to force and violence which is repugnant to our objective of peace. If any machinery can be set up to ensure that nations comply with their covenant to renounce war, such machinery must be sought primarily in the economic sphere.[36]

[33] See Claude, *Swords into Plowshares*, p. 218; Oppenheim, *International Law*, vol. 1, p. 132; Stone, *Legal Controls*, pp. 285, 293; and Hindmarsh, *Force in Peace*, p. 16.

[34] Cf. Brosche, "Arab Oil Embargo," pp. 312-313; and Goodrich, Hambro, and Simons, *Charter*, p. 41.

[35] *Swords into Plowshares*, p. 236.

[36] John Foster Dulles, "Practicable Sanctions," in *Boycotts and Peace*, ed. Clark, p. 21.

The economic weapon, conceived not as an instrument of war but as a means of peaceful pressure, is the great discovery and the most precious possession of the League. Properly organised, it means the substitution of economic pressure for actual war. . . .[37]

The dominant concern of the drafters of the UN Charter was "to save succeeding generations from the scourge of war"; it was not to save them from economic pressure; it was not to depoliticize the world; and it was not to eliminate all forms of coercion. The fact that subsequent Charter provisions refer to the "threat or use of force," "threat to peace," "breach of the peace," and "acts of aggression" did not mean that the drafters wanted to proscribe all forms of intense coercion. It meant that they wanted to prohibit war whether it was legally so defined or not. To get bogged down in the technicalities and intricacies of the Charter while losing sight of this preeminent and overriding concern with war is to obfuscate rather than clarify the meaning of the Charter. And a fourth reason to doubt the assertion that the peaceful settlement provisions of the Charter were intended to prohibit the use of embargoes, boycotts, and other means of economic pressure is that the regulation of trade had long been regarded as among the sovereign rights of an independent state. If the drafters of the Charter had intended to proscribe such an important right, it seems reasonable to assume that they would have done so in a more explicit and forthright way.

In sum, the proposition that economic pressure is incompatible with the peaceful settlement provisions of the UN Charter is highly questionable. The assertion that this proposition is "beyond doubt" is itself doubtful.

GATT

At first glance the provisions of GATT would seem to restrict severely the legal authority of GATT members to use trade to promote foreign policy objectives, at least with respect to other GATT members. The agreement contains a general prohibition on the use of import and export controls (Article XI) and forbids trade policies that discriminate between GATT members (Article I). As Gardner points out, however, the agreement is full of exceptions that "make it extremely difficult to discern any coherent guidelines for national policy." He then adds:

And, what is more to the point, all of these principles are effectively vitiated by a subsequent GATT article (XXI) which declares that nothing in the GATT shall be construed "to prevent any contracting

---

[37] Anton Bertram, "The Economic Weapon as a Form of Peaceful Pressure," *Transactions of the Grotius Society* XVII (1931):139-174.

party from taking any action which it considers necessary for the protection of its essential security interests. . . .[38]

This "security" provision would seem to provide a rather large loophole, permitting just about any kind of economic statecraft imaginable.[39]

In sum, there are very few clear-cut and generally accepted legal prohibitions on the use of economic techniques of statecraft. After surveying the legal restrictions relevant to boycotts, J. Dapray Muir came to the following conclusion:

> About all that can be said at present with respect to the status of the boycott under international law is that a number of countries and commentators have suggested that it *ought to be* prohibited by law. But there is a vast gulf between law that is and law that ought to be.[40]

More or less the same thing could be said about most other forms of economic statecraft. The thorny question of what the law should be remains to be addressed.

What Should Be the Law?

Rather than answering this question directly, the discussion that follows will focus on desirable criteria for evaluating proposed changes in international law with respect to economic statecraft.

1. *War prevention comes first*

Priority should be given to war prevention. It is possible to imagine more harm being done by a nonmilitary technique of statecraft, such as a massive and sustained oil embargo, than by a military invasion by a small army of, say, three soldiers; but such mental gymnastics must not cause us to lose sight of the fact that war is the most important problem facing mankind. The threat of sudden planetary catastrophe does not come from nonmilitary techniques of statecraft. To equate—or even to compare—economic warfare with military warfare is to risk obfuscating the fundamental need to prevent war. Not only has this need dominated the international organization process in the twentieth century, not only is this the fundamental purpose of the United Nations, it is the basic imperative of the nuclear age. Indeed, "the prevention of acts of violence," as Fenwick points out, is "the immediate and most urgent, and in that sense the primary objective of international, as of municipal law."[41]

---

[38] Gardner, "Hard Road," p. 565.

[39] Cf. Muir, "Boycott," pp. 34-38.

[40] Ibid., p. 36. Cf. Friedmann, *Changing Structure*, p. 271.

[41] Fenwick, *International Law*, p. 219. Cf. Grenville Clark and Louis B. Sohn, *World Peace Through World Law* (Cambridge: Harvard University Press, 1958), pp. xi-xii.

The purposes of the United Nations include encouraging respect for human rights, promoting international cooperation in solving economic and social problems, and developing "friendly relations among nations based on respect for the principle of equal rights and self-determination of peoples" (Article 1). The maintenance of international peace and security, however, is the primary purpose of the organization. This "question of the order of priority of purposes is of practical importance, since they are not clearly consistent with each other in all respects."[42] When one of the subsidiary purposes is in conflict with the primary purpose, the former should give way to the latter. Thus, the prime criterion for evaluating proposed legal constraints on economic statecraft should be the likely effects on international peace and security. If a legal proscription on all economic pressure would be a useful way to prevent war, it should be seriously considered; if, however, such a rule would make it harder to control war, hesitancy is in order. Of course, in making such a judgment some conception of the causes of war is implied. Much of the discussion in the United Nations and by international law commentators seems to assume that the best way—or at least one way—to prevent war is to minimize the amount of pressure or coercion in the world. This line of reasoning can be challenged on grounds of both feasibility and desirability, as will be demonstrated in discussion of the next two criteria.

2. *Feasibility is important*

An important criterion for judging any proposed change in international law is feasibility. "Law can progress," Charles de Visscher points out, "only if it does not deceive itself as to the realities it seeks to order."[43] A similar view is expressed in Arnold Toynbee's observation that "life and law must be kept closely in touch, and, as you can't adjust life to law, you must adjust law to life."[44] The question of the feasibility of proposed legal constraints on economic statecraft will be discussed with reference to coercive effects, politics, and interdependence.

Should efforts to maintain international peace and security focus on the policy instruments used or on the effects produced? The work most frequently cited by those proposing legal constraints on economic statecraft is McDougal and Feliciano's *Law and Minimum World Public Order*. In determining the lawfulness of a given action, these authors argue that "the relevance of the kinds of instruments utilized . . . is rather limited," while "the effects achieved by the employment of coercion constitute a factor of the highest relevance" (p. 196). This leads them to conclude that "a first step toward minimum public order" in the world is a prohibition on

---

[42] Goodrich, Hambro, and Simons, *Charter*, p. 26.

[43] De Visscher, *Public International Law*, p. 102.

[44] Arnold J. Toynbee, "The Lessons of History," in *Peaceful Change*, ed. C.A.W. Manning (New York: Macmillan, 1937), p. 36. Cf. Bull, *The Anarchical Society*, p. 92.

the use of "intense coercion" in most instances *regardless of the policy instrument used to produce such effects* (pp. 258-259).

Ignoring for the moment the desirability of ridding the world of all forms of intense coercion, the feasibility of such an undertaking is questionable. Grenville Clark and Louis Sohn's *World Peace Through World Law* may be viewed as utopian by some, but compared with the approach of McDougal and Feliciano, Clark and Sohn appear pragmatic, prudent, and realistic. Whereas McDougal and Feliciano want to to regulate *all* forms of intense coercion, Clark and Sohn suggest that it would be "wise for this generation to limit itself to the single task of preventing international violence or the threat of it" (p. xiii), leaving to later generations the solution of a broader range of problems. *Nonviolent* intense coercion is both prevalent and permissible in most domestic societies. It occurs in families, in businesses, churches, and schools every day. The wisdom of advocating a degree of legal regulation of intense coercion on the international level that goes beyond that in most civil societies is not self-evident. To label such a proposal as a "*first* step toward *minimum* public order" can only make one wonder what McDougal and Feliciano would regard as "the *last* step toward *maximum* public order"!

An additional line of argument suggesting the wisdom of emphasizing policy instruments rather than their coercive effects is derived from Thomas Schelling's discussion of the war limitation process.[45] Schelling argues that limits on war are likely to be more effective if they are simple rather than complex, discrete rather than continuous, qualitative rather than quantitative, and obvious rather than subtle. Schelling uses this line of reasoning to show that a distinction between nuclear and nonnuclear weapons is likely to be a more useful way to delimit permissible uses of force than distinctions in terms of motivation, usage, or effects. Analogous logic suggests that attempts to regulate war are more likely to gain general acceptance, and thus be more effective, if they focus on the instruments of statecraft rather than their effects. "No shooting" is simple; "no intense coercion" is complex. "No bombs" is discrete; "no intensive coercion" is continuous. "No soldiers" is qualitative; "no intense coercion" is quantitative. (E.g., how much intensity is too much?) "No military force" is obvious; "no intense coercion" is less so. In short, neither "intensity"— a matter of degree —nor "coercion"—a vague and subjective matter— has the kind of salience that is likely to make "intense coercion" a useful place to draw the line with respect to relations among states. Comparatively speaking, the distinction between military and nonmilitary instruments of statecraft is simpler, more discrete, less quantitative, and more obvious. Even if one were to grant the premise that all intensive coercion is bad,

---

[45] *Strategy of Conflict*, pp. 257-266.

it does not follow that the best place to draw the line is with respect to effects rather than instruments. As Ian Brownlie points out in a similar context, the jurist "must rely on concepts which can be applied successfully in practice."[46]

The proposal of McDougal and Feliciano, however, is mild relative to proposals to ban all forms of pressure and/or coercion. At least they admit that some coercion is inevitable and confine their recommendations to *intense* coercion[47] When the United Nations General Assembly solemnly declares *any* form of interstate pressure to be a violation of international law, such acts may be dismissed as mere political rhetoric; but when scholars suggest that such declarations may have some binding force, the implications are more ominous.[48] When a writer observes that a prohibition on the threat or use of any kind of political or economic pressure would be "a mere illusion and utopian ideal," one is reassured that feasibility is being considered. But when the same writer later in the same article declares that "as far as Article 2(3) and Chapter VI of the [UN] Charter are concerned, it is beyond doubt that any kind of pressure is contrary to the principle of pacific settlement of disputes,"[49] this reassurance evaporates. Power is not distributed evenly in the international system, and one can understand and sympathize with small countries' resentment of this fact. It does not follow, however, that attempts to change this state of affairs by legal fiat are feasible. As Werner Levi succinctly observes:

> It is one thing to make legal rules for the game of politics. It is quite another to legislate politics out of existence. To ban all forms of political and economic pressure from international relations is tantamount to banishing reality.[50]

Similar comments could be made about the need for international law to recognize and adjust to the fact of international interdependence. Assertions of a legal right to absolute or nearly absolute political and economic independence are simply incompatible with life in the "global village." Every nation must take the policies of other countries into account in formulating its own policies. None is free to ignore the rest of the world. If some of the more sweeping views of intervention were to be taken

[46] *International Law*, p. 436. Cf. p. 435.

[47] See pp. 127-128, 197.

[48] Bowett, "International Law," p. 90; Lillich, "Economic Coercion," pp. 111-112; Paust and Blaustein, "Arab Oil Weapon," pp. 130-131; and Brosche, "Arab Oil Embargo," p. 309.

[49] Brosche, "Arab Oil Embargo," pp. 303, 316.

[50] Levi, *Law and Politics*, p. 83. For similar comments see also Stone, *Aggression and World Order*, p. 105; Schwebel, "Aggression," pp. 453-454; and Lincoln Bloomfield, "Law, Politics and International Disputes," *International Conciliation*, no. 516 (January 1958).

literally, this state of affairs would seem to be illegal. The attempt to legislate the fact of interdependence out of existence is not only certain to fail; it is likely to undermine respect for international law in general. Attempts to bring about an international utopia by legal fiat may actually generate a reversion to the law of the jungle.[51] The disenchantment of powerful countries with the United Nations is already discernible.

3. *The desirability of pressure*

The case against attempts to abolish all forms of coercion, pressure, and politics from international relations does not rest solely on the infeasibility of such efforts. Even if it were feasible to do so, it would not be desirable. The potentially constructive role of coercion, pressure, and politics in promoting the goals expressed in the UN Charter can be elucidated in terms of the closely related problems of pacific settlement and peaceful change. Whereas the former emphasizes disputes *within* the legal order, the latter has to do with disputes *about* the legal order.[52]

Would a ban on all forms of economic pressure promote or impede the peaceful settlement of disputes? In answering this question, it is necessary to understand the basic logic of the peaceful settlement approach. The fundamental assumption of this approach is that war is a technique for settling international disputes. The problem, according to the logic of pacific settlement, "is to find, develop, institutionalize, and persuade states to use other methods for the solution of their differences. War can be eliminated only by the provision of a functional equivalent."[53] The logic of pacific settlement thus does not seek to abolish pressure, coercion, or politics, but only to channel them into nonviolent forms of statecraft. This line of reasoning implies that war is to be discouraged by encouraging alternative means of settling disputes and that a prohibition on a functional equivalent to war is likely to increase the probability of war.

Robin Renwick has pointed out that in responding to an international crisis, governments frequently find themselves considering "three broad options: (a) to do nothing; (b) to consider taking some form of military action; (c) to seek to impose economic penalties."[54] To the extent that the likely alternative to economic pressure is military pressure, it is not obvious that a legal ban on both is the most effective way to maintain or promote international peace and security. Two eminent legal scholars have argued that attempts to prohibit nonviolent means of exerting pressure may actually make resort to war more likely:

[51] Stanley Hoffmann refers to "the old Kantian notion, that when there is unfeasibility, impossibility, there can be no obligation." (*Duties Beyond Borders* [Syracuse, N.Y.: Syracuse University Press, 1981], p. 156.)

[52] Claude, *Swords into Plowshares*, pp. 222-223.

[53] Ibid., p. 218.

[54] *Economic Sanctions*, p. 1.

Neither is there a good reason for a summary condemnation of boycotts . . . on the ground that such boycotts are contrary to the idea of pacific settlement of international disputes. . . . [We] must not be misled by a juxtaposition and implicit equal condemnation of economic and military force. In a world in which physical violence through wars proper has not become a matter of the past, there is an obvious element of exaggeration in the attempts to treat a peaceful form of struggle or resistance as war. Peace, in the sense of the absence of any form of competition, friction, or struggle, is a superficial idea—both within the state and outside it. International peace does not mean absence of international friction, or rivalries, or conflicting ambitions for the realization of men's will to power. It means that competition and conflicts of interest must find a solution by means other than war in its technical legal meaning. International peace does not mean that states will not behave in their mutual relations in a foolish, unfair, or immoral manner, or that such conduct will not be visited by retaliation of a similar nature. In a community from which war in its technical sense has been eliminated and which has not reached the state of moral perfection, pacific means of pressure are unavoidable. To prohibit them would mean to court the more radical remedy of war.[55]

* * *

It can even be argued that as long as . . . [the] liberty to resort to war itself survives, it would be a disservice to international peace, and to international law, to prohibit resort to . . . lesser degrees of force [such as embargoes and boycotts]. For such prohibition may tend to drive states to seek to vindicate their claims by war, in circumstances when they might otherwise well have been content with measures less disturbing to international order.[56]

Such arguments suggest that, far from being incompatible with pacific settlement, economic pressure is one of the functional equivalents to war that this approach seeks to encourage.

Peaceful change has been described not only as one of the fundamental problems of international law, but as "probably the fundamental question of any system of law." Any legal system must provide mechanisms for "peacefully adapting the law to changed conditions." Any legal system that fails to provide such alternatives to violent change "bears in itself the germs of its own destruction. It is in itself an incentive to violence."[57] Thus, the logic of peaceful change is basically the same as that of pacific settlement: it emphasizes functional equivalents to war. The only difference

[55] Lauterpacht, "Boycott," pp. 139-140.
[56] Stone, *Legal Controls*, p. 288.
[57] H. Lauterpacht, "The Legal Aspect," in *Peaceful Change*, ed. Manning, pp. 136-137.

is that whereas in the one instance war is viewed as a way of settling disputes, in the other instance it is seen as a way of promoting international change. The logic of peaceful change could be summarized as follows: Peaceful change means alterations in the status quo; "most alterations in the status quo require some kind of pressure to bring them about"; there-fore, the "manipulation of pressure and means of coercion short of actual resort to hostilities" may be necessary in order to bring about change without war.[58] From such a perspective, economic pressure is to be wel-comed as a peaceful alternative to war rather than condemned as a means of pressure similar to war. Richard Gardner cites Cordell Hull's belief that "if goods can't cross borders, armies will" as an argument *against* eco-nomic statecraft.[59] The logic of pacific settlement and peaceful change, however, suggests the need to revise Hull's aphorism and its implications along the following lines: "In order to discourage armies from crossing borders, it is wise to provide a functional equivalent, such as economic statecraft."

International lawyers sometimes seem to view international politics as comparable to sin—a necessary evil to be tolerated only because of the lack of feasible ways to eliminate it.[60] From this standpoint the legal prohibitions on the threat or use of force in the United Nations Charter lead to the logical next step of prohibiting the use of economic pressure and from there to a ban on all forms of international pressure. Such a viewpoint implicitly denies the socially constructive role of pressure and/ or coercion in settling disputes, promoting international change, balancing contending forces, adjusting international differences, and equilibrating the international system. When de Visscher observes that "the nineteenth century was the classic age of reprisals, as of all measures of so-called pacific coercion,"[61] such as embargoes and boycotts, it is worth pondering the possibility of a connection between this fact and the following comment by Stone:

It was the series of equilibrations produced by the statecraft of nineteenth century leaders which made possible, without any major war for a century, the emergence of the modern politico-economic and technological structure of the world, and the rise to self-help and self-assertion of the great peoples of Asia and Africa. It is neither

[58] The phrases in quotation marks are from Frederick Sherwood Dunn, *Peaceful Change* (New York: Council on Foreign Relations, 1937), pp. 84, 128. Cf. Arnold Wolfers, *Discord and Collaboration* (Baltimore: Johns Hopkins Press, 1962), p. 107.

[59] "Hard Road," pp. 567-568.

[60] For incisive discussions of the tendency to denigrate politics and to idealize legal proc-esses, see Claude, *Power and International Relations*, pp. 243-271; and Bloomfield, "Law," pp. 258, 289, 303, 315.

[61] *Public International Law*, p. 287.

necessary nor possible, in order to escape from its more evil consequences, for our age to plunge into a vacuum of statecraft.[62]

The process of civilization, as Quincy Wright has pointed out, is marked
not so much by the elimination of political controversy as by a tendency
for military techniques to decrease in importance while propaganda, economic pressure, and diplomacy increase in importance in the settling of
such controversies.[63]

Law is neither the only nor the most effective way to limit violence in
social processes; "instead, politics is the device which has proved most
useful."[64] The United Nations Charter was not intended to eliminate politics from international relations and has not done so in practice. "The
greatest potential contribution of the United Nations in our time," according to Claude, lies "in helping to improve and stabilize the working
of the balance of power system. . . . The immediate task, in short, is to
make the world safe for the balance of power system, and the balance
system safe for the world."[65] It is possible that encouraging the use of
nonmilitary techniques of statecraft would be a constructive step toward
both goals.[66] Any serious proposal for a legal ban on nonmilitary techniques
of statecraft should at least address this possibility.

4.   *Legitimacy of the rule-making process*

If law is to be effective, it must flow from a process perceived to be
legitimate if not by all parties subject to it, at least by all the most powerful
parties. No one would argue that the current legal order is perfectly just
or that it is so perceived. Many contemporary states, especially in the
Third World, played little or no role in establishing this legal order. Rich
and powerful states, especially European states, formulated these rules in
ways that are no doubt biased toward their interests. History, however,
cannot be undone; reform of the international legal order must start from
the existing situation. If old rules are to be abandoned or replaced with
new rules, it is desirable that this be done through processes that are likely
to be perceived as legitimate by all the major power centers. If dissatisfied
Third World states try to use their overwhelming voting power in the United
Nations General Assembly to rewrite international law, they not only will
fail, but may well weaken respect for international law in general—a

---

[62] *Aggression and World Order*, p. 106.

[63] *A Study of War*, pp. 854-860.

[64] Claude, *Power and International Relations*, p. 265.

[65] Ibid., p. 284.

[66] There is no such thing as a completely nonviolent or nonlethal technique of statecraft.
Compared to military techniques, however, propaganda, diplomacy, and economic statecraft
are all relatively nonviolent and less likely to have lethal effects, *ceterus paribus*.

prospect unlikely to be in their own long-run best interests.[67] The best way to revise international law is through the long, hard bargaining processes used in the Law of the Sea negotiations. Such processes require patience and compromise, but they are more likely to yield enduring results than unrealistic resolutions by the General Assembly. If economic statecraft is to be legally regulated it must be done with the consent and cooperation of the world's leading economic powers.

5. *Recognition of the roles and responsibilities of powerful states*

Not every principle embodied in the UN Charter is spelled out in the Charter. One such principle is that "Great Powers," i.e., those with relatively large military capabilities, have special responsibilities for the maintenance of international peace and security. This principle, which evolved from the Concert of Europe, is reflected in both the League of Nations and the United Nations.[68] The Charter was based on recognition of the unequal distribution of power among nations and tends to reflect the power structure existing in 1945. The United Nations was not an attempt to eliminate power from interstate relations or to radically redistribute power among the members. It was primarily an attempt to harness the existing power structure so as to maintain international peace and security. From this perspective, declarations that all forms of interstate pressure are incompatible with the principles of the Charter appear rather far-fetched.

Claims that the Charter implies a prohibition on pressure arise mostly from the statement in Article 2(1) that the United Nations "is based on the principle of sovereign equality of all its Members." Small, newly independent states have seized upon this principle in order to make the United Nations the guarantor of their sovereignty and independence. "On the international plane," one writer asserts, "the principle of national sovereignty is superior to all others, and the Charter declares that it be subordinated to none."[69] Actually, the Charter neither makes nor implies any such declaration. On the contrary, the point of the Charter—indeed, the point of international law in general—is to deny the supremacy of state sovereignty as a guide for international conduct.[70] The "equality" implied by the Charter is not in terms of territory, wealth, or power; it refers to equality before the law.[71] This does not imply a prohibition on political

---

[67] On the abuse of General Assembly powers in this respect, see Gardner, "Hard Road," p. 570; Stone, *Aggression and World Order*, pp. 151-183; and *Conflict Through Consensus*, pp. 87-175.

[68] Claude, *Swords into Plowshares*, pp. 21-80, 154. Cf. Articles 23, 27, 47, 86, 108, and 110 of the UN Charter.

[69] Buchheit, "Nonviolent Coercion," p. 67.

[70] Fenwick, *International Law*, pp. 125-126, 298; Levi, *Law and Politics*, pp. 39-40; and Goodrich, Hambro, and Simons, *Charter*, pp. 37-38.

[71] Goodrich, Hambro, and Simons, *Charter*, p. 37; L. Oppenheim, *International Law*, 8th ed., vol. 1, ed. H. Lauterpacht (London: Longmans, Green & Co., 1955), pp. 23, 263, 275; and Fenwick, *International Law*, pp. 268-270.

or economic pressure in international relations, and it does not imply that states are or ought to be politically equal. The Charter does indeed pay lip service to the principle of "sovereign equality" of states, but the main purpose of the United Nations was not intended to be the glorification of national sovereignty. The primary purpose was intended to be getting the Great Powers, especially the United States, to accept responsibility for the maintenance of international peace and security.[72] In a sense, this principle is prior to and more important than the particular mechanisms for fulfilling this responsibility spelled out in the Charter.

A second fundamental principle implied, but not explicitly stated, in the Charter is recognition of the special nature of, and grave dangers associated with, conflict among Great Powers. This principle is most clearly reflected in the right of the five permanent members of the Security Council to veto decisions of that organ. "The security scheme of the Charter," observes Claude, "was conceived as an arrangement for collective action against relatively minor disturbers of the peace, in cases where the great powers were united in the desire to permit or take action."[73]

Recognition that disputes between great powers are a distinguishable category of especially dangerous interstate relations helps to clarify a potential conflict between the functions of international law and those of economic statecraft. It has been argued that "one principle function of international law is to facilitate the process of international communication, especially in periods of crisis."[74] From this perspective the attempts by Third World countries to embody prohibitions on economic statecraft in international law may be interpreted as signals to rich and powerful states. These signals are intended to tell the powerful states that Third World states resent the uneven distribution of power in the world and the intended or unintended intrusions of powerful states into what the Third World states regard as affairs that should be under their control. If the use of international law for this purpose were costless, it could be argued that such signals contribute to furthering the principles of the Charter. Unfortunately, the costs of this particular use of international law as a signaling device may be rather high. Economic statecraft is an important means by which Great Powers can signal other Great Powers about the intensity of their views on particular issues. It is a way of identifying and helping other states to identify what Great Powers regard as their vital interests. If military means of sending such signals—force and threats of force—are ruled out, it is essential to recognize the importance of providing some alternative means

---

[72] Claude, *Swords into Plowshares*, pp. 73, 77.

[73] Claude, *Power and International Relations*, p. 162. For discussion of the significance of the veto in the UN Charter, see Claude, *Power and International Relations*, pp. 156-168; and *Swords into Plowshares*, pp. 71-73, 141-162.

[74] Falk, *Status of Law*, p. 13n. Cf. William D. Coplin, "International Law and Assumptions about the State System," *World Politics* XVII (July 1965):617.

for Great Powers to say "I really mean it." The Carter grain embargo, for instance, was a way for the United States to signal the Soviet Union that further steps in Southwest Asia could generate a superpower confrontation that neither wanted. It is doubtful that diplomacy or propaganda could have been as effective in conveying such a signal. In short, superpowers exist, they have vital interests, and any military confrontation between them is likely to endanger global peace and security. Any instrument of statecraft that is helpful in avoiding superpower confrontations can thus be viewed as contributing to furtherance of the primary purpose of the United Nations—i.e., the maintenance of international peace and security. The question, then, is whether it is more important to avoid misunderstanding between Great Powers and small powers or between Great Powers and other Great Powers. Both common sense and the UN Charter suggest that the latter is the more dangerous situation and should be given priority. Thus, the international signaling function of economic statecraft may be more important than the international signaling function of international legal constraints on such measures. Recognition of this possibility, furthermore, is completely consistent with the basic principles of the UN Charter.

In sum, there are very few clear-cut, legally binding international norms regulating the use of economic statecraft. There is a large body of international opinion, mostly in communist and Third World states, that favors the regulation and perhaps prohibition of such measures. Judged in terms of the criteria suggested here, however, the case for broad legal bans on economic statecraft is not compelling.

The reader of the preceding chapters of this book will no doubt be struck by a major incongruity between the conventional wisdom concerning the effectiveness of economic statecraft and arguments in favor of legal constraints on such measures. Whereas the conventional wisdom depicts economic techniques as weak and ineffective means to coerce other states, the case for strengthening legal controls rests on assertions that such measures "can be used to subjugate one nation to the will of another,"[75] can pose "a genuine threat to the sovereignty of the target state,"[76] can be so effective as to "amount to aggression,"[77] "may in certain circumstances be very effective instruments of national policy,"[78] can "impair a nation's sovereignty and give rise to . . . humiliation and lasting damage,"[79] or are the "real force" with which target states can be "effectively controlled

[75] Boorman, "Economic Coercion," p. 270.
[76] Buchheit, "Nonviolent Coercion," p. 68.
[77] Schwebel, "Aggression," pp. 451-452.
[78] Brownlie, *International Law*, p. 435.
[79] Buchheit, "Nonviolent Coercion," p. 66.

and their sovereignty turned into an empty formula.''[80] Thus, while students of international politics denounce economic techniques as so futile as to raise questions about the judgment of policy makers foolish enough to use them, many international lawyers denounce such measures as so devastatingly effective that they should be outlawed.

INTERNATIONAL MORALITY AND ECONOMIC STATECRAFT

The realms of international morality and legality overlap only partially. Thus, any particular instance of the use of economic statecraft may be neither illegal nor immoral, both illegal and immoral, illegal but not immoral, or immoral but not illegal. The question of the morality of economic statecraft must therefore be considered separately.

The analytical perspective of the statesman employed in assessing the effectiveness and utility of economic statecraft can easily be misconstrued to imply that employing such techniques is justifiable if their utility is relatively high. This is true—indeed, it is tautological—if the values of the statesman are taken as the standard of justification. The values of the statesman, however, may be evil. Thus, to assert that economic statecraft had relatively high utility and effectiveness in promoting Hitler's goal of preparing for World War II is not to say that this was a morally justifiable undertaking. Although judging the consequences of a foreign policy undertaking may be relevant to assessing its morality, it is not equivalent to a moral judgment. Utility is one thing; morality is another.

Traditional political philosophy has usually confined itself to the realm of domestic society; therefore, not much international moral theory exists. Indeed, the whole matter of whether and how moral principles should be applied to international relations is highly controversial. No attempt to resolve these controversies will be made here. Instead the discussion will focus on the implications of alternative moral perspectives for the practice of economic statecraft and on analytical problems that must be addressed in applying moral principles to particular instances. The intent is not to settle the question of the morality of economic statecraft but rather to set the parameters within which fruitful thinking about this problem can take place.

Alternative Moral Perspectives

Before considering the traditional schools of thought with respect to international morality, it is useful to identify some pitfalls commonly found in popular—and sometimes in scholarly—discussions of economic state-

[80] Levi, *Law and Politics*, p. 80. Cf. McDougal and Feliciano, *Law*, p. 190.

craft. These approaches are labeled "pitfalls" because they seem to lie outside the boundaries within which productive debate can occur.

PITFALL 1: ALL FORMS OF ECONOMIC STATECRAFT ARE IMMORAL

The assertion that any and all uses of economic statecraft are immoral cannot withstand even cursory analysis. Such a position would require one to argue that the Allies should have allowed unrestricted trade with Germany during World War II, that free trade in dangerous drugs should be allowed, that all tariffs are immoral whether discriminatory or not, and that all state trading, including the Louisiana Purchase, is unjustifiable. No serious attempt to argue such a position is known to this writer. The fruitful question for debate, then, is not whether economic statecraft *per se* is morally justifiable, but rather what conditions, if any, set limits on the justifiable use of such techniques.

PITFALL 2: ONLY DISINTERESTED USAGE OF SUCH TECHNIQUES IS PERMISSIBLE

Discussions of foreign aid are especially prone to imply that aid is morally deficient if the interests of the donor are being furthered by the transactions. Thus, foreign aid is often categorized as given either in the "national interest" of the donor or for "humanitarian" reasons. If all pursuit of self-interest were immoral or if international politics were primarily a zero-sum game, this might be a defensible approach. In a world of overlapping interests, however, it is quite possible that aid and trade transactions are mutually beneficial for all parties. Although any given instance of aid or trade might be immoral, this cannot be inferred from the fact that advantages are being sought by one or more of the parties concerned.

PITFALL 3: POLICIES EMBODIED IN UNITED NATIONS RESOLUTIONS OR STATEMENTS BY REPRESENTATIVES OF WEAK STATES ARE MORALLY SUPERIOR TO THOSE OF STRONG STATES[81]

To depict the approach to foreign aid embodied in United Nations resolutions as based on humanitarianism and moral principles while describing the approach of the United States as based on furthering the "national interest" is at best misleading. Weak Third World states use United Nations resolutions to advance their "national interests" now just as the United States did in the 1950s, when it could count on majority support. The United Nations approach may or may not be morally superior to that of

---

[81] Cf. Ohlin, *Foreign Aid Policies Reconsidered*, pp. 13-14; Ian M. D. Little, *Economic Development: Theory, Policy, and International Relations* (New York: Basic Books, 1982), pp. 112-113; and Claude, *Swords into Plowshares* pp. 28, 63, 126-127.

the United States, but it is no less political and no less reflective of "national interests" as perceived by statesmen.

Charles Beitz has identified two major schools of thought regarding the morality of statecraft.[82] The first, which he labels moral skepticism, is associated with Machiavelli, Bodin, Hobbes, and the postwar "realists," such as Hans Morgenthau. This intellectual tradition emphasizes "national interests" in international relations and denies "the existence of any controlling universal rules in relations between states."[83] This perspective, which Beitz regards as the dominant Anglo-American tradition, provides little or no basis for condemning the morality of economic statecraft.

The second school of thought, which Beitz refers to as "the morality of states," is associated with Pufendorf, Vattel, Locke, Bentham, and John Stuart Mill. This perspective emphasizes state autonomy, nonintervention, and self-determination and asserts that states are subject to moral rules in their dealings with each other. States are viewed as having the same right to moral autonomy that individuals have in domestic society. Recognizing, however, the lack of an international authority comparable to the state in domestic society, this approach allows for more self-help "in order to compensate for the absence of a common enforcer of law."[84] This approach provides many grounds for moral objections to the practice of economic statecraft—or any other kind of statecraft. If "sovereignty," "intervention," and "self-determination" are interpreted broadly, almost any interstate influence attempt is subject to moral censure. This general philosophical orientation is related to the prohibitions on intervention and pressure in recent resolutions of the United Nations General Assembly. Of course, the self-help emphasis in this approach does provide a possible rubric under which some kinds of economic pressure could be justified, e.g., redress for an injury inflicted by another state.

Beitz criticizes the "morality of states" perspective on two grounds. First, he denies that states deserve the same moral status as individuals; and second, he objects to the absence of a principle of distributive justice in the "morality of states" position.[85] Consequently he suggests the need for a third approach, which he labels "cosmopolitan," based on the contractarian views of John Rawls.[86]

---

[82] *Political Theory and International Relations* (Princeton: Princeton University Press, 1979), pp. 3-66; and "Bounded Morality: Justice and the State in World Politics," *International Organization* XXXIII (Summer 1979):406-410.

[83] *Political Theory*, p. 3. The question of whether particular theorists belong in Beitz's categories will not be addressed here. For purposes of this discussion Beitz's characterizations of the schools of thought are used merely to give rough approximations of different intellectual approaches.

[84] "Bounded Morality," p. 408.

[85] Ibid., pp. 408-409; *Political Theory*, pp. 65-66.

[86] *A Theory of Justice* (Cambridge: Harvard University Press, 1971).

Since Rawls' *Theory of Justice* is considered to be a major statement of the principles of social justice—perhaps *the* major statement of the twentieth century—it is worth considering the implications of his approach for the practice of economic statecraft. Rawls' basic approach is to ask what principles of social justice rational persons would choose behind a "veil of ignorance." The veil of ignorance prevents people from knowing which society, race, sex, socioeconomic group, or generation they will belong to (pp. 118-150). From this "original position" Rawls derives two basic principles of justice. The first is that each person should have "an equal right to the most extensive basic liberty compatible with a similar liberty for others" (p. 60). This principle concerns equal treatment before the law, free speech, voting rights, and so on. The second principle is that "social and economic inequalities are to be arranged so that they are both: (a) to the greatest benefit of the least advantaged, . . . and (b) attached to . . . positions open to all under conditions of fair equality of opportunity" (p. 302).

The question here is not the validity of Rawls' principles of justice, but rather their implications for the practice of economic statecraft. Determining such implications is complicated by the fact that Rawls concentrates his attention on "self-contained" national communities and pays very little attention to international relations. In an age when the phrase "global village" has become a cliché, Rawls' neglect of the international dimension of justice constitutes a major flaw in his analysis. (It is ironic that *A Theory of Justice* was published the same year that Harold and Margaret Sprout published *Toward a Politics of the Planet Earth*!)[87] The few comments Rawls offers about statecraft do not seem to provide a basis for sweeping moral condemnation of economic statecraft. Even war—if it is just—is permissible in Rawls' scheme. Thus, he notes that the means employed in the conduct of war "must not destroy the possibility of peace or encourage a contempt for human life that puts the safety of . . . mankind in jeopardy." A just state, he argues, "is not moved by the desire for world power or national glory; nor does it wage war for purposes of economic gain or the acquisition of territory. These ends are contrary to the conception of justice that defines a society's legitimate interest" (p. 379). This last comment about the legitimacy of ends could be interpreted to imply that states should never seek such ends by any means. Such an inference, however, does not seem to be consistent with the rest of Rawls' argument and was probably not intended by Rawls. It is not the pursuit of economic gain or territory *per se* that is wicked, but rather the use of war as a means

[87] For criticisms of Rawls' failure to treat international relations more seriously, see Brian Barry, *The Liberal Theory of Justice* (London: Oxford University Press, 1973), pp. 128-133; Robert Amdur, "Rawls' Theory of Justice: Domestic and International Perspectives," *World Politics* XXIX (April 1977):452-461; and Beitz, *Political Theory*.

to such ends. Economic gain may be pursued through international trade, and territory may be acquired through purchase. It is difficult to believe that Rawls intended to imply that such uses of economic statecraft were illegitimate uses of state power.

Policy and Cosmopolitanism

Rawls' principles of justice are quite general and leave room for usage of a broad spectrum of economic techniques of statecraft. As Beitz points out, the cosmopolitan perspective "leaves open the question of what concrete moral requirements apply to states," "does not entail any particular political program," and does not specify what "political strategies are needed to implement cosmopolitan principles." Such questions depend on "hypotheses from the empirical study of international political economy."[88] The difficulty of applying such principles to the complex realities of international politics will be illustrated in the following discussion of helping the poor, intervention, dependence, and maintaining order.

HELPING THE POOR

The global policy implications of Rawls' principle of distributive justice seem at first to be staggering. The proposition that social and economic inequalities are justified only to the extent that such inequalities benefit the least advantaged segments of society might be interpreted as requiring a massive international redistribution of wealth. Such an interpretation easily leads to assertions that economic techniques such as "monetary and trade reforms, debt cancellation, and . . . massive development aid" are not merely morally permissible but morally obligatory.[89]

Specific policy inferences, however, must be approached with caution. Before policies for helping the poor can be specified, alternative policy responses must be evaluated. And this in turn depends on how the problem is defined. If the problem is primarily one of capital shortage, foreign aid might seem to be in order; but if the capital shortage is due to hostile governmental attitudes toward private foreign investment, deliberate withholding of aid to provide incentives for the government in the poor country to improve the foreign investment climate might be a more effective way to attack the problem. If the problem is primarily one of starvation and malnutrition, food aid might seem to be appropriate; but if the starvation and malnutrition are caused by inadequate incentives for agricultural production in the poor country, food aid might further weaken such incentives and intensify the problem. If the problem is primarily that of poverty created

[88] "Bounded Morality," pp. 409-410.
[89] Amdur, "Rawls' Theory," p. 455.

and maintained by participation in the international capitalist economy, rich capitalist countries might seem to be obligated to sever trade with poor countries; but if the problem is caused by insufficient trade with rich countries, such measures would be inappropriate. If the problem is excessive population growth despite a sincere and well-planned governmental population control policy, massive aid might be beneficial; but if the problem is caused by the absence of attempts to control population growth, aid may magnify the problem. Foreign aid may discourage savings, encourage inflation, discourage self-help, and encourage uneconomic projects.[90] This is not to say that such effects are inevitable or even probable, but the possibility of such effects must at least be taken into account. Foreign aid does not *necessarily* benefit the poor; more aid (like more salt) is not necessarily better than less; and nonaid may help the poor more in certain situations. Even if the Rawlsian principle of distributive justice is extended to international relations, the specific policy implications for economic statecraft must be determined in the context of particular cases and in terms of particular theories about the causal effects of various techniques.

It is important to note that Rawlsian principles can even be used to justify international inequality to the extent that such inequality is beneficial to the least advantaged. Serious arguments have been advanced by at least one author to the effect that the gap between rich and poor countries benefits the poor—at least to some extent.[91] Such arguments should not be ignored in formulating moral judgments about the need for international redistribution of wealth. The gap, after all, could be eliminated by impoverishing the rich without enriching the poor; but it is not obvious that the cause of social justice would thereby be advanced.

Although Rawls' two principles of justice are of fundamental importance, they are in a sense secondary to the prior specification of "primary social goods," i.e., the values in terms of which rational persons choose the two principles of justice. Of the "primary social goods," self-respect is the most important in Rawls' view. It has been argued that if international inequality undermines the self-respect of the least advantaged, the case for

[90] For arguments to the effect that foreign aid may actually be detrimental to the poor, see the following: U.S. Senate, *Foreign Aid Program: Compilation of Studies and Surveys*, prepared under the direction of the Special Senate Committee to Study the Foreign Aid Program, Study No. 7, "American Private Enterprise, Foreign Economic Development, and the Aid Programs," prepared by the American Enterprise Association, 85th Cong., 1st sess., 1957, Senate Doc. 52, pp. 539-618; Milton Friedman, "Foreign Economic Aid: Means and Objectives," *Yale Review* XLVII (June 1958):500-516; Banfield, *American Foreign Aid Doctrines*; and P. T. Bauer, *Equality, the Third World and Economic Delusion* (Cambridge: Harvard University Press, 1981).

[91] Herman Kahn, *World Economic Development: 1979 and Beyond* (Boulder, Colo.: Westview, 1979).

wealth redistribution is strengthened.[92] Although this is an important point, the potential implications of the self-respect line of argument are many. Receiving aid, after all, often weakens self esteem. This, of course, depends on the form of aid, the conditions attached, the perceived donor, the amount, and so on; but the essential point is that one cannot say *a priori* whether foreign aid will enhance or undermine the self-respect of the recipient.[93] It is not even obvious that stringless aid would be less demeaning than aid with strings. If strings are viewed as a normal condition of aid given among equals, e.g., the Marshall Plan, then the absence of strings may be seen as a paternalistic act that weakens self-esteem. Just as children are told that when they grow up they will no longer be protected from the coercive effects of laws, treating poor countries with "kid gloves" may be tantamount to telling them that they are not considered "grown up" countries.[94] Pressure and coercion do not necessarily weaken self-respect—the idea that "the Marine Corps builds men" is not entirely a matter of false advertising. The question of whether the Rawlsian emphasis on self-respect calls for more aid, less aid, stringless aid, or aid with strings cannot be answered without reference to specific circumstances.

INTERVENTION

In the "morality of states" perspective, nonintervention is of fundamental importance. Since almost any kind of international economic relationship is likely to infringe on a state's "economic independence," autarky is an appealing policy from this perspective. The cosmopolitan approach, however, places less emphasis on the moral significance of state boundaries and makes intervention morally permissible if carried out in accordance with Rawlsian principles of justice. Thus, strings on aid intended to ensure that the poor really benefited would be quite appropriate— perhaps even morally obligatory.[95]

Beitz suggests that if the "target state is just, or is likely to become just if left free from external interference," cosmopolitan principles would prohibit "conditional bilateral aid."[96] This, however, is tantamount to a ban on all bilateral aid, since all aid involves strings if only in the form of a vague and unspecified obligation to reciprocate in some way. Even

---

[92] Amdur, "Rawls' Theory," pp. 448-450.

[93] Of course, it may be permissible to sacrifice self-esteem in the short run in order to strengthen it in the long run.

[94] If aid transactions are viewed as social exchanges, the importance of strings is even clearer. Strings specify means by which the recipient may at least partially discharge the debt incurred by accepting aid. The surest way to humiliate someone is to give a gift but refuse to let the other party reciprocate. See Mauss, *The Gift*; and Dillon, *Gifts and Nations*.

[95] See Beitz, *Political Theory*, pp. 83-92; and Amdur, "Rawls' Theory," pp. 452-458.

[96] Beitz, *Political Theory*, pp. 91-92.

though both parties may deny the existence of such an obligation, each knows that it exists.[97] Some kinds of strings may be more morally acceptable than others, but to declare all strings—including the implicit ones—morally unacceptable is to prohibit all forms of foreign aid.

Since World War II the most important kind of American economic intervention has been carried out in the name of anticommunism. Rawlsian principles provide a strong basis for justification of such interventions. For Rawls, the first principle, concerned primarily with basic political liberties, takes priority over the second principle, concerned with distributive justice. Since communist countries have an atrocious record of protecting basic liberties, economic intervention to prevent communist takeovers has at least a *prima facie* moral justification. Indeed, since the first principle takes priority over the second, economic deprivations that conflicted with the second principle might be justifiable if carried out in order to preserve basic liberties.[98] This is not to say that every intervention in the name of anticommunism is justified; it is merely to note the relationship of Rawls' principles to such a rationale. The need to examine the circumstances of each case remains.

DEPENDENCE

Dependency is a deceptively simple concept. It is simple in the sense that it can be succinctly defined in terms of the opportunity costs of severing a relationship. The higher the costs, the greater the dependency. This concept, which has a pedigree several centuries old,[99] is deceptive in that opportunity costs and their implications are easily misunderstood. For example, dependency is not a phenomenon that exists independently of the value system of the dependent actor. In this sense actors are at least partially responsible for their own dependency. Thus, the United States is dependent on Arab oil imports in the sense that forgoing them would involve costs. Although this state of affairs is frequently bemoaned, what is often overlooked is that Americans could free themselves from this dependency overnight by simply lowering the value they place on operating private automobiles. Greedy people, with a large number of intense desires, as the Stoic philosophers long ago pointed out, are prime candidates for

[97] See Mauss, *The Gift*.

[98] "It may also be that a proper understanding of the moral basis of the nonintervention rule permits the exercise of non-military forms of influence over a society when it seems likely to reduce distributive injustice (and, perhaps, when various other conditions are met as well)." (Beitz, "Economic Rights and Distributive Justice in Developing Societies," *World Politics* XXXIII [April 1981]:324.) Since the preservation of basic liberties takes precedence over distributive justice, it is obvious that intervention for such purposes should be included among the "various other conditions" that might justify "non-military forms of influence."

[99] Baldwin, "Interdependence and Power."

dependency status.[100] The moral implications of dependency would therefore seem to depend on the moral status of the values responsible for
dependence. Envy, lust for power, and material greed might have a lower
status than the primary social goods discussed by Rawls.

The most important requirement for assessing the moral status of dependency, however, is a clear understanding of the inherent relationship
between the gains from trade and dependence.[101] The gain from trade is
simply another label for the opportunity costs of forgoing trade. There is
no possibility of realizing the benefits of the division of labor without
simultaneously becoming at least somewhat dependent with respect to some
goods and some other actors. This fundamental aspect of social life is
sometimes obscured by contemporary discussions of international dependence. Indeed, "dependency" has acquired many of the unsavory moral
connotations that have made "exploitation" and "imperialism" nearly
useless as vehicles of scientific communication.

Beitz, for example, observes that economic dependence "can best be
understood by comparing it with the political imperialism associated with
the colonial period, of which economic dependence is alleged to be a lineal
descendent."[102] This approach, however, is almost sure to lead to a profound misunderstanding of the relationship between economic dependence
and the division of labor. Contrary to Beitz, economic dependence can
best be understood by depicting it as an inevitable consequence of the
division of labor.[103]

It is true, of course, that when two parties are mutually dependent, the
less dependent party may be able to coerce the more vulnerable party. It
is also true that the less vulnerable party (i.e., the less dependent party)
may use this power to manipulate the terms of trade in its favor; but it is
seldom recognized that an adverse change in the terms of trade necessarily
decreases the more vulnerable party's gains from trade and therefore weak-

[100] Epictetus, *The Discourses and Manual*, trans. P. E. Matheson (Oxford: Clarendon
Press, 1916).

[101] Hirschman, *National Power*, pp. 3-19.

[102] *Political Theory*, p. 116.

[103] Beitz never provides an explicit definition of dependence or interdependence, although
both concepts figure prominently in his analysis. He relies "for the sake of discussion" on
the views of contemporary "dependency theorists" based largely on recent Latin American
writings. This is unfortunate since this school of thought not only is unrepresentative of
mainstream social science thinking on the subject but is also rather weak in its intellectual
foundations. For further discussion of "dependency" (or *dependencia*) theorists, see Little,
Economic Development, pp. 218-266; Baldwin, "Interdependence and Power," pp. 492-
495; Tony Smith, "The Underdevelopment of Development Literature: The Case of Dependency Theory," *World Politics* XXXI (January 1979):247-288; Robert A. Packenham,
"The New Utopianism: Political Development Ideas in the Dependency Literature," *Working
Paper* no. 19, Latin American Program, Woodrow Wilson International Center for Scholars,
Washington, D.C., 1978; and Knorr, *Power of Nations*, pp. 239-309.

ens its dependency, *ceterus paribus*. One cannot have it both ways. If international trade results in zero or negative gains from trade for poor countries, they cannot be depicted as vulnerable to a trade cutoff. Their vulnerability arises precisely from the fact that trade is valuable to them. This is not to say that economic dependence is never morally wrong; it is only to suggest that the relationship between distributive justice and economic dependence is considerably more complex (and in some ways more simple!) than Beitz implies.[104]

Rawls himself recognizes the inextricable relationship between dependence and the division of labor and bans neither from the just society. He notes that "a well ordered society does not do away with the division of labor" and that, although some of the more demeaning forms of dependency should be eliminated, "when work is meaningful for all, we cannot overcome, *nor should we wish to*, our dependence on others."[105] Although Rawls is not referring to international relations here, there is no reason to believe that extension of his line of reasoning would prohibit a global division of labor. Certain forms of dependency are, of course, demeaning to the human spirit; but the just society need not and should not forgo all of the advantages of the division of labor. Dependency, *per se*, is not morally offensive to anyone who accepts the ancient assumption that human beings are social animals.

ORDER AND JUSTICE

The question of international justice cannot be isolated from the question of international order. In an unjust world the principle of justice requires change; but in a dangerous world the principle of order constrains both the rate of change and the choice of instruments for promoting change. Thus, there is a continuing tension between the two principles.[106]

Redistributing wealth among states vividly illustrates this tension. There is virtually no way to strengthen the economies of Third World countries without simultaneously enhancing their military potential.[107] The implications of this for international order are not self-evident, but they should be addressed when arguments for redistribution are put forth. The cosmopolitan perspective rightly questions the moral significance of state boundaries, but this does not mean that states can be ignored in assessing the morality of any particular case.

In sum, economic statecraft—like any other set of foreign policy instruments—can be used for good or evil. As with warfare, the general rule

---

[104] Cf. Beitz, *Political Theory*, pp. 146-147.

[105] *A Theory of Justice*, p. 529. Italics added. Beitz ignores this passage in discussing dependence and interdependence. (*Political Theory*, pp. 116-121, 143-153.)

[106] For a discussion, see Bull, *The Anarchical Society*, pp. 77-98.

[107] See Knorr, *Military Power and Potential*; and Little, *Economic Development*, p. 332.

that the means used should be proportional to the ends pursued governs the use of economic techniques. Particular instruments—like particular military weapons—are morally offensive under almost any circumstances. Such measures might include traffic in dangerous drugs, slave trading, and so on. For most economic techniques of statecraft, however, moral status must be determined in the context of the policy-contingency framework in which they are used or contemplated. Preparation for unjust wars, attempts to take unfair advantage of another country, actions that make the target state less just, or pursuit of any other goal unbecoming a just state are unlikely to be morally permissible uses of economic statecraft. But preparing for a just war, attempting to deter one country from taking unfair advantage of another, helping a state to become more just, or pursuit of other goals suitable for a just state are likely to be permissible, perhaps even obligatory, under some circumstances.

CHAPTER 12

CONCLUSION

Ignorance is preferable to error; and he is less
remote from the truth who believes nothing, than he
who believes what is wrong.
(Thomas Jefferson, *Notes on the State of Virginia*)

* * *

Better know nothing than half-know many things.
(Friedrich Wilhelm Nietzsche,
Thus Spake Zarathustra)

* * *

It is better to know nothing than to know what
ain't so.   (Josh Billings, *Proverb*)

Economic statecraft has been practiced for centuries. Regardless of whether use of such techniques has increased recently or not, improved understanding of such phenomena is long overdue. Development of knowledge about economic statecraft, at least since 1945, has been retarded by the conventional wisdom that such measures have little utility. One of the primary goals in the previous chapters has been to demonstrate the inadequacies of this conventional wisdom. Much of the discussion therefore resembles what Stanley Hoffman has called a "wrecking operation."[1] Such operations are intended to generate healthy skepticism with respect to the conventional wisdom and thereby to clear the way for new ways of thinking.

Wrecking operations, as the quotations in the headnote of this chapter indicate, are legitimate contributions to knowledge; but they are no substitute for new theories or sets of generalizations about which economic techniques are likely to work under what circumstances; and readers of the preceding chapters may well be wondering what the author proposes as a replacement for the conventional wisdom about economic statecraft. While the desire for a substitute for the conventional wisdom is understandable, premature generalization may do more harm than good. The implication of the line of argument developed in the foregoing chapters is that what is needed is more qualification, more patience, more rigor, and more caution in generalizing about economic statecraft. Most of the cases discussed here were chosen not because they are representative of typical instances of economic statecraft but rather because of the frequency with

---

[1] Stanley Hoffmann, ed., *Contemporary Theory in International Relations* (Englewood Cliffs, N.J.: Prentice-Hall, 1960), p. 171.

which they are cited by the conventional wisdom. Such a case selection strategy is well suited for testing the adequacy of the conventional wisdom, but it is less useful for generalizing about typical cases.

The second main goal of this book has been to provide an analytical framework within which reliable knowledge about economic statecraft can be developed to replace the conventional wisdom. Although this framework has been applied to a number of cases, none is studied with the thoroughness and rigor required of a definitive case study. The rationale for the case studies in this book is closer to what has been called a "plausibility probe."[2] Such studies are intended to test the plausibility of a particular approach in order to determine whether more ambitious use of the approach is likely to be worthwhile. If the plausibility probes had indicated that application of the analytical framework developed here was likely to lead to the same conclusions as the conventional wisdom, further research would not seem worthwhile. In virtually every case examined, however, there was reason to suspect that thorough and rigorous application of the framework developed here would lead to conclusions significantly different from those of the conventional wisdom.

The basic idea underlying the proposed approach is that economic techniques should be analyzed in much the same way as other techniques of statecraft. Although the basic principles of the approach have been developed with economic statecraft in mind, they should be equally applicable to the study of diplomacy, propaganda, and military statecraft. The analytical principles elucidated in the foregoing chapters can be condensed into a set of guidelines that should help in avoiding the more common pitfalls in evaluating the utility of economic techniques of statecraft:

1. *Targets and goals are usually multiple.*

The single most important step in describing an actual or potential influence attempt is careful determination of who is trying to influence whom with respect to what. Oversimplified views of the structure of goals and targets is the most frequent cause of underestimation of the utility of economic statecraft.[3]

2. *Success is usually a matter of degree.*

Neither perfect success nor perfect failure is likely. Simple dichotomies categorizing the outcomes of influence attempts in terms of "success" or "failure" can be highly misleading.

3. *Alternatives matter.*

Information about the likely utility of a given tool of statecraft acquires significance only by comparison with alternative policy instruments. As-

---

[2] Eckstein, "Case Study and Theory in Political Science."

[3] For an example of oversimplified treatment of goals and targets, in which most cases are analyzed in terms of a single goal and a single target, see Hufbauer and Schott, *Economic Sanctions in Support of Foreign Policy Goals.*

sertions that economic statecraft will not work should be accompanied by suggestions as to what policy option is likely to work better.

4. *Some things are more difficult than others.*

A moderate degree of success in accomplishing a difficult task may seem more impressive than a high degree of success in accomplishing an easy task. In assessing statecraft, as in judging diving contests, scores should be adjusted for the level of difficulty. "Don't bite off more than you can chew" is a recipe for *seeming* to be successful, but it is not necessarily a demonstration of superior chewing ability.[4] In capability analysis the size of the bite is not a tactical matter; it is a given.

5. *Images matter.*

The pursuit of symbolic foreign policy goals is not necessarily an indication of weakness, frivolity, or excessive emotionalism. Foreign policy makers usually behave as if others were watching—and rightly so!

6. *The bases of power are many and varied.*

Economic policy instruments may work through noneconomic power bases. Foreign aid may successfully project a commitment to defend the recipient regardless of the economic effects of the aid, and trade restrictions may successfully convey a threat to invade even when their economic impact is nil. Economic sanctions need not bite in order to work.[5]

7. *Comparing our costs with theirs is not very helpful.*

The costs of the power wielder should be compared with the costs of his other policy options. Comparing the costs to the power wielder with the costs imposed on the target is likely to be quite misleading.

8. *Imposing costs for noncompliance is a measure of success.*

To make the target of an influence attempt pay a price for noncompliance is to be at least partially successful. Thus, the relevant question is not merely whether compliance was forthcoming, but also whether costs for noncompliance were imposed.

9. *Costs have their uses.*

Other things being equal, it is always desirable to minimize costs; but other things are not always equal. The selection of a costly method of conveying a signal may add credibility to the signal. Thus, a statesman interested in demonstrating resolve may want to avoid the less expensive means of communication. When outcomes are the same, cheaper is better; but under some circumstances, the costliness of the medium enhances the credibility of the message.[6]

The policy maker or policy analyst who keeps these nine points in mind when estimating the actual or potential utility of economic statecraft should

[4] Cf. ibid., pp. 76-77.
[5] Cf. ibid., pp. 80-81.
[6] Cf. ibid., pp. 81-82.

at least be able to avoid the more common difficulties of making such estimates.

To say that economic statecraft is more useful than the current conventional wisdom would have one believe is not to say that such measures always or usually work. It may well be that most techniques of statecraft work rather poorly most of the time, but this does not obviate the need to differentiate among various policy alternatives.

Does the argument in this book suggest that increased use of economic techniques of statecraft would be desirable? Not necessarily. Decisions as to whether or how to use economic statecraft must be rooted in careful scrutiny of the particular case at hand. Scholarly argument, as Jacob Viner has pointed out, usually needs to be tempered by "information, wisdom, judgment, measurement-of-a-kind of things not scientifically measurable, [and] compassion for the weaker segments of mankind" if the "final result is to be reasonably applicable to particular cases." Viner was suspicious of facile leaps from academic analysis to policy prescription. He believed that academic scholars could most usefully contribute to public policy not by prescribing detailed policies for particular cases but rather by providing tools "for the organization of knowledge and for bringing values to bear on public issues," by exploring "conflicts between principles," and by searching out "the importance of degree, relation, and proportion" with respect to public issues.[7] It is in this spirit that the preceding chapters have been written.

The argument in this book does suggest the need for increased understanding of the nature, implications, and consequences of economic statecraft. In a world in which the stakes of statecraft have risen astronomically, better understanding of all techniques of statecraft becomes imperative. If, indeed, statesmen are to choose war, this choice should be the result of reasoned assessment of alternative courses of action rather than the result of inadequate understanding of the range of policy options available to them. Reasonable people may differ with respect to the utility of war as an instrument of policy, but there is little to be said in defense of unnecessary wars. Few today would argue that Thomas Jefferson should have acquired the Louisiana Territory by war rather than by purchase. It would be a pity—perhaps a global disaster—if a contemporary American president were to resort to war solely because the nature, implications, and consequences of economic statecraft had been misrepresented to him by his advisors. In the nuclear age, elucidation of alternatives to military statecraft becomes especially important.

[7] Viner, "The Intellectual History of Laissez Faire," pp. 62-63. For a similar view, see George and Smoke, *Deterrence in American Foreign Policy*, pp. 616-642, esp. p. 628. For examples of the kind of policy advice that would have appalled Viner, see Hufbauer and Schott, *Economic Sanctions*, pp. 76-85.

Policy science focuses on the means by which statesmen may pursue their goals. Stanley Hoffmann has warned that this approach runs the risk of becoming "a study of manipulation, through excessive emphasis on the skills of policy-making," of developing a "fascination with the strategies of power" and the "tools which decision-makers use," and of slipping into "the unsavory task of justifying the decisions" of statesmen. Whether the attempt at policy science in this book exemplifies such dangers is for others to judge. Although Hoffmann warns against the risks associated with policy science, he does not deny the value of this approach. He notes that one of the roles of scholarship is "to help the policy-makers understand the situations and the alternatives among which they will have to choose."[8] Better understanding of the nature, implications, and consequences of economic statecraft should contribute to that end.

[8] *Contemporary Theory*, pp. 11-12.

BIBLIOGRAPHY

BOOKS

Adler-Karlsson, Gunnar. *Western Economic Warfare, 1947-1967: A Case Study in Foreign Economic Policy.* Stockholm: Almqvist and Wiksell, 1968.

Alexander, Robert J. *The Tragedy of Chile.* Westport, Conn.: Greenwood Press, 1978.

Allison, Graham T. *Essence of Decision.* Boston: Little, Brown, 1971.

Anderson, Charles W. *Statecraft: An Introduction to Political Choice and Judgment.* New York: John Wiley, 1977.

Anderson, Frank Maloy, and Hershey, Amos Shartle, eds. *Handbook for the Diplomatic History of Europe, Asia, and Africa, 1870-1914.* Washington, D.C.: Government Printing Office, 1918.

Angell, Sir Norman. *The Foundations of International Polity.* London: William Heinemann, 1914.

Aron, Raymond. *Peace and War: A Theory of International Relations.* Garden City, N.Y.: Doubleday, 1966.

Bailey, Thomas A. *The Art of Diplomacy: The American Experience.* New York: Appleton-Century-Crofts, 1968.

————. *A Diplomatic History of the American People.* 10th ed. Englewood Cliffs, N.J.: Prentice-Hall, 1980.

Baldwin, David A. *Economic Development and American Foreign Policy: 1943-62.* Chicago: University of Chicago Press, 1966.

————. *Foreign Aid and American Foreign Policy: A Documentary Analysis.* New York: Praeger, 1966.

Banfield, Edward C. *American Aid Doctrines.* Washington, D.C.: American Enterprise Institute, 1963.

Barry, Brian. *The Liberal Theory of Justice.* London: Oxford University Press, 1973.

Baskir, Lawrence M., and Strauss, William A. *Chance and Circumstance: The Draft, the War, and the Vietnam Generation.* New York: Alfred A. Knopf, 1978.

Bauer, P. T. *Equality, the Third World and Economic Delusion.* Cambridge: Harvard University Press, 1981.

Baumont, Maurice. *The Origins of the Second World War.* Translated by Simone de Couvreur Ferguson. New Haven: Yale University Press, 1978.

Beitz, Charles R. *Political Theory and International Relations*. Princeton: Princeton University Press, 1979.

Benham, Frederic. *Economic Aid to Underdeveloped Countries.* New York: Oxford University Press, 1961.

Bernstein, Marver H. *The Politics of Israel: The First Decade of Statehood*. Princeton: Princeton University Press, 1957.

Blau, Peter M. *Exchange and Power in Social Life*. New York: John Wiley, 1964.

Blechman, Barry M., and Kaplan, Stephen S. *Force Without War: U.S. Armed Forces as a Political Instrument*. Washington, D.C.: Brookings Institution, 1978.

Boulding, Kenneth E. *A Primer on Social Dynamics: History as Dialectics and Development*. New York: Free Press, 1970.

Boulding, Kenneth E., and Mukerjee, Tapan, eds. *Economic Imperialism*. Ann Arbor: University of Michigan Press, 1972.

Brierly, J. L. *The Law of Nations*. 6th ed. Edited by Humphrey Waldock. Oxford: Oxford University Press, 1963.

Brodie, Bernard. *War and Politics*. New York: Macmillan, 1973.

Brown, William Adams. *The United States and the Restoration of World Trade*. Washington, D.C.: Brookings Institution, 1950.

Brownlie, Ian. *International Law and the Use of Force*. London: Oxford University Press, 1963.

Brzezinski, Zbigniew. *Power and Principle: Memoirs of the National Security Adviser, 1977-1981*. New York: Farrar, Straus, Giroux, 1983.

Buchanan, Norman S., and Ellis, Howard S. *Approaches to Economic Development*. New York: Twentieth Century Fund, 1955.

Bull, Hedley. *The Anarchical Society*. New York: Columbia University Press, 1977.

Butterfield, H. *The Statecraft of Machiavelli*. London: G. Bell, 1940.

Callahan, Patrick; Brady, Linda P.; and Hermann, Margaret G., eds. *Describing Foreign Policy Behavior*. Beverly Hills, Calif.: Sage, 1982.

Callières, François de. *On the Manner of Negotiating with Princes*. Translated by A. F. Whyte. Notre Dame, Ind.: University of Notre Dame Press, 1963.

Camps, Miriam. *The Management of Interdependence: A Preliminary View*. New York: Council on Foreign Relations, 1974.

Carr, Edward Hallett. *The Twenty Years' Crisis: 1919-1939*. 2d ed. London: Macmillan, 1946.

Carter, Jimmy. *Keeping Faith: Memoirs of a President*. New York: Bantam, 1982.

Catlin, G.E.G. *The Science and Method of Politics*. New York: Alfred A. Knopf, 1927.

Cecco, Marcello de. *Money and Empire*. Oxford: Basil Blackwell, 1974.

Chapman, Margaret, and Marcy, Carl, eds. *Common Sense in U.S.-Soviet Trade*. Washington, D.C.: American Committee on East-West Accord, 1983.

Chill, Dan S. *The Arab Boycott of Israel*. New York: Praeger, 1976.

Clark, Evans, ed. *Boycotts and Peace*. New York: Harper, 1932.

Clark, Grenville, and Sohn, Louis B. *World Peace Through World Law*. Cambridge: Harvard University Press, 1958.

Claude, Inis L., Jr. *Power and International Relations*. New York: Random House, 1962.

———. *Swords into Plowshares*. 4th ed. New York: Random House, 1971.

Clausewitz, Carl von. *On War*. Edited and translated by Michael Howard and Peter Paret. Princeton: Princeton University Press, 1976.

Cline, Ray S. *World Power Assessment: A Calculus of Strategic Drift*. Boulder, Colo.: Westview, 1975.

Coffin, Frank M. *Witness for Aid*. Boston: Houghton Mifflin, 1964.

Cohen, Benjamin J., ed. *American Foreign Economic Policy: Essays and Comments*. New York: Harper and Row, 1968.

Cohen, Stephen D. *The Making of United States International Economic Policy: Principles, Problems, and Proposals for Reform*. New York: Praeger, 1977.

Crucé, Émeric. *The New Cyneas*. Translated by Thomas Willing Balch. Philadelphia: Allen, Lane and Scott, 1909.

Cunningham, William. *The Growth of English Industry and Commerce in Modern Times*. 3d ed. 2 vols. Cambridge: Cambridge University Press, 1903.

Dahl, Robert A. *Modern Political Analysis*. 1st and 3d eds. Englewood Cliffs, N.J.: Prentice-Hall, 1963 and 1976.

Dahl, Robert A., and Lindblom, Charles E. *Politics, Economics, and Welfare: Planning and Politico-Economic Systems Resolved into Basic Social Processes*. New York: Harper and Row, 1953.

Dam, Kenneth W. *The GATT: Law and International Economic Organization*. Chicago: University of Chicago Press, 1970.

David, Wade Dewood. *European Diplomacy in the Near Eastern Question, 1906-1909*. Urbana: University of Illinois Press, 1940.

Delaisi, Francis. *Political Myths and Economic Realities*. London: Noel Douglas, 1925.

Destler, I. M. *Making Foreign Economic Policy*. Washington, D.C.: Brookings Institution, 1980.

Deutsch, Karl W. *The Analysis of International Relations*. 2d ed. Englewood Cliffs, N.J.: Prentice-Hall, 1978.

Diamond, William. *The Economic Thought of Woodrow Wilson*. Baltimore: Johns Hopkins Press, 1943.

Dillon, Wilton S. *Gifts and Nations*. The Hague: Mouton, 1968.

Dolan, Edwin G. *TANSTAAFL*. New York: Holt, Rinehart, and Winston, 1971.

Dorfman, Joseph. *The Economic Mind in American Civilization*. 4 vols. New York: Viking Press, 1946.

Doxey, Margaret P. *Economic Sanctions and International Enforcement*. 1st and 2d eds. New York: Oxford University Press, 1971 and 1980.

Dunn, Frederick Sherwood. *Peaceful Change*. New York: Council on Foreign Relations, 1937.

Eagleton, Clyde. *International Government*. Rev. ed. New York: Ronald Press, 1948.

Epictetus. *The Discourses and Manual*. Translated by P. E. Matheson. Oxford: Clarendon Press, 1916.

Falk, Richard A. *The Status of Law in International Society*. Princeton: Princeton University Press, 1970.

Feis, Herbert. *The Road to Pearl Harbor*. Princeton: Princeton University Press, 1950.

Fenwick, Charles G. *International Law*. 4th ed. New York: Appleton-Century-Crofts, 1965.

Finlay, David J.; Holsti, Ole R.; and Fagan, Richard R. *Enemies in Politics*. Chicago: Rand McNally, 1967.

Fontaine, Roger W. *On Negotiating With Cuba*. Washington, D.C.: American Enterprise Institute, 1975.

Freedman, Robert Owen. *Economic Warfare in the Communist Bloc: A Study of Economic Pressure Against Yugoslavia, Albania, and Communist China*. New York: Praeger, 1970.

Friedmann, Wolfgang. *The Changing Structure of International Law*. New York: Columbia University Press, 1964.

Friedrich, Carl Joachim. *Inevitable Peace*. Cambridge: Harvard University Press, 1948.

Gaddis, John Lewis. *Strategies of Containment*. New York: Oxford University Press, 1982.

Gardner, Richard N. *Sterling-Dollar Diplomacy in Current Perspective*. Expanded ed. New York: Columbia University Press, 1980.

George, Alexander L.; Hall, David K.; and Simons, William R. *The Limits of Coercive Diplomacy*. Boston: Little, Brown, 1971.

George, Alexander L. and Smoke, Richard. *Deterrence in American Foreign Policy: Theory and Practice*. New York: Columbia University Press, 1974.

Gilbert, Felix. *To the Farewell Address: Ideas in Early American Foreign Policy*. Princeton: Princeton University Press, 1961.

Gilmore, Richard. *A Poor Harvest: The Clash of Policies and Interests in the Grain Trade*. New York: Longman, 1982.

Gilpin, Robert. *U.S. Power and the Multinational Corporation: The Political Economy of Foreign Direct Investment*. New York: Basic Books, 1975.

———. *War and Change in World Politics*. Cambridge: Cambridge University Press, 1981.

Goldmann, Kjell, and Sjostedt, Gunnar, eds. *Power, Capabilities, Interdependence*. London: Sage, 1979.

Goodrich, Leland M.; Hambro, Edvard; and Simons, Anne Patricia. *Charter of the United Nations: Commentary and Documents*. 3d and rev. ed. New York: Columbia University Press, 1969.

Greenstein, Fred I. and Polsby, Nelson W., eds. *Handbook of Political Science*. Reading, Mass.: Addison-Wesley, 1975.

Gurr, Ted Robert. *Why Men Rebel*. Princeton: Princeton University Press, 1970.

Harrison, Anthony. *The Framework of Economic Activity: The International Economy and the Rise of the State*. London: Macmillan, 1967.

Harvey, Mose L. *East West Trade and United States Policy*. New York: National Association of Manufacturers, 1966.

Hawtrey, R. G. *Economic Aspects of Sovereignty*. London: Longmans, Green, 1930.

Heckscher, Eli F. *Mercantilism*. Rev. ed. 2 vols. Translated by Mendel Shapiro. New York: Macmillan, 1955.

Heilperin, Michael A. *Studies in Economic Nationalism*. Geneva: Librairie E. Droz, 1960.

Hemleben, Sylvester John. *Plans for World Peace Through Six Centuries*. Chicago: University of Chicago Press, 1943.

Hindmarsh, Albert E. *Force in Peace*. Cambridge: Harvard University Press, 1933.

Hinsley, F. H. *Power and the Pursuit of Peace*. London: Cambridge University Press, 1963.

Hirschman, Albert O. *A Bias for Hope: Essays on Development in Latin America*. New Haven: Yale University Press, 1971.

———. *The Passions and the Interests*. Princeton: Princeton University Press, 1977.

———. *National Power and the Structure of Foreign Trade*. Berkeley: University of California Press, 1945; expanded ed., 1980.

Hoffmann, Stanley, ed. *Contemporary Theory in International Relations*. Englewood Cliffs, N.J.: Prentice-Hall, 1960.

———. *Duties Beyond Borders*. Syracuse, N.Y.: Syracuse University Press, 1981.

Holsti, K. J. *International Politics: A Framework for Analysis*. 3d and 4th eds. Englewood Cliffs, N.J.: Prentice-Hall, 1977 and 1983.

Holzman, Franklyn D. *International Trade under Communism—Politics and Economics*. New York: Basic Books, 1976.

Homans, George C. *Social Behavior: Its Elementary Forms*. Rev. ed. New York: Harcourt Brace Jovanovich, 1974.

Hufbauer, Gary Clyde and Schott, Jeffrey J. *Economic Sanctions in Support of Foreign Policy Goals*. Washington, D.C.: Institute for International Economics, 1983.

Huntington, Samuel P. *The Common Defense*. New York: Columbia University Press, 1961.

Iklé, Fred C. *How Nations Negotiate*. New York: Harper and Row, 1964.

Jervis, Robert. *The Logic of Images in International Relations*. Princeton: Princeton University Press, 1970.

————. *Perception and Misperception in International Politics*. Princeton: Princeton University Press, 1976.

Johansen, Robert C. *The National Interest and the Human Interest*. Princeton: Princeton University Press, 1980.

John, Martin L., ed. *Propaganda in International Affairs*. Philadelphia: Annals of the American Academy of Political and Social Science, 1971.

Jordan, Hamilton. *Crisis: The Last Year of the Carter Presidency*. New York: G. P. Putnam's Sons, 1982.

Kagan, Donald. *The Outbreak of the Peloponnesian War*. Ithaca, N.Y.: Cornell University Press, 1969.

Kahn, Herman. *World Economic Development, 1979 and Beyond*. Boulder, Colo.: Westview, 1979.

Kaplan, Jacob J. *The Challenge of Foreign Aid: Policies, Problems, and Possibilities*. New York: Praeger, 1967.

Kaufman, Burton Ira, ed. *Washington's Farewell Address: The View from the 20th Century*. Chicago: Quadrangle Books, 1969.

Kemp, Murray C. *The Pure Theory of International Trade*. Englewood Cliffs, N.J.: Prentice-Hall, 1964.

Keynes, John Maynard. *The General Theory of Employment, Interest, and Money*. New York: Harcourt, Brace, 1936.

Kindleberger, Charles P. *Power and Money: The Economics of International Politics and the Politics of International Economics*. New York: Basic Books, 1970.

Kissinger, Henry. *The White House Years*. Boston: Little, Brown, 1979.

Knorr, Klaus. *Military Power and Potential*. Lexington, Mass.: D. C. Heath, 1970.

————. *On the Uses of Military Power in the Nuclear Age*. Princeton: Princeton University Press, 1966.

————. *The Power of Nations: The Political Economy of International Relations*. New York: Basic Books, 1975.

Knorr, Klaus, and Patterson, Gardner, eds. *A Critique of the Randall Commission Report on United States Foreign Economic Policy.* Princeton: International Finance Section and Center of International Studies, 1954.

Knorr, Klaus, and Trager, Frank N., eds. *Economic Issues and National Security.* Lawrence: Regents Press of Kansas, 1977.

Krasner, Stephen D. *Defending the National Interest.* Princeton: Princeton University Press, 1978.

Kuznets, Simon. *Economic Growth of Nations.* Cambridge: Harvard University Press, 1971.

Langer, William L. and Gleason, S. Everett. *The Undeclared War, 1940-1941.* New York: Harper, 1953.

Lasswell, Harold D. *Politics: Who Gets What, When, How.* New York: Meridian Books, 1958.

————. *World Politics and Personal Insecurity.* New York: McGraw-Hill, 1935.

————. *World Politics Faces Economics.* New York: McGraw-Hill, 1945.

Lasswell, Harold D., and Kaplan, Abraham. *Power and Society: A Framework for Political Inquiry.* New Haven: Yale University Press, 1950.

Lasswell, Harold D.; Lerner, Daniel; and Spier, Hans, eds. *Propaganda and Communication in World History.* 3 vols. Honolulu: University Press of Hawaii, 1979, 1980.

Lauren, Paul Gordon, ed. *Diplomacy: New Approaches in History, Theory, and Policy.* New York: Free Press, 1979.

Lentner, Howard H. *Foreign Policy Analysis: A Comparative and Conceptual Approach.* Columbus, Ohio: Charles E. Merrill, 1974.

Levi, Werner. *Law and Politics in the International Society.* Beverly Hills, Calif.: Sage, 1976.

Lewis, W. Arthur. *The Theory of Economic Growth.* Homewood, Ill.: Richard P. Irwin, 1955.

Lillich, Richard B., ed. *Economic Coercion and the New International Economic Order.* Charlottesville, Va: Michie, 1976.

Liska, George. *The New Statecraft: Foreign Aid in American Foreign Policy.* Chicago: University of Chicago Press, 1960.

Little, Ian M. D. *Economic Development: Theory, Policy, and International Relations.* New York: Basic Books, 1982.

Losman, Donald L. *International Economic Sanctions: The Cases of Cuba, Israel and Rhodesia.* Albuquerque: University of New Mexico Press, 1979.

Machiavelli, Niccolò. *The Prince and the Discourses.* New York: Modern Library, 1950.

Machlup, Fritz. *Essays on Economic Semantics.* Englewood Cliffs, N.J.: Prentice-Hall, 1963.

Malthus, Rev. T. R. *Definitions in Political Economy, preceded by An Inquiry into the Rules Which Ought to Guide Political Economists in the Definition and Use of Their Terms; with Remarks on the Deviations from these Rules in their Writings*. London: John Murray, 1827.

Mandelbaum, Michael. *The Nuclear Revolution: International Politics Before and After Hiroshima*. Cambridge: Cambridge University Press, 1981.

Manning, C.A.W., ed. *Peaceful Change*. New York: Macmillan, 1937.

March, James, ed. *Handbook of Organizations*. Chicago: Rand McNally, 1965.

Marshall, Alfred. *Principles of Economics*. 9th (variorum) ed. 2 vols. New York: Macmillan, 1961.

Mason, Edward S. *Foreign Aid and Foreign Policy*. New York: Harper and Row, 1964.

Mauss, Marcel. *The Gift*. Translated by Ian Cunnison. Glencoe, Ill.: Free Press, 1954.

McDougal, Myres S., and Feliciano, Florentino P. *Law and Minimum World Public Order*. New Haven: Yale University Press, 1961.

McGowan, Patrick J., and Shapiro, Howard B. *The Comparative Study of Foreign Policy: A Survey of Scientific Findings*. Beverly Hills, Calif.: Sage, 1973.

Merritt, Richard L., ed. *Foreign Policy Analysis*. Lexington, Mass.: Lexington Books, 1975.

————, ed. *Communication in International Politics*. Urbana: University of Illinois Press, 1972.

Mersky, Roy M., ed. *Conference on Transnational Economic Boycotts and Coercion*. 2 vols. Dobbs Ferry, N.Y.: Oceana, 1978.

Mikesell, Raymond F. *United States Economic Policy and International Relations*. New York: McGraw-Hill, 1952.

Mill, John Stuart. *Principles of Political Economy*. New ed. London: Longmans, Green, 1923.

Millikan, Max F., and Rostow, W. W. *A Proposal: Key to an Effective Foreign Policy*. New York: Harper, 1957.

Milward, Alan S. *War, Economy and Society, 1939-1945*. Berkeley: University of California Press, 1977.

Montgomery, John D. *Foreign Aid in International Politics*. Englewood Cliffs, N.J.: Prentice-Hall, 1967.

Moran, Theodore H. *Multinational Corporations and the Politics of Dependence: Copper in Chile*. Princeton: Princeton University Press, 1974.

Morawetz, David. *Twenty-Five Years of Economic Development, 1950 to 1975*. Baltimore: Johns Hopkins Press, 1977.

Morgenthau, Hans J. *Politics Among Nations*. 3d ed. New York: Alfred A. Knopf, 1964.

Muir, Ramsay. *The Interdependent World and Its Problems*. Boston: Houghton Mifflin, 1933.

Myrdal, Gunnar. *Against the Stream: Critical Essays on Economics*. New York: Pantheon, 1973.

Nagel, Jack H. *The Descriptive Analysis of Power*. New Haven: Yale University Press, 1975.

Nelson, Joan M. *Aid, Influence, and Foreign Policy*. New York: Macmillan, 1968.

Nelson, Walter Henry, and Prittie, Terence C. F. *The Economic War Against the Jews*. New York: Random House, 1977.

Nicolson, Harold. *Diplomacy*. 3d ed. New York: Oxford University Press, 1963.

Northedge, Fred S. *The Use of Force in International Relations*. New York: Free Press, 1974.

Ohlin, Goran. *Foreign Aid Policies Reconsidered*. Paris: Organization for Economic Cooperation and Development, 1966.

Oppenheim, Felix E. *Political Concepts: A Reconstruction*. Chicago: University of Chicago Press, 1981.

Oppenheim, L. *International Law: A Treatise*. 7th ed. 2 vols. Edited by H. Lauterpacht. London: Longmans, Green, 1952.

––––––. *International Law*. 8th ed. 2 vols. Edited by H. Lauterpacht. London: Longmans, Green, 1955.

Osgood, Robert E., and Tucker, Robert W. *Force, Order, and Justice*. Baltimore: Johns Hopkins Press, 1967.

Packenham, Robert A. *Liberal America and the Third World: Political Development Ideas in Foreign Aid and Social Science*. Princeton: Princeton University Press, 1973.

Parsons, Talcott, and Bales, Robert F. *Family, Socialization and Interaction Processes*. Glencoe, Ill.: Free Press, 1955.

Pastor, Robert A. *Congress and the Politics of U.S. Foreign Economic Policy, 1929-1976*. Berkeley: University of California Press, 1980.

Patterson, Gardner. *Discrimination in International Trade: The Policy Issues, 1945-1965*. Princeton: Princeton University Press, 1965.

Pincus, John. *Economic Aid and International Cost Sharing*. Baltimore: Johns Hopkins Press, 1965.

––––––. *Trade, Aid, and Development*. New York: McGraw-Hill, 1967.

The Political Economy of American Foreign Policy. New York: Henry Holt, 1955.

Prange, Gordon W. *At Dawn We Slept: The Untold Story of Pearl Harbor*. New York: McGraw-Hill, 1981.

Qualter, Terence H. *Propaganda and Psychological Warfare*. New York: Random House, 1962.

Ranney, Austin, ed. *Political Science and Public Policy*. Chicago: Markham, 1968.

Ransome, Harry Howe, ed. *An American Foreign Policy Reader*. New York: Thomas Y. Crowell, 1965.

Rawls, John. *A Theory of Justice*. Cambridge: Harvard University Press, 1971.

Renwick, Robin. *Economic Sanctions*. Cambridge: Harvard University Center for International Affairs, 1981.

Richardson, J. Henry. *British Economic Foreign Policy*. London: George Allen and Unwin, 1936.

Rosenau, James N. *Calculated Control as a Unifying Concept in the Study of International Politics and Foreign Policy*. Research Monograph No. 15, Princeton University Center of International Studies, February 10, 1963.

————, ed. *International Politics and Foreign Policy: A Reader in Research and Theory*. Rev. ed. New York: Free Press, 1969.

Rosenau, James N.; Thompson, Kenneth W.; and Boyd, Gavin, eds. *World Politics: An Introduction*. New York: Free Press, 1976.

Rostow, W. W. *The Stages of Economic Growth: A Non-Communist Manifesto*. Cambridge: Cambridge University Press, 1960.

Rothschild, K. W., ed. *Power in Economics: Selected Readings*. Middlesex: Penguin, 1971.

Royal Institute of International Affairs. *International Sanctions*. London: Oxford University Press, 1938.

Russell, Bertrand. *Power: A New Social Analysis*. New York: W.W. Norton, 1938.

Russell, Frank M. *Theories of International Relations*. New York: D. Appleton-Century, 1936.

Russett, Bruce M. *No Clear and Present Danger: A Skeptical View of United States Entry into World War II*. New York: Harper and Row, 1972.

Sabine, George H. *A History of Political Theory*. Rev. ed. New York: Henry Holt, 1950.

Samuelson, Paul. *Economics*. 10th ed. New York: McGraw-Hill, 1976.

Schelling, Thomas C. *Arms and Influence*. New Haven: Yale University Press, 1966.

————. *International Economics*. Boston: Allyn and Bacon, 1958.

————. *The Strategy of Conflict*. Cambridge: Harvard University Press, 1960.

Schmitt, Bernadotte E. *The Annexation of Bosnia, 1908-1909*. Cambridge: Cambridge University Press, 1937.

Schumpeter, Joseph A. *History of Economic Analysis*. New York: Oxford University Press, 1954.

Schwarzenberger, Georg. *Economic World Order?* Dobbs Ferry, N.Y.: Oceana, 1970.

Semmel, Bernard. *The Rise of Free Trade Imperialism: Classical Political Economy, the Empire of Free Trade, and Imperialism, 1750-1850.* Cambridge: Cambridge University Press, 1970.

Sharp, Gene. *The Politics of Nonviolent Action*. 3 vols. Boston: Porter Sargent, 1973.

Sigmund, Paul E. *The Overthrow of Allende and the Politics of Chile, 1964-1976*. Pittsburgh: University of Pittsburgh Press, 1977.

Silberner, Edmund. *La Guerre dans la Pensée Économique du XVIᵉ au XVIIIᵉ Siècle*. Paris: Librairie du Recueil Sirey, 1939.

―――. *The Problem of War in Nineteenth Century Economic Thought*. Translated by Alexander H. Krappe. Princeton: Princeton University Press, 1946.

Simon, Herbert A. *Administrative Behavior*. 3d ed. New York: Free Press, 1976.

―――. *Models of Man*. New York: Wiley, 1957.

Smith, Adam. *An Inquiry into the Nature and Causes of the Wealth of Nations*. Edited by Edwin Canaan. New York: Modern Library, 1937.

Snyder, Glenn H., and Diesing, Paul. *Conflict Among Nations: Bargaining, Decision Making, and System Structure in International Crises*. Princeton: Princeton University Press, 1977.

Snyder, Richard C., and Furniss, Edgar S. *American Foreign Policy: Formulation, Principles, and Programs*. New York: Rinehart, 1954.

Sprout, Harold, and Sprout, Margaret. *The Ecological Perspective on Human Affairs: With Special Reference to International Politics*. Princeton: Princeton University Press, 1965.

―――. *Foundations of International Politics*. Princeton: D. Van Nostrand, 1962.

―――. *Toward a Politics of the Planet Earth*. New York: Van Nostrand, 1971.

Spykman, Nicholas John. *America's Strategy in World Politics*. New York: Harcourt, Brace, 1942.

Stawell, F. Melian. *The Growth of International Thought*. London: Thornton Butterworth, 1929.

Stent, Angela. *From Embargo to Ostpolitik: The Political Economy of West German–Soviet Relations, 1955-1980*. Cambridge: Cambridge University Press, 1981.

Stevens, Robert Warren. *Vain Hopes, Grim Realities: The Economic Consequences of the Vietnam War*. New York: Franklin Watts, 1976.

Stone, Julius. *Aggression and World Order*. Berkeley: University of California Press, 1958.

———. *Conflict Through Consensus: United Nations Approaches to Aggression*. Baltimore: Johns Hopkins Press, 1977.

———. *Legal Controls of International Conflict*. New York: Rinehart, 1954.

Stourzh, Gerald. *Benjamin Franklin and American Foreign Policy*. 2d ed. Chicago: University of Chicago Press, 1969.

Strack, Harry R. *Sanctions: The Case of Rhodesia*. Syracuse, N.Y.: Syracuse University Press, 1978.

Taussig, F. W. *State Papers and Speeches on the Tariff*. Cambridge: Harvard University Press, 1893.

Tedeschi, James T., ed. *The Social Influence Processes*. Chicago: Aldine-Atherton, 1972.

Thucydides. *The History of the Peloponnesian War*. Translated by Crawley. New York: Modern Library, 1951.

———. *The History of the Peloponnesian War*. Translated by Rex Warner. New York: Penguin, 1972.

Tucker, Robert W. *The Inequality of Nations*. New York: Basic Books, 1977.

Vance, Cyrus. *Hard Choices: Critical Years in America's Foreign Policy*. New York: Simon and Schuster, 1983.

Van Dyke, Vernon. *Political Science: A Philosophical Analysis*. Stanford: Stanford University Press, 1960.

Viner, Jacob. *International Economics*. Glencoe, Ill.: Free Press, 1951.

———. *The Role of Providence in the Social Order*. Philadelphia: American Philosophical Society, 1972.

———. *Studies in the Theory of International Trade*. New York: Harper, 1937.

———. *Trade Relations Between Free Market and Controlled Economies*. League of Nations Pub. II. Economic and Financial, 1943. II.A.4.

Visscher, Charles de. *Theory and Reality in Public International Law*. Translated by P. E. Corbett. Princeton: Princeton University Press, 1957.

Wallace, William. *The Foreign Policy Process in Britain*. London: Royal Institute of International Affairs, 1975.

Walters, F. P. *A History of the League of Nations*. London: Oxford University Press, 1952.

Watson, Adam. *Diplomacy*. New York: McGraw-Hill, 1983.

Weber, Max. *The Theory of Social and Economic Organization*. Translated by A. M. Henderson and Talcott Parsons and edited by Talcott Parsons. New York: Free Press, 1947.

Weintraub, Sidney, ed. *Economic Coercion and U.S. Foreign Policy:*

Implications of Case Studies from the Johnson Administration. Boulder, Colo.: Westview, 1982.

Welch, William. *American Images of Soviet Foreign Policy*. New Haven: Yale University Press, 1970.

Welles, Sumner. *Seven Decisions that Shaped History*. New York: Harper and Row, 1951.

Whitton, John B., ed. *The Second Chance: America and the Peace*. Princeton: Princeton University Press, 1944.

Wight, Martin. *Power Politics*. Edited by Hedley Bull and Carsten Holbraad. New York: Holmes and Meier, 1978.

Wilcox, Clair. *A Charter for World Trade*. New York: Macmillan, 1949.

Wilczynski, Jozef. *The Economics and Politics of East-West Trade*. New York: Praeger, 1969.

Wiles, P.J.D. *Communist International Economics*. Oxford: Basil Blackwell, 1968.

Wilkinson, David O. *Comparative Foreign Relations: Framework and Methods*. Belmont, Calif.: Dickenson, 1969.

Wolf, Charles Jr. *Foreign Aid: Theory and Practice in Southern Asia*. Princeton: Princeton University Press, 1960.

Wolfers, Arnold. *Discord and Collaboration*. Baltimore: Johns Hopkins Press, 1962.

Wolfers, Arnold, and Martin, Laurence W., eds. *The Anglo-American Tradition in Foreign Affairs*. New Haven: Yale University Press, 1956.

Wright, Quincy. *The Study of International Relations*. New York: Appleton-Century-Crofts, 1955.

————. *A Study of War*. 2d ed. Chicago: University of Chicago Press, 1965.

Wu, Yuan-li. *Economic Warfare*. New York: Prentice-Hall, 1952.

Yergin, Daniel. *The Shattered Peace: The Origins of the Cold War and the National Security State*. Boston: Houghton Mifflin, 1978.

Young, Oran. *The Politics of Force*. Princeton: Princeton University Press, 1968.

Zimmern, Sir Alfred. *The Greek Commonwealth*. 5th ed. London: Oxford University Press, 1931.

ARTICLES, PAPERS, AND SPECIAL STUDIES

Adler-Karlsson, Gunnar. "The U.S. Embargo: Inefficient and Counterproductive." *Aussenwirtschaft* XXXV (June 1980):170-187.

Alchian, Armen A. "Cost." *International Encyclopedia of the Social Sciences*, vol. 3. New York: Free Press, 1968.

Allen, Robert Loring. "Economic Warfare." *International Encyclopedia of the Social Sciences*, vol. 4. New York: Free Press, 1968.

Amdur, Robert. "Rawls' Theory of Justice: Domestic and International Perspectives." *World Politics* XXIX (April 1977):438-461.

Amerongen, Otto Wolff von. "Commentary: Economic Sanctions as a Foreign Policy Tool?" *International Security* V (Fall 1980): 159-167.

Aron, Raymond. "Ideology in Search of a Policy." *Foreign Affairs* LX (1982):503-524.

Bachrach, Peter, and Baratz, Morton S. "Two Faces of Power." *American Political Science Review* LVI (December 1962):947-952.

Baer, George W. "Sanctions and Security: The League of Nations and the Italian-Ethiopian War, 1935-1936." *International Organization* XXVII (Spring 1973):165-179.

Baldwin, David A. "Analytical Notes on Foreign Aid and Politics." *Background* X (May 1966):66-90.

———. "The Costs of Power." *Journal of Conflict Resolution* XV (June 1971):145-155.

———. "Economic Power." In *Perspectives on Social Power*, edited by James T. Tedeschi, pp. 395-413. Chicago: Aldine, 1974.

———. "Foreign Aid, Intervention, and Influence." *World Politics* XXI (April 1969):425-447.

———. "Interdependence and Power: A Conceptual Analysis." *International Organization* XXXIV (Autumn 1980):471-506.

———. "International Aid and International Politics." *Public Administration Review* XXIX (January-February 1969): 94-99.

———. "The International Bank in Political Perspective." *World Politics* XVIII (October 1965):68-81.

———. "Inter-Nation Influence Revisited." *Journal of Conflict Resolution* XV (December 1971):471-486.

———. "Money and Power." *Journal of Politics* XXXIII (August 1971):578-614.

———. "Power Analysis and World Politics: New Trends Versus Old Tendencies." *World Politics* XXXI (January 1979): 161-194.

———. "Power and Social Exchange." *American Political Science Review* LXXII (December 1978):1229-1242.

———. "The Power of Positive Sanctions." *World Politics* XXIV (October 1971):19-38.

———. "Thinking about Threats." *Journal of Conflict Resolution* XV (March 1971):71-78.

Ball, George W. "The Case Against Sanctions." *New York Times Magazine*, September 19, 1982.

Baloyra, Enrique A. "Madness of the Method: The United States and Cuba." In *Latin America, the United States, and the Inter-American*

System, edited by John D. Martz and Lars Schoultz, pp. 115-144. Boulder, Colo.: Westview, 1980.

Barber, James. "Economic Sanctions as a Policy Instrument." *International Affairs* LV (July 1979):367-384.

Beitz, Charles R. "Bounded Morality: Justice and the State in World Politics." *International Organization* XXXIII (Summer 1979):405-424.

————. "Economic Rights and Distributive Justice in Developing Societies." *World Politics* XXXIII (April 1981):321-346.

Bergsten, C. Fred; Keohane, Robert O.; and Nye, Joseph S. "International Economics and International Politics: A Framework for Analysis." *International Organization* XXIX (Winter 1975):3-36.

Berman, Harold J. "A Reappraisal of U.S.-U.S.S.R. Trade Policy." *Harvard Business Review* XLII (July-August 1964):139-151.

Bertram, Anton. "The Economic Weapon as a Form of Peaceful Pressure." *Transactions of the Grotius Society* XVII (1931):139-174.

Bialer, Seweryn, and Afferica, Joan. "Reagan and Russia." *Foreign Affairs* LXI (Winter 1982-83):249-271.

Bienen, Henry, and Gilpin, Robert. "Economic Sanctions as a Response to Terrorism." *Journal of Strategic Studies* III (May 1980):89-98.

————. "An Evaluation of the Use of Economic Sanctions to Promote Foreign Policy Objectives, with Special Reference to the Problem of Terrorism and the Promotion of Human Rights," a report prepared for the Boeing Corporation, April 2, 1979.

Blau, Peter M. "Interaction: Social Exchange." *International Encyclopedia of the Social Sciences*, vol. 7. New York: Free Press, 1968.

Blessing, James A. "The Suspension of Foreign Aid: A Macro-Analysis." *Polity* XIII (Spring 1981):524-535.

Bloomfield, Lincoln. "Law, Politics and International Disputes," *International Conciliation*, no. 516 (January 1958).

Blum, Yehuda Z. "Economic Boycotts in International Law." In *Conference on Transnational Economic Boycotts and Coercion*, edited by Roy M. Mersky, vol. 1, pp. 89-99. Dobbs Ferry, N.Y.: Oceana, 1978.

Bonn, M. J. "How Sanctions Failed." *Foreign Affairs* XV (January 1937):350-361.

Boorman, James A. III. "Economic Coercion in International Law: The Arab Oil Weapon and the Ensuing Juridical Issues." In *Economic Coercion and the New International Economic Order*, edited by Richard B. Lillich, pp. 255-281. Charlottesville, Va.: Michie, 1976.

Bornstein, Morris. "Economic Sanctions and Rewards in Support of Arms Control Agreements." *American Economic Review* LVIII (May 1968):417-427.

Boulding, Kenneth E. "The Economics of Human Conflict." In *The Nature of Human Conflict*, edited by Elton B. McNeil, pp. 172-191. Englewood Cliffs, N.J.: Prentice-Hall, 1965.

Boulding, Kenneth E., and Gleason, Alan H. "War as an Investment: The Strange Case of Japan." In *Economic Imperialism*, edited by Kenneth E. Boulding and Tapan Mukerjee, pp. 240-261. Ann Arbor: University of Michigan Press, 1972.

Bowett, Derek W. "International Law and Economic Coercion." In *Economic Coercion and the New International Economic Order*, edited by Richard B. Lillich, pp. 89-103. Charlottesville, Va.: Michie, 1976.

Brosche, Hartmut. "The Arab Oil Embargo and United States Pressure Against Chile: Economic and Political Coercion and the Charter of the United Nations." In *Economic Coercion and the New International Economic Order*, edited by Richard B. Lillich, pp. 285-317. Charlottesville, Va.: Michie, 1976.

Buchheit, Lee C. "The Use of Nonviolent Coercion: A Study in Legality Under Article 2(4) of the Charter of the United Nations." In *Economic Coercion and the New International Economic Order*, edited by Richard B. Lillich, pp. 41-69. Charlottesville, Va.: Michie, 1976.

Callahan, Patrick. "Commitment." In *Describing Foreign Policy Behavior*, edited by Patrick Callahan, Linda P. Brady, and Margaret G. Hermann. Beverly Hills, Calif.: Sage, 1982.

Carswell, Robert. "Economic Sanctions and the Iranian Experience." *Foreign Affairs* LX (Winter 1981-1982):247-265.

Cerf, Jay H. "We Should Do More Business with the Communists." In *American Foreign Economic Policy*, edited by Benjamin J. Cohen, pp. 305-314. New York: Harper and Row, 1968.

Chenery, Hollis, and Strout, Alan. "Foreign Assistance and Economic Development." *American Economic Review* LVI (September 1966):679-733.

Clarke, D. G. "Zimbabwe's International Economic Position and Aspects of Sanctions Removal." *Journal of Commonwealth and Comparative Politics* XVIII (March 1980):28-54.

Cleveland, H. Van B. "Economics as Theory and Ideology." *World Politics* VI (April 1954):289-305.

Cohen, Bernard C. "Foreign Policy." In *International Encyclopedia of the Social Sciences*, vol. 5. New York: Free Press, 1968.

Cohen, Bernard C., and Harris, Scott A. "Foreign Policy." In *Handbook of Political Science*, vol. 6: *Policies and Policymaking*, edited by Fred I. Greenstein and Nelson W. Polsby, pp. 381-437. Reading, Mass.: Addison-Wesley, 1975.

Combs, Jerald A. "Embargoes." In *Encyclopedia of American Foreign*

Policy, 3 vols., edited by Alexander de Conde. New York: Charles Scribner's, 1978.

Condliffe, J. B. "Economic Power as an Instrument of National Policy." *American Economic Review* XXXIV (March 1944):305-314.

Converse, Elizabeth. "The War of All Against All." *Journal of Conflict Resolution* XII (December 1968):471-532.

Coplin, William D. "International Law and Assumptions about the State System." *World Politics* XVII (July 1965):615-634.

Corden, W. M. "Tariffs and Protectionism." In *International Encyclopedia of the Social Sciences*, vol. 8. New York: Free Press, 1968.

Dahl, Robert A. "The Concept of Power." *Behavioral Science* II (July 1957):201-215.

———. "Power." In *International Encyclopedia of the Social Sciences*, vol. 12. New York: Free Press, 1968.

Domínguez, Jorge I. "Cuban Foreign Policy." *Foreign Affairs* LVII (Fall 1978):83-108.

———. "Taming the Cuban Shrew." *Foreign Policy*, no. 10 (Spring 1973), pp. 94-116.

Doxey, Margaret. "International Sanctions: A Framework for Analysis with Special Reference to the U.N. and Southern Africa." *International Organization* XXVI (Summer 1972):525-550.

———. "The Making of Zimbabwe: From Illegal to Legal Independence." *The Year Book of World Affairs* XXXVI (1982): 151-165.

———. "Sanctions Revisited." *International Journal* XXXI (Winter 1975-1976):53-78.

Dulles, John Foster. "Practicable Sanctions." In *Boycotts and Peace.* Edited by Evans Clark. New York: Harper, 1932.

Earle, Edward Mead. "Adam Smith, Alexander Hamilton, Friedrich List: The Economic Foundations of Military Power." In *Makers of Modern Strategy: Military Thought from Machiavelli to Hitler*, edited by Edward Mead Earle, pp. 117-154. Princeton: Princeton University Press, 1943.

Eckstein, Harry. "Case Study and Theory in Political Science." In *Handbook of Political Science*, vol. 7: *Strategies of Inquiry*, edited by Fred I. Greenstein and Nelson W. Polsby, pp. 79-137. Reading, Mass.: Addison-Wesley, 1975.

Frey, Frederick W. "On Issues and Nonissues in the Study of Power." *American Political Science Review* LXV (December 1971):1081-1101.

Friedman, Milton. "Foreign Economic Aid: Means and Objectives." *Yale Review* XLVII (June 1958):500-516.

Friedmann, Wolfgang. "Intervention and International Law." In *Intervention in International Politics*, edited by Louis G. M. Jaquet, pp.

40-68. The Hague: Netherlands Institute of International Affairs, 1971.

Gaddis, John Lewis. "The Rise and Fall of Détente." *Foreign Affairs* LXII (Winter 1983-1984):354-377.

Gallagher, John, and Robinson, Ronald. "The Imperialism of Free Trade." *The Economic History Review* VI (1953):1-15.

Galtung, Johan. "On the Effects of International Economic Sanctions: With Examples from the Case of Rhodesia." *World Politics* XIX (April 1967):378-416.

―――. "On the Meaning of Nonviolence." *Journal of Peace Research*, no. 3 (1965), pp. 228-257.

―――. "Pacifism from a Sociological Point of View." *Journal of Conflict Resolution* III (1959):67-84.

Gardner, Richard N. "The Hard Road to World Order." *Foreign Affairs* LII (April 1974):556-576.

George, Alexander L. "Case Studies and Theory Development: The Method of Structured, Focused Comparison." In *Diplomacy: New Approaches in History, Theory, and Policy*, edited by Paul Gordon Lauren, pp. 43-68. New York: Free Press, 1979.

Georgescu-Roegen, Nicholas. "Utility." *International Encyclopedia of the Social Sciences*, vol. 16. New York: Free Press, 1968.

Gilpin, Robert. "Economic Interdependence and National Security in Historical Perspective." In *Economic Issues and National Security*, edited by Klaus Knorr and Frank H. Trager, pp. 19-66. Lawrence: Regents Press of Kansas, 1977.

―――. "The Political Economy of the Multinational Corporation: Three Contrasting Perspectives." *American Political Science Review* LX (March 1976):184-191.

Glad, Betty. "Jimmy Carter's Management of the Hostage Conflict: A Bargaining Perspective," paper presented at the American Political Science Association Meeting, New York, 1981 (mimeo).

Gonzalez, Edward. "The United States and Castro: Breaking the Deadlock." *Foreign Affairs* L (July 1972):722-737.

Gouldner, Alvin W. "The Norm of Reciprocity." *American Sociological Review* XXV (April 1960):161-178.

Graham, Frank D. "Economics and Peace." In *The Second Chance: America and the Peace*, edited by John B. Whitton. Princeton: Princeton University Press, 1944.

Grieve, Muriel J. "Economic Sanctions: Theory and Practice." *International Relations* XIII (October 1968):431-443.

Haberler, Gottfried. "The Liberal International Economic Order in Historical Perspective." In *Challenges to a Liberal International Economic Order*, edited by Ryan C. Amacher, Gottfried Haberler, and

Thomas D. Willett, pp. 43-65. Washington, D.C.: American Enterprise Institute, 1979.

Harsanyi, John C. "Measurement of Social Power, Opportunity Costs, and the Theory of Two-Person Bargaining Games." *Behavioral Science* VII (January 1962):67-80.

Hermann, Charles F. "Instruments of Foreign Policy." In *Describing Foreign Policy Behavior*, edited by Patrick Callahan, Linda P. Brady, and Margaret G. Hermann. Beverly Hills, Calif.: Sage, 1982.

Hermann, Margaret G., Hermann, Charles F., and Hutchins, Gerald L. "Affect." In *Describing Foreign Policy Behavior*, edited by Patrick Callahan, Linda P. Brady, and Margaret G. Hermann. Beverly Hills, Calif.: Sage, 1982.

Hitch, Charles J. "National Security Policy as a Field for Economics Research." *World Politics* XII (April 1960):434-452.

Hoffmann, Fredrik. "The Functions of Economic Sanctions: A Comparative Analysis." *Journal of Peace Research*, no. 2 (1967), pp. 140-160.

Holsti, K. J. "The Study of Diplomacy." In *World Politics*, edited by James N. Rosenau, Kenneth W. Thompson, and Gavin Boyd, pp. 293-311. New York: Free Press, 1976.

Hosoya, Chihiro. "Miscalculations in Deterrent Policy: Japanese-U.S. Relations, 1938-1941." *Journal of Peace Research*, no. 2 (1968), pp. 97-115.

Huntington, Samuel P. "Trade, Technology, and Leverage: Economic Diplomacy." *Foreign Policy*, no. 32 (Fall 1978), pp. 63-80.

Hurewitz, J. C. "The Middle East: A Year of Turmoil." *Foreign Affairs* LIX (1981):540-577.

Hyde, Charles Cheney, and Wehle, Louis B. "The Boycott in Foreign Affairs." *American Journal of International Law* XXVII (January 1933):1-10.

Hyland, William G. "U.S.–Soviet Relations: The Long Road Back." *Foreign Affairs* LX (1982):525-550.

International Bank for Reconstruction and Development. *World Bank Atlas*, 1972.

————. *World Development Report, 1982*. New York: Oxford University Press, 1982.

Joffe, Josef. "Europe and America: The Politics of Resentment (cont'd)." *Foreign Affairs* LXI (1983):569-590.

Kaiser, Robert G. "U.S.–Soviet Relations: Goodbye to Détente." *Foreign Affairs* LIX (1981):500-521.

Katzenstein, Peter J. "Domestic Structures and Strategies of Foreign Economic Policy." *International Organization* XXXI (Autumn 1977):879-920.

Kindleberger, Charles P. "U.S. Foreign Economic Policy, 1776-1976." *Foreign Affairs* LV (January 1977):395-417.

Klitgaard, Robert E. *National Security and Export Controls*, Rand Corporation Report, R-1432-1-ARPA/CIEP, April 1974.

———. "Sending Signals." *Foreign Policy*, no. 32 (Fall 1978), pp. 103-106.

Knight, Frank H. "Some Fallacies in the Interpretation of Social Cost." *Quarterly Journal of Economics* XXXVIII (August 1924):582-606.

Knorr, Klaus. "International Economic Leverage and Its Uses." In *Economic Issues and National Security*, edited by Klaus Knorr and Frank N. Trager. Lawrence: Regents Press of Kansas, 1977.

———. "On the International Uses of Military Force in the Contemporary World." *Orbis* XXI (Spring 1977):5-27.

Kuznets, Simon. "Aspects of Post-World War II Growth in Less Developed Countries." In *Evolution, Welfare, and Time in Economics: Essays in Honor of Nicholas Georgescu-Roegen*, edited by A. M. Tang, E. M. Westfield, and James E. Worley, pp. 39-65. Lexington, Mass.: Lexington Books, 1976.

Lauterpacht, H. "Boycott in International Relations." *British Yearbook of International Law* XIV (1933):125-140.

———. "The Legal Aspect." In *Peaceful Change*, edited by C.A.W. Manning. New York: Macmillan, 1937.

Letiche, J. M. "The History of Economic Thought in the *International Encyclopedia of the Social Sciences*." *Journal of Economic Literature* VII (June 1969):406-425.

Levine, Herbert S.; Rushing, Francis W.; and Movit, Charles H. "The Potential for U.S. Economic Leverage on the USSR." *Comparative Strategy* I (1979):371-404.

Levi-Strauss, Claude. "The Principle of Reciprocity." In *Sociological Theory*, edited by Lewis A. Coser and Bernard Rosenberg, pp. 84-94. New York: Macmillan, 1957.

Lipton, Michael. "Aid Allocation When Aid is Inadequate: Problems of the Non-Implementation of the Pearson Report." In *Foreign Resources and Economic Development*, edited by T. J. Byres, pp. 155-182. London: Frank Cass, 1972.

Loring, David C. "The Fisheries Dispute." In *U.S. Foreign Policy and Peru*, edited by Daniel A. Sharp, pp. 57-118. Austin: University of Texas Press, 1972.

Lowenthal, Abraham F. "Cuba: Time For a Change." *Foreign Policy*, no. 20 (Fall 1975), pp. 65-86.

Lyons, Gene M.; Baldwin, David A.; and McNemar, Donald W. "The 'Politicization' Issue in the U.N. Specialized Agencies." *Proceedings of the Academy of Political Science* XXXII (1977):81-92.

March, James G. "An Introduction to the Theory and Measurement of Influence." *American Political Science Review* XLIX (June 1955):431-451.

McKinlay, R. D., and Little, R. "A Foreign Policy Model of U.S. Bilateral Aid Allocation." *World Politics* XXX (October 1977):58-86.

McLellan, David S., and Woodhouse, Charles E. "The Business Elite and Foreign Policy." *Western Political Quarterly* XIII (March 1960):172-190.

Merritt, Richard L. "Transmission of Values Across National Boundaries." In *Communication in Interntional Politics*, edited by Richard L. Merritt. Urbana: University of Illinois Press, 1972.

Millar, T. B. "On Writing About Foreign Policy." In *International Politics and Foreign Policy: A Reader in Research and Theory*, edited by James N. Rosenau. Rev. ed. New York: Free Press, 1969.

Miller, Judith. "When Sanctions Worked." *Foreign Policy*, no. 39 (Summer 1980), pp. 118-129.

Morgenthau, Hans. "A Political Theory of Foreign Aid." *American Political Science Review* LVI (June 1962):301-309.

Muir, J. Dapray. "The Boycott in International Law." In *Economic Coercion and the New International Economic Order*, edited by Richard B. Lillich, pp. 21-38. Charlottesville, Va.: Michie, 1976.

Nagel, Jack H. "Some Questions about the Concept of Power." *Behavioral Science* XIII (March 1968):129-137.

Olson, Richard Stuart. "Economic Coercion in International Disputes: The United States and Peru in the IPC Expropriation Dispute of 1968-1971." *Journal of Developing Areas* IX (April 1975):395-414.

―――. "Expropriation and International Economic Coercion: Ceylon and the 'West' 1961-65." *Journal of Developing Areas* XI (January 1977):205-225.

―――. "Economic Coercion in World Politics: With a Focus on North-South Relations." *World Politics* XXXI (July 1979):471-494.

Oppenheim, Felix E. "The Language of Political Inquiry: Problems of Clarification." In *Handbook of Political Science*, vol. 1: *Political Science: Scope and Theory*, edited by Fred I. Greenstein and Nelson W. Polsby, pp. 283-335. Reading, Mass.: Addison-Wesley, 1975.

Paarlberg, Robert L. "Lessons of the Grain Embargo." *Foreign Affairs* LIX (Fall 1980):144-162.

Packenham, Robert A. "The New Utopianism: Political Development Ideas in the Dependency Literature." *Working Paper*, no. 19, Latin American Program, Woodrow Wilson International Center for Scholars, Washington, D.C., 1978.

―――. "Political-Development Doctrines in the American Foreign Aid Program." *World Politics* XVIII (January 1966):194-235.

Paust, Jordan J., and Blaustein, Albert P. "The Arab Oil Weapon—A Threat to International Peace." In *Economic Coercion and the New International Economic Order*, edited by Richard B. Lillich, pp. 123-152. Charlottesville, Va.: Michie, 1976.

Pechman, Joseph A. "Making Economic Policy: The Role of the Economist." In *Handbook of Political Science*, vol. 6: *Policies and Policymaking*, edited by Fred I. Greenstein and Nelson W. Polsby, pp. 23-78. Reading, Mass.: Addison-Wesley, 1975.

Perroux, François. "The Gift: Its Economic Meaning in Contemporary Capitalism." *Diogenes*, no. 6 (Spring 1954), pp. 1-19.

Petras, James, and Morley, Morris. "Chilean Destabilization and Its Aftermath: An Analysis and a Critique." *Politics* XI (November 1976):140-148.

Pinder, John. "Economic Diplomacy." In *World Politics: An Introduction*, edited by James N. Rosenau, Kenneth W. Thompson, and Gavin Boyd, pp. 312-336. New York: Free Press, 1976.

Porter, Richard C. "Economic Sanctions: The Theory and the Evidence from Rhodesia." *Journal of Peace Science* III (Fall 1978):93-110.

"A Report of the Commission on United States-Latin American Relations." In *The Americas in a Changing World*. New York: Quadrangle, 1975.

Riker, William H. "Some Ambiguities in the Notion of Power." *American Political Science Review* LVIII (June 1964):341-349.

Rosenau, James N. "Comparative Foreign Policy: Fad, Fantasy, or Field?" *International Studies Quarterly* XII (September 1968):296-329.

Rosenfeld, Stephen S. "Testing the Hard Line." *Foreign Affairs* LXI (1983):489-510.

Rosenstein-Rodan, Paul N. "International Aid for Underdeveloped Countries." *Review of Economics and Statistics* XLIII (May 1961):107-138.

Russett, Bruce M. "Pearl Harbor: Deterrence Theory and Decision Theory." *Journal of Peace Research*, no. 2 (1967), pp. 89-105.

Saint Brides, Lord. "The Lessons of Zimbabwe-Rhodesia." *International Security* IV (Spring 1980):177-184.

Schelling, Thomas C. "American Aid and Economic Development: Some Critical Issues." In *International Stability and Progress*, pp. 121-169. New York: American Assembly, 1957.

———. "American Foreign Assistance." *World Politics* VII (July 1955):606-626.

———. "National Security Considerations Affecting Trade Policy." In *United States International Economic Policy in an Interdependent World*, papers submitted to the Commission on International Trade and Investment Policy, Compendium of Papers, 3 vols., vol. 1, July 1971, pp. 723-737.

———. "The Strategy of Inflicting Costs." In *Issues in Defense Economics*, edited by Roland N. McKean, pp. 105-127. New York: National Bureau of Economic Research, 1967.

Schreiber, Anna P. "Economic Coercion as an Instrument of Foreign Policy: U.S. Economic Measures Against Cuba and the Dominican Republic." *World Politics* XXV (April 1973):387-413.

Schwebel, S. M. "Aggression, Intervention and Self-Defense in Modern International Law." *Recueil des Cours* (1972-II), pp. 411-498.

Shneyer, Paul A., and Barta, Virginia. "The Legality of the U.S. Economic Blockade Under International Law." *Case Western Reserve Journal of International Law* XIII (Summer 1981):451-482.

Simon, Herbert A. "Notes on the Observation and Measurement of Political Power." *Journal of Politics* XV (November 1953): 500-516.

Smith, Tony. "The Underdevelopment of Development Literature: The Case of Dependency Theory." *World Politics* XXXI (January 1979):247-288.

Snyder, Glenn H. "The Security Dilemma in Alliance Politics." *World Politics* XXXVI (July 1984):461-495.

Stepan, Alfred. "The United States and Latin America: Vital Interests and the Instruments of Power." *Foreign Affairs* LVIII (1980):659-692.

Strange, Susan. "International Economics and International Relations: A Case of Mutual Neglect." *International Affairs* XLVI (April 1970):304-315.

Swanson, Dean. "Specificity." In *Describing Foreign Policy Behavior*, edited by Patrick Callahan, Linda P. Brady, and Margaret G. Hermann. Beverly Hills, Calif.: Sage, 1982.

Tatu, Michel. "U.S.-Soviet Relations: A Turning Point?" *Foreign Affairs* LXI (1983):591-610.

Taubenfeld, Rita Falk, and Taubenfeld, Howard J. "The 'Economic Weapon': The League and the United Nations." *Proceedings of the American Society of International Law* LVIII (1964):183-205.

Toynbee, Arnold J. "The Lessons of History." In *Peaceful Change*, edited by C.A.W. Manning, pp. 27-38. New York: Macmillan, 1937.

Viner, Jacob. "Economic Thought: Mercantilist Thought." In *International Encyclopedia of the Social Sciences*, vol. 4. New York: Free Press, 1968.

———. "The Intellectual History of Laissez Faire." *The Journal of Law and Economics* III (October 1960):45-69.

———. "Power Versus Plenty as Objectives of Foreign Policy in the Seventeenth and Eighteenth Centuries." *World Politics* I (October 1948):1-29.

Walinsky, Louis J. "Coherent Defense Strategy: On the Case for Economic Denial." *Foreign Affairs* LXI (Winter 1982-1983): 272-291.

Wallensteen, Peter. "Characteristics of Economic Sanctions." *Journal of Peace Research*, no. 3 (1968), pp. 248-267.

Wardle, H. Newell. "Gifts." *Encyclopedia of the Social Sciences*, vol. 3. New York: Macmillan, 1937.

Whitton, John B. "Institutions of World Order." In *The Second Chance: America and the Peace*, edited by John B. Whitton. Princeton: Princeton University Press, 1944.

Williams, Benjamin H. "The Coming of Economic Sanctions into American Practice." *American Journal of International Law* XXXVII (July 1943):386-396.

UNITED STATES GOVERNMENT PUBLICATIONS

Commission on Foreign Economic Policy. *Report to the President and the Congress*. Washington, D.C.: Government Printing Office, 1954.

―――. *Staff Papers*. Washington, D.C.: Government Printing Office, 1954.

Committee to Strengthen the Security of the Free World. *The Scope and Distribution of United States Military and Economic Assistance Programs*. Washington, D.C.: Government Printing Office, 1963.

Composite Report of the President's Committee to Study the United States Military Assistance Program. 2 vols., August 17, 1959.

Gray, Gordon. *Report to the President on Foreign Economic Policies*. Washington: Government Printing Office, 1950.

International Development Advisory Board. *A New Emphasis on Economic Development Abroad: A Report to the President of the United States on Ways, Means and Reasons for U.S. Assistance to International Development*, March 1957.

―――. *Partners in Progress*, A Report to the President, March 1951.

U.S. Agency for International Development, Statistics and Reports Division. *U.S. Overseas Loans and Grants and Assistance from International Organizations*, special report prepared for the House Foreign Affairs Committee, 1965-1982.

U.S. Congress, Joint Committee on the Economic Report. *Hearings: Foreign Economic Policy*. 84th Cong., 1st sess., 1955.

U.S. Congress, Joint Economic Committee. *Cuba Faces the Economic Realities of the 1980s*, Committee Print. 97th Cong., 2d sess., 1982.

U.S. Congress, Office of Technology Assessment. *Technology and East-West Trade*. November 1979.

―――. *Technology and East-West Trade: An Update*. May 1983.

U.S. House of Representatives, Committee on Foreign Affairs. *An As-*

sessment of the Afghanistan Sanctions: Implications for Trade and Diplomacy in the 1980's, report prepared by the Congressional Research Service, Committee Print. 97th Cong., 1st sess., 1981.

————. *Hearings: East-West Relations in the Aftermath of Soviet Invasion of Afghanistan.* 96th Cong., 2d sess., 1980.

————. *Hearings: Rhodesia and United States Foreign Policy.* 91st Cong., 1st sess., 1969.

————. *Hearings: Sanctions as an Instrumentality of the United Nations—Rhodesia as a Case Study.* 92d Cong., 2d sess., 1972.

————. *Hearings: United States and Chile During the Allende Years, 1970-1973.* 93d Cong., 2d sess., 1975.

————. *Hearings: United States–Western European Relations in 1980.* 96th Cong., 2d sess., 1980.

U.S. House of Representatives, Committee on International Relations. *Hearings: Extension of the Export Administration Act of 1969*, part I. 94th Cong., 2d sess., 1976.

U.S. Senate, Committee on Agriculture. *Hearings: Economic Impact of Agricultural Embargoes.* 97th Cong., 2d sess., 1982.

U.S. Senate, Committee on Banking, Housing, and Urban Affairs. *Hearings: U.S. Embargo of Food and Technology to the Soviet Union.* 96th Cong., 2d sess., 1980.

U.S. Senate, Committee on Finance. *U.S. International Trade Strategy: Hearings Before the Subcommittee on International Trade.* 96th Cong., 2d sess., 1980.

U.S. Senate, Committee on Foreign Relations. *Hearings: East-West Trade.* 88th Cong., 2d sess., 1964.

————. *Hearings: Economic Relations with the Soviet Union.* 97th Cong., 2d sess., 1982.

————. *Hearings: U.N. Sanctions Against Rhodesia—Chrome.* 92d Cong., 1st sess., 1971.

————. *Hearing: U.S. Foreign Policy Objectives.* 96th Cong., 2d sess., 1980.

————. *The Premises of East-West Commercial Relations: A Workshop Sponsored by the Committee on Foreign Relations and Congressional Research Service*, Committee Print. 97th Cong., 2d sess., 1982.

————. *United States Foreign Policy*, "Economic, Social, and Political Change in Underdeveloped Countries and Its Implications for United States Policy," a study prepared by the Center for International Studies, Massachusetts Institute of Technology, Committee Print. 86th Cong., 2d Sess., 1960.

————. *United States Foreign Policy*, "Worldwide and Domestic Economic Problems and their Impact on the Foreign Policy of the United

States," a study prepared by the Corporation for Economic and Industrial Research, Committee Print. 86th Cong., 1st sess., 1959.

U.S. Senate. *Foreign Aid Program: Compilation of Studies and Surveys*, prepared under the direction of the Special Senate Committee to Study the Foreign Aid Program. 85th Cong., 1st sess., 1957, Senate Doc. 52.

U.S. Senate, Special Committee to Study the Foreign Aid Program. *Foreign Aid*. Report no. 300, 85th Cong., 1st sess., 1957.

DISSERTATIONS

Blessing, James A. "The Suspension of Foreign Aid by the United States, 1948-1972." Ph.D. dissertation, State University of New York at Albany, 1975.

Cumes, J.W.C. "Foreign Economic Policy: A Study of the Use of Economic Means to Promote Foreign-Policy Objectives Since 1919, with Special Reference to Australia." Ph.D. dissertation, University of London, 1951.

Osgood, Theodore Kent. "East-West Trade Controls and Economic Warfare." Ph.D. dissertation, Yale University, 1957.

Simpson, Janice Catherine. "The Position in International Law of Economic Measures of Coercion Carried on Within a State's Territory." Ph.D. dissertation, University of Chicago, 1935.

Wan, Henry York, Jr. "A Contribution to the Theory of Trade Warfare." Ph.D. dissertation, Massachusetts Institute of Technology, 1961.

INDEX

CPSIA information can be obtained at www.ICGtesting.com
Printed in the USA
LVOW06s0823171115

462945LV00004B/26/P

9 780691 101750